Web-Based Instruction

Web-Based Instruction

Badrul H. Khan
EDITOR

Educational Technology Publications
Englewood Cliffs, New Jersey 07632

Library of Congress Cataloging-in-Publication Data

Web-based instruction / Badrul H. Khan, editor.
    p. cm.
    Includes bibliographical references and index.
    ISBN 0–87778–296–2 (hardcover).—ISBN 0–87778–297–0 (softcover)
    1. World Wide Web (Information retrieval system) 2. Internet
(Computer network) in education. 3. Computer-assisted instruction.
I. Khan, Badrul Huda.
LB1044.87.W43   1997
025.06'37—dc21   96–52250
                                                      CIP

Printed in the United States of America.

Library of Congress Catalog Card Number:
96–52250.

International Standard Book Numbers:
0–87778–296–2 (hardcover).
0–87778–297–0 (softcover).

First Printing: February, 1997.

This book is dedicated to my late parents:

Mr. Lokman Khan Sherwani &
Mrs. Shabnom Khanam Sherwani
of
Khan Manzil, Pathantooly, Chittagong, Bangladesh

Acknowledgments

I wish to express my appreciation to the authors of the chapters included in this volume. Their cooperation and timely submission of manuscripts made the publication of this book a reality. I would like to thank Lawrence Lipsitz and the staff at Educational Technology Publications for their editorial assistance. I would also like to thank William Milheim and Steve Malikowski for reviewing the original outline of the book. I would like to thank my colleagues and students for their encouragement, support, comments, and suggestions. I would especially like to thank my students who designed an online course entitled Web-Based Instruction which is based on the chapters of this book and other relevant resources. You can visit these students via the Web (http://www.utb.edu/~edtech/courses/wbi.html). Finally, I would like to thank my wife, Komar Khan, and my son, Intisar Khan, who sometimes stayed up late to support and encourage me while I was working on this book.

Preface

As the Internet is fast emerging, its World Wide Web is becoming an increasingly powerful, global, interactive, and dynamic medium for delivering instruction. More and more institutions are using the Web to provide instruction and training. Increasing numbers of these institutions offering Web-based courses are recognizing the fact that the Web is a viable medium of learning and instruction.

The Web, as a medium of learning and instruction, has the potential to support the creation of well-designed resources, such as Web-based instruction (WBI). During the summer of 1996, I decided to offer a graduate course entitled "Web-Based Instruction (WBI)" as a selected topics course in educational technology. While searching for appropriate textbook(s) and relevant resources on WBI, I cross-posted a message to several listservs requesting information about WBI. After posting the message, several people replied with information scattered all over the Internet regarding WBI. However, many respondents felt there was a tremendous need for the compilation of information on WBI. Out of necessity, I began to compile relevant materials on WBI for my students, which in turn led me to think about producing a book on WBI.

With encouragement from Lawrence Lipsitz of Educational Technology Publications and several colleagues, I decided to edit a book on WBI. As we all know, the Web is a very new instructional medium. Researchers and practitioners involved in WBI belong to diverse areas of our social systems. As the editor of this book, I took an open and democratic approach to solicit contributions. I sent e-mail messages to potential authors and also cross-posted a message to several listservs, soliciting contributions for the book. As a result, I put together this comprehensive book on WBI by incorporating works of talented individuals with unique backgrounds from around the globe.

The purpose of this book is to provide readers with information related to design, development, delivery, management, and evaluation aspects of WBI. This book is divided into five main sections, including: introduction to Web-based instruction; Web-based learning environments and critical issues; designing Web-based instruction; delivering Web-based instruction, and case studies of Web-based courses.

Badrul H. Khan
November, 1996

Table of Contents

SECTION III
DESIGNING WEB-BASED INSTRUCTION

SECTION IV
DELIVERING WEB-BASED INSTRUCTION

SECTION V
CASE STUDIES OF WEB-BASED COURSES

Web-Based Instruction

SECTION I

Introduction to Web-Based Instruction

1

Web-Based Instruction (WBI): What Is It and Why Is It?

Badrul H. Khan

For many years, visionaries and futurists have been telling us that one day we would have quick and easy online access to all of the world's information. Well, the future has arrived; [it's] called the World Wide Web (WWW) and its growth in the past few years has been phenomenal. Already the Web is showing us how global networks will transform education.

—Greg Kearsley, 1996

Introduction

While growing up in Bangladesh during the 1970s, I used to dream about having access to well-designed learning resources that were only available to students in industrialized countries. In the '70s, it was unthinkable that we might have equal access to those resources. In the '90s, it has become a reality. Now, we are blessed with the emergence of the World Wide Web, commonly known as the Web, as one of the most important economic and democratic mediums of learning and teaching at a distance. As the Internet is rapidly emerging, the Web has become an increasingly powerful, global, interactive, and dynamic medium for sharing information. The Web provides an opportunity to develop new learning experiences for students not possible previously (Alexander, 1995). As a result, students from around the globe can enjoy equal access to the many learning resources available on the Web.

As the Information Age evolves, our society is undergoing massive changes that have tremendous impact on our educational systems. Advances in information technology, coupled with the changes in society, are creating new paradigms for education. Participants in this new educational paradigm require rich learning environments supported by well-designed resources (Reigeluth & Khan, 1994). The Web, as a medium of learning and instruction, has the potential to support the creation of these well-designed resources.

Web-Based Instruction (WBI)

Web-based instruction (WBI) can be viewed as an innovative approach for delivering instruction to a remote audience, using the Web as the medium. According to Smith and Ragan (1993), "Instruction is the delivery of information and activities that facilitate learners' attainment of intended, specific learning goals" (p. 2), and the medium is the physical means by which the instructional message is communicated. Designing and delivering instruction on the Web requires thoughtful analysis and investigation of how to use the Web's potential in concert with instructional design principles (Ritchie & Hoffman, chapter 16). The following definition of WBI incorporates the issues raised above:

> *Web-based instruction (WBI) is a hypermedia-based instructional program which utilizes the attributes and resources of the World Wide Web to create a meaningful learning environment where learning is fostered and supported.*

A WBI learning environment should include many resources, support collaboration, implement Web-based activities as part of the learning framework, and support both novices and experts (Sherry & Wilson, chapter 7). In this chapter, a WBI program is discussed in terms of various components and features that can be conducive to learning environments.

Components are integral parts of a WBI system (Banathy, 1992). *Features* are characteristics of a WBI program contributed by those components. Components, individually and jointly, can contribute to one or more features. For example, *e-mail* (component) in a WBI program can provide *asynchronous communication* (feature) to students and the instructor. Likewise, *e-mail, listservs, newsgroups, conferencing tools, etc.* (components) can jointly contribute to the creation of a virtual community (feature) on the Web. Some WBI features that are contributed by WBI components are listed in the Appendix. Features and their relevant components listed in the Appendix are by no means static. As the Web matures, new components will become available for WBI, and the existing components will improve with time. As a result, new features will be available to enrich WBI learning environments.

WBI Components

Various WBI components are clustered into the following general categories. Please note that within the scope of this chapter, it is not possible to discuss the functions of all the various components that might constitute a WBI program. However, several chapters in this book address many of these components (please use the book index to locate them).

1. **Content Development**
   (a) Learning and instructional theories
   (b) Instructional design (ID)
   (c) Curriculum development

2. **Multimedia Component**
   (a) Text and graphics
   (b) Audio Streaming (e.g., Real Audio)
   (c) Video Streaming (e.g., QuickTime)
   (d) Graphical User Interface (GUI)—uses icons, graphics, windows and a pointing device, instead of a purely character-mode interface (Tittel & Gaither, 1995). Microsoft Windows and MacOS are examples of GUIs.
   (e) Compression technology (e.g., ShockWave)

3. **Internet Tools**
   (a) Communications Tools
      (i) Asynchronous: e-mail, listservs, newsgroups, etc.
      (ii) Synchronous: text-based (e.g., Chat, IRC, MUDs, etc.) and audio-video (e.g., Internet Phone, Cu-SeeMe, etc.) conferencing tools.

     (b) Remote Access Tools (Logging in to and transferring files from remote computers.)
        (i) Telnet, File Transfer Protocol (ftp), etc.

     (c) Internet Navigation Tools (Access to databases and Web documents.)
        (i) Gopher, Lynx, etc.

     (d) Search and Other Tools
        (i) Search Engines
        (ii) Counter Tool

4. **Computers and Storage Devices**
     (a) Computer platforms running Unix, DOS, Windows and Macintosh operating systems.
     (b) Servers, hard drives, CD ROMs, etc.

5. **Connections and Service Providers**
     (a) Modems
     (b) Dial-in (e.g., standard telephone line, ISDN, etc.) and dedicated (e.g., 56kbps, T1, E1 lines, etc.) services
     (c) Gateway Service Provider, Internet Service Providers, etc.

6. **Authoring Programs**
     (a) Programming languages (e.g., HTML—HyperText Markup Language, VRML—Virtual Reality Modeling Language, Java, Java scripting, etc.)
     (b) Authoring Tools (easier to use than programming languages)
     (c) HTML Converters and Editors, etc.

7. **Servers**
     (a) HTTP servers, HTTPD software, Web site, URL—Uniform Resource Locator, etc.
     (b) Common Gateway Interface (CGI)—a way of interacting with the http or Web servers. CGI enables such things as image maps and fill-out forms to be run (http://www.sp.ph.ic.ac.uk/htmlinfo.html).

8. **Browsers and Other Applications**
     (a) Text-based browser, graphical browser, VRML browser, etc.
     (b) Links (e.g., hypertext links, hypermedia links, 3-D links, imagemaps, etc.)
     (c) Applications that can be added to Web browsers such as plug-ins.

WBI Features

A well-designed WBI program can provide numerous features conducive to learning and instruction. These features can encompass pedagogical, technological, organizational, institutional and ethical issues related to distance education on the World Wide Web as discussed by Hill (chapter 8). The more components a WBI program integrates, the more features it is able to offer.

WBI features can be divided into two categories: (1) *key features* and (2) *additional features*. *Key features* are inherent to the Web and are integral to WBI design. They are available for the designers to incorporate within WBI lessons. In contrast, *additional features* are dependent on the quality and sophistication of WBI design. The effectiveness of additional features largely depends on how well the key features are incorporated into the design of WBI. The following are examples of some key features and additional features:

1. **Key Features**
   Interactive, multimedial, open system, online search, device-distance-time independent, globally accessible, electronic publishing, uniformity world-wide, online resources, distributed, cross-cultural interaction, multiple expertise, industry supported, learner-controlled, etc.

2. **Additional Features**
   Convenient, self contained, ease of use, online support, authentic, course security, environmentally friendly, non-discriminatory, cost effective, ease of coursework development and maintenance, collaborative learning, formal and informal environments, online evaluation, virtual cultures, etc.

Both key features and additional features are listed in the Appendix to this chapter, beginning on page 11, in their respective order. These features are discussed in relation to their contributing components and their importance to WBI learning environments. Each feature is described in terms of its capabilities and possible limitations.

Conclusion

As the Information Age evolves and technical advances make resources more accessible, the Web will be a viable medium to facilitate learning. WBI has the ability to provide rich learning environments in a global, democratic, and interactive manner. WBI design requires careful consideration of the Web's potential in relation to instructional design principles. An understanding of capabilities of WBI components and features can facilitate the design of meaningful learning environments and relevant learning opportunities.

References and Suggested Readings

Alexander, S. (1995). Teaching and learning on the World Wide Web (http://www.scu.edu.au/ausweb95/papers/education2/alexander/).

Andrews, D. H., & Goodson, L. K. (1980). A comparative analysis of models of instructional design. *Journal of Instructional Development, 3*(4), 2–16.

Banathy, B. H. (1991). *Systems designs of education: A journey to create the future.* Englewood Cliffs, NJ: Educational Technology Publications.

Banathy, B. H. (1992). *A systems view of education: Concepts and principles for effective practice.* Englewood Cliffs, NJ: Educational Technology Publications.

Berge, Z. L., & Collins, M. P. (Eds.). (1995). *Computer-mediated communication and the online classroom* (Vols. 1–3). Cresskill, NJ: Hampton Press.

December, J., & Randall, N. (1995). *The World Wide Web 1996 unleashed* (3rd ed). Indianapolis, IN.

Dede, C. (1996). The evolution of constructivist learning environments: Immersion in distributed, virtual worlds. In B. G. Wilson (Ed.), *Constructivist learning environments: Case studies in instructional design* (pp. 165–175). Englewood Cliffs, NJ: Educational Technology Publications.

Dick, W., & Carey, L. (1996). *The systematic design of instruction* (4th ed.). New York: Harper Collins Publishers.

Donders, O., Eek, M., & Remmers, E. (1995). World Wide Web and its potential for self-guided learning (http://www.to.utwente.nl/ism/online95/campus/library/online95/online95.htm).

Duchastel (1996). Design for Web-based learning. *Proceedings of the WebNet-96 World Conference of the Web Society*. San Francisco.

Duffy, T. M., & Jonassen, D. H. (Eds.). (1992). *Constructivism and the technology of instruction: A conversation*. Hillsdale, NJ: Lawrence Erlbaum Associates.

Gagné, R., Briggs, L., & Wager, W. (1992) *Principles of instructional design* (4th ed.). New York: Harcourt, Brace, Jovanovich.

Harasim, L., Hiltz, S. R., Teles, L., & Turoff, M. (1995). *Learning networks: A field guide to teaching and learning online*. Cambridge, MA: MIT Press.

Hiltz, S. R. (1994). *The virtual classroom: Learning without limits via computer networks*. Norwood, NJ: Ablex Publishing.

Hiltz, S. R. (1995). Impacts of college-level courses via asynchronous learning networks: Focus on students (http://www.njit.edu/njIT/Department/CCCC/VC/Papers/Async_Learn/Philly.html).

Hughes, K. (1994). Entering the World Wide Web: A guide to cyberspace (http://www.eit.com/web/www.guide/).

Jonassen, D. H. (1996). *Computers in the classroom: Mindtools for critical thinking*. Englewood Cliffs, NJ: Prentice-Hall.

Kearsley, G. (1996, Winter). The World Wide Web: Global access to education. *Educational Technology Review, 5*, 26–30.

Kemp, J. E., Morrison, G. R., & Ross, S. M. (1994). *Designing effective instruction*. New York: Merrill.

Khan, B. H., Murphy, K., & Lopez, C. (1996, March). Models for collaborative teaching/learning at a distance (pp. 524–527). In R. Robin, J. D. Price, J. Willis, & D. A. Willis (Eds.), *Technology and Teacher Education Annual, 1996*. Charlottesville, VA: Association for the Advancement of Computing in Education.

Khan, B. H. (1995, March/April). Obstacles encountered during stages of the educational change process. *Educational Technology, 35*(2), 43–46.

Khan, B. H., & Reigeluth, C. M. (1993, June). Educational systems design: An integrated, disciplined inquiry in the nation's schools of education. *Educational Technology, 33*(6), 36–40.

Kilby, T. (1996). What is Web-based training? (http://www.clark.net/pub/nractive/alt1.html).

Kinzie, M. B. (1996). Frog dissection via the World Wide Web: Implications for widespread delivery of instruction. *Educational Technology Research and Development, 44*(2), 59–69.

Leshin, C. B., Pollock, J., & Reigeluth, C.M. (1992) *Instructional design strategies and tactics*. Englewood Cliffs, NJ: Educational Technology Publications.

Lin, X. D., Bransford, J. D., Hmelo, C. E., Kantor, R. J., Hickey, D. T., Secules, T., Petrosino, A. J., Goldman, R., & The Cognition and Technology Group at Vanderbilt. (1995). Instructional design and development of learning communities: An invitation to a dialogue. *Educational Technology, 35*(5), 53–63.

McGreal, R. (1996). Roy's list of a dozen things that can go wrong in a World Wide Web course or even worse. *The Distance Educator, 2*(2), p. 6.

McManus, T. F. (1996). Delivering instruction on the World Wide Web (http://www.edb.utexas.edu/coe/depts/ci/it/projects/wbi/wbi.html).

Murphy, K., Khan, B., Knupfer, N., & Cifuentes, L. (1997, February). Implementing online student-to-student distance dialogue: Adding depth to local course offerings. Paper accepted for presentation at the Annual Meeting of the Association for Educational Communications and Technology (AECT), Albuquerque, NM.

New Brunswick Distance Education, Inc. (1995). Learning on the Web (http://cnet.unb.ca/lotw/page020.html).

Reigeluth, C. M. (Ed.). (1983). *Instructional design theories and models: An overview of their current status*. Hillsdale, NJ: Lawrence Erlbaum Associates.

Reigeluth, C. M. (1995). Educational systems development and its relationship to ISD. In G. J. Anglin (Ed.), *Instructional technology* (pp. 84–93). Englewood, CO: Libraries Unlimited.

Reigeluth, C. M., & Khan, B. H. (1994, February). Do instructional systems design (ISD) and educational systems design (ESD) really need each other? Paper presented at the Annual Meeting of the Association for Educational Communications and Technology (AECT), Nashville, TN.

Rheingold, H. (1993). *The Virtual community*. Reading, MA: Addison-Wesley.

Romiszowski, A. J. (1981). *Designing instructional systems*. East Brunswick, NJ: Nichols.

Schwier, R. A., & Misanchuk, E. R. (1993). *Interactive multimedia instruction*. Englewood Cliffs, NJ: Educational Technology Publications.

Sherry, L. (1996). Raising the prestige of online articles. *Intercom, 43*(7), 24–25, 43.

Shotsberger, P. G. (1996). Instructional uses of the World Wide Web: Exemplars and precautions. *Educational Technology, 36*(2), 47–50.

Smith, P. L., & Ragan, T. J. (1993). *Instructional design*. New York: Macmillan Publishing Company.

Spiro, R. J., Feltovich, P. J., Jacobson, M. J., & Coulson, R. L. (1992). Cognitive flexibility, constructivism, and hypertext: Random access instruction for advanced knowledge acquisition in ill-structured domains. In T. M. Duffy & D. H. Jonassen (Eds.), *Constructivism and the technology of instruction: A conversation* (pp. 57–75). Hillsdale, NJ: Lawrence Erlbaum Associates.

Stancil, D. D. (1995). The Virtual lab: Engineering the future (http://www.ece.cmu.edu/afs/ece/class/projects/badelt/www/virtual-lab.html).

Tittel, E., & Gaither, M. (1995). *60 minute guide to Java*. Foster City, CA: IDG Books Worldwide, Inc.

Valauskas, E. J., & Ertel, M. (1996). *The Internet for teachers and school library media specialists*. New York: Neal-Schuman Publishers.

Willis, J. (1995). A recursive, reflective, instructional design model based on constructivist-interpretivist theory. *Educational Technology, 35*(6), 5–23.

Wilson, B. G. (1995). Metaphors of instruction: Why we talk about learning environments. *Educational Technology, 35*(5), 25–30.

Wiggins, R. (1995). *Growth of the Internet: An overview of a complicated subject* (http://www.msu.edu//staff/rww/netgrow.html).

Wilson, B.G. (Ed.). (1996). *Constructivist learning environments: Case studies in instructional design*. Englewood Cliffs, NJ: Educational Technology Publications.

Acknowledgment

I would like to thank Brent Wilson, Lorraine Sherry, and Marisa Nelson for their critical reading of this chapter. I would also like to thank my students and colleagues for their review of this chapter.

The Author

Badrul H. Khan is Assistant Professor and Coordinator of the Educational Technology graduate program at the University of Texas at Brownsville.

e-mail, World Wide Web
khanb@utb1.utb.edu
http://www.utb.edu/~khanb/khan.html

Appendix
Features and Components Associated with WBI Learning Environments

Features	Components*	Relationship to WBI
Interactive	Internet tools, hyperlinks, browsers, servers, authoring programs, instructional design, etc.	WBI students can interact with each other, with instructors, and online resources. Instructors and experts may act as facilitators. They can provide support, feedback, and guidance via both synchronous and asynchronous communications. Asynchronous communication (i.e., e-mail, listservs, etc.) allows for time-independent interaction, whereas synchronous communication (i.e., conferencing tools) allows for live interaction.
Multimedial	Browsers, authoring programs, Web-based conferencing tools, etc.	A WBI course can be designed to address all students' learning styles by incorporating a variety of multimedia elements, such as text, graphics, audio, video, animation, etc. For WBI courses, students can browse through libraries, museums, and archives, or consult experts from around the globe. However, use of text based browsers (e.g., Lynx) limits users to only textual materials. Limited bandwidth and large file sizes also limit the speed of downloading multimedia elements used in WBI.
Open System	Internet and World Wide Web	WBI is an open system. Learners have the freedom to move outside their environment, as opposed to a closed system (e.g., book, CD-ROM), where they are confined to areas pre-determined by the designer. An open system fosters more user control. However, it is more difficult to design an open system because the designer agrees to give up a certain amount of control to the user (Jones & Farquhar, chapter 28). There is a potential for chaos and entropy in poorly designed open learning environments because learners are apt to diverge from their original task when they have too many choices (Wilson, 1995).
Online Search	Search engines, gophers, etc.	Students in a WBI course can use a searchable course glossary (Goldberg, chapter 37). They can also use search engines to find relevant online resources related to course content and research projects. Students are able to link to Web site documents by indexing words found in the title, the body of text, or by counting the number of times words occur in the text (Maddux, chapter 35).

* The components included in the Appendix do not strictly follow component categories provided earlier in this chapter. Please note that the Appendix does not provide an inclusive list, but offers some examples of components that contribute to the different features.

Features	Components	Relationship to WBI
Device, Distance, and Time Independent	Internet and World Wide Web	Students can enroll in a WBI course from anyplace in the world (distance-independent) using any computer platform (device independent) at any time of the day or night (time independent). A WBI course developed on one platform can be read or viewed on other platforms.
Globally Accessible	Computers, modems, connections, Internet service providers, servers, browsers, etc.	Information and resources from around the world can be accessed by anyone from anywhere in the world as long as he or she has a computer with an Internet connection. It is important to realize that not everyone has this access (McManus, 1996), and that some access can be only text based. For WBI courses, students can browse through libraries, museums, and archives, or consult experts around the globe. The rapid access to resources can promote higher levels of student involvement and motivation. However, file size and transfer speed are limiting factors. Limited bandwidth means slower performance for sound, video and graphics. Speed problems can make WBI less efficient and less effective.
Electronic Publishing	E-mail, listervs newsgroups, servers, HTML editors, authoring tools, etc.	The Web provides an easy mechanism for electronic publishing. Both instructors and students are able to author and publish their work to a global audience. The posting of student projects, papers, and other student work may be used for modeling, discussion, or review in WBI (Bannan & Milheim, chapter 50). Students' ability to publish their work on the Web serves as a powerful motivating force, which leads to improved effort and self-esteem (Kearsley, 1996). Another benefit is that students can be supported through interactive peer reviews from the global educational community (Sherry, 1996).
Uniformity World-Wide	Internet and World Wide Web	The open standard of the Web allows anyone in the world to create and post Web documents using common scripting language and standard Internet addresses. The Web uses a common scripting language called HTML, which is extremely flexible and functional across all platforms, and is accessible to all users world-wide. The Uniform Resource Locator (URL) addressing system is also widely accessible over the Internet. Having a consistent URL address structure makes Web browsing easier for WBI students. This open standard makes it easier for instructors to develop WBI courses. As more and more WBI courses are developed, students will have alternative options to take the courses they want. Before taking a WBI course, students can view both course and instructor information (if provided by the course).

Features	Components	Relationship to WBI
Online Resources	Internet and World Wide Web	The Web provides instant and unlimited access to online resources. These resources can be up-to-the-minute and archival. Access to new developments and discoveries is immediately available to the learner (Donders, Eek, & Remmers, 1995). The latest updated entry is usually indicated within the Web page. This feature provides instructors with access to information sources that are more dynamic, enabling them to incorporate recent examples into course materials (Butler, chapter 57). WBI students, instructors and experts are able to publish previously authored documents on their own WBI course archives, making them available for worldwide use of resources.
Distributed	Internet tools, hyperlinks, databases, servers, CD-ROMs, etc.	The multimedia documents now available on the Web are spread over hundreds of network servers all over the world. The Web is distributed because there is no centralized control, and anyone can be an information publisher (http://cnet.unb.ca/lotw/page016.html). These multimedia resources are easily attainable and provide a variety of materials so that learning becomes more relevant for all users (Kearsley, 1996). All the materials on the Web can be downloaded and printed (some restrictions may apply) from any WBI course and any other Web sources.
Cross-cultural Interaction	Internet and World Wide Web	WBI provides a medium that allows students and instructors to communicate online with sources from all over the world. Not only do students benefit from multi-perspective views of subject matter, but they also serve as representatives of their own cultures. The ability to explore and learn about distant cultures and civilizations is facilitated through the Internet. Learners are not limited to individual authors', editors', or instructors' points of view.
Multiple Expertise	Internet and World Wide Web	WBI courses can take advantage of sources available on the Web that are provided by experts from various fields. The electronic community can provide a variety of perspectives from outside experts to guest lecturers (Bannan & Milheim, chapter 50). Experiences and instruction that come directly from the sources and experts represented on the Web can tremendously benefit students.

Features	Components	Relationship to WBI
Industry Supported	Hardware, software, browsers, search engines, educational Web sites, etc.	WBI developers can access information about almost any hardware and software on the Web because the companies that produce these materials have their own Websites. Many of the Internet applications can be downloaded free of charge from companies' Websites. Students can, therefore, download appropriate software for WBI courses. In most cases, educational enterprises are allowed to use the software with little or no cost. Companies may also contribute to the Web through product development or sponsorship of educational sites.
Learner-Controlled	Internet tools, authoring programs, hyperlinks, instructional design, etc.	The Web facilitates a democratic learning environment by permitting the learner to influence what is learned, how it is learned, and the order in which it is learned. (Schwier & Misanchuk, 1993). The filtered environment of the Web allows students the choice to actively participate in discussion or simply observe in the background. WBI puts students in control so they have a choice of content, time, feedback and a wide range of media for expressing their understandings (Relan & Gillani, chapter 4). This facilitates student responsibility and initiative by promoting ownership of learning. The learner-control offered by WBI is beneficial for the inquisitive student, but the risk of becoming lost in the Web and not fulfilling learner expectations can be a problem and will require strong instructional support (Duchastel, 1996).
Convenient	Internet tools, hyperlinks, forms, browsers, modems, connections, Internet service providers, etc.	WBI courses can be convenient to students, instructors and institutions. Students can register, do coursework, conduct research, and communicate with the instructor via the Internet without having to physically travel. Instructors can update course materials with relative ease, provide guidance and support, both synchronously and asynchronously, without being confined to a classroom and office hours. Institutions' online support systems can administer students' enrollment, tuition and course grades via the Internet so that operational and employment costs are minimized. However, accessing the Web, downloading multimedia files, and adjusting to a new medium can sometimes be challenging.
Self-contained	Internet and World Wide Web	A WBI course can be totally self-contained, that is, it can be taken completely online. It can be designed to be all-inclusive, requiring no resources outside the Web. Students can log on anytime they wish, access all resources, take quizzes and exams, and receive results. It allows learners to meet their own special needs in a self-paced and self-assessing environment.

Features	Components	Relationship to WBI
Ease of Use	A standard point and click navigation system. Common User Interface, Search Engines, Browsers, Hyperlinks, etc.	A well-designed WBI course with intuitive interfaces can anticipate learners' needs and satisfy the learners' natural curiosity to explore the unknown. This capability can greatly reduce students' frustration levels and facilitate a user-friendly learning environment. However, delays between a learner's mouse click and the response of the system can contribute to the frustration level of users. The hypermedia environment in a WBI course allows students to explore and discover resources which best suit their individual needs. While this type of environment facilitates learning, it should be noted that learners may lose focus on a topic due to the wide variety of sources that may be available on a WBI course. Also, information may not always be accessed because of common problems related to servers such as connection refusal, no DNS entry, etc.
Online Support	E-mail, listservs, 1-800 number, FAQ, fax, etc.	A WBI course can provide the learner with online resources that aid in instruction or serve as information facilitators if students encounter unanticipated technical problems or questions on the course content.
Authentic	Internet and World Wide Web	WBI courses can be designed to promote authentic learning environments by addressing real world problems and issues relevant to the learner. "The most significant aspect of the Web for education at all levels is that it dissolves the artificial wall between the classroom and the 'real world'" (Kearsley, 1996). Kearsley (1996) emphasizes that accessibility to world wide information brings realism and authentic learning experiences to teachers and students, regardless of their educational level.
Course Security	Servers, authoring programs, Internet service providers, gateway service providers, etc.	Only instructors or designated individuals can modify or alter information on a WBI course with the proper password. If an institution prefers, it can make a WBI course accessible to only those who are enrolled and have assigned passwords. This limited accessibility enables both students and instructors to send and receive homework, assignments, reports and exams confidentially. It is important for both instructors and students to take precautionary measures in sending their materials to the correct address. McGreal (1996) notes that a confidential memo to a student could be inadvertently posted to the entire class or it could get copied by a student and appear on alt.newsgroup.

Features	Components	Relationship to WBI
Environmentally Friendly	Internet and World Wide Web	The Web can promote environmentally sound educational practices. Supplying course materials and instruction to students via the World Wide Web helps reduce the physical and environmental burdens imposed by student travel. Students are able to take WBI courses without traveling to the campus; this reduces the degree of traffic pollution.
Non-discriminatory	E-mail, newsgroups, listservs, MUDs, chat, IRC, etc.	The Web can facilitate a democratic medium which makes WBI accessible to all users regardless of their location, age, ethnicity, gender, language, physical limitations, etc. The shared, filtered environment of the Web also affords anonymity so that communication and interaction are less inhibitive. Users feel more secure while actively participating in WBI projects. Non-native speakers may feel more confident about posting their work or comments because they have time to process their thoughts before posting (http://cnet.unb.ca/lotw/page020.html). It is important to note that WBI courses offered in multilingual formats will be very helpful to students, especially those whose native languages are not written in English characters.
Cost-Effective	Internet and World Wide Web	WBI can be cost-effective for students, instructors, and institutions. Students' traveling, parking, and text book costs are minimized. Instructors do not need to print syllabi or handouts. Institutions' operating costs decrease because the cost of physical facilities and maintenance is minimized. WBI students do not need to use physical classroom facilities, nor do they need to crowd parking facilities if they have computers with Internet connections at home. However, the initial cost of computer equipment and connectivity may be prohibitive for some people.
Ease of Coursework Development and Maintenance	HTML, editors, authoring tools, servers, etc.	WBI uses common scripting language called Hyper Text Markup Language (HTML). HTML tags are easy to learn. There are many translators available that will add tags to the text. However, it is important to have a working knowledge of HTML in order to do simple trouble shooting (Descy, chapter 33). Web authoring tools are also very easy to use and require no technical expertise on the part of the course designer (Goldberg, chapter 37). Ease of coursework development tools allows instructors more time to concentrate on developing innovative and creative WBI lessons. *(Continued)*

Features	Components	Relationship to WBI
		(*Continued*) Ease of coursework maintenance benefits both instructors and students. The instructor can update WBI course information with relative ease. This "scaleable" quality makes it easy for instructors to customize their coursework by adding or deleting lessons or messages so they can meet the needs of all their students. This feature facilitates instruction so that quality of lessons continuously improves and up-to-date information is readily available. Course materials such as handouts, syllabi and the necessary resources for WBI class projects can be downloaded. Due to the ever-changing nature of the Web, many links may become obsolete because they are no longer active. It is important to include links in WBI that are consistently updated and/or a visitor counter that indicates a large amount of traffic (Voithofer, chapter 38).
Collaborative Learning	Internet tools, instructional design, etc.	Collaborative learning emphasizes cooperative efforts among faculty and students. This learning process stresses active participation and interaction on the part of both instructors and students (Hiltz, 1995). WBI creates a medium of collaboration, conversation, discussions, exchange, and communication of ideas (Relan & Gillani, chapter 4). The sharing of knowledge and resources engages students in higher level thinking skills, which promote active and interactive learning from multiple perspectives (Harasim, Calvert & Groenboer, chapter 18). WBI facilitates cooperative learning which extends beyond the classroom to potentially every classroom that is connected to the Internet (Relan & Gillani, chapter 4).
Formal and Informal Environments	Home pages, hyperlinks, computers, modems, connections, Internet service providers, etc.	WBI courses can support both formal and informal environments. Formal environments are instructor driven. The instructor provides the course syllabus, times for weekly "cyberlectures," assignments, references and related resources (McLellan, chapter 22). Informal environments are more student-centered where students submit their assignments, engage in discussion, and post anecdotes on the class listserv (McLellan, chapter 22).
Online Evaluation	Forms, e-mail, database, etc.	Online evaluation for WBI includes both assessment of learners and evaluation of the instruction. A variety of evaluation and assessment tools can be incorporated into a WBI course. Individual testing, participation in group discussions, questions and portfolio development can all be used to evaluate students' (*Continued*)

Features	Components	Relationship to WBI
		(*Continued*) progress (Rasmussen, Northrup & Lee, chapter 43). A WBI course can have a facility that allows students to submit instructor evaluations to the appropriate departments in an institution. A WBI course can also have a facility that allows students to submit comments about the design and delivery of the course to the instructional designer. The grades from students' quizzes, assignments, exams, and projects can be stored on a database. These grades would be available online to students once they have entered their password (Goldberg, chapter 37).
Virtual Cultures	Listservs, newsgroups, e-mail, multi-user	WBI extends the boundaries of traditional classroom learning (Relan & Gillani, chapter 4). The following are some of the virtual features that can be incorporated into WBI:
		Virtual Community: The Web fosters community building and networking. It serves as an environment for students to engage in a wide range of discussion topics with their peers and leading authorities in their field and creates a broader audience for their work other than the instructor (McLellan, chapter 22).
		Virtual Classroom: A virtual classroom creates an environment where online resources are used to facilitate collaborative learning among students, between students and instructors, and between a class and a wider academic and non-academic community (Hiltz, 1995).
		Virtual Office Hours: E-mail and newsgroups are some of the new methods of holding office hours. Instructors and students can also set up real-time question and answer sessions via Web based conferencing tools (Willis & Dickinson, chapter 9).
		Virtual Library: Students in WBI courses can use various Web-based virtual libraries on a variety of subjects. The World Wide Web Virtual Library (hosted on http://www.w3.org/) represents a massive, collaborative effort to gather and present information on a wide range of subjects (December & Randall, 1995).
		Virtual Field Trips: Learners are fully immersed in an interactive computer generated environment. Students can explore existing places or things to which they would otherwise not have access.
		Virtual Lab: Virtual labs provide students with an opportunity to get real-type lab experiences. This enhances the flexibility of laboratory education, and introduces students to the new paradigm of remote experimentation (Stancil, 1995).

2

The Evolution of the World Wide Web as an Emerging Instructional Technology Tool

David M. Crossman

Introduction

In 1957, at Syracuse University, a professor teaching a basic instructional technology course in which I was a student speculated that, "One day, we will have an instructional technology that will permit the display of information in any medium, on any subject, in any order, at any time." Most of us chuckled. After all, he was almost as young as we were, and was, no doubt, overwhelmed by his own enthusiasm. Surely this would not happen in my lifetime. I was underwhelmed.

In December of 1990, after a decade of preliminary work at the European Particle Physics Laboratory in Geneva, Switzerland, Tim Berners-Lee and his colleagues ran the first version of the World Wide Web. It was put up on the Internet at large in the summer of 1991.

Thus, in 33 years such a technology did emerge. Developed first to provide a way in which physicists could communicate more easily and more rapidly with each other, virtually every institution of any kind is scrambling to develop a "home page" and a presence on the Web. Led first by the military and major universities and research centers, the locus of Web activity has shifted to the commercial sector. Now, virtually every business from General Motors to the local pizza parlor advertises itself in cyberspace.

The prophecy of 1957 has been realized. The World Wide Web does provide information "...in any medium, on any subject, in any order, at any time." We might importantly add, "...in *any place*," since cyberspace permits information to be accessed virtually anywhere.

In mid-1996, as this chapter is being written, almost 40 years have passed since I sat in that classroom. In all of that time, no technology has emerged as rapidly as the World Wide Web. Not only is it on the lips of every educator and business person, but also the Web is common knowledge in virtually every walk of life. We are all rushing to put up home pages, and to share our lives, whether prudently or not, with the rest of the world. Many feel that the Web is the most important technology of our time.

Growth of the Web

Since 1991, when the Web was first released onto the Internet at large, extraordinary growth has taken place. In 1993, not only did the President and Vice President of the United States

19

come online with their own home pages, but also the Mosaic browser, developed by Marc Andreesen and his colleagues at the National Center for Supercomputing Applications at the University of Illinois, grew immensely. In 1994, the World Wide Web eclipsed telnet to become the second most popular service on the Net. In 1995, the Web surged forward to become the service with the most traffic on NSFNet, exceeding ftp-data for the first time. At roughly the same time, commercial e-mail providers such as CompuServe, America Online, and Prodigy began to provide Internet access.

In January of 1991, there were 376,000 hosts. In January of 1996, there were 9,472,000 hosts—an increase of 25 times. In January of 1991, there were 3,556 networks. In January of 1996, there were 93,671 networks—an increase of 26 times. Clearly, these figures will have to level off soon, but these figures cannot be viewed as anything but astonishing.

In 1995, the Internet was connected to 173 of 238 entities within the world. An entity is a geographical area identified by the ISO (International Standards Organization) two letter code, such as AF (Afghanistan). Thus, by June 15, 1995, 73% of the countries of the world were Internet connected to some degree (Landweber, 1996).

Although the Internet is widely thought to be controlled by no one, The Internet Society, founded in 1992 by Vinton Cerf, has made major contributions in encouraging the use of standard protocols, and, in particular, sponsoring workshops for connectivity in developing nations. Largely because of the efforts of the Internet Society staff, the Internet has become responsible for realizing the idea of the "global village" made famous by Marshall McLuhan. Cerf estimates that there will be 200 million computers on the Net by the year 2000 (Perry, 1996).

In Place of Space

The Web has a curious effect on space and time. Most students, and indeed most teachers, go to a particular place at a particular time for a particular class on a particular topic. The Internet in general and the Web in particular are gradually changing the ways in which we relate to those places.

Several years ago, in the loft of my Maine summer hideaway, I logged onto the AERA Committee C listserv devoted to Instruction and Learning. The topic was constructivism. Someone from Berkeley introduced an idea and inquired if there were others who could contribute. In a few minutes there was a response from the University of Edinburgh. In a few more, an educational researcher from the University of Graz in Austria commented. Then, someone from the University of Sydney. Finally, there was a long and thoughtful consideration of the issue from the University of Montreal. I sat transfixed! Here were four people who had never heard of each other, debating a professional issue of common concern—from the four corners of the earth! Magic! Howard Rheingold calls this a "virtual community" and has an excellent book of the same title (Rheingold, 1993). One of the interesting and lively debates I have had with my students this year is the question of the so-called "virtual community." Perhaps it is a real community, just one unconstrained by place and time. Thus it is with cyberspace. Our conventional ways of relating to space probably need to be examined. I maintain a lively e-mail correspondence with many students and colleagues all summer long from that little cottage in Maine. Many no doubt think I am slaving away in my office at the University. I'll never tell!

The Web as an Instructional Technology Tool

The growth of instructional technology has a fascinating history. The invention of the audio-cassette by Philips in 1962 put an easy-to-use recordable audio format in the hands of almost everyone. The development of the Beta format by Sony put a similar video format in the hands of millions. The subsequent development of VHS and the widespread sale of its manufacturing license by JVC made video commonplace. Indeed, even today when videodisc materials are available in a wide variety of formats—all superior to VHS—VHS prevails because it is such a widespread standard. For the same reason, the 35mm film cartridge format, developed by Leica in 1932, is used in all 35mm cameras today.

These technologies flourished for two reasons: (1) The format became standardized, and (2) the new technology was simpler to use.

So it is with the Web. The hypertext transfer protocol (http) is the standard form of the uniform resource locator used throughout the world. And so, a specific http form of URL will open a home page in Australia just as surely as another will open a requested page in Washington, D.C. Standardization provides this consistency of access. How about simplicity? Consider the Archie or Veronica search to locate appropriate ftp or gopher sites. Servers had to be found and parameters set. It was an awkward, complicated process. And it still is. The Web, fortunately, has bypassed all of that complexity. Through the use of a variety of search engines, such as Lycos, Infoseek, Yahoo, WebCrawler, and others, the simple entry of a key word or words yields a richness of information. Thus, the Web user has access to standardized protocols and simplicity of operation in addition to text, full color graphics and photography, full motion color video, and high fidelity sound. Is it any wonder that the Web is the fastest growing communication system in history?

Most students' first use of the Internet is e-mail. It is fast, it can be both written and read at one's convenience, and, provided one has institutional access, it is cheap (even totally free to the user). One also has a written record of correspondence that can be kept or deleted—or even printed!

For many students, e-mail has provided a way of communicating with faculty that is quite new. Thoughts can be composed at leisure and then sent. The reader enjoys the same convenience.

Gradually, some students have learned the operation of telnet, ftp, and gopher. Many have learned the advantages of Usenet and mailing lists. But all of this is text based and in black and white.

The World Wide Web is very different. Not only does it permit the use of most earlier Internet services, it is in color, deals easily with graphics and pictorial materials of all kinds, handles full motion video, and supports very high quality audio, all of which is accessible with commonly available hardware and software.

As the capabilities of the Web have become more widely known, understood, and applied, students and faculty have been quick to utilize its potential. Many have purchased computers and fast modems to access the Web at home. And many institutions have provided Web browsers in their computer laboratories, as well as providing SLIP drivers or PPP protocol software to facilitate home use.

I have just completed teaching a course dealing with many of the professional issues of instructional design and technology. During the course, we read William Mitchell's *City of Bits*, the complete text of which is available from the MIT Press (http://www-mitpress.mit.edu/). The chapters of the book are made available in hypertext, requiring that each student make specific access decisions as he or she reads (Mitchell, 1995).

In that same course, one student placed her term paper on a Web site, together with a rich variety of graphic and photographic material. Thus, the paper was available to every student with Web access. Others used e-mail to circulate bibliographic information to their classmates and me.

Common Knowledge: Pittsburgh

Clearly, schools must be connected before any electronic information flows in or out. Several years ago, I visited a school district near Pittsburgh which identified itself as being connected to the Internet. I was told to go to the school library. However, I found no terminals anywhere in the reading area. I asked a librarian who told me that the only connected machine was in the librarian's office. Investigation revealed that the occupant of the office had no idea of how to connect to the Internet. And, no students were permitted to touch it!

An example of an attempt to reverse this all-too-familiar situation is Common Knowledge: Pittsburgh, in the Pittsburgh Public Schools. This project, led by Professor Robert Carlitz of the Department of Physics & Astronomy at the University of Pittsburgh, is financed by the National Science Foundation and is a collaboration of the Pittsburgh Supercomputing Center, the University of Pittsburgh, and the Pittsburgh Public Schools. The project, now in its fifth year, has put Pittsburgh in a leadership position nationally, pointing the way to provide Internet access to city school districts. Efforts of this kind are flourishing throughout the country and are essential to provide public school access to the Web.

Concerns

Like most instructional technologies, the Web has both varied and unique characteristics. Equally, this remarkable communication system requires care in its use. It provides access to information in ways that are only now becoming real for many users. Larger than the largest library, the Web and its Internet parent carry more information than has ever before been gathered in any form. Remarkably, available search engines have provided very powerful access capabilities. So popular and important have these search engines become that several developed by faculty and students at Carnegie Mellon University and Stanford University and elsewhere have sold stock to the public, making large amounts of money for those individuals and institutions involved (Blumenstyk, 1996). As this chapter is being written, in mid-1996, Netscape has provided access on its home page to no fewer than 12 of these search engines.

In 1994, I secured a file requested by e-mail from a Brown University server (brownvm. brown.edu). In the body of the message I simply wrote, <list global>. In response to that request, I received a file 100 pages long identifying all known listservs. I repeated that request in 1996 and received a file 450 pages long, identifying listservs on every conceivable subject. Any of these thousands of listservs are available for subscription to anyone requesting them. The amount of information available is overwhelming.

Many teachers whose students use the Web are concerned about the question of authenticity and reliability of information on the Internet in general and the Web in particular. Even the most casual evening of Web surfing reveals incredible amounts of trivia, misinformation, bad manners, hostility, stupidity and other vagaries of humankind. Not unlike life. The Web, if anything, cries for critical thinking. Vinton Cerf, in the international publication of the Internet Society, *OnTheInternet*, writes:

> We truly must think about what we see and hear. We must evaluate and select. We must choose our guides. What better lesson than this to teach our young children to prepare themselves for a new century of social, economic and technological change?
>
> Let us make a new-century resolution to teach our children to think more deeply about what they see and hear. That, more than any other electronic filter, will build a foundation upon which truth can stand. (Cerf, 1996)

As an instructional technology, the Web is unique in its ability to not only carry a variety of media, but to do so from virtually anywhere, creating that "global village" we noted earlier. The Web permits the sharing of information as personal as one person to another or as public as one person to the entire world.

It has the potential to become the most comprehensive communication system ever developed. Clearly, the future is much more interesting than ever before.

References

Blumenstyk, G. (1996, May 10). Internet tools earn professors and students big winnings on Wall Street. *The Chronicle of Higher Education*, p. A28.

Cerf, V. G. (1996, April). *OnTheInternet*, 2(2), p. 37.

Landweber, L., (1996). *Connectivity table* (ftp://ftp.cs.wisc.edu/connectivity_table/).

Mitchell, W. J. (1995).*City of bits*. Cambridge, MA: The MIT Press (http://www-mitpress. mit.edu/).

Perry, J. (1996, April). Snappy dresser. Wine collector. Noted bon vivant. And father of the internet. *OnTheInternet*, 2(2), p. 37.

Rheingold, H. (1993). *The virtual community: Homesteading on the electronic frontier*. New York: HarperCollins.

Zakon, R. H. (1996). Hobbes' Internet timeline (http://info.isoc.org/guest/zakon/Internet/History/HIT.html).

Acknowledgment

I would like to thank Dr. Sandi Behrens of the Software Engineering Institute at Carnegie Mellon University for her careful reading of this chapter and her many helpful suggestions during its preparation.

The Author

David M. Crossman is Professor of Education, University of Pittsburgh, Pittsburgh, Pennsylvania.

e-mail, World Wide Web
   dmc+@pitt.edu/~idthp
   http://info.pitt.edu/~idthp

3

Web-Based Distance Learning and Teaching: Revolutionary Invention or Reaction to Necessity?

Alexander J. Romiszowski

A Systems Analysis of the Workplace of the Future

In order to try to make sense of the future into which we may be moving, we could do worse than to adopt the well-tried and tested "systems approach" for the design of a scenario of the educational and training systems of the future. As a first step in this process, we must perform a systems analysis of the "end-product" of the proposed new educational system, that is, the new type of "knowledge work" that it is postulated will become prevalent in the networked society of the 21st century.

The knowledge worker is somebody who earns a living by using knowledge in order to create new knowledge. The knowledge worker must have well developed capabilities of critical analysis in order to be able to select from the vast array of available information that which is of relevance and value, and a high measure of creativity in order to invent or develop the new knowledge that may offer a competitive advantage to his/her organization. In the future fast moving and open information society, this advantage will not last very long before the new knowledge becomes public knowledge and many people or organizations may act on it. Therefore, the task of knowledge workers is to continually renew the process of knowledge creation, thus keeping themselves, or their employers, ahead of the competition.

Such high levels of critical insight and creativity are what traditionally single out the exceptionally intelligent human beings from the rank and file. However, as computer software becomes more capable and intelligent and replaces many of the routine tasks formerly performed by human beings, then maybe the only area of future occupation where human beings will excel will be in this form of creative knowledge work. The goal of the aspiring educated human being may therefore be focused ever more on the acquisition of the necessary skills to be a successful knowledge worker. The purpose of this chapter is to investigate in what way such a societal trend, if indeed it comes about, would affect education and training needs, processes, and, particularly, delivery systems as we move into the next century.

The basic conceptual model of a "system" is some "process," acting within some "context" from which it acquires resources or "inputs" and to which it delivers results or "outputs." In our case, the process component is our knowledge worker or, if we wish to take a broader view, an organization which is keeping abreast of its competition by engaging in knowledge work. The principal input to this process is the existing knowledge or information that has already been discovered, organized, and made available in meaningful and useful ways. However, the amount of information in the world in general is estimated to be doubling every few years. The more information there is, the more it tends to become difficult to find the specific information that may be of particular relevance to a particular activity or problem situation that we may be facing at a specific point in time. We are faced with the paradoxical situation of having to act more quickly in order to keep abreast of change, but, as the total amount of information available to us increases, finding the task of new knowledge generation more difficult and possibly slower than in the past.

If we now turn to the output side of our system, we see a similar dilemma. The expected output from knowledge work is some form of creative and unique solution or suggestion for "keeping ahead of the competition." We are faced with the paradoxical situation that all of us, as individuals or organizations, will be forced to adapt faster and more creatively to an ever changing environment in order to be able to survive and prosper. On the other hand, this very activity of rapid inventive knowledge generation and its implementation in order to keep abreast of change will contribute to the acceleration of the process of change within the environment, thus forcing us to adapt and invent still more.

We therefore see, both on the input and the output sides of our system, that the impact of new technologies, on the one hand, offers us tools with which to deal with the new challenges that a changing society or workplace presents and, on the other hand, those same technologies actually are responsible for the changes that are generating these new and ever changing challenges. Is there a danger that these forces for ever faster and greater change may lead society to a point where the whole system disintegrates? Such catastrophes happen in electrical, electronic, and other types of engineering systems when there is an absence of an effective control system.

The general systems theory principles of homeostasis and regulation suggest that a control system, to be effective, must be similar in complexity and variety to the system being controlled (Ashby, 1956). This implies that whatever regulatory systems exist in society as a whole, every process component must possess its own self-regulating mechanisms. For example, government legislation and controls cannot hope to control the directions of change in future society without the cooperation of the economically active organizations that compose the society. And these organizations are not fully "under control" if their key workers do not collaborate participatively toward the same set of global objectives. In short, the responsibility of the knowledge worker goes beyond the creation of new knowledge in order to deal successfully with environmental change, but encompasses also the judgment of which changes should be promoted and which should be controlled in order that the overall system does not get into a state of disequilibrium. How may the knowledge workers of the future develop the abilities to control change so that it may be beneficial to the majority of citizens as well as to the organization that employs them?

The often suggested answer to this sort of question is "through appropriate education and training." But what are the skills and competencies that the next generation of the world's citizens should master in order to become effective and responsible knowledge workers? And what are the key methodologies of the educational systems required by society in the 21st century in order to implement this new curriculum? In order to form a model of the curriculum, we once more start by conceptualizing the outcomes of this future educational process, that is, the key competencies of an effective knowledge worker.

Self-Directed and Just-in-Time Learning

One increasingly important competency in the future society will be "self-directed-learning." Much emphasis is being placed in modern school curricula on "learning to learn," as a response to the realization that in the future, learning will be a lifelong occupation, largely occurring outside of the formal educational institution (Benson, 1994). One area for lifelong learning, already evident in modern, highly computerized organizations, is the need to continually learn to use new tools for the accessing, processing, and transformation of information into new knowledge. These tools today typically take the form of software application packages. The very rapid rate of substitution of these tools and their increasing sophistication has led to a significant conceptual reorganization of the training function in such environments. The talk today is of "just-in-time training" (Carr, 1992; Goodyear & Steeples, 1992; Plewes, 1992). Just as the concept of just-in-time inventory control in business management signifies an attempt to keep stock levels very close to the levels of utilization, so that purchases are made just when required, so in the area of knowledge and skills acquisition through training, the just-in-time concept argues that the person who requires a new skill should learn it at the time when it is required and never before.

Just-in-time training, in its implementation, implies a high level of individualization and self-direction in the training and education processes, so that each individual may learn just what he or she needs at the time when he or she needs it. Almost by definition, this implies a radical change in the training delivery systems from place-based and time-fixed group instruction (characteristic of our conventional education in the past) to on-the-job distributed training that may be utilized, under learner-control, at any appropriate time or place. This, in turn, implies the use of technology-based training delivery systems (Benson, 1994).

The just-in-time training concept is congruent with the general principles of "performance technology." The identifying characteristic of the performance technology approach is to relate all training and education activity to its effect on relevant job-related performance that may be measured, tracked, and evaluated on a regular basis (Clark, 1994; Gilbert, 1978; Langdon, 1991). In the performance technology approach, training and education are but a part of the total armory of techniques for enhancing and maintaining human performance in the organization. Other techniques are: just-in-time information provision in the form of reference material or job aids; improved incentives; improved feedback on the results of performance; appropriate consequences (both rewards and punishments); and so on (Davies, 1994; Gilbert, 1978; Harless, 1992; Rossett, 1992). In the networked environments of modern organizations, and, increasingly, even in the home, access to information-sharing networks (including, but not exclusively, the Internet) is providing a medium capable of furnishing all manner of relevant information to the worker at the place of work, eliminating much previous travel to courses, conferences or libraries.

Self-Directed Knowledge Acquisition and Hypermedia

However, that is not the whole picture. On the input side, in order to perform as a creative knowledge worker, the person must first access the information that is available and relevant in order to put it to use. In order to facilitate this process, the information should be available in a well-organized form. The organization of vast amounts of information into meaningful structures is no easy task. The difficulty lies partly in the complexity of analysis required to come to conclusions about how best to organize and present subject matter to a variety of different user groups with different motives for using the information. It comes also from the sheer enormity of the task, given the vast amount of information which is generated every year. Finally, it comes from the difficulty of arranging access to the resulting vast libraries of information for the potential end-users.

A technology-based solution to these issues has appeared in the form of hypertext or hypermedia systems. The concept of a "universe of information" composed of electronically interlinked documents was suggested by computer scientists as early as Bush (1945). The concept was realized in practice by Englebart (1963) and Nelson (1965). However, it was only in the last decade or so that the large-scale implementation of the concept has resulted in practical hypertext systems becoming available to the public at large (Conklin, 1987; McAleese, 1989).

The World Wide Web is the latest embodiment of hypertext/hypermedia environments, allowing the practical implementation and use of hypertext environments to graduate from the relatively small stand-alone systems, previously developed with tools such as HyperCard or ToolBook, to much larger and universally available systems of structured information.

The Metacognitive Skills of Information Analysis

Another important aspect to consider is that of the skills and capabilities required by the knowledge worker in order to locate and assess the value of specific items that are "out there" in the expanding universe of information. The skills of locating information in a complex and vast library are not easy to master. However, the user can be helped by a combination of systems for the organization of information and for online help.

A second set of skills, also not that easy to master, is necessary for the analysis and evaluation of information, once it is located, to judge whether it is useful for the particular task which one is trying to accomplish. These are the "critical thinking skills" that most educational curricula attempt to develop, but at present only seem to succeed in actually doing with a small proportion of the population. However, as we move into the age of the knowledge worker and the knowledge organization, the importance of these skills will increase. We may even reach the situation in which only those human beings who can demonstrate a high level of skill in critical analysis will be likely to hold down a challenging and well-rewarded job. Therefore, improvement in the effectiveness of education in this area of skill-building is a critical issue.

Critical-analysis skills development is the area of research that has concerned many cognitive scientists in recent years. One aspect of the problem is concerned with making sense of the information available. However well-organized and well-communicated some of the information sources may become, it is unrealistic to expect that all information generated in the world of the future will be written by expert communicators, or be subjected to analysis and reorganization by instructional designers. It will often fall on the end-user to make sense of imperfectly structured and communicated information sources. Research on techniques of information analysis, such as Concept Mapping (not to be confused with Information Mapping, which will be discussed later) has demonstrated the potential for improving students' information analysis and comprehension skills (Novak, 1991; Young, 1994). These techniques are now being applied both to the improvement of electronic online communications by the incorporation of concept maps as a form of advance organizers, content guides or browsing tools in online information resources (Reader & Hammond, 1994; Schroeder, 1994), and to the development of improved skill in dealing with online study materials by special preparatory concept-map drawing exercises (Naidu & Bernard, 1992; Russell & Meikamp, 1994).

The Skills of Creative Problem Solving

Let us now move from the input-output (information and performance) considerations that we have been addressing once more to the "process"; that is, the activity of the knowledge worker when utilizing relevant available knowledge to create useful new knowledge. The role of the knowledge worker will be to add value to existing knowledge by transforming it into more application-specific knowledge that, for a time, will be the unique property of that individual or organization. This highlights yet one more critical set of thinking skills. In addition to the skills of analysis, used to identify relevant knowledge and the skills of evaluation to judge the usefulness of this knowledge for the task at hand, the knowledge worker must possess skills of synthesis, or the putting together of ideas in novel ways in order to create new ideas.

We are here using the terms of Analysis, Synthesis and Evaluation as used in Bloom's taxonomy of objectives in the cognitive learning domain (Bloom *et al.*, 1956) to describe the higher order outcomes of learning associated with creative or productive thinking. The fact that Bloom's taxonomy has been around for a long time as a theoretical construct for instructional designers does not imply that education and training systems necessarily always do a good job of developing these creative thinking skills. As we progress into the 21st century, however, the importance of appropriate strategies and methodologies for the development of these three categories of creative thinking skill will become increasingly important. It may be argued that this is where the core curriculum of any basic schooling system should focus its attention in the future.

The above-mentioned observation, that educational systems may not always do a good job in the area of higher-order thinking skills, should not be taken to imply that there is no known methodology or technology appropriate for their development. Many successful programs for the development of critical thinking skills have been developed and implemented. Analysis of such programs reveals that they tend to have certain characteristics in common. They tend to use "experiential learning" techniques. That is, they tend to set up learning situations which present a problem or a complex task for the learners to deal with and then encourage and assist the learners to draw general conclusions and establish general principles that may explain or predict across a range of similar situations (Romiszowski, 1981; Steinaker & Bell, 1979). One teaching methodology that is particularly successful in the development of critical thinking is the case study method. This typically puts the student in an experiential learning situation of having to deal with a real or simulated problem situation. Study of the specific case then leads to a discussion in which general principles and concepts that underlie the case are identified and then tested out on other case examples for verification of their general validity. Other techniques used for the development of critical thinking include small-group discussions, simulation games, project-based work, and collaborative problem-solving activities. It may be noted that most of the techniques known to work in this type of learning situation involve small-group interaction, in-depth discussion, a lot of interchange of ideas between the participants, and an approach to the conduct of the teaching/learning activity that is flexible, collaborative, and "conversational." Another term that is often associated with this group of instructional techniques is "experiential" learning (Romiszowski, 1984).

The Areas of Competency, and Related Technologies

To summarize so far, we note that the mix of key competencies that are required by tomorrow's knowledge workers involve performance-related competencies, not only in terms of successful and creative solutions of novel problems but also in terms of efficient and rapid learning of the use of new tools and techniques that are constantly appearing in the job environment. In this area, the relatively older traditions of instructional design continue to be relevant and useful. It is possible to identify specific knowledge and skills required in order to master the tools of the job. The one difference is that as the tools are replaced at ever greater frequency, the emphasis in the teaching/learning process is on quick, just-in-time learning. The emphasis is also on not learning the details of utilization of a tool if some sort of on-the-job reference or performance support system proves to be adequate.

On the input side, the skills of information access, location, analysis, and evaluation are of importance. Here we may see the need for better information provision through better structuring and online support of tomorrow's electronic libraries, through better authoring of the materials to be included in these libraries, and also through improving the skills of our citizens in dealing with complex and vast libraries of information accessible over networks from a distance.

In the middle, between input and output, is the process that transforms existing knowledge into new knowledge. This is seen as the major point of importance in future educational provision for the citizens of a highly technological and networked society. In this area, the relatively well established methodologies of experiential learning and reflective learning are seen as the best available models at this time.

Delivery Technologies for the Future Curriculum
Electronic Performance Support Systems

Let us now consider some of the technologies and some of the methodologies that may be of particular relevance in each of the areas of critical competence that we have identified. To start with the output side of our picture, the performance technology approach to design typically uses a mix of instructional materials and reference or job aid materials to support the performer in the job situation. In future networked societies, it will be ever more common to find that both the training materials and reference materials are in fact electronically stored and distributed. This performance-support software that may be either stand-alone, for example a CD-ROM disc accessed on an individual personal computer, or may be networked from some central server to many users. This trend to online performance support is a natural tendency, not only because of the potential benefits that electronic delivery and control of learning and reference materials may have, but also because in the networked society or job environment, the computers and networks are already there for other reasons and it is both economical and convenient to use the same tools and distribution systems for learning and reference materials. As this tendency developed, we have recently seen the birth of a new form of instructional technology, which has gained the name "Electronic Performance Support Systems" (Gery, 1991; Milheim, 1992; Stevens & Stevens, 1995).

An Electronic Performance Support System, or EPSS, is an integrated system of training and reference materials, possibly some software tools, such as special-purpose spreadsheets or simulation "shells" for testing out hypotheses, and whatever else may help to both develop and maintain the performance of persons carrying out a particular set of tasks. This integrated system of job-related information is delivered to those persons, online, as part of the software that supports their job, by means of a general purpose computer/workstation that typically performs other job-related functions as well.

In many current applications of EPSS, the delivery medium is a local area network of computers owned by the employing organization. But, as the EPSS philosophy spreads (as it undoubtedly will) to supporting human performance in more general areas of activity, not necessarily linked to a persons' principal employment, but maybe to their hobby interests (e.g., auto maintenance) or home activities (e.g., parenting), such online support systems will increasingly be available as publicly accessible services on the Web. And many organizations, as they turn to the Web as an alternative method of networking within the organization (through the creation of Intranets within the Internet) the Web will become the vehicle for delivering job-related EPSS to the workers.

Multimedia, Hypermedia, and the Web

On the "input" side of our picture, growth in the provision of hypertext and hypermedia systems and the implementation of powerful networks (such as the Internet and the promised future information superhighways) points the way in which technology is leading us in relation to the organization, storage and distribution of information to end-users. Although we are not yet there, the promise is that in a short time, most citizens of the world will be in a position to economically access just about any information in the world. Although the technology enthusiasts may be a little over optimistic in terms of timelines, the signs are that we are heading towards much cheaper and more democratic access to the world's stores of information.

Whether this trend will mean an improvement in how society actually uses information is yet to be seen. The evidence from countries where multiple channels of television are normally available is that most citizens use only a few of these channels on a regular basis. If today the typical USA resident regularly uses only four or five out of the forty or fifty channels that are piped to the household, what may be the position some years down the line when 500 channels are available in every house? Will the citizens still be using five out of the 500 on any regular basis? And if a proportion of the channels is made available either for education or public access information distribution as opposed to entertainment, what is the likelihood that if people choose to access these channels, they will benefit as much as they hoped to in terms of identifying useful information, understanding it, and learning how to use it in practice? Not only will the average citizen require an above-average level of skill in navigating through information networks and identifying points which are worth paying attention to among the so many that are not, but also, the networks of information must be so organized that an average citizen without a superhuman capability of information analysis will indeed have the capabilities of identifying what is out there and which parts of it are of relevance and value.

Most hypertext and hypermedia products have, to date, been "stand-alone" systems, in that although they offer the end-user the possibility of "browsing," or "navigating" a particular knowledge domain in a flexible, learner-directed manner, that browsing is limited to the information documented in a particular CD-ROM or other media package. The vision of Nelson (1973, 1980, 1987) and other hypermedia enthusiasts, of a global system of interlinked information sources that ultimately would provide access to all the world's information resources for all the world's citizens, remained a theoretical construct until very recently. Indeed, attempts in the USA to implement the beginnings of such a system in the mid 1980s, under the name of the "Education Utility" (Gooler, 1986) failed miserably. Now, a decade later, spurred by the explosive growth of the Internet, the concept is entering the realms of practical implementation and use. The World Wide Web, now the preferred manner of accessing the information resources of the Internet, is a hypertext system that allows the contributors of information to create links between their contributions and any of the other documents, or "sites," existing in the system, and allows the Internet users to navigate freely from one site to another by simply clicking on the highlighted indicators of existing links.

How close are we today to realizing Nelson's dream of universal democratic access to the world's information resources? Perhaps not as close as some people would have us believe. There are several reasons for this. One that immediately springs to mind, especially in the context of a discussion taking place in nations such as Indonesia, Brazil, Russia, or Angola, where the telecommunication infrastructure is not as developed or as freely accessible as in, say, Europe, Australia, Singapore, or the USA, is the time and resources that will have to be spent in order to make today's emerging technologies truly available and affordable on a worldwide basis.

A second, more easily overlooked, reason is that even in the technologically "developed" nations, the currently existing infrastructure is not up to coping with the traffic that will result from exponentially expanding use of the Internet, both in terms of information providers and end-users. Already there are signs of the system being over-extended, particularly at certain times of the day. Continuing growth in the size of information resources and the volume of end-user traffic must be accompanied by proportional growth in the capacity of the networks to carry the traffic. This is a not an insignificant investment, even for the richer developed nations.

A third, yet more easily overlooked, reason for caution is the limited capacity of the end-users to find their way through an "exploding universe" of information in an effective and efficient manner. Finding relevant information in conventional libraries has always been problematic and difficult. The advent of hypertext has introduced an additional set of "micro" problems to the previously existing "macro" issues of information search and retrieval. In addition to previous difficulties of finding relevant documents (books, papers, articles), the reader is faced with difficulties in finding relevant information within the document. One major user problem in many currently available hypertext systems is described as the "lost in hyperspace" effect (Edwards & Hardman, 1989; Yankelovich *et al.*, 1988). The readers navigate in a non-linear pattern from one "node" of information to another, following potentially interesting or relevant "links," and soon lose their bearings, as if in a maze, unclear as to where they have arrived in the domain of study and why they are there. The undisputed technical advantages of making information more easily and more democratically available are to some extent undermined by human skill limitations on effectively using such an information network.

Whereas the responses to the two earlier cited reasons lie in the domains of the technology itself (coupled to economic and political decisions as regards necessary financial resources), the solutions to this third reason lie within the domain of the social and cognitive sciences and the related technologies of communication and education. One future area of work for the instructional systems design and development professional will be in the area of online information systems, to help solve both the "macro" issues of information systems design from the human engineering viewpoint and the "micro" issues of the design of nonlinear, browsable, hypermedia documents that are understandable and really useful to the end-user.

The "macro" level of design will draw strongly on existing techniques for the organization of information libraries, coupled to innovative techniques of providing "librarian support" to the end-user by automated means. This is one of the few areas in which artificial intelligence research has so far produced tangible products, in the form of "expert systems" that effectively and efficiently replicate the user-help capabilities of the skilled librarian (Bailey, 1992; Denning & Smith, 1994; McCrank, 1993; Morris, 1991). These new developments are now beginning to be applied to the design of "search engines" for use in global networks such as the Internet (Price-Wilkin, 1994; Valauskas, 1995).

The "micro" level of design will focus on the principles and procedures for the development of "hyperdocuments" of various types, especially as relates to the organization of information so that it is of the maximum value to the maximum range of possible end-users and, at the same time, organized so that readers may freely navigate from one detailed item of information to another while always maintaining a clear vision of the "big picture" and their position within it. Among the many attempts to develop authoring techniques for this purpose, the structured writing methodology named "Information Mapping" is an early development (Horn, 1969, 1973) that has proven its power in many contexts (Romiszowski, 1976), and has continued to mature and grow in versatility (Horn, 1989; Romiszowski, 1986).

Computer Mediated Communication (CMC)

At the middle of our systems diagram (the knowledge workers themselves and their process of critical and creative thinking), a technology that holds much promise is Computer-Mediated-Communication (CMC). CMC is a much broader concept than "computer conferencing." It includes any form of organized interaction between people, utilizing computers or computer networks as the medium of communication. The attractions of CMC for future educational systems are many. First of all, it is yet one more and particular versatile approach to the delivery of "distance education." There are powerful political, economic, and social arguments that support the extended use of distance education methods in the future.

However, there are other characteristics of CMC that are of value even if the educational process is not or should not be carried out at a distance. For example, the "asynchronous" nature of interpersonal communication in a computer network, where individuals read messages and then respond in their own time, taking as long as they need to think out their responses, holds promise in certain contexts as compared to more conventional approaches to group discussion (Romiszowski & Corso, 1990; Romiszowski & DeHaas, 1989). Although face-to-face meetings may have advantages in terms of interpersonal and social contact, non-verbal communication and so on, they also have disadvantages. They are held in "real time," which apart from possibly making it difficult or impossible for some people to participate due to other commitments or geographical distance, also may limit in some cases the amount of planning and analysis or the amount of participation that individuals who do attend may have time for. They may also limit participation due to various forms of personal inhibition.

CMC is probably the fastest growing area of educational technology research and development at the moment(Romiszowski & Mason, in press). However, we still are not in a position to be able to design CMC systems that will effectively implement particular group-learning strategies with the same amount of confidence that we have when designing a computer-based instruction package or a set of online reference materials as job-performance aids for a project geared towards the mastery of certain job skills. Nor are we yet as knowledgeable or skillful in the use of CMC as we are beginning to be in the organization of meaningful networks of information within the electronic communication networks that are beginning to link all parts of the world. Of the three areas that we have identified, the CMC area is the most promising for the development of the reflective thinking and creative planning skills that are required to close the gap between information and performance in knowledge work. However, for the time being, we know little about how to implement CMC for the effective development of creative thinking skills.

It is in the area of CMC, therefore, that the greatest need exists for research and development on the design and development of creative-thinking training programs. Once more, here we meet an interesting paradoxical problem to resolve. On the one hand, we have identified the critical thinking, or creative problem solving, area as being of paramount importance for the knowledge worker of the future and, therefore, ultimately, for the employability of the human race. We have also identified the types of teaching-learning techniques that seem to be most effective in this area. These tend to be experiential exercises followed by interpersonal interaction in small groups, and with facilitators to guide the group towards useful conclusions.

The small-group-discussion teaching-learning methodologies have always been relatively expensive, as they involve small groups of students at one place and time with highly skilled and experienced group facilitators. In the future, with falling technology costs and all manner of distance education hardware/software systems appearing on the market at economical prices, the small group learning methodology will appear as a luxury that we can afford to use but sparingly. Yet it is exactly this methodology that we currently know how to use effectively for the development of critical-thinking skills. The paradoxical situation, therefore, is that in the changing technological and economical climates as we move into the 21st century, we may get less and less of what we need more and more.

As the impact of technology on society is at least partly to blame for this paradoxical problem, it would be appropriate if we could find a solution to the problem within that same technology. Over the last few years, a number of research studies have been performed to investigate the utilization of the case study methodology within computer networks as opposed to small-group meetings (Romiszowski, Grabowski, & Damadaran, 1988; Romiszowski, Grabowski, & Pusch, 1988; Romiszowski, 1990; Romiszowski & Chang 1992, 1995). The results of these studies will not be repeated in detail here. However, it is important to highlight two emerging conclusions. First, if properly planned and implemented, computer-mediated conversations may be just as effective as small-group discussions for the development of a wide range of higher-order decision-making and planning skills. Second, the key to the design of effective instructional CMC environments may be found in the application of a scientific theory of conversation. In addition to Instructional Technology, Performance Technology, and Information Technology, the field should develop and apply a Conversation Technology.

Conclusion: The Real Meaning and Importance of Networks

A principal tenet underlying the structure and content of this book is that the global network of computers, enabled by the Internet and currently most effectively embodied in the World Wide Web, is a major revolutionary force that is reshaping the educational and training scenario. However, one may also observe that the COMPUTER NETWORK is merely a technological device to link together human beings into collaborative CONVERSATIONAL NETWORKS, where they can exchange ideas and share materials, often stored and presented as hypertext or hypermedia INFORMATION NETWORKS. But the object of the whole exercise is ultimately to help individuals to build their own (and to enable them to help others build their own) CONCEPTUAL NETWORKS of interrelated ideas, strategies, and theories. These are the networks that are essential for the processes of critical analysis and evaluation of existing knowledge and the creative synthesis of new knowledge: the essential components of knowledge work, the key to employability and professional satisfaction in the future "networked society."

We may therefore argue that due, at least in part, to the technological networking of society in general, and the world of work in particular, the mix of essential human intellectual "survival skills" is of necessity changing. The employable adult of the future must develop the skills of thinking critically and reflectively, both using and creating new knowledge structures or networks. The known effective learning strategies for the development of such skills involve intensive interaction not only with content structured into knowledge networks, but with other people (both "masters" and other "apprentices") who have an interest in the specific knowledge domain. These interactions should have the characteristics of conversations between members of a network of people with common interests. As other impacts of technology on society lead to such effects as globalization and diversification, the members of any common-interest network tend to be widely scattered. Therefore, the need emerges for cost-effective media that may enable the human network to converse and in the process (incidentally) to access relevant information sources. From these needs spring the real causes for the growing importance of technology-based communication networks, such as the World Wide Web in education. A true case of necessity being the mother of invention.

References

Ashby, W. R. (1956). *An introduction to cybernetics*. London, UK: Chapman and Hall.

Bailey, C. W., Jr. (1992). The Intelligent Reference Information System Project. A merger of CD-ROM, LAN, and Expert System Technologies. *Information Technology and Libraries*, *11*(3).

Benson, G. M., Jr. (1994). The lifelong learning society: Investing in the new learning technology market sector. Stephentown, NY: Learning Systems Engineering. ERIC Document ED375809.

Bloom, B. *et al.* (1956). *Taxonomy of educational objectives, Handbook 1: The cognitive domain*. New York: Longman.

Bush, V. (1945). As we may think. *Atlantic Monthly, 176*(1), 101–8.

Carr, C. (1992). *Smart training: The manager's guide to training for improved performance.* New York: McGraw-Hill.

Clark, R. C. (1994). Hang up your training hat. *Training and Development, 48*(9), 61–63.

Conklin, J. (1987). Hypertext: An introduction and survey. *IEEE Computer, 20*(9), 17–41.

Davies, I. K. (1994). Process re-design for enhanced human performance. *Performance Improvement Quarterly, 7*(3).

Denning, R., & Smith, P. J. (1994). Interface design concepts in the development of ELSA, an intelligent electronic library search assistant. *Information Technology and Libraries, 13*(2), 133–47.

Dorsey, L. T. *et al.* (1993). Just-in-time knowledge performance support: A test of concept. *Educational Technology, 33*(11).

Edwards, D. M. & Hardman, L. (1989). Lost in hyperspace: Cognitive mapping and navigation in hypertext environments. In R. McAleese (Ed.), *Hypertext: Theory into practice.* Norwood, NJ: Ablex.

Egan, K. (1972). Structural Communication: A new contribution to pedagogy. *Programmed Learning and Educational Technology, 9*(2), 63–78.

Egan, K. (1976). *Structural Communication.* Belmont, CA: Fearon.

Englebart, D. (1963). A conceptual framework for the augmentation of man's intellect. In P. W. Howerton & D. C. Weeks, *Vistas in information handling, Vol 1: The augmentation of man's intellect by machine* (pp. 1–29). Washington, DC: Spartan Books.

Gayeski, D. M. (1995). DesignStation 2000: Imagining future realities in learning systems design. *Educational Technology, 35*(3), 43–47.

Gilbert, T. F. (1978). *Human competence: Engineering worthy performance.* New York: McGraw-Hill.

Gery, G. (1991). *Electronic performance support systems.* Boston: Weingarten Publications.

Gery, G. (1995). Attributes and behaviors of performance centered systems. *Performance Improvement Quarterly, 8*(1).

Goodyear, P., & Steeples, C. (1992). IT-based open learning: Tasks and tools. *Journal of Computer Assisted Learning, 8*(3) 163–86.

Gooler, D. D. (1986). *The education utility: The power to revitalize education and society.* Englewood Cliffs, NJ: Educational Technology Publications.

Harless, J. (1992). Wither performance technology? *Performance and Instruction, 31*(2), 4–8.

Hodgson, A. M. (1974). Structural communication in practice. In A. J. Romiszowski (Ed.), *APLET yearbook of educational and instructional technology—1974/75.* London, UK: Kogan Page.

Horn, R. E. (1969). *Information Mapping for learning and reference.* Lexington, MA: Information Resources, Inc.

Horn, R. E. (1973). *Introduction to Information Mapping.* Lexington, MA: Information Resources, Inc.

Horn, R. E. (1989). *Mapping hypertext.* Lexington, MA: The Lexington Institute.

Langdon, D. (1991). Performance technology in three paradigms. *Performance and Instruction, 30*(7), 1–7.

McAleese, R. (1989). *Hypertext: Theory into practice.* Norwood, NJ: Ablex.

McCrank, L. J. (1993). Reference expertise: Paradigms, strategies, and systems. *Reference Librarian, 40.*

Milheim, W. D. (1992). Performance support systems: Guidelines for system design and integration. *Canadian Journal of Educational Communication, 21*(3), 243–52.

Morris, A. (1991). Expert systems for library and information services: A review. *Information Processing and Management, 27*(6), 713–24.

Naidu, S., & Bernard, R. M. (1992). Enhanced academic performance in distance education with concept mapping and inserted questions. *Distance Education, 13*(2), 218–33.

Nelson, T. H. (1965). The hypertext. Paper presented at the 1965 Congress of the International Federation for Documentation. Washington, DC: International Federation for Documentation, *Abstracts*, p. 80.

Nelson, T. H. (1973). A conceptual framework for man-machine everything. Montvale, NJ: *AFIPS Conference Proceedings*.

Nelson, T. H. (1980). Replacing the printed word: A complete literary system. In S. H. Livingston (Ed.), *Information Processing 80*. Amsterdam: North Holland.

Nelson T. H. (1987). *Literary machines*. San Antonio, TX: Nelson.

Novak, J. (1991). Clarify with concept maps. *Science Teacher, 58*(7), 44–49.

Pask, G. (1976). Conversational techniques in the study and practice of education. *British Journal of Educational Psychology, 46.*

Pask, G. (1984). Review of Conversation Theory and a protologic (or protolanguage). *Educational Communication and Technology, 32*(1), 3–40.

Plewes, T. J. (1992). Workforce trends, workplace trends: How they dictate a changing education and training strategy. Paper presented at the "Work Now and in the Future" Conference, Portland, Oregon, November 1992. ERIC Document ED352493.

Price-Wilkin, J. (1994). A gateway between the World Wide Web and PAT: Exploiting SGML through the Web. *Public Access Computer Systems Review, 5*(7), 5–27.

Reader, W., & Hammond, N. (1994). Computer based tools to support learning from hypertext: Concept mapping tools and beyond. *Computers and education, 22*(1–2), 99–106.

Romiszowski, A. J. (1976). *A study of individualized systems for mathematics instruction at post-secondary levels*. Ph.D. Thesis. University of Loughborough, UK.

Romiszowski, A. J. (1981). *Designing instructional systems*. London, U.K: Kogan Page.

Romiszowski, A. J. (1984). *Producing instructional systems*. London, UK: Kogan Page.

Romiszowski, A. J.(1986). *Developing auto-instructional materials*. London, UK: Kogan Page.

Romiszowski, A. J. (1990). The Case Method, interactive media, and instructional design. Proceedings of the 7th. International WACRA Conference. Needham, MA: World Association for Case Method Research and Application.

Romiszowski, A. J., & Chang, E. (1992). Hypertext's contribution to computer-mediated-communication: In search of an instructional model. In M. Giardina (Ed.), *Interaction multimedia environments* (pp. 111–130). Heidelberg: Springer-Verlag.

Romiszowski, A. J., & Chang. E. (1995). Hypermedia networks for case-study discussions in distance education. Paper presented at the World Conference on Distance Education, Birmingham, UK.

Romiszowski, A. J., & Corso, M. (1990). Computer-mediated seminars and case studies: Possible future trends for in-service training and development by means of interactive distance education. Paper presented at 15th World Conference on Distance Education, Caracas, Venezuela.

Romiszowski, A. J., & DeHaas, J. (1989). Computer-mediated communication for instruction: Using e-mail as a seminar. *Educational Technology, 29*(1).

Romiszowski, A. J., Grabowski, B.L., & Damadaran, B. (1988). Structural Communication, expert systems, and interactive video: A powerful combination for a non-traditional CAI approach. *Proceedings of AECT National Conference*. Washington, DC: AECT.

Romiszowski, A. J., Grabowski, B. L., & Pusch, W. S. (1988). Structural Communication: A neglected CAI methodology and its potential for interactive video simulations. Paper presented at the ADCIS Annual Conference.

Romiszowski, A. J., & Jost, K. (1989). Computer conferencing and the distance learner: Problems of structure and control. Paper presented at the 1989 University of Wisconsin Conference on Distance Education.

Romiszowski, A. J., & Mason, R. (in press). Research on computer mediated communication. Chapter for D. Jonassen (Ed.), *Handbook of research on educational communication and technology*. New York: Macmillan.

Rossett, A. (1992). Performance technology for instructional technologists: Comparisons and possibilities. *Performance and Instruction, 31*(10), 6–10.

Russell, R., & Meikamp, J. (1994). Creativity training: A practical teaching strategy. *Proceedings of Annual Conference of the American Council on Rural Special Education*, Austin, TX. ERIC No. ED369621.

Schön, D. A. (1983). *The reflective practitioner: How professionals think in action*. London, UK: Temple Smith.

Schön, D. A. (1987). *Educating the reflective practitioner*. San Francisco, CA: Jossey-Bass.

Schroeder, E. E. (1994). Navigating through hypertext: Navigational technique, individual differences, and learning. *Proceedings of R & D Section*, 1994 AECT Conference, Nashville, TN.

Steinaker, N. W., & Bell, M. R. (1979). *The experiential taxonomy: A new approach to teaching and learning*. New York: Academic Press.

Stevens, G. H., & Stevens, E. F. (1995). *Designing electronic performance support tools*. Englewood Cliffs, NJ: Educational Technology Publications.

Valauskas, E. J. (1995). *Britannica Online*: Redefining encyclopedia for the next century. *Database, 18*(1) 14–18.

Yankelovich, N. G., *et al.* (1988). Issues in designing a hypermedia document system: The intermedia case study. In S. Ambron & K. Hooper (Eds.), *Interactive multimedia* (pp. 33–86). Redmond, VA: Microsoft Press.

Young, M. M. (1994). Cognitive reengineering: A process for cultivating critical thinking skills in RNs. ERIC Document No. ED379299.

The Author

Alexander J. Romiszowski is Professor, Department of Instructional Design, Development, and Evaluation, Syracuse University, Syracuse, New York.

e-mail
    alexromi@sued.syr.edu

SECTION II

Web-Based Learning Environments and Critical Issues

4

Web-Based Instruction and the Traditional Classroom: Similarities and Differences

Anju Relan and Bijan B. Gillani

In recent times, "traditional instruction" has been considered a major cause of a dysfunctional and even an obsolete educational system (Banathy, 1994; Reigeluth, 1994). Such criticisms have escalated as multimedia and telecommunications technologies continue to evolve and advance, with promises of providing the learner with a richer, more meaningful education relevant for the future workplace and learning environments. Amidst this technological revolution, a new medium has emerged: the World Wide Web, which continues to grow at an unprecedented pace, captivating both young and adult users. In educational literature, the term "Web-based instruction" has seen frequent usage, and on account of its novelty, is interpreted broadly as any form of instructional delivery in which the World Wide Web is included as a tool. In a similar vein, "traditional instruction," in lay terms, is viewed as an instructional environment which, among other characteristics, encourages passive learning, ignores the individual needs of students, and underserves the development of problem solving and other higher order intellectual skills (Hannum & Briggs, 1982).

"Web-based instruction" and "traditional" approaches to instruction are usually juxtaposed to highlight their seemingly inherent incompatibilities. The intent of this chapter is to elaborate upon the two pedagogical environments and highlight their differences and similarities via a discussion of instructional strategies practiced in each.

Traditional Instruction

In a systematic study and analysis of classroom practices continuing over a century, Cuban (1993) describes classroom instruction as a model stretching from a teacher centered to student centered curriculum. The author observes that in a teacher centered curriculum:

a. teacher talk exceeds student talk;

b. instruction occurs frequently with the whole class; small group or individual instruction occurs less often;

c. use of class time is largely determined by the teacher;

41

   d. teachers look upon the textbook to guide curricular and instructional decision making; and

   e. classroom furniture is arranged into rows of desks or chairs facing a chalkboard.

In a student centered curriculum, on the other hand, "students exercise a substantial degree of responsibility for what is taught, how it is learned, and for movement within a classroom" (Cuban, 1993, p. 7). Thus, at this end of the spectrum of classroom practices:

   a. student talk is equal or greater than teacher talk;

   b. most instruction occurs in small groups;

   c. students help choose the content to be organized and learned;

   d. teachers permit students to determine partially or completely the rules of behavior, classroom rewards and punishment;

   e. varied instructional materials are used independently or in small groups determined by the group or the individual; and

   f. furniture is arranged so that students can work in groups or individually.

Cuban proposes that the teacher centered model was in place by 1916 in most schools, with traces of the student centered curriculum evident in smaller and private schools. In spite of several pedagogical shifts and criticisms levelled against formal education in the last five decades, Cuban concludes that, "there has yet been no clustering of research findings or written observations to challenge the picture of the enduring dominance of a teacher centered curriculum ..." (p. 235).

We consider the criteria that Cuban uses above to describe even student centered instruction as epitomizing the essential elements of "traditional instruction." To the criteria proposed by him, we would add the following to construct an interpretation:

   a. Spatial and temporal structures that learners must adhere to in the learning process are firmly in place. Generally, learning is geographically compartmentalized—physical spaces are assigned for the purpose of learning: the classroom, the lab, and playground, field trips. The compartmentalization of the learning space is extended to a temporal and sequential structure, e.g., disciplines are taught within designated time slots, in a fixed sequence.

   b. Physical presence of the student and teacher in a classroom is a requirement for learning to occur, in spite of the relatively brief interaction that occurs between a student and the teacher during a regular school day.

During his research on effective schools, Goodlad (1984) described a typical scenario which explicates what we consider as "traditional classroom instruction":

> Not "how" but "what" to learn dominated consistently. Teachers and children were busy "covering" what was set forth in the textbooks and workbooks. Children, either as individuals or in groups, were not seeking solutions to problems identified by them as important and meaningful. Instead, they were moderately busy on assignments predetermined by teachers. In general, the subject matter studied appeared to be remote from the daily concerns and interests of the children ... While the children were not bubbling with excitement, they appeared not to be completely bored either. (pp. 13–14)

Why is "traditional instruction" largely devoid of cognitively powerful instructional strategies? Cuban (1993) asserts that many effective classroom practices are difficult to integrate and implement within the structural frameworks in which "traditional instruction" occurs, and are the cause of the stability of traditional classroom practices. These include the arrangement of school space, organization of content and students into grade levels, fifty minute periods, and large classrooms. In the following section, we propose that the repertoire of effective methods is vastly improved via effective use of the World Wide Web in instructional delivery (namely, via Web-based instruction). The attributes of the World Wide Web have the capability of enabling teachers to design innovative instruction in spite of seemingly immutable structures in place.

Web-Based Instruction

We define WBI as the application of a repertoire of cognitively oriented instructional strategies implemented within a constructivist (Lebow, 1993; Perkins, 1991) and collaborative learning environment, utilizing the attributes and resources of the World Wide Web. The instructional strategies may be designed using the World Wide Web in any of the following ways:

- as a resource for the identification, evaluation, and integration of a variety of information;

- as a medium of collaboration, conversation, discussions, exchange, and communication of ideas;

- as an international platform for the expression and contribution of artistic and cognitive understandings and meanings; and

- as a medium for participating in simulated experiences, apprenticeships, and cognitive partnerships

Just as traditional instruction (whether teacher centered or student centered) is executed within the structural patterns which are in place, WBI is situated within different contextual assumptions. First, it is assumed that the learner has access to the World Wide Web at all times, and is allowed to explore it in a self-determined or guided sequence. Second, WBI would function best in a constructivist environment, indeed; the use of the medium in any other way would defeat its purpose in the instructional process. Third, the teacher "dethrones" him/herself as the disseminator of information, and becomes a facilitator for finding, assessing, and making meanings from the information discovered from a variety of media. Fourth, learning occurs in an interdisciplinary fashion without regard to the attainment of learning objectives within a fixed time.

Given the above set of assumptions, we provide some examples of the kinds of projects WBI might include, while contrasting it with traditional instruction, and conclude with a set of generalities based on the strategies used in the examples.

1. Traditional classrooms are space bound; learning occurs within a physical boundary—for example, a classroom, a school, field trips, and various other locations. WBI extends the boundaries of learning, so that it can occur in the classroom, from home, and in the workplace. Having permanent access to a multitude of learning resources regardless of one's geographical location allows continuity in learning and encourages uninterrupted reflection about a topic, and revision of one's thesis. As an example, Susan's sixth grade has begun a project exploring the issues surrounding air quality and its effect on people. In class she worked on exploring the chemical pollutants released

by the automobile. While walking home, she is struck by the layer of smog in the horizon. Curious to find out what it is composed of, she reaches home, logs on to the World Wide Web, and conducts a search on smog, air pollution, and the long term effects on population. The resources she finds are from major universities, environmental groups, agencies, and newspapers located all over the world. She skims through the resources, selects some to read, creates bookmarks of the ones she would like to share in class, and goes back to school the following day with a self-generated hypothesis on how the problem of air pollution can be resolved locally.

2. WBI may be employed to promote experiential learning, or learning "on site," so that the process of learning is integrated with the real world. Several expeditions by scientists and professionals have elicited student participation from schools. Students vicariously experience the excursion/expedition via photographs, activity logs, interaction with participants, and classroom activities based on the topic. As an example: Excerpt taken from GlobaLearn (http://www.globalearn.org):

> In March, 1996, students all over the country will log onto the Internet, direct a live expedition and help unravel one of the greatest mysteries of all time. Their teachers, for the first time, will put away textbooks and use a learning adventure to satisfy curriculum requirements. MayaQuest is a two-part, kid-directed expedition led by adventurer Dan Buettner. Its goal is to engage an online audience to help explain 9th century collapse of the ancient Maya civilization. Last spring, some 40,000 teachers used the program in their classrooms. During February the MayaQuest team cycled through Central America carrying laptop computers, a satellite dish and a connection to the Internet. Kids and online explorers voted on team decisions, explored 21 Maya sites and were virtually on hand for several major discoveries. Then these kids actually helped archaeologists answer questions.

3. WBI offers a new sensibility and means of social interaction engineered towards learning. Cooperative learning as an effective learning strategy has been studied and practiced extensively (Johnson & Johnson, 1990). With WBI, cooperative learning extends beyond one classroom to potentially every classroom that is connected to the Internet! Students have the potential of discussing, problem solving, querying their own peers as well as knowledgeable adults in a particular field. For example, during the MayaQuest expedition (http://www.mayaquest.mecc.com), students are able to ask questions of expert archeologists, as well as cooperatively solve problems posed by project coordinators. While traditional instruction tends to discourage social interaction, WBI is designed for collaboration and interaction which can be effectively employed towards learning. This type of social interaction fosters a different sense of accountability among students.

4. The predominant source of content shifts from the textbook and the teacher to a more varied source of information. Further, the nature of content becomes dynamic, versus the static texts published on a certain date. Students who have performed extensive research on topics may also contribute to the content on the topic. Finally, the impact of such a diverse resource of content cannot be overlooked in its ability to prod the learner to use highly developed metacognitive skills to glean, review, assess, select, and integrate this content meaningfully, with the facility of collaborative discourse, synchronous or asynchronous, simultaneously available on the World Wide Web.

5. A noteworthy attribute of the World Wide Web is the presentation of content in a hypertext format, which allows the user to pursue a sequence of content entirely based on his/her volition. This presents a colossal shift to the student in

gaining a control of learning which is characteristically absent from a traditional classroom. The cognitive advantages of hypermedia have been discussed extensively elsewhere (e.g., Jonassen, Myers, & McKillop). WBI not only allows the learner to partake of the infinite content available on the World Wide Web, but also to contribute to it and represent his or her own understandings and meanings in hypermedia formats. One can find numerous examples of student projects on school Web pages across the curriculum (for examples, see http://www.classroom.net)

6. The World Wide Web is increasingly promoting the concept of distance education, which has thus far been a cumbersome and expensive process. Numerous courses are offered remotely, where the learner enjoys the flexibility of time and content, and is able to obtain individualized feedback on assignments. The ability of the instructor and students to communicate privately or collectively in a synchronous or asynchronous manner lends a new dimension to the design of instructional strategies.

7. Individualization and student choice also acquire a different set of dimensions with the World Wide Web. Students have a choice of content, time, resources, feedback, and a variety of media for expressing their understandings. For example, while content was designated by the instructor from a textbook and library media in traditional instruction, it acquires a different meaning on the World Wide Web. Content can be information as well as the interpretations of information by experts, novices, and students. It can be in the form of research reports, arguments, journalistic accounts, and essays. Content is not only represented through text and graphics, but in any multimedia format. Similarly, feedback is not restricted to that of the instructor, but includes collegial responses from learners in various geographical locations.

Web-Based Instruction, Traditional Instruction, and Changing Conceptions of Learning

The traditional approaches of learning have lately been questioned in their ability to provide the learner with "rich" rather than "minimalist" environments (Perkins, 1996), and with "authentic" experiences of learning which are meaningful to the learner in some intrinsic manner. These notions have led educators of think of learning as being "situated" (Brown, Collins, & Duguid, 1989); for example, "...knowledge is no longer simply an individual acquisition, but resides also in groups or communities that share a situatedness" (Damarin, 1983, p. 27). The World Wide Web enables an environment in which such "learning communities" (Lin *et al.*, 1996) can be created, and rich, authentic experiences provided. Just as the application of hypertext and hypermedia created novel modes of learning and contributed to the restructuring of an instructional environment (e.g., the creation of constructivist ways of learning), the World Wide Web has the power to generate novel learning strategies which will eventually be embedded in cognitive, social, and cultural contexts.

References

Banathy, B. (1994). Designing educational systems: Creating our future in a changing world. In C. M. Reigeluth & R. J. Garfinkle (Eds.), *Systemic change in education* (pp. 27–34). Englewood Cliffs, NJ: Educational Technology Publications.

Barsanti, B. English literature Website (http://www.computek.net./public/barr/ barr.html).

Brown, J. S., Collins, A., & Duguid, P. (1989). Situated cognition and the culture of learning. *Educational Researcher, 18*(1), 32–42.

Classroom Connect (http://www.classroom.net).

Cuban, L. (1993). *How teachers taught* (2nd ed.). New York: Teachers College Press.

Damarin, S. (1993). Schooling and situated knowledge: Travel or tourism? *Educational Technology, 33*(10), 27–32.

English Literature Web Site (http://www.computek.net./public/barr/barr.html).

GlobaLearn (http://www.globalearn.org).

Goodlad, J. (1976). Schooling today. In J. S. Golub (Ed.), *Facing the future* (pp. 3–22). New York: McGraw-Hill Book Company.

Goodlad, J. (1984). *A place called school.* New York: McGraw-Hill Book Company.

Hannum, W., & Briggs, L. (1982). How does instructional system design differ from traditional instruction? *Educational Technology, 22*(1), 9–14.

Johnson, D., & Johnson, R. (1990). *Cooperative learning and achievement.* In S. Sharon (Ed.), *Cooperative learning theory and research* (pp. 22–37). New York: Praeger.

Jonassen, D. H., Myers, J. M., & McKillop, A. M. (1996). From Constructivism to Constructionism: Learning with Hypermedia/Multimedia rather than from it (pp. 93–106). In B. G. Wilson (Ed.), *Constructivist learning environments: Case studies in instructional design.* Englewood Cliffs, NJ: Educational Technology Publications.

Lin, X., Bransford, J. D., Hmelo, C. E., Kantor, R. J., Hickey, D. T., Secules, T., Petrosino, A. J., Goldman, S. R., & The Cognition and Technology Group at Vanderbilt. (1996). Instructional design and the development of learning communities (pp. 203–220). In B. G. Wilson (Ed.), *Constructivist learning environments: Case studies in instructional design.* Englewood Cliffs, NJ: Educational Technology Publications.

Lebow, D. (1993). Constructivist values for instructional systems design: Five principles for a new mindset. *Educational Technology Research and Development, 41*(3), 4–16.

Perkins, D. N. (1991). Technology meets constructivism: Do they make a marriage? *Educational Technology, 31*(5), 18–23.

Perkins, D. N. (1996). Foreword: Minds in the 'hood. In B. G. Wilson (Ed.), *Constructivist learning environments: Case studies in instructional design* (pp. v–viii). Englewood Cliffs, NJ: Educational Technology Publications.

Pitsco Company. Ask an expert (http://www.usa.net/~pitsco/pitsco/ask.html).

Reigeluth, C. M. (1994). Introduction: An imperative for systemic change. In C. M. Reigeluth & R. J. Garfinkle, (Eds.), *Systemic change in education.* Englewood Cliffs, NJ: Educational Technology Publications.

Wilson, B. G. (1996). Introduction: What is a constructivist learning environment? In B. G. Wilson (Ed.), *Constructivist learning environments: Case studies in instructional design* (pp. 3–10). Englewood Cliffs, NJ: Educational Technology Publications.

The Authors

Anju Relan is Director, Instructional Design and Technology Unit, School of Medicine, University of California at Los Angeles.

e-mail
   arelan@ucla.edu
   http://www.mednet.ucla.ed~/dept./som/edr/IDTUtap.htm

Bijan B. Gillani is Associate Professor and Coordinator of the Graduate Program in Educational Technology Leadership, School of Education, California State University, Hayward.

e-mail, World Wide Web
   bgillani@csuhayward.edu
   http://edschool.csuhayward.edu/bgillani/bijan.html

5

Interactive Multimedia and Web-Based Learning: Similarities and Differences

John Hedberg, Christine Brown, and Michael Arrighi

Introduction

The nature of the relationship between the teacher and learner continues to change as developments in technology allow them not only to communicate in various ways, but also to access and generate a wide range of resources. The delivery format influences the way information can be represented, accessed, and manipulated by the teacher or learner. The learner can now elect to be the information user or information producer. This chapter explores the similarities and differences between bounded and unbounded resource material from the learner's perspective as information user or information producer.

The Teacher and Learner in a Technology Framework

In the course of this discussion we will apply a framework which relates teachers to learners along three main axes—time, place, and group size, as indicated in Figure 1. This representation acknowledges the work of Norman (1995) and Stanford (1996). At one extreme, we have the typical classroom, where the teacher and learner share the same space at the same time, and learners may work individually or in groups. At the other extreme, the teacher and learner are at different venues, communicate asynchronously, and learners may or may not congregate to share their experiences or collaborate/cooperate with learning tasks. The ability for teachers and learners to find a position somewhere along that continuum has been largely facilitated by developments in information technology—a field which incorporates communications, computer, and audiovisual technologies.

The multitude of ways the teacher and learner can communicate and the time and feedback quality of those communications largely determine the success of the teacher/learner relationship and the learning outcomes. The move to provide electronic services through fiber optics directly into the home supports the ability to communicate using video, sound, and text. Future growth in open learning study offered commercially is likely to increasingly require ca-

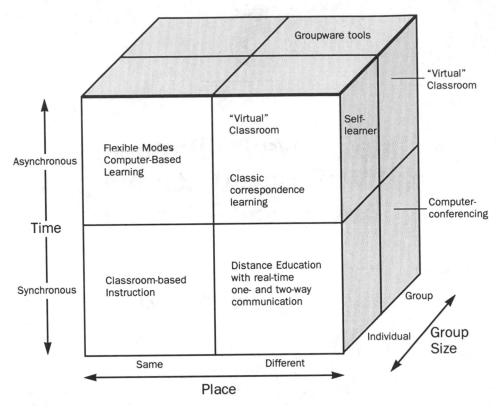

Figure 1. Factors which relate teachers and learners.

pability to move files and information between people in different locations and could become one aspect of the development of domestic interactive multimedia distribution.

We believe that a real-time video communications link between each communicating party is not really necessary within normal constraints. It is amazing what learning can occur off-line when two people delay their individual communications to times which are more convenient to them. Here, the important consideration is that information can be communicated employing a variety of visual and verbal forms as required. This can be achieved over cheaper types of connections that some of the engineers are proposing. Synchronicity or real-time communications should be subservient to the quality of the information exchanged and the appropriateness of its clarity and representation. Good communications need not be instantaneous!

The Learner as User or Producer

Typically, the learner has been regarded as the recipient of information. With developments in educational software and the proliferation of both bounded interactive multimedia titles on CD-ROM and unbounded resources on the Web, the learner usually occupies the role of software user. When the activities of the learner are regarded as the central focus in education (Schank & Cleary, 1995) and emphasis is placed on what he or she is actually doing when using the software, the question can then be asked: Should the learner be a software user or a software *producer*?

As a software user, his or her actions may encompass the full range of activities offered by software designers, from passive guided direction in prescriptive environments through to simulations and open active gathering and reconstruction of multimedia resources. What he or she learns and how widely he or she uses that knowledge, skill, or strategy is a function of the context of program use—the learner extracts from a program what sense he or she makes of it, not what use the designer intended.

> . . . the coherence of the learner's experience in this situation is not tied in essential ways to the instructional designer's intent (no matter how detailed or explicit these intentions are spelled out as instructional objectives) nor to the instructional plan built into the instructional system. Rather, the coherence of the learner's instructional experience is tied to the sense that such a learner constructs out of the actual situation (of which the instructional system is just a part). (Streibel, 1991, p. 123)

If the learner is a software *producer*, the next question to ask is: Why is the learner producing interactive multimedia software? If his or her focus is on the development of an interactive multimedia *product*—whether a CD-ROM title or a Web page—then the emphasis will be on learning about interactive multimedia production as a body of knowledge with an accompanying set of skills—a situated and authentic activity which synchronizes learning and doing, yet an activity in which the acquisition of content knowledge is a fringe benefit. This equates with designer as learner (Jonassen & Reeves, in press). In this context, the cognitive load of many production tools may be very high and require substantial time to "polish" the outcome.

If the learner's emphasis is on the learning which occurs through the *process* of interactive multimedia construction—learner as designer (Jonassen & Reeves, in press)—then the nature of the product is far less important than the knowledge construction process which the learner experiences along the way. Less emphasis is placed on the refinement of production skills and more emphasis is placed on student-initiated design and development with just-in-time skill support. When the focus is upon the process, the cognitive load of the construction tool(s) should be minimal to permit the learner to focus on knowledge construction.

The relationship between the activities of teaching and learning, and interactive multimedia and Web page development as a mechanism to assist learning, can be seen in Table 1.

The key activities of teaching and learning do not equate with teacher and student. Both teachers and students are involved in the activities of learning and of teaching, especially in a cooperative or collaborative situation. The distinction is made between use of bounded and unbounded educational interactive multimedia material such as CD-ROM titles and Web resources, and student production of interactive multimedia. Within the latter category, the reason for production then distinguishes between a focus on product development for purposes of publishing, and a focus on the significance of the construction process. In this chapter, we will confine the discussion to the learner as a software user (Model A) and as a producer with a process focus (Model C).

Table 1. Cross-grid of teaching vs. learning, use vs. production.

	Use	**Production**	
	(Model A)	*For Product* (Model B)	*For Process* (Model C)
Teaching	Teaching through the use of IMM and Web Products	Teaching About IMM and Web Page Production	Teaching with IMM Web Page Construction Tools
Learning	Learning Through Use of these Products	Learning About IMM and Web Page Production	Learning with IMM and Web Page Tools

Concept of Static or Dynamic Information Sources

The advent of interactive multimedia in its present form of integrated digital forms of representation has enabled individuals to produce software using a variety of different ways of representing and combining their ideas. Teachers may present their students with a world of highly interactive and visually stimulating resources. The ability to access unbounded or dynamic information is what primarily distinguishes Web-based instruction (WBI) from instruction using interactive multimedia materials on bounded delivery vehicles such as CD-ROMs.

The CD has become a favored platform in computer-based learning methodology. However, many digital forms or formats of representation, such as frames, movies, and floating notebooks, can now be integrated with the Web, so the distinction between these two delivery vehicles is blurring. Governments and other funding agencies will tend to support whatever is deemed the most cost-effective. Costs for bounded media production are generally higher, due to labor and hardware requirements to produce and market a commercial product. A CD-ROM, once authored, is immutable, but may offer high quality resources in a structured context. Web products can be altered instantaneously and can be used remotely and universally from home/office/classroom.

There are a number of important attributes of interactive multimedia, however it is delivered, that need to be discussed in order to focus upon the nature of the resources accessed by the learner.

Information Representation

Information in a multimedia world can be presented in new and different ways. This may seem simplistic, but it is an important consideration when designing or evaluating products and should not be overlooked. Imagine the student who sees a set of figures and cannot understand the underlying trend. A set of numbers which fluctuate with no obvious pattern may hide the fact that the underlying trend is upwards. Simply converting these numbers to a graph will reveal a new aspect of the information which is difficult to see otherwise. Similarly, viewing a map of the land or a spatial layout may actually provide an understanding of problems which are not evident in a straight text-based description of the issue.

If someone is to seek out information in a complex field, he or she can be presented with something that approximates the real task. Thus, through visual links, we can create an environment that allows the user to explore and undertake a range of tasks which closely mirror those of the real world. In this way, we do not have to be constrained by verbal descriptions of visual activities. While most instructors have been long espousing the importance of sight in the learning process, often the sight is used to view words rather than visuals. Significant cognitive load is removed from the user when we can convert to a world in which the actual process is learned as the task unfolds. A better cognitive fidelity is achieved between the learning task and real-world tasks.

The planned nature of CD-ROM production usually ensures that authoritatively-sourced and therefore, to some degree, validated content has an inherent structure which remains stable no matter when it is accessed by a user. None of these features in a global sense characterize information available on the Web. The initial euphoria associated with access to unbounded and largely unstructured information on the Web is dissipating among information seekers, who are tiring of a tabloid format—where we have all headlines and no text. Web "books" are no longer being judged by their bit-laden covers. Serious users want to search the contents and indices as quickly as possible before "buying into" a time consuming, link-hopping series of clicks. Mechanically user-friendly, the Web, nevertheless, is a smorgasbord of information which either may not be available next time access is attempted, may no longer exhibit the same form, or may not provide information sources to encourage students to acknowledge the origin and development of ideas. Virtual Classrooms are filled by the proliferating input of culturally biased lesson plans and intuitive interfacing. Meanwhile, the student still asks: 'So what do I do with all this information?'

Solutions to the problems of validity and constancy of information are emerging. The development of Listservers like *Heproc* (http://rrpubs.com/heproc/index.htm) quickly guide users to targeted home pages and provide subscription facilities to dedicated news arenas which deliver daily email updates on demand to the "latest" dedicated Websites. Gophers and FTP accessing, like *Gopher Jewels* (http://www.einet.net/GJ/index.html), have become more sophisticated. Through them, the frustration of browser fatigue is alleviated. These tools quickly retrieve accredited papers and articles that are not substantially outdated by "publication" time.

Access and Navigation

A related component of representation is access to information. Creating access to information, especially using "hyper" links, can create new meanings not previously considered possible.

Using interactive CD-ROM multimedia to model the knowledge base and to give the user freedom to interact with it gives autonomy back to the user. Rather than provide a set of pre-designed sequences that assume one learning model, a more interactive approach can be developed by giving the user a bounded information landscape and the tools necessary to explore and investigate the information. Package designers have used a variety of techniques to help users around such bounded information packages. These include:

- use of color to identify the area or main path;

- the position of elements in the screen to indicate their relationship to the underlying metaphor or the separation of positional navigation choices from the functional options (e.g., separation of the movement from help and explanation functions);

- simple use of contextual clues, regular use of a standard format of basic word style format to indicate links with other sources of information;

- written directions which appear in separate areas or windows to understand the underlying information structure;

- simplified mnemonics or preferably the use of icons to provide standard and immediately comprehensible support for navigation or learning;

- the development of visual and text based search strategies and links to maps which show learning path choices;

- enabling user path maps to be modified, highlighting the paths which have been travelled;

- creating new links by the user using a series of tools which enable the package to be modified, either by adding new information or by adding new hypertext linkages based on the student's own conceptual maps.

The unbounded Web is a virtual universe expanding like that of the real world. No one can give a true audit of its guesstimated 50 million pages, claimed by some to double in number every six months. Its saving grace is that the existing nightmare of quickly finding the constituent research from within this mass is being mellowed by a friendly growth of increasingly more sophisticated search engines.

In essence, we have at our fingertips an uninhibited access to infinite information, and with it, never-before imagined global interactivity with like-minded spirits. And the best is yet to come, because emerging technology is developing compatible bonding of the Web with CD-ROMs through software that, in unison, packages information access tools such as audiovisual, aural, and textual imports into "courseware."

Interactivity and Control

Clear information representation and access facilitate the user's ability to find and manipulate much of the available information. Many proponents of the use of interactive multimedia talk about the interactivity involved in the exciting dynamic programs. However, this can sometimes be a trap. Allowing the user to simply choose between a set of options or turn pages of cute animations is not interactivity. Nor can it be claimed that it is user control. It is important that the user is required to think before a response is possible. Consider a typical arcade video game—only a few control buttons are provided, but the user can make a character jump, flail a sword, etc. This means that the choice and its consequence are part of the interactivity and intrigue of the game. It is the "stuff" which creates high engagement. However, adventure games often proceed along a time and movement axis which allows the user very little control over the direction the adventure might take. While this may be appropriate for a game, this type of movement through a learning environment might be very constricting and would frustrate rather than engage learners.

Used effectively, the technology can allow users to interact in ways that the designers of the system did not plan, and well designed interactive multimedia materials make it unnecessary to structure materials in advance for the user. Effective student use of unstructured materials, however, will depend on access, understanding, and available tools. Flexible access to the information caters to a broad range of users. Clear understanding of the metaphors used to structure information permits the user to clearly identify the mental model of the information provider, and thus glean deeper meaning from that structure. The use of cognitive tools such as word processors, spreadsheets, and multimedia authoring systems permit the user to extract, create, organize, and orchestrate information his or her own way when solving personally meaningful tasks.

Howard Gardner's (1983) vision carries a responsibility applicable to the Web that: "There are two salient problems in the design of multimedia documents: informing and guiding the computer user through a complex body of information, and the creation of a visual design rhetoric appropriate for interactive computer displays..." (cited by Lynch, 1994). Research in this arena substantially points to an imperative need for a restructuring of education policy to ensure that students become creative in their thinking, that they shed the still extant burden of rote "learning." But in the process, the pitfall of information overload must be avoided (Turoff, 1995).

It would be premature to posit an evaluation of the Web as learning tool—it may well take another decade to arrive at definitive theories in this context. Its potential for improving the quality of life for the masses is clear, but there is little doubt that corporate sectors and sociopolitical engineers have a vested interest in its mechanics. It behooves educators universally to be vigilant, so ensuring that this vehicle is not to be driven by such entities. Failing this, we can anticipate an isolated tier of humanity perpetually imprisoned in that category for which Nicholas Negroponte has coined the label: *The Digitally Homeless.*

The geographic, temporal, and technological links between teacher and learner, the bounded or dynamic nature of resources, and the degree to which the learner can access and manipulate those resources all converge when we look at education from the *learner's* perspective.

The Learner as User

Learning theory has influenced the structure of interactive multimedia CD-ROMs along an instructivist to constructivist continuum (Figure 2). There are many fine examples of software at points on this scale which, when viewed collectively, indicate a number of trends. For the software user, as you move towards the constructivist end of the spectrum, there is an increase in the potential for group interaction as the nature of tasks becomes more complex and learner generated. Group work with CD-ROMs means fewer workstations are required for each class of students, but this student-to-hardware ratio gain is usually offset by an increased need for teacher/peer support, due to the more complex nature and varied duration of tasks.

The range and extent of user interaction with the data in the software increases as the user is given more freedom to navigate, access, determine the format of information representation, and manipulate the data using cognitive and metacognitive tools. All this freedom to access and manipulate data is presented in an information landscape which provides context and support structures. The landscape can be quite extensive and extensible if the aim is to cater to users with a broad range of background knowledge. This degree of flexibility of use means that inbuilt support will tend to be either very situation specific, such as an example, or very generic, indicating potential strategies for software use.

Constructivist software need not be used by a group; however, the individual user in this more democratic environment needs to display the motivation and metacognitive skills of a self-regulated learner to gain maximum benefit from the software without peer support. The group provides a discussion forum for suggestions, ideas and debate, a multitude of

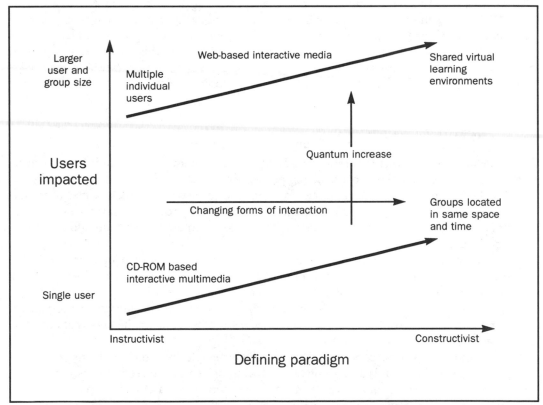

Figure 2. Comparing the impact and relationships between interactive (CD-ROM based) multimedia and Web-based delivery.

learning and problem solving strategies to share, and immediate personal feedback on all communication channels (auditory, visual, body language). Such group benefits are only achieved once group members have acknowledged the need to refine such skills as negotiation and collaboration.

The limitations on the information base are primarily its permanent nature. Once you have solved all inherent problems within a fixed landscape, no matter how creative and advanced the data management and manipulation tools, there is no new data with which to work, and no regular update of information to note current trends. As a "microworld" in which to explore and develop skills in information transformation and interpretation, CD-ROMs provide high quality material with support. As such, they are an excellent environment in which to develop these skills, particularly when there is the opportunity to combine inbuilt support with real-time personal group benefits.

The complete freedom of the Web environment suggests that the user is operating entirely within a constructivist framework. Closer examination indicates the same spectrum of instructivist to constructivist activities can be offered, but within generally shorter time periods and with less defined borders. A single user engaged in a drill and practice exercise on the Web unwittingly shares a similar experience with countless other Web users accessing the same material. As we move towards the constructivist end, differences begin to emerge between groupwork on the Web and real-time groupwork using a CD-ROM. The group on the Web may be extremely large, asynchronous, at varied locations, and fluctuating due to transient membership. This limits spontaneous group interaction, but increases the opportunity for group members to take time to reflect on issues. The changing nature of the group also permits the infusion of new ideas.

Web users generally experience material of a lower quality than that which is stored on fixed commercial media, and the nature of the interactivity is not as powerful; however, applets (using technologies such as Java) are increasingly addressing this issue and may provide a rich source of highly specific interaction and targeted learning. Of course, Web material is more readily updated, so the user will be able to use the tools provided through applets to monitor trends in current data.

The Learner as Producer

When the individual learner is permitted to occupy the role of interactive multimedia producer with a focus on the knowledge construction process, he or she is publishing for personal viewing. All the information searching, discussion with peers, mistakes, re-makes, media production, screen construction, and linking are vital elements of the process the learner experiences. Immediately, he or she must take an active approach to the appraisal, accumulation, and generation of relevant resources.

Low level authoring tools, which place fewer demands on cognitive load than high level production tools, permit the learner to rapidly construct a series of screens. These may undergo many revisions before the underlying structure and interrelationships among concepts are perceived. By externalizing this evolving body of knowledge in multimedia format, the constructor can brainstorm, reflect, revise, and reconstruct what he or she knows at any stage in the overall process.

This building process is not initially driven by principles of interface design, or awareness of a target audience. It is a self-motivated process, driven by the learner's desire to clearly express a concept, usually one screen at a time. The learner has a chance to play with combinations of relevant media, which are either self-generated or personally selected to express ideas in different ways. As concepts are described with increased depth of understanding, clearer interrelationships and overarching concepts may emerge. Eventually the program may develop a coherent architecture with clear navigation. The constructor generates feedback each time he or she reviews and reflects upon the structure and content of his or her multimedia knowledge base.

A finished product is not important in this process. Frequently at the end of a period of construction, the learner can simply explain how he or she would publish his or her ideas in a sophisticated design. The implementation of this design may no longer matter—the learner is ready to move on.

A teacher watching the evolution of ideas is quickly able to identify what the learner understands well, and what has yet to be clarified. The more clearly a learner understands something, the more simply he or she can explain it. Great detail and complexity through a "cut and paste" exercise does not necessarily indicate comprehension of the detail. The knowledge construction process for an individual learner can be ongoing. Document editing, linking, and synthesis may continue. As the body of information and its associated structure lose coherence for the constructor, he or she must begin the process of restructuring to incorporate new information. The inner processes of assimilation and accommodation are externalized.

Interactive multimedia construction to facilitate the learning process need not be a solitary exercise. Groups of learners may also construct interactive multimedia to process information. Several features of the group process distinguish it from that experienced by the individual:

- the need for group skills such as collaboration and cooperation;
- an increased demand for both hardware and software to meet the increased capacity of a group to generate and construct resources;
- numerous opportunities to discuss material, and to learn through teaching other group members;
- valuable feedback from group members; and
- development of interpersonal skills.

Interactive multimedia construction offers the learner many advantages. It is an active process which is personally meaningful and promotes deep processing of knowledge. It facilitates the development of a wide range of associated social, technical, and problem-solving skills, permits knowledge representation in a range of media forms, and allows the learner to engage in a long term process. Many skills may be anchored and integrated within one context prior to their transfer to other situations. Teachers have the opportunity to observe the thinking processes of learners, rather than checklist outcomes, which may lack a meaningful context.

High levels of hardware and software resources are required to support the learner as constructor, and considerable flexibility in timetabling can unsettle those teachers who prefer set management procedures. Without the personal experience of the knowledge construction process, many teachers would not anticipate the needs of the learners, or be able to maximize their support of learners.

Authoring tools for the construction of Web documents currently offer a page metaphor with hypertext as the dominant link structure. The brainstorming process tends to be more "top-down" than the screen metaphor of more traditional low level multimedia authoring tools such as HyperStudio. For the individual learner constructing his or her own network of Web pages, the resource bank is as large as the Web itself, and the support network equally voluminous, through bulletin boards and countless sites which model different ways to present information. Web authoring for learning offers several advantages over authoring for more fixed media such as CD-ROM:

- information is constantly updated;

- less equipment is required for production;

- there is currently less requirement for high level graphics, though this is rapidly changing; and

- the Web itself provides a constantly updated source of design models for the structuring of large bodies of information.

Disadvantages of Web document construction as a learning process are the current limitations of low level authoring tools, which constrain user creativity through severe limitations on screen layout, the lack of constancy of linked information sites, and the dominance of text in the English language.

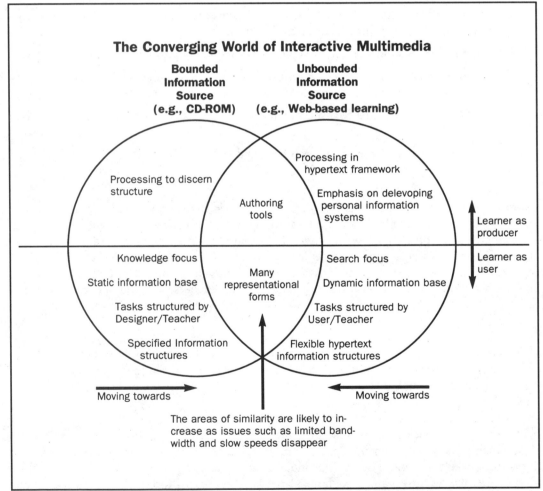

Figure 3. Reducing the differences and increasing the similarities.

Conclusions

Learners using bounded or unbounded resources need to acquire a common set of skills in information appraisal, selection, organization, structuring, and communication of ideas in the solution of meaningful tasks. The nature (instructivist to constructivist) and source of these tasks (whether teacher or learner generated) help determine their relevance, complexity and ability to promote a deeper orientation to learning than simple rote learning.

Learners as knowledge constructors share some fundamental features, whether working individually or in groups, on traditional screen based structures or within more of a Web page hypertext architecture. They develop diverse skills in data/media selection, generation, organization, orchestration, and restructuring. The opportunity to share the results of construction labor with others permits these active learners to gain feedback as to whether their level of understanding is sufficient to facilitate meaningful communication of ideas to others. The means of information representation is as unique as the individual or group. Interactivity resides in both the recursive construction process and within interpersonal communications. It no longer relates to the ability of a user to manipulate data within a fixed structure. The ultimate in interactivity is the process of knowledge construction. The additional skills demanded of the learner as producer deal with resource management and increased metacognitive awareness of what is largely a self-regulated process.

The distinction between user and producer blurs with the ability on the Web to use applets to manipulate and re-present dynamic information. Essentially the user can create a personalized framework to access and manipulate Web information—potentially the Web becomes tailored as his or her own personal information system.

It is expected that the current seemingly different worlds of these two technologies will increasingly coalesce and the differences will largely be determined by the cost of access rather than the technology's physical form. In Figure 3, we present our synthesis of these two delivery vehicles in the light of the learner as information user or producer.

The fundamental difference between the bounded and unbounded resource banks resides in the essential nature of group activities. Authoring tools for both systems are coalescing in the development of more specific cognitive tools, and forms of representation on CD-ROM are increasingly appearing on the Web. The significance of change facilitated by Web developments is the move to the Virtual Classroom. The challenge for educators within this context is to devise better metacognitive tools to support the group process of learning.

References

Cuban, L. (1994). The promise of the computer. In C. Huff & T. Finholt (Eds.), *Social issues in computing: Putting computing in its place.* New York: McGraw-Hill.

Gardner, H. (1983). Frames of mind: *The theory of multiple intelligences.* New York: Basic Books.

Jonassen, D. H., & Reeves, T. C. (in press). Learning with technology: Using computers as cognitive tools. In D. Jonassen (Ed.), *Handbook of research on educational technology.* New York: Macmillan.

Korcuska, M. (1996). Software factories for active learning environments. In P. Carson & F. Makedon (Eds.), *Educational multimedia and hypermedia 96: Proceedings of EdMedia 96 World Conference on Educational Multimedia and Hypermedia* (pp. 360–325).

Lynch, P. J. (1994). Visual design for the user interface: Design fundamentals. *Journal of Biocommunications, 21*(1), 22–30.

Norman, K. L. (1995). *Teaching in the switched on classroom: An introduction to electronic education and hypercourseware,* Chapter 1, Engines for educators (http://www.lap.umd/SOC/Ch1/Ch1.html).

Ornstein, A. C. (1992). *Secondary and middle school teaching methods.* New York: HarperCollins.

Schank, R. C., & Cleary, C. (1995). *Engines for education*. Hillsdale, NJ: Lawrence Erlbaum Associates.

Stanford, D. (1996). Interactive multimedia in education. In C. McBeath & R. Atkinson (Ed.), *The learning superhighway, new world, new worries: Proceedings of the 3rd International Interactive Multimedia Symposium* (pp. 28–37).

Streibel, M. J. (1991). Instructional plans and situated learning. In G. J. Anglin (Ed.), *Instructional technology: Past, present, and future* (pp. 119–132). Englewood, CO: Libraries Unlimited.

Turoff, M. (1995). Designing a virtual classroom. *International Conference on Computer Assisted Instruction*. National Chiao Tung University, Hsinchu, Taiwan (http://www.njit.edu/njIT/Department/CCCC/VC/Papers/Design.html).

The Authors

John Hedberg, is Associate Dean and Head, Graduate School of Education, Faculty of Education, University of Wollongong, Australia.

e-mail, World Wide Web
    John_Hedberg@uow.edu.au
    http//:www.uow.edu.au

Christine Brown, is a Lecturer, Faculty of Education, University of Wollongong, Australia.

e-mail, World Wide Web
    Christine_Brown@uow.edu.au
    http//:www.uow.edu.au

Michael Arrighi, is Research Associate IMM; Ph.D. Candidate, Faculty of Education, University of Wollongong, Australia.

e-mail, World Wide Web
    Michael_Arrighi@uow.edu.au
    http//:www.uow.edu.au

6

Effective Dimensions of Interactive Learning on the World Wide Web

Thomas C. Reeves
and Patricia M. Reeves

Introduction

The World Wide Web has attracted the attention of people around the world, including that of educators and trainers. Despite all the interest, little research evidence exists to support claims for the effectiveness of Web-based instruction (WBI). Before collecting such evidence, it is essential to define the dimensions of interactive learning that can be enabled via the World Wide Web. Further, an analysis of the critical dimensions of WBI is required to guide program development, implementation, and evaluation. Accordingly, this chapter presents a model of interactive learning via the World Wide Web based upon research and theory in instructional technology, cognitive science, and adult education.

The proposed model includes ten dimensions of interactive learning on the World Wide Web, including (1) pedagogical philosophy, (2) learning theory, (3) goal orientation, (4) task orientation, (5) source of motivation, (6) teacher role, (7) metacognitive support, (8) collaborative learning, (9) cultural sensitivity, and (10) structural flexibility. This set of ten dimensions is by no means exhaustive, and enhancements to strengthen its utility are expected. Nonetheless, this model addresses a fundamental misunderstanding, i.e., what is unique about WBI is not its rich mix of media features such as text, graphics, sound, animation, and video, nor its linkages to information resources around the globe, but the pedagogical dimensions that WBI can be designed to deliver. In short, the World Wide Web is only a vehicle for these dimensions. Although WBI may be more efficient or less costly than other vehicles, it is the learning dimensions that will determine its ultimate effectiveness and worth (Clark, 1994).

Each of the ten dimensions in this model is presented as a two-ended continuum with contrasting values at either end. Of course, the world is rarely dichotomous and there is more complexity involved in learning than any one of these dimensions represents. However, the individual dimensions themselves are not as important as the arrays across the ten dimensions that represent the instructional designs of various WBI sites.

Pedagogical Philosophy

← ——— →

Instructivist   Constructivist

The debate between instructivist and constructivist approaches to teaching and learning continues throughout education and training (Kafai & Resnick, 1996). At the risk of over-simplifying this issue, the "pedagogical philosophy" dimension ranges from a strict instructivist structure to a radical constructivist one. Instructivists stress the importance of objectives that exist apart from the learner. Once objectives are identified, they are sequenced into learning hierarchies, generally representing a progression from lower to higher order learning, and direct instruction is designed to address each of the objectives in sequence. Little emphasis is put on learners per se, who are viewed as passive recipients of instruction or treated as empty vessels to be filled with learning. Instructivists espouse an objectivist epistemology that defines knowledge as separate from knowing. They believe that reality exists regardless of the existence of sentient beings, humans acquire knowledge about this reality in an objective manner through the senses, learning consists of acquiring truth, and it can be measured precisely with tests.

By contrast, constructivists emphasize the primacy of the learner's intentions, experience, and cognitive strategies. According to constructivists, learners construct different cognitive structures based upon their previous knowledge and what they experience in different learning environments. It is paramount for constructivists that learning environments be as rich and diverse as possible. Instead of an empty vessel, the learner is regarded as an individual replete with pre-existing knowledge, aptitudes, motivations, and other characteristics that are difficult to assess, much less accommodate. Direct instruction is replaced with tasks to be accomplished or problems to be solved that have personal relevance for learners. With regard to epistemology, constructivists believe that knowledge does not exist outside the minds of human beings and that what we know of "reality" is individually and socially constructed based on prior experience. Rather than truth, learning consists of acquiring viable strategies that meet one's objectives, and at best, learning can be estimated only through observation and dialogue. Many WBI sites are based upon instructivist (tutorial) structures rather than constructivist (tool) approaches, but there are other sites that function primarily as resources for learners engaged in constructing their own knowledge representations.

Learning Theory

← ——— →

Behavioral   Cognitive

The design of WBI should be based upon sound learning theories. Although there are many learning theories, two that dominate instructional design are behavioral and cognitive psychology. These two theories are often juxtaposed, and thus the "learning theory" dimension has behavioral psychology at one end of the continuum and cognitive psychology at the other. Behavioral psychology continues to underlie most interactive learning systems, including WBI. According to behaviorists, the critical factors in learning are not internal states, but observable behavior, and instruction involves shaping desirable behaviors through the arrangement of stimuli, responses, feedback, and reinforcement. A stimulus is provided, usually in the form of a short presentation of content. Next, a response is demanded, often via a question. Feedback is given as to the accuracy of the response, and positive reinforcement is given for accurate responses. Inaccurate responses result in a repetition of the original stimulus or a modified (often simpler) version of it, and the cycle begins again.

Cognitive psychologists, by contrast, place more emphasis on internal mental states than on behavior. A cognitive taxonomy of internal learning states includes simple propositions, schema, rules, general rules, skills, general skills, automatic skills, and mental models (Kyllonen & Shute, 1989). Cognitivists claim that a variety of learning strategies, including memorization, direct instruction, deduction, drill and practice, and induction, are required in any learning environment depending upon the type of knowledge to be constructed by the learner. The World Wide Web appears to be a powerful vehicle for the delivery of learning environments grounded in cognitive learning theory, and futurists like Dede (1996) are exploring this frontier.

Goal Orientation

←───→

Sharply Focused   General

The goals for education and training can range from sharply focused ones (e.g., following medical trauma protocols) to general, higher-order ones (e.g., developing patient rapport). Hence, the goal orientation dimension of WBI varies in degree of focus from sharp to broad. Cole (1992) maintains that some knowledge "has undergone extensive social negotiation of meaning and which might most efficiently and effectively be presented more directly to the learner" (p. 29). In such cases, direct instruction, perhaps in the form of a Web-based tutorial, may suffice. Other knowledge is so tenuous, creative, or of a higher level that WBI that promotes inductive learning is much more appropriate. Advanced learning environments might include a blend of direct instruction with opportunities to use technology as a cognitive tool (Jonassen & Reeves, 1996). For example, progressive medical schools already place beginning students in clinical settings while providing them with pedagogical support to learn basic knowledge and skills as needed via the Internet (Brandau & Chi, 1996).

Task Orientation

←───→

Academic   Authentic

A basic tenet of adult learning theory (andragogy) is that the context of learning is enormously important to adults (Beder, 1989; Merriam, 1993). Contemporary cognitive learning theories also emphasize the importane of context (cf. Brown, Collins, & Duguid, 1989). The "task orientation" dimension has academic tasks at one end and authentic tasks at the other. Most existing examples of WBI employ academic tasks, but WBI can be designed to focus on authentic tasks relevant to learners. Consider the design of a WBI site for adult basic education. An academic design would depend heavily on having the learners complete traditional academic exercises, such as identifying parts of sentences. By contrast, an authentic design would engage the adults in practical activities such as preparing job applications, thereby situating practice and feedback within realistic scenarios. Cognitive learning theory indicates that the ways in which knowledge, skills, and attitudes are initially learned affect the degree to which these abilities can be used in other contexts. If knowledge, skills, and attitudes are learned in a context of use, they will be used in that and similar contexts. Otherwise, it is left up to learners to generate connections between problems and solutions. WBI should be designed to support the transfer of knowledge and skills whenever possible.

Source of Motivation

←───→

Extrinsic   Intrinsic

Motivation is a primary factor in any theory or model of learning. Every new educational technology promises to be intrinsically motivating, and the World Wide Web is no exception

(Perelman, 1992). The "source of motivation" dimension ranges from extrinsic (i.e., outside the learning environment) to intrinsic (i.e., integral to the learning environment). Intrinsically motivating instruction is elusive regardless of the delivery system, but some proponents seem convinced that WBI will motivate learners automatically, simply because of the integration of music, voice, graphics, text, animation, video, and a user-friendly interface. Multimedia studies indicate that learners soon tire of these media elements (Reeves, 1993a), and it should be obvious that motivational aspects must be consciously designed into WBI as rigorously as any other pedagogical dimensions.

Teacher Role

←——→

Didactic   Facilitative

WBI can be designed to support different roles for teachers, e.g., the traditional didactic role of the instructor as "sage on the stage" or the facilitative role as "guide on the side." Accordingly, the "teacher role" continuum ranges from didactic to facilitative. A quarter century ago, Carroll (1968) told us that "By far the largest amount of teaching activity in educational settings involves telling things to students..." (p. 4). Little has changed since then, despite much discussion of a shift in the teacher's role from a didactic one to that of a facilitator. Part of the problem is that educational technology research continues to be focused on how the computer can be used to present information and judge learner input (neither of which computers do well) while asking learners to memorize information and later recall it on tests (which computers do with far greater speed and accuracy than humans). It is time to assign cognitive responsibility to the part of the learning system that does it best, i.e., the learner (Jonassen & Reeves, 1996). The World Wide Web may be the ideal vehicle for this transformation. The learner should be responsible for recognizing and judging patterns of information, organizing data, constructing alternative perspectives, and representing new knowledge in meaningful ways, while the computer should perform calculations, store information, and retrieve it upon the learner's command. When the World Wide Web is used by learners as a cognitive tool, the teacher is a coach or even a collaborator in the knowledge construction process.

To date, most WBI sites are designed to support didactic roles, e.g., professors may put a syllabus and other materials for traditional courses on the Web so that students have easier access to those materials. In the near future, with technical advances such as Java and Shock-Wave enabling the development of "applets" for data visualizations and complex interactions that support student learning, WBI can be designed to provide learners with course content as well as assignments and problems to solve, with the teachers or trainers playing the roles of facilitators, coaches, mentors, and guides.

Metacognitive Support

←——→

Unsupported   Integrated

Metacognition refers to a learner's awareness of objectives, ability to plan and evaluate learning strategies, and capacity to monitor progress and adjust learning behaviors to accommodate needs (Flavell, 1979). In short, metacognitive skills are the skills one has in learning to learn. The "metacognitive support" dimension has unsupported at one end of the continuum and the integrated at the other. Imagine WBI designed to challenge learners to solve complex problems such as troubleshooting electrical circuit boards. Metacognitive support integrated into such a site could provide learners with recapitulations of their troubleshooting strategies at any point in the problem-solving process. Much research and development remains before WBI regularly includes sophisticated metacognitive support, but the potential is enormous. The construction of Web-based portfolios is another example of how support for reflection and metacognition might be provided for WBI.

Collaborative Learning Strategies

Unsupported   Integral

WBI can be designed to ignore or promote collaborative learning, i.e., some sites require co-operative learning whereas others make no provision for its support. The "collaborative learning" dimension ranges from a complete lack of support for collaboration to the inclusion of collaborative learning as an integral feature. Cooperative and collaborative learning refer to instructional methods in which learners work together in pairs or small groups to accomplish shared goals. When WBI is structured to foster cooperative learning, learners can benefit both instructionally and socially. Given an appropriate instructional design, two or more learners working together via the World Wide Web might accomplish more than an isolated learner because the interactions between the learners may be just as important for learning as the interactions between the learners and the WBI.

Cultural Sensitivity

Insensitive   Respectful

All instructional systems have cultural implications. For example, whereas constructivist pedagogy advocates questioning on the part of learners, "why?" questions may be inappropriate in some cultures. Although it is unlikely that WBI can be designed to adapt to every cultural norm, sites should be designed to be as culturally sensitive as possible. The "cultural sensitivity" dimension ranges from insensitive to respectful. Few WBI sites have been developed in which cultural sensitivity is integral to their design, whereas more than a few are culturally insensitive. For example, WBI that uses icons such as a pointing hand to indicate direction may violate a cultural taboo by representing a dismembered body part in certain African cultures. At the very least, WBI should accommodate the diverse ethnic and cultural backgrounds among the learners expected to use it. Better yet, the sites should build upon the diversity in the populations where these programs will be used so that the overall learning environment is enhanced.

Structural Flexibility

Fixed   Open

Interactive learning environments can be "fixed" or "open" with respect to time and/or place. "Fixed" systems, still dominant in U. S. education, are usually limited to specific places, e.g., a classroom or laboratory, at specific times, e.g., the ubiquitous 50-minute class period. "Open" systems can be used by the learner independent of time and/or place constraints, e.g., print-based independent study materials mailed to learners. The World Wide Web provides opportunities for more open (asynchronous) learning, although some Web-based learning events are temporally fixed (synchronous), e.g., MOOs or MUDs. Major questions remain about whether or how the World Wide Web can be used to break the hegemony of the fixed instructional modes that limit pedagogical innovation in traditional academic settings. To date, most of the World Wide Web sites developed for education and training simply supplement traditional "fixed" approaches to teaching and learning. The rapid growth of the Internet and the high bandwidth capabilities of the World Wide Web mean that interactive learning can be designed for delivery anytime, anywhere to anyone with a personal computer and a high-speed modem.

Applying the Model

As a starting point defining the critical variables incorporated within WBI, this model has applications in research, design, implementation, and evaluation. Figure 1 illustrates one possible use of the model in terms of differentiating between different forms of WBI.

WBI A in Figure 1 was designed by higher education faculty to provide support for undergraduate chemistry courses. Its instructional design includes for direct tutoring and drill-and-practice, using principles of behavioral psychology to stimulate and reinforce learning of formulas and other discrete knowledge. The teacher's role is primarily facilitative because the

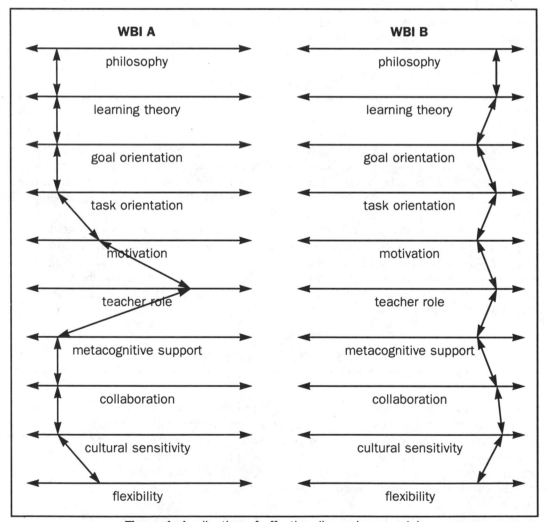

Figure 1. Application of effective dimensions model.

computer has assumed the major share of direct teaching. It provides little accommodation for individual differences or metacognitive support. No collaboration is supported, and no attention has been paid to cultural issues in the design of this site.

WBI site B is a constructivist program about HIV/AIDS for adult healthcare practitioners, available on the World Wide Web. An elaborate scenario is the focus of learner activity. There are no right answers to solving the problems presented in the scenario. Teachers are collaborators in the intrinsically motivating quest to solve real problems. Site B does make special allowances for individual differences, and provides for high levels of learner control and collaborative learning. Finally, the designers of this site have consciously attempted to make the program reflect the multicultural population in the hospitals where it will be used.

Conclusion

Many are predicting that the World Wide Web will revolutionize instruction and dramatically improve the effectiveness of education and training. If the Web is to live up to its promise, we must strive to understand the basic dimensions that WBI can (and cannot) accommodate. The proposed model is by no means comprehensive and complete, and we view it as a starting point for others to critique, modify, and improve. Accordingly, a World Wide Web site <http://itech1.coe.uga.edu/Reeves.html> providing other perspectives on this model has been developed by a team of graduate students in the Department of Instructional Technology at The University of Georgia.[1] Further review and comments are welcome.

References

Beder, H. (1989). Purposes and philosophies of adult education. In S. B. Merriam & P. M. Cunningham (Eds.), *Handbook of adult and continuing education* (pp. 37–50). San Francisco: Jossey-Bass.

Brandau, D. T., & Chi, X. (1996, June). The development of a computer-mediated academic communication system. In P. Carlson & F. Makedon (Eds.), *Educational telecommunications '96* (pp. 46–50). Boston, MA: AACE.

Brown, J. S., Collins, A., & Duguid, P. (1989). Situated cognition and the culture of learning. *Educational Researcher, 18*(1), 32–41.

Carroll, J. B. (1968). On learning from being told. *Educational Psychologist, 5,* 4–10.

Clark, R. E. (1994). Media will never influence learning. *Educational Technology Research and Development, 42*(2), 21–29.

Cole, P. (1992). Constructivism revisited: A search for common ground. *Educational Technology, 32*(2), 27–34.

Dede, C. (1996). The evolution of constructivist learning environments: Immersion in distributed, virtual worlds. In B. G. Wilson (Ed.), *Constructivist learning environments: Case studies in instructional design* (pp. 165–175). Englewood Cliffs, NJ: Educational Technology Publications.

Flavell, J. H. (1979). Metacognition and cognitive monitoring: A new area of psychological inquiry. *American Psychologist, 34,* 906–911.

Jonassen, D. H., & Reeves, T. C. (1996). Learning with technology: Using computers as cognitive tools. In D. H. Jonassen, (Ed.), *Handbook of research on educational communications and technology* (pp. 693–719). New York: Macmillan.

---

[1]The World Wide Web site about "Higher Education and the World Wide Web" was initially prototyped in the Spring of 1996 by a team of graduate students (Saada Al-Ghafry, Lisa Bennett, Peggy Leland, David Noah, and Charles Padgett) and further developed by David Noah and Tom Reeves in the Summer of 1996.

Kafai, Y., & Resnick, M. (Eds.). (1996). *Constructivism in practice: Designing, thinking, and learning in a digital world.* Mahwah, NJ: Lawrence Erlbaum Associates.

Kyllonen, P. C., & Shute, V. J. (1989). A taxonomy of learning skills. In P. L. Ackerman, R. J. Sternberg, & R. Glaser (Eds.), *Learning and individual differences: Advances in theory and research* (pp. 117–163). New York: W. H. Freeman and Company.

Lajoie, S. P., & Derry, S. J. (Eds.). (1993). *Computers as cognitive tools.* Hillsdale, NJ: Lawrence Erlbaum Associates.

Lewis, L. H. (1989). New educational technologies for the future. In S. B. Merriam & P. M. Cunningham (Eds.), *Handbook of adult and continuing education* (pp. 613–627). San Francisco: Jossey-Bass.

Merriam, S. B. (Ed.). (1993). *An update on adult learning theory.* San Francisco: Jossey-Bass.

Perelman, L. J. (1992). *School's out: Hyperlearning, the new technology, and the end of education.* New York: William Morrow.

Reeves, T. C. (1993a). Research support for interactive multimedia: Existing foundations and future directions. In C. Latchem, J. Williamson, & L. Henderson-Lancett (Eds.), *Interactive multimedia: Practice and promise* (pp. 79–96). London: Kogan Page.

Reeves, T. C. (1993b). Pseudoscience in computer-based instruction: The case of learner control research. *Journal of Computer-Based Instruction, 20*(2), 39–46.

The Authors

Thomas C. Reeves is Professor, Department of Instructional Technology, The University of Georgia, Athens, Georgia.

e-mail, World Wide Web
treeves@coe.uga.edu
http://itech1.coe.uga.edu/reeves.html

Patricia M. Reeves is a doctoral student, Department of Adult Education, The University of Georgia, Athens, Georgia.

e-mail
preeves@coe.uga.edu

7

Transformative Communication as a Stimulus to Web Innovations

Lorraine Sherry and Brent Wilson

Traditional school learning tends to be didactic. In the transmission model of communication, the instructor-as-expert delivers instruction to the students. The student is supposed to process the information mentally, much as a computer follows an algorithm to carry out an information processing sequence. School learning is usually a structured, individual activity in which time, place, topics, and activities are fixed, and the instructor determines the pace of the lesson (Norman, 1993).

Herein lies the problem. People are not machines; they are social, perceptual creatures whose preferred way of learning is experiential. People often work well in small groups, sharing their knowledge and collaborating to perform complex tasks. They do best when learning is practical, situated, and context-dependent. And, when the learning is self-paced rather than instructor-paced, learners are able to pause and reflect on what they have learned. An ideal learning environment would maintain the substance of traditional, structured instruction, while achieving some of the flexibility and informality of learning experiences out of school.

Transformative Communication

As the Web extends learning beyond classroom walls to learning communities, so must roles and concepts of teaching and learning be restructured. Pea (1994) describes two alternatives to the transmission model of communication: the ritual view, in which representations of shared understandings are communicated within a group of learners to perpetuate tradition, and the transformative view, which combines elements of the transmission and ritual views. In the transformative view, the communication between teacher and taught is generative: Instructors learn along with their students. As a result, instructors and students alike are transformed as learners by the process of communication. Through such collaborative discourse within the learning community, a two-way dynamic system comes into being. The active learning that occurs then begins to push the frontiers of knowledge.

> It takes significant effort for an instructor to understand what students are thinking about new learning topics. They may well develop new understandings of the subject domain by seeing how students have spontaneously come to think about it and what surprising inferences they may draw. (Pea, 1994, p. 290)

Instructors participate actively in the learning process by contributing interventions or providing distinctive tasks that help students transfer knowledge to new contexts. This becomes crucial when the community of learners is dispersed in time and space, and is engaging in computer-mediated communication within a computer-supported learning environment. The instructor's role now includes designing an infrastructure for constructive discourse and negotiation of meaning among the students—an environment that supports not only transmission of information and management of roles and activities, but also social support for the efforts of the members of the learning community.

The shift from instructor-dominated instruction to transformative communication has important implications for the instructor's teaching style, epistemology, and concept of the students as an audience. The focus is now on the learner and authentic problems, rather than on a structured curriculum.

First, the instructor is no longer "in charge"—the instructor's role is no longer authoritarian, but rather, that of a facilitator. This can be very threatening to instructors who desire to exert total control over the learning process.

Second, the process of instruction lends itself to an awakening within the students—a realization that the instructor is not the sole authority or repository of answers, and that the answers to real problems aren't as simple as they might seem! This begins to stimulate deeper understandings within the student, at the same time as it could perhaps make an ambitious instructor feel irrelevant to the learning process.[1]

And, third, the students are no longer just drawing on classroom resources, but are accessing an unlimited number of people, activities, and knowledge databases through the Web. Thus, they are able to present and disseminate polished products that they have created themselves.

Just as this process may threaten traditional instructor roles, it also liberates students and communities of learners. Many barriers of time and space are removed for instructors and students who live in impoverished learning environments. They now can draw on resources from around the globe and form a more global perspective on their learning experiences. Moreover, they begin to engage in cumulative knowledge building and reflection, resulting in a shared base of experiences and understandings.

The downside to this is that a gap may begin to form between the technological "haves" and "have nots," as the use of technology exacerbates the economic differences between school districts (Ravitch, 1987). Moreover, if the technology is implemented without a concurrent change in pedagogy, the use of the Web will not guarantee learning any more than a campus library guarantees learning. Unless the local culture supports the shift in teaching and learning styles, both technically and philosophically, innovative learning environments are set up for failure (Gross *et al.*, 1970; Teasley, 1996).

Developing Supports

Any innovative project requires ongoing evaluation, revision, and support until the innovation becomes part of the culture. Web-based instruction involves creating an environment where resources are available and collaboration is supported, where Web-based activities are incorporated into an overall learning framework, and where novices and experts alike are supported. This is not easy! In our own research (Lawyer-Brook & Sherry, 1996), we have found that creating online helpdesks, manning them with technology support people, and providing toll-free telephone numbers for online help do not of themselves constitute an adequate learner support environment. People will go to friends whom they perceive as experts, or to a user's group

---

[1]It can also pose a problem for students who resist technology on grounds of principle, believing that the technology influences their lives in negative ways.

where there is collegial exchange and cooperation, rather than seeking advice from an unknown person at the other end of the line.

The same type of failure may occur as we try to enculturate graduate students into using e-mail communications between regular meetings of classes and seminars, even if a learner support environment is provided and the department is ostensibly committed to educational technologies as its professional focus (Wilson, Ryder, McCahan, & Sherry, 1996).

Ellsworth (1991) recommends using electronically mediated communications for adult learners because it is a new avenue for learning that provides interaction that is not time specific, allowing for quick feedback on homework and assignments. However, in our own experience, we have found that the learning curve is steep; there is also the danger of a "funnel effect" in which the more vociferous members of the class dominate the discussion while others gradually drop out; and then the class ends. As a result, the whole concept of quarterly or semesterly classes is called into question. We suggest that the use of e-mail as a lifelong habit needs to be infused throughout the whole university culture, and used as a tool throughout the entire curriculum, not just as a "one-time-shot" for a few specific classes.

This leads to two further questions:

- What kinds of communication are transformative?

- What do we need in a learner support environment?

When learning occurs by instructors and students alike, not in clearly directed, controlled terms, but by expanding the frontiers of knowledge, we are dealing with transformative communication. Some key indicators that transformative communication is happening are:

- The student teaches the instructor something he or she didn't know before about the technology or about the content.

- The student goes beyond the textbook or the lecture to reveal differences of opinion among the experts.

- More emphasis is placed upon finding support or backing for a position than on conforming to authority.

- Students participate in setting the agenda for the class by helping to choose content or learning methods, or both.

- Students are calling the instructor's attention to valuable learning resources.

- Students are having conversations with knowledgeable people the instructor doesn't know.

- While the instructor helps establish expectations and sets a clear assessment standard, the students collaboratively guide much of their own learning.

- The instructor finds himself or herself saving student work—not merely as examples of student work, but as content resources for future reference.

When groups of people gather together to provide mutual support and scaffolding for learning and performance, we are dealing with an effective support environment for a learning community. Some key indicators of an effective learner support environment are:

- Students are solving their own problems and sharing their solutions with others.

- Students are making presentations to classmates, announcing the finding of a solution to a common problem.

- Solutions to common problems are codified and shared with succeeding groups.

- Effective learning resources are found, "stolen," or developed, and are made available to the entire learning community.

- Students are encouraged and rewarded for taking initiative.

- Students are made to feel that their unique strengths are valued, and that they have something to offer the larger learning community.

- Technical supports are "multiply encoded" via print resources, online resources, and person-to-person hand-holding.

- The cultural values of learner support are reflected in the formal rules and reward structure of the organization.

- The informal culture encourages risk-taking and innovation, and inclusion of diverse needs.

These features become especially important in Web-based instruction, since its activities tend to be less structured than traditional instruction.

Levels of Structure in Web-Based Instruction

In our experience, we have worked with a continuum of instructional activities and learner support environments, ranging from unstructured to highly structured, each with its advantages and disadvantages, each appropriate to the situation. Table 1 illustrates some typical activities.

Table 1. Typical activities for Web-based instruction.

Unstructured	Graduate students participating in e-mail discussions in seminars.
	Creating individual student home pages.
Very loosely structured	A team building a departmental home page.
	A team using e-mail conferencing to build a shared knowledge base.
Mostly structured	A team participating in a case-based instruction project or competition.
Structured	A class building an annotated bibliography, with assigned roles and literature format, to be placed on the Web.

Please note: We are not attempting to generalize these types of activities to a set of principles. We began by "just doing it"—engaging students in loosely structured activities. Later on, as we gained more comfort and expertise with computer-supported learning environments, authentic problems, and student-directed learning, we tried some more structured activities such as case-based instruction. In general, our unstructured activities tended to lead to irregularly dispersed knowledge with varying levels of expertise, whereas our structured activities tended to lead to convergent outcomes with a more commonly shared knowledge base.

In unstructured activities such as building student home pages or participating in e-mail conferences, where individuals decide on the sophistication of a project or their level of participation in a discussion group, we have found erratic differences in learning outcomes among participants. Some members became experts in certain areas while others remained novices. Some people book advantage of the technology while others held back.

Some members served in critical support roles, keeping the community together, while others placed stress on group functioning.

In the loosely structured activity of building a school home page, expertise was still irregularly distributed and developed at different rates for each individual in the learning community. However, "the group became a self-organizing system with members contributing their unique expertise and, in turn, learning new skills and extending the group's common knowledge base" (Sherry & Myers, 1996, p. 203). A common knowledge base emerged from the active dialogue of our design team as we took a reflective, critical look at our own activities while seeking to understand and apply concepts and techniques that were needed to carry out an authentic task. Although the collaborative efforts of the team sometimes resulted in differences of opinion, we found, like Ferraro and her colleagues (1995), that negotiation and resolution of conflict often resulted in a better product. Collaboration allowed our team members to fully explore the possible alternative courses of action and restructure our knowledge accordingly.

In the spring of 1996, six students in our program participated in the 1996 Virtual ID Case Competition,[2] a Web-based case study experience with six universities participating. There were no right answers and as many opinions as there were teams (and judges!). The jigsaw method (Brown & Palincsar, 1989) allowed each student to research an aspect of the case and to contribute individual sections to the final, collaboratively written case study. Hence, the resulting knowledge base was totally shared, and each individual member attained much of the shared expertise of the entire group.

Finally, more highly structured activities tend to have a standard format and a fixed learning goal in mind. An example of this was the creation of an annotated bibliography of readings related to cognition and instruction, in which each student was required to submit synopses of three readings to both the instructor and an editor. After each synopsis was reviewed, revised, and resubmitted, it was added to the class's Web page.[3] In such cases, the Web becomes a new medium, but the activity is not radically new or interactive.

Thus, a whole range of activities may be appropriate, depending on the needs of the situation, the prior knowledge and repertoire of skills of the audience, and the learning support available to students. A committed instructor will explore different activities, adding bit by bit to his or her own storehouse of strategies, as different opportunities present themselves. Gradually, such activities may be assimilated into the teaching strategies of the department or school, where they are more generally adopted and institutionalized.

"Which activity do I use when?," you may ask. That depends upon your comfort level with the technology and the instructional model, your own experience and skills, and the mental and emotional capital (energy and time) that you are willing to invest in the innovation. Sometimes these activities are initially done outside of the normal curriculum, which means that students get no academic credit for them. Even within courses, such innovations involve an element of unrewarded risk-taking for the instructor. A few high-achieving students and early-adapter instructors end up doing most the work. The true payoff is found in the satisfaction that some people get out of helping others, or the sense of belonging to a group that has developed a shared culture, shared values, and a shared vision. However, by advertising your group's successes and showing that learning outcomes are indeed achieved, you will find that these innovations gradually become integrated into the normal curriculum.

Having decided upon an appropriate activity, you may then ask, "How can I support an environment in which the learner assumes more direction and control over the learning goals,

---

[2]URL: http://teach.virginia.edu/go/ITcases
[3]URL: http://www.cudenver.edu/public/education/edschool/cog/cog.html

content, and methods?" To start, you must shift your focus from teaching to support, and envision your class, team, or group as a learning community. Wilson and Ryder (1996) suggest that, though learning can happen in a variety of ways, a common pattern of mutually supportive interaction will tend to emerge in learning communities, outlined by the following seven steps:

- Articulate the learning need. A community member becomes aware that he or she lacks certain knowledge or skills, or just has a simple desire to know something.

- Seek help in a group forum. The community maintains a public forum such as a distribution list or conference, where help may be found.

- Engage in a help consultation. Community members help one another, drawing on a variety of resources—human, archived questions, search tools, performance supports, or instruction.

- Assess learning. Typically, a combination of self-assessment and consensual agreement is used.

- Share the solution with the group. A restatement of the original problem and its solution may be helpful.

- Archive the interaction or restated solution for future reference. This information should be stored in a public location for future access by any group member.

- Repeat this process, or any part, if necessary to support learning.

Through collaborative activities and experiences, the team becomes cohesive, and develops into a dynamic learning community. This is most likely to happen when you use the Web to its best advantage—for information access, communication, collaboration, and sharing—and not for linear presentations, convergent learning outcomes, or high-level interactivity.

The ultimate concept of Web-based instruction is to set up a structure where all members of the learning community come to share knowledge and skills, to learn how to access necessary resources, to create new knowledge, and to disseminate it throughout both the local and global learning community. Needless to say, this is a very value-laden concept. Not every instructor is willing to surrender control, to give up the idea of being the information provider. Web-based instruction is bound to upset the existing system; it will either force change or cause resistance. By bringing new capabilities into existing instruction, however, the Web is redefining the rules and expanding the frontiers of curriculum and instruction.

References

Brown, A., & Palincsar, A. S. (1989). Guided, cooperative learning and individual knowledge acquisition. In L. B. Resnick (Ed.), *Knowing, learning, and instruction*. Hillsdale NJ: Lawrence Erlbaum Associates.

Ellsworth, J. H. (1991, May). *Electronically mediated learning among adults*. Paper presented at the National Conference on the Adult Learner, Columbia, SC (ERIC Document Reproduction Service No. ED 337 704).

Ferraro, A., Rogers, E., & Geisler, C. (1995). *Team learning through computer supported collaborative design*. Paper presented at the CSCL'95 Conference, Indianapolis, IN (http://www-cscl95.indiana.edu/cscl95/ferraro.html).

Gross, N., Giaquinta, J. B., & Bernstein, M. (1970). Failure to implement a major organizational innovation. In M. W. Miles & W. W. Charters, Jr. (Eds.), *Learning in social settings.* Boston, MA: Allyn & Bacon.

Lawyer-Brook, D., & Sherry, L. (1996, March). *Creating Connections: An Internet training program for rural K–12 instructors.* Paper presented at the Seventh National Conference on College Teaching and Learning, Jacksonville, FL (http://www.cudenver.edu/~lsherry/ejvc.html).

Norman, D. A. (1993). *Things that make us smart.* Reading, MA: Addison-Wesley.

Pea, R. D. (1994). Seeing what we build together: Distributed multimedia learning environments for transformative communications. *The Journal of the Learning Sciences, 3*(3), 285–299.

Ravitch, D. (1987). Technology and the curriculum. In M. A. White (Ed.), *What curriculum for the information age?* Hillsdale, NJ: Lawrence Erlbaum Associates.

Sherry, L., & Myers, K. M. M. (1996). Developmental research on collaborative design. In *Proceedings of the 43rd Annual Conference of the Society for Technical Communication* (pp. 199–204). Arlington, VA: Society for Technical Communication.

Teasley, U. H. (1996, February). *Factors affecting instructors' decisions about use and non-use of computers: Administrative actions.* Paper presented at the meeting of the Association for Educational Communications and Technology, Indianapolis, IN.

Wilson, B., & Ryder, M. (1996). *Dynamic learning communities.* Manuscript in preparation (http://www.cudenver.edu/~bwilson/DLC.html).

Wilson, B., Ryder, M., McCahan, J., & Sherry, L. (1996, February). *Cultural assimilation of the Internet: A case study.* Paper presented at the meeting of the Association for Educational Communications and Technology, Indianapolis, IN (http://www.cudenver.edu/~bwilson/assim.html).

The Authors

Lorraine Sherry is a doctoral student at the University of Colorado at Denver, and Research Associate, RMC Research Corporation, Denver, Colorado.

e-mail, World Wide Web
lsherry@carbon.cudenver.edu
http://www.cudenver.edu/~lsherry

Brent Wilson is Associate Professor at the University of Colorado at Denver.

e-mail, World Wide Web
bwilson@carbon.cudenver.edu
http://www.cudenver.edu/~bwilson

8

Distance Learning Environments Via the World Wide Web

Janette R. Hill

Distance learning consists of instruction through print or electronic communications media to persons engaged in learning in a place or time different from that of the instructor(s) or other students (Moore, Cookson, & Donaldson, 1990). From its beginnings with pen and paper in correspondence study in England (Sherow & Wedemeyer, 1990), distance learning has incorporated several technologies to meet the "media" requirement, including radio, television, and computers. Computer technologies have been used in a variety of ways to meet various needs: chat groups, electronic mail, and, most recently, the World Wide Web.

Of the methods incorporating computer technologies, the Web holds the greatest potential for promoting interaction by, and engagement of, the learner (Shotsberger, 1996). A concern often associated with distance learning is the lack of learner interaction. The capabilities afforded by the Web (e.g., animation, audio, chat, graphics, and video) make active learning in distant learning environments possible.

Several Web sites have been developed to provide learners with access to instructional resources from a distance (see, for example, http://www.utexas.edu/world/instruction/index.html). These sites range from those posting course materials such as syllabi, class notes, and review materials (see, for example, *Computers in the Classroom*; http://seamonkey.ed.asu.edu/ emc300/ index.html) to sites which immerse the learner in activities, promoting interaction, involvement, and engagement (Shamp, 1996; Shotsberger, 1996). While sites such as the Virtual Hospital (http://indy.radiology.uiowa.edu/VirtualHospital.html) and the Virtual Language Lab (http://philae.sas.upenn.edu/) portray high-end use of the technological and pedagogical techniques for the Web, they are currently the exception rather than the rule. Most course-based or learning sites simply post course materials. Use of the Web as merely an "electronic book" falls far short of the potential the medium affords. As with other distance learning initiatives, the Web has substantial potential for moving instruction away from a repository model to one where *active learning* can occur (Filipczak, 1995; Howard-Vital, 1995; Shotsberger, 1996).

The purpose of this chapter is to discuss issues, prospects, and challenges associated with creating distance learning environments via the Web. While learning via the Web is a central focus of this text, in this chapter, the issues are discussed in broad terms. The reader is encouraged to look to other chapters for specific information on particular issues.

Distance Learning Issues and the World Wide Web

Design, development, delivery, and technological considerations become relevant when creating a distance learning environment via the Web. Three primary Web attributes make creating Web-based learning environments challenging: access to multimedia, asynchronicity, and "required" reading.

Access to multimedia expands the range of resources the learner can use to participate in the learning process. The asynchronous nature assists in self-directed learning through flexible scheduling; both the learner and the instructor decide when and where to access course materials and other resources. While some interaction may take place in synchronous mode, access traditionally follows a "when convenient for you" model.

"Required" reading is created by the information displayed on the screen, whether instructor or student generated. The dynamically created messages can take several forms, from text to audio and video files to animation (Harris, 1994). Keeping up with the required "reading," as well as interpretations of the media, can be a significant challenge.

The unique attributes, along with the general nature of the Web, generate issues beyond those associated with all distance learning environments. General distance learning issues, as well as specific Web issues, are presented using a framework established by Schrum (1995), which includes four areas for consideration: pedagogical, technological, organizational, and institutional. As the "proper" use of technology is a discussion with any innovation introduced into a learning environment (Reed & Sork, 1990; Schrum, 1995), ethical issues are also considered.

Pedagogical

Pedagogical issues relate to teaching and learning. A fundamental pedagogical issue pertains to the importance of the medium in distance learning environments. As pointed out by Winn (1990), the medium often drives the methodology, creating constraints on instruction. While one could argue that this is no different than face-to-face (i.e., "traditional") learning environments, the reliance on the technology for delivery of instruction increases the constraints exponentially. The incorporation of several pedagogical methodologies and strategies in the distance learning environment can aid in breaking the constraints (see, for example, Joyce & Weil, 1996).

The impact of distance learning on the learner is another major issue. A complaint often voiced by learners in distance learning environments is that they feel isolated and unconnected. Developing strategies that empower the learner, encouraging both cooperative and independent work as well as interaction, can be used to overcome this limitation (Davie & Wells, 1991; Schrum, 1992; Senecal, 1995; Smagorinsky & Fly, 1993; Wolcott, 1995).

Several unique issues arise related to pedagogy and the Web. Information overload is one issue. Working in an environment that is filled with multiple media can lead to feelings of being overwhelmed. This may be closely related to the issue of dissonance often associated with hyperlinked environments (Marchionini, 1988). Ways to assist the learner in overcoming the "lost in hyperspace" phenomena should be incorporated into the course.

Timing is another issue. In addition to being multi-level, Web environments are also "multi-speed" (Romiszowski in Harris, 1994, p. 181). Learners have the capability of accessing materials over time; as such, they can also engage in activities over time. This can lead to feelings of a lack of overall cohesiveness, presenting a considerable challenge for establishing themes for interaction and discussion (Harris, 1994; Schrum, 1992).

Technological

Technological issues are concerns related to the hardware and software used in distance learning environments. Issues such as bandwidth, speed of communication lines, intuitive software applications, and costs all fall under this category (Hannafin, Hill, & Land, in press). With a heavy reliance on a computer, modem and network connection, access to hardware is a substantial issue. Without access, interaction in a Web environment is not possible. This leads to a closely associated issue: cost. While the learner may choose to purchase the necessary equipment (or have to), the costs associated with this decision are not insignificant (Hannafin, Hill, & Land, in press).

Even if access and costs are not issues, other technological challenges may arise. Use of computer technologies is not yet widespread. This creates a situation where "technology novices" are enrolled in Web courses. Intimidation by, and fear of, the equipment are issues which must be considered (Boston, 1992). How to use the equipment, as well as the software, is an associated concern.

Perhaps the biggest challenge associated with the technological side of the Web are the frustrations that often accompany technological difficulties. In addition to frustrations created from lack of knowledge in relation to hardware and software, frustrations can also mount from an inability to connect to the network or in the need to wait while information downloads to the desktop (Schrum, 1992). Not only is it aggravating, it can also be expensive. This is an issue for everyone involved in Web environments.

Organizational

Organizational issues pertain to the preparation of the distance learning course. Planning for the course is one major issue falling under this category. Course planning and preparation are important activities within the context of distance learning (Schrum, 1995; Wolcott, 1995). Challenges faced within a traditional learning environment are magnified as the facilitator must think several weeks or months ahead in order to produce the site and materials, as well as enabling access to the tools needed to use the materials.

Schrum (1995) discusses several other organizational issues that should be considered during the planning and preparation phases of course design, including how much of the course will rely on Web-related interactions and the type of assignments and interactions to be included in the course. Each needs to be considered prior to the implementation of a Web-based course.

Another issue in the organizational category is ongoing support. While planing and preparing for the course are important, continued support, both technological and human-based, throughout a course is vital if the course is to maintain momentum and be successful. The support needed is a constant challenge throughout a Web course (Boston, 1992).

Providing a mechanism that will ensure cohesiveness is another organizational issue. Organizing the course so there is a sense of continuity is important. It will assist both the learner and the instructor in maintaining a sense of continuity, as well as aid in community-building. One feature of the Web that makes this issue less debilitating than with other distance learning technologies is the ease with which pages can be updated and revised. Daily updates and revisions to a Web site are quite feasible. However, a caution must be issued: While it is easy to make changes to the environment, too much change can potentially be distracting for the learner. A Web page template should be established and adhered to in order to minimize learner dissonance.

Institutional

Institutional issues are policy-related concerns generally decided by the organization involved in the distance learning implementation. These organizations include the institution delivering the instruction as well as the one receiving the instruction from a distance. Concern such as faculty development, promotion and tenure, course credit, payment, course validity, evaluation and support fall under this area (Boston, 1992; Schrum, 1995).

A major issue associated with institutional/policy decisions is the amount of time it takes for faculty to prepare for Web courses. Not only is it "prep" work for a new course, it is also getting to know the equipment and how it works, as well as staying on-top of technological updates. Schrum (1995) recommends at least one semester of reduced time to assist the faculty member in preparing.

Ethical

Ethical considerations in a distance learning environment act as a foundation for several areas presented thus far. Ethical issues need to be considered in any process in which learners "... are engaged in a process to change another person in some way and any effort to change a person has the potential to cause harm" (Reed & Sork, 1990, p. 30). The following are issues falling under this category: admission; intake and retention of students; course development and presentation; program and course marketing; program and course administration; learner/facilitator interaction; and program, course, and learner evaluation.

All issues related to distance learning must be considered when deciding to initiate a learning environment at a distance. The more planning and up-front work that is completed, the easier it will be for all participants (learners, facilitators, technicians, instructors) to positively experience distance learning.

Web-Based Distance Learning Environments: Prospects and Challenges

One of the goals in creating a distance learning environment is the desire to create a community of learners. This is different from establishing an educational environment. In an educational environment, learners may have some interaction, but collaboration and active learning are not emphasized as they are in a learning environment. The creation of a virtual community will add to the support needed in a distance learning environment to move it toward becoming an environment for learning (Dede, 1995).

Harasim (1990) shares several visions of the use of electronic technologies in learning environments. The ability of the Web to reach remote learners makes it a viable option for all types of learners (kids, single parents, graduate students, etc.) across all grade levels. The Web has the ability to create an active learning environment, one which affords the learner opportunities to engage and think. The Web also opens the world in terms of the people who can be reached and the resources that can be gathered.

Many challenges are associated with creating meaningful learning environments via the Web. These range from technological challenges in keeping ahead of the technology growth to ethical concerns related to access and evaluation.

A significant challenge in using the Web for instruction is the lack of understanding associated with emerging information systems (Hill & Hannafin, 1996). Conventional school activities help to shape "compliant" thinking (McCaslin & Good, 1992). This engenders learners who lack the orientation, mental models, and strategies (or capabilities for creating them) for these open-ended learning environments, where divergent thinking, multiple perspectives, and independent thinking are critical (Hannafin, Hall, Land, & Hill, 1994; Hill, Lebow, Driscoll, & Rowley, 1994; Howard-Vital, 1995). Adjusting the ways we teach to foster divergent thinking and multiple perspectives may assist learners in using these environments effectively and with minimal disorientation.

As the Web and other interactive technologies continue to grow, the need for research also expands (Duchastel, 1991). Several questions (Schrum, 1992) can be considered for researching distance learning environments, including:

- In what ways do educators who learn in this manner [the Web] integrate the technology into their professional work?

- What is the nature of communication and interaction online, and in what ways is it similar or different from other communications? (p. 50)

Harris (1995) advocates the use of a collaborative model to create "telecollaborative" projects. *Science Connections*, a distance learning project implemented at the Learning and Performance Support Laboratory at the University of Georgia, incorporated substantial collaborative efforts across institutions (universities and K–12 schools) as well as across groups (professors, teachers, pre-service teachers, and students). As of this writing, the project is not complete; however, the prospects for creating and implementing these types of environments via the Web are promising (Luetkehans, Hill, & Hagan, 1996).

Conclusion

The Web is a technology that has clear potential for creating a learning-centered environment, bridging gaps between distance learning and traditional learning environments. As the educational use of Web-based technologies becomes widespread, distinctions between distance education and classroom-based education may become less apparent.

References

Boston, R. L. (1992). Remote delivery of instruction via the PC and modem: What have we learned? *The American Journal of Distance Education, 6*(3), 45–57.

Davie, L. E., & Wells, R. (1991). Empowering the learner through computer-mediated communication. *The American Journal of Distance Education, 5*(1), 15–23.

Dede, C. (1995, July). The transformation of distance education to distributed learning. *InTRO* (http://129.7.160.78/InTRO.html).

Duchastel, P. (1991). *Research directions for interactive information technologies*. Unpublished manuscript.

Filipczak, B. (1995). Putting the learning into distance learning. *Training, 32*(10), 111–112, 114–118.

Hannafin, M., Hall, C., Land, S., & Hill, J. (1994). Learning in open-ended environments: Assumptions, methods, and implications. *Educational Technology, 34*(8), 48–55.

Hannafin, M. J., Hill, J. R., & Land, S. (in press). Student-centered learning and interactive multimedia: Status, issues, and implications. *Contemporary Education*.

Harasim, L. (1990). Computer learning networks: Educational applications of computer conferencing. *Journal of Distance Education, 1*(1), 59–70.

Harris, J. (1994). Telecommunications training by immersion: University courses online. *Machine-Mediated Learning, 4*(2&3), 177–185.

Harris, J. (1995). Organizing and facilitating telecollaborative projects. *The Computing Teacher, 22*(5), 66–69.

Hill, J. R., & Hannafin, M. J. (1996). Cognitive strategies in the use of a hypermedia information system. *ETR&D*. Manuscript submitted for publication.

Hill, J. R., Lebow, D., Driscoll, M. P., & Rowley, K. (1994, April). *The effect of generative teaching on students' metaphors for learning*. Paper presented at the annual meeting of the NCIC (American Educational Research Association), New Orleans, LA.

Howard-Vital, M. R. (1995). Information technology: Teaching and learning in the twenty-first century. *Educational Horizons, 73*(4) 193–196.

Joyce, B., & Weil, M. (1996). *Models of teaching* (5th ed.). Boston: Allyn and Bacon.

Luetkehans, L., Hill, J. R., & Hagan, T. (1996). Science connections: Problem solving at a distance. In M. P. Driscoll (chair), *Proceedings of Getting It Together: Collaboration in Distance Education*. Conference held at the Florida State University, Tallahassee.

Marchionini, G. (1988, November). Hypermedia and learning: Freedom and chaos. *Educational Technology, 28*(11) 8–12.

McCaslin, M., & Good, T. (1992). Compliant cognition: The misalliance of management and instructional goals in current school reform. *Educational Researcher, 21*(3), 4–17.

Moore, M. G., Cookson, P., & Donaldson, J. (Eds.). (1990). *Contemporary issues in American distance education*. New York: Pergamon Press.

Reed, D., & Sork, T. J. (1990). Ethical considerations in distance education. *The American Journal of Distance Education, 4*(2), 30–43.

Schrum, L. (1992, December). Professional development in the information age: An online experience. *Educational Technology, 32*(12), 49–53.

Schrum, L. (1995). *Teaching at a distance: Strategies for successful planning and development*. Unpublished manuscript.

Senecal, M. (1995, February). Interactivity: A matter of give and take. *UNESCO Courier* (2), 16–18.

Shamp, S. A. (1996). *Instruction on the Web* (http://www.grady.uga.edu/techexpo/).

Sherow, S., & Wedemeyer, C. A. (1990). Origins of distance education in the United States. In D. R. Garrison & D. Shale (Eds.), *Education at a distance: From issues to practice* (pp. 7–22). Malabar, FL: Robert E. Krieger Publishing Company.

Shotsberger, P. G. (1996, March/April). Instructional uses of the World Wide Web: Exemplars and precautions. *Educational Technology, 36*(2), 47–50.

Smagorinsky, P., & Fly, P. K. (1993). The social environment of the classroom: A Vygotskian perspective on small group process. *Communication Education, 42*(2), 159–171.

Winn, B. (1990). Media and instructional methods. In D. R. Garrison & D. Shale (Eds.), *Education at a distance: From issues to practice* (pp. 53–66). Malabar, FL: Robert E. Krieger Publishing Company.

Wolcott, L. L. (1995). The distance teacher as a reflective practitioner. *Educational Technology, 35*(1), 39–43.

The Author

Janette R. Hill is Assistant Professor of Educational Technology, University of Northern Colorado, Greeley, Colorado.

e-mail, World Wide Web
hill@edtech.univnorthco.edu
http://www.edtech.univnorthco.edu/coe/epsat/edtech/professors/hill/janette.html

9

Distance Education
and the World Wide Web

Barry Willis and John Dickinson

Distance education takes place when a teacher and student(s) are separated by physical distance and technology (i.e., audio, video, data, and print), often in combination with face-to-face communication, is used to bridge the instructional gap.

Without exception, effective distance education programs begin with careful planning and a focused understanding of course requirements and student needs. Appropriate technology can only be selected once these elements are understood in detail. There is no mystery in the way effective distance education courses and programs develop. They don't happen spontaneously; they evolve over time through the creative efforts of dedicated teacher-trainers in tandem with appropriate technology, and through an insightful understanding of the content to be developed and the learners for which it is intended.

Asynchronous computer tools such as the World Wide Web offer the teacher-trainer a number of course preparation and delivery options. Before exploring specific applications of the World Wide Web in the context of distance education, we will contrast the learning environment confronted by the distant teacher-trainer with that of the traditional instructor.

In the traditional instructional setting, teacher-trainers rely on a number of visual and unobtrusive cues to assess the learners' level of familiarity and understanding of the course content. A quick glance, for example, reveals those who are attentively taking notes, pondering difficult concepts, or enthusiastically preparing to respond to the instructor's questions. The same quick glance reveals those who are tense, frustrated, confused, tired, or bored.

Learners who are enthusiastic, fully engaged in the class and attentive to the questions posed by the instructor reveal something quite different from those who are withdrawn, and who arrive without class materials or receptive attitudes. Again, alert instructors factor these unobtrusive cues into class planning and delivery.

The effective teacher-trainer consciously and subconsciously receives and analyzes these visual cues with great subtlety and clarity. As a result, the delivery of information, and often the course content itself, is adapted to meet the unique mix of learner moods, characteristics, and needs at any one time. This process of visually receiving information, processing it, and adapting teaching behavior accordingly is so rapid and automatic that few teacher-trainers spend time thinking about it. To them, having an instinctive feel for their students is just "good teaching."

In reality, however, while natural instinct may help, it is the dynamics at play in and around the instructional setting that increase teacher effectiveness. For example, a well designed learning environment offers both instructors and learners many spontaneous opportunities for interaction outside of the instructional setting. Perhaps they talk between sessions or at the work place, meet informally on an assignment over lunch, or share mutual interests. Merely living in the same community provides a common frame of reference that leads to broader understanding and a sense of shared experience.

Finally, face-to-face interaction takes place without any technological link. Communication is spontaneous and free flowing, without the distraction of manipulating switches, anticipating potential technical difficulties, or relying on a piece of equipment linking teacher and students for purposes of communication and feedback.

In contrast, the challenges faced by the distant teacher are imposing. The teacher-trainer must, for example:

1. **Look at the course in a new way.** Few with distant teaching experience would downplay the importance of adapting traditionally delivered courses to the unique instructional environment confronted with distance education. In many cases, the more comfortable the instructor is in teaching in a traditional setting, the more difficult it is to face the reality that significant re-thinking and adaptation will be required for effective distant course delivery.

2. **Shift from the role of content provider to content facilitator.** To use a concert analogy, the traditional instructor serves as lead soloist, while the distance educator is the conductor and concert master. Proficiency here requires undisputed mastery of the subject being taught as well as an ability to draw on the varied backgrounds and hidden talents of the students.

3. **Gain comfort and proficiency in using technology as the primary teacher-student link.** In most distance education contexts, technology is the critical link between the teacher and students. Effective use of this link requires a working understanding of delivery system strengths and weaknesses, as well as related utilization strategies. This understanding, in turn, leads to the technical competence and confidence needed to effectively teach at a distance.

4. **Learn to teach effectively without the visual control provided by direct eye contact.** Distant teachers have few, if any, visual cues. Even the visual cues that do exist are filtered through technological devices such as video monitors. The effortless flow of stimulating teacher-class conversation can feel contrived and lacking in dynamism when spontaneity is altered by technical requirements and distance. Unless one uses a real-time visual medium such as television, the teacher receives no visual information from the distant sites. The teacher never really knows if, for example, students are asleep, talking among themselves, or even in the room. Separation by distance also affects the general rapport among students.

5. **Develop an understanding and appreciation for the distant students' lifestyle.** Living in different communities, geographic regions, states, or even countries deprives the teacher and students of a common community link or reference point. Often, the students' realm of experience, living conditions, and culture are foreign to the instructor, or even other class participants. To be effective, the instructor must gain an understanding of the students, either through first-hand observation or discussion with colleagues experienced with the target learner group. Instructional applications of the World Wide Web are many and varied. The World Wide Web offers teacher-trainers a number of opportunities to effectively use technology without some of the pitfalls inherent in other technical delivery systems. Specific distance education applications of the World Wide Web can be broken down into content delivery, program support, and enhanced interaction.

Content Delivery

Content delivery may be improved in areas where multimedia and interactive environments can be used to simulate situations or experiments that are difficult or expensive to duplicate for large numbers of learners. Areas such as architecture, chemistry, and forestry provide opportunities for these types of simulations. The advantage of the World Wide Web in these areas is that it can help delivery of these environments to learners located at a distance from the teacher-trainer.

Program Support and Enhanced Interaction

A traditional videotape or even an interactive video delivery method does not allow the learner to interact with the instructor in a natural way, so that office hours or out-of-class questions are sometimes more difficult. In addition, it rarely allows the learner to interact with other learners. The World Wide Web can be used to facilitate important interactive activities between the teacher-trainer and learner. For example:

- *"Virtual" office hours*: The World Wide Web, e-mail, and newsgroups are some Internet methods of holding office hours. Desktop interactive video through the Internet is an emerging technology that can allow real-time question and answer sessions.

- *Learner-to-learner interaction*: The Internet can be used to enhance communication among learners. They can work on assignments and team projects together by using newsgroups for group discussions and e-mail for working on questions or assignments that are not of interest to the entire class. Another important benefit for this type of interaction for distance education is that the learners are often distributed over many time zones or have different job schedules, so the asynchronous nature of newsgroups and e-mail is essential to allow an entire class to participate in discussions.

- *Web-based testing and performance evaluation*: Since the World Wide Web can be interactive, it can be used to create individual tests, to give and evaluate these tests, and to communicate all evaluations back to the learner. This could be used to customize the evaluation to the learner, making the evaluation process a valuable learning process. The teacher-trainer would need to be integrated into this evaluation process. If this were done correctly, it would be a major change in the traditional teach-test cycle.

- *Enhanced inter-institutional collaboration*: One of the opportunities that the World Wide Web provides is a sharing of teaching materials that has rarely been possible before. Course materials finalized in the form of a book have been shared for years, but now detailed course materials such as syllabi, class notes, assignments, laboratory experiments, and even learner-learner discussions can be shared between institutions by both teacher-trainers and learners across the Internet. This sharing will enable collaboration on courses in a way never before possible.

- *Program administration and marketing*: If more of the product for a course is available for viewing, it will be easier for others to decide whether it is worthwhile or not. For a class that is fully World Wide Web integrated, prospective learners will be able to view the class syllabi and textbook as before, but they will also be able to view materials such as detailed class notes and learner-learner class discussions from previous terms. This will enhance the marketability of the best World Wide Web courses.

Is the World Wide Web Going to Make Distance Education Better Than Traditional Education?

It is important to place the use of the World Wide Web in its proper perspective. The World Wide Web is a delivery technology that allows information to be distributed worldwide, using a generic interface that can be obtained by running programs that work on all computer platforms. These characteristics make it a valuable tool for distance education, but they also make it a valuable tool for traditional education. So however powerful the educational tools become on the World Wide Web, traditional education will always have the additional feature of a live teacher-trainer. The World Wide Web will greatly improve distance education, but it won't eliminate traditional education.

The compensation mechanism for the creator of comprehensive World Wide Web educational materials is not yet in place. Without this mechanism, World Wide Web matcrials will be created slowly. The effort involved in creating World Wide Web material is extensive and often needs a team of content experts, graphic artists, and World Wide Web professionals to produce quality educational materials.

Can the World Wide Web Replace
Teacher-Trainers or Traditional Education?

In many ways, this is the central issue that has concerned faculty for years. While the concern is justified, the reality persists that the World Wide Web and other sophisticated technology-based delivery tools are effective educational tools, but no replacement for faculty.

For example, if a faculty member writes a good textbook, then it captures much of the knowledge known about a particular topic. The fact that many good textbooks exist has not lessened the importance of traditional education. While many people will be able to read a good textbook and learn most of the information about the topic, most will miss important points or remain confused or even not find the book interesting enough to complete. Any delivery method that is not completely interactive, no matter how well done, can allow the recipient to disconnect from the experience and to fail to learn or experience the expected knowledge. All of these points apply to the World Wide Web.

In Summary

Technology can do many wonderful things for the distant learner. As technology grows in sophistication, new opportunities present themselves that the skilled teacher-trainer and student can take advantage of. The World Wide Web is a sophisticated tool that puts a whole world of previously inaccessible information resources at the fingertips of the trained teacher and learner. Even with the World Wide Web, however, teacher guided interaction remains at the heart of most effective educational innovation. It will continue this way into the future. We see this as good for the teacher-trainer and the learner, as well as those involved with optimizing the resources available through the World Wide Web.

The Authors

Barry Willis is Director of Engineering Outreach and Professor of Education, University of Idaho, Moscow, Idaho.

e-mail, World Wide Web
   outreach@uidaho.edu
   http://www.uidaho.edu/evo

John Dickinson is Chairman and Professor of Computer Science at the University of Idaho.

e-mail
   dickinson@uidaho.edu

10

The World Wide Web in Education: Issues Related to Cross-Cultural Communication and Interaction

Betty Collis and Elka Remmers

Introduction: Does the Web Bring Cross-Cultural Communication and Interaction to Education?

The universality of the World Wide Web as a platform for communication and interaction relates certainly to its technical aspects and apparently to many characteristics of its available functionalities. Throughout the world, educationally oriented World Wide Web sites have been created, and traffic among these sites includes persons from countries around the globe. Does this mean, however, that the communication and interaction supported by those sites will have the same meaning and level of appropriateness to persons from different cultures and backgrounds? Will the World Wide Web make possible a breakthrough in cross-cultural communication and interaction in learning settings?

In this chapter we will briefly identify some of the key issues that have confronted the cross-cultural portability of educational software and the adaptation of courses for trans-border delivery, and suggest implications from these issues with respect to the cross-cultural use of a World Wide Web site for educational communication and interaction. We will present considerations that we feel to be especially important, briefly reflect upon these, and offer some preliminary suggestions for guidelines for World Wide Web sites to increase their potential for cross-cultural communication and interaction. We will conclude with a set of choices for the cross-cultural application of World Wide Web environments, each of which gives a different answer to the question: *Will the World Wide Web bring a new level of cross-cultural communication and interaction to education?*

World Wide Web Sites and Cross-Cultural Use: Some Basic Categories

In order to draw lessons for the World Wide Web from earlier experiences with the cross-cultural portability of education software and trans-border courses, we first need some definitions and categories. "Culture" can be defined in many ways (see, for example, Roblyer, Dozier-Henry, & Burnette, 1996); for our purposes we take it to mean the language, behaviors, and norms that characterize a group. "Language" includes not only its most obvious meaning, but also the usage variations within a language that set one group apart from another. Such variations relate to level and choice of vocabulary, and also to more subtle variations in tone and style of language use. Behaviors and norms relate to the sorts of interactions that are expected in a given group, as well as those which would make group members uncomfortable. Thus, "cross-cultural use of educational World Wide Web sites" is not only a phenomenon relating to political borders, language groups, and geographical distances; there can be different cultures in a state or district or even in an institution which can also block communication and interaction among those within them.

With regard to educational World Wide Web sites, we can define two basic categories relevant to cross-cultural applications:

- *Category 1.* Sites made for one context and its culture, but visited by those from other contexts and cultures.

- *Category 2.* Sites made specifically for cross-cultural participation.

Many educational sites on the World Wide Web are in the first of these categories; sites put up by a school, a department, a regional support center, for example, which are targeted for local use but, because of the nature of the World Wide Web and the pervasiveness of its search engines, are found and visited by many outside of the target group. The second category also has many exemplars, including sites representing educational network services which focus on cross-cultural (or cross-national) pairings of schools; sites for institutions serving students in widespread locations; and (particularly in Europe) sites representing multi-national educational partnerships and programs. Such sites may vary widely in the extent to which they reflect cross-cultural differences in their design and maintenance.

Lessons from Experience

Categories 1 and 2 have their parallels in terms of educational software and courses for transborder student populations. Educational software portability has been studied for more than two decades, generally in the context of increasing the chance that a software product made for one context and culture will be used in others. In 1987 and 1988, for example, the Commission of the European Communities brought together educational software experts from throughout Europe to find paths towards more-portable educational software and the creation of a common market for these adaptable programs. Among the barriers confronting these goals were:

- Problems of human language and vocabulary.

- Problems of differences in educational cultures and environments.

- Teaching-style differences.

- Problems relating to the ergonomics of different human languages in terms of their display and handling by computers.

- Technical problems relating to platforms, operating systems, and the lack of standard interfaces and module libraries. (Ballini & Poly, 1988)

In the ensuing years, problems relating to technical standardization and to the technical handling of some aspects of language translation have been substantially reduced, but problems relating to pedagogical and cultural issues, as well as distribution bottlenecks, continue, resulting in relatively little development of a cross-cultural market for educational software made originally for a particular local context, analogous to Category 1 World Wide Web sites (Collis, 1996). The cost and complexity of bringing multi-national educational software development teams together and sustaining their cooperation has been a natural limit on Category 2 software development. Only a handful of (English-language) software development companies, with multi-national distribution networks, have succeeded in marketing CD-ROMs of multimedia resource materials on a trans-border basis, with titles of a generic nature (famous paintings, famous composers, etc.).

Based on various analyses of factors affecting the cross-cultural portability of educational software (see, for example, Aston & Dolden, 1994), guidelines have emerged not only for software design but also for course design for cross-cultural participation via communication technologies. In Europe, for example, the "TeleScopia Project" has focused on the adaptation of courses for trans-European delivery, including via World Wide Web sites, and generated guidelines such as the following:

- *Communication and interaction.* In cross-cultural contexts, do not assume that more communication and interaction is better than less, especially when such activities cause burdens for the participants.

- *Language.* When communication and interaction are used, be particularly sensitive to cultural differences in terms of communication styles (i.e., who should initiate comments or questions, who should moderate, the extent to which disagreement or debate is expected, who should decide to terminate a line of communication, the level of formality considered appropriate in interaction between instructor and students, etc.).

- *Content.* Choose course content where the cross-cultural aspects are either of minimal relevance (thus highly specialized professional courses or courses relating to a common trans-border phenomenon such as learning to use the Internet) or courses where the cross-cultural aspects are integral to the content (i.e., learning a foreign language, international business issues, etc.).

- *Representation form.* Consider the use of visualizations to replace or supplement text, but be alert to cultural differences in the acceptability and interpretability of various aspects of visualization.

(For a longer list of guidelines, and a discussion, see Collis, Parisi, & Ligorio, 1996.)

These experiences have direct relevance to the consideration of educational World Wide Web sites and their cross-cultural potential.

Implications for Educational World Wide Web Sites

The World Wide Web has profoundly expanded the opportunities for cross-cultural communication and interaction through its remarkable trans-border range and acceptance. Now, through a single, standardized user interface, locally developed learning resources not only can be made more conveniently accessible to their target audiences, but at the same time available to anyone else who can access the World Wide Web. Thus, in theory, all Category 1 resources on the World Wide Web are candidates for cross-cultural use. Similarly, more and more educational sites will be made with cross-cultural participants in mind from the start, partly because the World Wide Web now makes widespread access feasible, and partly because the World Wide Web is itself stimulating cross-cultural exchanges through its worldwide attractiveness. Thus, both educational and commercial motivations are accelerating the appearance of "Category 2" World Wide Web sites.

Given this potential, what are important implications for World Wide Web sites in terms of their cross-cultural use? Based on the previous experience with educational software and trans-border courses, and our own current work (see the Notes at the end of this chapter), we offer the following ideas:

Interaction and Communication

We must be alert to the fact that there are substantial cross-cultural differences in interaction and communication beyond the actual words being said. Any organizational setting develops its own culture, with norms and expectations relating to aspects such as the degree of formalism and centrality in communication patterns (Woolliams & Gee, 1992). A hyperlinked environment emphasizing user choice may not be consistent with a hierarchically oriented culture. Hyperlinking may also not be optimal for persons with certain learning styles or needs, such as field-dependent persons and those with strong task-orientations. Such characteristics are partially a function of the individual him- or herself, but are also influenced by the broader cultural setting (Sellin & Winters, 1996). However, there appears to be little specific research done on instructional design for hyperlinked learning environments for cross-cultural use. Cross-cultural teams of instructional design theorists are not much known. Perhaps the World Wide Web will stimulate this.

Preliminary guidelines for World Wide Web sites? For Category 1 sites, it seems best to try to fit local norms for tone and style of communication and interaction. Those who "visit" the sites from outside should be respectful of these local norms, and as much as possible try to understand and work within them. Appropriateness in terms of how people address and ask requests of each other is interpreted differently in different cultures; we must not assume that our own interpretation should be appreciated elsewhere.

For Category 2 sites, a careful analysis must be done from the start as to the degree, type and extent of communication and interaction that is most appropriate for the participants. Well-structured communication, moderated by someone with appropriate standing for all participants, may be best for those who for cultural as well as other reasons do not wish to participate in wide-ranging or informal discussions. Also, the increasing accessibility of audio and video real-time communication via the World Wide Web may not be of benefit to cross-cultural sites because of tone-and-style discrepancies in communication norms, as much as because of time-zone differences.

Language

Language is a critical issue. Should we recommend that Category 1 World Wide Web sites remain in their local languages and Category 2 World Wide Web sites be in a globally accepted common language? For Category 1, would this mean that only those who speak the local language can benefit from the local resources? Automatic language translation is becoming available for World Wide Web sites (for a limited set of languages) but will not be more than automatic in terms of the richer and more-subtle aspects of language and thus not likely to satisfy educational requirements. For Category 2 sites, what should the common language be? English? Chinese? Because English is now, for socio-economic reasons, the dominant language on the World Wide Web does not mean that this should be taken for granted, or even that it will remain the case a decade from now. Will the World Wide Web in time accelerate English as the international *lingua franca*, or will it force monolingual English speakers to finally have to work in a second language; for example, Chinese?

Preliminary guidelines for World Wide Web sites? We suggest for Category 1 sites to perhaps have two levels of access, the major one for local use, making full and rich use of local language and situations; and a second, summary level for cross-cultural use, where language impact is reduced as much as possible to facilitate translation, and where a subset of links is selected that leads to materials with possible cross-cultural interest. For Category 2 sites, we suggest working with partners where a common agreement on language can be established or for whom multiple-language versions of at least some parts of the World Wide Web site can be supported. Do not make the assumption that an English-language site will be adequate for all those who can read English. It might be best if those who write World Wide Web sites in English for cross-cultural access are multilingual themselves, as they are likely to be more sensitive to sentence construction and word order and choice than monolingual native-English speakers. Sites for cross-cultural use should be pilot-tested on persons with different mother tongues, perhaps being cross-translated at least two times and adapted based on any difficulties in understanding that occur (Itzkan, 1993).

Content and Purpose

For Category 1 sites, content and purpose should be shaped by local needs; if these happen to also be of use to the outside world, the World Wide Web can make it possible for the resources to be shared. However, in the future, it may be wise for local sites to operate as intranets rather than being on the Internet itself, both to reduce some of the overflow of World Wide Web use, but also to remove the need to be concerned about outside visitors, if these are not particularly wanted (as may be the case in terms of a site to support a particular course, where admission to the course is not being offered via the Internet). For Category 2 sites, the determination of content and purpose is much more critical. What can and should be done via a cross-cultural site? Perhaps the guidelines from the TeleScopia Project, mentioned earlier with respect to trans-border course participation, are most pertinent: Choose either a focus on "culturally neutral" resources or on resources that make explicit and rich use of the cross-cultural potentiality of the World Wide Web.

Preliminary guidelines for World Wide Web sites? If a local site is unlikely to be of much value to outside visitors, consider mounting the site on an intranet (with links to the Internet World Wide Web), so that in time, educational materials on the World Wide Web itself are predominantly oriented toward at least cross-cultural sharing. Or, alternatively, make only a "sampler" available for cross-cultural visitors. For Category 2 sites developed with cross-cultural uses as a goal, choose, as much as possible, focuses that either transcend or exploit cross-cultural differences. Topics that transcend cultures include those that are (relatively) culturally neutral (such as elementary electric circuits) and also those that develop a built-in culture of their own (such as the Internet and the World Wide Web, reflecting what might be called "technology's built-in cultural bias," Roblyer, Dozier-Henry, & Burnette, 1996). In addition, topics that exploit cross-cultural differences should reflect this exploitation in the design and conduct of the World Wide Web site, to avoid the site being dominated by the language or worldview of any one of the site participants.

Visualizations

To overcome some of the problems of language for cross-culturally oriented World Wide Web sites, the use of visualizations seems a good response. As World Wide Web sites continually improve in their multimedia capabilities (and as local network access slowly catches up to these improvements), it may seem a self-evident guideline that sites become more and more visual. Bradsher (1996), for example, tells how Japanese students got around language problems in getting to know students in other lands by creating World Wide Web pages showing photos of food choices for a balanced meal in their country. The evolution of graphic user interfaces, the worldwide acceptance of the icons used in the Windows environment and now in World Wide Web browsers, suggests that visualizations will become part of an international *lingua franca* for educational World Wide Web sites. But, as usual, such solutions are never as simple as they might appear. We know that the design of user interfaces for international use requires the same cultural sensitivity as the design of communication and interaction, (Nielsen, 1990), and that the interpretability and acceptability of visualizations, as well as the use of visualizations themselves in learning settings, is subject to considerable cross-cultural variation.

Preliminary guidelines for World Wide Web sites? For sites in Category 1, specific links to a carefully selected subset of visual resources may be a strategy for offering accessibility to outside visitors, an excellent way to share some local experiences and settings without dealing directly with the language issue. For Category 2 sites, however, visuals should be carefully chosen to fit the common culture of the site participants, even if this results in a site that looks "boring" to those outside of the partnership or perhaps one that makes little use of visuals at all, the reverse.

Three Answers: Is the World Wide Web Leading to an Increase in Cross-Cultural Communication and Interaction?

On one hand, the answer to this question appears to be an unqualified "yes." The World Wide Web is vibrant with cross-cultural activity (although mainly in the Category 1 context rather than that of Category 2 because of the extra effort needed to organize cross-cultural partnerships or distribution settings). This would seem to imply that there is no doubt that the World Wide Web is leading to an increase in cross-cultural communication and interaction. On the other hand, looking more closely and reflecting on our past experience with other forms of cross-cultural activities in education, we see three different answers to our question:

Superficial

One answer is that we will be seeing superficial rather than meaningful cross-cultural experiences. Many more Category 1 sites will be available, which visitors may drop into and which may broaden awareness of cross-cultural differences for those who visit. However, such awareness is likely to be superficial, especially with language and curriculum differences serving as barriers to any deep understanding of the resources and persons available. Similarly, Category 2 sites made "for the world" will be mounted, especially by those wishing to sell their presence internationally, but without careful analysis of cross-cultural needs and differences. The World Wide Web equivalent of the international superficiality of advertisements for Coca-Cola, Marlboro cigarettes, and Benetton fashions will be the result: A kind of cross-cultural communication, to be sure, but educationally superficial.

Homogeneous

Another answer may be that a sincere effort will be made to offer worthwhile educational opportunities to persons outside of one's own setting, but the homogeneous nature of this home setting will not be questioned. For example, a native-English speaking site author may never question the assumption that his or her site be offered to the world in English. A site produced by an institution or a publisher will not question the norms and approach of the sponsoring organization, but will see the World Wide Web as a way to bring these to a broader market. The motivation in the homogeneous answer is not that of the superficial cola commercial, but of the missionary; through this new channel we can bring our insights and beliefs to those who were not fortunate enough before to be able to take advantage of them. The homogeneous answer, when it occurs as a well-meaning parochialism, is perhaps more dangerous to real cross-cultural understanding than the superficial answer.

Multi-Cultural

Here, an awareness of and respect for the "deep structures" of different cultures (Roblyer, Dozier-Henry, & Burnette, 1996), including of one's own, serves as a base and filter for what a site developer assumes the outside world wants and needs. Given this awareness, the World Wide Web makes possible interaction and communication in ways that can make use of trans-cultural technologies and at the same time try to respect local cultures and institutions. It is here that we feel the most promising "answer" to the contribution of the World Wide Web to cross-cultural understanding can occur. But like all most-promising answers, it is also the most challenging to achieve, requiring both a multicultural worldview and a large dose of wisdom. The four sets of considerations we discussed earlier, with respect to care for culturally different expectations for communication and interaction, for sensitivity with respect to language assumptions, for content that is either culture-transcendent or culture-saturated, and for increased utilization of appropriate visualizations, appear to be both common sensical and reinforced by previous experiences with cross-cultural acceptance of other forms of learning materials.

Thus, of the three possible answers to the question "Will the World Wide Web increase cross-cultural communication and interaction in education?" we suspect that the superficial answer is already the most common and will lead to a dissipation of the potential of the World Wide Web for cross-cultural understanding, while the homogeneous may be the most dangerous, leading to a sort of well-meaning colonization of the World Wide Web around the norms of the culture most favored to dominate access. The multi-cultural is what we hope to contribute to.

For examples associated with our own work, see:

Collis, B. (1996). *Online Learning Course Site*. Enschede, NL: Faculty of Educational Science and Technology (http://www.to.utwente.nl/ism/online96/campus.htm).

TechNet (1996). *TechNet Finland WWW-Services*. Dipoli Lifelong Learning Institute. Helsinki, Finland: Helsinki University of Technology (http://www.dipoli.hut.fi/org/TechNet/TNF/telecom/EuroProprog.html); see material related to the EuroPro and ECOLE projects.

References

Aston, M., & Dolden, B. (1994). Logiciel sans frontiéres. *Computers & Education, 22*(1/2), 1–8.

Ballini, D., & Poly, A. (1988). European methodology for the development of educational software programs. *Euryclée Info, 3,* 3–10.

Bradsher, M. (1996). Making friends in the global village: Tips on international collaborations. *Learning and Leading with Technology, 23*(6), 48–50.

Collis, B. (1996). The evolution of educational software portability. In D. Ely (Ed.), *Educational media and technology yearbook 1996* (pp. 38–76). Englewood, CO: Libraries Unlimited.

Collis, B., Parisi, D., & Ligorio, M. B. (1996). Adaptation of courses for trans-European tele-learning. *Journal of Computer Assisted Learning, 12,* 47–62.

Itzkan, S. J. (1993). *Student recommendations for global networking in schools.* A report from the First Global Classroom Youth Congress, Washington, DC, June 28–29, 1993. Available on the Internet from the World Future Society, c/o Seth J. Itzkan (rsch281c@cl.uh.edu).

Nielsen, J. (Ed.). (1990). *Designing user interfaces for international use.* Amsterdam: Elsevier.

Roblyer, M. D., Dozier-Henry, O., & Burnette, A. P. (1996). Technology and multicultural education: The 'uneasy alliance.' *Educational Technology, 36*(3), 5–12.

Sellin, R., & Winters, E. (1996). *Cross cultural communication: Tips for those who develop material for translation* (http://www.bena.com/ewinters/xculture.html).

Woolliams, P., & Gee, D. (1992). *Accounting for user diversity in configuring online systems. Online Review, 16*(5) (http://sunrae.uel.ac.uk/hci/int/papers/online.html).

The Authors

Betty Collis and Elka Remmers are with the Faculty of Educational Science and Technology, University of Twente, The Netherlands.

e-mail, World Wide Web
collis@edte.utwente.nl
http://www.twente.nl/ism/online95/campus/rooms/Collis/home.html

E.Remmers@student.utwente.nl
http://Mat075207.student.utwente.nl/~elka/

11

The Role of Motivation in Web-Based Instruction

Richard Cornell and

Barbara L. Martin

Introduction

Launching headfirst into Web-based instruction is not for the timid, be they students or instructors. Numerous challenges are posed when delivery of instruction is via the Web, either through the World Wide Web or using an intranet. Challenges related to Web-based instruction include: student and teacher degree of acceptance, prior participant knowledge, attitude toward technology, content level, degree of interactivity, amount of difficulty in using the system, ease of accessibility into the system, and teacher and student ability and availability to communicate. These challenges portend a potentially serious problem, *motivation*. While motivation problems affect learners, it is not uncommon that *instructors* also experience them.

Motivation Defined

Martin and Briggs (1986) state that "motivation is a hypothetical construct that broadly refers to those internal and external conditions that influence the arousal, direction, and maintenance of behavior" (p. 201). Motivation is actually an umbrella term that encompasses a myriad of terms and concepts (such as interest, curiosity, attribution, level of aspiration, locus of control, etc.); the theories and ideas can be related to individual or environmental and social influences of motivation.

According to Keller (1983), motivation "refers to the magnitude and direction of behavior.... it refers to the *choices* people make as to what experiences or goals they will approach or avoid, and to the *degree of effort* they will exert in that respect" (p. 369). Keller uses these two concepts, choices and effort, to illustrate (a) the reasons a person approaches or avoids a task and (b) how to design instruction to make a task more interesting (Martin & Briggs, 1986).

Motivation in Distance Education

Distance educators have long been concerned about motivation. Some estimate that as many as 30–50% of all students who start a distance education course drop out before finishing (Moore & Kearsley, 1996). Research has found three factors indicative of student success in completing a distance education course (Armstrong *et al.*, 1985; Billings, 1989; Moore & Kearsley, 1996). They are: intention to complete the course, early submission of work, and completion of other distance education courses. These factors can help identify students who may not be motivated to complete a course so that appropriate support can be made available to them.

Other components that may influence student motivation are: (a) course design, (b) the degree of interaction that is provided and available, and (c) the role of the site facilitator. Some general considerations designing effective distance courses that are motivating include organizing the course into short, self-contained segments, providing frequent summaries and reviews, and linking the content to real-life work or issues with a high degree of transfer from learning to everyday life (Moore & Kearsley, 1996).

Regarding interaction, students typically prefer to interact with the instructor, other students, and the instructional media by asking questions, giving presentations, and having discussions rather than listening to a lecture or having limited involvement and interaction (Martin & Bramble, 1996). The student study guide can play a role in creating student involvement by providing students with specific questions to answer and assignments to complete. In addition, it is the responsibilty of the instructor to provide adequate and immediate feedback to students to keep them on track and facilitate their completion of the course.

While Web-based distance education generally does not have a site facilitator, a facilitator can be crucial in promoting interaction and can serve to humanize or to personalize the instruction. Other ways that instruction can be humanized is to provide pictures of students and the instructor to each other (Cortell *et al.*, 1995), have each student meet with the instructor at least once during the course (if feasible), and to make plans for teleconferences and other forms of synchronous interaction.

Student Motivation

The question remains as to why some students remain highly motivated, while others do not. There will always be students who turn in assignments in advance of their peers, while others may not turn in anything. The problem of those latter students is more critical when the assigned work is done via the Web. Unlike traditional face-to-face instruction, when Web-based instruction is delivered at a distance, there is no one in an authority role to ask the students for their assignments. Teacher and students are removed from one another and, most likely, in time as well; clearly the case in asynchronous learning.

Identifying the Unmotivated Student

If a student lacks motivation, one or more conditions might prevail:

1. While most of the students turn in assignments with regularity, the unmotivated student is typically late or provides no response to required work.

2. Repeated messages to the student remain unanswered or, if a reply is given, it typically contains reasons why the student has not completed the work.

3. If taking on and off-campus classes, the student makes no effort to communicate with the instructor, even to the point of avoidance when both are in relative proximity.

4. The student's peers will occasionally make comments about the situation.

These are signs that something is amiss with the student and his or her progress through the class. While the same may be said for students enrolled in traditional classroom instruction, inaccessibility between the Web-based student and instructor is a major hindrance toward subsequent resolution of the problem. The instructor faced with unmotivated students may accept the notion that, in any class, there are those who lack the drive to succeed.

While we do not recommend that instructors spoon-feed every student, we do not alternatively suggest that students on a failing path be left to fend totally for themselves. Rather than ignore the unmotivated student, follow-up with that individual is recommended. To assume that students who turn in work late or not at all are unmotivated is fallacious.

Causes for a Lack of Student Motivation

1. Family illness may have befallen the student; a spouse or children are having problems; the workload at the office or plant has dramatically increased; electricity or telephone service to the home has been cut off or interrupted.

2. The student is unprepared to deal with the content being delivered, especially if such discussion occurs on the Web, wherein each student has a responsibility to participate.

3. The student is required to participate electronically, but lacks funds to afford the purchase of resources required for participation in the class.

4. The student encounters initial difficulty in using the hardware or software systems and is embarrassed to seek help.

5. A phobia about technology may exist, yet the student may not disclose such fears.

6. The instructor assumes that students have sufficient background and knowledge.

7. There have been interpersonal difficulties between the student and the instructor or peers, in which case, reluctance to participate is not uncommon.

8. The student uses English (or language of the country in which instruction is taught) as a second language but must depend upon it as his or her primary learning tool.

9. The novelty has worn off, especially when instruction delivered is followed by limited access to required resources at school, home, or work.

10. The student sees no connection between what is being taught via the Web and his or her goals, needs, or desires.

11. More time and energy is put into socialization than academics.

12. The student is engaged in education primarily because of some external or internal pressure sources.

Possible Solutions

A number of possible interpersonal interventions are available to instructors who are dealing with unmotivated students:

1. Get to know the students. Accomplish this through face-to-face communication, and through student submission of individual *biographies* in which students are encouraged to be forthcoming about themselves and their prior experiences.

2. Have students provide their photographs, phone numbers, and e-mail addresses.

3. If a student is experiencing motivation or other problems, do not wait until mid-semester to communicate with the student.

4. While it seems obvious, do not communicate with the unmotivated student on a public forum such as the listserv or Web.

5. Accept that no matter what intervention strategies are undertaken, there will be those students whom the instructor will not be able to reach.

6. If unsuccessful in reaching an unmotivated student, invite him or her to drop by to discuss the problem, at a mutually convenient time.

7. Avoid confrontation, sarcasm, or put downs. An honest expression of concern for the student's well-being will often turn the situation around.

8. If a face-to-face meeting cannot be arranged, use regular mail, e-mail, or whatever other method it takes to communicate.

9. Failing these strategies, inform the student in a more formal manner that he or she is in academic jeopardy.

10. Share such communication with your department chair or colleagues, as well as the student records office.

Course Design Considerations

Keller's Motivational-Design Model

Keller (1983) has developed a motivational-design model for designing motivational materials and courses that can be adapted for designing Web-based courses. There are four categories in the model: interest, relevance, expectancy, and satisfaction. Interest refers to establishing and maintaining curiosity and learner arousal. Relevance refers to linking the learning situation to the need and motives of the learner. Expectancy refers to the causes that an individual attributes to his or her behavior and the likelihood that a person will repeat or approach a similar task. Satisfaction is defined as continuing motivation, the desire to continue in the pursuit of similar goals.

Keller and Burkman (1993) make several assumptions related to motivational message design. First, they assume that stimulating student motivation is part of the courseware designer's responsibility. Second, motivation to learn is a means, not an end; that is, it is intended to be used to stimulate learners. Third, designing motivating instruction can be a systematic process. Fourth, motivation must be considered in all parts (beginning, middle, and end) of the design process. And, finally, motivation and effectiveness are related.

Keller and Burkman present numerous principles of motivational design strategies in each of the four categories that may promote motivation. Some of the key principles related to Web-based instruction follow:

Variation and Curiosity

1. Make changes in the organization and presentation of content to stimulate attention and curiosity. For example, use discovery based instructional strategies.

2. Provoke mental conflict by introducing problems to be solved and contradictory facts. For example, send the students to different Web pages with differing opinions on a topic that is being studied.

3. Engage in intranet-based competitions between students in the class as well as those located in other classes or at other institutions.

4. Develop a diversity of Web-based products which appeal to differing learning styles.

Relevance
1. Build a strong relationship between what is being learned and the objectives of the course.

2. Show how the instruction relates to what the learner already knows.

3. Show how the instruction relates to the student's future goals.

4. Adapt course requirements to the learning style of the students.

5. Be an enthusiastic instructor who is also in the process of learning new things.

Challenge Level
1. Include a student study guide with the following:
   a. advance organizers to show students where they are going and how to get there.
   b. the goals and performance requirements.
   c. student selected goals and learner options for activities.

2. Provide opportunities for students to interact with the instructor, other students, and the instructional materials.

3. Provide short segments of instruction.

4. Provide frequent summaries and reviews.

5. Provide frequent confirmational and corrective feedback.

6. Have students submit work early in the course.

7. Ask students to overtly state their intention to finish the course.

Positive Outcomes
1. Provide the opportunity for students to use the new skills and knowledge learned during the course.

2. Reward accomplishment by using positive feedback.

3. Use extrinsic rewards (games with points, privileges, or tokens) to sustain motivation.

4. Share work done on Web with others, especially those at other institutions.

5. Encourage collaboration between students as they develop Web-based assignments.

Positive Impression
1. Make the initial perception of print courseware seem easy, rather than difficult. For example, teach students how to use appropriate search strategies to navigate the Web.

2. Make the instructional text well organized.

3. Make the physical attributes of the product consistent with learner expectations through instruction related to good graphic and text design principles, i.e., use of white space, complementary colors and background, limited use of large visuals, plain typeface and font, etc., in the materials produced for the course.

4. Use graphics, pictures, maps, charts, etc., that make the information easier to understand and to hold the students' attention.

5. The most effective pictures include people, are in color, and include novelty and drama.

6. Organize a Web contest to be judged by a panel of technologists who have an interest in both the mechanics of Web design as well as the aesthetics.

Readable Style
1. Use active voice and action verbs.

2. Use sentences that are moderate length.

3. Vary the vocabulary.

Early Interest
1. Create interest in the instruction as early as possible.

2. Provide opportunities early in the instruction to interact with others and with the instructional materials.

The Unmotivated Instructor

At the outset, it was stated that motivation problems also affect instructors. Unmotivated instruction has complex reasons which underly it, but when such a situation does occur, it impacts not only the instructor, but also the entire class.

Reasons for Instructor Lack of Motivation

1. Instructors view change differently. Early adapters in particular seem to thrive on change, while others react negatively whenever something alters their routine.

2. Administrators mandate that the instructor will adapt his or her present course so that it may be delivered using Web-based instructional techniques.

3. The change in technologies, especially those formerly used, dictates that the instructor get with it technologically lest he or she be labeled a traditionalist.

4. The instructor has been given inadequate time to obtain new skills to accommodate the revised instructional approach.

5. Little or no incentive has been offered to the instructor to make an effort at using Web-based instructional methods.

6. The instructor is techno-phobic.

7. "I see no reason why I should have to adapt new methods to teaching what I know works...after all, the students learn the material. Besides, I tried using technology once and everything went wrong."

Little wonder instructors bring such feelings toward the use of Web-based instruction—no one wants to risk looking foolish by embarking on such an adventure unless there is a strong safety net.

How to Motivate the Unmotivated Instructor

The following may help an unmotivated instructor design a course for delivery via Web-based instruction:

1. *Re-tool* establishes the wrong mind-set. The possibilities and constraints of teaching via the Web are quite different from those used in traditional classroom delivery. If the class is destined for Web delivery, consider it an opportunity to rethink the entire class from beginning to end, addressing not only *the methods* to be employed but also the *content*.

2. Seek the opportunity to redesign the course well ahead of the time it is due to be taught. Teaching a Web-based course is not just a re-do of what has been taught in the past. Suggest to the department chair that using the Web will require the acquisition of a new set of teaching skills, including sufficient time to search for sources on the Web, locate those not on the Web, and integrate them into the course design.

3. Realize that using the Web to deliver instruction will, at least initially, *take far more time, not less*; that the time communicating with students will *increase disproportionately* as compared with time spent in the traditional classroom.

4. Use this new teaching assignment as a means to obtain a new computer to conduct the class via the Web. An upgraded home computer might be negotiated—for that is where far more time communicating with students will be spent, rather than in the office.

5. Identify who among the students is skilled in using the Web for other purposes and let them assist. Admit a learning deficit (related to the technology) to the class as, *together, we will all learn how to use this new method of instruction*.

6. Find others who have also been asked to teach via the Web. Join them as they learn the techniques, or ask for their insights if they have prior Web-based teaching experience.

7. If the institution has asked you to teach via the Web, it is likely that it has a faculty development center or office of instructional resources. Within these facilities is a team of experts able to assist.

Summary

We have examined motivation from a variety of perspectives, beginning with definition, and moving into elements of causal relationships as to why student motivation levels vary, not only between and among those in the class, but within the individuals as their circumstances change over the course of a semester.

Course design can influence student motivation. Instructors should pay attention to the following: how to provide variety and stimulate curiosity, make the course relevant and challenging, and provide positive outcomes. Additionally, courses should be designed to create a positive first impression, be readable, use graphics and pictures that are relevant and useful, provide cues to the learners, and stimulate early interest so that students will be more likely to complete the course.

Finally, we have addressed the problem of motivation, or the lack thereof, in instructors. Like students, instructors are vulnerable to the forces which impact them, and the inability to deal with change is high among the factors which frequently lead to lessened levels of instructor motivation. The pressure to adapt to new and emerging technologies in instruction will not abate; if anything, it will increase with dramatic speed.

References

Armstrong, M., Toebe, D., & Watson, M. (1985). Strengthening the instructional role in self-directed learning activities. *Journal of Continuing Education in Nursing, 16*(3), 75–84.

Billings, D. M. (1989). A conceptual model of correspondence course completion. In M. G. Moore & G. C. Clark (Eds.), *Readings in distance learning and instruction, 2*. University Park, PA: ACSDE.

Cortell, R., Fernandes, M., & Foshee, N. (1995). The message was the medium. In R. A. Cornell & K. Murphy (Eds.), *An international survey of distance education and teacher training: From smoke signals to satellite II* (pp. 142–152). Orlando, FL: University of Central Florida, and Paris: International Council for Educational Media.

Keller, J. M. (1983). Motivational design of instruction. In C. M. Reiguluth (Ed.), *Instructional design theories and models: An overview of their current status* (pp. 386–434). Hillsdale, NJ: Lawrence Erlbaum Associates.

Keller, J., & Burkman, E. (1993). Motivation principles. In M. Fleming & W. H. Levie (Eds.), *Instructional message design: Principles from the behavioral and cognitive sciences* (pp. 3–53) (2nd ed.). Englewood Cliffs, NJ: Educational Technology Publications.

Martin, B. M., & Bramble, W. J. (1996). Designing effective video training instruction: The Florida Tele-training Project. *Educational Technology Reserach and Development*, 44(1), 85–99.

Martin, B. M, & Briggs, L.J. (1986). *The affective and cognitive domains: Integration for instruction and research*. Englewood Cliffs, NJ: Educational Technology Publications.

Moore, M. G., & Kearsley, G. (1996). *Distance education: A systems view*. Belmont, CA: Wadsworth.

The Authors

Richard Cornell is Associate Professor, Instructional Systems, University of Central Florida, Orlando, Florida.

e-mail, World Wide Web
  cornell@pegasus.cc.ucf.edu
  http://pegasus.cc.ucf.edu/~cornell/

Barbara L. Martin is Visiting Associate Professor at the University of Central Florida.

e-mail
  barbarm@pegasus.cc.ucf.edu

12

Emerging Roles for Instructors and Learners in the Web-Based Instruction Classroom

Paul G. Shotsberger

Introduction

As Web-based Instruction (WBI) becomes more collaborative and interactive, it is important to consider the emerging roles of WBI instructors and learners in this rapidly evolving educational environment. These roles will be discussed in the context of three key issues for interactive WBI. First, to what extent must instructors formalize and/or tailor the use of WBI interactive tools and methods in order to ensure learner involvement? Second, what is the appropriate blend of synchronous and asynchronous contact required to support WBI learners, and to what extent will they require face-to-face training in the use of collaboration tools such as shared workspaces? Third, what is the role of the instructor in fostering a sense of community among learners in a virtual WBI classroom? Proposed responses to these issues are illustrated using a WBI system designed for training mathematics teachers in applying the National Council of Teachers of Mathematics (NCTM) *Professional Standards for Teaching Mathematics* (1991) in their classrooms.

Background

At the University of North Carolina at Wilmington, we have developed a WBI site called INSTRUCT, which stands for Implementing the NCTM School Teaching Recommendations Using Collaborative Telecommunications. INSTRUCT is intended to be a self-sustaining vehicle for delivering in-service teacher training and facilitating teacher licensure renewal. INSTRUCT contains a training module, which is a multimedia version of the NCTM Standards for Teaching Mathematics (NCTM, 1991), an area containing mathematics-related World Wide Web resources, a meeting area for synchronous conversations, a threaded discussion area for asynchronous communications, and an option for sending e-mail.

Each trainee is expected to participate in online review and discussion of INSTRUCT materials, resulting in the application of Standards principles in their mathematics lessons. INSTRUCT training provides North Carolina high school mathematics teachers with (1) personal experience with applying the innovations and practices contained in the NCTM Standards for Teaching Mathematics, (2) the capacity to employ effectively the resources of the World Wide

Web for supporting instruction, (3) the opportunity to collaborate with colleagues at other schools using computer telecommunications, (4) the ability to be involved in in-service training and support during the course of the school year, and (5) licensure renewal credit for their participation in the project.

Some Issues

Formalizing and Tailoring the Interactive Environment

Research on computer tutors and microworlds indicates that if the use of options for investigation and experimentation depends on user initiative, it is likely the tools will not be employed (e.g., Lewis, Bishay, & McArthur, 1993). Similarly, Schrum (1996) points out that for telecommunications, "Freedom to explore and investigate individually is important, but some structured activities and minimal weekly requirements are also essential." However, Moore (1992) notes the danger of increasing what he terms *transactional distance* between users by imposing a highly structured environment in distance education. The question then becomes how much formalism should be introduced into the WBI environment, and to what extent does this formalism needs to be tailored to individual learners?

Successful WBI depends on the presence of self-directed learning, which could be considered both a component and a result of WBI. Eastmond (1995) believes that self-direction in distance education is a function not only of the individual learner, but also the instructional facilitator and the sponsoring institution. Learners should be given the opportunity to interact, to reflect, and to apply their learning experientially, but it is unreasonable to expect these kinds of outcomes without clear guidance in the use of interactive methods. In her work with computer conferencing, Harasim (1993) has found that "...the application of intentional design to online environments yielded important benefits for collaborative learning, such as facilitating active participation, peer interaction, and divergent thinking" (p. 124). Harasim (1993) and Eastmond (1995) have suggested ways in which instructors and institutions might organize an online learning environment to better communicate expectations and encourage interaction:

1. Publishing preliminary materials that stress learner involvement frequency to heighten interactivity.

2. Posting asynchronous messages specifically intended to promote conversation.

3. Communicating one-on-one with learners to encourage interaction or ask about difficulties.

4. Assigning varying roles to learners, such as presenter, discussant or discussion moderator.

5. Using smaller work groups to accomplish tasks, avoiding sole reliance on large group format for meetings and discussions.

The INSTRUCT design provides an example of how the form of WBI interaction can be specified while simultaneously allowing for individual differences among learners. INSTRUCT participants are given assignments designed to inject some aspect of each of the six standards into actual classroom lessons. An intentional by-product of these assignments is to encourage the need for sustained interaction and collaboration among learners and instructors (Honey & McMillan, 1994). Teachers are therefore given the opportunity to discuss lesson ideas in synchronous meetings using Netscape Chat before having to complete a lesson plan on their own. However, the format of these synchronous meetings can change as learners become more accustomed to collaborating with each other.

Initially, teachers would be encouraged to brainstorm in large-group meetings, as this format represents a less threatening means of collaboration. Later, instructors could encourage large-group meetings to be followed by private "chats" between those participants teaching the same subject area in order to promote more in-depth sharing of ideas. Once teachers are comfortable with this more intimate form of collaboration, instructors can introduce the concept of team teaching a lesson, wherein the teachers would plan and execute the same lesson, conduct the lesson in their individual classrooms, and then compare outcomes during meetings and discussions with other INSTRUCT participants. This type of approach to structuring the WBI learning environment can also serve to enhance the feeling of community among users, as discussed in a later section.

Synchronous and Asynchronous: What's the Right Mix?

Brush *et al.* (1993) identify some important aspects of distance performance support systems intended for instruction:

> ...a support system for distance instruction would need to aid in the delivery of the content of the training, to provide a mechanism for interaction between instructors and students, to offer options for feedback about assignments and projects, and to give the program staff alternatives for evaluating the training and maintaining quality control over activities. (p. 39)

Moore (1992) warns against dependence on one-way communication in distance education systems, which tends to promote *transactional distance* between users. Guskey (1986) elaborates on the need for promoting interaction among participants involved in instruction, noting in particular that teachers require the opportunity to share ideas and concerns with others before making changes in their instructional practices.

As noted in the previous section, INSTRUCT's design integrates aspects of groupware, or software intended to support group interaction, to expand its use beyond being simply a storehouse of instructional material. Mandviwalla and Olfman (1994) suggest that users employing groupware should have the capability to meet synchronously or asynchronously, as appropriate, and the tools for carrying out these interactions should be contained in a single system. But the question arises. To what extent can/should these technologies be blended, and what will be the requirement for face-to-face training in order for users to employ such a complex learning environment?

Each of INSTRUCT's six Standards for Teaching Mathematics is designed to take approximately two and one-half weeks each to complete. Of the time teachers are expected to spend online covering each standard, only about 25 percent of that time is actually spent browsing the hypermedia material. Approximately 50 percent of the time is spent in synchronous meetings such as those detailed in the previous section. The remaining 25 percent of the online time is spent searching a collection of mathematics-related Web resources intended to support instruction, as well as filling out each standard's Check for Understanding form, which evaluates the teacher's grasp of the standard through the use of multiple choice, fill-in-the-blank, and free-response questions.

Despite the large proportion of time INSTRUCT learners spend in synchronous interaction, the reality of WBI is that this time is necessarily limited; therefore, unanswered questions will remain from the online meetings. Further, in a number of cases, hypermedia material of one professional standard is linked to material of a previous standard, and so teachers are prompted to reflect on connections between standards, raising the potential for follow-on questions or comments. Thus, the asynchronous communication option provides concurrent, on-going support for open-ended discussion and debate concerning the standards during formal training. Scardamalia and Bereiter (1993) urge that for asynchronous communication:

The flow of information must allow for progressive work on a problem, with ideas remaining active over extended periods of time and revisited in new and unexpected ways. (p. 38)

INSTRUCT's discussion option benefits learners by affording them the opportunity to be involved in more long-term discussions about issues raised in the NCTM Professional Standards, by facilitating the sharing of news and other items of interest between colleagues, and by affording users continual access to previous communications via discussion histories. Additionally, an overall goal of INSTRUCT is to provide a means for teacher collaboration once formal training is completed. The threaded discussion area is ideal for teachers to propose their own topics for discussion and contribute to them at their leisure throughout the school year.

The presence of sophisticated collaboration tools and the expectation that both synchronous and asynchronous options will be employed by WBI users begs the question of training needed for effectively employing such a complex environment. As Eastmond (1995, p. 90) points out, "...participating on a computer conference presupposes a level of knowledge and skill with computer telecommunications that not all [users] share." In the case of INSTRUCT, it is likely that some of the teachers who would be using the site would have no prior experience even with simple telecommunications tools such as electronic mail. Therefore, all INSTRUCT training is preceded by limited face-to-face staff development in both navigating the Web and participating in online meetings and discussions. The hope is that the initial inconvenience of face-to-face training will reap benefits later as users are able to participate in many different WBI courses.

Fostering a Sense of Community

Mention has already been made of Moore's (1992) concern that transactional distance needs to be minimized in distance education. Stated more positively, the question becomes: What is the best way to create a virtual community from a group of individuals separated by (to a greater or lesser extent) time and space? In the area of teacher training, one of the direct benefits of face-to-face workshops is the sense of community and self-worth teachers derive from taking part in professional training with colleagues from other schools (Guskey, 1986). With regard to INSTRUCT, if learners are not comfortable with expressing their feelings and opinions about making changes in their classroom instruction, it is likely that any potential long-term benefit of the WBI will be lost. Brush *et al.* (1993) observed that for their performance support system, "...the formation of cohort groups of teachers was important not only to operate the program efficiently but also to produce ongoing benefits to the teachers after they have completed the program" (p. 40).

Gunawardena (1995) has made an important connection between social presence theory (Short *et al.*, 1976) and computer-mediated communication (CMC). A major finding of Gunawardena's research points to the crucial role of the instructional facilitators of computer conferences in creating a sense of community and collaboration among users. Needless to say, given the text-based environment of many conferencing or discussion tools and the resulting lack of cues that tend to regulate social interaction, the task of mediating group activity while promoting some kind of kinship among learners is challenging in the extreme.

Hiltz (1994) found that when students were asked to advise faculty concerning the instructor's role in distance instruction, three basic principles emerged for establishing and maintaining a learning community: Be responsive, be competent online, and organize the interaction. Specifically, instructors were exhorted to be flexible in their presentations and activities, to provide frequent and directed questions and responses, to acknowledge comments made by students, to encourage "lurkers" to contribute to the group, and to provide periodic updates and reviews of discussions. Regarding the last point, it is important to understand that even if a WBI such as INSTRUCT is employing tools like Netscape Chat, which provides meeting scripts for archival purposes, or a threaded discussion software such as WWWBoard, the historical records generated by these programs do not relieve the instructor of the responsibility to provide a cogent summary of the previous week's activities. To the extent that these summaries can be personalized to include the names of contributors and recognition for ideas and suggestions, the communal nature of the group will be enhanced.

In one sense, the role of instructional facilitator in WBI is analogous to that of the student modeling problem in computerized intelligent tutoring systems (ITS). In his seminal article, VanLehn (1988) identifies four primary decision areas for the ITS model: advancement of the learner to the next higher level of instruction, the need to offer unsolicited advice, problem generation, and adaptation of explanations. Similar to the situation of the WBI instructor, the ITS student model must make its decisions based on limited information, usually only keystrokes or mouse-clicks, without the availability of the rich data provided by nonverbal cues. In order to reduce the burden on the student model, VanLehn (1988) and others (e.g., Bull & Pain, 1995) have suggested the use of a *glass box* model which would open up the model to inspection by the student, allowing learners the opportunity to participate interactively in the diagnosis of their own understanding and the determination of the next actions of the ITS.

For WBI, this *glass box* approach would translate into a more open WBI architecture. As with INSTRUCT, WBI design should ensure that all participants have access to a wide range of communications options, both synchronous and asynchronous, that can be used in large-group, small-group, and one-on-one settings. Learners should have full access to information about the instructional goals and strategies of the WBI, as well as their progress through the learning objectives. There should also be an understanding, cultivated by the WBI instructor, that learners are welcome to provide feedback or requests for mid-course corrections at any time. An open architecture would certainly not decrease the mediation load on the WBI instructor; however, the alternative of having to support effective student learning in an interactive but reduced-cue environment is at best a difficult proposition. An open WBI environment that promotes communication and collaboration can result in learners becoming part-owners in the instruction, greatly enhancing their sense of online community.

Summary

The roles of WBI instructors and learners were considered within three central issues for interactive WBI: Formalizing and tailoring the interactive environment, blending synchronous and asynchronous communications, and fostering a sense of community among learners. As the World Wide Web matures and computer collaborative tools become more sophisticated, the topics addressed here will only grow in significance. Given the rapid pace of change in the first half of the 1990s, we can scarcely imagine what the future holds for WBI instructors and learners.

References

Brush, T., Knapczyk, D., & Hubbard, L. (1993). Developing a collaborative performance support system for practicing teachers. *Educational Technology, 33*(11), 39–45.

Bull, S., & Pain, H. (1995). "Did I say what I think I said, and do you agree with me?" Inspecting and questioning the student model. In J. Greer (Ed.), *Proceedings of AI-ED 95* (pp. 501–508). Charlottesville, VA: Association for the Advancement of Computing in Education.

Eastmond, D. V. (1995). *Alone but together: Adult distance study through computer conferencing.* Cresskill, NJ: Hampton Press.

Gunawardena, C. N. (1995). Social presence theory and implications for interaction and collaborative learning in computer conferences. *International Journal of Educational Telecommunications, 1*(2/3), 147–166.

Guskey, T. R. (1986, May). Staff development and the process of teacher change. *Educational Researcher, 15*, 5–12.

Harasim, L. (1993). Collaborating in cyberspace: Using computer conferences as a group learning environment. *Interactive Learning Environments, 3*(2), 119–130.

Hiltz, S. R. (1994). *The virtual classroom: Learning without limits via computer networks.* Norwood, NJ: Ablex.

Honey, M., & McMillan, K. (1994). Case studies of K–12 educators' use of the Internet: Exploring the relationship between metaphor and practice. *Machine-Mediated Learning, 4*(2&3), 115–128.

Lewis, M. W., Bishay, M., & McArthur, D. (1993). The macrostructure and microstructure of inquiry activities: Evidence from students using a microworld for mathematical discovery. In P. Brna, S. Ohlsson, & H. Pain (Eds.), *Proceedings of AI-ED 93* (pp. 169–176). Charlottesville, VA: Association for the Advancement of Computing in Education.

Mandviwalla, M., & Olfman, L. (1994). What do groups need? A proposed set of generic groupware requirements. ACM *Transactions on Computer-Human Interaction, 1*(3), 245–268.

Moore, M. G. (1992). Distance education theory. *American Journal of Distance Education, 5*(3), 1–6.

National Council of Teachers of Mathematics (1991). *Professional standards for teaching mathematics.* Reston, VA: NCTM.

Scardamalia, M., & Bereiter, C. (1993). Technologies for knowledge-building discourse. *Communications of the ACM, 36*(5), 37–41.

Schrum, L. (1996). Two federally supported rural telecommunication models for professional development and instructional improvement. In *Technology and Teacher Education Annual.* Charlottesville, VA: Association for the Advancement of Computing in Education.

Short, J., Williams, E., & Christie, B. (1976). *The social psychology of telecommunications.* London: John Wiley & Sons.

VanLehn, K. (1988). Student modeling. In M. C. Polson & J. J. Richardson (Eds.), *Foundations of intelligent tutoring systems.* Hillsdale, NJ: Lawrence Erlbaum Associates.

The Author

Paul G. Shotsberger is Assistant Professor, Mathematical Sciences Department, University of North Carolina at Wilmington

e-mail, World Wide Web
shots@cms.uncwil.edu
http://www.cms.uncwil.edu/~shots

13

Faculty Incentives for the Preparation of Web-Based Instruction

Vicki Williams and Karen Peters

But First, the Disincentives

No comprehensive discussion of faculty incentives would be truly meaningful without an initial discussion of the disincentives. As idealistic as academics can be, faculty must identify, accept, and overcome, or redefine, disincentives before investing time or energy in the development of instruction for the Web or any other delivery system beyond lecture and chalkboard. Sadly, faculty face more disincentives than incentives.

Foremost in the mind and critical to the future of each and every tenure-track assistant or associate professor are promotion and tenure (P&T) activities. Without a doubt, this process serves as a strong incentive for research and an equally strong disincentive for instructional innovation. If lecture and transparencies produce even moderate success in the classroom, they are the weapon of choice, since they leave more time for publishing and committee meetings. Rethinking and redesigning instruction takes time and careful contemplation.

A quick study of the profile of attendees at instructional technology seminars typically shows a number of non-tenured faculty members who are enthusiastic about utilizing the World Wide Web. However, it is primarily tenured professors who actually invest the time to redesign their courses and are willing to risk peer criticism. Only full professors have the luxury of teaching. Murray (1992) and Bowen (1985) found that faculty prefer incentives such as release time, travel funds, development funds, or encouragement from senior-level administrators and department heads. Untenured faculty seldom receive any of these incentives to innovate and renovate the learning and teaching environment.

Why is the promotion and tenure process such a disincentive? Basically, it has to do with the time required to design, develop, and implement instruction and to create the new learning environment. It is not uncommon for an hour of Web instruction to require 200 hours of design and development (d&d).

This d&d also requires a broad range of skills. A Web-based curriculum project may require the skills of an instructional designer, a graphics artist, a digital video technician, an instructional programmer, an audio technician, and a Webmaster or server manager. If faculty members must acquire any of these new skills in order to carry out their vision, entire weeks and months can be swallowed up without a significant product to demonstrate. How many journal articles could be published in the same amount of time? One must ask, "What are my priorities, teaching and learning or keeping my position?"

One solution would be for faculty members with similar subject course responsibilities to collaborate and pool their expertise and resources. This way, the workload could be shared and the product designed to accommodate both courses. Unfortunately, many faculty members are uncomfortable working with colleagues and are more accustomed to working alone. While not so in many smaller institutions, the current atmosphere in major research universities is still competitive, not collaborative. Why? P&T asks, "What have you done?" and not "What have you and your colleagues done?"

Of course, if faculty members can find a source to fund the design and development of an innovative teaching and learning project, then they might be able to buy some release time and satisfy P&T requirements at the same time. However, while there are many sources of grants for these types of projects (e.g., AT&T and the Alfred P. Sloan Foundation), the competition for funds is intense.

Finally, faculty must overcome the "just tell me what to do" student attitude. Regardless of the planning and implementation invested in the most innovative Web-based curriculum, some students are accustomed to being spoon fed and prefer to be told what to do. Their lack of interest and enthusiasm in something that has taken so much time and effort is not encouraging.

With so many disincentives, why would anyone choose to redefine the learning environment he or she creates for his or her students? When asked that question, the faculty at Penn State responded from several perspectives, including an administrative task perspective and an instructional perspective.

Now, the Good Part: Incentives

What Faculty Members Say

Dr. David L. Passmore (1996):
> The incentives for a faculty member for designing a Web-based course? Simple. Increased productivity and efficiency. Productivity increases, because the faculty member can reach more students who are at too great a distance for traditional University Park based instruction. Efficiencies are provided by lowering costs and logistics of materials distributions.

Dr. Gerry Santoro (1996):
> By developing Web-based courses, faculty can create an interactive learning environment that changes the tired old paradigm of instruction from one of "shoveling knowledge" at the students to one of guiding students through collaborative learning experiences.
>
> A Web-based course is effectively "published" to the world, enhancing the faculty member's status as an instructor, and allowing their work to be utilized and recognized internationally.

Another faculty member, Dr. Charles W. Heuser, Jr. (1996) responds:
> I have taught the course Horticulture 138 for a number of years. It is what I call an "information inventory" course. It requires the students to learn a lot of information about a very extensive number of plants used in the landscape industry. When I first started teaching this course, I changed it to a lecture format with the use of a large number of slides. One lecture may have up to 80 slides. It was important for the students to know the aesthetic features of the plants they were learning. While the slides were an improvement, I still felt this was not the best method for the course. There was no way for the students to review the extensive slide library I was using.
>
> Putting the slides in the library did not work, as the students did not use them. When the possibility of using the Web to teach my course became available, I knew I had found my answer. I was now able to provide information and pictures to my students at a pace

to fit their needs. My incentive for using the Web-based instruction was simply to provide the students the best possible method for them to learn the subject matter.

Incentives for developing Web-based instruction can be broken down into administrative and support benefits, instructional benefits, and individual benefits. The administrative benefits include efficiency of time, scheduling benefits, distributive assignments, ease of documentation of student participation, and faculty reflection. The instructional benefits include allowing students more time to assimilate and reflect on the information, more creative classroom activities, a better environment to accommodate flexibility in learning styles, and more authentic learning environments. The individual benefits include increased exposure and collaborative opportunities.

Administrative

Although the up front time required to develop Web-based instruction may seem an inefficient use of time, once the course is developed, faculty need only to update and manage the site. This frees faculty to spend time on other academic activities, such advising and publishing.

Time wasted in scheduling (and sometimes re-scheduling) office appointments with students will also be reduced. Faculty are able to establish virtual office hours, open a Web-chat line and be "available" for students' questions or concerns while doing other work. E-mail is another medium for addressing questions and concerns. Students have the option of e-mailing their instructors at any time and receiving quick responses to their inquiries. Instructors can set regular times to check and respond to the e-mail messages, promising a 24–48 hour turn around.

Instructional

Using the asynchronous environment of the Internet for instruction allows students more time to assimilate and reflect on the information. As noted above, the horticulture students can review photographs of plants as many times and at any time they please. They are not limited to the restrictions of the conventional classroom. Less assertive students may feel more at ease responding on their own than in front of an entire class.

Web-based Instruction opens a world of opportunity for more creative classroom activities. Classroom activities become almost personalized as students search for related information on the subject matter. Students can build and share information sources; virtual meetings such as classroom chats and class list-servs can enhance collaboration and cooperation among students.

A Web-based environment offers a better environment to accommodate flexibility in learning styles. What is a learning style? Claxton and Ralston (1978) define "learning styles" as a student's consistent way of responding to and using stimuli in the context of learning. Keefe (1987) states that learning styles are characteristic cognitive, affective, and physiological behaviors that serve as relatively stable indicators of how learners perceive, interact with, and respond to the learning environment. Kegan (1982) has noted that personality development and preference to learn occurs in the context of interactions between the individual and his or her environment, rather than internal or innate processes alone.

The focus, therefore, has been to look at what characteristics the group has in common and developing a program to fit those similarities. Instructors are able to identify only a few elements of their students' learning styles through observation. Each of the models advocates acknowledging and accepting diversity among individuals. The impression is that instructors should adapt instruction to the ways in which individuals, not groups, learn. This is not a very viable solution. If the instructor is to ensure that he or she reaches the most learners, he or she should develop and plan a variety of tasks that cater to various learning styles, not the assumed style of the group.

Learning grows out of what interests the learner, not the teacher. The Web offers an excellent environment to support a number of learning style differences. Faculty can create a learning environment that challenges each style of student to pursue a topic further, gather different perspectives on an issue, and really accomplish a learner centered goal.

Hummel (1993) brought out the demand for authenticity, real-world relevance, and utility from education and the need for problems from real situations with appropriate levels of complexity. Rosove (1972) indicates that much of what interests a learner is the "stuff" in his or her own environment. The Web is a great tool to create more authentic, meaningful learning environments.

Conclusion

Web-based Instruction is a marvelous new tool for learning and teaching, but faculty members face many obstacles to its effective integration in instruction. Although it appears that disincentives far outweigh incentives, the desire to improve learning environments spurs many instructors to utilize the Web's capabilities to their fullest. Web-based Instruction is not a solution to every instructional problem, but it adds another powerful delivery medium to the faculty toolkit.

References

Bowen, Z. (1985). Faculty incentives: Some practical keys and practical examples. *New Directions for Higher Education, 13*(3), 33–43.

Claxton, C. S., & Ralston, Y. (1978). *Learning styles: Their impact on teaching and administration*. (Report No. 10). Washington, DC: George Washington University, Clearinghouse on Higher Education (ERIC Document Reproduction Service No. ED 167 065).

Heuser, C. W. Jr. (1996). In an electronic mail message on June 27, 1996.

Hummel, H. G. K. (1993). Distance education and situated learning: Paradox or partnership? *Educational Technology, 33*(12).

Keefe, J. W. (1987). *Learning style theory and practice*. Reston, VA: NASSP Publications.

Kegan, R. (1982). *The evolving self* (p. 7). Cambridge, MA: Harvard University Press.

Murray, S. F. (1992). *Determining faculty attitudes toward incentives and rewards* (ERIC Document Reproduction Service No. ED 349 058).

Passmore, D. L. (1996). In an electronic mail message on June 22, 1996.

Rosove, P. (1972). The integration of humanism and education. *Educational Technology, 12*(1), 10–18.

Santoro, G. (1996). In an electronic mail message on June 25, 1996.

The Authors

Vicki Williams is an Instructional Designer with Educational Technology Services at Pennsylvania State University.

e-mail, World Wide Web
vqw@psu.edu
http://ets.cac.psu.edu/homes/Williams

Karen Peters is a Faculty Development Specialist with Educational Technology Services at Pennsylvania State University.

e-mail, World Wide Web
kmp138@psu.edu
http://ets.cac.psu.edu/homes/Peters

14

Facilitating Change: A Process for Adoption of Web-Based Instruction

M.M. Jennings and D.J. Dirksen

The tremendous growth in the use of technology has created challenges for education (Dirksen & Tharp, 1996). In many cases, being able to utilize the technologies available to us has become a necessity rather than a matter of choice. In order to help youth to be better prepared to work in this information age, educators are beginning to integrate technology within their instruction. "If we anticipate a future when more students need more learning, there is only one way to meet that need without diminishing the quality of students' learning experiences: We must change the way we deliver education" (Twigg, 1993, p. 11). Web-based instruction provides one alternative for helping students to be better prepared for the demands of today's society.

The challenge, and it is a challenge, is to assist educators in making the change. The diffusion of instructional technologies into the public school system has been laboriously slow and in many cases ineffective (Cuban, 1986). Yet individual educators have adopted many of these technologies and localized change has taken place. Whether formally or informally, educators who have instigated change have taken on the role of mentor and change facilitator. Those who understand the change process and systematically incorporate procedures that facilitate change while introducing new innovations will be more effective in promoting the adoption of the Innovation.

What is the change process? How does one go about diffusing an innovation? In this chapter we cite two empirically tested models which are available potential blueprints for change: Diffusion of Innovation (Rogers, 1995) and the Concerns-Based Adoption Model (CBAM) (Hall & Hord, 1987). Diffusion of Innovation describes how innovations are initially adopted by groups of people that fall within what Rogers (1995) calls "adopter categories." CBAM offers a series of three diagnostic procedures which can be used to evaluate the concerns of individuals and their use of the innovation. The results of these diagnostic procedures can then be used to systematically direct any related interventions that are needed to facilitate the adoption process. Diffusion of Innovation and CBAM research will be discussed in this chapter and examples of implementation completed at the University of Northern Colorado (UNC) will be included. For a more in-depth review of diffusion research and CBAM, please see the original authors' books as cited in the References.

Rogers defines diffusion as "The process by which an innovation is communicated through certain channels over time among members of a social system" (1995, p. 5). He has determined a continuum of categories into which people fall in relation to their use of an innovation. A small percentage of people are "innovators." These people are described by Rogers as venturesome because they are the first to try new products and processes. Their role in the

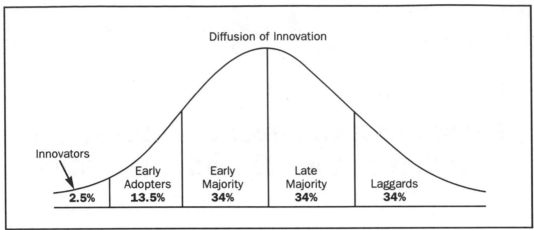

Figure 1. Adopter categorization on the basis of innovativeness
(from *Diffusion of Innovation*, 4th ed., p. 262, by E. M. Rogers).

diffusion of innovation process is to take the innovation outside of the initial concept system where it is passed to "early adopters." The early adopter is the most important category of adoption for diffusion of an innovation because at this stage the innovation will begin to be utilized and accepted. Acceptance of an innovation by this group will be most likely include acceptance by the "early majority" group.

The early majority component of the bell curve (see Figure 1) is more deliberate and thoughtful in its acceptance of something new than the two previous groups. Its acceptance, however, means that the innovation has become commonplace. The fourth adopter category is the "late majority." This group is not easily convinced of the usefulness of an innovation. Peer pressure often plays a part in its adoption decision. The last group Rogers calls "laggards." He stresses that this term should not be thought of in a negative manner. These people are simply traditionalists who take time to accept the new over the tried and true.

In addition to innovators who unknowingly help activate the diffusion process, there are "change agents" whose focus is to facilitate the adoption of an innovation by a system. A change agent is an individual who tries to influence the acceptance or rejection of new innovations. Oftentimes a change agent will identify an "opinion leader" from the early adopter category who is willing to help in the diffusion process. An opinion leader is a respected member of the group who other members look to for leadership. Promotional efforts by an opinion leader is an effective and concrete promotional tool for facilitating change.

One more important concept related to innovation adoption is "critical mass." "Critical mass occurs at the point at which enough individuals have adopted an innovation so that the innovation's further rate of adoption becomes self-sustaining" (Rogers, 1995, p. 313). At this point it is difficult, if not impossible, to impede an innovation. For change agents who wish to introduce Web-based instruction, it is important to find educators who are technology literate opinion leaders in the early adopter category of their particular field. These people will help facilitate the change process.

Diffusion of Innovation in Action

The College of Education at the University of Northern Colorado (UNC) is in the process of bringing all of its faculty online. To facilitate this process, surveys and interviews were used to identify those faculty members to whom their peers looked for direction in the use of technology. Once these opinion leaders were identified, their natural leadership was exploited to influence the adoption of technology as an instructional and professional development tool. It is the desire of the college to model technology use within the classroom as well as for professional development. The primary opinion leader identified within the college was given release time to teach special seminars for faculty members. These hands-on training sessions were designed to help faculty members begin to adopt and integrate the use of computers within their teaching.

The diffusion of innovation process is working at UNC. The mentoring process that was initiated at the faculty level has filtered down to student use as well. Early adopter faculty members have begun to integrate technology within their classes and students are seeing first hand how technology can be incorporated within instruction. Students are encouraged to use the technology for their in-class presentations and within their own teaching in several types of field experiences. Some of the recent teacher graduates and student teachers are skilled enough that they are becoming change agents within the public schools to which they are assigned. They are helping cooperating and other teachers within the building to not only use the technology as a simple tool for teaching, but to understand the value of the technology for learning.

Where Diffusion of Innovation is the macro-approach to understanding adoption of an innovation, the Concerns-Based Adoption Model is the micro-approach to facilitating change.

Concerns Based Adoption Model (CBAM)

The CBAM model includes three diagnostic dimensions: "Stages of Concern" (SoC), "Levels of Use" (LoU), and an "Innovation Configuration Map" (ICM). There are seven levels within

---

6   REFOCUSING: The focus is on exploration of more universal benefits from the innovation, including the possibility of major changes or replacement with a more powerful alternative. Individual has definite ideas about alternatives to the proposed or existing form of the innovation.

5   COLLABORATION: The focus is on coordination and cooperation with others regarding use of the innovation.

4   CONSEQUENCE: Attention foouooc on impaot of the innovation on student in his/her immediate sphere of influence. The focus is on relevance of the innovation for students, evaluation of student outcomes, including performance and competencies, and changes needed to increase student outcomes.

3   MANAGEMENT: Attention is focused on the processes and tasks of using the innovation and the best use of information and resources. Issues related to efficiency, organizing, managing, scheduling, and time demands are utmost.

2   PERSONAL: Individual is uncertain about the demands of the innovation, his/her inadequacy to meet those demands, and his/her role with the innovation. This includes analysis of his/her role in relation to the reward structure of the organization, decision making, and consideration of potential conflicts with existing structures or personal commitment. Financial or status implications of the program for self and colleagues may also be reflected.

1   INFORMATIONAL: A general awareness of the innovation and interest in learning more detail about it is indicated. The person seems to be unworried about himself/herself in relation to the innovation. She/he is interested in substantive aspects of the innovation in a selfless manner such as general characteristics, effects, and requirements for use.

0   AWARENESS: Little concern about or involvement with the innovation is indicated.

Figure 2. Stages of concern about the innovation (from Hall & Hord, 1987, p. 60).

the Stages of Concern that describe the intensity of the feelings and perceptions of the individual adopting the innovation. There are eight Levels of Use which describe the behaviors associated with an individual's use of the innovation. Specific behaviors are associated with each Level of Use. Finally, Innovation Configuration Maps are visual/word maps that describe how the innovation is currently being used or how it can be adapted, or mutated from the original.

Stages of Concern

SoC has been used extensively in concerns research involving a variety of innovation adoption situations. According to Hall and Hord (1987), the process of change can be more successful if the "concerns" of the individual are considered. The concept of concerns has been defined as: "The composite representation of the feelings, preoccupation, thought, and consideration given to a particular issue or task" (Hall, George, & Rutherford, 1979, p. 5). The SoC Questionnaire (SoCQ) provides a quantitative measure of the intensities of the seven Stages of Concern dimensions (see Figure 2 on previous page).

Levels of Use

Levels of Use provides key information for understanding and describing implementation and diffusion of an innovation. Data collected from LoU interviews provide useful insights about staff development, evaluation, planning and facilitation for leaders and change facilitators. By evaluating and categorizing the levels of use, appropriate interventions can

VI	**RENEWAL:** State in which the user reevaluates the quality of use of the innovation, seeks major modifications of or alternatives to present innovation to achieve increased impact on clients, examines new developments in the field, and explores new goals for self and the system.
V	**INTEGRATION:** State in which the user is combining own efforts to use the innovation with related activities of colleagues to achieve a collective impact on clients within their common sphere of influence.
IVB	**REFINEMENT:** State in which the user varies the use of the innovation to increase the impact on clients within immediate sphere of influence. Variations are based on knowledge of both short- and long-term consequences for clients.
IVA	**ROUTINE:** Use of the innovation is stabilized. Few if any changes are being made in ongoing use. Little preparation or thought is being given to improving innovation use or its consequences.
III	**MECHANICAL USE:** State in which the user focuses most effort on the short-term, day-to-day use of the innovation with little time for reflection. Changes in use are made more to meet user needs than client needs. The user is primarily engaged in a stepwise attempt to master the tasks required to use the innovation, often resulting in disjointed and superficial use.
II	**PREPARATION:** State in which the user is preparing for first use of the innovation.
I	**ORIENTATION:** State in which the user has recently acquired or is acquiring information about the innovation and/or has recently explored or is exploring its value orientation and its demands upon user and user system.
0	**NON-USE:** State in which the user has little or no knowledge of the innovation, no involvement with the innovation, and is doing nothing toward becoming involved.

Figure 3. Levels of use of an innovation (from Hall & Hord, 1987, p. 84).

be designed for each user. According to Hall and Hord (1987), Levels of Use focuses on the behaviors that are, or are not, exhibited in relation to the innovation (see Figure 3 on previous page). The Levels of Use definitions presented in Figure 3 include three "nonuse" descriptions and five "use" descriptions.

Innovation Configuration Map

Innovations tend to be adapted and, in many cases, mutated by their users. It is often difficult to predict how an innovation will be utilized by the end user. An Innovation Configuration Map (ICM) address this implementation problem by "mapping" out acceptable as well as probable behavior patterns with the innovation.

Hall and Hord (1987) have developed a procedure for mapping the different ways an innovation may be used. The primary task in developing an ICM is to identify if and how the innovation is being used. Then, based on this information, a continuum from "ideal" to "no use" is created. The overall goal of IC Mapping is to develop a word map which identifies optimal conditions as well as adaptations and mutations of the innovation. The result is a concept map of the innovation. See Figure 4 for a one page sample of an ICM that was developed for integrating technology within the classroom.

I. ALL DAY IN THE CLASSROOM
    A. Teacher
        1. Technology is utilized throughout the day by the teacher. [*teacher application, all*]

Consistent reliance on and seamless integration of technology.	Applies selected integration emphasis	Goes through motions with bits and pieces of technology.	Non-use
Completed Integration *(a)*	*Selected Application* *(b)*	*Parts & Pieces* *(c)*	*Nothing* *(d)*
Technology is integrated without conscious effort into instructional activities throughout the day.	Selected technologies are utilized appropriately throughout the day.	Technology use is limited to curricular requirements.	
• Teacher incorporates technology into learning activities.	• Selected technologies are incorporated into instruction.	• The teacher incorporates those pieces of technology that are required by the curriculum.	
• Transitions between activities are well organized, quickly performed, and do not interrupt flow of work.	• The teacher relies on support materials when using technology.	• The teacher uses those technologies which are most compatible with his or her teaching style.	
• Technology is used to facilitate learning activities using a variety of student activity levels.	• Teacher facilitates learning using specific technologies with which the teacher is comfortable.	• Use of technology is focused on curricular demands.	
• Use of technology is focused on meeting the learner's needs.	• Use of technology is focused on the skills of the teacher.		

Figure 4. Innovation configuration map.

ICMs provide new insights into the innovation and its implementation which helps to clarify the multiple forms that an innovation may take and act as a guide for facilitating the change process. They provide word pictures of the different ways in which the innovation can be used and form a basis for judgments about the effectiveness of an innovation.

CBAM in Action

The mentoring approach for technology use with student teachers at UNC, as mentioned earlier, is currently being evaluated using the CBAM diagnostic procedures. In the most recent evolution of this study, cooperating teachers were asked to participate. Initial correlations indicate that the mentoring of the technology use by the cooperating teacher and the confidence and knowledge level of the technology use by the student teacher has a profound effect on the student teacher's use of technology within the classroom. In some cases, the preservice student teacher left the university with a routine level of use for using the technology as a teaching tool and was able to help the cooperating teacher develop technology use skills. Those students placed with cooperating teachers who were at a routine level of use themselves were able to take an active role within their schools, becoming change facilitators for promoting the adoption of technology as a teaching tool.

Conclusions

It is important to understand that change takes time, effort, and commitment from all of the parties involved. Successful implementation is much more likely to occur when change agents enlist the help of opinion leaders and actively address the individual concerns related to technology use by the current and potential users. Change is a process, not one single event (Hall & Hord, 1987).

References

Cuban, L. (1986). *Teachers and machines: The classroom use of technology since 1920.* New York: Teachers College Press.

Dirksen, D. J., & Tharp, D. (1996). Utilizing CBAM to promote systemic change: The use of instructional technologies in the classroom. *Technology and Teacher Education Annual 1996.* Charlottesville, VA: Association for the Advancement of Computing in Education.

Hall, G. E., George, A., & Rutherford, W. (1979). Measuring stages of concern about the innovation: A manual for the use of the SoC questionnaire. (Report No. 3032). Austin: The University of Texas at Austin, Research and Development Center for Teacher Education (ERIC Document Reproduction Service No. ED 147 342).

Hall, G. E., & Hord, S. M. (1987). *Change in schools: Facilitating the process.* Albany, NY: State University of New York Press.

Rogers, E. M. (1995). *Diffusion of innovation* (4th ed.). New York: The Free Press.

Twigg, C. (1993). Can education be "productive"? *EDUCOM Review, 28*(6), 10–12.

The Authors

M. M. Jennings, is a Graduate Assistant and Computer Lab Manager, Educational Psychology, Statistics and Technology, University of Northern Colorado.

e-mail
    jennings@edtech.univnorthco.edu

D. J. Dirksen, is a Doctoral Candidate and Graduate Assistant, Educational Psychology, Statistics, and Technology, University of Northern Colorado.

SECTION III

Designing Web-Based Instruction

15

Cognitive Flexibility Hypertexts on the Web: Engaging Learners in Meaning Making

David H. Jonassen, Dean Dyer,
Karen Peters, Timothy Robinson,
Douglas Harvey, Marsha King,
and Pamela Loughner

Introduction

More than twenty years ago, Ted Nelson (1974) conceived of an electronic hypertext called Xanadu that would interconnect all of the world's literature, so that scholars and learners could have immediate access to any of the world's stored literature. For years he sought to develop a commercially viable version of Xanadu, realizing that such an endeavor would require highly distributed computing facilities. Now, Nelson's dream is coming true. Xanadu is emerging in the form of the World Wide Web, a distributed network of computers storing multimedia files that are all interlinked by a formal hypertext mark-up language (HTML). The World Wide Web is a mega-hypertext that has the potential for interlinking all of the world's electronically stored information.

Hypertext is a natural medium for information access. If a user has a query, he or she is able to use sophisticated search engines to manipulate an even more sophisticated indexing system to locate information on any topic he or she chooses. Using hypertext links as access structures, users may also browse through related documents to acquire information on any subjects at any time. Access structures provide visual, structural cues that can signal the structure of text and facilitate access to it (Waller, 1982), but are those cues sufficient for engaging and supporting learning (i.e., meaning making)? If not, do we need richer learning models for structuring hypermedia?

Many think not, because in the mid-1990s, the Web is being promoted as the latest technological revolution and panacea in many educational contexts. Public schools and universities are converting much of their instruction to the Web sites with the promise of providing on-demand, anytime, anywhere instruction. As this Web-based instruction is being implemented, an important emergent issue is whether hypertext and hypermedia can support learning adequately through its system of access structures. Is providing access to

119

information sufficient for learning? Probably not. If the Web is to become more than a giant library or a commercial trading place, we need to explore how to represent and structure user interactions to facilitate learning. The process of transforming the information that is accessed into personal knowledge (what we call learning) requires that users possess and be able to articulate an information need, and that they consciously relate the information that they are accessing to what they already know in an effort to reconceive what they know. When learners have information needs and are able to articulate those needs in terms of an information query, a hypertext can be extremely effective in supporting information access. However, learning from hypertext relies on learners being able to integrate what they are finding with what they already know into some kind of coherent, conceptual scheme (Jonassen, 1988). For most learners, that process requires support. For instance, what happens when learners are unable to formulate meaningful information queries? They need to be able to articulate information needs—a reason, purpose, or goal for accessing information. The most powerful purposes are to answer a question, resolve a discrepancy or conflict between what is known and what is encountered, satiate a curiosity, ponder a puzzlement, or reconcile a perturbation; that is, to make sense out of something that doesn't make sense. So, in order to support meaningful learning on the World Wide Web, better models for providing a purpose, engaging learners, and structuring learners' interactions are needed.

Conceptual models for structuring hypertext are evolving (Jonassen & Mandl, 1990). Contemporary instructional design, undergirded by a constructivist epistemology (Jonassen, 1991), has provided numerous models for designing problem- or project-based learning environments (Duffy & Jonassen, 1992), such as anchored instruction (Cognition and Technology Group at Vanderbilt, 1991, 1993), cognitive flexibility theory (Spiro, Feltovich, Jacobson, & Coulson, 1991), goal-based scenarios (Schank, 1994), and case-based learning environments (Jonassen, in press a). In all of these kinds of environments, learners' information needs are prompted by presenting them with authentic problems or conundrums that they find interesting. Solving the problem requires knowledge that they need to learn, which requires that they seek out information, differing interpretations, or a variety of support systems.

These rich environments promote study and investigation within authentic (i.e., realistic, meaningful, relevant, complex, and information-rich) contexts; encourage the growth of student responsibility, initiative, decision making, and intentional learning; cultivate an atmosphere of cooperative learning among students and teachers; utilize dynamic, generative learning activities that promote high level thinking processes (i.e., analysis, synthesis, problem solving, experimentation, creativity, and examination of topics from multiple perspectives) to help students integrate new knowledge with old knowledge and thereby create rich and complex knowledge structures; and assess student progress in content and learning to learn through realistic tasks and performances (Grabinger, 1996). Two of the most critical features of learning environments are integration and comprehensiveness (Hannafin, 1992), the process of linking new knowledge to old and modifying and enriching existing knowledge and increasing the number of access points to that information.

Among the richest and best researched of these models, cognitive flexibility theory is probably the most adaptable to a hypertext environment (Spiro & Jehng, 1990), such as the World Wide Web. Cognitive flexibility theory is a conceptual model for designing learning environments that is based upon cognitive learning theory. Its intention is to facilitate the acquisition of advanced knowledge to serve as the basis for expertise in complex and ill-structured knowledge domains. Cognitive flexibility theory uses hypertext to rearrange "instructional sequences, for multiple dimensions of knowledge representation, for multiple interconnections across knowledge components, and so on. Features like these correspond nicely to well known

properties of hypertext systems, which facilitate ... multiple linkages among content elements"
(Spiro *et al.*, 1991, p. 67).

Cognitive Flexibility Theory

Cognitive flexibility theory was developed to overcome sources of misunderstanding among
learners and to promote advanced knowledge acquisition. The sources of misunderstanding include reductive bias—an oversimplified understanding of important concepts, especially in
knowledge domains that are conceptually complex (Feltovich, Spiro, & Coulson, 1989). So
much instruction oversimplifies the content that it seeks to transmit, because its designers believe that it is impossible to convey appropriate levels of complexity to novices who have inadequate prior knowledge structures. Concepts have to be simplified in order to make them
understandable—in order to build on the limited, relevant world knowledge that is possessed
by novices. So, our instruction filters out the complexity that exists in most applied knowledge
domains, causing shallow understanding of domain knowledge to develop.

This simplification process is accomplished by employing simplified prototypic examples,
cases, and analogies. These are easier to conceptualize and implement in most learning environments. So, content is organized in prepackaged knowledge structures that communicate the
reliability and regularity of the content. But the knowledge that results from this approach is
also pre-packaged and rigid and is therefore not easily adapted to learning contexts outside the
immediate instructional context (Spiro, Vispoel, Schmitz, Samarapungavan, & Boerger, 1987).

A belief implied by pre-packaging knowledge (and most traditional principles of
instructional design) is that knowledge is context- and content-independent, that knowledge
or skills, once acquired, easily transfer to different contexts. Cognitive flexibility theory,
on the other hand, accentuates the role of context, because information acquired in a real-
world context is better retained, the learning that results is more generative, higher order,
and more meaningful, and the transfer of that learning is broader and more accurate (Spiro
et al., 1991).

Designing instruction for advanced knowledge domains is also difficult because often the
domain knowledge is ill-structured. Ill-structured knowledge results from ill-defined concepts,
which tend to have variable attributes and ambiguous criteria. Traditional designers typically
treat categories or constructs as regular and well-structured. depicting them as taxonomies that
reliably distinguish classes of events. However, events and phenomena in the real world tend
to be more ill-defined. They tend to have few general principles that can predict most of the
cases or determine appropriate action. There are no prototypic cases, or they are misleading,
and certain aspects of cases are differentially important in different contexts, so each case appears novel because of the interactions of effects (Spiro *et al.*, 1987, 1988).

In order to overcome these sources of misunderstanding, cognitive flexibility theory tries
to avoid oversimplifying instruction (Spiro *et al.*, 1988). Hypertexts designed using cognitive
flexibility theory stress the conceptual interrelatedness of ideas and their interconnectedness in
the link structure. Cognitive flexibility hypertexts reflect the complexity that normally faces
practitioners, rather than treating practical, professional problems as simple, linear sequences
of decisions.

In order to do that, cognitive flexibility hypertexts provide multiple representations of
content. Traditional instructional design practice believes that there is a single, best way to
conceive knowledge; that is, there is a single schema or concept that best describes any object
or event. That best method is revealed by task analysis. However, in order to comprehend the
complexity of the real world, learners should understand and personally reconcile its different
interpretations. Transfer of acquired knowledge to novel situations, which is essential in prob-

lem solving, requires the understanding of these multiple mental representations that are best achieved through the instructional use of multiple analogies. "It is only through the use of multiple schemata, concepts, and thematic perspectives that the multi-faceted nature of the content area can be represented and appreciated" (Jacobson, 1990, p. 21). Cognitive flexibility theory intentionally represents multiple perspectives or interpretations of the content that it seeks to teach. The theory borrows a rich metaphor of "criss-crossing the landscape" from Ludwig Wittgenstein for physically describing this process. The learner criss-crosses the intellectual landscape of the content domain by looking at it from multiple perspectives or through multiple themes.

Like most constructivist approaches to learning, cognitive flexibility theory emphasizes case-based instruction. Rather than basing instruction on a single example or case, it is important that a variety of cases be used to illustrate the content domain. The more varied these cases are, the broader the conceptual bases that they are likely to support. And these cases should be authentic, requiring the same thinking that is required in real-world contexts. The ill-structuredness of any knowledge domain is best illustrated by multiple perspectives or themes that are inherent in many cases. The extensive use of multiple cases also supports a variety of applied contexts for the acquisition of knowledge.

In the process of reconciling multiple perspectives on authentic cases, learners must construct their own interpretation of the truth. Rather than instructors transmitting objective knowledge and requiring learners to encode those representations, learners should be responsible for constructing their own knowledge representations in order to adapt and use them in novel situations.

Finally, cognitive flexibility hypertexts support complexity. Rather than instructors mapping oversimplified models onto the learner, the learner needs to recognize the inconsistencies in that knowledge by applying it in different contexts or relating it to different perspectives while it is being learned. Cognitive flexibility theory conveys this complexity by presenting multiple representations of the same information and different thematic perspectives on the information. In order to construct useful knowledge structures, learners need to compare and contrast the similarities and differences between cases.

Implementations of Cognitive Flexibility Theory on the World Wide Web

At Penn State, we have been exploring the implications of cognitive flexibility theory for structuring Web-based learning environments. The following learning environments are being developed to test the utility and efficacy of cognitive flexibility theory on the Web.

Understanding Instructional Design

Since cognitive flexibility theory focuses on learning in complex and ill-structured domains, understanding the field of instructional design seems like a very appropriate content domain for examining cognitive flexibility theory. With a deluge of design models and theories, instructional design offers many themes and perspectives with which to view instructional cases. Instructional design represents an archetypal example of ill-structured problem solving, because most design problems have vaguely defined or unclear goals, unstated constraints, multiple solutions or solution paths, no consensual agreement on the appropriate solution, and multiple criteria for evaluating solutions (Jonassen, in press b).

The intended audience for the Web cognitive flexibility hypertext on instructional design is novice instructional design students. It would also be suitable as a case study review for new instructional designers.

The goal of the hypertext is to expose the users to 15 actual instructional design cases, the different themes and perspectives involved, and how the themes and perspectives within each problem are related. By being presented with varying themes and perspectives, the users will reflect on their current practices and understanding of instructional design as they attempt to produce their own solutions to the instructional problems.

The assessment will consist of three actual instructional design cases. The user must pick one case and design a solution(s) for the case. Additionally, the user will be asked to reflect on and write a brief synopsis on what (if anything) has changed in his or her understanding of instructional design.

Themes relevant throughout various instructional design cases in the hypertext are:

- autonomy and independence;

- logistical support tools (how do the support tools assist in the analysis and synthesis of information?);

- social and psychological dimensions;

- context dependency (meanings are altered by the context of other themes with which they occur); and

- strategic initiatives.

The example case that follows will show how these themes relate to individual cases. Themes are listed on the bottom of each page in the case. Upon selecting a theme, the user is linked to a page explaining how the selected theme is relevant to that specific case (see Figure 1). Although every case does not include every theme, there is considerable overlap. Throughout

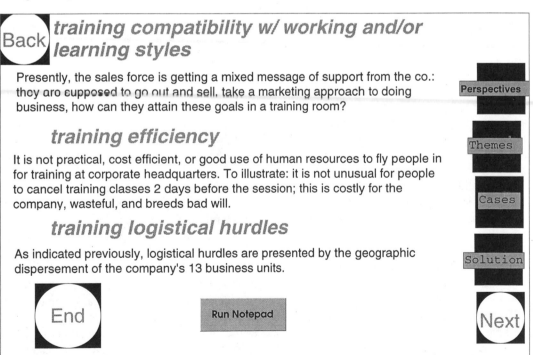

Figure 1. A theme page for the SERV-U case. This page explains how various themes relate to the case.

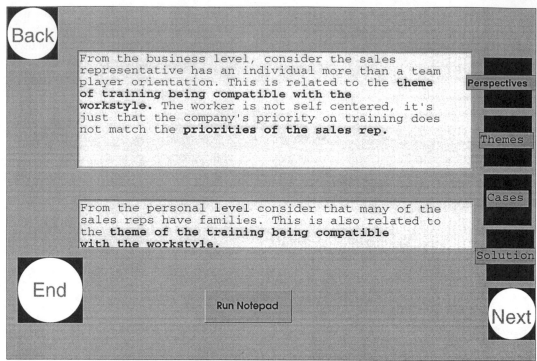

Figure 2. A perspectives page for the SERV-U case. From this page, the user can link to further perspectives, themes, or back to the case itself.

each case there are also hotwords or phrases that link to the themes and perspectives pages (see Figure 2). With the browser navigation tools and the designer's footers and hot words, the user should be able to criss-cross between cases, perspectives, and themes within our designed pages. When the user wanders into the Web (which he or she is encouraged to do), criss-crossing is limited to the browser's functions.

Perspectives were built around the "players" in each case; anyone who had any effect at all on the problem and/or the outcome. The perspectives are listed on the bottom of each page in the case. Upon selecting a perspective, the user will be brought to a page explaining how the selected perspective is relevant to the that specific case. At the bottom of this page, the user then has a choice of going back to the case, or viewing other cases sharing similar perspectives. In addition to the players, at any time the user can click on a button to view a page on industry players or major theories (such as Gagné, Briggs, Jonassen, Merrill, and Reigeluth, or a page on constructivism, objectivism, situated learning theory, symbolic interaction theory, and so on).

From the specific case pages, the user is also capable of viewing possible solutions to the problem at hand. We tried to present multiple solutions, if possible. There are hotwords and phrases within the solutions linking to perspectives, themes, industry players, and major theories.

Let's look at an example. The first case is an actual case presented to a distance education design class at Penn State Great Valley. The case deals with a computer services company. The company provides service for other companies that have mainframe computers. For the sake of anonymity, we'll call the company SERV-U. Specific services marketed by SERV-U include: helpdesk services, which companies call directly with an 800 number, and services management.

Traditionally, SERV-U had been a "break/fix" company, meaning that their primary function was response to service calls. However, the newer, more sophisticated systems being used by companies are part of the reason that SERV-U has adopted a proactive rather than reactive approach to doing business. It is also significant to note that the training style at SERV-U is evolving away from the "closing the deal on the spot" focus and moving toward a marketing approach that recognizes and responds to customer needs. These are two important factors encouraging SERV-U's commitment to ongoing, relevant training for its sales force.

SERV-U has a decentralized structure with 20 business units located in various cities throughout the United States. Each business has an area sales director and over a dozen salespeople with varying degrees of skill and experience. That's over 250 people in field sales.

SERV-U has a list of training considerations the company wanted developed into a menu from which the employees could choose, according to the priority of need. Some of the desired courses include:

- hiring skills;

- proposal development: basic and advanced;

- strategic planning;

- the "SERV-U Way," comprising total quality management, problem solving, and other elements;

- laptop PC training;

- presentation skills;

- communication skills;

- training on financials (how to determine if the client is profitable, etc.); and

- product training.

The major challenge facing the company is the lack of human resources to conduct an ambitious training program with over 20 geographically disparate locations. The current policy is to bring the sales force to one central location twice a year for one week of intensive training. During the sessions, sales people get "beeped" or their portable phones ring, and they leave the training session. Some just leave every hour on the hour to check their messages, with little attention paid to the training. The result is an untrained sales force and nascent complaints on customer service related issues. SERV-U invested heavily in some teleconferencing equipment; however, the same scenario happened at the dispersed training locations, also. There seems to be no camaraderie among the sales force, no team spirit; everyone is out for himself or herself.

The company is open to making an investment in alternative training methods if it gets a good return on investment. A point for instructional designers is that the company had clearly stated that any training program will fail unless there is embedded accountability from those who receive instruction.

Up until this point, the case can be presented in a strictly linear print format, as has been done here. One of the themes in this case is *social and psychological dimensions*. If the user follows this link, he or she will find that the sales representatives' individualistic attitudes have been identified. This may lead the user to explore the sales representative perspective, where he or she will find out that the rep's job is *commission driven*. "Commission driven" is a hot phrase linked to the theme of *logistical support*. The current training programs' delivery methods are not compatible with the *working styles* of their sales representatives. These reps make their living on commission, earning an average of $5,000 per commission, the client tells us. Of course, a phone call from a potential client is more important than a training class! "Working styles" is another hot phrase linked to the theme of social and psychological dimensions in that the sales reps' lives are pretty hectic. Most have families with whom they would prefer to spend any available free time.

There are a variety of ways in which this case can be solved. The actual designers who worked on this case decided that the most critical problem was that salespeople could not come together for training. Instruction was placed on video and audio, so that the salespeople could use the instruction when they had time. If they were interrupted, they could pick up where they left off in the lesson. Assessment was now handled through written correspondence. There were still training sessions conducted at the teleconferencing facilities, but the time was reduced from two weeks to only a few days.

This case shows a sample of the issues that must be carefully considered by the instructional design team in order to come up with a viable solution to the problem. The cases are authentic, real world instructional problems of the types that instructional designers face in their jobs. Not only are the contexts authentic, but so are the tasks expected of the learner. The users are not asked to name the phases of the design process; they are asked to design. Multiple perspectives are explored within each case. These differing perspectives force the user to evaluate conflicting information and synthesize these positions into a personal position, just as an instructional designer needs to balance the perspectives of various stakeholder groups. The cases and perspectives are contextually rich because of the inherent complexity of the domain. For all these reasons, cognitive flexibility hypertexts are a natural medium for teaching instructional design.

Environmental Issues

The College of Earth and Mineral Sciences, as part of its mission of serving the people of the Commonwealth, has developed collections of teaching and learning resources within our areas of expertise. Among these materials is a cognitive flexibility hypertext that focuses on issues of biodiversity, land use and control, and conflict resolution styles as they have emerged in the controversy surrounding the reintroduction of the Mexican grey wolf into wilderness areas of the American Southwest.

The wolf-reintroduction Web site (see Figure 3) allows the learner to examine the reintroduction issue from the perspectives of a half dozen or so people who actually will be affected by the wolves. We identified various issues interwoven through their comments: local vs. national control of the land, consumption vs. conservation, cooperation vs. confrontation. From the pages that explain these issues, the Web-site visitor can link to specific comments that exemplify the point of view under discussion.

The same set of interviews—audio clips and transcripts—can be sorted according to at least the four thematic issues identified above. In this way, the learner has flexible options about how he or she traverses and understands the information space. If the learners are thorough about following all of the links on each page, by the time they have finished, they will have seen and heard the same material via three or four different organizing themes, thereby criss-crossing the landscape in three or four directions. The wolf-reintroduction hypertext does not tell learners how to interpret the jumble of voices, but does suggest ways of looking at and listening to the opinions expressed.

An important design goal of the wolf site is to prompt visitors to actively construct their own meaning from the viewpoints represented. We ask the visitors to register their own opinions on the reintroduction question by voting yes or no and explaining their decision (see Figure 4). When they do this, they are shown the current tally of yes and no votes and can read the explanatory comments of other visitors. This is an attempt to gently prod them to process the varying viewpoints, assign some value to each, and come to a conclusion, however tentative. While it is certainly possible for visitors to ignore the voting and simply listen to the var-

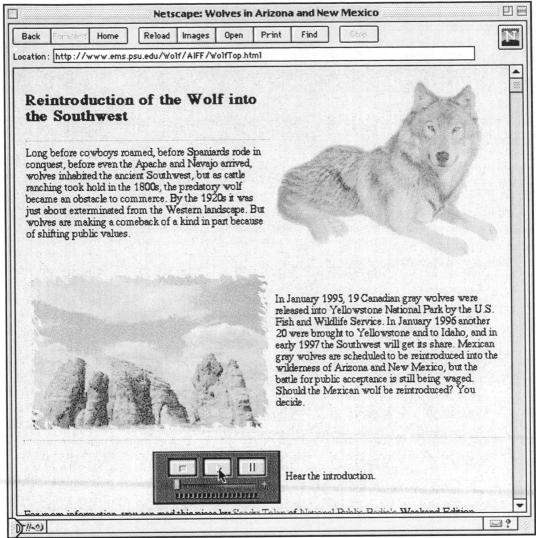

Figure 3. The Wolf-Reintroduction Web site.

ious characters in the site, it is expected that most people will want to join the discussion and register their own opinion.

The wolf-reintroduction hypertext supports the acquisition of advanced knowledge in a complex and ill-structured domain. The issue of re-introducing wolves into habitats they once occupied is very complex, and it does not seem to have a neat, logical structure. Since the question does involve identifiable themes, it seems to be a good candidate for presentation via a cognitive flexibility hypertext.

Two additional cases that focus on conservation vs. development, central control vs. local control, and cooperation vs. confrontation themes are being devloped. A real-life local issue is the selection of a route for U.S. Route I-99, a proposed interstate highway currently in the planning stages. Local landowners and environmental groups are actively debating the alternatives with the Pennsylvania Department of Transportation. People on all sides of the

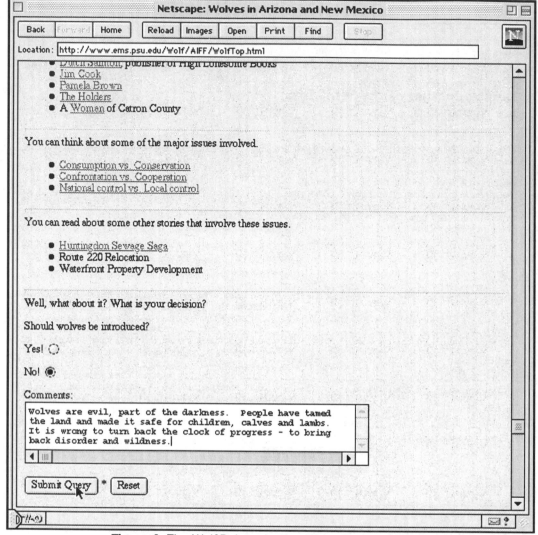

Figure 4. The Wolf-Reintroduction Web site (continued).

debate are participating in the route selection process in ways that clearly involve the three central issues in the wolf debate. The hypertext will allow users to examine arguments for and against the various alternative routes, and make their own decisions. The decisions of previous users will be presented along with the decision of the Department of Transportation.

Students at central Pennsylvania's Huntingdon Area Middle School have become involved in environmental protection activities around their community, and in the process, have learned much about the three central themes in the wolf debate. They have succeeded in affecting change through cooperation with the state and local authorities, learning which government agency has authority over what area. They have learned how much effort and money goes into environmental protection infrastructure like sewage systems, and the arguments for not spending the money and effort. Our hypertext links will allow the user to follow the activities of the students as they uncover pollution and work through government agencies and funding sources to solve the problem. The user will learn how the same three themes affected the students' approach to their challenges.

Environmental issues are excellent candidates for flexibility hypertexts. Multiple perspectives prevail, and few solutions will please the majority. Cognitive flexibility theory represents a useful model for educating the public about these and similar issues prior to voting.

Understanding Sexual Harassment

A cognitive flexibility hypertext is being developed to support a teaching unit on sexual harassment for first-year students in a speech communications class, entitled Gender Roles in Communication. Traditional instructional strategies, such as lecture and class discussion, were perceived to be less than optimal in helping students understand the complex nature of sexual harassment and to recognize the types of sexual harassment they might encounter in their lives. It was decided that a case-based approach in the form of a cognitive flexibility hypertext might be more effective, as it would allow for a variety of situations to be presented in an authentic context, and stimulate reflection by the students.

The main goals for the hypertext are to help students recognize when they are the victim of sexual harassment, to help students become more aware of how their own actions may contribute to an environment conducive to sexual harassment, and to help students develop the ability to develop an appropriate course of action if they should encounter a situation involving sexual harassment.

In order to achieve these goals, a flexibility hypertext was selected because it can reflect the complexity of the issue of sexual harassment as well as to promote transfer of that knowledge. The hypertext was guided by the belief that the themes and perspectives surrounding sexual harassment should be interconnected throughout the cases, and that the cases needed to be authentic, believable, and perceived as real-life problems to first-year university students. Finally, the learning task and tools should promote reflection by the learner, and the program's interface should be easy to use.

The World Wide Web was selected because there was a desire to allow for the full version of the hypertext to link to Internet based resources (such as the university policy on sexual harassment and other pages related to gender studies). The use of frames allows users to easily use the program by allowing the case information and perspectives to be separated from navigational controls.

From a central menu, students may choose from among six sexual harassment cases (see Figure 5) which explore issues relevant to undergraduate students, including:

- professor makes a comment in class;

- student meets with an advisor;

- (Work Study) supervisor makes sexual advances;

- professor asks student out;

- three students working together; and

- student walks past group (of other students).

Some of the cases explore interactions between university personnel and students, while others involve interactions between students. Some cases explore rather straightforward situations (e.g., sexual advances), while others deal less obvious situations which may involve sexual harassment (e.g., classroom comments). The scenarios were written in such a way as to allow students, regardless of gender, to identify with several perspectives in the case. For each scenario, differing viewpoints, including those of friends, university personnel, and legal counsel

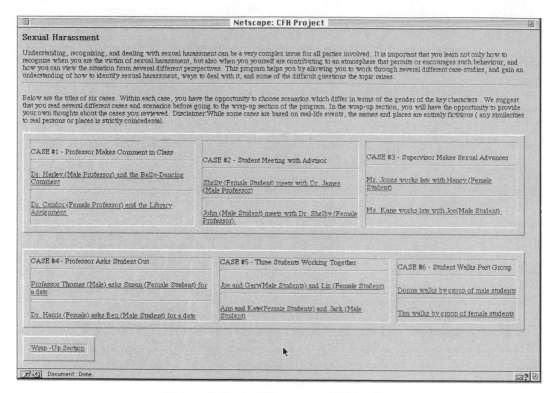

Figure 5. Sexual Harassment Web site.

are made available to help the student better understand the given situation. It is the perspectives which allow for the criss-crossing of themes across cases.

Let's look at an example. In one scenario, a student's expression of wanting the freedom to research his or her own interests and express ideas freely in class, despite an apparently hostile attitude on the part of the professor, is the primary issue. It raises the issue of individual freedom versus the control of a person in authority, and the user may choose to follow a link to a page which goes into more depth on the issue of freedom vs. control. From there, links are available to similar perspectives in other cases (see Figure 6). For example, a link is made to a perspective in a scenario which involves a student's desire to enter a building via the front doors vs. the rude comments made by a group of students sitting outside the entrance. In both instances, one person's freedom of choice is being curtailed by the fact that someone else appears to have control of the situation. The criss-crossing from case to case allows the learners to develop a sense for the recurring themes that surround sexual harassment cases. Those recurring themes include freedom vs. control, inclusion vs. exclusion, society vs. individual, reality vs. perception, and avoidance vs. confrontation. These themes are intertwined with various realms, e.g., psychology, ethics, constitutional law, to name a few, to explore sexual harassment more fully.

In the conclusion section, students are allowed to choose the questions they want to answer from a variety of options. One question asks learners to assume the role of a victim in one of the scenarios and explain how they would have responded in the situation. Another question asks students to select and explore a recurring theme through publicized cases of sexual harassment. Yet another question asks students to examine their behavior to de-

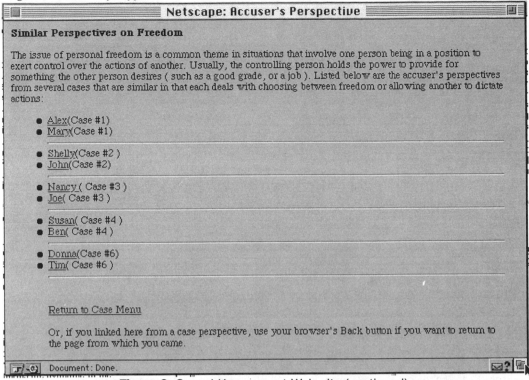

Figure 6. Sexual Harassment Web site (continued).

termine if actions they may have exhibited in the past could have contributed to a situation of sexual harassment.

Summary

Each of these hypertexts was designed to exploit the interconnectivity of hypertext and to reflect the conceptual model described in cognitive flexibility theory. These hypertexts were designed to avoid oversimplifying the ill-structured content domains. Clearly, instructional design, environmental issues, and sexual harassment possess multivariate perspectives. This natural complexity needs to be conveyed by the instruction in order to avoid the reductive belief that these domains are simple with predictable beliefs. So, each of the hypertexts provides multiple representations of content. The information available to the student in each case is varied.

All three hypertexts provide multiple cases as the basis for instruction. The knowledge, perspectives, and information are all case-driven, so that any information is provided by the hypertext only in the context of a case. What results should be context-dependent knowledge. So, understanding instructional design is not likely to transfer to the legal implications of sexual harassment, which has its own intricacies. The importance of a clinical context for the acquisition of instructional design, environmental, and harassment knowledge cannot be overstated. Knowledge is best acquired in relevant situations that are likely to be encountered by the student as a practitioner (Brown, Collins, & Duguid, 1989). The cases provided in all of these hypertexts are real cases. The problems encountered and the reasoning required to solve those cases are dependent upon the knowledge domains. In all of the hypertexts, learners are required to construct their own understanding. They are not told what the right answers or right perspectives are. In attempting to solve cases, learners build complex schemata that consists of procedural (how to) knowledge rather than an amalgamation of unrelated facts. This procedural knowledge is more readily transferable.

From a design perspective, it is important to note that the link structures of the hypertext are conceptual and not referential. Links take learners to alternate perspectives and conceptions of the events being explored. This is what makes cognitive flexibility theory such a powerful model for structuring hypertext.

Publication deadlines have precluded the completion of empirical validation of these hypertexts. Research on flexibility theory has found no differences in reproductive memory between learners studying traditional, single-perspective materials and those studying flexibility hypertexts, but that learners studying flexibility theory materials are better able to transfer the principles to novel, unrelated cases (Jacobson, 1990; Spiro *et al.*, 1987). Our testing program anticipates similar findings.

References

Brown, J. S., Collins, A., & Duguid, P. (1989). Situated cognition and the culture of learning. *Educational Researcher, 18*(1), 32–42.

Cognition and Technology Group at Vanderbilt (CTGV). (1991). Technology and the design of generative learning environments. *Educational Technology, 31*(9), 34–40.

Cognition and Technology Group at Vanderbilt (CTGV). (1993). Designing learning environments that support thinking. In T. M. Duffy, J. Lowyck, & D. H. Jonassen (Eds.), *Designing environments for constructive learning* (pp. 9–36). Berlin: Springer-Verlag.

Coulson, R. L., Feltovich, P. J., & Spiro, R. J. (1989). Foundations of a misunderstanding of the ultra-structural basis of myocardial failure: A reciprocation network of oversimplifications. *Journal of Medicine and Philosophy, 14*, 109–146.

Duffy, T. M., & Jonassen, D. H. (Eds.). (1992). *Constructivism and the technology of instruction: A conversation.* Hillsdale, NJ: Lawrence Erlbaum Associates

Feltovich, P. J., Spiro, R. J., & Coulson, R. L. (1989). The nature of conceptual understanding in biomedicine: The deep structure of complex ideas and the development of misconceptions. In D. Evans & V. Patel (Eds.), *The cognitive sciences in medicine.* Cambridge, MA: MIT Press.

Feltovich, P. J., Coulson, R. L., & Spiro, R. J., (1986). *The nature and acquisition of faulty student models of selected medical concepts: Cardiovascular impedance.* Paper presented at the annual meeting of the American Educational Research Association, Montreal.

Grabinger, R. S. (1996). Rich environments for active learning. In D. H. Jonassen (Ed.), *Handbook of research on educational communications and technology.* New York: Macmillan.

Jacobson, M. J. (1990). *Knowledge acquisition, cognitive flexibility, and the instructional applications of hypertext: A comparison of contrasting designs for computer-enhanced learning environments* (Doctoral dissertation, University of Illinois).

Jonassen, D. H. (1988). Designing structured hypertext and structuring access to hypertext. *Educational Technology, 28*(11), 13–16.

Jonassen, D. H. (1991). Objectivism vs. constructivism: Do we need a new paradigm? *Educational Technology Research and Development, 39*(3), 5–14.

Jonassen, D. H. (in press a). Scaffolding diagnostic reasoning in case-based learning environments. *Journal of Computing in Higher Education.*

Jonassen, D. H. (in press b). Instructional design models for well-structured and ill-structured problem solving learning outcomes. *Educational Technology Research and Development.*

Jonassen, D. H., & Mandl, H. (1990). *Designing hypermedia for learning.* Heidelberg: Springer-Verlag.

Nelson, T. (1974). *Dream machines.* South Bend, IN: The Distributors.

Schank, R. C. (1994). Goal-based scenarios. In R. C. Schank & E. Langer (Eds.), *Beliefs, reasoning, and decision making*. Hillsdale, NJ: Lawrence Erlbaum Associates

Spiro, R. J., Coulson, R. L., Feltovich, P. J., & Anderson, D. K. (1988). *Cognitive flexibility theory: Advanced knowledge acquisition in ill-structured domains*. Tech Report No. 441. Champaign, IL: University of Illinois, Center for the Study of Reading.

Spiro, R. J., Feltovich, P. L., Jacobson, M. J., & Coulson, R. L. (1991). Cognitive flexibility, constructivism, and hypertext: Random access instruction for advanced knowledge acquisition in ill-structured domains. *Educational Technology, 31*(5), 24–33.

Spiro, R. J., & Jehng, J. C. (1990). Cognitive flexibility and hypertext: Theory and technology for the non-linear and multi-dimensional traversal of complex subject matter. In D. Nix & R. J. Spiro (Eds.), *Cognition, education, and multimedia: Explorations in high technology*. Hillsdale, NJ: Lawrence Erlbaum Associates.

Spiro, R. J., Vispoel, W., Schmitz, J., Samarapungavan, A., & Boerger, A. (1987). Knowledge acquisition for application: Cognitive flexibility and transfer in complex content domains. In B. C. Britton (Ed.), *Executive control processes*. Hillsdale, NJ: Lawrence Erlbaum Associates.

Waller, R. (1982). Text as diagram: Using typography to improve access and understanding. In D. H. Jonassen (Ed.), *The technology of text: Principles for structuring, designing, and displaying text*. Englewood Cliffs, NJ: Educational Technology Publications.

The Authors

David H. Jonassen is Professor of Instructional Systems at Pennsylvania State University, University Park, Pennsylvania.

e-mail
  jonassen@psu.edu

Dean Dyer, Karen Peters, Timothy Robinson, Douglas Harvey, Marsha King, and Pamela Loughner are doctoral students at Pennsylvania State University, University Park, Pennsylvania.

16

Incorporating Instructional Design Principles with the World Wide Web[1]

Donn C. Ritchie and
Bob Hoffman

Instruction and the Internet

Instruction can be defined as a purposeful interaction to increase learners' knowledge or skills in specific, pre-determined ways. In this context, simply publishing a World Wide Web page with links to other digital resources does not constitute instruction. Instructional sequences typically embrace seven common elements: motivating the learner, specifying what is to be learned, prompting the learner to recall and apply previous knowledge, providing new information, offering guidance and feedback, testing comprehension, and supplying enrichment or remediation (Dick & Reiser, 1989). With forethought, each of these events can be incorporated in instruction designed for delivery on the World Wide Web.

Motivating the Learner

Since leaving a Web page is as easy as clicking the mouse button, Web page designers have focused much of their efforts on identifying what attracts and retains the attention of the casual browser. The use of graphics, color, animation, and sound have long been used as external stimuli to motivate learners, and each of these techniques can be applied to accomplish similar purposes on Web pages. Some organizations highlight Web pages with yearly, weekly, and even daily awards for aesthetically pleasing, technically innovative, and generally creative pages.[2] These examples provide new developers with easy access to see what attracts and holds a user's attention. It should be noted, however, that simply adding color, graphics, or animation doesn't ensure motivating pages. Like the use of multiple fonts and styles when the Macintosh was first introduced, excess is often counterproductive. Examples of unattractive Web sites are also numerous. They can be found through general browsing or by accessing specific locations that compile this information.[3]

---

[1]This chapter is based on a previous article published in R. Robin, J. D. Price, J. Willis, & D. A. Willis (Eds.), *Technology and Teacher Education Annual, 1996*. Charlottesville, VA: Association for the Advancement of Computing in Education.

[2]http://www.highfive.com/, http://wings.buffalo.edu/contest/, http://toocool.com/, http://www.capstudio.com/ippa/award.html, http://www.thoughtport.com/spinnWebe/features/awards.html

[3]http://turnpike.net/metro/mirsky/Worst.html

How can Web-based instruction be created to motivate the learner? First, developers should consider more than perceptual arousal. Attention, and thereby motivation, can also be stimulated through inquiry arousal, in which learners encounter a problem, contradictory information, or mystery to be resolved. Other methods to increase motivation include establishing the relevance or value of what users are to learn (e.g., by linking to organizations, job positions, or sites that include related topics), or by increasing the learners' confidence in being able to complete their learning task (e.g., by linking to examples of completed projects or providing easy practice activities).

Identifying What Is to Be Learned

In most cases, it is important to let learners know early in a lesson what they will be responsible for knowing or doing by the end of the instruction (unless employing methods such as discovery or problem based learning). This helps learners focus on factors the instructor deems salient. With the tendency of users to free associate while Web "surfing," in which their attention (and learning) may be distracted from desired outcomes, it is crucial for Web-based instructional developers to help learners keep their instructional goals in mind. While it may be true that learning often occurs serendipitously, users engaged in Web-based instruction can too easily spend valuable time in unpurposeful browsing or simply becoming distracted by following links to external sources which have been incorporated to contextualize the material.

Listing outcomes or expectations as students access an instructional page is one method to help focus learners on expected outcomes. Unfortunately, links to external sources may too easily allow learners to forget the purpose of the instruction. To help reduce this problem, designers should judiciously include external links only to those locations which offer strong support to the instruction.

Reminding Learners of Past Knowledge

Cognitive psychologists generally agree that for information to be retained in long-term memory, learners must associate or link the new information with some related information already stored in long-term memory (Gagné, 1985).

Web pages have an advantage over many other forms of instructional delivery in their ability to offer multiple links from any one location. Multiple links provide learners, who may have diverse backgrounds or knowledge, the ability to choose salient associations to remind them of previously gained knowledge. In the spreadsheet example, links could be made to pages describing machines which manipulate numbers (such as adding machines, calculators, and even abacuses), pages that remind students of different mathematical properties or functions, or pages that provide examples as to when spreadsheets may be used (such as for creating budgets, calculating payments for the purchase of a car, or charting the stock market). By identifying similarities, differences, or experiences between their existing knowledge structures and the to-be-learned information, students will more quickly grasp and assimilate the new information.

To ensure that salient links are created to remind learners of existing knowledge, it is important for the designer to gain an understanding of the learners. Questions to which the designer may want to find answers include: What characteristics do the learners share? How do they differ? What is a typical member like? What is their prior knowledge in this content area? What misconceptions do learners have? Do learners come to the course with preconceived attitudes?

Requiring Active Involvement

Most educators agree that for learning to take place, the learner must actively process and make sense of the information presented. Generally speaking, a more active learner will integrate knowledge more readily than a passive learner. Unfortunately, thoughtful, active learning seldom occurs through simple engagement with the Web. While it is true that users make decisions as to which links to pursue, too often would-be learners merely browse superficially, then jump to another site.

How can instructional designers increase the possibility that learners actively process information? One way is to require them to develop an artifact of their learning. Dodge (1995) summarizes eight specific strategies based on work by Marzano (1992) that can be assigned to ensure that learners produce artifacts of their knowledge. These strategies include requiring learners to compare, classify, induce, deduce, analyze errors, construct support, make abstractions, or analyze perspectives that they encounter in the course of their Web activities. Another related strategy is to prompt users to construct alternative representations of the information they encounter (Sticht, 1992).

Providing Guidance and Feedback

Guidance and feedback can be provided to users either during their exploration of Web materials or afterward, by critiquing the artifacts or representations of their exploration. Most links on Web pages are shown by highlighted and underlined text in which the text itself serves as a descriptor for the topic of that link. Users of Web pages will tell you, however, that often these descriptors or the links they represent turn out to be misleading or even irrelevant. This may be partially due to the lack of relationship denoted in the link's name or descriptor. A more meaningful system would be to use words such as "definition," "example," or "non example" when teaching concepts or principles; "definition" or "mnemonic" when teaching facts; and "shortest path" or "alternative path" when teaching a procedure.

A second method to provide both guidance and feedback can occur when users are required to make an informed choice among alternatives after engaging a segment of instruction. If these choices are designed to determine appropriate or inappropriate responses by the learner, pages linked to their answers can be used to either reinforce the correct response or explain the rationale of an incorrect answer and guide the user to a more appropriate answer or other remediation.

A third, more complex method uses CGI (Common Gateway Interface) codes to provide learners with detailed information and alternative choices. With CGI scripts, information that students place into online text fields, buttons, or check boxes can be compared to preset answers in a database or text file. Feedback can provide individual students with a deeper explanation of the consequences of their choices and active links which guide them to additional information. CGI scripts can also be written to capture variables from students, store them, and access this information at a later date.

Testing

To ensure that students have integrated the desired knowledge, learning needs to be assessed. This can be done either on or off line, through objective or subjective tests, or through development of products or artifacts of their learning.

Online testing can be constructed with CGI scripts similar to those described above for guidance and feedback, in which information is gathered from students, compared to established criteria in text or database files, and assigned grades and/or other feedback. This can be automated for objective tests, or saved in files for instructor critique if more open-ended questions are used.

Developing learning artifacts can also be done online if students are provided with the capabilities of constructing their own Web pages. For example, they could be required to create a

WebQuest (Dodge, 1995). WebQuests are inquiry-oriented activities in which users, constrained by specific tasks, access the Web to acquire, integrate, extend, or refine their knowledge.

Providing Enrichment and Remediation

The final step in many instructional programs is to provide learners with either remediation in areas where comprehension is lacking, or enrichment to extend students' knowledge. Both CGI scripts and direct linking of pages can be used to implement these features.

Although remediation may consist of no more than recycling students back through instructional material, it can also be designed to provide parallel forms of instruction with alternative methods of information presentation, additional practices and links to contextualize the information, and alternate tests. Enrichment may consist of related links to relevant topics, or additional ideas to explore. Whether enrichment or remediation is offered, links should be constructed to help ensure that learners receive relevant, specific information matched to their knowledge or skill.

Summary

The emergence of the World Wide Web, with its easy-to-use graphical interface, has dramatically altered the way in which people access information and think about computers. Methods in which we deliver and receive instruction may also be on the brink of a new frontier. Venturing into this new dimension, however, will require thoughtful analysis and investigation of how to use the Web's potential in concert with instructional design principles. If these two forces can be integrated, it may produce a distributed, instructional medium with characteristics unlike previous methods of distance learning.

References

Dick, W., & Reiser, R. (1989). *Planning effective instruction.* Englewood Cliffs, NJ: Prentice-Hall.

Dodge, B. (1995). *Some thoughts about WebQuests* (http://edWeb.sdsu.edu/courses/EDTEC596/ About_WebQuests.html).

Marzano, R. J. (1992). *A different kind of classroom: Teaching with dimensions of learning.* Alexandria VA: Association for Supervision and Curriculum Development.

Rumble, G. (1986). *The planning and management of distance education.* London: Croom Helm.

Sticht, T. (1992). *Functional context education.* San Diego, CA: Applied Behavioral and Cognitive Sciences, Inc.

The Authors

Donn C. Ritchie is Associate Professor, Department of Educational Technology, San Diego State University, San Diego, California.

e-mail, World Wide Web
dritchie@mail.sdsu.edu
http://edweb.sdsu.edu/people/DRitchie/DRitchie.html

Bob Hoffman is Assistant Professor, Department of Educational Technology, San Diego State University, San Diego, California.

e-mail, World Wide Web
Bob.Hoffman@sdsu.edu
http://edweb.sdsu.edu/people/rhoffman/rhoffman.html

17

Designing a Web-Based Electronic Performance Support System (EPSS): A Case Study of *Literacy Online*[1]

Jamie Reaves Kirkley and
Thomas M. Duffy

A Day in the Life of Using *Literacy Online*. . . .

Mary is a volunteer tutor working with an adult learner in a literacy program. She needs ideas for her next lesson with her learner. She goes to the public library to get onto the World Wide Web and the *Literacy Online* Web site. She reads about a teaching strategy where one uses a student's interests as a basis for teaching. She finds a learning activity showing how to use the newspaper sports section as a teaching tool. After printing out the strategy and lesson, she then replies to an e-mail sent to her from another tutor asking how to deal with learning disabilities. Mary relies on this Web-based system to provide resources, support, communication, and tools to help her improve her performance as a volunteer literacy tutor.

Introduction

Although the Web is used in many areas of business and higher education, declining access costs and increased computer power are making it more accessible for groups such as K–12 and adult education. Educators are using it to build collaborative networks of information, resources, and people across the world. This means that Web sites can now be designed to serve as electronic performance support systems (EPSSs) for people in education and other fields.

This article describes the rationale, design, and development of a Web-based EPSS to support the needs of adult literacy teachers and tutors.

The Uses of EPSS Systems

EPSSs in Business

The traditional EPSS is a computer application or series of applications that provides integrated information, tools, and methodology electronically, on demand, at the moment of

---

[1]The Web site discussed in this chapter is located at: http://www.thinkshop.edu/al

need (Gery, 1991). The purpose of this type of system is to support the performance of a job or task. It serves as a type of toolkit, providing integrated resources to help the user meet specific needs.

An EPSS is designed to provide tools, resources, and support systems designed to fit specific environments. Depending on what is needed in the environment, it might contain a database of resources and information, a coaching and guidance system providing assistance with certain tasks, such as making decisions, methods for communicating with colleagues, simulations of job tasks, job aids, and administrative tools such as project management software. EPSSs often contain common computer tools, such as word processors, electronic mail, databases, and spreadsheets. These tools can be customized to store and provide information as well as enabling one to create and manipulate it.

Early EPSSs often focused on technology rather than job performance (Raybould, 1995). Now the view is shifting to systems that focus on enabling one to perform specific job-related tasks (Hudzina *et al.*, 1996; Gery, 1995). EPSSs are usually integrated directly into a person's working environment for greater convenience and usability (Barker & Banerji, 1993; Laffey, 1995). Guidance is provided when it is needed and in the context of the working environment. This means that learning is not something that is done outside of a person's activities, but instead in the context of the activities themselves. Raybould (1995) indicates that 85–90 percent of a person's job knowledge is learned on the job, so being able to learn in the context of one's job is an important rationale for EPSSs.

The following example illustrates how EPSSs provide training and support in the context of the job. A customer service representative (CSR) needs to make a decision about whether a customer should receive an increase in her credit card limit. The CSR uses an EPSS system designed specifically for this task. He opens a guidance system that not only trains and helps him make the decision, but gives him resources such as the company policies and procedures manual and access to the customer's payment history. As he goes through the various steps of the decision making program, he learns not only how to make decisions about making credit increases, but also how those decisions are made based on specific information. He also uses various tools, such as databases and spreadsheets, to look up information and make calculations. After making the decision, he opens a word processing program, chooses the appropriate form letter, and mails it to the customer. This type of integrated support system is an example of a job-integrated EPSS. It provides training as well as information, tools, and support.

EPSSs in Education

Although EPSSs have been used in the business world for some time, their use in education is a more recent development. EPSSs are often self contained systems that can be expensive to develop and maintain. But with the advent of inexpensive and readily available technologies, educational systems are now able to design and use them as never before. Whereas the task of an EPSS in the business world is usually to support worker performance and job training, an education EPSS is more concerned with supporting learning and the tasks associated with learning. Law (1994) describes this type of system as a form of "cognitive training wheels." This type of EPSS serves to support learning, as well as the process of teaching.

Collis & Verwijs (1995) discuss several examples of how software is being used in education to support learning and performance. Some EPSSs have been developed specifically for use in education, while others have been adapted from the business world. These hybrid EPSSs offer educational resources as well as integrated tools such as databases, communication systems, and guidance systems. One example discussed is the "The Teacher, Learner, and Administrator Toolkit." This system contains seven types of activities: telecommunicating, accessing and developing resources, planning and scheduling, accessing and developing strategies, recording, evaluating, and reporting. It also contains a Toolchest with a wordprocessor, paint program, databases of materials, and a database of student information. Like a business EPSS, the Toolkit provides resources as well as common computer tools. As computer technologies become more inexpensive and easier to use, educational organizations can more readily design systems to directly support teaching and learning.

Web-Based EPSSs

The World Wide Web, with its vast collection of networked information and resources that can be accessed all over the world, provides an excellent foundation for building educational EPSSs. Increasingly, Web sites are being developed to support groups of people with specific interests.

To provide further support, Web-based applications such as browsers often contain tools to support communication, collaboration, and learning. Some examples of tools are electronic mail, electronic whiteboards, and Internet phone. These tools are enabling people from across the world to communicate, collaborate, and share resources.

Companies and organizations are now building their own internal Web systems called Intranets that work in conjunction with the Internet and World Wide Web. Intranets use the best of Web technologies and often provide performance support. They enable workers to access information via internal Web pages that contain text, graphics, audio, and video. Company manuals, production records, and other types of information can be accessed by those with an appropriate password. Intranets serve as an example of how Web technologies are being used to create EPSSs in the business world.

By combining content with tools, Web based EPSSs can be built to serve the needs of educators. One example of a resource-based Web site that serves educators is the "The Pathways to School Improvement Web Site (http://www.ncrel.org/sdrs/pathways.htm)." This site targets K–12 educators and provides resources on topics related to school improvement, such as assessment and leadership. Created by the North Central Regional Educational Laboratory, it provides papers written by various education authors as well as case studies about teachers.

Although this Web site mainly serves as a collection of resources, other sites often provide tools for communicating and exchanging ideas. *Literacy Online* is an example of a Web-based EPSS that provides communication and idea exchange as well as access to information and resources. Before describing the system, it is important to understand the context of why adult literacy tutors and teachers need performance support.

Designing *Literacy Online*

Research and Needs Analysis

Before designing this Web based EPSS, the design team conducted research and a needs analysis to determine: (1) the feasibility of the system; (2) how it would support the needs of teachers and tutors; (3) what type of information would be provided; and (4) the overall design of the interface.

The team interviewed adult literacy tutors, teachers, and administrators from four different programs across the nation and two nationally known researchers in the field of adult literacy. From the research, the team found that literacy programs spend about $250 per student per year, while public schools spend about $4000 per student per year (Mikulecky, 1989). This lack of funding translates into a variety of problems for many adult literacy programs, including minimal money to pay for support staff, training, materials, and communication among literacy providers. Tutors typically have minimal support services and resources. This creates a need not only for training but also for quality teaching resources and ongoing guidance.

Most literacy instruction is provided by part-time teachers and volunteers who have little formal or on-the-job training (Mikulecky, 1989). Generally, volunteer tutors receive 10 to 20 hours of training before they begin working with some of the most challenging learners (Newman & Beverstock, 1990). Many tutors do not receive further training.

The team also conducted a needs analysis with a volunteer literacy program. The program coordinator and several tutors were interviewed. From the needs analysis, the team identified the following issues to be most prevalent:

- Tutors often do not receive adequate training. Generally, tutors receive less than 20 hours of training; there is often no further training. We also found that the training tutors receive often emphasizes how to tutor the non-reader, which makes up only three percent of population in the United States. Therefore, specific teaching methods and strategies for mid-level readers are not addressed, and tutors have to learn these on their own. Tutors often deal with specialized problems, such as auditory, visual, or reading disabilities. They rarely receive training or special assistance to teach them to work with special problems.

- Mentoring is an important part of the tutor's ongoing education. Tutors often do not have adequate support services to assist them. Therefore, they often rely on each other for guidance. Yet this is difficult, since they tutor at different times and places and do not meet with each other on a regular basis.

- Tutors often have difficulties developing effective teaching strategies and learning activities. Since many do not receive adequate training, they have little knowledge of the various types of teaching methods and learning activities. For example, a tutor may be trained to use a phonics teaching method. Even if a learner is not responding well to this method, the tutor may keep using it because he or she does not know another method to use.

Based on the needs analysis, the system was designed to support literacy teachers and tutors in the following ways:

- Help them learn to develop effective lesson plans to meet their immediate teaching needs (many tutors said what they needed most were good lessons and activities).

- Provide access to teaching materials and resources.

- Help them become more effective teachers by providing information about a variety of teaching strategies.

- Provide opportunities for communication and collaboration so they could talk to other tutors and develop mentoring relationships.

Design Considerations
To Use the Web or Not to Use the Web...

When designing Web based EPSSs, it is important to consider the following:

- Is the system feasible?

- What type of guidance, support, and information should be provided?

- How should the interface be designed to accommodate users?

- Which tools should be incorporated to support the goals of the users?

- How can usability testing become part of the design and redesign process?

These questions guided the design of *Literacy Online*. First, the design team had to determine whether a computer-based or Internet-based system would work best. They had considered building a stand-alone computer-based system, but this would have required a huge financial investment from literacy providers. It also would have lacked certain tools and capabilities, such as the ability to reach and connect people all over the world.

Building this system on the Web offered distinct advantages and disadvantages. However, there were many more advantages. The first advantage was that a large amount of resources were readily available. There are many information resources already online that can be repackaged to use with learners. For example, the famous Pueblo Colorado Consumer Reports are all online. They can be used by a tutor to teach a learner how to be a smart consumer. There are brochures on a wide range of life skills-related topics, such as how to buy a car or shop wisely for food. By using these as a basis for instruction, tutors can help learners improve reading skills as well as life skills.

The Web provides a system that can be reached by a large population. With literacy providers, teachers, tutors, and learners spread out geographically, the Web provides a path to a central place that serves as a home site for this group of educators. Since there is no one agency sponsoring adult literacy education, this central Web site becomes an important way to connect people and resources.

Another advantage of using the Web was the ability to easily update and add information. With technologies such as CD-ROMs, information is permanent and static until a new CD-ROM is issued. With the Web, information can be updated and changes made without a huge investment in time and resources.

Yet another advantage was that the Web, with its graphics and hyperlinks, is fairly easy to use. It has a fairly simple point-and-click navigation system, where the user moves a mouse to point to and click on something such as a graphic to navigate the system. Ease of use is important since many teachers and tutors are not proficient Web users or even computer users.

Since computer capabilities of the various literacy providers vary greatly, it was important to design a system that offered easy access, a standard, built-in set of tools, and communication capabilities such as e-mail and newsgroups. Web browsers often contain a built in set of tools that can be used for communication and collaboration. E-mail and newsgroups are now built into many Web browsers. Without tools for Internet access, much of the communication and collaboration would not be available to teachers and tutors. These tools greatly facilitate the mentoring process that tutors use to gain advanced skills.

One disadvantage of using the Web was that the majority of people do not have access to it. However, that is changing quickly. CommerceNet/Nielsen reported that 13 percent of Americans had used the Web in March/April 1996. This is up from eight percent in August 1995. Computer companies are now making specialized, inexpensive computers whose sole function is to access the Internet. As computer technologies become faster and cheaper over time, more people will be able to afford to access the Internet. Many literacy programs do not have the necessary funding for adequate computer equipment and Internet access. However, public libraries are beginning to offer Internet access as part of their services. Since many literacy programs are located in libraries, this will be a convenient service for teachers and tutors.

Before designing the system, the team conducted a survey to determine if there was a sufficient number of tutors and teachers with access to justify starting the system. Surveys were sent to various literacy-related listservs and national agencies. It was determined that there was enough of a population to start it, and the number of people using it has grown quickly over a short time.

There is always one difficult design consideration when using the Web. That is deciding what type of interface to use and how to design it so that the maximum number of people can use it with ease. Since this population is not one that can take advantage of high-end graphics, it was important to keep the design simple. The site was redesigned several times to take advantage of graphics and frames. However, after discovering difficulties with navigation, it was redesigned to provide a much simpler interface. The new design is also more considerate of people using modem connections, which take longer to access and download images.

As the system was developed and redesigned, it was tested by various tutors and teachers. Usability testing continues to be an important part of the interface design process as well as the content development.

Designing *Literacy Online* to Meet the Needs of Teachers and Tutors

To meet the needs of literacy teachers and tutors, *Literacy Online* provides resources and tools that assist and train in the context of doing the job (see Figure 1). A tutor may go to the Web site to find a quick lesson plan for tonight's meeting. Or she may read about how to use a certain teaching strategy and see how it was used by another "expert" tutor. Communication tools provide further opportunities for learning through mentoring and collaboration.

Literacy Online provides information for several types of literacy providers—adult basic education, English as a Second Language, family literacy, and workplace literacy. Each section contains teaching issues, learning activities developed by tutors and teachers, Web resources, a showcase of student work, and discussion groups. These sections are described below. Although the site mainly consists of text, the future plan is to incorporate audio and video where appropriate.

- **Teaching Issues**
  Learning about and applying new teaching strategies is an important priority for tutors and teachers. *Literacy Online* provides tutors with information on various teaching strategies and opportunities to talk with others. Case studies form an important part of this section. They contain stories about expert tutors and the strategies they have used.

- **Learning Activities**
  Learning activities, or lesson plans, are intended to support and demonstrate certain strategies. They serve to reduce one of the major problems that arises in any teaching environment—inadequate guidance for the teacher to begin engaging the student. Schön (1987) found that while working with teachers and helping them adopt a theoretical position consistent with the concept of the reflective practitioner, it is important to use a script consistent with that theory to help learners enter that framework for thinking. This helps them begin to adopt the model of a reflective practitioner and think about their own teaching process.

- **Resource Materials**
  Teachers and tutors are constantly looking for resources and information on various topics. *Literacy Online* provides links to other Web resources that would be useful to teaching and learning.

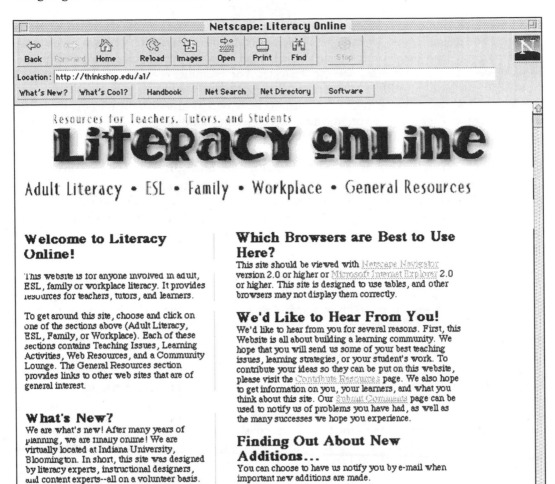

Figure 1. *Literacy Online* Web site

- **Collaborating with Experts and Other Tutors**
  Interaction with peers and experts is an important part of any learning environment (Rogoff, 1990). A Vygotskian perspective states that it is important for lesser skilled persons to have an expert scaffold learning within the zone of proximal development (ZPD). Through this scaffolding, the learner gradually builds skills and knowledge with help from someone with more capability (Vygotsky, 1978). For a new tutor, this other person is most likely a more experienced tutor. One of the most important ways that tutors learn is through social interaction. Teachers and tutors often rely on each other for assistance and advice. However, due to time and distance constraints, they do not often get the chance to talk with colleagues or experts. It is difficult to form a community of learners when there is no physical place in which they normally gather, when they are spread over large geographical areas, and when there is no organizational mechanism in place to facilitate the interactions. By providing tutors with tools through which they can interact with each other and experts, they can develop a learning community that is not possible without computer-mediated communication.

It is important to note that various sections of the Web site are strategically connected by hyperlinks. For example, the Teaching Issues section contains information on how to use real-world problems as a basis for designing curriculum. This is linked to a case study, which presents stories of how tutors used specific strategies. For example, one case study is a story of how one tutor used nutrition and consumer shopping to help her student learn to better feed her family. The case study is linked to a learning activity that gives details on how to do this as well as other Web resources on nutrition and consumer shopping.

The Theory Guiding the Design

The design team used the constructivist principles of Cunningham, Duffy, and Knuth (1993) to guide the design and development of *Literacy Online*. These principles provided a framework for design as well as serving as a basis for facilitating teaching and learning. Some of the principles are listed below, with statements on how the system supports those principles for teachers and tutors.

- **Embed learning in realistic and relevant contexts.**
  Tutors and teachers are using this EPSS on the job, which makes their learning realistic and relevant. It meets their practical needs (e.g., finding a lesson plan for tonight's meeting) as well as helping to develop and mentor them as teachers.

- **Embed learning in social experience.**
  The system creates a collaborative environment in which tutors can communicate electronically with the adult literacy community, which includes experts, administrators, teachers, tutors, and students.

- **Provide experience with the knowledge construction process.**
  As tutors construct lesson plans, they make decisions about what overall strategies or approaches and activities they use. *Literacy Online* gives them access to such information, but does not make decisions for them. It also enables them to contribute their own ideas to the Web site. Tutors can contribute their own learning activities and strategies to the system, and the best activities and strategies are added as content to the *Literacy Online* Web site.

- **Provide experience in and appreciation for multiple perspectives.**
  Since teachers, tutors, and others are collaborating and helping to build the site, the system contains the ideas and views of many.

These constructivist principles were used by the design team to guide the philosophy of the design and development of *Literacy Online*. These principles are also embedded within much of the content of the system in order to encourage and facilitate a constructivist teaching and learning environment.

Conclusion

This article demonstrates how EPSSs can be designed on the Web to support teaching and learning performance. The Web provides an open and fluid environment which can be used to take advantage of many resources and tools that can be accessed by people from across the world. By organizing content, resources, and tools into an EPSS, people can participate in "knowledge networking." Harasim *et al.* (1995) defined this as "self directed learning and growth through the pursuit of information." As people use these systems in context of teaching and learning, they can learn new skills that are practical and relevant to both.

The Web offers a unique teaching and learning environment. As it becomes more sophisticated and more accessible, we will see these both businesses and education designing and using Web based EPSS systems.

References

Barker P., & Banerji, A. (1993). Case studies in electronic performance support. Paper presented at AI-ED August 93: World Conference on Artificial Intelligence in Education, Edinburgh, Scotland.

Carpenter, A., & Provorse, C. (1994). *The world almanac of the USA*. Mahwah, NJ: Funk & Wagnalls.

Collis, B., & Verwijs, C. (1995). A human approach to electronic performance and learning support systems: Hybrid EPSSs. *Educational Technology, 35*(1), 5–21.

CommerceNet/Nielsen Internet Survey Home Page (http://www.nielsenmedia.com/commercenet/exec.html).

Cunningham, D., Duffy, T., & Knuth R. (1993). The textbook of the future. In C. McKnight, A. Dillon, & J. Richardson (Eds.), *Hypertext: A psychological perspective*. New York: Ellis Harwood.

Gery, G. (1991). *Electronic performance support systems*. Boston: Weingarten Publishers.

Gery, G. (1995). Attributes and behaviors of performance-centered systems. *Performance Improvement Quarterly, 8(1)*, 47–93.

Harasim, L. *et al.* (1995). *Learning networks: A field guide to teaching and learning online*. Cambridge, MA : MIT Press.

Hudzina, M., Rowley, K., & Wager, W. (1996). Electronic performance support technology: Defining the domain. *Performance Improvement Quarterly, 9*(1), 36–48.

Laffey, J. (1995). Dynamism in electronic performance support systems. *Performance Improvement Quarterly, 8*(1), 31–46.

Law, M. (1994). Electronic performance support systems: "Cognitive" training wheels for the acquisition of skilled performance. ERIC Document ED371734.

Mikulecky, L. (1989). *Second chance: Basic skills education*. Washington, DC: US Department of Labor.

Newman, A., & Beverstock, C. (1990). *Adult literacy: Contexts and challenges*. Newark, DE: International Reading Association.

Raybould, B. (1995). Performance support engineering: An emerging development methodology for enabling organizational learning. *Performance Improvement Quarterly, 8*(1), 7–22.

Rogoff, B. (1990). *Apprenticeship in thinking: Cognitive development in social context*. New York: Oxford University Press.

Schön, D. (1987). *Educating the reflective practitioner*. San Francisco: Jossey-Bass.

Sprout, A. (1995). The Internet inside your company. *Fortune, 132*, 161–64.

Sticht, T. (1982). *Basic skills in Defense*. Alexandria, VA: Human Resources Research Organization.

Vygotsky, L. (1978). *Mind in society. The development of higher psychological processes*. Cambridge, MA: Harvard University Press.

Acknowledgments

The authors would like to acknowledge the following people for their contributions to the design and development of *Literacy Online*: Larry Mikulecky, Anabel Newman, Sonny Kirkley, Candace Bertotti, Lindsay Bennion, Ron Saito, Tom Benjey, and all the teachers and tutors who shared information about their own experiences.

The Authors

Jamie Reaves Kirkley is a Doctoral Student, Department of Language Education and the Department of Instructional Systems Technology, School of Education, Indiana University, Bloomington, Indiana.

e-mail
 jkirkley@indiana.edu

Thomas M. Duffy is Professor, Department of Instructional Systems Technology, School of Education, Indiana University, Bloomington, Indiana.

e-mail
 duffy@indiana.edu

18

Virtual-U: A Web-Based System to Support Collaborative Learning

Linda Harasim, Tom Calvert, and Chris Groeneboer

Introduction

Virtual-U is a World Wide Web-based networked learning environment customized for the design, delivery, and enhancement of post-secondary education. One of the main design goals is to provide a flexible framework to support advanced pedagogies based on principles of active learning, collaboration, multiplicity, and knowledge building, varied content areas, including the sciences and the arts, and varied instructional formats, including seminars, tutorials, group projects, and labs (Harasim 1995). The framework consists of tools to support core activities, including course design, individual and group learning activities, knowledge structuring, class management, and evaluation.

The design of Virtual-U builds on advanced research in online education, engineering, and human-computer interface design. It was decided to base it on World Wide Web tools, since these support the desired client-server architecture and are widely available. However, the tools are evolving rapidly and as a result, successive versions of Virtual-U are being implemented to take advantage of new features as they become available. This does not have a major impact on the basic functionality which supports the collaborative learning pedagogy, but it does affect the user interface design and the "look and feel" of the system.

Educational Principles and Models of Learning

The main goal is to shape Virtual-U into a learning environment by structuring and organizing online interactions based on principles of active and collaborative learning, multiple perspectives, and knowledge building. Collaborative or group learning refers to instructional methods whereby students are encouraged or required to work together on academic tasks. While there are important differences among various theoretical and practical understandings of collaborative learning (Damon & Phelps, 1989), all distinguish collaborative learning from the traditional 'direct transfer' model in which the instructor is assumed to be the sole source of knowledge and skills. Unlike the teacher-centered models that view the learner primarily as a passive recipient of knowledge from an expert, collaborative or group learning is based upon a learner-centered model that treats the learner as an active participant. The conversations (verbalizing), multiple perspectives (cognitive restructuring), and arguments (conceptual conflict resolution) that arise in cooperative groups may explain why collaborative groups facilitate greater cognitive development than the same individuals achieve when working alone (Sharan, 1980; Slavin, 1980; Stodolsky 1984; Webb, 1982, 1989).

Knowledge building is a learning strategy in which active articulation, sharing, and organizing of ideas and information into individual and group knowledge structures is encouraged. Koschmann *et al.* (1993) note that as knowledge is complex, dynamic, and interactively related, it is critical that instruction promote multiple perspectives, representations, and strategies. Scardamalia and Bereiter (1993) distinguish between knowledge reproduction strategies (copy-delete summarization) and knowledge building strategies which

> are, by contrast, focussed centrally on understanding...In this view, learning—like scientific discovery and theorizing—is a process of working toward more complete and coherent understanding. The kind of discourse that supports such learning is not discourse in which students display or reproduce what they have learned. It is the kind of discourse that advances knowledge in the sciences and disciplines. It is the discourse of 'conjectures and refutations' as Popper called it. (pp. 37–38)

History of Online Education

Research and field experience generated over the past decade indicate that computer networking, especially computer conferencing, can effectively support post-secondary course delivery entirely or partially online, with significant user satisfaction, and with low rates of attrition (Harasim *et al.*, 1995; Hiltz, 1990, 1993; Kaye, 1991; Mason, 1989). Online delivery of courses can enrich and expand traditional educational activities and outcomes; perhaps more importantly, networking has demonstrated the potential to support entirely new types of educational interaction and outcomes. There are, nonetheless, important constraints and challenges.

The Early Challenges of Online Education

One of the earliest field experiments in online course delivery was at the Ontario Institute for Studies in Education (OISE) in the mid-1980s. At that time, there were no models, theoretical or practical, to guide course design and delivery online. Pioneering those first online courses (graduate courses and a non-credit professional development course for teachers) involved conceptualizing, designing, and delivering courses entirely online, using a computer conferencing system to connect students who were geographically distributed. The educational approach taken reformulated collaborative learning activities for a networked environment characterized by five key attributes: an asynchronous, place-independent, many-to-many, text-based computer-mediated system (Harasim, 1989, 1990). These five attributes have subsequently proven to be both constraints and opportunities for enabling effective collaborative learning online. The educational design, tested and refined by ongoing research, has proven robust and effective in over ten years of iterations and has been adopted by educators and institutions worldwide.

Educational Outcomes

Analysis of data collected over ten years of application of this approach to graduate and undergraduate courses, delivered both entirely and partially online, indicates important outcomes, such as active participation, peer interaction, multiple perspectives and divergent thinking. Problems associated with collaborating online, especially as related to information management and lack of educational supports, were also identified.

Significant outcomes of the experience with online collaborative course design were:

- Active learning: specifically, active participation by students.

- Interactive learning: specifically, in peer-to-peer discussion and exchange.

- Multiple perspectives: specifically, through input from all the other online students as well as the instructor.

- Metaphor: e.g., a spatial metaphor to ease the transition from traditional face-to-face classrooms to structured online classrooms.

System-generated data showed a high volume and number of conference messages written by the students. Students regularly input large amounts of original text, generating a rich database of information. Not only was the overall volume of messaging high in the online classes, but it was fairly evenly distributed among the students in each class. Most students participated most of the time, sending several messages each week. The major factor supporting the participation noted by students was the increased access opportunities offered by the asynchronous, place-independent environment.

Group interaction was also motivating to students. Student interviews and feedback comments emphasized that the group interaction was intellectually stimulating and fun, and that they worked harder and produced higher quality work online. The online courses developed, in varying degrees, strong communities of friendship.

Students also reported that they appreciated the exposure to a diverse range of perspectives in the group learning design: Online students read input from all other students, rather than only the ideas of the instructor and a few students. Student interaction was not only significant in term of message volume, but also in quality of intellectual content.

In the early weeks of online discussion, many students reported communication anxiety and feeling 'lost in space'; nonetheless, they soon learned how to direct their comments to the appropriate conference space. Students reported that the existence of conferences for different topics and types of activities helped to orient them to the course curriculum and facilitated their navigation through the conferencing system.

These early field studies on networked learning environments suggest that it is important that participants form mental models of the "spaces" where they are working—the virtual seminar, the virtual discussion group, the virtual laboratory, the café for social interactions, etc. (Feenberg, 1993; Harasim, 1993b). This is important if they are to apply appropriate "social factors" to their interactions.

Problems

While research has demonstrated the potential of networked technologies to support active collaborative learning and interaction (Harasim, 1990, 1993), important problems were also identified. Until recently, online course delivery was based on generic networking tools such as e-mail, computer conferencing, or newsgroups. The use of generic networking tools has imposed significant overhead on the user, since these tools were not designed specifically to support educational activities (Feenberg, 1993; Harasim, 1993; Smith, 1988).

Key problems in using generic networking environments for education included the lack of tools to support instructional activities such as course design and group design, and the lack of tools to support key learning strategies such as knowledge building and multiple representations of ideas and knowledge structures (Harasim, 1990, 1991, 1993a).

There was an urgent need to create network environments specially customized for education, which could facilitate easy adoption and adaptation (tailoring of individual courses) by the educators and which provide embedded tools to support specific instructor and learner activities. There was also a need for the development of discipline specific tools, to expand the types of course content that could be delivered over networks, especially those related to mathematics and lab-science instruction, and to the cultural and fine arts.

Virtual-U

Based on the decade of field research in online course delivery described above, the design and development of the system now known as Virtual-U was initiated in 1994. The goal was to provide a flexible framework to support advanced pedagogies based on principles of active learning, collaboration, multiplicity, and knowledge building, varied content areas including the sciences and the arts, and varied instructional formats including seminars, tutorials, group projects, and labs (Harasim, 1995). The framework consists of tools to support core activities including course design, individual and group learning activities, knowledge structuring, class management, and evaluation.

The attention to pedagogy is what distinguishes Virtual-U from other virtual universities. The Web has typically been used as a publishing environment characterized by a correspondence course model or a broadcast model of learning in which faculty post lecture notes or students post assignments online.

Design Directions

The designers and implementors of Virtual-U comprise a multidisciplinary team of educators, HCI specialists, engineers, computing scientists, database designers, instructional designers, implementors, instructors, learners, and researchers. The initial design is based on networked multimedia workstations (PCs or Macs) and a unix server. The decision was made to build on widely available World Wide Web tools, since there is active interest in developing these tools for multiple platforms. Thus, the students and instructors using Virtual-U need only a Netscape browser on their workstation because all of the Virtual-U software resides on a central server. The major components of the system include the architecture, campus spaces, and tools, all of which contribute to shaping the environment specifically for online learning.

Web-Based Client-Server Architecture

The architecture is a hybrid distributed-star configuration consisting of a central server, a set of local servers, and a set of networked multimedia workstations in which local servers may also communicate with each other directly. Multimedia resources and specialized knowledge are distributed throughout the system (and beyond). In order to use the system, the student activates the browser and contacts the server World Wide Web address. A security system allows registered students to access materials for the course in which they have enrolled. Users can also link directly to other World Wide Web resources.

The conferencing system is based on a structured file system. This works well for a limited number of users, but for large scale deployment it will be reimplemented with a database structure. The user interface and the tools available are evolving as the Web-based tools evolve. The use of Java and other software makes it possible to play animations and simulations, which greatly enhances the potential content for specialized areas such as laboratory experiments and dance instruction.

Spatial Metaphor

Until recently, online learning environments were completely text based; much like reading prose, the participants formed their own imagery of the virtual environments. With multimedia which provide 2-dimensional images of 3D scenes, and even video or animation, it is possible to provide the students with explicit cues which help them orient themselves, both in terms of navigating around the virtual environment as well as in setting social norms as to the appropriate behavior expected in each virtual space.

The approach is to use a spatial metaphor in which users navigate using images of university buildings, offices and study areas (Figure 1). While the key spaces are instructional, such

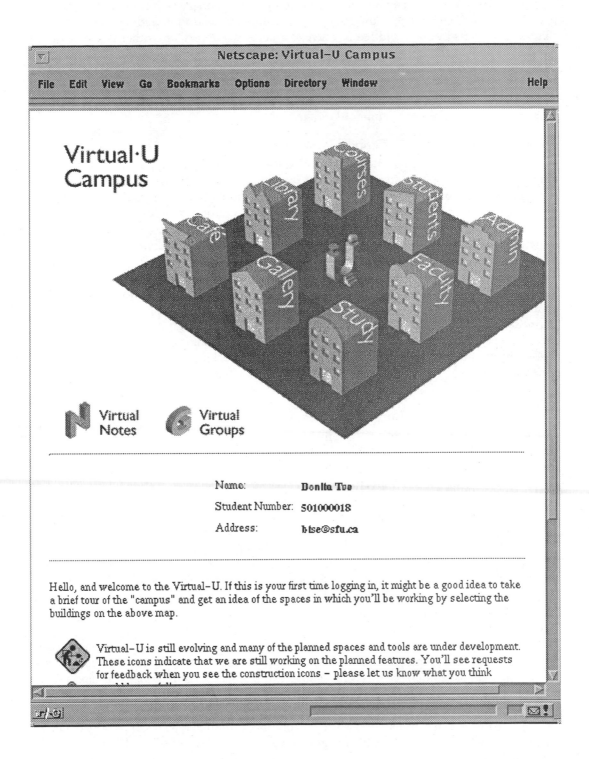

Figure 1. Virtual-U navigation is supported by a spatial metaphor.

as virtual classrooms for seminars and discussion groups and spaces for team projects, labs, etc., the Virtual-U environment also includes spaces for academic advice, for administrative activities such as registration and fee payment, for access to library and other information resources (including an art gallery) and for social interchange (the virtual cafe).

While a spatial metaphor may be helpful during a transitional stage, more experienced users sometimes find that it gets in the way of efficiency. Therefore, users are provided with five ways of navigating Virtual-U and accessing tools: spaces (graphic imagery), a navigation map, menus, a control panel, and hot-key alternatives.

Functional Components to Support New Pedagogies

Another major component of Virtual-U is the set of tools to support core activities including course design, individual and group learning activities, knowledge structuring, class management, and evaluation. Tools to support course design include a course structure tool and a group design tool. The course structure tool consists of a template for the course syllabus. Instructors fill in the template, obviating the need for knowledge of HTML in constructing the syllabus. The group design tool facilitates the shaping of conferences for effective online collaboration and communication.

Virtual Groups, a Web-based conferencing system designed and developed by the Virtual-U team, mediates online group interaction (Figure 2). The annotation tool and the tool for creating concept maps provide ways of organizing ideas and structuring knowledge. The hypermedia environment also supports knowledge structuring through hyperlinks and multiple media, namely, text, graphics, images, video, and sound. An online grade book assists in class management, and evaluation is supported by the polling facility, conference logs, and logs of usage statistics.

Initial Experience with Virtual-U

Current pilot course offerings on Virtual-U include two communication courses which focus on student-moderated online seminars, project teams, debates, and projects which involve inquiry, goal-setting, group dynamics, analysis, and reflection; an engineering course (with a virtual lab component), and various courses from business, education, and computer science. The results of data captured from user reports and usage statistics are being applied to the next iteration of Virtual-U development.

An iterative method of development for Virtual-U has worked well because feedback and newly available technology can be incorporated early on. For example, on the Web, the sense of 'place' users reported experiencing with previous versions of computer conferencing systems was lost. With the release of Netscape 2.0, new features such as frames, multiple windowing, and Java support were adapted to provide context. The message list in a conference can now be accessed in one window, a particular message selected, and the contents of the message displayed in another window.

Other refinements, such as easier navigation and multiple views of conference discussions, are contributing to development of this new generation of Web-based conferencing systems. For example, conference messages can be text, graphics, or animation—the next version of the conferencing system allows HTML in the body of a message. The need for a submit form for submitting work to the server has also been identified.

In addition, multimedia forms of collaboration and conferencing are being explored, such as real-time video conferencing, image conferencing (shared white boards, many of which include video), and 3D real-time messaging using Worlds Chat. As multimedia communication becomes increasingly possible over networks, there is a need to identify which media are most

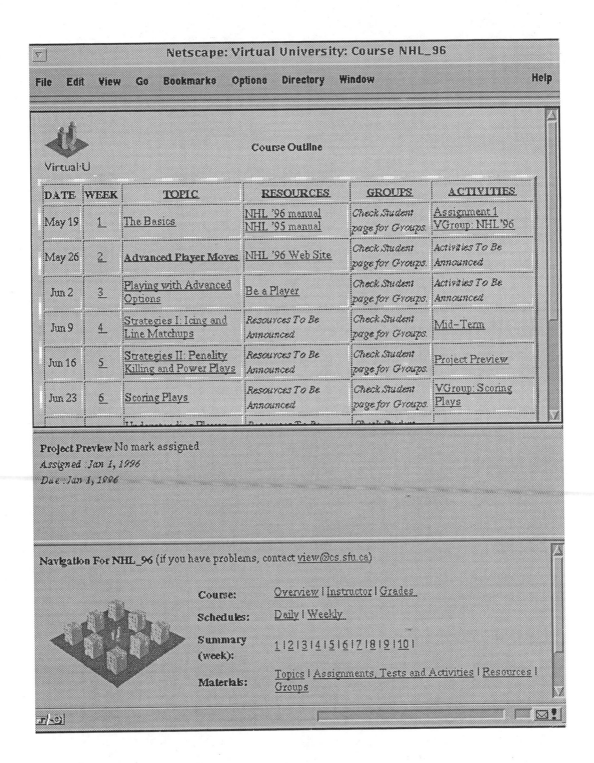

Figure 2. The course structuring tool supports course authors in structuring.

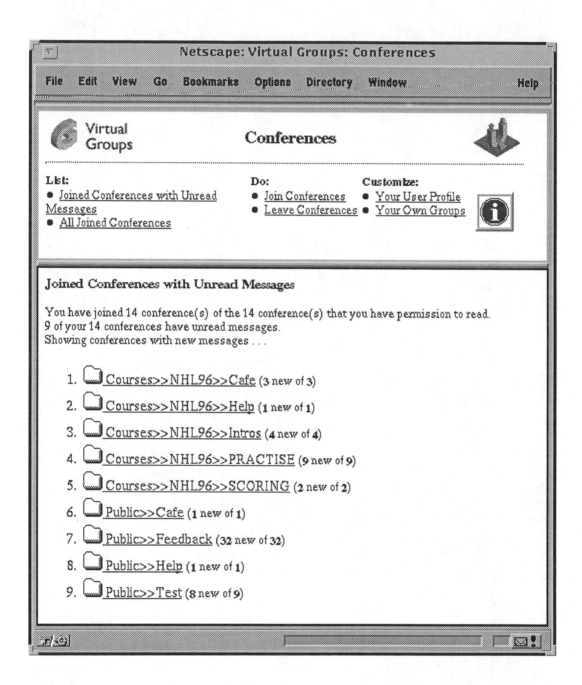

Figure 3. The interface to Virtual Groups, a Web-based conferencing tool.

effective for which educational activities. Appropriate and effective use of powerful broadband networks is critical. It is also imperative that tools be developed to assist educators and learners in designing and integrating multimedia products into the virtual learning environments.

Efforts in developing a virtual lab and a virtual art gallery have met with initial success and will continue to evolve. Currently an online dance course is being developed. This project raises many interesting issues and challenges for technology regarding how certain some types of instruction can be done online.

Conclusions

Observations from the use of early versions of Virtual-U suggest that a spatial metaphor is necessary to provide a sense of place and that it provides a useful mental model to assist navigation. The nature of the cues that can best support this metaphor range from text to explicit 3D spaces, and these are being investigated. Significant activity continues in further customizing the Web space into a learning environment by developing advanced teacher and learner tools. Specific embedded supports to facilitate course design, collaborative learning, knowledge building, and visualization tools are currently underway.

References

Cohen, E. G. (1984). Talking and working together: Status, interaction, and learning. In P. L. Peterson, L. C. Wilkinson, & M. Hallinan (Eds.), *The social context of instruction* (pp. 171–187). New York: Academic Press.

Damon, W., & Phelps, E. (1989). Critical distinctions among three approaches to peer education. *International Journal of Educational Research*, 13(1), 9–19.

Feenberg, A. (1993). Building a global network: The WBSI executive education experience. In L. Harasim (Ed.), *Global networks: Computers and international communication*. Cambridge, MA: MIT Press.

Harasim, L. (1989). Online education: A new domain. In R. Mason & T. Kaye (Eds.), *Mindweave: Computers, communications, and distance education* (pp. 50–62) Oxford: Pergamon Press.

Harasim, L. (1990). Online education: An environment for collaboration and intellectual amplification. In L. Harasim (Ed.), *Online education: Perspectives on a new environment* (pp. 39–66). New York: Praeger Publishers.

Harasim, L. (1991). Designs and tools to augment collaboration in computerized conferencing systems. In J. Nunamaker & R. Sprague (Eds.), *Proceedings of the Hawaiian International Conference on Systems Science, Vol. IV, Organizational Systems and Technology Track* (pp. 379–385).

Harasim, L. (1993a). Collaborating in cyberspace: Using computer conferences as a group learning environment. *Interactive Learning Environments*, 3(2), 119–130.

Harasim, L. (1993b). Networlds: Networks as social space. In L. Harasim (Ed.), *Global networks: Computers and international communication*. Cambridge, MA: MIT Press.

Harasim, L. (1995). The virtual university: New approaches to higher education in the 21st Century. Keynote Address to the Australian Society for Computers in learning in Tertiary Education Conference (ASCILITE'95), Melbourne, Australia.

Harasim, L., Hiltz, R., Teles, L., & Turoff, M. (1995). *Learning networks: A field guide to teaching & learning online*. Cambridge, MA: MIT Press.

Hiltz, S. R. (1990). Evaluating the virtual classroom. In L. Harasim (Ed.), *Online education: Perspectives on a new environment* (pp. 133–185). New York: Praeger Publishers.

Hiltz, S. R. (1993). *The virtual classroom: A new option for learning via computer networking*. Norwood, NJ: Ablex.

Koschmann, T., Myers, A., Feltovich, P., & Barrows, H. (1994). Using technology to assist in realizing effective learning and instruction: A principled approach to the use of computers in collaborative learning. *Journal of the Learning Sciences, 3*(3), 227–264.

Kaye, A. (1991). Computer networking in distance education: Multiple uses, many models. In A. Fjuk & A. E. Jenssen (Eds.), *Proceedings of the Nordic Electronic Networking Conference* (pp. 43–51). Oslo, Norway.

Mason, R. (1989). An evaluation of CoSy on an Open University course. In R. Mason & A. Kaye (Eds.), *Mindweave: Communication, computers, and distance education.* Oxford: Pergamon Press.

Scardamalia, M., & Bereiter, C. (1993). Technologies for knowledge-building discourse. *Communications of the ACM, 36*(5), 37–41.

Sharan, S. (1980). Cooperative learning in small groups: Recent methods and effects on achievement, attitudes, and ethnic relations. *Review of Educational Research, 50*(2), 241–71.

Slavin, R. E. (1980). Cooperative learning. *Review of Educational Research, 50*(2), 315–42.

Smith, R. C. (1988). Teaching special relativity through a computer conference. *American Journal of Physics, 56*(2), 142–147.

Stodolsky, S. S. (1984). Frameworks for studying instructional processes in peer work-groups. In P. L. Peterson, L. C. Wilkinson, & M. Hallinan (Eds.), *The social context of education* (pp. 107–124). New York: Academic Press.

Webb, N. (1982). Group composition, group interaction, and achievement in cooperative small groups. *International Journal of Educational Psychology, 74*(4), 475–84.

Webb, N. (1989). Peer interaction and learning in small groups. *International Journal of Educational Research, 13*(1), 21–29.

Acknowledgments

This work was supported in part by the TeleLearning Network of Centres of Excellence, by the B. C. Innovation Fund, and by contracts from FPM Systems and CANARIE Inc.

The Authors

Linda Harasim is Professor, School of Communication, Simon Fraser University, Burnaby, British Columbia, Canada.

e-mail, World Wide Web
   linda@telelearn.ca
   http://fas.sfu.ca/telelearn/homepages/harasim/harasim.htm

Tom Calvert is Professor, Schools of Computing Science, Engineering Science and Kinesiology, at Simon Fraser University, Burnaby, British Columbia, Canada.

e-mail, World Wide Web
   tom@sfu.ca
   http://fas.sfu.ca/cs/people/Faculty/Calvert/

Chris Groeneboer is a Research Associate, Virtual-U Project, School of Computing Science, Simon Fraser University, Burnaby, British Columbia, Canada.

e-mail, World Wide Web
   groen@cs.sfu.ca
   http://fas.sfu.ca/cs/People/

19

An Event-Oriented Design Model for Web-Based Instruction

Thomas M. Welsh

Introduction

One of the challenges for instructional designers charged with the task of suggesting the best use of an instructional medium such as the World Wide Web is the inevitable and incessant rate of change of information technologies. At an unprecedented rate, educators the world over are experiencing drastic increases in the use of the Web by their institutions, along with astounding changes in the Web itself (Kearsley, Lynch, & Wizer, 1995; Shotsberger, 1996). As of this writing, the estimated number of Web sites in the world was 366,590, up from approximately 100,000 in August, 1995, while the estimated number of people using the Internet was 63,276,218 (NeTree, 1996). The size of the Web was doubling every five months (Gray, 1995). At the author's institution, increases in faculty, student, and staff use of the Web have mirrored that of the world as a whole. While these are only rough estimates (indeed, generating statistics on such an amorphous and dynamic system as the Internet is a daunting task at best; Orenstein, 1995), they lead to several assumptions about the Web which can be held with great confidence:

- The capabilities of the World Wide Web will continue to expand at an astounding rate.

- Expansion of the Web's capabilities will lead to ever more sophisticated and data-intensive uses, resulting in a continued taxing of the network infrastructures of educational institutions, municipalities, and the Internet as a whole.

With this in mind, those designing instruction that uses the Web as the primary means of communication between class participants need instructional development models that take into account the current and future capabilities of the Web, as well as its evolving limitations. This chapter presents an Event-Oriented Design model (EOD) for Web-based instruction that acknowledges these issues. Based on the Rogers (1983) discussion of characteristics found to affect the rate of adoption of an innovation by organizations, four key criteria were deemed essential for ultimate adoption by the de facto designers of WBI, faculty members themselves. Any instructional design model for WBI must meet the following criteria:

1. It must be *systematic*, and therefore useful as a standard online course development methodology.

2. It must be *adaptable* to different educational disciplines and to differing pedagogical orientations.

3. It must be *technology independent*, incorporating technologies in wide use for instruction, as well as new technologies such as the Web.

4. It must be *useful in traditional contexts* so faculty can recognize the benefits of the design approach in instructional contexts other than WBI.

Components of Event-Oriented Design

The EOD model involves consideration of three elements that draw from the fields of distance education and instructional design. These are asynchronous vs. synchronous learning (Romiszowski, 1994), specification of performance objectives and the determination of instructional strategies for meeting objectives (Gagné, Briggs, & Wager, 1992), and specification of information technologies best suited to meet instructional goals in distance contexts. In the EOD model, first a *course* is conceptualized as a series of individual *modules*. Each module is com-

Table 1. Full synchronous, limited synchronous, and asynchronous instructional events.

Event	Traditional Classroom Environment	Web-Based Instruction
Full Synchronous	• Typical class session attended by instructor and students	• Entire class meets via Web-based chat forum. Class participants participants present ideas to class using text or audio, or potentially video-based real time communication tools.
Limited Synchronous	• Student group meet outside of class time to complete assignments.	• Student group meet in Web-based chat forum to complete group assignments posted to the Web. Two students meet in Web chat forum to discuss issues or tutor each other.
	• Instructor meets with individual students or student groups during office hours.	• Instructor holds regular Web office hours where chat forum is used with individual students and student groups to provide tutoring, feedback, etc.
Asynchronous	• Student completes individual homework assignments involving primarily the tasks of reading and/or some form of personal expression such as writing. When homework involves a product, student turns in product to instructor at next class session.	• Students download assignments and information resources from class Web site. Instructor receives written work and provides feedback via e-mail.
	• Library is used to access information resources.	• Students access relevant worldwide information resources through annotated links suggested by instructor and other students.

prised of a series of instructional *events*, each of which results in students meeting specific performance objectives.

Next, each instructional event is analyzed to determine the *type of event* it is. Some events are "full synchronous," in that they involve all class participants and the instructor. Some events are "limited synchronous," in that they involve two or more members of the class. Some events are "asynchronous," in that they involve only one individual at a given point in time. Table 1 offers examples of these events as manifested in traditional classroom and Web-based contexts.

It is important to note that synchronous events, either limited or full, generally consume greater bandwidth and involve more sophisticated uses of information technology than asynchronous events (Berge, 1995). For example, when students correspond with an instructor asynchronously via e-mail, information is sent one way with little regard as to the speed of the exchange. It makes little difference whether a message sent arrives in five seconds or 10 minutes. However, when students use a synchronous Web-based chat forum to converse with an instructor, packets of text are exchanged in rapid-fire succession as students and instructor replicate the type of dialogue that would take place face to face. The speed at which information is transferred takes on greater importance as both parties are engaging in a continuous dialogue. This taxes both local and worldwide network infrastructures. Servers can become overburdened, individual packets of information comprising a message can be lost en route, and local and regional networks can become busy, all resulting in potential failure of the instructional event. This scenario becomes exacerbated with more bandwidth-intensive activities such as the exchange of digital video images.

In addition to data transmission limitations, synchronous events impose psycho-social conditions which can both enhance and detract from the instructional event. Berge (1995) discusses the social aspects of synchronous computer conferencing and their potential effects on the exchange. The effects of humor, sarcasm, informality, member roles, and other elements of group dynamics in electronically mediated communication environments can result in unintended consequences. Therefore, it is important that course designers recognize the potential pitfalls when deciding on synchronous events for Web-based instruction. They must weigh the benefits of real time dialogue against the limitations that network infrastructures and electronically mediated group interaction impose. In short, before specifying synchronous events for Web-based instruction, first consider asynchronous options.

After the types of events that comprise an instructional module are determined, Web-based information technologies are chosen based on how well-suited they are to enable events. In many cases, several technologies may be available for a specific event. For example, in the case of an asynchronous instructional event where the learner is given a case study assignment and responds to issues, the information could be presented to the learner either as an HTML page or as a word processing file that must be downloaded. It is also possible to present case information to the learner in audio format that is downloaded; however, this strategy would be far more data-intensive. Subsequently, the learner could respond to the assignment by completing an HTML form contained within a Web page, by using a word processor and sending the file to the instructor as an enclosure, or by simply typing responses directly into an e-mail message. In any case, the instructional event is the same—an asynchronous event where information is provided and a response is made by the student. The choice of Web-based technologies best suited to enable the event should be based on ease of use for student and instructor, available network capacity, hardware and software, and specific attributes of the available technologies. For example, while presenting information to students in audio format is far more complex and data-intensive than presenting the same information as HTML text, it may be determined that this is a reasonable trade-off due to the beneficial characteristics of audio.

In each case, the instructor must choose the technology *best suited* to enable an event from the many technologies available.

In summary, designing for WBI using the EOD model involves the following steps:

1. Specify instructional goal and performance objectives of the course using traditional instructional design methods.

2. Sequence performance objectives and chunk them into a series of instructional modules, each of which results in students meeting objectives. While instructional modules need not be equal in duration or scope, parallel structuring can establish a comfortable rhythm for the students and instructor.

3. Divide each module into a series of instructional events.

4. For each event, specify event type; full synchronous, limited synchronous, or asynchronous.

5. For each event, specify appropriate Web-based technology(ies) to enable the event. Care should be taken to choose only from Web-based technologies available to the instructor and all students.[1]

Table 2. Performance objective and instructional events for one
module of a contemporary American history course.

Module: Effect of the Bay of Pigs Invasion on US/Soviet Relations

Performance Objective: Learner will be able to describe three outcomes of the Bay of Pigs invasion on US/Soviet relations in no more than 2–3 pages and support personal opinion by citing relevant course-related texts.

Instructional Events:

1. Learner reads chapters 2–4 of *Bay of Pigs* text.

2. Learner writes 3–5 questions that he/she wants answered in class.

3. Learner attends class where the following occurs:

   A. Instructor makes presentation

   B. Instructor facilitates discussion among students where questions are asked and answered.

   C. Instructor makes announcement regarding assignment of 2–3 page paper and answers questions.

4. Learner works individually on assignment.

5. Learner turns assignment in to instructor.

6. Instructor grades assignment and provides feedback.

7. *If necessary, instructor meets with learner during office hours.*

8. *If necessary, learner meets with other students to discuss course, etc.*

---

[1] The EOD model assumes that Web-based technologies will continue to evolve. For example, at this writing, Web-based chat forums and whiteboards are available only as plug-ins and helper applications for Web browsers. However, they are anticipated to be included in the next release of several Web browsers. As technologies that better enable events come available, they should replace older, less reliable or user-friendly technologies.

6. For each event, develop Web-based content where needed and define procedures that ensure smooth completion of the event.

7. Engage in formative evaluation and pilot testing as necessary to verify that each event, as well as the course as whole, is robust pedagogically and procedurally.

An Example of Event-Oriented Design for WBI

The example on the previous page illustrates the use of the EOD model for one module of a contemporary American history course. Because space limitations preclude discussion of each step in the EOD model, this example emphasizes steps three through five, where events and event types are specified and appropriate technology enablers are defined. Table 2 specifies the instructional events for this module.

Table 3. Events and Technology Enablers.

Event	Technology Enabler
1. Learner reads chapter 2–4 of *Bay of Pigs* text.	*World Wide Web*—Learner can order book through bookstore online. With proper copyright clearance, text from book can be posted to course Web site.
2. Learner writes 3–5 questions that he/she wants answered	*E-mail*—Learner writes questions in e-mail. Sends them to instructor via e-mail to meet requirements.
3. Learner attends class where the following occurs: **A.** Instructor makes presentation **B.** Instructor facilitates discussion among students where questions are asked and answered and answered. **C.** Instructor makes announcement regarding assignment of 2–3 page paper and answers questions.	*World Wide Web chat forum*—At a predetermined time, instructor and students all access the chat forum available through the course Web site. Instructor and students present and discuss by typing text on the page. Students pose their questions in forum. The text of the entire chat session is automatically saved for future access by students. The text of the chat then becomes a resource for student access through the Web page.
4. Learner works individually on assignment.	*Word processor or e-mail*—Learner writes paper.
5. Learner turns assignment in to instructor.	*E-mail*—Learner e-mails the assignment to instructor.
6. Instructor grades assignment and provides feedback.	*E-mail/World Wide Web chat forum*—Instructor grades assignment and provides feedback by annotating student's text.
7. *If necessary, instructor meets with learner during office hours.*	*World Wide Web chat forum*—Instructor is "in office" on course Web chat forum page during predetermined office hours. Instructor can "meet" with many students, not just one. Frequently asked questions can be posed to Web site.
8. *If necessary, learner meets with other students to discuss course, etc.*	*World Wide Web forum*—Students can meet together in chat forums (or "breakout rooms") whenever they wish.

Each of these eight events can be successfully replicated, and in some cases enhanced, in a WBI learning environment. Table 3 describes step four in the EOD model, where Web-based technologies are used to enable each instructional event in one module, and, in some cases, enhance it.[2]

Why Web-Based Instruction Should Also Be Applicable to Traditional Instructional Contexts

Many see the World Wide Web as the next great alternative to traditional instruction. Indeed, given recent developments in telecommunications technology, Web-based instruction can replicate, virtually, all the key learning activities that occur in traditional classroom-based and distance education environments (Romiszowski, 1994). While there are limitations, as with other distance education technologies (Laney, 1996), in the degree to which it can replicate traditional instructional events, WBI can be an enhancement over traditional classroom-based and distance education environments.

However, just as with past distance education technologies, the World Wide Web should not be seen as a panacea to the problems that afflict traditional education, but as an alternative, more or less useful depending on the educational context. As Simonson (1995, p. 12) argues, technology should be used, "to make the experiences of distant and local learners positive and equivalent." Traditional education will not disappear overnight. While educators are confronted with the need to teach courses in multiple instructional contexts, models such as EOD give them the means to plan for these contexts within the scope of one design effort. The key to effective WBI design is to determine how to best replicate the beneficial things that occur in traditional classroom and distance education environments, as well as improve upon the limitations of these environments by using the information resources and interaction capabilities of the Web.

Once an instructor has completed the seven steps involved in designing a course using the EOD model, it is a relatively simple matter to enable the same events in a more traditional campus environment. This is one of the strengths of the EOD model. A course developed under the model can be engineered so that the same events occur in a traditional context using technologies appropriate for the context. For example, it is possible to review Table 3 under the premise that the instructional context is a more traditional campus environment. In this case, the same set of events can be enabled using the technologies available in the classroom and on campus. While the technology enablers listed in Column 2 of the table will be different, the events themselves will be the same.

Conclusion

Some will argue that the EOD model demotes the role of technology to that of implementation vehicle, that it precludes one from thinking about how technology can influence strategy, and that Web-based instruction should not seek to virtually recreate the classroom but should be a means to change our notions of teaching and learning. While these points are well taken, there is an equally valid point that educators (especially in post-secondary institutions) are being called upon to implement specific courses in different contexts. One instructor may deliver one section of a course to remote students via the Web while delivering another section of the same course to a local population using non-Web-based technologies. In this case, models such

---

[2]The technologies listed are not the only ones that can be used to enable events. Other technologies can be incorporated if they serve to better enable an event. The technology is a means to an end, not an end in itself.

as EOD provide a strategy for undergoing a single design effort that can be implemented regardless of context.

While technology can, and should, influence thinking about pedagogy, technology should not be its master. Simonson (1995) reminds us that instructional media are, primarily, vehicles for the exchange of ideas. If the EOD model results in Web-based instruction that replicates the best instruction occurring in traditional settings, it can be deemed successful. If it results in a reassessment of what constitutes effective instruction, even better.

References

Berge, Z. (1995). Facilitating computer conference: Recommendations from the field. *Educational Technology, 35*(6), 22–30.

Gagné, R., Briggs, L., & Wager, W. (1992) *Principles of instructional design* (4th ed.). New York: Harcourt, Brace, Jovanovich.

Gray, M. (1995). Measuring the growth of the Web (http://www.mit.edu/ people/mkgray/growth/).

Kearsley, G., Lynch, W., & Wizer, D. (1995). The effectiveness and impact of on-line learning in graduate education. *Educational Technology, 35*(6), 37–42.

Laney, J. D. (1996). Going the distance: Effective instruction using distance learning technology. *Educational Technology, 36*(3), 51–54.

NeTree. (1996). *Internet statistics—Estimated* (http://www.netree.com/ netbin/Internetstats/).

Orenstein, R. (1995). *Irresponsible Internet statistics generator* (http://www. anamorph.com/docs/stats/ stats.html).

Rogers, E. (1983). *Diffusion of innovations.* New York: The Free Press.

Romiszowski, A. (1994). Telecommunications and distance education. In D. Ely & B. Minor (Eds.) *Educational media and technology yearbook* (pp. 159-163). Englewood, CO: Libraries Unlimited.

Shotsberger, P. G. (1996). Instructional uses of the World Wide Web: Exemplars and precautions. *Educational Technology, 36*(2), 47–50.

Simonson, M. (1995). Does anyone really want to learn at a distance? *TechTrends, 40*, p. 12.

The Author

Thomas M. Welsh is Assistant Professor of Instructional Technology, California State University, Chico, California.

e-mail
   twelsh@oavax.csuchico.edu

20

Learner-Centered Web Instruction for Higher-Order Thinking, Teamwork, and Apprenticeship

Curtis Jay Bonk and Thomas H. Reynolds

During the upcoming decade, we will undoubtedly see momentous advances in Web-based instruction (WBI), spurred by new developments in the information superhighway, the design of innovative World Wide Web technology tools and features, and the growing acceptance of learner-centered instructional principles and techniques (American Psychological Association (APA), 1995). Chronicling the "common" Web-based instructional techniques in existence today will likely appear limited when compared to approaches that supersede them in the 21st century. In order to extend the half-life of this chapter, therefore, our goals are three-fold:

- ground current examples of Web-based instructional techniques, tools, and practices in learner-centered pedagogy;

- provide a menu of Web-appropriate alternative instructional strategies for creative and critical thinking as well as cooperative learning; and

- raise the discussion of WBI to issues of learning apprenticeships and student perspective taking.

The Learner-Centered Movement

The learner-centered movement has encouraged instructors to create challenging and novel environments that help learners link new information to old, seek meaningful knowledge, and think about their own thinking. Important to WBI, learning is now deemed heavily influenced by social interactions and environmental factors such as culture, technology, and instructional practices (APA, 1995). As educators and researchers increasingly accept Vygotsky's (1978) views that the social plane is the origin of all mental activity and growth (Brown & Palincsar, 1989; Chang-Wells & Wells, 1993; Salomon 1988), student learning is increasingly analyzed in a social context. From this sociocultural perspective, meaning is seen as a negotiation and knowledge building process within a learning community (Bonk & King, 1995; Brown, Ash, Rutherford, Nakagawa, Gordon, & Campione, 1993; Koschmann, 1994; Scardamalia & Bereiter, 1994; Tharp & Gallimore, 1988; Wells & Chang-Wells, 1992). The World Wide Web is one such learning community wherein learner-centered instructional techniques have exhibited significant promise.

167

Wagner and McCombs (1995) recently pointed out that distance education technologies such as the World Wide Web offer ideal possibilities for placing students at the center of one's learning environment. In fact, in the most successful online courses and global networks, students are assuming significant instructional roles (e.g., offering tips and helping construct new knowledge) that transform traditional teaching practices and student learning opportunities (Harasim, 1993).

The asynchronous communication of the World Wide Web offers students a palette of online information resources (e.g., movies, instructor notes, expert reports, course updates, interactive experiments, electronic libraries, reference rooms, assignments, quizzes, readings, student products, and self-selection task options) (Harasim, Hiltz, Teles, & Turoff, 1995) as well as new routes for student social interaction and dialogue (e.g., voice and text chat tools, virtual whiteboards, public text pointing devices, teacher or expert commentary options, debate forums, student opinions, peer knowledge bases, and transcripts of previous student interactions) (Bonk, Medury, & Reynolds, 1994; Bonk, Reynolds, & Medury, 1996; Fetterman, 1996, in press). It is the premise of this chapter that as these interactive resources and tools materialize on the Web, the importance of one's instructional selections coincidingly rise in salience. Consequently, any instructional guidelines provided here should prove useful and timely for future Web instructors.

The Web is a tool for "assisting in learning" (see Tharp & Gallimore, 1988), not simply an extension of or substitution for traditional teaching practices (Fetterman, in press). As assisters of learning, instructors manage and structure tasks, model and demonstrate ideas, provide questions and feedback, coach or scaffold learning, encourage students to articulate beliefs and ideas, foster student reflection and self-awareness, push student exploration and application of skills, and directly instruct when appropriate (Bonk & Kim, in press; Collins, Brown, & Newman, 1989; Rogoff, 1990; Tharp, 1993). During this learning assistance, learners browse, build, link, juxtapose, and reflect on new knowledge. While most WBI ideas about learning assistance appear to be speculative and untested, a myriad of innovative and exciting pedagogical strategies are emerging for WBI as we head into the next millennium.

Alternative Web-Based Instruction Strategies:
Creative, Critical, Cooperative

The status of the World Wide Web as an alternative instruction delivery mechanism will soon focus educator and researcher attention on how WBI classes foster student creative processes, critical thinking, and small group work. As such, there are literally hundreds of instructional approaches available for Web instructors to promote idea generation, planning, organization, critique, and reflection on the Web; far too many to detail here. Though still somewhat broad in scope, this chapter focuses on ideas for enhancing creative and critical thinking, followed by a brief account of instructional approaches for cooperation and collaboration on the Web.

Creative Thinking on the Web (See Table 1)

If creativity requires students to sense gaps in information, make guesses and hypotheses, test and revise ideas, and communicate results (Torrance, 1972), what better tool is there than the Web? Web browsing tools now exist to explore and search for information, dynamically view the results of one's choices, and send these findings to instructors and peers. As indicated earlier, the teacher's role here involves managing the distribution of these self-selection activities (Harasim *et al.*, 1995), as well as scaffolding them with comments and suggestions that guide and intellectually support learner achievement during various learning quests (Teles, 1993). Apparently, the Web may be the ideal tool to nurture students' willingness to take risks, commitment to task, curiosity, openness to experience, broad interests, originality, imaginative play, intuition, attraction to novelty and complexity, artistic ability, metaphorical thinking, problem finding, elaboration of ideas, and breaking away from the norm; all of which are key attributes of creative people (Davis, 1992; Starko, 1995; Young, 1985).

Researchers such as Davis (1992), Perkins (1986), and de Bono (1994) have championed instructional techniques that address students' divergent or creative thinking. In WBI, chat boxes, windows, and conferencing options might embed a number of creative thinking op-

Table 1. Summary of suggested creative thinking techniques for the Web.

1. Brainstorming: Focus on (1) quantity or more ideas; (2) the wilder the better; (3) no evaluation; and (4) building on, combining, improving, and hitchhiking on ideas is sought. (e.g., What are ways schools can be more effective?)
2. Reverse Brainstorming (Davis, 1992; Starko, 1995). (e.g., What are ways schools can be less effective?)
3. Assigning Thinking Roles in Role Plays. (e.g., In restructuring Shields Elementary School, I want to consider how the World Wide Web might play a more central role in instruction. For this discussion, you will randomly be assigned one of the following roles: summarizer, judge, connector, mentor, warrior, mediator, inventor, watchdog, debator, improver, commentator, idea squelcher, idea generator, questioner, devil's advocate, optimist, etc.)
4. Creative Writing: Telling Tall Tales, Story Starters, Forced Response Wrap Arounds, Newsletters, Cartoons, Object Obituaries, Jokes, Riddles, Object Talking (Golub, 1994). (e.g., "I visited a school yesterday that was real inspiring in terms of their instructional approaches and incorporation of technology in education. In this school, I saw 500 computers all fiber optically networked to....John, can you continue this story?")
5. Simulations and Role Plays. (e.g., We are going to simulate a school restructuring meeting. You will each be assigned one of the following roles: parent, teacher, administrator, politician, student, real estate agent, professor of education, community leader, corporate executive, etc.)
6. What If, Just Suppose, and Rearrange the Facts Exercises. (e.g., What if you were put in charge of Littlefeat Elementary School? Or: Just suppose that your local high school received a $3 million grant for restructuring and you were the curriculum director. What would you do...?)
7. Metaphorical Thinking, Analogies, Forced Associations, Synectics (Davis, 1992). (e.g., This school is like a ____ (for example, a prison, museum, monastery, a beehive, etc.)? Or: An effective teacher is like a ____ (for example, a tour guide, surveyor, orchestra conductor, mechanic, baker, artist, etc.)?)
8. Free Writing, Diaries, Personal Journal Logs, Wet Inking. (e.g., After viewing this film on learner-centered schools, I want you to jot down some reflective notes for no more than ten minutes on a school you have observed that embodied many of these principles. Try to write down the first things that enter your minds, no matter how silly or unrelated they may seem.)
9. Idea-Spurring Questions, Checklists, or Cards (Davis, 1992). (e.g., Think about the Web site you have created on learner-centered schools. What can you do to improve it? What can you add? What can you delete? Modify? Combine? Make bigger? Make smaller? Reverse? Rearrange? Minimize? etc.)
10. Semantic Webbing, Mapping, Linking, Chaining, Free Association Exercises. (e.g., With the word "effective schools" in the middle of a semantic map, I want you to suggest any attributes and characteristics related to this concept that you think of.)

tions. For instance, in a course on school restructuring, the instructor might use conferencing tools and interactive chat windows to begin the course with a simple brainstorming or reverse brainstorming exercise intended to loosen students up (Starko, 1995). To further promote interactivity and creative license among participants, students might be assigned thinking-related roles within these forums (e.g., summarizer or commentator) (Bonk & Smith, 1996). Importantly, such role assignment has proven effective in both electronic mail and computer conferencing systems when used to discuss critical course issues or controversial case vignettes (Bonk, Appelman, & Hay, 1996). Starter activities such as "telling tall tales" (Golub, 1994) are additional ways the instructor can initiate an imaginative electronic discussion on a topic and have everyone add to it with his or her own unique perspective.

One longitudinal study of asynchronous environments found that these interactive conferences and discussions tend to be more extended and engaging for students than traditional lecture-based instruction (Chong, 1996). According to Harasim *et al.* (1995), the anonymity of pen names and pseudo-roles during electronic discussions encourages student idea experimentation and risk taking disclosures. Students' assigned roles, as noted in Table 1, might parallel occupational choices or societal interests. Though roles might be randomly assigned or based on order of entry into the conversation, with the careful task structuring and instructor scaffolding, such interactive simulations and role plays can become common discourse activities on the Web.

Thoughtful planning also impacts the successful use of Web-based hypermedia environments, since students and instructors often want to instantly capture and replay video sequences and problem vignettes in order to locate additional information or view situations from alternative perspectives (The Cognition and Technology Group at Vanderbilt, 1991). Innovative use of such resources by Web instructors might spur additional curiosity and dissonance by continually rearranging key features of a predicament or situation with a series of "just suppose" and "what-if" exercises. Though relatively simple, these exercises help students break from their current mental set and find new insights (Davis, 1992).

Other creative thinking techniques for the Web might include student free writing or metaphorical thinking on a key course topic such as "effective schools." Afterwards, students' free writing and metaphors of effective schools might be compared to lists generated by previous or current course participants. Similar writing tasks, such as student private journal logs or diaries of Web explorations, also can spark creativity. Additional encouragement for divergent thought and ideas when writing might come from idea-spurring questions, cards, and checklists strategically inserted into Web activities by the instructor.

As Web software becomes more sophisticated, proposals from students on specific topics (e.g., how to create effective schools) might eventually be entered in attribute webs or interactive ferris wheels (Lyman, 1992; McTighe, 1992) and then randomly spun to juxtapose ideas from alternate wheels to help students discover other angles and viewpoints. Or perhaps software tools might take student ideas and automatically add them to idea webs or semantic maps being constructed by a class on the World Wide Web. As such tools for creative thought emerge, WBI may help students challenge the rules, exercise one's "risk muscle" (von Oech, 1983), discover new patterns and relationships, improvise, and add details to one's work. Despite these extensive divergent thinking avenues, enhancing critical thinking pathways may be an equally strong dimension of the web.

Critical Thinking on the Web (See Table 2)

Besides impacting creative thinking and general problem solving processes, some WBI techniques directly enhance student evaluation of materials and resources. According to leading thinking skill proponents (Beyer, 1988; Ennis, 1989; Paul, 1990; Presseisen, 1986), critical thinking is used to select information, evaluate potential solutions, determine the strength of an argument, recognize bias, and draw appropriate conclusions.

Whereas semantic webs and free association exercises are creative devices, most graphic organizers facilitate critical thinking since they help students sort out the hierarchy and logical flow of ideas. Student mapping of Web-based conferencing discussion threads is just one relatively simple and useful application of this idea. Other Web-based instructional activities that have students create or modify spatial representations of information (e.g., Venn diagrams or concept maps) provide opportunities for students to display knowledge depth and overall conceptual understanding (Angelo & Cross, 1993).

Table 2. Summary of suggested critical thinking techniques for the Web.

1. Graphic Organizers: Flowcharts, Models, Concept Maps, Venn Diagrams, Decision-Making Trees, Sequence Charts. (e.g., I want you to draw a Venn diagram comparing traditional and learner-centered instruction as well as detailing areas of overlap between the two, if any.)
2. Voting or Ranking Methods, Nominal Group Process. (e.g., Please categorize and rank the ideas on the list we generated while brainstorming ways to create more effective elementary schools in the United States.)
3. Plus, Minus, Interesting (PMI), Pros and Cons (de Bono, 1994). (e.g., Record the positives, negatives, and interesting aspects on your Web readings for this week.)
4. Minute Papers, Reflection Logs, Think Sheets, Guided Questioning. (e.g., What was the muddiest point of the instructor Web notes on school restructuring?) (Angelo & Cross, 1993)
5. K-W-L (de Bono, 1994). (What did you already **k**now about school restructuring? What do you still **w**ant to know about school restructuring? What did you **l**earn in this part of the course or in your Web explorations about school restructuring?)
6. Summing Up: Summaries, Abstracts, Reviews, Index Cards, Outlines, Nutshelling. (e.g., I want you to summarize one school restructuring article or homepage you read during the past week while browsing the Web.)
7. Critiques, Rebuttals, Replies, Rejoinders. (e.g., I want you to critique an article you found on the Web related to school restructuring and also write a potential rebuttal to the original author(s).)
8. Mock Trials, Debates, Examining Both Sides of Argument, Force Field Analysis. (e.g., Please list three arguments for and three arguments against moving from traditional instruction to APA's 14 learner-centered principles in your local high school.)
9. Case-Based Reasoning: Case A, Case B; Case and Commentaries; Cumulative Cases; Critical Instances, Problem Vignettes. (e.g., After reading and replying to the first case on school restructuring at Thoroughgood High, wherein the authors admitted it took five years of careful planning, I want you to read the follow-up case on New Beginner Middle School, where restructuring efforts just began last year. Then we will reply to the following questions . . . as well as those you want to discuss.)
10. Categorization Schemes, Taxonomies, Comparison and Contrast Matrices. (e.g., After immersing yourself in the articles you find on the Web related to school restructuring, I want you to categorize or classify these articles into a coherent and useful organizational scheme or matrix.)

Another critical thinking method with strong ties to creative thinking activities is the use of voting methods. The nominal group process (Bonk & Smith, 1996), for example, is often used to rank and categorize student brainstormed ideas. According to Harasim *et al.* (1995), since voting methods help students appreciate peer rankings of assignments and class ideas, it is both motivational for the students and insightful for the instructor. As networlds (Harasim, 1993) evolve, these voting results may highlight where participant opinions and ideas are similar as well as vastly different according to age, gender, and geographic locale.

Besides idea ranking, various writing-to-think activities are extremely useful in fostering student reflection and critical evaluation (Applebee, 1984; Greene & Ackerman, 1995). Students on the Web might list the plus, minus, and interesting (de Bono, 1994) aspects of an assignment or topic, jot down the muddiest or most interesting points of a lesson (Angelo & Cross, 1993; Craig, 1995), or record prior experiences and incoming knowledge on a topic. Critiques, abstracts, rebuttals, conferencing debates, guided question reflection logs, and case analyses also fall within the realm of critical thinking writing activities. Embedding these opportunities for reflection and summarization helps solidify student learning and restructure student knowledge (Bonk, Mulvaney, Reynolds, & Dodzik, 1996; Hidi & Anderson, 1986; Winograd, 1984).

Any activity wherein students identify main points, search for cause and effect, find patterns and relationships, rank ideas, develop timelines, build taxonomies or categorization schemes, draw comparisons and contrasts, examine costs versus benefits, or interlink ideas, certainly is a worthwhile exercise in critical thought. And, as noted below, such activities are even more intellectually valuable when students work in teams.

Cooperative and Collaborative Learning on the Web (See Table 3)

Given that team products can be displayed to the world, online learning environments such as the World Wide Web offer extensive opportunities for collaboration and cooperative learning (Harasim, 1990; Riel, 1990, 1993). Simple structures for cooperative learning in the traditional classroom have students turning to their partner and sharing ideas. Applying this concept to the Web, students might be assigned Web-partners for e-mailing their thoughts and ideas regarding questions raised by the instructor or one's peers. Or, perhaps, a learning team might share its ideas regarding interesting or complex classroom queries in a round robin fashion and then summarize its ideas for the entire class.

Another easy-to-implement and effective conferencing idea is the use of starter and wrapper roles to initiate and summarize discussion, respectively (Bonk, Appelman, & Hay, 1996). This activity could be embedded within satellite conferences or electronic cafes (for additional information on conferencing tools, see the chapter by Malikowski in this text or Chong, 1996).

As mentioned earlier, giving students roles for discussion also enhances their processing of material and the overall sense of interdependence and accountability among group members. Incorporating Johnson and Johnson's (1992) structured controversy approach on the Web may prove especially useful in addressing debatable or sensitive topics. In this method, pairs of students are assigned pro and con sides of a topic. Next, they become experts on the assigned topic by reading material referenced on the Web. After forming their opinions, groups argue out their sides of the topic and then switch roles and eventually come to a compromise position written up for the instructor.

A number of other generic cooperative learning methods are amenable to the Web. For instance, Group Investigation (Sharan & Sharan, 1976) and "Coop Coop" (Kagan, 1992) both involve students selecting topics and dividing these up into mini-topics for individual explorations. Later, this individual work is compiled and presented in a final report or presentation, wherein the instructor is the referee or critic (Harasim *et al.*, 1995). To foster further reflection

Table 3. Summary of suggested cooperative learning techniques for the Web.

1. Partner Activities: Turn to Your Partner and: Share/Check Work/Review/Discuss, Think/Pair-Share, Peer Review/Edit and Conferences, Peer Interviews, Tell and Retell. (e.g., Please share with your assigned e-mail partner your brainstormed lists regarding how schools can be made more effective.)
2. Round robins and Round tables (Kagan, 1992). (e.g., I want your suggestions for handling the school restructuring case we just read. In a roundrobin fashion, I want each person in your group to add one idea and then pass the list on the next person in the group until your group has exhausted each individual's ideas. Then you are to rank the top five ideas of your group.)
3. Asynchronous Conferencing: Electronic Cafes, Satellite Conferences, Discussions Groups, Electronic Conference Starter(s) and Wrapper(s). (e.g., Listed below are the 15 discussion topics on school restructuring selected by the class. Please sign up to start or initiate discussion for one of these weeks and also sign up to be a wrapper of the class discussion for another week.)
4. Synchronous Conferencing. (e.g., This week we will be discussing school restructuring in a real-time conference with three well-known school principals. After this discussion, small groups will be formed to summarize the issues facing restructuring across these situations.)
5. Structured Controversy (Johnson & Johnson, 1992). (e.g., Pairs of students will be assigned to pro and con sides of a debate on any secondary school restructuring based on constructivist philosophy. After one week, these roles will be reversed. Next, a consensus paper will be written by your group.)
6. Group Investigation, Jigsaw, Coop Coop (Kagan, 1992). (e.g., We will divide school restructuring concerns into elementary, middle, secondary, and college levels. In groups of 4–5 students at each level, each student will select a minitopic in which to become an expert and share his or her findings with the group. Minitopics will be combined into a joint group composition or product.)
7. Value Lines and Graphs. (e.g., This week we will debate the utility of the APA's (1995) 14 learner centered principles. First of all, student teams will rate the worth they place on each of these principles from 1 (low) to 10 (high) a value line. After the debate, each group will reconsider its ratings of these principles on a new value line.)
8. Project-Based Learning. (e.g., Each group of 4–5 students will create blueprints for the ideal high school. In your work, please detail your basic principles or tenets, goals and objectives, potential funding sources, timeline, implications, budget, marketing plans, etc.)
9. Gallery Tours (Kagan, 1992). (e.g., Each of the five cooperative groups in this class will create a Web page to display its ideal school. Peers, public school principals, and education professors will provide detailed feedback and later rate your Web pages.)
10. Other Group Activities: Team Competitions, Panel Discussions, Symposia, Debates, Team Concept Webs, Picture Making Exercises, Buzz Groups. (e.g., Panel discussions will be established based on areas where you feel you have gained some expertise during this course and where significant questions have been raised. Individual points will be awarded for depth, clarity, logic, and creativity.)

and dialogue, each cooperative team might be forced to indicate its views or positions on a World Wide Web value line both before and after such cooperative projects.

The capabilities of the World Wide Web to display student text, graphics, animation, and sound may make it the ideal project-based learning (PBL) forum (Savery & Duffy, 1996; Williams, 1992). Gallery tours of student PBL products on the Web encourage student pride and ownership in the work. In addition to PBL, interactive activities such as panel discussions, symposia, team concept webs, and student team competitions might prove to be the real WBI success stories of the next century. Displays of course projects and team ideas from geographically and culturally diverse peers on the World Wide Web, nevertheless, will be confronted with questions concerning project organization, ownership, and assessment. Such considerations aside, the ultimate benefit here may be enhanced student collaboration processes as well as access to and interaction with mentors and peers on the Web.

Apprenticeship and Perspective Taking

As instructional strategies proliferate on the Web, course instructors must become conscious of how to apprentice student learning and enhance their perspective taking (Bonk, Appelman, & Hay, 1996; Harasim, 1993; Riel, 1993). However, fostering these opportunities remains the most culturally significant but least appreciated possibility of WBI.

A cognitive apprenticeship is a powerful instructional approach for building student thinking and teamwork skills. In accordance with this approach, the conferencing and collaboration technologies of the Web bring students into contact with authentic learning and apprenticing situations. Experts and learning guides might be available on the Web through "ask-an-expert," electronic mentorships, tutoring, informal peer interactions, student work groups, and other access to network resources (Harasim *et al.*, 1995). Dialogue processes between students and adult guides are hypothesized to move the learner from novice status to greater knowledge and skill of the discipline (Collins, 1990; Lave, 1991; Lave & Wenger, 1991; Rogoff, 1990). In recent electronic mentoring projects, student reception of ongoing feedback and support from meteorologists, explorers, or environmentalists brought students into contact with the community of practice and involved them in genuine data collection and reporting (Edelson, Pea, & Gomez, 1996; The GLOBE Program, 1995; Ruopp, Gal, Drayton, & Pfister, 1993; Songer, in press; Sugar & Bonk, 1995). As these expert resources multiply the pedagogic potential of every Web-based classroom, thoughtful consideration of one's instructional selections becomes increasingly crucial.

While instructors in WBI weigh the opportunities for cognitive apprenticeship, they might simultaneously consider how this teaching venue increases opportunities for students to take the position of another, since this skill is central to human intelligence (Bonk, 1990; Mead, 1934; Selman, 1971). The shared or common space (Schrage, 1990) created on the World Wide Web with conferencing tools, chat boxes, virtual whiteboards, opinion polls, and bulletin boards is prime real estate for cultivating knowledge negotiation and the gradual building of inter-subjectivity among participants. Given the emergence of such tools and resources, instructors must begin to locate and appropriately use strategies of instruction that tap into this perspective taking power source and push students to new heights of interpersonal understanding and global diversity appreciation.

Conclusions

With WBI, students now have new learning partners and learning materials for discovering, producing, and synthesizing knowledge. Given the endless WBI possibilities for higher-order thinking, teamwork, and apprenticeship, there is perhaps no issue with more immediate ramifications than elaborating on Web-based instructional techniques and practices today. In fact, educational historians and cultural anthropologists may treat the proliferation of World Wide Web instructional tools and techniques as one of the most significant cultural advances of the next century!

References

American Psychological Association (1995). *Learner-centered psychological principles: A framework for school redesign and reform*. Washington, DC: American Psychological Association.

Angelo, T. A., & Cross, K. P. (1993). *Classroom assessment techniques: A handbook for college teachers* (2nd ed.). San Francisco: Jossey-Bass.

Applebee, A. N. (1984). Writing and reasoning. *Review of Educational Research, 4,* 571–595.

Beyer, B. K. (1988). *Developing a thinking skills program*. Boston, MA: Allyn & Bacon.

Bonk, C. J. (1990). A synthesis of social cognition and writing research. *Written Communication, 7*(1), 136–163.

Bonk, C. J., Appelman, R., & Hay, K. E. (1996). Electronic conferencing tools for student apprenticeship and perspective taking. *Educational Technology, 36*(5), 8–18.

Bonk, C. J., & Kim, K. A. (in press). Extending sociocultural theory to adult learning. In M. C. Smith & T. Pourchot (Eds.), *Adult learning and development: Perspectives from educational psychology*. Mahwah, NJ: Lawrence Erlbaum Associates.

Bonk, C. J., & King, K. S. (1995). *Computer conferencing and collaborative writing tools: Starting a dialogue about student dialogue*. Proceedings for the First International Conference on Computer Support for Collaborative Learning (CSCL). Bloomington, IN: Indiana University (http://www-cscl95.indiana.edu/cscl95).

Bonk, C. J., Medury, P. V., & Reynolds, T. H. (1994). Cooperative hypermedia: The marriage of collaborative writing and mediated environments. *Computers in the Schools, 10*(1/2), 79–124.

Bonk, C. J., Mulvaney, M., Reynolds, T. H., & Dodzik, P. (1996). *Exploring how writing shapes thinking through alternative assessment of knowledge structure change*. Manuscript submitted for publication.

Bonk, C. J., Reynolds, T. H., & Medury, P. V. (1996). Technology enhanced workplace writing: A social and cognitive transformation. In A. H. Duin & C. J. Hansen (Eds.), *Nonacademic writing: Social theory and technology* (pp. 281–303). Mahwah, NJ: Lawrence Erlbaum Associates.

Bonk, C. J., & Smith, G. S. (1996). *Alternative instructional strategies for critical and creative thought in the accounting curriculum*. Manuscript submitted for publication.

Brown, A. L., Ash, D., Rutherford, M., Nakagawa, K., Gordon, A., & Campione, J. C. (1993). Distributed expertise in the classroom. In G. Salomon (Ed.), *Distributed cognitions: Psychological and educational considerations* (pp. 188–228). New York: Cambridge University Press.

Brown, A. L., & Palincsar, A. S. (1989). Guided, cooperative learning and individual knowledge acquisition. In L. Resnick (Ed.), *Cognition and instruction: Issues and agendas*. Hillsdale, NJ: Lawrence Erlbaum Associates.

Chang-Wells, G. M., & Wells, G. (1993). Dynamics of discourse: Literacy and the construction of knowledge. In E. A. Forman, N. Minick, & C. A. Stone (Eds.), *Contexts for learning: Sociocultural dynamics in children's development* (pp. 58–90). New York: Oxford University Press.

Chong, S. M. (1996). *Models of asynchronous computer conferencing for collaborative learning in large section college classes*. Manuscript submitted for publication.

Cognition and Technology Group at Vanderbilt (1991). Technology and the design of generative learning environments. *Educational Technology, 31*(5), 34–40.

Collins, A. (1990). Cognitive apprenticeship and instructional technology. In L. Idol & B. F. Jones (Eds.), *Educational values and cognitive instruction: Implications for reform*. Hillsdale, NJ: Lawrence Erlbaum Associates.

Collins, A., Brown, J. S., & Newman, D. (1989). Cognitive apprenticeship: Teaching the crafts of reading, writing, and mathematics. In L. B. Resnick (Eds.), *Knowing, learning, and instruction: Essays in honor of Robert Glaser*. Hillsdale, NJ: Lawrence Erlbaum Associates.

Craig, J. (1995). *Minute papers in a large class*. Technical Report #7(2), Teaching Resources Center. Bloomington, IN: Indiana University.

Davis, G. A. (1992). *Creativity is forever* (3rd ed.). Dubuque, IA: Kendall/Hunt Publishing.

de Bono, E. (1994). *De Bono's thinking course: Revised edition* (3rd ed.). New York: Facts On File.

Edelson, D. C., Pea, R. D., & Gomez, L. (1996). Constructivism in the collaboratory. In B. G. Wilson (Ed.), *Constructivist learning environments: Case studies in instructional design* (pp. 151–164). Englewood Cliffs, NJ: Educational Technology Publications.

Ennis, R. (1989). Critical thinking and subject specificity. *Educational Researcher, 18*(3), 4–10.

Fetterman, D. M. (1996). Videoconferencing online: Enhancing communication over the Internet. *Educational Researcher, 25*(4), 23–27.

Fetterman, D. M. (in press). Ethnography in the virtual classroom. *Practicing Anthropologist*.

The GLOBE Program (1995). *The GLOBE Program* (http://www.globe.gov). Washington, DC: National Oceanic and Atmospheric Administration.

Golub, J. N. (1994). *Activities for the interactive classroom*. Urbana, IL: National Council of Teachers of English.

Greene, S., & Ackerman, J. M. (1995). Expanding the constructivist metaphor: A rhetorical perspective on literacy research and practice. *Review of Educational Research, 65*(4), 383–420.

Harasim, L. (1990). Online education: An environment for collaboration and intellectual amplification. In L. Harasim (Ed.), *Online education: Perspectives on a new environment* (pp. 39–64). New York: Praeger.

Harasim, L. M. (1993). Networlds: Networks as a social space. In L. M. Harasim (Ed.), *Global networks: Computers and international communication* (pp. 15–34). Cambridge, MA: MIT Press.

Harasim, L., Hiltz, S. R., Teles, L., & Turoff, M. (1995). *Learning networks: A field guide to teaching and learning online*. Cambridge, MA: MIT Press.

Hidi, S., & Anderson, V. (1986). Producing written summaries: Task demands, cognitive operations, and implications for instruction. *Review of Educational Research, 56*, 473–493.

Johnson, D. W., & Johnson, R. T. (1992). Encouraging thinking through constructive controversy. In N. Davidson & T. Worsham (Eds.), *Enhancing thinking through cooperative learning* (pp. 120–137). New York: Teachers College Press.

Kagan, S. (1992). *Cooperative learning*. San Juan Capistrano, CA: Kagan Cooperative Learning.

Koschmann, T. D. (1994). Toward a theory of computer support for collaborative learning. *Journal of the Learning Sciences, 3*(3), 219–225.

Lave, J. (1991). Situating learning in communities of practice. In L. B. Resnick, J. M. Levine, & S. D. Teasley (Eds.), *Perspectives on socially shared cognition* (pp. 63–82). Washington, DC: American Psychological Association.

Lave, J., & Wenger, E. (1991). *Situated learning: Legitimate peripheral participation*. New York: Cambridge University Press.

Lyman, F., Jr. (1992). Think-pair-share, thinktrix, thinklinks, and weird facts: An interactive system for cooperative learning. In N. Davidson & T. Worsham (Eds.), *Enhancing thinking through cooperative learning* (pp. 169–181). New York: Teachers College Press.

McTighe, J. (1992). Graphic organizers: Collaborative links to better thinking. In N. Davidson & T. Worsham (Eds.), *Enhancing thinking through cooperative learning* (pp. 182–197). New York: Teachers College Press.

Mead, G. H. (1934). *Mind, self, and society.* Chicago, IL: The University of Chicago Press.

Paul, R. (1990). *Critical thinking: What every person needs to know to survive in a rapidly changing world.* Rohnert Park, CA: Center for Critical Thinking and Moral Critique.

Perkins, D. N. (1986). *Knowledge as design.* Hillsdale, NJ: Lawrence Erlbaum Associates.

Presseisen, B. Z. (1986). *Critical thinking and thinking skills: State of the art definitions and practice in public schools.* Paper presented at the annual convention of the American Educational Research Association, San Francisco, CA.

Riel, M. (1990). Cooperative learning across classrooms in electronic learning circles. *Instructional Science, 19,* 445–466.

Riel, M. (1993). Global Education through learning circles. In L. Harasim, (Ed.), *Global networks.* Cambridge, MA: MIT Press.

Rogoff, B. (1990). *Apprenticeship in thinking: Cognitive development in social context.* New York: Oxford University Press.

Ruopp, R., Gal, S., Drayton, B., & Pfister, M. (Eds.). (1993). *LabNet: Toward a community of practice.* Hillsdale, NJ: Lawrence Erlbaum Associates.

Salomon, G. (1988). AI in reverse: Computer tools that turn cognitive. *Journal of Educational Computing Research, 4*(2), 123–139.

Savery, J. R., & Duffy, T. M. (1996). Problem-based learning: An instructional model and its constructivist framework. In B. G. Wilson (Ed.), *Constructivist learning environments: Case studies in instructional design* (pp. 135–148). Englewood Cliffs, NJ: Educational Technology Publications.

Scardamalia, M., & Bereiter, C. (1994). Computer support for knowledge-building communities. *Journal of the Learning Sciences, 3*(3), 219–225.

Schrage, M. (1990). *Shared minds: The technologies of collaboration.* New York: Random House.

Selman, R. (1971). Taking another's perspective: Role-taking development in early childhood. *Child Development, 42,* 1721–1734.

Sharan, S., & Sharan, Y. (1976). *Small-group teaching.* Englewood Cliffs, NJ: Educational Technology Publications.

Songer, N. (in press). Can technology bring students closer to science? In K. Tobin & B. Fraser (Eds.), *The international handbook of science education.* The Netherlands: Kluwer.

Starko, A. J. (1995). *Creativity in the classroom: Schools of curious delight.* New York: Longman.

Sugar, W. A., & Bonk, C. J. (1995). *World Forum communications: Analysis of student and teacher interactions.* Proceedings for the Association for Educational Communications and Technology, Anaheim, CA (also ERIC Document Reproduction Service No. ED 383341).

Teles, L. (1993). Cognitive apprenticeship on global networks. In L. M. Harasim (Ed.), *Global networks: Computers and international communications* (pp. 271–281). Cambridge, MA: MIT Press.

Tharp, R. (1993). Institutional and social context of educational reform: Practice and reform. In E. A. Forman, N. Minick, & C. A. Stone (Eds.), *Contexts for learning: Sociocultural dynamics in children's development* (pp. 269–282). New York: Oxford University Press.

Tharp, R., & Gallimore, R. (1988). *Rousing minds to life: Teaching, learning, and schooling in a social context.* New York: Cambridge University Press.

Torrance, E. P. (1972). Teaching for creativity. *Journal of Creative Behavior, 6,* 114–143.

von Oech, R. (1983). *A whack in the side of the head: How to unlock your mind for innovation.* New York: Warner Books.

Vygotsky, L. S. (1978). *Mind in society.* Cambridge, MA: Harvard University Press.

Wagner, E. D., & McCombs, B. L. (1995). Learner-centered psychological principles in practice: Designs for distance education. *Educational Technology, 35*(2), 32–35.

Wells, G., & Chang-Wells, G. L. (1992). *Constructing knowledge together: Classrooms as centers of inquiry and literacy.* Portsmouth, NH: Heinemann.

Williams, S. M. (1992). Putting case-based instruction into context: Examples from legal and medical education. *Journal of the Learning Sciences, 2*(4), 367–427.

Winograd, P. (1984). Strategic difficulties in summarizing texts. *Reading Research Quarterly, 19*, 404–425.

Young, J. G. (1985). What is creativity? *The Journal of Creative Behavior, 19*, 77–87.

Acknowledgments

We would like to thank Jamie Kirkley, who helped create the URL related to this article (see: http://cee.indiana.edu/bobweb.html). We also are grateful to Padma Medury and Robert Fischler for their timely editorial advice and suggestions concerning this manuscript.

The Authors

Curtis Jay Bonk is Assistant Professor, Department of Counseling and Educational Psychology, Indiana University, Bloomington, Indiana.

e-mail, World Wide Web
    CJBonk@Indiana.Edu
    http://copper.ucs.indiana.edu/~cjbonk

Thomas H. Reynolds is Assistant Professor, Department of Educational Curriculum and Instruction, Texas A&M University, College Station, Texas.

e-mail
    TomR@Tamu.Edu

21

A Motivational Framework for Web-Based Instruction

Philip Duchastel

Introduction

Motivation is one of the weakest links in our study of learning and design processes as they apply to instruction. It is believed, however, that motivation, particularly in its manifestation as interest, will become more and more central to Web-based learning as the true richness of the Web and its multimedia potential are realized. This chapter examines interest and motivation models as they apply to WBI in order to establish a framework that will guide design approaches for WBI.

Intrinsically motivated action, including that which is focused on learning, is undertaken out of interest (Deci, 1995). Students can and do engage in learning activities for extrinsic motives as well (self-esteem, family favor, the promise of future rewards, etc.), but it is generally recognized that intrinsic motivation is far superior, for it deals with the inherent topic of learning. In this respect, interest is both a goal and a means within education. It is a goal in that one of the functions of education is to stimulate interest in what are considered to be the social values of the day (these being the basis of curricular decisions); and it is a means of attaining other educational goals, such as conceptual and skill development.

Motivational Context

Motivational factors of a psychological nature often condition the relation that a student will have with instruction (e.g., fear of failure or ridicule, personal expectations, etc.), but these generally act in an overall context of schooling rather than in a specific instructional setting. Nevertheless, they do impact the learning environment and need to be considered in the design of an educational system, as suggested by a recent set of principles to that effect adopted by the American Psychological Association (APA, 1993).

It remains that the World Wide Web (the Web) is thought of as inherently interesting, particularly by those who have had ample exposure to it. This is essentially why the Web, as an instructional resource, is seen as such a boon for learning. Where does this interest arise from? Is it the enduring novelty, the sense of control, the richness of information, the interaction possibilities, the multimedia attractiveness, or what? And, then, there is also the troublesome side of the Web: Its fickleness and general anarchy can trap one into a surfing mode that can sap interest in a specific topic and generate unending competition for attention.

Our challenge as instructional designers faced with this new and powerful information and communication tool is how to turn it into a useful and attractive learning environment, or more precisely, how to make use of it in these terms, given that no one controls the Web. The fascination of users with the Web makes this challenge largely one of motivation, indeed one of channeling interest into productive avenues.

A challenge that educators have struggled with, and continue to do so, is that of making learning easy and fun for learners of all ages. The issue is partly one of content to be learned (the curriculum issue) and partly one of method of instruction, where technologies can greatly assist in livening things up. The Web addresses both, as we shall see.

One goal in the next generation of instructional design theories must certainly be to overcome this notion, still all too prevalent (particularly within the student population), that succeeding at learning is largely a struggle. We will have achieved a true milestone in instructional design theory when this view falls into disfavor through the design of successful and appealing learning environments.

Interest within WBI

The richness of information found on the Web makes it an intrinsically interesting place to frequent (somewhat like a well stocked and well appointed bookstore). What is the secret of the Web's success in this respect? That is the question addressed here; later, we will explore how to take advantage of this motivational punch to facilitate learning. The aim of this section is to consider some of the motivational concepts that have been advanced in psychology and education in order to gradually weave a motivational framework that will help us capture the Web's impact as well as outline design strategies to capitalize on this impact.

At a very general level, people differ in their tendency to engage in and enjoy effortful cognitive endeavors, what is known in psychology as the need for cognition (Cacioppo *et al.*, 1966). Individual differences are thus at play in this realm. Likewise, environmental differences will determine cognitive motivation: Two types of interest have been distinguished and studied (Renninger *et al.*, 1992; Tobias, 1993), the first being situational interest, generated by the local factors of the situation (novelty, intensity...), the other being topic interest, referring to people's long-lasting interest in certain favored topics, which varies widely across people. All these interact of course, particularly in an information-rich environment.

Situational differences can be of tremendous importance in their impact on how the task of learning is perceived by the students and hence on how they approach learning. European and Australian researchers in particular have explored these issues in terms of depth of learning (e.g., Biggs & Coilis, 1982; Marton *et al.*, 1984). The general conclusion from this line of inquiry is that students vary in their orientation to learning, at times adopting a meaning orientation, where the goal is to delve into a topic and come to grips with it, and at other times simply doing with a reproducing orientation focused on a superficial approach of learning in order to parrot back the information on a test. Naturally, situational factors, such as the nature of an anticipated test, will affect the approach adopted, with radical impact on motivation, particularly in terms of the intrinsic-extrinsic aspect. All this is of some concern to design for WBI.

More directly tied to the world of instructional design are two theories that influence motivational views: Keller's ARCS model (1983) and Malone's framework for intrinsically motivating instruction (1981).

The ARCS model considers four factors in motivation to learn: attention, relevance, confidence, and satisfaction (the first letter of these four words make up the acronym for the model). WBI provides amply for the first two factors but may be problematic for the latter two.

Gaining and sustaining attention is easy on the Web, given the wealth of informative resources that are being made available and given the richness of multimedia design strategies that are used to attract attention. In fact, one problem in this area is precisely the richness of the Web, with its potential for distraction. One of the strategies suggested by Keller and Suzuki (1988) for designing motivating courseware of the traditional kind is to avoid dysfunctional attention-getting effects, but that is only possible when one controls student interaction, which is generally not the case in WBI. Task focus thus becomes a crucial design element for WBI in order to keep student Web interaction on task.

Relevance, the second factor in ARCS, is very much a matter of alignment with one's topic interests and perceived usefulness for long-term goals. It can thus relate to intrinsic or to extrinsic motivators, depending on the content of the instructional task. One certain advantage of WBI in this respect is its potential to help shift relevance from extrinsic to intrinsic. Once again, the richness of the Web comes into play here, leading to an enhancement of the possibilities of finding personally relevant resources that match the learning outcomes set by the particular WBI resource being used.

Confidence and satisfaction, the last two ARCS factors, relate to student perceptions of being able to achieve success and feelings about the achieved outcomes. They generally act on task persistence over time more than on the moment-to-moment task interaction as it unfolds, and, as such, are less controlled in WBI. On the positive side, the sense of learner-control offered by WBI can be a definite plus for the curious student, but the danger of getting lost in the vastness of the Web and not properly fulfilling learning expectations can be a very real one and will require proper instructional support (Duchastel, 1996). Additionally, traditional software strategies such as matching the difficulty level to the student's progress or providing adequate reinforcement for progress are more tenuous in the open environment of WBI. The very richness of the Web does, however, provide natural consequences in terms of satisfaction at finding interesting and relevant resources for learning, which somewhat tempers these dangers.

Turning now to the Malone model, we see a somewhat different set of concerns, even though there is much overlap. Malone (1981) studied why computer games are captivating and then extrapolated to see how those same factors can be used to make learning with computers more fun. His model involves three factors: challenge, fantasy, and curiosity (CFC), which together combine to create intrinsically motivating instruction.

Challenge is provided for by explicit goals, particularly so when they are personally meaningful ones, and by uncertain outcomes. Fantasy involves immersing the learner in an interesting setting that invites involvement, perhaps an adventure setting or perhaps a realistic one, such as a baseball game or a business venture, and so on. Fantasy can be either extrinsic (merely an interesting setting for some learning activity) or more usefully, intrinsic, whereupon the setting is intimately tied into what is being learned (e.g., a lemonade stand as a fantasy for learning basic economics principles).

Challenge and fantasy are closely associated with instructional games and simulations, and, as such, are not directly related to WBI. Indeed, the Web remains for now an information-rich but process-poor learning resource (Duchastel & Turcotte, 1996), where interactive processes are still sparse and technically limited. That, of course, will change in time, particularly with Java-like languages that offer efficient interactivity. Fantasy in particular may well become a central feature of WBI as VRML becomes economically feasible and populates the Web with interactive virtual reality worlds. Even now, though, the richness of the Web can encourage challenge and fantasy, although building on these factors remains largely dependent on general learning environment design principles for WBI (Duchastel, 1996).

Malone's third factor, curiosity, is more closely tied into intrinsic motivation and also more relevant to current WBI because it can capitalize on the information richness of the Web.

Malone emphasizes cognitive curiosity much in the style of Berlyne (1960), whose notion of epistemic (knowledge-oriented) curiosity underlies much of the information exploration that goes on within the world of the Web. Challenge is involved here within the cognitive realm, the idea being to challenge preconceptions, bring out inconsistencies, and reveal incompleteness of one's knowledge. It is Jean Piaget's theory of assimilation-accommodation that comes to mind in this context (see Duchastel, 1990, for instructional design implications of this approach).

In summary, both Keller's ARCS model and Malone's CFC model provide interesting dimensions to consider in better understanding why WBI can be intrinsically motivating and in seeking to enhance this aspect in the design of WBI. Another well-known model within education, Wlodkowski's (1993) instructional motivation model, should be mentioned, even if it may be somewhat less applicable to WBI. Indeed, this model is much broader in that it emphasizes instructor-student interaction factors and delivery factors; however, it too has some elements that relate to design, particularly content selection factors, which can lead to practical strategies to enhance intrinsic interest.

Design Space

The motivational factors reviewed in the previous section provide a general framework for thinking about WBI, but it is premature to consider designing an explicit motivational model for WBI, which is itself evolving rapidly. At this point, it is only possible to provide some directions of thinking that may help WBI designers manipulate the design space at their disposal.

As we consider the technology of the Web and what it makes possible, we see two strong motivational aspects, beyond those discussed above, that it emphasizes. The first is called the effin factor and deals with the effort-to-interest relationship evident in our dealings with information search activities. The other is the communicative aspect of the Web, whereby interchange is enhanced in support of collaborative learning.

The effin factor (Duchastel, 1996) captures the positive relationship between the inherent interest a person sees in a topic and the effort the person is willing to devote to an information search in support of exploring the topic. The Web generally reduces the effort needed (despite search and navigation difficulties), thereby encouraging exploration. This fact should be taken advantage of in WBI through the design of active, discovery-oriented, open learning instructional strategies rather than simply replicating within this new medium the more controlled and focused strategies that CBT is known for. It is even suggested that a fully task-driven instructional strategy (similar in tone to the familiar problem-based learning paradigm of professional education—Savery & Duffy, 1996) replace the more traditional content-driven strategy of high-school and college instruction (Duchastel, 1997). Collaborative learning through interchange on the Web flows in the same direction of open learning, and likewise should be taken advantage of in WBI.

Perhaps the crucial question is that of content. Given that the Web is a storehouse of information and resources and that it is ever-evolving, how do we come to decide what to focus on in WBI? In other words, how narrowly or how broadly do we set the learning tasks for our audiences? At an even deeper level is a questioning of the very curriculum decision-making that takes place in contemporary education (see, for instance, Schank & Cleary, 1994, for a general critique, and Anderson, 1995, for a critique in the area of mathematics). The information richness of the Web only exacerbates this issue.

Conclusion

WBI, because of its richness and because of its motivational impact, will strongly impact education. This is particularly true at the intermediate levels of schooling (high school and college) where education is perhaps most difficult and delicate for the students.

On the one hand, the growing wealth and diversity of resources on the Web promise to bring to the educational scene more real-world instructional content, thus influencing content-selection decisions. A growing awareness of the interplay between what is learned and how it is learned will also likely impact instructional design theory, if not learning theory itself.

On the other hand, we may well see a tremendous growth in informal and out-of-class learning, even though the formal program of schooling will continue to frame learning activities and evaluation standards. As argued elsewhere (Duchastel & Turcotte, 1996), the impact of this growth will see itself realized in a potential shift of power in the classroom (when the instructor is no longer necessarily the expert) with a concomitant shift in the role of the teacher towards a greater emphasis on guidance and mentoring.

Thus, the potential of WBI in creating a new motivational framework for learning is to be welcomed and used to strive towards the goal of making learning fun. Only then will learning environment design be considered successful!

References

American Psychological Association (1993). *Learner-centered psychological principles: Guidelines for school redesign and reform.* Washington, DC: APA and the Mid-Continent Regional Educational Laboratory.

Anderson, J. R. (1995). *Learning and memory. An integrated approach.* New York: John Wiley & Sons.

Berlyne, D. (1960). *Conflict, arousal, and curiosity.* New York: McGraw-Hill.

Biggs, J., & Coilis, K. (1982). *Evaluating the quality of learning. The SOLO Taxonomy.* New York: Academic Press.

Cacioppo, J., Petty, R., Feinstein, J., & Jarvis, B. (1996). Dispositional differences in cognitive motivation: The life and times of individuals varying in need for cognition. *Psychological Bulletin, 119,* 197–253.

Deci, E. (1995). *Why we do what we do: The dynamics of personal autonomy.* New York: Putnam's.

Duchastel, P. (1990). Assimilatory tools for informal learning: Prospects in ICAI. *Instructional Science, 19,* 3–9.

Duchastel, P. (1994). Learning environment design. *Journal of Educational Technology Systems, 22*(3), 225–233.

Duchastel, P. (1996). Design for Web-based learning. *Proceedings of the WebNet-96 World Conference of the Web Society,* San Francisco.

Duchastel, P. (1997). A Web-based model for university instruction. Submitted for publication (http://www.crim.ca/~pduchast/model.html).

Duchastel, P., & Turcotte, S. (1996). On-line learning and teaching in an information-rich context. *Proceedings of the Ineti96 International Conference,* Montréal, Canada.

Harasim, L., Hiltz, S., Teles, L., & Turoff, M. (1995). *Learning networks.* Cambridge, MA: MIT Press.

Keller, J. (1983). Motivational design of instruction. In C. Reigeluth (Ed.), *Instructional design theories and models: An overview of their current status.* Hillsdale, NJ: Lawrence Erlbaum Associates.

Keller, J., & Suzuki, K. (1988). Use of the ARCS motivation model in courseware design. In D. Jonassen (Ed.), *Instructional designs for microcomputer courseware.* Hillsdale, NJ: Lawrence Erlbaum Associates.

Malone, T. (1981). Toward a theory of intrinsically-motivating instruction. *Cognitive Science, 4,* 333–369.

Marton, F., Entwistle, N., & Hounsell, D. (1984). *The experience of learning.* Edinburgh: Scottish Academic Press.

Renninger, K., Hidi, S., & Krapp, A. (1992). *The role of interest in learning and development.* Hillsdale, NJ: Lawrence Erlbaum Associates.

Savery, J., & Duffy, T. (1996). Problem-based learning: An instructional model and its Constructivist framework. In B. Wilson (Ed.), *Constructivist learning environments: Case studies in instructional design.* Englewood Cliffs, NJ: Educational Technology Publications.

Schank, R., & Cleary, C. (1994). *Engines for education.* Hillsdale, NJ: Lawrence Erlbaum Associates (http://www.ils.nwu.edu/~e_for_e/index.html).

Tobias, S. (1993). *Interest and prior knowledge.* Paper presented at the annual meeting of the American Educational Research Association, Atlanta, GA.

Wilson, B. (Ed.). (1996). *Constructivist learning environments: Case studies in instructional design.* Englewood Cliffs, NJ: Educational Technology Publications.

Wlodkowski, R. (1993). *Enhancing adult motivation to learn.* San Francisco: Jossey-Bass.

About the Author

Philip Duchastel is Program Professor of Technology, Fischler Center for the Advancement of Education, Nova Southeastern University, Ft. Lauderdale, Florida.

e-mail, World Wide Web
   duchaste@fcae.nova.edu
   http://www.nova.edu/~duchaste

22

Creating Virtual Communities Via the Web

Hilary McLellan

The Internet, and especially its World Wide Web, offers tremendous resources for education. Vice President Al Gore has described the Internet as "highways of the mind." Concomitantly, the Internet offers *highways for learning*. However, a better metaphor is to think of the Internet as a gathering place for *virtual communities*, including virtual learning communities.

Virtual Learning Communities

Just as a classroom where teacher and students are physically present develops into a community, however temporary, over the course of a semester, classes taught via the Internet become virtual learning communities, communities unbounded by physical space. According to Howard Rheingold (1993), "Virtual communities are social aggregations that emerge from the Net when enough people carry on those public discussions long enough, with sufficient human feeling, to form webs of personal relationships in cyberspace" (p. 9). Rheingold further explains that, "People in virtual communities use words on screens to exchange pleasantries and argue, engage in intellectual discourse, conduct commerce, exchange knowledge, share emotional support, make plans, brainstorm, gossip, feud, fall in love, find friends and lose them, play games, flirt, create a little high art and a lot of idle talk. People in virtual communities do just about everything people do in real life, but we leave our bodies behind. You can't kiss anybody and nobody can punch you in the nose, but a lot can happen within those boundaries. To the millions who have been drawn into it, the richness and vitality of computer-linked cultures is attractive, even addictive" (p. 3).

Schrage's Model

How to create a virtual community that supports learning? Schrage (1991) offers a model that highlights the importance of collaboration. According to Schrage, the goal should be to create a *shared experience* rather than *an experience that is shared*. An experience that is shared is passive. A shared experience is one that is participatory—a conversation or a discussion, as opposed to a speech, a lecture, or a television broadcast. Schrage theorizes that electronic environments such as the Internet and groupware offer immense potential as a context for supporting collaboration. He explains, "The well-crafted collaborative environment integrates the intellectual virtues of print, the video appeal of television, and the information-manipulating powers of the personal computer. Carefully calibrated collaborative media are self-contained but able to work productively with a larger network" (p. 26).

It is essential to define collaboration, since this is the premise for the virtual learning community. Schrage offers this definition: "Collaboration is the process of shared creation: two or more individuals with complementary skills interacting to create a shared understanding that none had previously possessed or could have come to on their own. Collaboration creates a shared meaning about a process, a product, or an event. In this sense, there is nothing routine about it. Something is there that wasn't there before. Collaboration can occur by mail, over the phone lines, and in person. But the true medium of collaboration is other people" (p. 40). Furthermore, collaboration is a *purposive* relationship based on a desire or need to solve a problem, create, or discover something within a set of constraints. Schrage emphasizes that, "The issue isn't communication or teamwork, it's the creation of value" (p. 39).

Schrage presents a model of collaboration composed of thirteen design themes: (1) competence; (2) a shared, understood goal; (3) mutual respect, tolerance, and trust; (4) creation and manipulation of shared spaces; (5) multiple forms of representation; (6) playing with the representations; (7) continuous but not continual communication; (8) formal and informal environments; (9) clear lines of responsibility but no restrictive boundaries; (10) decisions do not have to be made by consensus; (11) physical presence is not necessary; (12) selective use of outsiders for complementary insights and information; and (13) collaboration's end.

Implementing Schrage's Model

Recently, I taught a graduate course on Information Design via the Internet (World Wide Web, listserv, electronic mail) that was designed on the basis of Schrage's model of collaborative communities. This course served 25 masters degree students across the western United States and Canada as part of a graduate program in Library and Information Management at Emporia State University.

The following discussion will explain how this class conformed to Schrage's model. As the class progressed, emergent activities on the part of students fortuitously reinforced the implementation of this model, testifying to its value for Internet-based education.

Competence

The course was based on competence with the technology underlying the course delivery—computers, modems, communications software. Some students possessed more experience, so they shared their expertise, raising the level of competence for all. Special effects pioneer John Dykstra, who has worked on such films as Star Wars, discusses the vital importance of collaboration in his work: "Now you're both trying to create something you *don't* know. So you get a communal mind going; you want to get people's minds to interact as components of a larger mind—one person's logical sense, one person's visual sense, another person's acoustic sense. You get a communal brain. What matters is not just the individual talents but the ability to integrate them" (quoted in Schrage, 1991, pp. 37–38). Similarly, in the Internet-based class on Information Design, all the participants, including the instructor, were attempting to create a new form of education, something unknown. Also, a communal mind developed, with people's competences proving highly complementary and synergistic.

A Shared, Understood Goal

The class and its subject matter provided the goal, which was shared by all the students: to learn about information design through a new, experimental learning process that highlighted technology skills. This goal encompassed all of the themes that Schrage identified: problem-solving, creating, discovering, and creating value.

Mutual Respect, Tolerance, and Trust

As any educator knows, this element of Schrage's model should be fundamental to all educational contexts and experiences. In practice, the teacher can set the tone, but occasionally problems can arise, often due to a single individual—someone who is not listening to others or who seems to need to know all the answers, to have the last word, creating his or her own debilitating barriers to learning while turning off and even intimidating other students. The Internet context can draw out these tendencies in a few students, more so than a face-to-face learning environment. In these instances, the teacher must continually reinforce the collaborative premise of the virtual learning community.

In some ways, the Internet context creates a level playing field for diverse students, thereby diminishing sources of intolerance and mistrust. One student in the Information Design class commented that in the Internet format, topics were "distilled down to their intellectual component, with all extraneous variables removed." These extraneous variables include race, gender, different abilities, and appearances. It is important to note that the Internet format is not a panacea, but it can filter out some "noise" factors that interfere with communication and learning.

Creation and Manipulation of Shared Spaces

In the Information Design class, the listserv provided a shared space that all could share in creating. Beyond that, students could identify the URLs for World Wide Web sites relevant to class topics and assignments, thereby providing pointers to the larger shared space of the World Wide Web itself. Some students added such URLs to their own Web pages as a resource for all the students in the class; as part of this class, each student created two Web pages, and some already had established their own Web pages.

Multiple Forms of Representation

Multiple forms of representation were central to the content of this course on Information Design, which covered the following topics: (1) Graphic Design; (2) Maps. Representing Spatial Information; (3) Scientific Visualization and Virtual Reality; (4) Verbal Information Design: Learning to Give, Take, and Use Instructions; (5) Narrative Information Design; (6) Metaphors and Symbols in Information Design; (7) Audio Information Design; and (8) Information Design in Advertising and the Entertainment Industry.

Illustrations were featured along with text on the Web page "Cyberlectures," providing multiple forms of representation. This is something that can be applied to any kind of subject matter. Additionally, it might be possible to consider links to other Web pages as an actual form of representation unto itself—representing hypertextual information structures. And certainly the Web pages featured in these links, containing text, images, and, increasingly, other components, such as audio and multimedia, support the inclusion of multiple forms of representation.

Playing with the Representations

Learning activities that feature playing with different representations can be very valuable (McLellan, 1996). Different learners may be more attuned to different types of representations, so that by implementing activities that features different representations, different learners benefit from some activities more than they do from other activities, featuring less personally relevant representations. At the same time, all learners get practice shifting between different representations, different points of view (Marks-Tarlow, 1995).

The Information Design class featured a Web page design assignment that specifically centered upon playing with representations: A map transformation assignment. The assignment was specified as follows: A map is a graphic representation of all or a part of the surface of the earth. Using the idea of a map as a point of departure, design a personal map plotting your daily route from where you live to where you work (or some other trip that you make frequently). Consider incorporating elements associated with a map such as a legend or a compass. Use any media to carry this out. Now transform this map information into words: Write the formal directions that you would give someone to get from one place to another. Now prepare another written description, this time an intuitive, personal description of this event, this journey across space.

Continuous but Not Continual Communication

Communication was continuous throughout the time span of the class. Students could log on to the listserv and the class Web pages whenever it suited their schedules. However, it was very important for students to participate in the listserv dialogue on a regular basis. One student fell behind and submitted many of her assignments near the end of the class, so that they were out of sync with the discussion that centered around each of those assignments. It is essential to establish effective communication at the beginning of the class, and even before the class gets underway, about logistics and about class requirements, expectations, and resources.

Formal and Informal Environments

In this class, the course pages implemented by the instructor on the World Wide Web acted as the formal environment. This formal space featured the syllabus, weekly "cyberlectures," assignments, references, and related resources. The course listserv served as an informal space. This perceived distinction was made clear by the fact that some students were willing to share very personal information on the listserv, but did not want this kind of information anywhere on the Web where it would be accessible to the entire world.

The listserv provided the primary "community" space. Students submitted their assignments to the listserv, together with discussions, jokes, and anecdotes. This class featured more assignments than a traditional class, specifically short assignments that were smaller in scale and relatively informal, in keeping with the listserv format. Assignments were designed to support the possibility of wide-ranging discussions, which, indeed, resulted.

In contrast to much traditional teaching, the virtual community context centered around the listserv provided greater interaction between students as well as the opportunity for students to see each other's homework and respond to it, creating a more dynamic learning experience. Students of all kinds benefit from having a broader audience for their work than just the teacher, a broader dialogue about ideas and insights.

Clear Lines of Responsibility but No Restrictive Boundaries

Clear lines of responsibility were established through the framework of the syllabus and the implementation of the class. Many of the class assignments centered around exploring resources on the World Wide Web; as a result, the boundaries of exploration were broad and unrestricted. The hypertextual structure of the World Wide Web makes it fundamentally unrestrictive, providing a valuable resource for implementing this dimension of Schrage's model.

Decisions Do Not Have to Be Made by Consensus

In an educational context such as the Information Design class, the instructor is the final arbitor in decision-making. However, it is valuable to have students take ownership of the class by helping to determine certain things, such as options for discussion topics, helping classmates determine how to solve technical problems, and ideas for carrying out assignments.

The instructor must pay close attention to student input, which can illuminate problems and needed clarifications. Some student input will deal with technical issues and with getting oriented to the class. But other student input builds upon the structure put forward by the instructor. This needs to be encouraged, supported, and put to use where it proves useful. Student expertise and ideas can be very useful in enhancing the quality of the virtual learning community.

Physical Presence Is Not Necessary

The lack of physical presence did not prove a barrier in the Information Design class. However, a Web page was established for this class that featured brief student biographies, together with photographs and e-mail addresses. This helped students to attach faces to the other participants in the virtual community of the class. In addition, students were asked to introduce themselves informally on the listserv at the beginning of the class. A photograph of the instructor was included on the class home page so that students would have a face to connect to this member of the virtual community.

Rheingold (1993) reports that, "Some people—many people—don't do well in spontaneous spoken interaction, but turn out to have valuable contributions to make in a conversation in which they have time to think about what to say. These people, who might constitute a significant proportion of the population, can find written communication more authentic than the face-to-face kind" (p. 23). Indeed, this proved to be true in the Information Design class. One student in particular who was reportedly very shy in face-to-face classes became quite loquacious in the virtual community context of the Internet-based class.

One student in the Information Design class reported afterward that he got to know students far better in this class than in person-to-person meetings that took place in on-site classes and other forums. This corresponds to Rheingold's assessment that the Internet is a place where "people often end up revealing themselves far more intimately than they would be inclined to do without the intermediation of screens and pseudonyms" (p. 27).

Related to this, Biocca (1995) has discussed the notion of "social presence"—the sense of being present in a social encounter with another person. Social presence can be achieved "virtually," at a distance, as is well demonstrated by the telephone call. The two speakers are at different physical locations, but they feel fully present with each other in the context of the conversation. Increasingly, the sense of social presence extends to virtual communities on the Internet, such as the class described here. This phenomenon of social presence on the Internet is documented in both Howard Rheingold's book *The Virtual Community* (1993) and Sherry Turkle's book, *Life on the Screen* (1995). Turkle explains, "In cyberspace, we can talk, exchange ideas, and assume personae of our own creation. We have the opportunity to build new kinds of communities, virtual communities, in which we participate with people from all over the world, people with whom we converse daily, people with whom we may have fairly intimate relationships but whom we may never physically meet" (pp. 9–10).

Selective Use of Outsiders for Complementary Insights and Information

While outsiders were not utilized directly in the Information Design class, outside information came from the textbooks and the wealth of resources available on the Internet, in particular the World Wide Web. Instructors need to adapt their teaching to include the Web resources—and other Internet resources —as a supplement to textbooks. This proved to be an extremely valuable dimension of the Information Design class.

It would be very easy to get input from outsiders in an Internet-based class via electronic mail, and increasingly, Web-based video featuring desktop video software like CU-SeeMe, increasingly powerful and versatile Web browsers, digital cameras, and other technologies.

Collaboration's End

The class ended with the end of the semester. The temporary virtual community dissolved. But at the same time, lasting bonds were established, expanding and strengthening the wider community of library and media specialists. One student who traveled to another city to attend a weekend intensive class reported that students at that location who had been classmates in the Information Design class implemented via the Internet were very hospitable, inviting her to stay at their homes and to go out to dinner with them.

Conclusion

This chapter has described an Internet-based class that was based around a model of a collaborative virtual community. Michael Schrage proposes that "Language isn't just a medium of communication, it's a tool for collaboration," and indeed, that is true. The Internet itself is a powerful tool for both communication and collaboration. Its full potential remains to be tapped. Science fiction writer William Gibson (1996), who coined the term "cyberspace," recently mused, "I imagine that the World Wide Web and its modest wonders are no more than the test pattern for whatever the 21st century will regard as its equivalent medium." The Information Design class discussed here was surely that—a test pattern for future Internet-based education. As such, it provides some useful guideposts for better models down the cyberspace highway.

References

Biocca, F. (1995, May). *Presence*. Presentation presented for a workshop on Cognitive Issues in Virtual Reality, VR '95 Conference and Expo, San Jose, CA.

Burke, G., & McLellan, H. (1996). The Algebra Project: Situated learning inspired by the Civil Rights movement. In H. McLellan (Ed.), *Situated learning perspectives* (pp. 263–278). Englewood Cliffs, NJ: Educational Technology Publications.

Gibson, W. (1996, July 14). The Net is a waste of time: And that's exactly what's right about it. *New York Times Magazine*, 30–31.

Marks-Tarlow, T. (1995). *Creativity inside out: Learning through multiple intelligences*. Reading, MA: Addison-Wesley.

McLellan, H. (1996). 'Being digital': Implications for education. *Educational Technology, 36*(6), 5–20.

Moses, R. P., Kamii, M., Swap, S. M., & Howard, J. (1989). The Algebra Project: Organizing in the spirit of Ella. *Harvard Educational Review, 59*(4), 423–443.

Rheingold, H. (1993). *The virtual community*. Reading, MA: Addison-Wesley

Schrage, M. (1991). *Shared minds: The new technologies of collaboration*. New York: Random House.

Turkle, S. (1995). *Life on the screen*. New York: Simon & Schuster.

Wilde, J., & Wilde, R. (1991). *Visual literacy: A conceptual approach to graphic problem solving*. New York: Watson-Guptill Publications.

The Author

Hilary McLellan is a partner in McLellan Wyatt Digital, Emporia, Kansas.

e-mail, World Wide Web
   71643.2064@compuserve.com
   http://tech-head.com

23

Web-Based Learning Activities for Children

Steve Hackbarth

The World Wide Web has emerged rapidly to become the premier electronic medium. Its attributes match those of print, audio, video, and computer, but with the addition of vast scope (content and geography). This scope enhances communications, information retrieval, and sharing, and consequently appeal. In K–12 classrooms having reliable access to the Web, teachers may consider it as a viable option among other readily available media. The primary purpose of this chapter is to describe the sorts of activities that may effectively exploit attributes of the Web.

Evolution of Mediated Instruction

Much effort has been expended throughout this past century to produce instructional materials and programs that incorporate sound pedagogy. "Basal readers" have been designed to teach children in a systematic manner with increasingly complex grammar and vocabulary. Math and science series of textbooks have been developed across the grades to ensure that students learn essential concepts and methods as needed to advance toward the mind set of experts. Teacher guides, templates, and related materials have ensured effective and efficient delivery of well-integrated curriculums.

Advances in computer-based learning (CBL) programs these past few decades have also been marked by efforts to help students progress through largely state-mandated spiral curriculums. Thus, we teachers may select programs suitable for virtually every student in every subject. Categories of programs range from tutorial and simulation to reference and practice. Integrated learning systems (ILSs) provide assessment, guidance, instruction, and evaluation. Application programs—word processing, database management, spreadsheet, graphics, draw and paint, multimedia—promote creative analyses of information and syntheses of knowledge (Hackbarth, 1996b; Jonassen, 1996).

Current content, clear exposition, and logical organization have been hallmarks of good instructional programs, whether mediated by text or teacher. Published materials that have failed to meet these and other stringent criteria generally have not survived state selection committees.

Usher in the New Age. Trade book publishers, bolstered by constructivists, have been successful in discrediting basal readers and in stimulating demand for "quality literature" with "authentic language" and "real life" content (mirroring the worst and best of children's TV).

Textbooks, videos, computerized instructional programs, integrated learning systems, and everything else that smacks of "systematic direct instruction" has been attacked as being in violation of students' integrity and constructivists' assumptions about learning (Duffy & Jonassen, 1992; Wilson, 1996).

How opportune that the World Wide Web has dawned just in time to serve constructivist as well as more traditional ideals. Though driven heavily by commercial interests that used to make educators wince, the Web appears to have been welcomed into schools with less resistance than that experienced by Whittle Communications' Channel One, with its offer of free video equipment in exchange for airing 10 minutes of ads per hour. PBS executive Hall Davidson (1996) observed that "If a toy were being sold with the same veracity as the Web is sanguinely portrayed in the media, there would be people in jail by morning" (p. 22).

Nevertheless, amid national and regional mandates for schools to "get wired," and generous corporate and government offers of "seed money," teachers of every philosophical persuasion are being urged (pushed) to adapt their curriculums to incorporate Web-based learning activities. Davidson (1996) challenged us to acknowledge that: "It will take time for the young millionaires of the Net to bankroll instructional methodology for their new medium. . . . With no cyber version of PBS to balance the merchants, we as Ednetizens will just have to do it ourselves" (p. 22). Following are hints as to how we may proceed.

Definitions

Que's Computer User's Dictionary (Pfaffenberger, 1993) defines a "network" as: "A computer-based communications and data exchange system created by physically connecting two or more computers" (p. 419). *Que's* definition of "local area network" (LAN) is: "The linkage of personal and other computers within a limited area by high-performance cables so that users can exchange information, share expensive peripherals, and draw on the resources of a massive secondary storage unit, called a *file server*" (p. 359). A "wide area network" (WAN) "uses high-speed, long-distance communications networks or satellites to connect computers over distances greater than the distances—one or two miles—traversed by local area networks" (p. 655). So then, what are the Internet and its World Wide Web?

The "Internet" is defined as: "A system of linked computer networks, worldwide in scope, that facilitates data communication services such as remote login, file transfer, electronic mail, and distributed newsgroups" (Pfaffenberger, 1993, p. 330). *The Random House Personal Computer Dictionary* (Margolis, 1996) defines the World Wide Web quite simply as: "A system of Internet servers that support specially formatted documents . . . in a language called *HTML (HyperText Markup Language)* that supports links to other documents, as well as graphics, audio, and video files" (p. 523).

Laurie Quinlan (in press) provides us with a more colorful description:

> Picture the ever-changing patterns of a kaleidoscope and the childlike fascination with the shifting motifs. When all the parts are put together just right, the toy becomes a window into a magical world. The relatively simple device reveals colorful images of diamonds, snowflakes, and fireworks. Like the kaleidoscope, the World Wide Web reflects the ever-changing views of society. The vast array of words and images fascinates users of all ages. Yet within the simplicity of its use is a complexity of implications, especially for the classroom teacher.

No wonder that when I asked my fourth grade students to write about what sorts of activities they would like to do with computers this coming year, as many listed "accessing the Internet" as "playing games." So what are the attributes of this new medium that might be contributing to its headline-making popularity and to claims that it can transform schooling?

Attributes of the Web

Does the World Wide Web have distinctive (beyond teachers and multimedia CD-ROMs, for examples) attributes ("affordances") that permit design of uniquely superior learning activities? In *The Educational Media and Technology Yearbook 1997* (Hackbarth, in press-c), I suggest that the Web appears to be distinctive in the following five respects.

- It provides economical access to people and multiformat information in ways unmatched by any other combinations of media.

- Much content on the Web cannot be found in any other format, except the authors' originals.

- The Web permits the work of individuals, such as teachers and students, to be shared with the world.

- It is a powerful, flexible resource, in some ways (e.g., global hypermedia links) unlike any others, that students are likely to encounter and rely on in the workplace.

- Students approach the Web with eager anticipation and awe, knowing that it is at the cutting edge of technology used by their most progressive peers and by successful adults.

Greg Kearsley (1996) elaborated on attributes of the Web as follows:

> The most significant aspect of the Web for education at all levels is that it dissolves the artificial wall between the classroom and the "real world." . . . With the Web . . . students can find original materials and collect first-hand information themselves. . . . The second powerful aspect . . . is that it provides an easy mechanism for students (and teachers) to make their work public . . . . Furthermore, students can examine the work of others . . . , [which] allows for global comparisons, collaborations and competition. . . . A third aspect . . . is that it provides an easy way to create and distribute multimedia materials. . . . Finally, . . . students . . . can include links to the source material in their work . . . . [And they can] include input fields in a Web document [to] collect data or comments from everyone who visits. (pp. 28–29)

The above few core attributes alone are sufficient to open up possibilities for the systemic, systematic design, development, and conduct of productive learning activities not previously feasible, many perhaps not even possible. As WBL advances, we may expect to see sites where teachers hold online "live" office hours and provide 3D, stereo, "face-to-face" (videoconferencing) homework help (Todd, 1996). The technology has arrived; only teacher incentives and reliable, equitable access lag far behind. Thus, WBL can incorporate the best senses of "interactivity" long associated with good CBL, and may expand to include some of those "real-time," if not "proximal-space," inter-human senses that are so much a part of quality education.

Systematic Design of WBL Activities

The Web is a rich repository of information as well as a flexible medium of communication. Reference to instructional design models reveals considerations that typically precede selection of media (Braden, 1996; Dick & Carey, 1996; Dills & Romiszowski, 1997; Hackbarth, in press-b; Kemp, Morrison, & Ross, 1994; Reiser & Dick, 1996; Romiszowski, 1993; Salisbury, 1996). Elsewhere, I outlined the following (5 phase, 18 step) ID model in a linear format, relying on text (1996b, pp. 20–27) and a graphic (in press and below) to express its space/time lived dynamics.

Phase I. **DIAGNOSE**
>
> Step 1. Figure out what students need to know.
> Step 2. Assess what they already know. (See Figure 1.)

Phase II. **DESIGN**
>
> Step 3. Design tests of learning achievement.
> Step 4. Identify effective instructional strategies.
> Step 5. Select suitable media.
> Step 6. Sequence learning activities within the program.
> Step 7. Plan introductory activities.
> Step 8. Plan follow-up activities.

Phase III. **PROCURE**
>
> Step 9. Secure materials at hand.
> Step 10. Obtain new materials.

Phase IV. **PRODUCE**
>
> Step 11. Modify existing materials.
> Step 12. Craft new materials.

Phase V. **REFINE**
>
> Step 13. Conduct small-scale test of program.
> Step 14. Evaluate procedures and achievements.
> Step 15. Revise program accordingly.
> Step 16. Conduct classroom test of program.
> Step 17. Evaluate procedures and achievements.
> Step 18. Revise in anticipation of next school term.

Although the above has a linear structure, later steps surely inform earlier ones. Thus, at any point we may have to "take a few steps back" to revise our assessments, tests, procedures, materials, and yes, even our objectives. With respect to the process of designing programs that incorporate WBL activities, not utterly unlike designing programs that employ other media, the necessities for flexibility, creativity, reflective thinking, and end user (teacher/student) involvement remain essential. I stand by my Alex Romiszowski-inspired conclusions of over a decade ago (1986):

> Instructional systems design does not provide easy answers to complex questions about the value-laden enterprise of education in "developed" nations, nor does it do so in the rural villages of those less fortunate. Its prime virtues are that it makes explicit how to go about identifying genuine problems wherever encountered, and details how to proceed towards their amelioration based on the best information and resources available. Again, it is not a recipe and can never replace critical judgement or creativity. An ISD procedure that incorporates the elements of systematic planning and local self determination best ensures that the resulting programs will provide lasting benefits to the people of all nations. (p. 37)

From the graphical representation of my zig-zag (phenomenological, stream of action/consciousness) "2D2PR" model (see Figure 2), it can be seen that this essentially linear process includes ongoing evaluation and reflection, and revision within earlier phases as illuminated by progress in later phases. Thus, at any point we may decide to reconceive objectives and priorities, abort a project in favor of a more promising solution, or implement an alternative.

The Computer Literacy Assessment Tool

Name _____ M F _____ Class _____ Date _____

A. How do you feel about books? Please circle one.

I hate them.　　I don't like them.　　I don't care.　　I like them.　　I love them.

B. How do you feel about television programs? Please circle one.

I hate them.　　I don't like them.　　I don't care.　　I like them.　　I love them.

C. How do you feel about computers? Please circle one.

I hate them.　　I don't like them.　　I don't care.　　I like them.　　I love them.

D. How skillful are you in the use of computers? Please circle one.

No skill　　Little skill　　Medium skill　　Much skill　　Expert

E. Please describe your access to computers.

I have no access to computers at home. _____

I have access to the following computer(s) at home. _____

F. For what purposes do you use computers (at home and at school)?

1.	5.
2.	6.
3.	7.
4.	8.

G. Please list some things that computers help us (children and adults) to do.

1.	5.	9.
2.	6.	10.
3.	7.	11
4.	8.	12

H. Please write all the words you know that have to do with computers.

1.	11.	21.
2.	12.	22.
3.	13.	23.
4.	14.	24.
5.	15.	25.
6.	16.	26.
7.	17.	27.
8.	18.	28.
9.	19.	29.
10.	20.	30.

I. Please write on the back of this form what you would like to do with computers this year.

Figure 1. During the first week of class, I administer the above timed *Computer Literacy Assessment Tool* to my upper elementary school children (three minutes for each section F–H). Thus, I get a quick glimpse both at what they know already and at what they want to learn about computers. A second administration at the end of the year provides information about changes in attitudes and gains in knowledge.

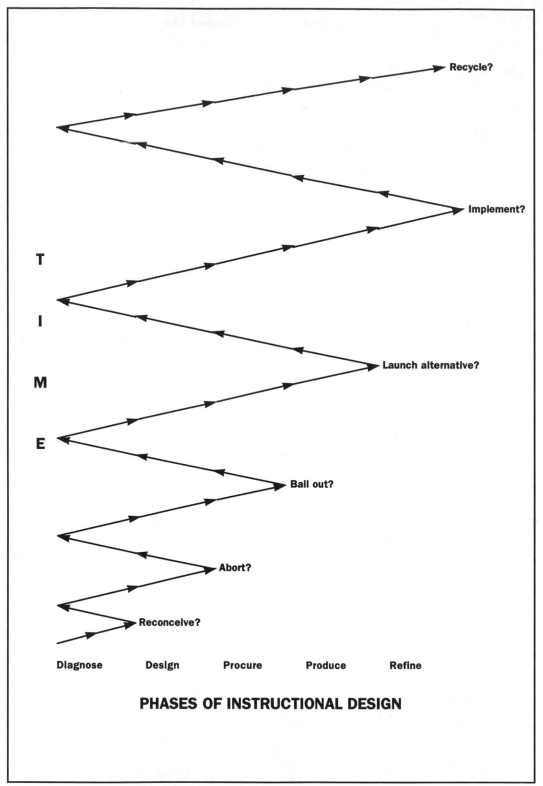

Figure 2. A zig-zag model of instructional design.

Ongoing evaluation and revision are implied from the phenomenological perspective I have adopted here, because that is the nature of mature, reflective human consciousness (though we all benefit from having good training and tools, and by being reminded to be more careful and thorough). And though we may tend to select fruitless pursuits grounded in bias and error, the harsh realities of time constraints, finances, and accountability serve well to nudge us to make adjustments or seek alternative routes more responsive to the evolving landscape of education.

Addressing challenges of constructivist thinking, with its calls for a new "hypermedia design model" based on "cognitive flexibility theory," Thomas Fox McManus (1996) concluded that these significant insights deal "mostly with the pursuit of intermediate and expert knowledge in complex and ill-structured learning domains. If [the] learning domain is simple or well-structured, [we] might want to consider using a more traditional ISD model." Katherine Cennamo, Sandra Abell, and Mi-Lee Chung (1996) observed that in the design of materials in accord with constructivist thinking generally, in the design of (whether the knowledge domain is simple or complex):

> instructional designers should be guided by, but not limited to, the decisions required by traditional instructional design models. With a knowledge of the questions inherent in each stage of traditional instructional design models, designers can examine the data that evolve through the construction of instructional materials, and make decisions in collaboration with the client, based on shared assumptions about the content and teaching/learning process. (p. 47).

Again, models of instructional design surely should allow for the possibility that solutions to problems inherent in teaching and learning are not always instructional in nature, Web-based or otherwise. For example, it now is commonly recognized that achievement is best ensured within a climate of high expectations, where rules of conduct are consistently enforced, and where parents are encouraged to take active roles (Shanker, 1995).

Varieties of WBL Activities

As we plan our instruction, selecting suitable media based largely on contextual considerations that include educational aims, student characteristics, pedagogical strategies, and budget, we envision the sorts of activities that might effectively exploit attributes of the Web. Elsewhere (in press-c), I describe three closely interrelated categories of Web-based learning activities—communications, informational retrieval, and information sharing. Varieties of computer-based instruction (e.g., tutorial, simulation) are covered in Hackbarth, 1996b. Here I introduce Judi Harris's classification scheme for online "activity structures" (1995a, b, c, d, e, f; 1995–96; http://mac246.ed.uiuc.edu/activity-structures).

Interpersonal Exchanges are Harris's first of three general groupings of "educational telecomputing activities." Examples she describes fall into subcategories of keypals, global classrooms, electronic appearances, electronic mentoring, question-and-answer services, and impersonations (1995c).

- Keypals. These activities include informal e-mail correspondence over an extended period of time as well as participation in discussion groups (listservs, newsgroups, bulletin boards, forums) and Internet Relay Chat (IRC).

- Global classrooms. Here students in one class correspond as a group with students in another about a topic of mutual interest.

- Electronic appearances. Special guests may be invited to post responses to students' queries on listservs or newsgroups, or may engage in a brief exchange of e-mail.

- Electronic mentoring. Students explore topics of interest by corresponding via e-mail with volunteers having greater expertise, whether a professional or merely a more advanced student.

- Question-and-answer services. Various educational institutions, governmental agencies, professional organizations, and commercial enterprises respond to questions posed by students.

- Impersonations. Subject matter experts pose as historical figures, well-known authors, world leaders, scientists, etc., and respond to students' inquiries accordingly.

Information Collections are Harris's second genre of online activities. These include information exchanges, database creation, electronic publishing, tele-fieldtrips, and pooled data analyses (1995b).

- Information exchanges. Book reviews, weather conditions, nature observations, etc., are shared among students and teachers via e-mail and Web pages.

- Database creation. Data are collected from a variety of participants and organized into databases for further study.

- Electronic publishing. Related articles are collected, edited, and placed on an Internet Gopher or Web server.

- Tele-fieldtrips. Missed the boat? No problem. Let the travelers know what you're interested in via e-mail, then watch a Web site for their reports.

- Pooled data analyses. Data collected from several sources are combined and then examined to find patterns and trends.

Problem-Solving Projects round out Harris's classification scheme. Examples are: information searches, parallel problem-solving, electronic process writing, serial creations, simulations, and social action projects (1995a).

- Information searches. Students are presented with, or may pose, problems to solve, and are given a variety of sources to explore, including online.

- Electronic process writing. Students post their essays and poems online and receive suggestions from others, including published authors.

- Sequential creations. Here, students draft a document (perhaps multimedia) and challenge another school to elaborate. The process may be cycled around the globe.

- Parallel problem-solving. Students at several sites work independently and then share their methods and findings.

- Virtual gatherings. Students and teachers from around the globe engage in Internet Relay Chat (IRC), or an e-mail—arranged simultaneous gathering "in spirit," at a set time, usually to discuss a set topic.

- Simulations. Students collaborate online in recreating historical events, designing environments, and manipulating variables within hypothetical economic, political, and ecological systems.

- Social action projects. Participants stage global telethons to raise money for worthwhile causes.

Judi Harris has collected detailed descriptions of "Sample Curriculum-Based K–12 Educational Telecomputing Projects" and has made them available (http://www.ed.uiuc.edu/Activity-Structures/web-activity-structures.html).

The above projects can be made responsive both to traditional views of direct instruction and to constructivists' challenges to focus more attention on the design of open-ended learning environments, those for which objectives are less readily prespecified and measured. Thomas Duffy and Anne Bednar (1992) characterized the latter as:

> rich contexts, authentic tasks, collaboration for the development and evaluation of multiple perspectives, and abundance of tools to enhance communication and access to real-world examples and problems, reflective thinking, modeling of problem solving by experts in the content domain, and apprenticeship mentoring relationships to guide learning. (p. 132)

My own vital concern for the *integration* of cognitive and affective dimensions of learning across the entire academic curriculum has led me to write in terms of "impassioned scholarly apprenticeship," contrasted with a mere "cognitive apprenticeship" that could be interpreted as being detached from the emotions or "objective" in its methods and conclusions. In an update of my doctoral studies (1996a), I concluded that:

> Special steps must be taken if students are successfully to investigate the world as embodied in the curriculum in the same spirit as they spontaneously expand the horizons of their daily lives. Engagement of students in the reflective investigation of particular phenomena by means of discipline-based methods might serve to foster this spirit of adventure. Teachers wishing to participate with their students in such inquiry . . . could:
>
> - Meditate upon the nature of knowledge, how it evolves, and of what value it is to learn.
> - Study the methods actually used to gain new knowledge and the criteria by which evidence and claims to truth are assessed in each subject area.
> - Design, implement, assess, and revise inquiry activities that their students are capable of engaging in fruitfully.
> - Encourage students' creative expression in the pursuit of personally significant knowledge that enhances efficacy within their daily lives.
> - Model the quest for knowledge in the service of humanity. (pp. 38–39)

Active engagement of students in scholarly apprenticeships that draw upon human, print, Web, and other resources may serve well to impart valuable insights into the nature of knowing, per se, and thus may serve as good preparation for those who ultimately contribute to the advance of knowledge.

Conduct of WBL Activities

How might WBL activities best be conducted? Again, not unlike most other activities, these may fit into four phases—prepare, perform, follow-up, and evaluate (Hackbarth, 1996b, p. 36):

Phase I. **PREPARE**

        Step 1. Review course components.
        Step 2. Practice presentation.
        Step 3. Procure equipment and materials.
        Step 4. Prepare facilities and personnel.

Phase II. **PERFORM**
>   Step 5. Provide orientation.
>   Step 6. Present lesson.
>   Step 7. Elicit responses.
>   Step 8. Provide feedback.

Phase III. **FOLLOW-UP**
>   Step 9. Review and refine.
>   Step 10. Expand on achievement.

Phase IV. **EVALUATE**
>   Step 11. Assess achievements.
>   Step 12. Assess program.

Of course, we must adapt such systematic procedures to suit our contexts, which in some respects are unique. For example, K–12 classroom instruction differs in many respects from adult distance education. However, the phases outlined above generally hold across students differing widely in age and motivations, and across subjects.

Ann Caputo (1994) provided the following summary list of recommendations for school use of online services.

- Use communications technology only to solve real problems, to help you to teach better and your students to learn more. Don't "jump on the electronic bandwagon just for the sake of the ride."

- For students below the fifth grade level, CD-ROM databases generally are more appropriate than online.

- Involve students and teachers in selection of services rather than imposing them from above.

- Sequence introduction of new technology so as not to overwhelm students. Start with realistic goals and expand on these as you and your students gain competence.

- Have student mentors serve as "search buddies" to those unfamiliar with efficient strategies for productively exploring online databases.

- Impress upon students the value of carefully planning their search strategies in advance.

- Encourage students to explore beyond standard sources that could just as well be obtained in local libraries.

- Challenge students to draw upon online services to answer questions and solve problems that concern them personally.

- Foster a spirit of collaboration among teachers, librarians, students, and administrators in making the best use of online services.

To this I would add notes of caution about picking up dangerous "keypals," disclosing your password, having your computer "infected" by "viruses," encountering foul language, observing pornographic visuals, and becoming victims of "cyberscams" (Mather, 1996; Ross & Bailey, 1996).

Evaluating Students' Achievements

Evaluation of what students learn has both process and product components. We administer tests primarily to determine how well students achieved the objectives set for, and with, them. We draw also upon conferences, direct observations of behavior, and portfolios. We note if students learned something of value not anticipated in the objectives, if they enjoyed the experience, and if they felt challenged to explore further on their own. We ask them to discuss with us and write in journals about the quality of our teaching and the value they perceive in what they have learned. Portfolios include both drafts and final products. For each piece, students express why they selected it and how they feel about it. Our own criteria for assessing the quality of work is made explicit, both in written form and in our conversations with students and their parents. We appreciate fully the fact that:

> Much of what we hope students will learn, and much of what they actually do learn, cannot. . . easily be anticipated. . . . [And we] don't let the existence of neatly written outcome objectives blind [us] to the importance of what students get out of the process, per se. Discovering the values of sharing and working collaboratively or experiencing the benefits of engaging in conflict resolution may well overshadow the significance of absorbing prescribed subject matter. (Hackbarth, 1996b, p. 21)

More explicit criteria for evaluating learning outcomes have been provided by David Jonassen (1996). Though he specified that these be applied primarily to products of "using a computer application program ['mindtool'] to engage learners in constructive, higher-order, critical thinking about the subjects they are studying" (p. iv), they may serve just as well in the context of WBL generally.

- **originality**—Do the products represent the student's original thoughts, or are they copied from sources or other students?

- **complexity**—How many ideas are represented, and are those ideas richly interconnected? How useful would that knowledge be in solving problems?

- **coherence**—Are the relationships that are expressed in the product meaningful and appropriate, and are they consistently used?

- **inference**—Are the students able to make hypotheses and conjectures based on the information in their products?

- **predictability**—Are the students able to solve the kinds of problems faced by citizens, consumers, and professionals in the field?

- **contextual relevance**—Do the learners' responses reflect representations of the contexts encountered in a field of study or in the real "tests" of life?

- **resource/tool use**—Do the students make effective use of the resources and tools that were made available during the activity and those commonly available in the real world?

- **repertoire of knowledge**—Did the students' responses call on a repertoire of knowledge and judgment in different forms, that is, a mix of declarative, structural, and procedural knowledge? (pp. 282–283)

Jonassen rightly added that: "The purpose of evaluation is to make a value judgment about students' performance, and that is something that can [should] never be completely objectified" (p. 283). The judged quality of that performance reflects as much on the teacher, curriculum, and context as it does on the students.

Summary and Conclusions

Maria Cornish and Brian Monahan (1996) summed up nicely the range of Internet-based learning activities:

> Educational professionals, elementary students, and parents all have an opportunity to gather information. Teachers can exchange lesson plans and information, participate in educational discussions, and consult researchers. Students can participate in interactive projects and improve their writing skills by communicating with students around the world. Parents are able to keep in close contact with the school and exchange information with one another via e-mail. They could also get assistance from specialists when available. (p. 56)

Odvard Egil Dyrli and Daniel Kinnaman (1996a) dilated enthusiastically on advantages of computer-based telecommunications to bring "immediacy and individualization to the school curriculum." In their own well-chosen words:

> Teachers and students can individualize learning according to their needs and interests by selecting from a host of online educational experiences such as keypals and electronic field trips. Teachers can also find up-to-date materials including articles, reports, surveys, databases, maps, diagrams, photographs, film clips, and sound bites—and bring them to the classroom at the very time they are needed. Users can connect to world-wide events as they are happening, communicate instantaneously with people on every continent, participate in cooperative online projects, and explore content themes interactively in an infinite variety of sequences. (p. 65)

Today's students and teachers have access to vast resources. Classrooms are filled with books, audiotapes, and videos. Nearby libraries and computer labs offer more opportunities for learning. The virtues of Web-based learning activities need to be assessed in relation to what they offer more effectively and efficiently than more traditional ones. Educators need to reflect on the merits and costs of e-mail versus snail mail and telephone, online browsing versus opening a book or viewing a video, singing and dancing versus sitting, hands-on experiences versus simulated ones. Much random exploration of online services can be justified in terms of students gaining familiarity with an exciting and empowering medium. However, time spent online needs to be made at least as productive in achieving aims of education as activities it displaces.

Two decades ago, in an assessment of the scope and promise of the then highly touted programmed instruction, George Kneller and I (1977) observed that:

> If the material base of our civilization is to be maintained and improved, a good deal of . . . knowledge must be transferred from generation to generation. Much may be transmitted by technological means . . . . But the moral and intellectual heritage of our civilization consists in large part of inexact knowledge, values, and works of art and thought. Such content is learned better through the active inquiry of the student, guided and encouraged by his [or her] teacher. . . , [because] education [in its richest sense is] a meeting of persons, in which the teacher personalizes knowledge, bringing it to life in his [or her] own way, and the student appropriates knowledge [from many sources], using it so that it both reflects and contributes to the growth of his [or her] own personality [as well as intellect and character]. (p. 186)

Surely, WBL activities can be crafted in such ways as to be integrated effectively into more human relation centered, inquiry-based, and open-ended curriculums that are responsive to the many challenges facing teachers today.

References and Related Readings

Armstrong, S. (1995). *Telecommunications in the classroom* (2nd ed.). Eugene, OR: International Society for Technology in Education.

Aronson, L. (1995). *HTML3 manual of style*. New York: Macmillan Computer Publishing.

Benson, A. C., & Fodemski, L. (1996). *Connecting kids and the Internet: A handbook for librarians, teachers, and parents*. New York: Neal-Schuman Publishers.

Berge, Z. L., & Collins, M. P. (Eds.). (1995). *Computer-mediated communication and the online classroom* (Vols. 1–3). Cresskill, NJ: Hampton Press.

Berge, Z. L., & Collins, M. P. (Eds.). (1996). *Wired together: The online k–12 classroom* (Vols. 1–4). Cresskill, NJ: Hampton Press.

Boe, T., Graubart, C., & Cappo, M. (1995). *World desk: A student handbook to Gopher and the World Wide Web*. Santa Cruz, CA: Learning in Motion.

Braden, R. (1996). The case for linear instructional design and development: A commentary on models, challenges, and myths. *Educational Technology, 36*(2), 5–23.

Burbules, N. C., & Callister Jr., T. A. (1996). Knowledge at the crossroads: Some alternative futures of hypertext learning environments. *Educational Theory, 46*(1), 23–50.

Burke, J. (1996). *Learning the Internet: A workbook for beginners*. New York: Neal-Schuman Publishers (also available is a *Powerpoint* "slide show disk").

Campbell, D., & Campbell, M. (1995). *The student's guide to doing research on the Internet*. Reading, MA: Addison-Wesley.

Caputo, A. (1994). Seven secrets of searching: How and when to choose online. *MultiMedia Schools, 1*(1), 29–33.

Cennamo, K. S., Abell, S. K., & Chung, M. (1996). A "layers of negotiation" model for designing Constructivist learning materials. *Educational Technology, 36*(4), 39–54.

Clark, D. (1995). *The student's guide to the Internet*. Indianapolis: Alpha Books.

Cornish, M., & Monahan, B. (1996). A network primer for educators. *Educational Technology, 36*(2), 55–57.

Cotton, E. G. (1996). *The online classroom: Teaching with the Internet*. Syracuse, NY: ERIC/EdInfo Press.

Crawford, L. (1995). Kids in cyberspace: A smart, safe guide to online services. *The Computing Teacher, 22*(6), 12–14.

Cuban, L. (1995). Déjà vu all over again? *Electronic Learning, 15*(2), 34–37, 61.

Cummins, J., & Sayers, D. (1995). *Brave new schools: Challenging cultural literacy through global learning networks*. New York: St. Martin's Press.

Davidson, H. (1996). Casting the Web. *Technology & Learning, 16*(6), 22.

Descy, D. E. (1995). Making a World-Wide Web page. *Tech Trends, 40*(5), 9–11.

Descy, D. E. (1996a). Evaluating Internet resources. *Tech Trends, 41*(4), 3–5.

Descy, D. E. (1996b). NCSA Mosaic, Netscape, and Java/HotJava!! *Tech Trends, 41*(1), 6–8.

Descy, D. E. (in press). The Internet and education: Privacy and pitfalls. *Educational Technology*.

Dick, W., & Carey, L. M. (1996). *The systematic design of instruction* (4th ed.). New York: HarperCollins.

Dills, C., & Romiszowski, A. J. (Eds.). (1997). *Instructional development paradigms*. Englewood Cliffs, NJ: Educational Technology Publications.

Duffy, T. M., & Bednar, A. K. (1992). Attempting to come to grips with alternative perspectives. In T. M. Duffy & D. H. Jonassen (Eds.), *Constructivism and the technology of instruction: A conversation* (pp. 129–135). Hillsdale, NJ: Lawrence Erlbaum Associates.

Duffy, T. M, & Jonassen, D. H. (Eds.). (1992). *Constructivism and the technology of instruction: A conversation*. Hillsdale, NJ: Lawrence Erlbaum Associates.

Dyrli, O. E. (1995). Personalizing politics. *Technology & Learning, 16*(3), 10.

Dyrli, O. E., & Kinnaman, D. E. (1995). Connecting classrooms: School is more than a place. *Technology & Learning, 15*(8), 82–88.

Dyrli, O. E., & Kinnaman, D. E. (1996a). Part 2: Energizing the classroom curriculum through telecommunications. *Technology & Learning, 16*(4), 65–70.

Dyrli, O. E., & Kinnaman, D. E. (1996b). Part 3: Teaching effectively with telecommunications. *Technology & Learning, 16*(5), 57–62.

Dyrli, O. E., & Kinnaman, D. E. (1996c). Part 4: Connecting with the world through successful telecommunications projects. *Technology & Learning, 16*(6), 57–62.

Dyrli, O. E., & Kinnaman, D. E. (1996d). Part 5: The changing face of telecommunications: What's next for schools? *Technology & Learning, 16*(7), 56–61.

Elliot, G. J., Jones, E., Cooke, A., & Baker, P. (1995). Making sense: A review of hypermedia in higher education. In H. Maurer (Ed.), *Educational multimedia and hypermedia, 1995: Proceedings of ED-MEDIA 95*. Charlottesville, VA: Association for the Advancement of Computing in Education.

Ellsworth, J. H. (1994). *Education on the Internet: A hands-on book of ideas, resources, projects, and advice*. Indianapolis: Sams Publishing.

Fetterman, D. M. (1996). Videoconferencing online: Enhancing communication over the Internet. *Educational Researcher, 25*(4), 23–27.

Frazier, D., with Kurshan, B., & Armstrong, S. (1995). *Internet for kids*. Alameda, CA: SYBEX.

Frazier, G., & Frazier, D. (1994). *Telecommunications and education: Surfing and the art of change*. Alexandra, VA: National School Boards Association.

Gardner, D. C., Beatty, G. J., & Sauer, D. (1995). *Internet for Windows: America Online edition*. Rocklin, CA: Prima Publishing.

Giagnocavo, G., McLain, T., & DiStefano, V. (1995). *Educator's Internet companion—Classroom Connect's complete guide to educational resources on the Internet*. Lancaster, PA: Wentworth Worldwide Media.

Hackbarth, S. (1986). Instructional systems design: An appropriate technology for developing nations. *Programmed Learning & Educational Technology, 22*, 35–38.

Hackbarth, S. (1996a). Confluent education: An analysis from the perspective of Merleau-Ponty's philosophy. In J. H. Brown (Ed.), *Confluence in education: Integrating consciousness for human change* (pp. 17–42). Greenwich, CT: JAI Press.

Hackbarth, S. (1996b). *The educational technology handbook: A comprehensive guide—Process and products for learning*. Englewood Cliffs, NJ: Educational Technology Publications.

Hackbarth, S. (in press-a). Exploiting educational features of commercial online services. In Z. L. Berge, & M. P. Collins (Eds.), *Wired together: Computer-mediated communication in K–12. Volume 1: Perspectives and instructional design*. Cresskill, NJ: Hampton Press.

Hackbarth, S. (in press-b). Logos, chaos, and legos: Multiple perspectives on modular design. *Educational Technology*.

Hackbarth, S. (in press-c). Web-based learning in the context of K–12 schooling. In R. C. Branch & B. B. Minor (Eds.), *The educational media and technology yearbook 1997*. Englewood, CO: Libraries Unlimited.

Halliday, C. M. (1995). *The trail guide to Prodigy: A rapid-reading reference to using and cruising the Prodigy online service.* Reading, MA: Addison-Wesley.

Harmon, C. (1996). *Using the Internet, online services, & CD-ROMs for writing research and term papers.* New York: Neal-Schuman Publishers.

Harris, J. (1995a). Educational telecomputing activities: Problem-solving projects. *Learning and Leading with Technology, 22*(8), 59–63.

Harris, J. (1995b). Educational telecomputing projects: Information collections. *Learning and Leading with Technology, 22*(7), 44–48.

Harris, J. (1995c). Educational telecomputing projects: Interpersonal exchanges. *Learning and Leading with Technology, 22*(6), 60–64.

Harris, J. (1995d). Knowledge-making in the information age: Beyond information access. *Learning and Leading with Technology, 23*(2), 57–60.

Harris, J. (1995e). Organizing and facilitating telecollaborative projects. *Learning and Leading with Technology, 22*(5), 66–69.

Harris, J. (1995f). *Way of the ferret: Finding and using educational resources on the Internet*, 2nd ed. Eugene, OR: International Society for Technology in Education.

Harris, J. (1995–96). Telehunting, telegathering, teleharvesting. *Learning and Leading with Technology, 23*(4), 36–39.

Heide, A., & Stilborne, L. (1996). *The teacher's complete & easy guide to the Internet.* Buffalo, NY: Trifolium Books.

Heinich, R., Molenda, M., Russell, J., & Smaldino, S. (1996). *Instructional media and technologies for learning* (5th ed.). Englewood Cliffs, NJ: Prentice-Hall.

Hill, J., & Buerger, B. (1996). Hypermedia as a bridge between education and profession. *Educational Technology Review,* Winter(5), 21–25.

Johnson, N. B. (1995). *Navigating the Internet with Prodigy.* Indianapolis, IN: Sams.net Publishing.

Jonassen, D. H. (1996). *Computers in the classroom: Mindtools for critical thinking.* Englewood Cliffs, NJ: Prentice-Hall.

Joseph, L. (1995). *World link: An Internet guide for educators, parents, and students*, 2nd ed. Columbus, OH: Greyden Press.

Junion-Metz, G. (1996). *K–12 resources on the Internet: An instructional guide.* Berkeley: Library Solutions Press.

Kaufeld, J. (1995). *America Online for dummies.* Indianapolis: IDG Books.

Kearsley, G. (1996). The World Wide Web: Global access to education. *Educational Technology Review,* Winter(5), 26–30.

Kemp, J. E., Morrison, G. R., & Ross, S. M. (1994). *Designing effective instruction.* New York: Merrill.

Kimeldorf, M. (1995). Teaching online—techniques and methods. *Learning and Leading with Technology, 23*(1), 26–31.

Kneller, G. F., & Hackbarth, S. L. (1977). An analysis of programmed instruction. *The Educational Forum, 41,* 181–187.

Krol, E., & Klopfenstein, B. (1996). *The whole Internet* (academic edition). Sebastopol, CA: O'Reilly & Associates.

Kurshan, B. (1996). Virtual communities: The Web of life and learning. *MultiMedia Schools, 3*(3), 24–26.

Lamb, A. C. (1996). *Spin your own Web site using HTML.* Evansville, IN: Vision To Action.

Lamb, A. C., & Johnson, L. (1995). *Cruisin' the information highway: Internet and the k–12 classroom.* Evansville, IN: Vision To Action.

Landeck, T. (1995). Curriculum and technology: Levels of integration. *Windows k–12 Classroom Resource, 1*(1), 14–15.

Laughon, S., & Hanson, W. R. (1996). Potholes on the Infobahn. *MultiMedia Schools, 3*(3), 14–23.

Leshin, C. B. (1995a). *Internet adventures: Visiting virtual communities: A step-by-step guide for educators.* Phoenix, AZ: XPLORA Publishing.

Leshin, C. B. (1995b). *Netscape adventures: Step-by-step guide to Netscape Navigator and the World Wide Web.* Phoenix, AZ: XPLORA Publishing.

Leshin, C. B. (1996). *Internet adventures: Step-by-step guide for finding and using educational resources.* Boston: Allyn & Bacon.

Linn, M. C., & Muilenburg, L. (1996). Creating lifelong science learners: What models form a firm foundation? *Educational Researcher, 25*(5), 18–24.

Maddux, C. D. (1996). Search engines: A primer on finding information on the World Wide Web. *Educational Technology, 36*(5), 33–39.

Margolis, P. E. (1996). *Random House personal computer dictionary*, 2nd ed. New York: Random House.

Mather, M. A. (1996). Exploring the Internet safely: What schools can do. *Technology & Learning, 17*(1), 38–46.

Maxymuk, J. (Ed.). (1996). *Finding government information on the Internet: A how-to-do-it manual.* New York: Neal-Schuman Publishers.

McClain, T. (1995). *Educator's Internet companion.* Lancaster, PA: Wentworth Worldwide Media.

McClain, T., & DiStefano, V. (1995). *Educator's World Wide Web tour guide.* Lancaster, PA: Wentworth Worldwide Media.

McClain, T., & DiStefano, V. (1996). *Educator's essential Internet training system.* Lancaster, PA: Wentworth Worldwide Media.

McKenzie, J. (1995). Beforenet and afternet. *MultiMedia Schools, 2*(3), 6–8.

McManus, T. F. (1996). Delivering instruction on the World Wide Web (http://www.edb.utexas.edu/coe/depts/ci/it/projects/wbi/wbi.html).

Meyers, E., & McIsaac, P. (1996). *Teachers guide to cyberspace.* New York: Impact II—The Teachers Network.

Miller, E. B. (1996). *The Internet resource directory for k–12 teachers and librarians, 95/96 edition.* Englewood, CO: Libraries Unlimited.

Milone Jr., M. N., & Salpeter, J. (1996). Technology and equity issues. *Technology & Learning, 16*(4), 38–47.

Mirabito, M. (1996). Establishing an online education program. *T.H.E. Journal, 24*(1), 57–60.

Moody, G. (1995). *The Internet with Windows.* Newton, MA: Butterworth-Heinemann.

Morville, P., Rosenfeld, L. B., & Janes, J. (1996). *The Internet searcher's handbook: Locating information, people, and software.* New York: Neal-Schuman Publishers.

O'Loughlin, L. (1995a). *Free stuff from America Online: Your guide to getting hundreds of valuable goodies.* Scottsdale, AZ: Coriolis Group Books.

O'Loughlin, L. (1995b). *Free stuff from CompuServe: Your guide to getting hundreds of valuable goodies.* Scottsdale, AZ: Coriolis Group Books.

Peters, M., & Lankshear, C. (1996). Critical literacy and digital texts. *Educational Theory, 46*(1), 51–70.

Pfaffenberger, B. (1993). *Que's computer user's dictionary*, 4th ed. Indianapolis: Que.

Pfaffenberger, B. (1995). *Que's computer & Internet dictionary*, 6th ed. Indianapolis: Que.

Pfaffenberger, B. (1996). *Publish it on the Web! Macintosh version.* Boston: AP Professional.

Pivovarnick, J. (1995). *The complete idiot's guide to America Online.* Indianapolis: Alpha Books.

Place, R., Dimmler, K., & Powell, T. (1996). *Educator's Internet yellow pages.* Englewood Cliffs, NJ: PTR Prentice Hall.

Pogrow, S. (1996). Reforming the wannabe reformers: Why education reforms almost always end up making things worse. *Phi Delta Kappan, 77,* 656-663.

Polly, J. A. (1996). *The Internet kids' yellow pages special edition.* Berkeley: Osborne McGraw-Hill.

Postman, N. (1995). *The end of education: Redefining the value of school.* New York: Knopf.

Powell, N. (1996). Ready to be a cybernaut? In E. Meyers & P. McIsaac (Eds.), *Teachers guide to cyberspace.* New York: Impact II—The Teachers Network.

Price, J. (1995). *The trail guide to America Online: A rapid-reading reference to using and cruising the America Online service.* Reading, MA: Addison-Wesley.

Quinlan, L. (1996). Customizing Web documents for the classroom: An example from Lakeville High School's advanced composition class. *Tech Trends, 41*(2), 27-30.

Quinlan, L. (in press). Creating a classroom kaleidoscope. *Educational Technology.*

Rakes, G. C. (1996). Using the Internet as a tool in a resource-based learning environment. *Educational Technology, 36*(5), 52-56.

Reigeluth, C. M. (1996). Of paradigms lost and gained. *Educational Technology, 36*(4), 58-61.

Reiser, R. A., & Dick, W. (1996). *Instructional planning: A guide for teachers.* Boston: Allyn & Bacon.

Roblyer, M. D., Dozier-Henry, O., & Burnette, A. P. (1996). Technology and multicultural education: The "uneasy alliance." *Educational Technology, 36*(3), 5-12.

Romiszowski, A. J. (1993). *New technologies in education and training.* East Brunswick, NJ: Nichols.

Ross, T. W., & Bailey, G. D. (1996). Creating safe Internet access. *Learning and Leading with Technology, 24*(1), 51-53.

Rosenfeld, L, Janes, J., & Kolk, M. V. (1996). *The Internet compendium: Guide to resources by subject.* New York: Neal-Schuman Publishers.

Rowland, R., & Kinnaman, D. (1995). *Researching on the Internet: The complete guide to finding, evaluating, and organizing information effectively.* Rocklin, CA: Prima Publishing.

Salisbury, D. F. (1996). *Five technologies for educational change: Systems thinking, systems design, quality science, change management, instructional technology.* Englewood Cliffs, NJ: Educational Technology Publications.

Salpeter, J. (1995). Quit blaming teachers. *Technology & Learning, 16*(3), 6.

Salpeter, J. (1996). Why NetDay? *Technology & Learning, 16*(7), 5.

Sanchez, B., & Harris, J. (1996). Online mentoring: A success story. *Learning and Leading with Technology, 23*(8), 57-60.

Schepp, D., & Schepp, B. (1995). Kidnet: *The kid's guide to surfing through cyberspace.* New York: HarperCollins.

Scigliano, J. A., Levin, J., & Horne, G. (1996). Using HTML for organizing student projects through the Internet. *T.H.E. Journal, 24*(1), 51-56.

Schofield, J. W. (1995). *Computers and classroom culture.* New York: Cambridge University Press.

Shafran, A. (1995). *The complete idiot's guide to CompuServe.* Indianapolis: Que.

Shanker, A. (1995). A reflection on 12 studies of education reform. *Phi Delta Kappan, 77,* 81-83.

Shotsberger, P. G. (1996). Instructional uses of the World Wide Web: Exemplars and precautions. *Educational Technology, 36*(2), 47-50.

Simpson, C. M. (1995). *Internet for library media specialists.* Worthington, OH: Linworth Publishing.

Spiro, R. J., Feltovich, P. J., Jacobson, M. J., & Coulson, R. L. (1992). Cognitive flexibility, constructivism, and hypertext: Random access instruction for advanced knowledge acquisition in ill-structured domains. In T. M. Duffy & D. H. Jonassen (Eds.), *Constructivism and the technology of instruction: A conversation* (pp. 57–75), Hillsdale, NJ: Lawrence Erlbaum Associates.

Starr, R. M. (in press). Delivering instruction on the World Wide Web: Overview and basic design principles. *Educational Technology.*

Starr, R. M., & Milheim, W. D. (1996). Educational uses of the Internet: An exploratory survey. *Educational Technology, 36*(5), 19–28.

Steen, D. R., Roddy, M. R., Sheffield, D., & Stout, M. B. (1995). *Teaching with the Internet: Putting teachers before technology.* Bellevue, WA: Resolution Business Press.

Steinberg, G. (1995). *Special edition using America Online.* Indianapolis: Que.

Todd, S. (1996). Going global: Desktop video conferencing with *CU-SeeMe. Learning & Leading with Technology, 24*(1), 57–61.

Tomei, L. A. (1996). Preparing an instructional lesson using resources off the Internet. *T.H.E. Journal, 24*(2), 93–95.

Tsikalas, K. (1995). Internet-based learning? *Electronic Learning, 14*(7), 14–15.

Tyre, T. (1995). Commercial online services: Benefits for educators. *T.H.E. Journal, 23*(1), 44–45.

Valauskas, E. J., & Ertel, M. (Eds.). (1996). *The Internet for teachers and school library media specialists: Today's applications, tomorrow's prospects.* New York: Neal-Schuman Publishers.

Wagner, R. (1995). *Inside CompuServe,* 3rd ed. Indianapolis: New Riders Publishing.

Warschauer, M. (1995). *E-mail for English teaching: Bringing the Internet and computer learning networks into the language classroom.* Alexandria, VA: TESOL Publications.

Wentworth Worldwide Media. (1996). *Educator's Internet companion: Classroom Connect's complete guide to educational resources on the Internet.* Lancaster, PA: Author.

Wentworth Worldwide Media. (1996). *Educator's World Wide Web tourguide,* rev. ed. Lancaster, PA: Author.

Wiggins, R. R., & Tittle, E. (1995). *The trail guide to CompuServe: A rapid-reading reference to using and cruising the CompuServe online service.* Reading, MA: Addison-Wesley.

Williams, B. (1995). *The Internet for teachers.* Indianapolis: IDG Books.

Willis, J. (1995). A recursive, reflective, instructional design model based on Constructivist-Interpretivist theory. *Educational Technology, 35*(6), 5–23.

Wilson, B. G. (Ed.). (1996). *Constructivist learning environments: Case studies in instructional design.* Englewood Cliffs, NJ: Educational Technology Publications.

Web K–12 Resources

The following annotated list of recommended Web sites of interest primarily to K–12 educators was compiled by *Laurie A. Quinlan*, Communications Instructor, Lakeville High School, Lakeville, MN. She graciously agreed to let me publish it here (with nonexclusive rights), and invited us all to contact her for updates (laurieq@vax1.mankato.msus.edu), and to read her K–12 teacher-oriented column in Tech Trends, an informative periodical included with our membership in the Association for Educational Communications and Technology (aect@aect.org).

AskERIC Home Page: http://ericir.syr.edu
> The Educational Resources Information Center (ERIC) provides a variety of services and products for educators at all levels.

B.E.S.T.: http://eyecatchers.com/eyecat/BEST
> Archive of the best educational sites on the World Wide Web.

Busy Teacher's Web Site: http://www.ceismc.gatech.edu/BusyT
> Reviews of educational materials on the Web, lesson plans, and classroom projects.

Classroom Connect: http://www.classroom.net
Provides information on Internet searching, educational conferences, school Web sites, and Web resources.

Education World: http://www.education-world.com
Archive of the best educational sites on the World Wide Web.

Educational Site of the Week: http://www.cyberstation.net/~may/surprise.htm
Every Wednesday, a new educational site is chosen, along with archives to past sites.

EdWeb: http://K12.cnidr.org:90
Online educational resources and information about trends in education.

GNA Teacher's Guide: http://uu-gna.mit.edu:8001/HyperNews/get/text/guide/index.html
Resources for online educators including databases, directories, hotlists, and periodicals.

Hotlist of K–12 Internet Sites: http://www.sendit.nodak.edu/k12
Index of elementary and secondary schools with Web sites.

InSITE: http://curry.edschool.Virginia.EDU/insite
Provides educational resources and discusses teacher education issues.

Instructional Technology Connections: http://www.cudenver.edu/~mryder/itcon.html
Excellent collection of LISTSERVs, e-journals, and k–12 links for teachers.

Kathy Schrock's Guide for Educators: http://www.capecod.net/Wixon/wixon.htm
A thorough list of resources arranged by discipline.

School.Net: http://k12.school.net
Provides links to online schools and information about educational uses of the Internet.

Teacher Tool Box: http://www.trc.org
Impressive list of resources for the k–12 curriculum.

Teacher's Edition Online: http://www.teachnet.com
Information on lesson plans, bulletin board ideas, and classroom themes and projects.

Web66: A K12 WWW Project: http://web66.coled.umn.edu
Information on setting up a server and finding k–12 resources.

World Lecture Hall Home Page: http://www.utexas.edu/world/lecture
Syllabi, assignments, lecture notes, exams, and calendars from many online courses. [See also /world/instruction/index.html.]

To these add:

American Federation of Teachers: http://www.aft.org
The rights and duties of teachers extend well beyond the classroom walls. Here we can read the pithy, influential "Where We Stand" columns of Albert Shanker. Also, we can explore issues of professional concern, and sign up to be "21st Century Teachers" technology mentors.

ArtsEdNet: http://www.artsednet.getty.edu
Information about "discipline-based arts education."

Berit's Best Sites for Children: http://www.cochran.com/theosite/ksites.html
Another regularly updated source.

CCCnet: http://www.cccnet.com
An interactive online k–12 curriculum, and a showcase for student projects.

CyberKids (and Cyberteens): http://www.woodwind.com:80/cyberkids
An online magazine with stories and articles by children.

Delivering Instruction on the World Wide Web:
http://www.edb.utexas.edu/coe/depts/ci/it/projects/wbi/wbi.html
Includes hardware and software requirements, *HTML* tutorials, discussion of design models, and links to other resources.

The Discovery Channel: http://www.discovery.com
   Billed as a "gateway to exploration and adventure."

Electronic Learning: http://scholastic.com/EL
   Describes top sites for educators.

Global SchoolNet Foundation: http://www.gsn.org
   A Microsoft-sponsored provider of information about educational uses of the Internet, and a host for school home pages.

Heritage Online: http://www.hol.edu
   Antioch University credit courses to help educators use the Internet.

History/Social Studies Web Site for K–12 Teachers: http://earth.execpc.com/~dboals/k–12.html
   Has lesson plans and links to other resources for teachers and parents.

Hot Sheet: http://www.tstimpreso.com/hotsheet
   Lists and provides links to popular sites by category—search engines, news, government, education, etc.

Impact II—The Teachers Network (TeachNet): http://www.teachnet.org
   A searchable database of award-winning classroom projects, funding opportunities, bulletin boards, and an introduction to the Web course.

Internet High School: http://www.caso.com
   Describes providers of online high school and equivalency courses, and The Internet University area lists college-level courses.

Judi Harris' Network-Based Educational Activity Collection:
http://mac246.ed.uiuc.edu/activity-structures
   A database of k–12 online projects, searchable by activity type and content area.

Judi Harris' Web-Based Activity Collection:
http://www.ed.uiuc.edu/Activity-Structures/web-activity-structures.html
   Has detailed descriptions of "curriculum-based k–12 educational telecomputing projects."

Kidscom: http://www.kidscom.com
   Describes Internet projects for children, in English, French, German, and Spanish.

KidsConnect: AskKC@iconnect.syr.edu
   A Microsoft-funded service for students wishing to pose questions. Now that should give parents and teachers a break! ;-)

KidLink: http://www.kidlink.org
   Helps link up keypals across the world.

KidsWeb: http://www.npac.syr.edu/textbook/kidsweb
   Links to Web sites of interest to children, the arts, sciences, social studies, reference, etc.

The Learning Resource Server: http://www.ed.uiuc.edu
   Goal of this University of Illinois College of Education site is "to provide resources that help learners move from *surfing* to *serving*. It has links to "real projects of teachers and students" and to "the work of researchers who are articulating new visions of what learning can be."

Ligature Gateway Academy: http://academy3.ligature.com
   Provider of Internet-based core curriculum for middle schools.

The Magellan Internet Guide: http://www.mckinley.com
   Permits limiting search to those Web sites that have been "rated and reviewed."

Media Literacy Project: http://interact.uoregon.edu/MediaLit/HomePage
   Describes resources that help develop critical thinking about media.

National Education Association: http://www.nea.org
   This is a prime reference for both professional and practical concerns. This site has links to k–12 newsgroups and listservs, and to the U.S. Teacher Corps, headquarters of the "21st Century Teachers" initiative that has been endorsed by President Clinton.

The Open University: http://www.open.ac.uk
  Describes course offerings at this leading distance education institution.

NASA's K–12 Internet Initiative: http://quest.arc.nasa.gov
  Provides guidance in educational uses of Internet.

Optical Data Corporation: http://www.infomall.org/Showcase/opticaldata
  Much about the company's products, but also has suggestions for educational uses of the Internet.

Possibilities! Science Education: http://kendaco.telebyte.com:80/billband/Possibilities.html
  Helps teachers integrate use of the Internet into the secondary science curriculum.

Scholastic Network: http://scholastic.com/network
  Has curriculum guides, projects, libraries.

SubmitAll: http://www.hometeam.com
  Provides site for free homepage and links your URL to search sites and directory services.

Top Ed Sites: http://www.pointcom.com
  Provides reviews of education-related Web sites.

Uncle Bob's Kids' Page: http://gagme.www.com/~boba/kids.html
  Best of the Web for children.

WebCATS: Library Catalogues on the World Wide Web
  Has links to "all" libraries with Web-based online public-access catalogues.

WebEd K12 Curriculum Links: http://badger.state.wi.us/agencies/dpi/www/WebEd.html
  Provides links to exemplary school Web sites.

World Wide Web Courseware Developers Listserv Home Page: http://www.unb.ca/web/wwwdev
  A source for developers of WBL activities, also lists Web-based "continuing education" courses in a wide variety of fields.

WWLib: http://www.scit.wlv.ac.uk/wwlib
  An indexed catalog of Web sites in the United Kingdom.

Yahoo Maps: http://maps.yahoo.com/yahoo
  Provides maps as per input of U.S. cities, streets, zip codes.

Yahooligans: http://www.yahooligans.com
  "Yet another hierachically organized oracle" for locating hot sites, but for 8–14 year olds.

Yahoo People Search: http://www.yahoo.com/search/people
  Provides telephone numbers and street addresses.

Keeping Up to Date

Regularly updated, annotated lists of books (!) about the Internet and its World Wide Web are available from:

  listserv@ubvm.cc.buffalo.edu

  message: Get newusers FAQ nettrain F=mail

  or for reviews, message: Get nettrain revs_1 nettrain F=mail

  Substitute 2, 3, 4, and 5 for the number one to obtain all five parts of the list.

  Another great source is The Unofficial Internet Book List:

  http://www.northcoast.com/savetz/booklist

Edupage is a summary of news items on information technology, provided online three times a week as a service of Educom, a consortium of colleges "seeking to transform education through the use of information technology." Written by John Gehl and Suzanne Douglas, it is available in English as well as several other languages. For translations and archives see: http://www.educom.edu, or e-mail: translations@educom.unc.edu.

InfoList for Teachers is another great source of Internet sites. It is a listserv-delivered, regularly updated publication by Rick Lakin, Yvonne Andres, Al Rogers, and Erica Rogers, and hosted by The Global Schoolnet Foundation.

http://www.electriciti.com/~rlakin

The Scout Report is a weekly online publication that describes Internet resources of interest to researchers and educators. It is prepared by Net Scout Services in the Computer Science Department, University of Wisconsin, and is sponsored by InterNIC, the National Science Foundation, AT&T, and Network Solutions, Inc.

http://rs.internic.net/scout_report-index.html
or e-mail: admin@ds.internic.net

Edupage, InfoList for Teachers, and *The Scout Report* may conveniently be received, along with other items of interest, by subscribing to the Minnesota Educational Media Organization's LISTSERV, **MEMO-net** (administrator **Don Descy**). Simply e-mail: listserv@vax1.mankato.msus.edu, leave the subject line blank (or type in a period, if needed), and type the message: subscribe memo-net Your Name

Videos about Web-Based Learning May Be Obtained from:

AECT: 1-202-347-7834; aect@aect.org

ASCD: 1-800-933-ASCD; 1-703-549-9110; member@ascd.org

Chip Taylor Communications: 1-800-876-CHIP; 1-603-434-9262; chiptaylor@chiptaylor.com

Educational Activities: 1-800-645-3739; 1-516-223-4666; edact@panix.com

Educational Video Network: 1-800-762-0060; 1-409-295-5767; pop123@tcac.com

ISTE: 1-800-336-5191; 1-503-346-4414; iste@oregon.uoregon.edu

PC-TV: 1-603-863-9322; 1-415-574-6233; 74774.13@compuserve.com

RMI Media Productions: 1-800-745-5480; rmimedia@aol.com

University of Delaware: 1-302-831-8162; podium@udel.edu

The Video Journal of Education: 1-800-572-1153; 1-801-566-6500; http://www.videojournal.com

Wentworth Worldwide Media: 1-800-638-1639; 1-717-393-1000; connect@wentworth.com

Winnebago: 1-800-533-5430; 1-507-724-5411; sales@winnebago.com

The Author

Steve Hackbarth is a computer specialist teacher at Public Schools 6 and 116, Manhattan, New York City.

e-mail
hackbarths@aol.com

24

Supporting Project-Based Collaborative Learning Via a World Wide Web Environment

Betty Collis

Project-Based Learning: Its Potential and Its Problems

Project-based tele-learning is defined as problem-oriented learning within the framework of a group project and using telematics support for the project activities. Collaborative learning in a problem-based context emphasizes inter- and intragroup interactions, where the students actively participate in the learning process while solving a problem as a group. Project-based instruction (see, for example, Blumenfeld, Soloway, Marx, Krajcik, Guzdial, & Palincsar, 1991) is a didactic strategy where not only problem-specific learning goals are involved, but also cognitive and social goals. Van Woerden (1991), for example, notes that project-based instruction in higher education involves a problem as a starting point, with the need to select and apply subject-specific knowledge for the solution of the problem; the contextualization of the project situation as preparation for further professional practice; the need for optimization of group-interaction skills; and the development of responsibility for one's own learning process. Kleijer, Kuiper, De Wit, and Wouters-Koster (1981) see four major characteristics of project-based instruction: self-responsibility for thinking and learning, awareness of social responsibility, thinking and acting from a scientific perspective but in a practical application, and relating both group process and product with professional practice.

Although agreement exists on the potential value of project-based learning, the success of the method depends on many variables whose handling is challenging to all those involved. Applications of communication and information technologies are being designed to support the need of project-based instruction and improve the efficiency of this instructional form in practice. Ryan and Koschmann (1994), for example, describe a variety of hardware and software tools including hypertext/hypermedia facilities, groupware and database facilities, LAN technologies and Internet links resulting in an electronically supported conversation facility, a teaching-case library, and a "clinical encounter simulation stack" to support project-based instruction in medical education. McManus and Aiken (1995) describe the integration of an intelligent tutor as a software coach to support the Jigsaw Methodology (a long-established didactical methodology for project-based instruction; see Aronson, Blaney, Stephan, Sikes, & Snapp, 1978) for groups of students in computer science. Szyperski and Ventre (1993) approach the support problem more generically, by defining and characterizing a class of applications for multi-party interactive multimedia and the network architecture needed to provide these applications, that can be employed in the support of project work. In their functional characterization of these applications, they emphasize the need for (a) a model of interaction, (b) a dataflow characterization, (c) an accessibility enforcement, and (d) event scheduling.

Despite many such research initiatives, however, project-based instruction remains a challenge for the instructor and the students. Particularly in a learning environment supported by telematic support so that students can work separately from each other in both time and place, the effectiveness of project-based tele-learning may get disturbed by loss of efficiency due to the number of telematic-based facilities that are difficult to control. Challenges are, in particular, with respect to (a) efficient support of communication, (b) efficient and effective access to appropriate (multi-media) information, and (c) efficient management of group processes and of the group's "memory" (Collis, Andernach, & van Diepen, 1996). The latter describe on-going work in the integration of shared workspace functionalities, e-mail and threaded computer conferencing functionalities, hyperlinked access to file-archives of course materials, and workflow-management tools within World Wide Web sites in different courses at the University of Twente. One of these courses can serve as a particular example of how World Wide Web functionalities can be combined in support of group-based project work.

"Online Learning": An Example of a Web-Based Course Emphasizing Collaborative Project Activity

The course "Online Learning" (to be renamed "Tele-Learning" in 1997) is an elective course for senior students in the Faculty of Educational Science and Technology at the University of Twente in The Netherlands. Students electing the course are specializing in the design and development of electronic media for learning support. In the 1996 version of the course, there were 33 students, from eight countries. English was used as the common language for the course, although only the instructor is a native-English speaker. The course is scheduled to meet face-to-face for eight two-hour sessions during the Spring term (March-May) and involves approximately 120 hours of time commitment from the students. The students come from a number of different programs with many different external commitments, and some attend the course entirely from a distance, via the Internet.

Relating directly to the objectives of the course is a collaborative learning activity, around which the project work is based. In 1994, this collaborative activity involved the students in the joint preparation of a course reader, working on teams with distant partners (specialists in other countries, invited by the instructor to join in the collaborative writing activity). In 1995, the collaborative activity was the adaptation of the 1994 reader into an updated version, making as full use as possible of the hyperlinking functionalities of the World Wide Web. In 1996, the collaborative activity was to create a "kiosk" of World Wide Web-based lesson materials for teachers, grouped around 14 different curriculum topics. In all cases, the major conceptual framework of the course was learning design of World Wide Web resources through the actual design and development of World Wide Web resources, in a social-contructivist atmosphere (Jonassen, 1995). From all three years, the students' final project is available as a World Wide Web site; in each year, the course as a whole has become more and more embedded in a World Wide Web environment itself. The fact that the busy and sometimes off-campus students have little time to meet with each other face-to-face to work collaboratively on their projects is a particular challenge for everyone involved.

These courses and the products of the students' collaborative project work can be seen at:

http://www.to.utwente.nl/ism/online94/
http://www.to.utwente.nl/ism/online95/campus/campus.html
http://www.to.utwente.nl/ism/online96/campus.htm

The course as seen from the students' perspective is described in Bos, Kikstra, and Morgan (1996) (available through the 1996 site under "Archive"). Other aspects of the course are also described in Collis (1996a, b) and in Collis, Andernach, and Van Diepen (1996).

Evolving the Use of World Wide Web Functionality for Project-Work Support

How can students work collaboratively on a complex project (in this case, involving the joint development of a World Wide Web resource) when it is difficult for them to arrange to meet face-to-face for their project-related tasks? In the 1994 and 1995 versions of the course, heavy use was made of e-mail with file attachments, computer conferencing, and joint access to a designated space (partition) on the server for each project group. The fact that all of these were separate environments, and also were separate from the World Wide Web environment in which the HTML files needed to be accessed, as well as from the HTML-editor environment in which the pages were created, caused a heavy strain on project management, not only for each of the groups, but also for the instructor, who had to conceptually integrate all the various activities of the groups as well as technically link all the pages that were produced into the final project sites. (In the 1996 kiosk, there are more than 800 student-made files involved. After the 1995 experience, the course was re-designed (or "pedagogically re-engineered;" Collis, 1996a), so that both the process of the course as well as the product of the course are all integrated into one World Wide Web site.

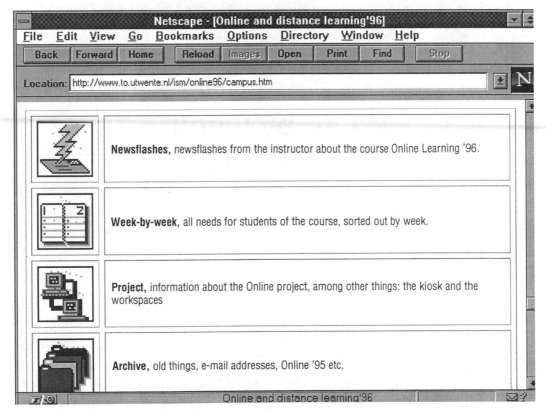

Figure 1. Main menu of course site for "Online Learning," 1996.

The 1996 Site: Integrated Support for Learning, Project Work, and Project Presentation

The main menu of the 1996 site is shown in Figure 1 on the previous page. The first of the options was used for message-type comments from the instructor, replaced at least every week (a banner message, run by a Java script, scrolling across the bottom of the home page, informed the students of the date and time when a new message occurred). The archive option took the students to a collection of reference materials for the course such as the course outline (the course is paperless; all materials are available through the World Wide Web site itself). The archive also serves as the entry to one-to-one communication among the class members and to other resources such as the previous versions of the course and the readers produced by the students during those versions. Most important to the project work, however, are the other two options. The Week-by-Week option is shown in Figure 2.

The Week-by-Week matrix serves an important role in integrating the theory and practice of the course. Each week a new interactive reading was inserted into the site, containing a large variety of external links as examples and extensions of the reading material itself. The reading material was also hyper-linked to the project-directions for the week (in the "Follow-Up" cells) and to the feedback given by the instructor to the group as a whole during each week.

Most interesting, however, for the support of project work was our use of a shared-workspace environment. The environment used is a tool produced by (and freely available from) the

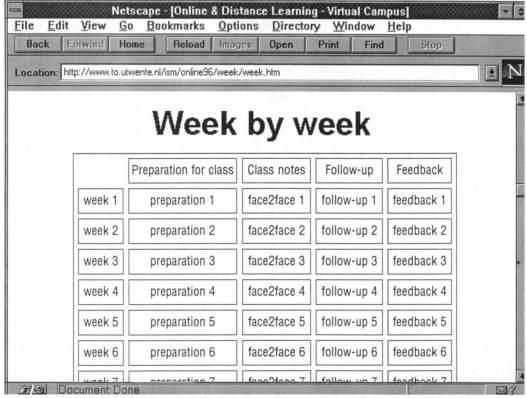

Figure 2. The "Week-by-Week" matrix, integrating course readings, outlines for face-to-face sessions, directions for project activities, and feedback.

GMD Institute in Bonn, Germany. The tool is called *"BSCW"*: *Basic Support for Collaborative Work* (http://bscw.gwd.de/Introduction/visitor.html).

BSCW supports the storage of various sorts of documents, text and word-processed files, hypertexts, audio, images, and video. It is World Wide Web-based, so using the environment is platform independent. Every group has its own workspace. BSCW keeps track of the events in the workspace, such as adding, reading and updating documents and of the agents involved in those events. Features such as various sorts of visualized file management functions (renaming, locking, "checking out a file," etc.) are also available. A particularly valuable aspect of BSCW is that group members can add remarks to their files, so that their groupmates can see at a glance what the intention or status of a newly-entered file might be.

In the "Online Learning" course, the students entered their workspaces directly from the main menu, via the "Project" option. After choosing this option and entering a new password, students saw the new menu of the BSCW, with icons for each of the 14 groups (and for the instructor). Choosing one's own workspace area yields a display such as the one shown in Figure 3.

Figure 3 shows a number of the very helpful functionalities of the shared workspace. Students can easily add any external or internal HTML file to the workspace, and can open and interact with the file, also from the workspace. This is a very helpful property, avoiding the need to move in and out of browser, directory, and communication environments in order to inspect new World Wide Web pages and give comments about them to one's groupmates. Sim-

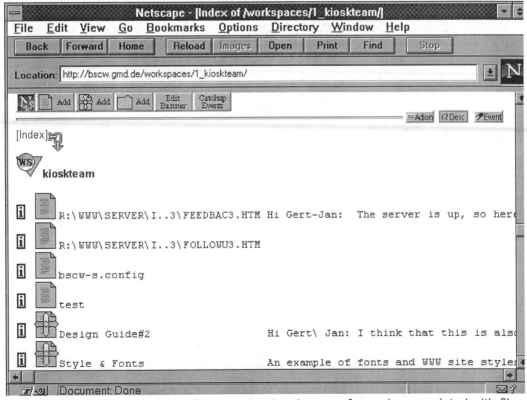

Figure 3. The BSCW shared workspace, showing the use of remarks associated with files.

ilarly, other types of files can also be opened and examined and commented upon, all from the same environment. (Actual editing of the various files cannot take place in this environment, however; files must be "checked out" to one's desktop, edited, and "checked in" again. These steps are simple, as they are well-supported by the BSCW tools.)

The workspace allows groups to create different workspace areas corresponding to each subdirectory or subfolder that they create. This function was very important for management as the number of files and versions of files increased. It was also very important for the instructor, who could give an instruction (via a "Follow-Up" cell in the "Week-to-Week" matrix) such as "Please put all your current versions of files in a folder 'Week x evaluation' so that I can come in this weekend, see what you are doing, and give you feedback on your current pages"). The message function lets the instructor conveniently add feedback directly to a file for the entire group to read, feedback that the group members can subsequently add to in their asynchronous communication with each other.

Among the other benefits of the shared-workspace environment was that it was integrated directly into the overall course site, with the standard navigation icons for the "Week-to-Week" matrix, to the Archive, and to the actual student product area (the "kiosk") always available, so that movement between all aspects of the overall course environment was integrated and easy. The World Wide Web functionality makes this possible.

For Further Development...

Although the results so far of this integrated World Wide Web course environment have been positive in terms of both student and instructor evaluations, there are many needs and improvements still required. In particular, the timeload on the instructor remains high and ever higher, with existing World Wide Web systems as with previous network support forms. The ease with which all the group members can communicate with each other and with the instructor is a two-edged sword: excellent for facilitating project work and collaboration but overwhelming for the instructor in terms of time for quality response. Administration and ongoing record keeping of all the group and individual student work is also demanding; in the 1997 version of the site, we are adding some data-collection tools to automate this to a certain degree. Communication support for threaded discussions, such as was available through our previously-used computer-conferencing environment, was not built into the 1996 site, but will be in the 1997 site, via newsgroup functionalities. Better interactivity will be built into the reading material of the course, via the use of cgi-forms and "magic cookie" types of data-passing, so that students can be challenged to give responses to the readings and external links, and the instructor can retain a record of these responses as well as tailor the feedback given to the responses. An authoring environment will be used to structure the weekly reading materials and offer different paths through the materials for students with different roles and interests within the groups (Horst *et al.*, 1996).

But it is the World Wide Web functionality that underlies all these possibilities. As the instructor of the course, and someone who believes strongly in the value of project work as a social-constructive approach to learning, I am excited about the possibilities that the World Wide Web offers. I am also sensitive to the need to look critically at those possibilities in terms of their overall contribution to project-based learning. Finding the indicators that help to focus in on the most profitable combination of tools and pedagogy for World Wide Web-based project learning is also the subject of a new interdisciplinary research project (1996–1999) which we have just launched (Collis & Widya, 1996).

References

Aronson, E., Blaney, N., Stephan, C., Sikes, J., & Snapp, M. (1978). *The Jigsaw classroom*. Beverly Hills, CA: Sage.

Blumenfeld, P., Soloway, E., Marx, R., Krajcik, J., Guzdial, M., & Palincsar, A. (1991). Motivating project-based learning: Sustaining the doing, supporting the learning. *Educational Psychologist, 26,* 369–398.

Bos, E., Kikstra, A., & Morgan, C. (1996). Multiple levels of use of the Web as a learning tool. In P. Carlson & F. Makedon, (Eds.), *Proceedings of ED-TELECOM '96* (pp. 31–36). Charlottesville, VA: AACE.

Collis, B. (1996a, June). *Pedagogical re-engineering: Design issues and implementation experiences with the World Wide Web as a learning environment*. Invited paper presented at ED-MEDIA/ED-TELECOM '96, Boston.

Collis, B. (1996b). *Tele-learning in a digital world: The future of distance learning*. London: International Thomson Computer Press (http://www.thomson.com/).

Collis, B., Andernach, T., & van Diepen, N. (1996). *The Web as process tool and product environment for group-based project work in higher education*. Paper submitted to WebNet '96 Technical Program, San Francisco.

Collis, B., & Widya, I. (1996). *Project-based tele-learning: Analysis, modeling, design, and evaluation*. Internal report, CTIT, University of Twente, Enschede, The Netherlands.

Jonassen, D. (1995). Supporting communities of learners with technology: A vision for integrating technology with learning in schools. *Educational Technology, 35*(4), 60–63.

Kleijer, H., Kuiper, R., De Wit, H., & Wouters-Koster, L. (1981). *Projectonderwijs tussen maatschappelijk idealisme en onderwijskundig alternatief* (Project-based education between social idealism and educational possibility). Amsterdam: SISWO.

McManus, M. M., & Aiken, R. (1995). Using an intelligent tutor to facilitate collaborative learning. In B. Collis & G. Davies (Eds.), *Innovating adult learning through innovative technologies* (pp. 49–64). Amsterdam: Elsevier Science.

Ryan, C., & Koschmann, T. (1994). The collaborative learning laboratory: A technology-enriched environment to support problem-based learning. In D. Foster (Ed.), *Recreating the revolution: Proceedings of the National Educational Computing Conference* (pp. 160–167). Eugene, OR: ISTE.

Szyperski, C., & Ventre, G. (1993). *A characterization of multi-part interactive multimedia applications*. Report with limited circulation. International Computer Science Institute, Berkeley, CA.

Horst, S. H., van der Martens, R. L., Portier, Sl. J., Valcke, M., & Weges, H. G. (1996). *Electronic course development with ILCE: From entry to delivery*. Heerlen, NL: Open University.

Van Woerden, W. (1991). *Het projectonderwijs onderzocht*. (Research into project-based education). Enschede: Febodruk.

The Author

Betty Collis is Associate Professor with the faculty of Educational Science and Technology, University of Twente, the Netherlands.

e-mail, World Wide Web
    collis@edte.utwente.nl
    http://www.to.utwente.nl/user/ism/collis/personal.htm

25

Designing Web-Based Instruction: A Human-Computer Interaction Perspective

Andrew Dillon and Erping Zhu

Introduction

The general interest in the World Wide Web as a medium for sharing and distributing textual and graphic information has brought about an increasing number of instruction-oriented Web sites and Web-based instructional pages. These range from offering supplemental (or even duplicate) instructional materials to students on campus to providing opportunities for off-campus individuals to complete courses via the World Wide Web. This chapter briefly discusses the design of Web-based instruction (WBI) from a human-computer interaction (HCI) perspective, raising issues which instructors and designers need to consider in the design of Web-based instruction, and suggesting ways in which instructors and designers can build optimal Web instructional sites and pages.

World Wide Web and Web-Based Instruction

The World Wide Web is a hypertext/hypermedia information and communication system on the Internet. The specific features of hypertext/hypermedia, such as linked nodes of information, multiple access paths to information, and if well designed, the ability to pursue information at increasing levels of detail, are considered to distinguish the new medium from the traditional print medium in several ways. The information in a hypertext/hypermedia system is supposedly non-linear and structured in chunks or nodes rather than in traditional paragraphs and sections (though similarities abound, and most empirical evidence suggests few readers of paper documents ever read in a linear fashion). The method of manipulation is scrolling and clicking with a mouse rather than turning pages by hand. Also, the size of the information space is largely hidden from the user. Because of these differences, the conventional and familiar model people use to interact with print medium may lose its effectiveness while interacting with electronic medium, and give rise to feelings of being lost or overwhelmed in the information space. These differences pose significant challenges as much as opportunities to designers of electronic documents in general and Web-based instruction in particular. Indeed, most of the empirical comparisons of hypermedia and paper have demonstrated that

221

there is a long way to go before the apparent advantages of the new medium can be turned to tangible benefits for learners (Dillon, 1996).

Instruction can be defined as a way of organizing and sequencing information in order to maximize the transfer of information from teacher to learner. The design of any instruction usually involves the use of instructional theories, design models, and strategies. Campbell, Hurley, Jones, & Stephens (1995), in their design of World Wide Web-based courseware, adopted the ASSURE model (Heinich, Molenda, & Russell, 1993) as a general framework for the course and Gagne's sequence of instructional events as a guide for evaluating the courseware. Alternatively, instruction can be designed and delivered using a problem-based instructional and learning model. In the problem-based learning model, learning starts with the presentation of a real world problem. Students, provided with instructors' guidance and resource materials, are encouraged to dive into the problem, construct individual understanding, and finally find the answer to the problem. In a traditional setting, students may expect such things in a course as weekly readings, assignments, instructor's lectures, class notes, tests, and exams. In a non-traditional setting, students may expect instructor's assistance, guidance, and scaffolding on individual or group work. No matter what theory or model of instruction is used, there are always certain expectations students have of a course. Because of these existing course-taking strategies in students and instructors, instruction usually possesses somewhat standard sequences including elements such as motivating the learner, explaining what is to be learned, helping the learner recall previous knowledge, providing instructional materials, providing guidance and feedback, testing comprehension, and providing enrichment (Dick & Reiser, 1989).

Most World Wide Web pages provide a very informal learning environment, in which people access information provided by various organizations, universities, and even individuals, and in which people attend to the selected information and explore subjects that are of interest to them. Generally speaking, the great majority of information on the Web belongs to this category. That is, Web sites are not instructional in the strict sense but are data sources. To qualify as Web-based instruction, the site surely has to possess certain instructional elements intentionally designed to maximize information transfer as mentioned above.

Human-Computer Interaction and Web-Based Instruction

The field of HCI comprises the study of the interaction between humans and computers with the general aim of informing the designer of more humanly acceptable technology. Since the field is multi-disciplinary in nature, there is no single theory that guides the study of human-computer interaction. However, traditional cognitive psychological views of the user have been dominant in the field, and the present chapter will use the information processing view of human cognition as a general theoretical framework to discuss issues in the design of Web-based instruction.

Within this framework, humans are considered to process information impinging on their sensory modalities on the basis of the bounded parameters of perception and knowledge stored in memory (Card, Moran, & Newell, 1983). As a limited processing system, humans actively attempt to automate repetitive cognitive acts through extraction of regularities in information available to them. Within this framework, learners are seen as active seekers and processors of information. Learners select and attend to environmental aspects, transform and interpret information, relating new information to previously acquired knowledge, and organize information to make it meaningful.

A further characteristic of HCI is its emphasis on empirical methods to determine the most reliable and valid guidelines for interface design. Popular views of the Web as an "information superhighway" or hypermedia as a "liberating technology" are considered unconvincing to most HCI practitioners without supporting evidence that users experience the Web as such. Indeed, recent HCI analysis of the information revolution suggest that user evaluation of most new technologies is very poorly carried out, and in the case of hypermedia in particular, Landauer (1995) claimed to be able to identify only nine scientifically acceptable evaluation studies ever being published in the literature on this subject, and the majority of these found the new technology to be poorer than paper for most users.

Issues in Designing Web-Based Instruction from an HCI Perspective

From an HCI perspective, several key issues emerge in the design of Web-based instruction: the tool, the learner, the tasks, and the environment (Shackel, 1991). In particular, focus must be on learners and their tasks. HCI professionals seek to ensure that learners (as users) can in fact interact with the technology in a manner that is effective, efficient, and satisfying. While not normally concerned with learning per se, HCI practitioners do seek to devise information technology that can be used appropriately by the intended users. In Web terms, this would mean ensuring readability of the screen, adequate support for navigation, task-relevant command structures, etc.

This brings us to an interesting perspective and one that is slightly out of favor among the current climate of Web-worship in higher education. The Web is just another technology through which instructors can reach learners and deliver instruction. There is nothing magical about this new technology that requires us to reinvent instructional design. After all, humans have not changed significantly as a result of the emergence of the Web, and the principles of information flow, feedback, formatting, detail, etc., that have been developed over the last few decades are still relevant and applicable in instructional design. What has changed is our ability to apply these principles over distributed learner populations with higher fidelity than previously.

From an HCI perspective, our first goal must be to understand users (learners) and the nature of their task in as much detail as possible so that we can develop information technology that will prove acceptable to them and efficient to their task. In other words, HCI professionals strive for a sufficient understanding of users, their characteristics and differences, and their knowledge of the subject domain and experience of the system. They need to conduct an adequate analysis of the task, users' relevant information, and skill needs in order to design a usable and efficient instructional system. For example, users with extensive domain knowledge may prefer fairly high density of information on the screen and fewer explanations of terminology, but users with little or no domain knowledge may prefer low information flow and more explanations. Therefore, our design should be based on such analysis, otherwise, it is less likely to meet users' needs and to achieve intended results. In the same manner, HCI ensures that human factors in interacting with computers are appropriately addressed in the design. If we know, for example, that users read better with positive polarity and high resolution screens, and are likely to suffer less navigation problems with information that maintains rather than violates conventional structures, then we can go some way towards ensuring that in terms of basic human factors, the Web-based tool meets minimum usability requirements.

However, such knowledge in itself is insufficient to guarantee learning will occur from using the system. It will only ensure that willing users are capable of interacting with the application in an efficient, effective and satisfying manner. Beyond this, HCI turns to instructional design for insights on how to take the well-designed or usable technology and apply instructional theory to its pedagogic use. Given the requirement for information to be perceived and processed before instruction can occur, HCI seeks to ensure the adequate perceptual and processing issues are addressed, while instructional theory can distinguish the pedagogic scenarios in which usable tools are applied in the design. In this manner, HCI seeks to ensure the ultimate usability and utility. This gives us a symbiotic relationship between two heretofore independent disciplines.

Conclusion

If we are to design usable and effective Web-based instruction, our interaction design must be compatible with the information processing characteristics of the human mind as well as users' models of the instructional system. From the human-computer interaction perspective, issues in the design of Web-based instruction are our understanding of the system's special features, the user's model of the instructional system, the learning task, the learner, and Web-based message design principles. Even with such knowledge, it is essential that the concept of learning is operationalized in a manner that renders it testable in the given context. Once operationalized, it must be tested on real learners performing real tasks, so that we may advance the state of WBI beyond mere presentation and hot-linking of text and graphics.

References

Campbell, J. K., Hurley, S., Jones, S. B., & Stephens, N. M. (1995). Constructing educational courseware using NCSA Mosaic and the World Wide Web. *Computer Networks and ISDN System, 27,* 877–896.

Card, S. K., Moran, T. P., & Newell, A. (1983). *The psychology of human computer interaction.* Hillsdale, NJ: Lawrence Erlbaum Associates.

Dick, W., & Reiser, R. A. (1989). *Planning effective instruction.* Englewood Cliffs, NJ: Prentice-Hall.

Dillon, A. (1996). Myths, misconceptions and an alternative perspective on information usage and the electronic medium. In J. Rouet *et al.* (Eds.), *Hypertext and cognition* (pp. 25–42). Mahwah, NJ: Lawrence Erlbaum Associates.

Gagne, R. M. (Ed.). (1987). *Instructional technology: Foundations.* Hillsdale, NJ: Lawrence Erlbaum Associates.

Heinich, R., Molenda, M., & Russell, J. D. (1993). *Instructional media and the new technologies of instruction (4rd ed.).* New York: Macmillan.

Landauer, T. (1995). *The trouble with computers: Usefulness, usability, and productivity.* Cambridge, MA: MIT Press.

McMillan, T. C., & Moran, B. P. (1985). Command line structure and dynamic processing of abbreviations in dialogue management. *Interfaces in Computing, 3,* 249–257.

Nielsen, J. (1993). *Usability engineering.* Boston: AP Professional.

Shackel, B. (1991). Usability: Context, framework, definition, design, and evaluation. In B. Shackel & S. Richardson (Eds.), *Human factors for informatics usability* (pp. 21–37). Cambridge, UK: Cambridge University Press.

The Authors

Andrew Dillon is Associate Professor, School of Library and Information Science, Indiana University, Bloomington, Indiana.

e-mail
   adillon@indiana.edu

Erping Zhu is a doctoral candidate, Instructional Systems Technology Department, at Indiana University.

e-mail
   zerping@indiana.edu

26

Designing Web-Based Instruction for Active Learning

S t e p h e n   J .   B o s t o c k

Introduction

Delivering educational content using the Web will not automatically improve learning. Consider some contrasting educational scenes involving the Web:

- Large numbers of students attend time-tabled classes where they sit alone at networked computers and read lecture notes from the screen for hours every week, printing some text for examination preparation. The tedium of listening to the lecture is replaced by the tedium of reading from the screen.

- Students pursuing a course attend scheduled sessions with networked computers where coaches are available. Through the browser interface, they access course documents, simulations and videos, forms for formative assessment, e-mail, and discussions. They search for additional materials around the world, and query tutors by e-mail. Assessments are research reports on subjects negotiated with a tutor. Written in small groups, they are submitted electronically and become Web resources for other students.

- Students use networked computers in an open access center and from home. They work singly or in groups on research projects on which they will not be examined. They search the Web for relevant data, courses and electronic discussions. A tutor is available to discuss searching, evaluating resources, and writing, but she is not a content expert. As students write reports, or assemble them by juxtaposing various Internet resources, their work automatically appears as Web pages. Other students' comments are made online and are appended to the pages.

The nightmarish first scene is traditional instruction by Web technology; broadcast via lectures is replaced with broadcast via the Web. Human contact is lost, students are isolated, and the educational experience is passive, limited, and alienating.

In the second scene, the Web is the major medium for both information retrieval and personal interactions with tutors and fellow students. Learning activities include reading multimedia Web pages of content, using interactive Web instruction, performing tasks to demonstrate competence and conducting research projects.

The third scene is de-schooled education mediated by the Web, fulfilling Illich's prediction of an educational network (Pickering, 1995). Though technically possible, this Utopia is culturally unlikely. It is useful for challenging assumptions about how new technologies should be used. My own teaching with the Web tries to avoid the first scene and develop the second while wondering about the third.

My readers could no doubt add some scenes of their own. How should we use this all-capable technology? To improve the quality of learning, increase the student/staff ratio or improve the balance sheet? As educational designers we can ask:

- What types of learning are we trying to achieve with computer based instruction?

- Does the Web have advantages over isolated personal computers for these types of learning?

- How do we design environments for such learning using the Web?

Active Learning

Active learning describes a process rather than a product. Why is the activity necessary or good? The constructivist psychology of learning describes the learning process as the internal construction of meaning in long term memory, building and reshaping personal knowledge through the experience of interactions with the world (Jonassen, 1994; Lebow, 1993). This requires the design of environments encouraging activities such as collaboration, autonomy in learning, critical reflection and authentic interactions with the real world (as opposed to an abstraction of the world in the mind of a teacher). This contrasts with common assumptions about learning being knowledge transfer from expert to novice.

The features of active learning (Grabinger & Dunlap, 1996) are:

A.   student responsibility and initiative to promote ownership of learning and transferable skills;

B.   intentional learning strategies, explicit methods of learning, reflection on learning processes, metacognitive skills;

C.   goal-driven, problem solving tasks and projects generating learning products of value;

D.   teachers as facilitators, coaches and guides, not sources of knowledge, requiring discussion between teachers and learners;

E.   authentic contexts for learning, anchored in real-world problems;

F.   authentic assessment strategies to evaluate real-world skills; and

G.   cooperative learning.

Instructional design involves identifying the learning activities in which learners need to engage and arranging the environment in which these can occur. As students in current educational contexts are primarily motivated by accreditation, it also involves assessment methods which will motivate active learning rather than superficial memorization for examination.

The Web

It is worth clarifying 'the Web.' Technically, the Web is a client/server information service based on HyperText Transfer Protocol. This provides a platform-independent global hyper-medium based on Web pages of HyperText Markup Language.

In addition, common Web browsers can access other Internet services such as telnet, e-mail and Usenet, blurring the distinction between these resources and the Web. Furthermore, browser add-ons can run applications (like ToolBook) delivered by the Web. We can continue to use authoring systems which are being adapted for Web-based Instruction. For example, Authorware and IconAuthor applications can be played with a browser add-on. With the development of Mobile Code languages like Java, add-ons are not needed and browsers are themselves interpreters for software distributed over the Web. ToolBook II will generate native HTML and Java. So there is a variety of ways of adding programs, and thus interactivity, to Web documents.

Most loosely, the Web is the user interface of a general purpose network computer (NC) capable of accessing all Internet services, displaying all media, and executing software, which may rival the isolated PC in education.

Network Computers in Education

Educational uses for personal computers are well known. To consider how network computers (NCs) might extend them, we can divide these uses into five types (Bostock, 1996):

1. **Data resources.** Although education is not merely information access, the quantity, quality and ease of access to information are important in designing a learning environment. The Web provides access to data of all types as the global hypermedium. The Web is the standard for providing access, alongside local CD-ROMs. The two are complimentary, and increasingly, the two will be seamlessly integrated: CD-ROMs' content is fixed while Internet data is current and extendible. NCs therefore extend PCs significantly as data resources.

   Of course, Web pages can be designed specifically as educational resources (e.g., Rosenberg's "Break of Day in the Trenches"), but they also give access to real world data, not data prepared by a teacher to support a particular view. "Information technology and access to data have made it possible to design active learning experiences involving activities based on what is done in the real world" (Hicks, 1995). The quality of this data varies. Real-world data is messy, incomplete, and needs to be understood in context. Evaluation of the quality of resources becomes an important part of the curriculum, rather than an irritation, and guidelines are being developed.

   Skills in finding and evaluating information are fundamental. Web access to information is provided through hypertext in lists of resources, virtual libraries, and querying search engines (Sangster, 1995).

2. **Tools.** Computers have been used as word-processors, spreadsheets, and so on to great effect in education. As in business, they can remove tedium from information processing, leaving time for more important learning activities. One advantage of NCs over PCs will be the ability to embed data in documents (or software objects in applications), not just from other local applications, but across the Web.

   More interesting is the ability of students to publish their work on the Web. Hybrid word-processors/browsers can create Web pages without HTML knowledge. Not just student home pages, but student work in final or draft form can be accessible to other students, tutors and the world. Web-publishing as a learning outcome motivates student learning and creativity. Students can be asked to evaluate others' work routinely. Group projects can create webs on various aspects of a topic (Landow, 1992).

3. **Simulations.** Simulations, games, modelling, microworlds, and programming languages are a range of applications sharing one feature: The learner programs the computer, not vice versa. These applications provide immediate, intrinsic feedback on the learner's actions (as opposed to a tutor's comments) and give direct interaction with

content, not in abstracted forms such as text, equations, or discussion. NCs make access to such resources as the Virtual Frog Dissection easy. Multi-user simulation games can be networked to extend realism. Simulation environments can be integrated with the Web (Neilson & Thomas, 1996), and generally, the Web allows educators to flexibly integrate different resources for different courses.

4. **Tutors.** The classic PC use in education is a substitute tutor. There is a range from the simplest, page-turning linear program learning, drill and practice, computer aided assessment, branching CAI with remediation, adaptive CAL, and, finally, Intelligent Tutoring Systems.

   Web pages and forms can be used to construct branching tutorials using multiple choice, equivalent to a HyperCard or ToolBook stack (Rowe, 1995). On a NC, the results of student entries and activities can be automatically e-mailed to tutors for monitoring or feedback. HTML has been extended for authoring, for example Super-CAL, Tutorial Markup Language and W3Lessonware. Intelligent tutors require Mobile Code, as difficult to develop for NCs as PCs.

5. **Communication.** Communication by e-mail is the single most common use of the Internet, and this can be integrated with the Web. Web pages can include "*mailto:*" links and browsers can be used to read and write e-mail and Usenet newsgroups. While global Usenet is a resource, groups local to a site can be used for discussion during a course.

   Computer Supported Co-operative Learning depends on networking and is increasingly integrated with the Internet. "Computer conferencing" systems are well established in distance education and some are integrated with e-mail. Using the Web for conferencing is experimental, but we can expect rapid development (Cunningham, 1996; Gould, 1995).

   Real-time conversation is supported in a simulated environment in Multi User Dimensions. They can simulate virtual classrooms for lectures and discussion, retaining familiar methods (McManus, 1995).

An Example

So much for principles; what of practice? Recently, I taught a new course about the Internet and Cyberspace to Arts and Humanities University students with basic Windows skills. Its aims were to develop skills in using the Internet, especially the Web, and understand issues concerning the Internet and society. There is an element of cheating: the Internet is the obvious, authentic medium for instruction about the Internet, but it illustrates general principles.

Many active learning characteristics imply favorable staff/student ratios for good teacher-learner communication. This course had 285 students, one tutor, and 12 junior academic coaches in computer rooms. Within resource restrictions and the University time-table of three hours per week, the course design promoted active learning using the Web as a major resource.

- The first weekly lecture was for orientation and motivation. Thereafter video compilations about issues were shown. Copies were placed in the library.

- All other media were accessed from NCs in timetabled sessions, with coaches on hand, or from public access NCs or from home. Course materials were on our local intranet and the Web. No paper was distributed. A course home page had news, a weekly schedule, and instructions for practical tasks and assigned work.

- Assessment was via eight practical tasks submitted by e-mail, a diary of work, and either a report on a search for, and evaluation of, Internet resources on a chosen subject (as a Web page), or an essay on an issue. An early draft could be submitted for comment.

- Students were encouraged to cooperate in the sessions and could collaborate in pairs on their report or essay.

- There were many Web pages of lecture notes and resource lists, including Internet guides and courses, particularly TONIC, which includes assessment quizzes.

- A CAL package introducing Internet tools and issues on the local network was included. Students were asked to summarize it at the start of the course.

- Students created personal home pages, adapting a template.

- A local Usenet newsgroup, with a long message life, was created for discussions.

- The tutor frequently used e-mail aliases for all students and for coaches, and they used his.

- Coaches provided open access 'surgeries' at lunch times.

- Students drew concept maps of their knowledge, using Courseworks or paper.

- Course evaluation included five Web forms, interviews with 50 students, assessment grades, and diary comments.

Conclusions

A full course evaluation is in progress. Simply placing lecture content on Web pages gives flexible access but makes no contribution to active learning. Web distribution did allow more flexibility in responding quickly to student concerns and external changes, but many students complained of too much reading from the screen, and few printed the Web pages. Web forms and the e-mail were essential for interactions between tutor, coaches and students. However, student collaboration was thin—only 24 collaborated in assignments and newsgroup contributions were relatively few. Most students appreciated the assessment methods and enjoyed researching a topic of their choice and creating a Web page. The great variation found in abilities and attitudes indicates the need for a range of media, with redundancy.

In the near future, technical advances will allow the course media, such as CAL and even video, to be accessed through the Web. While convenient for course administration and student access, this will have little effect on learning: "simply publishing a World Wide Web page . . .does not constitute instruction" (Ritchie & Hoffman, 1996). What is important is the mix of media and instructional design creating a rich environment for active learning, not tight Web integration. Interaction is a necessary ingredient for many media, and good Web-based courses will use e-mail, newsgroups, Web conferencing, and other media to achieve it.

References

Bostock, S. J. (1996, June). A critical review of Laurillard's classification of educational media. *Instructional Science, 24,* 71–88.

Cunningham, S. ERCIM W4G workshop on CSCW and the Web. *Graphics and visualization, 47* (http://orgwis.gmd.de/W4G/).

Grabinger, R. S., & Dunlap, J. C. (1995). Rich environments for active learning: A definition, *Alt-J, 3*(2), 5–34.

Gould, P. (1996, Feb). Conferencing on the Web. *CTI Biology Newsletter*, 24–25.

Hicks, J. (1995). Some active learning implications of the information era. *Active Learning, 2*, 39–41.

Jonassen, D. H. (1994). Thinking technology: Towards a Constructivist design model. *Educational Technology, 34*(3), 34–37.

Landow, G. P. (1992). *Hypertext*. Baltimore: Johns Hopkins University Press.

Lebow, D. (1993). Constructivist values for instructional systems design: Five principles towards a new mindset. *Educational Technology Research and Development, 41*(3), 4–16.

McManus, T. F. (1995, Aug. 15). Special considerations for designing Internet based instruction (http://ccwf.cc.utexas.edu/~McManus/special.html).

Neilson, I., & Thomas, R. (1996). Designing educational software as a re-usable resource. *Journal of Computer Assisted Learning 12*, 114–126.

Pickering, J. (1995) Teaching on the Internet is learning. *Active Learning, 2*, 9–12.

Ritchie, D. C., & Hoffman B. (1996, March 9). Using instructional design principles to amplify learning on the World Wide Web. *SITE 96 Conference* (http://edWeb.sdsu.edu/clrit/WWWInstrdesign/WWWInstrDesign.html).

Rowe, G. (1995). Teaching computer science on the World Wide Web. *International Journal of Computers in Adult Education and Training, 5*(1), 15–27.

Sangster, A. (1995). World Wide Web: What can it do for education? *Active Learning, 2*, 3–8.

The Author

Stephen J. Bostock is Director for Information Technology, Keele University, Staffordshire, England.

e-mail, World Wide Web
   stephen@cs.keele.ac.uk
   Home page: http://www.keele.ac.uk/depts/cs/Stephen_Bostock/sjbhome.html
   Supporting page: http://www.keele.ac.uk/depts/cs/Stephen_Bostock/wbi.html

27

Incorporating Interactivity and Multimedia into Web-Based Instruction

Bijan B. Gillani and Anju Relan

A great majority of instructional Web sites lack interactive multimedia capabilities that adhere to principles of instructional design. Educational Web sites that are multimedia enhanced generally include small sound and video files that must be downloaded and individually played with specialized helper applications. Today, with the advent of such multimedia technology as Java, JavaScripting, QuickTime Streaming, ShockWave, and cable modem technology, transmission of interactive instructional multimedia titles that are in accord with contributions of cognitive science is fast becoming a reality. The intent of this chapter is to first suggest an interactive Web-based instructional model (Gillani, 1994). Then, a practical description of incorporating multimedia into such a model is presented. Finally, basic design guidelines for effective interactive multimedia Web-based instruction (WBI) are discussed.

Interactive Web-based Instructional Model

Quality Web-based instructional programs must take into account how students learn. In recent years, there has been increasing interest in Vygotsky's theory of social cognitive development for instructional purposes (Gillani, 1994). Vygotsky (1978) argued that instruction is most efficient when students engage in activities within a supportive learning environment and when they receive appropriate guidance that is mediated by tools. Tools in such an interaction can be defined as cognitive strategies, a mentor, peers, computers, printed materials, or any instrument that organizes and provides information for the learner.

Each child's level of development suggests a range of tasks that can be effectively addressed with the help of scaffolding, or dynamic support, provided by tools. The lower limit of this range of learning tasks is marked by concepts and procedures already mastered by the student. The upper limit is marked by those tasks that the student would be able to accomplish only when provided with carefully designed interaction mediated by tools. The range between the lower limit of what the student knows and the upper limit of what the student has the potential of accomplishing defines what Vygotsky termed the zone of proximal development.

In Vygotsky's view, the role of instructional tools is to organize dynamic support to help children complete a task near the upper end of their zone of proximal development and then to systematically withdraw this support as the children move to higher levels of confidence (1987). The zone of proximal development defined as such can have profound implications for Web-based instruction.

Gillani (1994) has argued that internalization of concepts and cognitive processes within the zone of proximal development is acquired by a process that involves first observing behavior through modeling. Through these modeling interactions, the form and content of any new topic is gradually transferred from mentor to student. This does not imply that the child has mastered the behavior. On the contrary, the learning process now enters a more critical mediative stage where through questioning, exploring, and experimenting, the child guides his/her own principles of the task that was initially modeled. In other words, learning progresses from reliance on others to self-guidance or self-reliance. Finally, the child through self-guidance and generative abilities internalizes behavior that was modeled by the mentor.

Meaningful learning occurs when students learn to decode new information and to encode it with their prior information. David Ausubel (1968) proposed advance organizers as a cognitive strategy that links prior knowledge structure with new information. Therefore, effective instruction, as defined here, must include four phases: Advance Organizer, Modeling, Exploring, and Generating.

Furthermore, learning does not occur in isolation within a specific discipline where information is broken into bits and pieces. Rather, learning is viewed as holistic. In *Images of Mind*, Posner and Raichle (1994) have provided neurological evidence that although learning of elementary functions is localized, the human brain functions holistically when higher psychological activities are acquired. They have provided further evidence that the holistic function of the human brain during cognitive activities is under a hierarchical control. The components of such a hierarchy are thematically related. Partly, because of cognitive neuroscience findings, interest in an interdisciplinary approach to curriculum design has dramatically increased.

Unfortunately, the design of interdisciplinary curriculum has been based on shallow themes such as transportation. The problem with such superficial themes is that they do not take into account the student's developmental needs. Erikson (1959) has argued that there are certain developmental themes that children are subliminally concerned with during maturation. Some of these epigenetic themes are change, independence, dependence, fairness, judgment, patterns, and autonomy. Rather than selecting shallow themes for interdisciplinary curriculum, the suggestion is to select themes that are inherently part of the maturational process. Designing interdisciplinary instruction based on these epigenetic themes allows students to connect with the learning process naturally.

The contributions of Vygotsky's social cognitive theories, impact of neuroscience findings, and appropriate instructional themes stimulate a rethinking of interactive instructional design that is well suited for Web-based instructional models. However, such instructional design for the Web was not possible until frame technology was introduced with Netscape Navigator 2.0 in 1995.

Basically, frames enable the Web designer to create multiple, distinct, and independent viewing areas within the browser's window. In a frame based document, the traditional <BODY> tag is replaced with a <FRAMESET> tag which defines the layout of the browser window into frames. Each frame then becomes a window that can have its own URL (Uniform Resource Locator), scrollbar, and links to frames in the same document or other documents. Such internal connections among the frames of a browser enable the designer to create interactive links that can update and control the content of other frames (Graham, 1996).

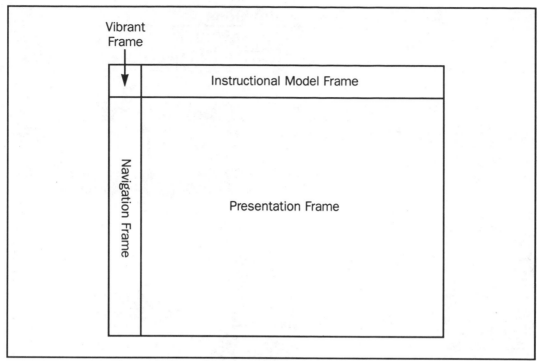

Figure 1. Use of frames for instructional design model.

Figure 1 illustrates the interactive nature of frames in interdisciplinary instructional design that has the potential of implementing cognitive theories as its theoretical foundation. It shows a schematic design where the browser window has been divided into four distinct viewing areas or frames: vibrant, instructional model, navigational, and presentation.

The four distinct areas can each represent one facet of the interactive model which was presented previously. The four learning stages as defined by Vygotsky's zone of proximal development can be inserted into the Instructional Model Frame. The contributions of interdisciplinary curriculum design can be represented in the Navigation Frame. The Presentation Frame is where the content for different phases of instruction in a specific discipline is displayed. The Vibrant Frame will be the tool that changes the thematic nature of instruction.

Figure 2 displays a Web-based instructional model that is a synergy of Vygotsky's social cognitive theories, neuroscience findings, and thematic instruction that are all embedded in frame technology. Let's briefly discuss each frame's function in Figure 2:

- The top right frame, Instructional Model, includes four buttons representing the four stages of learning as proposed by Vygotsky's zone of proximal development: Advance Organizer, Modeling, Exploring, and Generating. Each button in this frame updates and controls the content of the Navigation model.

- The left frame running down just below the Vibrant Frame is the Navigation Frame. This frame's content represents the interdisciplinary nature of instruction. However, its dynamic contents change in response to each button in the Instructional Model Frame. Depending on the nature of instruction, and the button that is clicked on in the Instructional Model Frame, various relevant disciplines appear in the Navigation Frame.

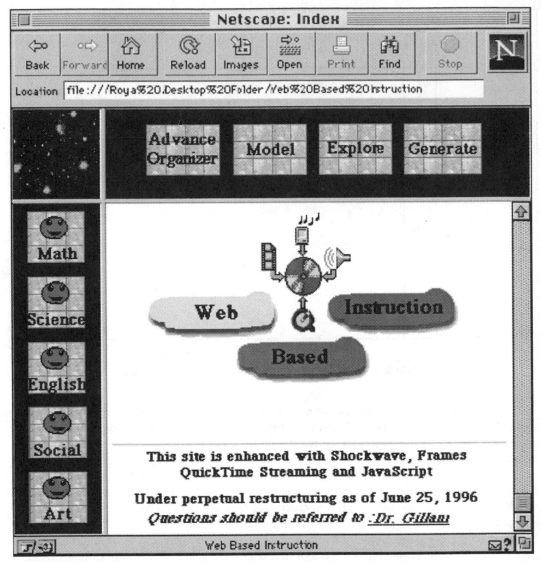

Figure 2. A social cognitive Web-based instructional model.

- The Presentation Frame displays dynamic instructional content. For example, if the lesson is in the second phase (Modeling), the menu items in the Navigation Frame may only show math, science, and art. When buttons representing different disciplines (math, science, and art) are clicked on in the Navigation Frame, a specific model for that discipline is displayed in the Presentation Frame. In the same fashion, if the lesson is in the third phase of instruction (Exploring), a different set of relevant disciplines for exploring appears in the Navigation Frame. Depending upon which button is clicked in the Navigation Frame, the Web will allow the student to explore the intended concept in the Presentation Frame.

- In the small top left area, Vibrant Frame, a QuickTime movie has been embedded which continuously shows a multimedia movie of the galaxy representing patterns. From an instructional perspective, this is the frame that determines the underlying themes for the contents. Each time the user clicks on it, a new theme will appear which changes the entire content of the lesson being presented.

Incorporating Interactivity and Multimedia into Instructional Web Sites

With the introduction of Netscape Navigator 2.0, the Web was transformed from being only a static display of files that was limited to text and graphics. Navigator 2.0 and its more recent descendant, Navigator 3.0, support a host of plug-ins that include such powerful interactive multimedia applications as Java, JavaScripting, ShockWave, and QuickTime Streaming. The reader will be provided with a general description of JavaScript and ShockWave as two examples of recent technologies that allow incorporating interactivity and multimedia into Web sites.

JavaScript

JavaScript is a full-feature object based scripting language. It is less powerful than Java programming language. However, JavaScript works quite effectively when it is embedded into HTML codes. With JavaScript, content is no longer static. Objects on the page (such as buttons, texts, and windows) can respond to user action directly because the codes that run the document are downloaded into the client's computer rather than coming from the server's script.

JavaScript was originally developed by Netscape with no relation to Java programming. However, when it became apparent that Java programming was going to dominate the Internet industry, Netscape pursued a partnership relationship with Sun's Java program and renamed it from LiveScript to JavaScript.

There are several salient features that make JavaScript a vigorous scripting language.

In comparison to Java, JavaScript is much more simple to learn. It is based on the syntax of Java. However, while Java may take months to master, JavaScript can be learned within a few weeks. It can easily be embedded into any HTML codes. The following is an example of how simple it is to include JavaScript into an HTML document:

```
<HTML>
<HEAD>
<TITLE.> WEB-BASED-INSTRUCTION<TITLE>
<SCRIPT LANGUAGE=3D" JavaScript">
< ! - - The main part of Script goes here, - - >
</Script>
</HEAD/>
<BODY>
< ! - - The body of the HTML goes here- - >
</BODY>
</HTML>
```

The most salient feature of JavaScript is that it is dynamic and functions on the client's side. JavaScript can be used to create programs that interact with the user without relying on CGI (Common Gateway Interface) programs which define how the browser, server, and script communicate. Because JavaScript is an interpretative language (not compiled), its codes can be embedded into HTML files and be interpreted on the fly. That is, when the file is transmitted to the user's side, the browser (e.g., Netscape) interprets the script and performs the intended function.

JavaScript is also object oriented. This means it is a method of building software that focuses on creating reusable data objects. These objects include window, dialog box, location, history, etc. What is important about JavaScript is that it can create its own objects or interact with objects that are included in the browser. Such interactions with objects allow developers to embed JavaScript in HTML documents for powerful programs that only advanced programs such as Java or C++ can provide.

The combination of simplicity, dynamic interaction, and object-oriented features allow developers to use JavaScript to create interactive Web-based instructional units that react to students' input rather than relying on the server's CGI script. For example, JavaScript can be used to create mathematical units that monitor and interact with students' input. It can be used to verify students' answers, their names, their scores, and text input such as their passwords. The capabilities of JavaScript are bound to make JavaScript an ideal tool for educators to create Web-based instruction that is far superior to the static capability of the Web document that is currently being practiced.

ShockWave

ShockWave is an example of compression technology for the Web. It was developed by Macromedia as a new way to compress large multimedia files. It is also designed to embed interactive multimedia titles created with Director or Authorware into HTML documents to be downloaded and played by Browsers. The most essential components of ShockWave technology for the Web are: Director (or Authorware), Afterburner, HTML Tag, and Plug-in.

Director is an authoring tool with extensive features that are used to create interactive multimedia units. Using its powerful Lingo (similar to HyperTalk Scripting Language), one can create complex multimedia units.

The main problem with incorporating Director movies into Web sites is their huge file size. To reduce file size and make Director movies Internet compatible, Macromedia engineers developed Afterburner, which is a post-compression technology.

During the compression process, Afterburner will alert the user to rename the Director movie by adding the ".DCR" (Director Compressed Resources) extension to the end of the original Director movie. After the process of compressing the Director movie is completed, its icon changes into a frying pan and can no longer be opened with the Director application. The compressed movie is called a ShockWave and can only be opened by placing it inside an HTML document using a new tag called <EMBED>.

Plug-in is the engine that allows Netscape and other browsers to play back multimedia units on the Web. The new technology allows third-party developers to embed their helper applications directly into the browser. Some of the plug-ins that are supported by Netscape Navigator are Adobe's Amber (Acrobat files), Macromedia ShockWave (multimedia), Paper's WebFX (VRML), and Apple's QuickTime Streaming (QuickTime).

Multimedia Design Guidelines for Web-Based Instruction

- Keep frames simple and be consistent in design of text graphics and sound. Simplicity and consistency eliminates cognitive overload.

- Do not distract the attention of the learner by providing unnecessary elements in a multimedia presentation. Use multimedia components to reinforce rather than distract from learning.

- Use multimedia components to cue the learner to important concepts and grab the learner's attention.

- Combine colors attractively to appeal to students. (For example, the color orange attracts attention, whereas the color blue creates a non-threatening environment.)

- Multimedia should convey information rather than be an art piece.

- Always keep the size of animation as small as possible.

- Dual encoding through the use of multimedia is an effective means of instruction.

References

Ausubel, D. P. (1968). *Educational psychology: A cognitive view*. New York: Holt, Rinehart, and Winston.

Erikson, E. H. (1959). Identity and the life cycle. *Psychological Issues Monograph*. Vol. 1. New York: International Universities Press.

Gillani, B. B. (1994). *Application of Vygotsky's social cognitive theory to the design of instructional materials*, unpublished dissertation, University of Southern California.

Graham, I. S. (1996). *HTML sourcebook: A complete guide to HTML 3.0*. New York: John Wiley & Sons.

Harpinski, R. (1996). *Beyond HTML*. Berkeley, CA: Osborne-McGraw-Hill.

Posner, M. I., & Raichle, M. E. (1994). *Images of mind*. NewYork: Scientific American Library.

Vygotsky, L. S. (1978). *Mind in society: The development of higher psychological processes*. Cambridge, MA: MIT Press.

The Authors

Bijan B. Gillani is Associate Professor and Coordinator of the Graduate Program in Educational Technology Leadership, School of Education, California State University, Hayward.

e-mail, World Wide Web
bgillani@csuhayward.edu
http://edschool.csuhayward.edu/bgillani/bijan.html

Anju Relan is Director, Instructional Design and Technology Unit, School of Medicine, University of California at Los Angeles.

e-mail, World Wide Web
arelan@ucla.edu
http://www.mednet.ucla.ed~/dept./som/edr/IDTUtap.htm

28

User Interface Design for Web-Based Instruction

Marshall G. Jones and John D. Farquhar

User Interface Design

In a computer based educational environment, user interface design refers to the creation of a seamless integration of content and control. This integration includes the physical layout of the information in the program and how the navigation of the program is conceptualized and implemented. Historically speaking, user interface design has long been the concern, and the domain, of the designers of system software (e.g., MS DOS, MS Windows, Windows 95, Mac OS) and application software designers (e.g., productivity software such as word processors, spreadsheets, or graphic programs). M. G. Jones (1995) provides a history of how the design focus on educational software has shifted from one focusing on screen design (Heines, 1984) to one focusing on user interface design (M. K. Jones, 1989; Jones, Farquhar, & Surry, 1995). For the purpose of context, suffice it to say that exponential growth in technology has fostered a move beyond linear tutorials.

Open Systems Versus Closed Systems

Today, educational software both functions and appears radically different from its not-that-much-earlier versions. Enormous multimedia applications provide users with seemingly endless paths, seemingly endless variations, and volumes and volumes of information. But the seemingly infinite material contained in educational multimedia applications is deceiving. For each and every one of these 600 MB programs is, in fact, finite. They are closed systems. They contain only what the designers and developers included. So while the learners have freedom to move within the environment, every choice that they can make has been predetermined by the designer.

World Wide Web pages are not stand-alone applications. They are documents written and formatted in Hyper Text Mark-up Language (HTML). The formatting of these pages is viewable only when they are "translated" by a World Wide Web browser (e.g., Netscape or Mosaic). And, as anybody who has ever surfed the World Wide Web knows, the type, version, and configuration of your browser makes a noticeable difference in how these pages look and perform. Additionally, the content of a World Wide Web course is potentially infinite. It is an open system. Links to sites not created by the designer can be provided for within the pages, or made by the user given knowledge of the address. While having an open system has its appeal, it can make designing for it extremely difficult, because in an open system, the designer agrees to give up a certain amount of control to the user.

Losing Control Within an Open System

Implementing a hypermedia program via the Web creates a loss of control over the standard concerns of display and interactive design. Unless you are delivering the content to a very specified and standard audience, you will not be able to identify the broad range of computer hardware platforms and configurations, operating systems, and browsers, as well as the myriad user settings available through each browser. You will not be able to limit your users to any particular path; they can access any page directly, given knowledge of the address. You will not know how your users will be using the materials. The digital information displayed on their screen can be printed, saved, or stolen. And, if you've allowed global access to your materials, you will know not whether your user is a native speaker of your language, a speaker of any language, an alien, etc.

This loss of control may suggest that user-interface design for Web-based products is completely futile. To the contrary, one can also argue that user-interface design is central and essential. Without consideration toward user preferences of perception and behavior, your product will become useless and unused. The design of open systems is simply more challenging. Let's consider how each issue of the open system affects design principles. Our discussion will consider two broad categories of concern: (1) the loss of technical control, and (2) the loss of curricular control.

Loss of Technical Control

The loss of technical control involves four architectural layers of Web technology. We will proceed through these concerns as if peeling through concentric shells, beginning with the outermost layer.

Layer 1: **Display Hardware.** Computer hardware limits the users to certain capabilities regardless of the software that they may be using. Basic screen resolutions will control the image size and grades of color. In fact, one can view and interact with Web materials using a monochrome monitor that virtually eliminates all of your artistically-crafted graphics. The users of such systems retrieve nothing but fixed-width alphanumeric characters.

Layer 2: **Connection Speed.** While the processor speed and total memory available will also contribute to interaction and display limitations, the component creating the greatest limitation to the most users is likely to be the speed and reliability of the connection to the network. The fastest and most reliable of connections challenge the most patient of users.

Layer 3: **Software.** Software that the user has installed affects the display and navigation of materials in quite different ways. While the use of different operating systems can impact the delivery of application-specific Web materials, this concern can be transparent and safely ignored in most instances. The use of different Web browsers is a much greater concern than the user's operating system. The features within the various browsers, while fairly standard, are often implemented in very different ways. For example, the all-important navigation buttons implemented along the Netscape Navigator toolbar are quite different in appearance and placement than those of the Microsoft Explorer browser. These inconsistencies are actually much more acceptable than differences in the way that browsers apparently interpret the HTML code. The position of text and graphics within the body of a page can be radically different, depending upon the type of browser used. The lack of standard interpretation of HTML causes the greatest concern for designers who desire control over the presentation of their work.

Layer 4: **User Settings.** The final loss of technical control of this open system can be found in the user settings. Depending upon the browser, users have control over the size of the window, font sizes, types, and colors of backgrounds and text among other settings. Nearly every control originally given to the designer is now in hands of the user. If the user has that much control, many designers may decide to give up all considerations toward the user. That, we believe, is a mistake.

Loss of Curricular Control

Open systems bring about a loss of control over many curricular issues as well as technical issues. Within an open system, users have greater freedom over the application of your materials.

The most obvious freedom given to the user in a hypermedia environment is the sequencing of information. Hypermedia, by definition, is the removal of a strict, linear, designer-driven sequence in order to allow for user-driven sequencing decisions. This abdication, however, does not remove responsibility from the designer to appropriately structure information. Instead, effective hypermedia requires greater consideration toward structure, display, and, consequently, user interface design.

Guidelines for the Interface Design of Web-Based Instruction

The design principles presented here fall into two areas. The first is an adaptation of user interface design principles developed by Jones and Okey (1995) as they apply to The Open System of Web-based Instruction. The second group is a list of standard HTML design suggestions filtered through the issues associated with Web-based instruction. These principles should be seen as a starting point for development, and a springboard for further research in the area.

1. **Provide structural cues.** The endless flow of information available on the Web creates a kind of "information vertigo." Arrange information in a non-threatening manner through techniques such as chunking, overviews, advance organizers, maps, and a fixed-display format. The consistent placement and style of section titles is one important cue to the structure of information.

2. **Clearly identify selectable areas.** Existing standards within Web browsing identify selectable areas visually with a royal blue color and interactively with changes of the cursor as the cursor is moved to a hot spot. Unless there is a good reason to violate this standard, use the royal blue color to indicate selectable areas and avoid the use of graphic maps which do not conform to these standards.

3. **Indicate selections made.** Users expect a system to register when a selection has been made. The HTML standard is to immediately change the royal blue selection color to a dark red upon selection. This feature notifies the user that the selection has been registered. While programmers of HTML can modify this color, we suggest that the standard be used.

4. **Indicate progress made.** A common support mechanism that the designer can provide is information describing the progress made. Such a "bread-crumbing" feature is another HTML standard. Links that have been accessed become a light red color. Unless you have reasons to remove such support, allow the standard to remain.

HTML Style Guidelines Applied to Web-Based Instruction

The following guidelines are HTML style recommendations which have been filtered through the issues inherent to user interface design. If you are unfamiliar with HTML style guides, you may find the sites listed in Table 1 to be a good place to start. As with the above interface design guidelines, these should be seen not as an end, but as a beginning place for further research and development.

A. **Provide multiple versions of your material.** A short page before the materials can offer a "dial up" version, with a text only version, or a version with smaller graphics, and a version for those with "big pipes" or direct network connections which contains larger graphics. This is illustrated nicely in "Pathways to School Improvement" (see Table 2).

B. **Offer help in configuring your learner's browsers.** While the addition of multimedia assets can offer users more variety in the information they see and deal with, it also requires that the learner has the correct "plug ins" or "helper application" installed on his or her machine. In the excellent PBS on the Internet program "Life on the Internet" (see Table 2), the designers provided users with a page which told them exactly which "plug ins" they would need. Links were provided to the sites where they could download Real Audio, Java, and other software to take full advantage of the material in the pages.

Table 1. Sites on interface design for World Wide Web pages.

Name of the Site	Author	Address or URL	Comments
Web Wonk	David Siegel	http://www.dsiegel.com/tips/index.html	A good site which raises issues and offers suggestions of various techniques.
Style Guideline for Online Hypertext	Tim Berners-Lee	http://www.w3.org/pub/WWW/Provider/Style/	Well written examination of the issues. Offers specific design recommendations.
A Practical Guide to HTML Publishing	Rick Reynolds	http://members.aol.com/Rick1515/index.htm	Fantastic links to HTML tools and style guidelines.
Web Style Manual	Patrick J. Lynch	http://info.med.yale.edu/caim/StyleManual_Top.HTML	Considered by many to be the best resource on HTML style.
Building Usable Web Pages: An HCI Perspective	Tim Comber	http://www.scu.edu.au/ausweb95/papers/hypertext/comber	A very good article dealing with the usability of Web pages.
Interface Design for Sun's World Wide Web site	Jakob Nielsen	http://www.sun.com:80/sun-on-net/uidesign	This is quite possibly the best site we have seen on user interface design on the World Wide Web. The research based guidelines are presented, and use of the World Wide Web for reporting the research is excellent.

C. **Keep pages short.** Short is relative. Sites such as Instructional Technology Research On-line (InTRO) publish research articles that are necessarily long (see Table 2). One should use as much text and information as needed, but research on the use of World Wide Web pages suggests that users do not like to scroll (Nielsen, 1996). Additionally, the longer the page, the longer it takes to load. The problem with making pages short is that people may choose to print out certain pieces of information, or download the entire contents of a group of pages. This can be handled by combining all of the pages into a single document that is labeled as being suitable for downloading or printing. Berners-Lee (1995) handles this nicely in his Web page style guide paper (see Table 2).

D. **Link to other pages, not to other points in the same page.** Jumping within the same page adds to the confusion of the learner. On very long pages, a jump to another section within a page may appear to be a jump to another page. If the learner goes to the "Back" button on the browser, then he or she can become lost.

E. **Select your links carefully; place your links carefully.** Nielsen (1996) says it best: "...if everything is highlighted, then nothing has prominence (emphasis in original)." The power of the World Wide Web is to offer links. But if too many links are offered, then confusion may set in for your learners. You may choose to prioritize or annotate your links for the users. The online magazine Slate (see Table 2) provides an interesting twist on the use of hypertext. In most of their articles, the related links are at the bottom of the page or at the end of the text they want you to read. This technique encourages people to read the entire passage, and helps organize the links for the user. Links placed within the passage can offer further information, clarification, and exploration opportunities for learners.

F. **Label links appropriately.** Many links are labeled quite cryptically. It is common to see links labeled like the following: "for more information on the migratory path of whales click **here**" (where **here** is the labeled link). HTML conventions make it possible to have entire sentences serve as a single hypertext link. Berners-Lee (1995) suggests that "...the thing-you-click is actually some kind of title for what it is when you click there." For example, "more information on **the migratory path of whales** is available" (where **the**

Table 2. URLs of cited pages.

Name of the Site	URL or Address	Description and techniques used
Pathways to School Improvement	http://www.ncrel.org/ncrel/sdrs/pathways.html	Multiple versions of a content provided for users with different connection speeds.
Life on the Internet	http://www2.pbs.org/internet/	Links provided to places to download plug-ins and helper applications needed to make the most of a particular site.
Instructional Technology	http://129.7.160.78/InTRO.html	Use of long text passages to publish research.
Style Guide for Online Hypertext	http://www.w3.org/pub/Provider/Style/	Example of combining contents from from multiple pages into a single page for the purpose of printing or downloading.
Slate	http://www.slate.come	An example of keeping hypertext links at the bottom of the page.

migratory path of whales is the labeled link). Additionally, your address or uniform resource locator (URL) can be an interface design issue (Nielsen, 1996). There are few URLs that people can remember. URLs such as www.cnn.com or www.mapquest.com are easy to remember and type into the location window of a browser.

G. **Keep important information at the top of the page.** People don't like to scroll (Nielsen, 1996). When learners come to a page, they are looking for interesting and important information. Give them the information they need and want in a hurry. Large static graphics at the top of a page may look nice, but if they take up the majority of the window's immediate viewable space, then you are likely wasting the space.

Conclusion

Much has been said in this chapter about the differences between closed and open systems and the inherent difficulties in designing open systems. The purpose of stating these differences is not to discourage people from using them, but to make the important point that designing instructional or educational materials for the Web is a starkly different proposition than designing traditional educational software.

References

Berners-Lee, T. (1995). Style guide for online hypertext (http://www.w3.org/pub/Provider/Style/All.html).

Heines, J. (1984). *Screen design strategies for computer-assisted instruction.* Bedford, MA: Digital Press..

Jones, M. G. (1995). Visuals for information access: A new philosophy for screen and interface design. In D. G. Beauchamp, R. A. Braden, & R. E. Griffin (Eds.), *Imagery and visual literacy* (pp. 264–272). Blacksburg, VA: International Visual Literacy Association.

Jones, M. G., Farquhar, J. D., & Surry, D. W. (1995). Using metacognitive theories to design user interfaces for computer-based learning. *Educational Technology, 35*(4), 12–22.

Jones, M. G., & Okey, J. R. (1995). Interface design for computer-based learning environments (http://129.7.160.78/InTRO.html).

Jones, M. K. (1989). *Human-computer interaction: A design guide.* Englewood Cliffs, NJ: Educational Technology Publications.

Nielsen, J. (1996). Interface design for Sun's World Wide Web site (http://www.sun.com:80/sun-on-net/uidesign/).

The Authors

Marshall G. Jones is Assistant Professor of Instructional Technology at Northern Illinois Unversity, DeKalb, Illinois

e-mail, World Wide Web
  mgjones@niu.edu.
  http://129.7.160.78/InTRO.html

John D. Farquhar is Assistant Professor of Instructional Technology at Pennsylvania State University, Harrisburg, Pennsylvania.

e-mail, World Wide Web
  jfarquhar@psu.edu
  http://www.hbg.psu.edu/~jxf18/

29

The Design of Distance Education Applications Based on the World Wide Web[1]

Barbara Pernici and
Fabio Casati

Introduction

In many organizations, the design of Web pages has been based on a bottom-up approach: The decision to provide information is made, the design (and graphical presentation) of single pages is the focus of the work, and then pages are linked to each other based on case by case decisions. On the other hand, in most World Wide Web applications, and in particular, within organizations, the type of information provided in a Web site is based on organizational data, in many cases already stored in an existing information system or at least available on paper. When designing the computer supported information system of an organization, the use of a systematic approach is quite established, yet in the case of Web sites, such an approach is not a common practice. The result of a lack of a systematic approach to designing World Wide Web sites is the well-known difficulty in retrieving the required information, and one of the consequences is the mostly navigational and "surfing" approach to the use of the Web. This problem is particularly critical in long-distance courses, where the user typically needs to visit the site for a long period of time, and with great attention.

In this chapter, we advocate the use of a methodological approach to the design of a long distance education application. We base our approach on the integration of techniques adopted for conceptual modeling of data, workflow (WF) conceptual design, and hypermedia design, structuring the approach in different phases for the consideration of conceptual and functional aspects first, and a systematic derivation of the structure of the site and of single Web pages from the initial conceptual design. The approach is illustrated by a site for distance education under development at Politecnico di Milano. The chapter is structured as follows: First, we describe our approach to the development of Web sites, and we present a case study for the development of a distance education course on database systems. Next, the Requirement-Analysis phase and requirement specification using Entity-Relationship (ER) and WF conceptual models are discussed. Then, the derivation of the structure of the Web

---

[1]Part of this work has been presented at the *Teaching and Learning on the World Wide Web Workshop*, Paris, May 1996.

site and "design in the small" of Web pages are illustrated. Finally, we close with remarks and some thoughts about future work.

A Systematic Approach to Design and Development of World Wide Web Applications

A systematic approach to information system design has been advocated, resulting in several design methodologies and models (Olle, Hagelstein, Macdonald, Rolland, Sol, Van Assche, & Verrijn-Stuart, 1988). Such methodologics traditionally concentrate on the first development phases, to capture the static and dynamic aspects to be supported by the information system. From several points of view, the development of a Web application has many characteristics in common with traditional information systems. However, there are some new characteristics typical of Web applications:

- the variety of access interfaces, which are not under control of the application developer; and

- the possibility of performing coordinated work through the Web.

A design methodology to develop Web applications, taking into consideration these different aspects, is essential in order to create applications fruitful to a great number of users, who may be visiting a site with different purposes and different technological capabilities. Advantages of having a well defined methodology include abstract conceptualization, improved interaction with the users, design for change, and systematic process development.

In developing online courses, the use of a well defined methodology is perhaps even more important than in ordinary Web applications. Here the focus is using a clear, logical structure to present the available material, without losing visitors in insignificant details or links which distract the attention of the user from the educational goals. The methodology we propose keeps the design of Web sites at the highest possible level of abstraction to force the developer to deeply analyze all conceptual issues before addressing low-level topics, such as links between HTML pages. Particular emphasis is put on the analysis of the characteristics of the expected user population, and in the semi-automatic derivation of Web pages. The methodology consists of the following four steps:

1. *Analysis of requirements*: The objectives of the site are defined.

2. *Specifications of requirements*: These include the modeling of the users who will visit the site, the representation of the data which constitute the *contents* of the site and of the data needed to process requests to the Web site (we will call this type of information *administration data*), and the representation of the patterns of user interaction of the sites.

3. *Design in the large*: The structure of the Web site is derived from the models defined in the specification phase.

4. *Design in the small*: Details concerning pages and links are defined, and graphical presentation is chosen.

In the following sections, we describe the case study which has been at the basis of our experimentation with the approach; it will be used throughout this chapter to exemplify the concepts that will be introduced.

Case Study: A Course on Database Systems

Experimentation has been performed on database courses, but the approach to site design has been generic with respect to the type of course to be supported. Available course material includes a set of slides, taken from lessons at universities, summer stages, or seminars. The main objective is to give students a complete course on database systems, including basic concepts as well as advanced issues. Users will mainly be part of the Computer Science degree course, but students from other degree courses and graduates are allowed to participate as well. The Web site should provide different access paths, targeted to the students' backgrounds and needs. At the end of every lesson module and at the end of the course, tests and exercises will enable the evaluation of each student's learning. This should be achieved mainly through automatic evaluation of the exercises. It is also planned that a tutor will be assigned to every registered student. Among the objectives of the Web site is support for instructors and researchers. In particular, researchers should be able to find materials on some hot research topics, as well as pointers to papers and other material.

Requirements Analysis and Specification

Requirements Analysis

Analyzing the site objectives and defining possible users is the very first step of the design process. In particular, there is the need to segment all potential visitors in order to understand the information and the functionalities to be provided for each category. Segmentation is performed according to two different criteria: student background/objectives and non-functional requirements.

Background/Objectives Segmentation

This segmentation has the purpose of determining which views of the existing material should be proposed to each type of visitor. By segmenting possible users, the designer can analyze the characteristics of the visitors and can offer a personalized access to each segment. Segmentation process can be *multilevel*: At first, users are segmented according to a certain factor (e.g., the degree course of a student). Then each of the segments is further divided into smaller groups by segmenting according to other factors (e.g., year in the degree course, or attendance in a specific course). In this way, the designer obtains a *segmentation tree*. At the end of the process, the leaves will represent the different categories for which the designer may want to offer a personalized access path. The goal of this phase is to identify the goals and needs for each user profile. In the database course example, the segmentation is shown in Figure 1.

Non-functional Requirements

For non-functional requirements, the segmentation process should relate hardware and software requirements, and connection speed. Hardware and software greatly differ when different countries are considered. Problems for connection speed are even higher: If we just want to serve our students on campus, we can expect fast connection with up-to-date, graphical browsers, including the required helper application. It is possible to use advanced multimedia features, and even non-standard HTML or Java, if we know which browsers are available in the university and available dialects. However, different access modalities should be provided for different clients. It is wise to provide pages readable by textual browsers and to make available some sub-courses for downloading, in order to be viewed locally.

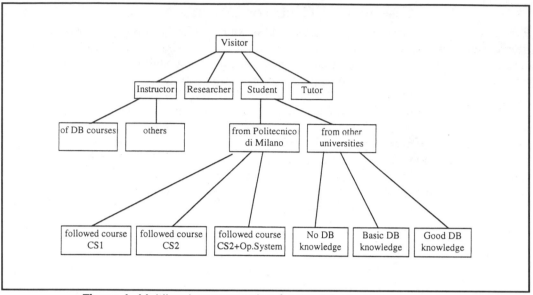

Figure 1. Multilevel segmentation for the DB course case study.

Requirements Specification

As mentioned above, requirements specification focuses mainly in representing the following characteristics:

- *data specification:* information to be provided and administration data;

- *process specification:* patterns of interactions with the World Wide Web application.

Data Specification

Setting up a Web site always requires a careful organization of the available data. Poorly organized (or missing) data often result in a deficient organization of the course, which causes disorientation in the users. Modeling with the E-R model helps one to understand the structure of complex data, and therefore helps in structuring its access by users from the navigational point of view. In particular, courses are usually characterized by a great amount of heterogeneous material. It is essential that the data have a clear and defined logical organization; otherwise, the visitor will get lost in the Web due to disorientation problems. In designing online courses, an important role is played by 'back-office' or administration data; that is, information on student visits. This information must be tightly coupled with the course contents in order to provide a 'personalized' access to students and for instructors and tutors to monitor the site. Most student 'back-office' data must not be directly mapped into HTML pages; on the contrary, they should not be displayed at all. Usually these data are used to generate pages (or sets of related pages) on-the-fly. For instance, in the database course example, student data are used to generate a page containing graded exercises, topics in which someone needs another lesson, and pointers to these lessons. The E-R diagram of the database course case study is depicted in Figure 2. Shaded areas indicate back-office (administration) data, while white areas are concerned with the contents of the courses.

Process Specification

Modeling the user access to the application is a basic step towards building a Web site focused on user needs, removing in these early design phases the constraint given by the im-

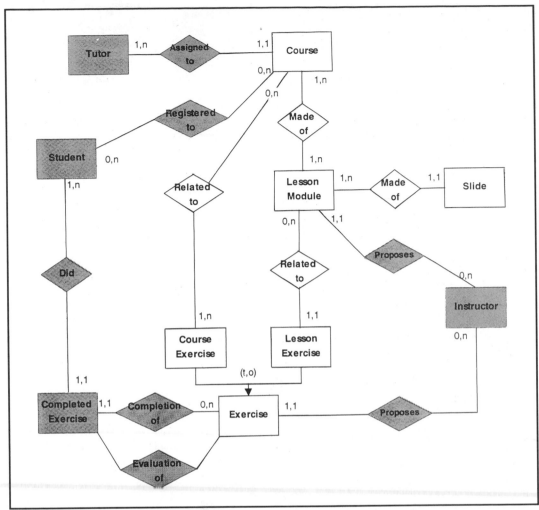

Figure 2. E-R diagram describing course data.

plementation. In fact, starting a project from the navigational structure has some major draw-backs. The problem is that the attention of the designer focuses on determining what are the possible links among available data. In this link-driven approach, it often happens that the vis-itor has too much (or too limited) freedom of navigating through data. In online courses, this is an even bigger problem, since the student might be tempted to 'surf' on the sea of available material rather than effectively follow the lessons.

In our methodology, therefore, the designer focuses on trying to determine the most ef-fective student behavior. User behavior may be specified by using *workflow* conceptual mod-els. These models simultaneously describe both manual and automatic actions (such as database updates).

In this early design phase, the designer should model the behavior of the student follow-ing the course independently from the specific aspects of the Web server connection. This forces the designer to try to capture the ideal student workflow. A workflow diagram repre-senting the student conceptual visit is depicted in Figure 3.

The basic assumption that will be made in the realization of the site is that this se-quence of tasks described in the workflow will be kept for each student, regardless of

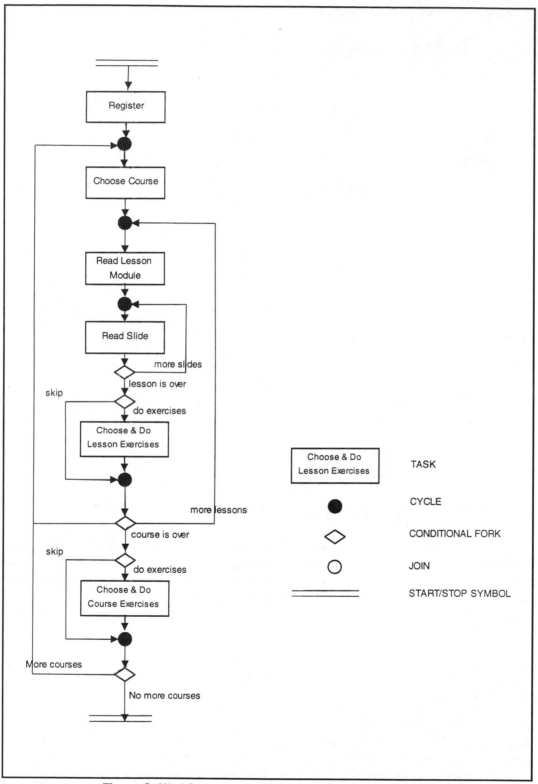

Figure 3. Workflow representing student conceptual visit.

whether the student takes a complete course at one time or leaves the system and then resumes the interaction. In both cases, the interaction with the student is in a state-dependent interaction pattern, with the system remembering the previous actions performed by that student.

Design

The design of a Web site is generally composed of two phases:

- *Design in the large:* The overall structure of the Web site is described by high level models that define links between logically related groups of information. Starting from the E-R diagram, and with the guidelines given by the workflow representation, it is possible to progressively derive (1) a description of the *navigational schema*, i.e., a schema that describes groups of logically related information, as well as access modalities to this information (e.g., through an index or a defined path), and (2) a HDM (Hypermedia Design Model; Garzotta, Paolini, & Schwabe, 1993) description of the Web site (a hierarchical description of links connecting the different information elements).

- *Design in the small:* the detailed project of the HTML pages is performed, focusing on presentation of aspects of each page. Design in the small is not discussed further.

Deriving the Navigational Schema

The *navigational schema* is obtained by adding semantics to the E-R links by analyzing the workflow models. Borrowing and extending concepts introduced in RMDM (Relation Management Data Model) diagrams (Isakowitz, Sthor, & Balasubramanian, 1995), we define the following link types:

- *menu:* information represented by the entity can be accessed via a menu;

- *sequence:* information represented by the entity can be accessed in a sequential way, controlled by the server, from the first to the last item;

- *trigger:* denote actions that represent interfaces between contents (course) data and administration data. Actions corresponds to services offered by the Web server.

In the DB course, for instance, we want to access courses by a menu, while lessons in a course are accessed in a sequential way. Besides entity and links, the RMDM also includes an entry point, representing the home page of the Web site. The RMDM derivation process takes advantage of the fact that the WF specification shows how a student accesses the different parts of the course.

These access modalities are represented in the workflow description by tasks representing user choices or by cycles, respectively; therefore, the transformation of choices and cycles in the workflow into the appropriate access to an entity in the navigational schema is the main aspect of the derivation process. For instance, the task *Choose Course* in the WF diagram causes a menu access to the *Course* entity to be inserted in the RMDM diagram, while the cycle involving the task *Read Slide* in the WF diagram causes a sequential access to the entity *Slide* to be inserted in the RMDM. The RMDM diagram of the DB course case study is depicted in Figure 4; the figure also includes links derived from WFs describing tutor and instructor visits. An algorithm for the semi-automatic derivation of an extended RMDM notation from the E-R and WF schemas is defined in Casati and Pernici (1996) with an example similar to our case study.

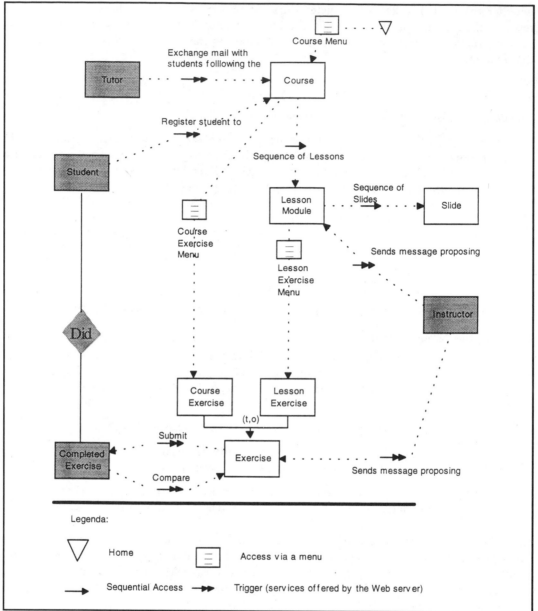

Figure 4. RMDM representation for the DB course case study.

Concluding Remarks and Future Work

A methodology and systematic development techniques for the design and implementation of distance education applications based on the World Wide Web have been presented. Initial design phases are based on conceptual design, and in particular on conceptual data modeling and on specification of interactions with different types of users through a workflow conceptual model. Particular attention has been paid to the problem of analyzing the characteristics of the population which is the target of the site. Segmentation criteria have been proposed for analyzing functional and non-functional requirements of the population.

Design techniques have been oriented towards a systematic derivation of Web pages from the conceptual schemas obtained in the first phases.

A case focusing on supporting interactions with database course students has been discussed. The course is currently under development at Politecnico di Milano (its completion is due in early 1997), and it will be used to support the classroom course on database systems at the engineering school.

We expect that the course will enable students to improve their learning by:

- providing a source to retrieve course material, in a personalized way;

- allowing interactions with other students and with tutors, besides ordinary classroom interaction with the instructor;

- providing means to test their learning, and to focus on aspects in which they feel weaker, with automatically generated study guidelines according to the results of the tests;

- allowing students who are unable to follow some lessons to keep their preparation up to date, in order to effectively follow the next classroom lessons; and

- offering the possibility to deepen their knowledge of subjects perhaps just briefly introduced in the classroom.

Implementation of techniques to achieve connection transparency is currently being studied by tracking students' visits, in order to let them continue from the point at which they left during the previous connection.

Future work will concentrate on providing a design support environment for the development of new applications. Tools to develop new courses based on the available schemas will be realized. In addition, advanced development environments focusing on the semi-automatic derivation of the structure of the Web pages from conceptual schemas will be experimented with and integrated with available tools supporting Web page production and with a DBMS to store WF support information.

The tools and the methodology should enable the delivery of Web-based courses with a common, consistent design for courses at the same university. We believe that this effort in delivering courses with a somewhat standardized structure would give students a consistent environment that can be effectively used to support their learning activity.

References

Casati F., Ceri S., Pernici B., & Pozzi G. (1995). Conceptual modeling of workflows. *Proc. of the Object-Oriented and Entity-Relationship Conf.*, LNCS Springer Verlag, Gold Coast, Australia.

Casati F., & Pernici B. (1996). A methodology for the design of World Wide Web sites and its application to distance education, *Proc. of SEBD '96*, Pisa, Italy.

Communications of the ACM. (1995, August). Special issue on designing hypermedia applications.

Garzotto F., Mainetti, L., & Paolini P. (1995, August). Hypermedia design, analysis, and evaluation issues. *Communications of the ACM.*

Garzotto F., Paolini P., & Schwabe D. (1993, Jan.). HDM: A model based approach to hypertext application design. *ACM Transactions on Information Systems.*

Isakowitz T., Sthor E., & Balasubramanian P. (1991, August). RMM: A methodology for structured hypermedia design. *Communications of the ACM.*

Olle T., Hagelstein J, Macdonald I., Rolland C., Sol H., Van Assche F., & Verrijn-Stuart, A. (1988). *Information systems methodologies.* Reading, MA: Addison-Wesley

Acknowledgments

Part of this work has been supported by a scholarship by Hewlett-Packard for the design of a World Wide Web site supporting advanced database courses.

The Authors

Barbara Pernici is a Professor, Dipartimento di Elettronica e Informazione, Politecnico di Milano, Italy.

e-mail, World Wide Web
pernici@elet.polimi.it
http://www.elet.polimi.it/people/pernici

Fabio Casati is a doctoral student Dipartimento di Elettronica e Informazione, Politecnico di Milano, Italy.

e-mail, World Wide Web
caseti@elet.polimi.it
http://www.elet.polimi.it/~casati/casati.html

30

Electronic Textbooks on the World Wide Web: From Static Hypertext to Interactivity and Adaptivity

Peter Brusilovsky, Elmar Schwarz, and Gerhard Weber

Introduction

The World Wide Web opens new ways of learning for many people. Now, educational programs and learning materials installed and supported in one place can be used by thousands of students from all over the world. However, most of the existing educational World Wide Web applications use the simplest solutions and are much weaker and more restricted than existing 'on-site' educational systems and tools. For many designers, the ideal form of educational World Wide Web material seems to be a static electronic copy of a regular textbook: chapter by chapter, page by page, picture by picture. Such "static electronic textbooks" have two major shortcomings. First, they are not interactive enough, i.e., students can only passively read the educational materials. Second, they are non-adaptive, i.e., students with different abilities, knowledge, and background get the same educational material in the same form. At the same time, interactivity is very important for any educational application as a prerequisite of active learning. Adaptivity is especially important for educational applications on the World Wide Web, which are expected to be used by very different classes of users without assistance of a human teacher (who usually can provide adaptivity in a normal classroom).

This chapter discusses the problems of developing interactive and adaptive "textbooks" on the World Wide Web. We present the system ELM-ART (Brusilovsky, Schwarz, & Weber, 1996), which is an intelligent interactive textbook to support learning programming in LISP. ELM-ART demonstrates how interactivity and adaptivity can be implemented in World Wide Web electronic textbooks (ET).

ELM-ART: Interactive Intelligent LISP Textbook on the World Wide Web

ELM-ART (ELM Adaptive Remote Tutor) is a World Wide Web-based system to support learning programming in LISP. ELM-ART is based on ELM-PE (Weber & Moellenberg, 1995) an Intelligent Learning Environment that supports example-based programming, intelligent analysis of problem solutions, and advanced testing and debugging facilities. ELM-ART provides all the course materials (presentations of new concepts, test, examples, and problems) in hypermedia form. It can be considered as an online adaptive ET with an integrated problem solving environment (we call it I^3 textbook, or intelligent, interactive, integrated textbook). ELM-ART differs from simple World Wide Web ET in two major aspects.

First, ELM-ART is interactive: All examples and problems (which are important components of any textbook) in ELM-ART are not just a static text as in other textbooks, but "live experience": Students can play with examples and solve problems interactively using World Wide Web fill-out forms. The fields of these forms are used to provide several kinds of input, such as the text of a problem solution, and the buttons are used to get several kinds of help and feedback from the system while examining an example or working at a problem:

- to ask the system to evaluate or to step a LISP expression which can contain any LISP functions learned in the introductory course;

- to request the most relevant case from the personal history (example or problem solution); and

- to request an intelligent diagnosis of the prepared solution.

Second, ELM-ART is adaptive. It "knows" the material it presents to a particular student and knows the current student level of knowledge about LISP. As a result, ELM-ART can help users to understand a particular section of learning material, and it supports them in learning and navigating the course material.

The next sections present interactive and adaptive features of ELM-ART in more detail.

Online Course Material

The course material in ELM-ART is provided on the World Wide Web in hypertext form. It consists of two main components: the textbook and the reference manual. The textbook (which is an online version of the normal printed LISP textbook used in the courses during the last few years) is hierarchically structured into units of different level: chapters, sections, and subsections. Each unit can be presented to the student as a World Wide Web "page," which shows the content of this unit (text and pictures) and various kinds of links from this unit to related elements of the course. All problem solving examples and problems are presented on separate "interactive" pages which use the possibilities of World Wide Web fill-out forms. The reference manual provides the reference access to the course material. Each "page" of the manual contains a brief explanation of one of the course concepts (which can be a special term, a LISP function, a data type, or a higher-level concept) and the links to the related course units and to related manual pages. Thus, the manual in ELM-ART also performs the roles of glossary and index of traditional textbooks.

Two kinds of links are used in the course: normal hierarchy links and content-based links. The hierarchy links connect a higher level unit (like a chapter) with all its sub-units (like sections in this chapter) and—in the other direction—each unit with its parent unit. Content-based links can be provided by ELM-ART because the system "knows" what is presented on each page of the course material, i.e., which concepts are introduced, presented, or summarized in each subsection, which concepts are demonstrated by each example, and which concepts are required to solve each problem. As a result, the system can provide cross-references between textbook and manual; for example, it can provide references from each textbook page (including example and problem pages) to corresponding manual pages for each involved concept. The links within the manual are also content-based links. The system "knows" the

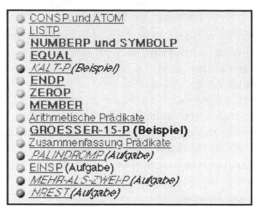

Figure 1. Example of adaptive annotation of links at the beginning of the course. The metaphor is traffic lights. Red (italic typeface) means not ready to be learned, green (bold) means ready and recommended, yellow means ready but not recommended.

pedagogical structure of the LISP domain and the relationships between various concepts. All these relationships are shown as links on the manual pages.

Adaptive Navigation Support

ELM-ART provides many more opportunities for browsing the course materials than traditional online textbooks. The negative side of it is that there is a higher risk for the student to get lost in this complex hyperspace. To support the student navigating through the course, the system uses *adaptive annotation*, an efficient adaptive hypermedia technique (Brusilovsky, 1996). Adaptive annotation means that the system uses visual cues (icons, fonts, colors) to show the type and the educational state of each link. Using the student model, ELM-ART can distinguish several educational states for each page of material (including problem, example, and manual pages): The content of the page can be known to the student, ready to be learned, or not ready to be learned (the latter example means that some prerequisite knowledge is not yet learned). The icon and the font of each link presented to the student are computed dynamically from the individual student model (Figure 1). They always inform the student about the type and the educational state of the node behind the link. Traffic lights are used as a metaphor. Red (italic typeface) means not ready to be learned, green (bold) means ready and recommended (part of the learning goal), yellow means ready but not recommended.

Adaptive Prerequisite-Based Help

The system knowledge about the course material comprises knowledge about what the prerequisite concepts are for any page of course material including example and problem pages. As a rule, the prerequisites are not shown directly. But, when the student has problems with understanding some explanation or example or solving a problem, he or she can request help (using a special button) and, as an answer to help request, the system presents an adaptively generated help page which shows annotated links to all pages where the prerequisite knowledge is presented.

Interactive Examples

An example in a textbook does not help very much if the user does not pay enough attention to it. That's why we want to provide an easy way for students to play with examples by integrating an enhanced evaluator into ELM-ART. This access is currently provided by transforming the text of any example into a link (Figure 2). When the user activates this link, the system loads the evaluator page, executes the example, and responds with the result or an error message (Figure 3). Employing the evaluator, the user can play with the given examples by modifying some pieces of code or by looking to step by step evaluation leading to a deeper understanding of the internal code evaluation strategy in LISP (Figure 3). Any occurring run-time error is explained by ELM-ART in more detail and more suitability for novices than common LISP interpreters do.

```
eine Liste erwartet und als Wert deren zweites Element liefert. Stellen
eine solche Funktion, die wir ZWEITES nennen. Dann liefert:

(ZWEITES '(BROT KAFFEE MILCH ZUCKER))

KAFFEE

(ZWEITES '(REST (BROT KAFFEE MILCH ZUCKER)))

(BROT KAFFEE MILCH ZUCKER)

(ZWEITES '())

NIL
```

Figure 2. Part of a page from the textbook concerning the problem "ZWEITES." Using the links, the examples are put into an interactive evaluator page where they can be modified and re-executed.

```
? (ZWEITES '(BROT KAFFEE MILCH ZUCKER))
(ZWEITES '(BROT KAFFEE MILCH ZUCKER))
 '(BROT KAFFEE MILCH ZUCKER)
 '(BROT KAFFEE MILCH ZUCKER) --> (BROT KAFFEE MILCH ZUCKER)
LIST --> (BROT KAFFEE MILCH ZUCKER)
 (REST (FIRST LIST))
  (FIRST LIST)
   LIST --> (BROT KAFFEE MILCH ZUCKER)
  (FIRST LIST) --> BROT
 (REST (FIRST LIST)) --> *ERROR*
(ZWEITES '(BROT KAFFEE MILCH ZUCKER)) --> *ERROR*
> Der Funktionsaufruf
> (REST BROT)
> ist fehlerhaft.
>
> Das REST-Konstrukt erwartet eine Liste als Argument.
>
> Das Argument ist aber ein Atom
> BROT

? (FIRST (REST '(BROT KAFFEE MILCH ZUCKER)))     [ Eval ][ Step ]
```

Figure 3: Evaluation of the first example of Figure 2.

Interactive and Intelligent Problem Solving Support

Any page describing a programming problem supports the user interactively in different ways. All problem pages provide an interface to the stepper to let the user to test the developed solution. If testing of a developed solution reports that it is still erroneous and the user is unable to find the error, he or she can try two forms of intelligent problem solving support: request a helpful example or invoke an intelligent program analyzer.

As ELM-ART is a system that supports example-based programming, it encourages the students to re-use the code of previously analyzed examples when solving a new problem. The hypermedia form of the course and, especially, similarity links between examples help the student to find the relevant example from his or her previous experience. An important feature of ELM-ART is that the system can predict the student's way of solving a particular problem and find the most relevant example from the individual learning history. This kind of problem solving support is very important for students who have problems with finding relevant examples. Answering the help request ("show example" on Figure 4), ELM-ART selects the most helpful examples, sorts them according to their relevance, and presents them to the student as an ordered list of hypertext links. The most relevant example is always presented first, but, if the student is not happy with this example for some reasons, he or she can try the second and the following suggested examples.

If the student failed to complete the solution of the problem, or if the student can not find an error which was reported by the testing component, he or she can ask the system to diagnose the code of the solution in its current state. As an answer, the system provides a sequence of help messages with more and more detailed explanation of an error (Figure 4). The sequence starts with a very vague hint what is wrong and ends with a code-level suggestion of how to correct the error or how to complete the solution. In many cases, the student can understand where the error is or what can be the next step from the very first messages and does not need

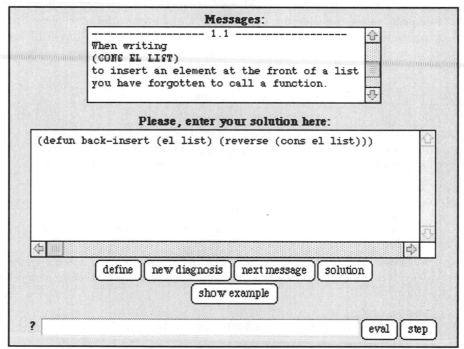

Figure 4. Form-based interface for problem solving support.

more explanations. The solution can be corrected or completed, checked again, and so forth. The student can use this kind of help as many times as required to solve the problem correctly. In this context, the ability to provide the code-level suggestion is a very important feature of ELM-ART as a distance learning system. It ensures that all students will finally solve the problem without the help of a human teacher.

Implementation of ELM-ART

The World Wide Web implementation of ELM-ART[1] is based on the Common LISP Hypermedia Server CL-HTTP (Mallery, 1994). CL-HTTP[2] is a fully featured HTTP server completely implemented in Common LISP. Since the original ELM-PE system was also implemented in Common LISP, CL-HTTP appears to be an optimal platform for our purposes. CL-HTTP offers a Common Gateway Interface[3] to handle incoming URLs from all over the world via the Internet. To enable the server to respond to a particular URL, this URL has to be associated to a response function implemented in LISP. Answering an incoming request, the server recognizes a URL, calls an associated function, and returns an HTML page which is generated by this function. With such an architecture, CL-HTTP is a very flexible and powerful tool for implementing intelligent applications on the World Wide Web. Since a LISP function is called to handle the request, any interactive or intelligent tool written in LISP can be connected to the World Wide Web with the help of CL-HTTP.

Conclusions and Future Work

The system ELM-ART described in this paper is an example of an interactive and adaptive ET implemented on the World Wide Web. ELM-ART provides remote access to hypermedia-structured learning material which includes explanations, tests, examples, and problems. Unlike traditional electronic textbooks, ELM-ART provides the learner with an adaptive interface, intelligent navigation support, adaptive help, and opportunities to play with examples, to solve problems, and to get intelligent problem-solving support. ELM-ART integrates the features of an electronic textbook, of a learning environment, and of an intelligent tutoring system.

We hope that methods we used in ELM-ART to represent knowledge about the subject, the interface, and the user, as well as adaptation techniques based in this knowledge, can be re-used for developing ET for different subjects on the World Wide Web (e.g., our team plans to use the same framework for implementing a World Wide Web textbook on statistics). We also want to investigate some advanced ways (i.e., JAVA) of adding interactivity to our ET. A first project is to port the adaptive LISP structure editor from ELM-PE to JAVA.

References

Brusilovsky, P. (1996). Methods and techniques of adaptive hypermedia. *User Models and User Adapted Interaction, 6*, p. 2.

Brusilovsky, P., Schwarz, E., & Weber, G. (1996). ELM-ART: An intelligent tutoring system on the World Wide Web. *Proceedings of Third International Conference on Intelligent Tutoring Systems, ITS-96*, Montreal

---

[1]ELM-ART URL: http://www.psychologie.uni-trier.de:8000/elmart

[2]http://www.ai.mit.edu/projects/iiip/doc/cl-http/home-page.html

[3]http://hoohoo.ncsa.uiuc.edu/cgi/

Mallery, J. C. (1994). A Common LISP hypermedia server. *Proceedings of the First International Conference on the World-Wide Web*, Geneva.

Weber, G., & Moellenberg, A. (1995). ELM-Programming-Environment: A tutoring system for LISP beginners. In K. F. Wender, F. Schmalhofer, & H. D. Böcker (Eds.), *Cognition and computer programming*. Norwood, NJ: Ablex.

Acknowledgments

Part of this work is supported by a grant from Alexander von Humboldt Foundation to the first author and by a grant from Stiftung Rheinland-Pfalz für Innovation to the third author.

The Authors

Peter Brusilovsky is Visiting Research Scientist, the School of Computer Science, Carnegie Mellon University, Pittsburgh, Pennsylvania.

e-mail, World Wide Web
plb@cs.cmu.edu
http://www.cs.cmu.edu/afs/cs.cmu.edu/user/plb/www/home.html

Elmar Schwarz is a graduate student, Department of Psychology, University of Trier, Germany.

e-mail, World Wide Web
schwarz@cogpsy.uni-trier.de
http://www.psychologie.uni-trier.de:8000/people/ESchwarz.html

Gerhard Weber is Associate Professor, Department of Psychology, University of Trier, Germany.

e-mail, World Wide Web
weber@cogpsy.uni-trier.de
http://www.psychologie.uni-trier.de:8000/people/GWeber.html

31

Moving Toward the Digital Learning Environment: The Future of Web-Based Instruction

Martin A. Siegel and Sonny Kirkley

There is a tsunami of data that is crashing onto the beaches of the civilized world. This is a tidal wave of unrelated, growing data formed in bits and bytes, coming in an unorganized, uncontrolled, incoherent cacophony of foam... None of it is easily related, none of it comes with any organizational methodology. (Wurman, 1996)

Introduction

If James Burke were writing today his award-winning television series, *The Day the Universe Changed*, he surely would choose a time in November 1993, when such an event occurred. A student team at the National Center for Supercomputing Applications (NCSA) at the University of Illinois released the first version of a graphical user interface to the World Wide Web, taking advantage of new Internet protocols developed at the CERN physics laboratory in Switzerland. No longer would the vision of the "information superhighway" be limited to 500 on-demand TV channels, gopher sites, and file transfer protocols. NCSA's Mosaic browser was followed by the commercial Netscape Navigator, revealing the power of integrated user-centered design. A multi-billion dollar industry was launched.

We now think of Internet information as the Web—interactive multimedia hypertext sites with dizzying graphics, digital sounds, and snappy animations. Its primary tool, the browser, shapes our thinking about the organization, presentation, and quality of information:

- information is not static; it is ever-changing and expanding;
- information is linked and "instantaneously" accessed;
- information is organized in multiple ways;
- information is produced by anonymous authors; it does not rely on established editorial or publishing practices; and
- information is screen-based; it is seen through a scrolling window and divided into "screen chunks."

But Roszak (1986) reminds us that information is not knowledge: "You can mass-produce raw data and incredible quantities of facts and figures. You cannot mass-produce knowledge, which is created by individual minds, drawing on individual experience, separating the significant from the irrelevant, making value judgments."

Education, too, is less about information acquisition and more about generative knowledge, which is the retention, understanding, and active use of knowledge. Such knowledge "does not just sit there but functions richly in people's lives to help them understand and deal with the world" (Perkins, 1992). From this perspective, education is less about training memories and more about educating minds; it is less about content *per se* and more about how to think about the content for solving authentic, real-world problems (Brooks & Brooks, 1993; Lebow, 1993; Moll, 1990; Savery & Duffy, 1995).

While current Web tools—browsers, voice chat, text chat, electronic mail, newsgroups, virtual white boards for collaboration, and so on—can support a problem-centered learning environment (as well as other teaching and learning models), the future of Web-based instruction will rely on design criteria that are theory-based, computer-imaginative, and user-centered.

Theory-Based Design

An underlying assumption of traditional education is that mastery of content presented by teachers or included in textbooks will result in the ability to solve diverse problems of the everyday world. We now know that this assumption is largely false (Bruer, 1993).

Even the most able students find it difficult to make appropriate connections between what they learn in school (the content of chemistry, biology, and government, for example) and understanding the nature of problems and their solutions outside of school (such as making recommendations about what to do with a community's declining land-fill space). These real-world or everyday problems (Sternberg, 1985) are different from the well-structured, single-solution textbook problems students solve in school. See Table 1.

A new paradigm, consistent with emerging models of Web-based instruction (Kirkley & Boling, 1995; Norman & Spohrer, 1996; Siegel & Sousa, 1994), is required to change the focus from content-centered to problem-centered learning. This paradigm—the *Digital Learning Environment*—incorporates the following features:

- A learner-centered and problem-based (rather than content-centered) instructional support system, in which learning is based upon analysis of a series of complex, real-world issues rather than upon memorization of facts and principles (Brown, Collins, & Duguid, 1989; Duffy & Jonassen, 1992).

- Safe settings for learning, in which making mistakes becomes as powerful a learning heuristic as employing successful problem-solving strategies in real-world contexts (Schank, 1994).

- A blurring of teacher and student roles, such that teachers model and demonstrate learning in problem-based settings, while students facilitate and manage their own learning environments (Duffy & Cunningham, 1996).

- Access to an integrated package of navigational, productivity, communication, collaboration, and knowledge/wisdom creation tools (Edelson, Pea, & Gomez, 1996; Harasim, Hiltz, Teles, & Turoff, 1995; Soloway, Guzdial, & Hay, 1994).

- Management tools that facilitate the development of student goals and activities as a collaboration between students, parents, and teachers, of which key components are alternative and traditional assessment practices (Farr & Tone, 1994; Reeves & Okey, 1996).

- Independence of any particular hardware or delivery system configuration (Siegel & Sousa, 1994).

Table 1. Real-world and school problems.

Characteristics of Real-world or Everyday Problems	Characteristics of School or Textbook-based Problems
• In the everyday world, the first and sometimes most difficult step in problem solving is recognition that a problem exists.	• The teacher or textbok signals that a problem exists.
• In everyday problem solving, it is often harder to figure out just what the problem is than to figure out how to solve it.	• The teacher or textbook provides the problem.
• Everyday problems tend to be ill-structured.	• The teacher or textbook defines the problem.
• In everyday problem solving, it is not usually clear just what information will be needed to solve a given problem, nor is it always clear where the information can be found.	• Needed information to solve school or text-based problems is found in the associated chapter or lecture; often parallel problems (examples) are solved for the student.
• The solutions to everyday problems depend on and interact with the contexts in which the problems occur.	• School or text-based problems are self-contained; little or no context is provided.
• Everyday problems generally have no one right solution, and even the criteria for what constitutes a best solution are often not clear.	• School or textbook-based problems have one right solution; textbook solutions are found in the back of the book—for every other problem!
• Solutions to important everyday problems have consequences that matter.	• Solutions to school or textbook-based problems have no consequences other than a grade.
• Everyday problem solving often occurs in groups.	• School or textbook-based problem solving often occurs alone.
• Everyday problems can be complicated, messy, and stubbornly persistent.	• School or textbook-based problems are clear, well-defined, and easily forgotten.

- An open, ever-changing, and ever-expanding information architecture (Siegel & Sousa, 1994), which has access to a global information network like the Internet, in contrast to a closed information architecture (e.g., book, diskette, videodisk, or a CD-ROM), which is finite and frozen in time.

Taken together, these features are designed to facilitate big concept, multi-disciplinary learning, and the development of authentic, cooperative problem-solving strategies. Learning how to learn in a domain is as important as accumulating facts and decontextualized information (Oshima, Bereiter, & Scardamalia, 1995; Riel, 1994). Moreover, changes in teacher and student behavior are promoted by direct training and collaboration embedded in tools that foster self-regulated behavior, metacognition, and the development of a community of learners and teachers (Harasim, 1993).

Computer Imaginative Design

When students use Internet resources for their classes, most interactions involve "pointing and clicking" as students navigate through hypermedia text and graphics. While this can be an absorbing experience in an ever-expanding, ever-changing, information-rich environment, we question its ultimate value as a learning tool. What is needed are new tools that create powerful instructional interactions that lead to deep conceptual insights as well as the development of sophisticated problem-solving and research skills. These instructional goals will be realized through the design and implementation of new Web tools linked to specific content areas. Tools in this new environment need to be more specialized than many tools we see today such as generic word processors. Simply using these specialized tools will help the learner better understand the knowledge domain in which the learner is working. For instance, a scientist's word processor for middle school might scaffold learners by helping them think through the process of justifying the findings of an experiment (Bonk, Hay, Cole, & Fischler, 1995; Edelson, Pea, & Gomez, 1996). Characteristic of the best tools will be an aspect of design we describe as "computer imaginative" (Siegel & Davis, 1986).

A design is computer imaginative if it exploits the strengths of the computer by creating possibilities that were not readily feasible in any other medium. Usenet, the Internet's asynchronous conferencing system, is an example of computer imaginative software; it takes advantage of a worldwide network of computers to facilitate global conferencing. Each day, as many as 40 million characters (equivalent to volumes A through G of the *Encyclopædia Britannica*) are distributed among 5,000 conferencing forums! It is difficult to imagine a global interactive communications system such as Usenet implemented in non-computer media.

"TimeWeb" Tool. At Indiana University's Center for Excellence in Education (http://cee.indiana.edu/), we are creating new Web tools (we call them "Wisdom Tools") to facilitate the goals of the Digital Learning Environment. Our first effort—the TimeWeb Tool—was designed to be a computer imaginative Web tool. In creating this tool, we considered whether it would be possible to portray, and more importantly, to construct information so that it contributes to deeper student insight and understanding of the content. How could we exploit the strengths of the Web medium to move beyond the "point and click" model of the browser or the hierarchical structure of bookmarks?

For example, imagine a history course with access to the TimeWeb Tool. Instead of viewing information in the usual hypermedia format, the same information could be plotted on a two-dimensional grid, with categories such as science, history, literature, art and music on the vertical-axis and time (in decades, years, months, etc.) on the horizontal-axis. Not only could students navigate through this timeline, comparing information found in one category with another, but they also could construct their own timelines. Web sites, individual pages, local files, graphics, animations, and sounds would be represented as icons on the two-dimensional time grid; clicking on an icon would take the student directly to that information. By manipulating the time scale and viewing time from varied resolutions (say, zooming into days or moving out to millennia), students would gain additional insights by noting changing patterns and relationships. The uses for this tool extend beyond the development of historical timelines, and it represents computer imaginative access and construction of information on the World Wide Web. For further information, see the Wisdom Tools site (http://wisdomtools.com/).

The Catalog Tool. Within higher education, students select courses from a bulletin or schedule of classes. Each entry includes the course title, section number, meeting times, and the instructor's name. The underlying assumption is that the student enrolls for the entire course for the designated semester or term. Already we are beginning to see course catalogs on the Web for Web-based instruction, and most of these catalogs lack computer imagination; that is, they imitate the medium of the paper-based catalog without taking advantage of the computer medium.

How might you design a computer imaginative catalog? Such a catalog would contain many features, but here are a few that would take advantage of the computer medium:

- The catalog would allow students to register for segments of a course and pay accordingly (this, of course, assumes that the Web-based course allows for open-entry enrollment and self-paced learning).

- The catalog would allow students to combine segments from one course with segments of another.

- The catalog would act as a "performance support system," making recommendations and performing as an academic advisor (the catalog would be linked to past student comments as well).

These features not only function as creative ways to exploit the Web medium, but they also respond to the needs of the end-user, and thus are characterized by learner-centered designs, the topic of the next section.

Learner-Centered Design

New Web-based instructional tools may be grounded in theory and characterized as computer imaginative, but if they do not adapt to the needs and capabilities of learners, they will be moderately useful at best or simply ignored at worst. Successful design requires an understanding of the technology, the person, and their mutual interaction (Kirkley & Boling, 1995; Norman & Draper, 1986; Soloway, Guzdial, & Hay, 1994).

There are three important considerations that affect the employment of Web-based tools in the learning environment:

- **Process versus product.** Tools such as word processors and spread sheets are designed to do a specific job; they are product oriented. The user merely supplies the input. The computer then takes over, processing it and returning the result to the user. That makes it very handy in business, where results are just what the user wants. Education, however, is often process oriented. The goal is not necessarily to get results in the fastest, most labor-saving way. Doing the task—going through the process—is often more important. In fact, obtaining the "correct answer" is often less significant than thinking about how the answer came about. The use of Web-based tools for education will need to accentuate the learning process.

- **Integration.** Any tool by itself may be useful. But combined with other tools, a powerful, integrated learning system is created. When using Web-based tools for instruction, we must be aware of possibilities for integration. An educational tool will be maximally useful only if it is smoothly and organically integrated with the learning process.

- **Training.** Students and teachers must have a clear understanding of how and when to use Web-based tools for instruction. "How" describes the tool's functions. "When" describes the context under which the tool is to be employed. All potential audiences—students, teachers, parents, administrators—must have a clear understanding of function and context. Embedded training and online discussion forums are two methods for these groups to gain this understanding.

Steps in the Creation of the Digital Learning Environment

For us to be able to implement the Digital Learning Environment requires several steps:

- **Building the environment.** Teachers and schools can implement the type of problem-based learning environment we have described without much outside intervention, and it can be done independently of technologies such as computers and the Web. However, using these technologies facilitates our activities (i.e., taking over some classroom management tasks) and enhances our capabilities (i.e., facilitating communication and collaboration over time and space) in ways that make the complexity of this learning environment more manageable.

- **Building tools.** As we become better at building these environments, we need to adapt or invent tools to better facilitate the learning environment and our activities within the environment. In most cases, this tool building is beyond the capabilities of a single school or district, but instead must come from business, universities, and government.

- **Training teachers, students, and parents.** The most critical component in the successful implementation of the Digital Learning Environment will be properly training teachers, students, and parents in how to manage and learn in this new kind of environment. This training must include both how and when to use the technology. It also must be ongoing. The traditional in-service training model in K–12 schools will no longer support the complexity of training for this environment.

- **Building the infrastructure.** Government, school districts, and business must work together to ensure that all learners and teachers have proper access to equipment and communication networks when it is needed. This includes access at school, at home and in the community (i.e., the local library).

- **Gaining community support.** Despite our best efforts, without community support it will be difficult to change the way in which we educate our children. Any type of change will meet resistance. These sweeping changes will require widespread support at both the local and national level. We are chiseling away at the very foundations of what adults expect of schooling and asking them to trust us and to spend large sums of money in the process. Ongoing community outreach must be part of our plan.

Because we are in the early stages of Web-based instruction, we are often more fascinated with the daily unveiling of new tools than with the ways teachers and students will use these tools to think about, as Richard Saul Wurman mellifluously described, "a tsunami of data... an unorganized, uncontrolled, incoherent cacophony of foam." We need to lessen our preoccupation with Web glitz and, instead, refocus our attention on the creation of the Digital Learning Environment. As this environment increases our command of the skills, knowledge, and wisdom we need, this capacity to lead us into creative use of a powerful new medium is surely the chief value and best destiny of Web-based instruction.

References

Bonk, C. J., Hay, K. E., Cole, S., & Fischler, R. B. (1995). *Building the infrastructure for student and teacher collaboration in an electronic community of elementary student weather forecasters.* Paper presented at the annual Hypermedia Conference, Bloomington, IN.

Brooks, J. G., & Brooks, M. G. (1993). *In search of understanding: The case for constructivist classrooms.* Alexandria, VA: Association for Supervision and Curriculum Development.

Brown, J. S., Collins, A., & Duguid, P. (1989). Situated cognition and the culture of learning. *Educational Researcher, 18*(1), 32–42.

Bruer, J. T. (1993). *Schools for thought: A science of learning in the classroom.* Cambridge, MA: The MIT Press.

Duffy, T. M., & Cunningham, D. J. (1996). Constructivism: Implications for the design and delivery of instruction. In D. H. Jonassen (Ed.), *Handbook of research on educational communications and technology*. New York: Macmillan.

Duffy, T. M., & Jonassen, D. H. (Eds.) (1992). *Constructivism and the technology of instruction: A conversation*. Hillsdale, NJ: Lawrence Erlbaum Associates.

Edelson, D. C., Pea, R. D., & Gomez, L. M. (1996). Constructivism in the collaboratory. In B. G. Wilson (Ed.), *Constructivist learning environments: Case studies in instructional design*. Englewood Cliffs, NJ: Educational Technology Publications.

Farr, R., & Tone, B. (1994). *Portfolio and performance assessment: Helping students evaluate their progress as readers and writers*. Fort Worth, TX: Harcourt Brace College Publishers.

Harasim, L. (1993). Collaborating in Cyberspace: Using computer conferences as a group. *Interactive Learning Environments, 3*(2), 199–130.

Harasim, L., Hiltz, S. R., Teles, L., & Turoff, M. (1995). *Learning networks: A field guide to teaching and learning online*. Cambridge, MA: MIT Press.

Kirkley, S., & Boling, E. (1995). *Learner-centered design: Software for the Information Age*. Paper presented at the annual convention of the Association for Applied Interactive Multimedia (AAIM), Asheville, NC (http://www.indiana.edu/~iirg/ARTICLES/AAIM/lcd.html).

Lebow, D. (1993). Constructivist values for instructional systems design: Five principles toward a new mindset. *Educational Technology Research and Development, 41*(3), 4–16.

Moll, L. C. (Ed.). (1990). *Vygotsky in education: Instructional implications of sociohistorical psychology*. New York: Cambridge University Press.

Norman, D. A., & Draper, S. W. (1986). *User centered system design: New perspectives on human-computer interaction*. Hillsdale, NJ: Lawrence Erlbaum Associates.

Norman, D. A., & Spohrer, J. C. (1996). Learner-centered education. *Communications of the ACM, 39*(4), 24–27.

Oshima, J., Bereiter, C., & Scardamalia, M. (1995). Information-access characteristics for high conceptual progress in a computer-networked learning environment. In J. L. Schnase & E. L. Cunnis (Eds.), *Proceedings of CSCL '95: The first international conference on computer support for collaborative learning* (pp. 259–267). Mahwah, NJ: Lawrence Erlbaum Associates.

Perkins, D. (1992). *Smart schools: From training memories to educating minds*. New York: The Free Press.

Reeves, T. C., & Okey, J. R. (1996). Alternative assessment for constructivist learning environments. In B. G. Wilson (Ed.), *Constructivist learning environments: Case studies in instructional design*. Englewood Cliffs, NJ: Educational Technology Publications.

Riel, M. (1994). Educational change in a technology-rich environment. *Journal of Research on Computing, 26*(4), 452–474.

Roszak, T. (1986). *The cult of information: The folklore of computers and the true art of thinking*. New York: Pantheon Books.

Savery, J. R., & Duffy, T. M. (1995). Problem based learning: An instructional model and its constructivist framework. *Educational Technology, 35*(5), 31–38.

Schank, R. C. (1994). Why hitchhikers on the Information Highway are going to have to wait a long time for a ride. *The Aspen Institute Quarterly, 6*(2), 28–58.

Siegel, M. A., & Davis, D. M. (1986). *Understanding computer-based education*. New York: Random House.

Siegel, M. A., & Sousa, G. A. (September, 1994). Inventing the virtual textbook: Changing the nature of schooling. *Educational Technology, 34*(7), 49–54.

Soloway, E., Guzdial, M., & Hay, K. (1994). Learner-centered design: The challenge for HCI in the 21st century. *Interactions, 1*(2), 36–48.

Sternberg, R. J. (1985). Teaching critical thinking, part 1: Are we making critical mistakes? *Phi Delta Kappan*, 67, 194–198.

Wurman, R. S. (1996). *Information architects*. Zurich, Switzerland: Graphis Press Corp.

The Authors

Martin A. Siegel is Director, Laboratory for Research & Development in Teaching and Learning, and Professor of Education, Center for Excellence in Education, Indiana University, Bloomington, Indiana.

e-mail, World Wide Web
  msiegel@indiana.edu
  http://cee.indiana.edu/folks/siegel.html

Sonny Kirkley is with the Laboratory for Research & Development in Teaching and Learning, Center for Excellence in Education at Indiana University, Bloomington, Indiana.

e-mail, World Wide Web
  ekirkley@indiana.edu
  http://cee.indiana.edu/folks/kirkley.html

32

A Web Site for Theories of Learning and Instruction

Greg Kearsley

About the TIP Data Base

The Theory Into Practice (TIP) project involves the development of a hypertext data base for theories of learning and instruction. The data base contains descriptions of 50 theories, which are linked to 18 major concepts and 18 task/content domains (see Tables 1 and 2). Each theory description includes the following sections: overview, scope/application, example, principles, and references. Relationships between theories (i.e., links) are identified by highlighted text within articles. These relationships can be connections between specific theories or to concepts that underly a number of theories. The theories are indexed in a number of ways, including content domain, type of learning, and task characteristics.

The TIP data base (http://gwis2.circ.gwu.edu/~kearsley) was primarily developed to make theories of learning and instruction more accessible to educators. Despite the wealth of theory available, practitioners seldom make use of it in their teaching activities and the design of curriculum. When asked why, most teachers and trainers explain that they find it difficult to identify which theories apply to the specific task or subject matter they are teaching. Since there are hundreds of theories, many of which are very extensive, it is not surprising that practitioners find it hard to isolate principles or findings that might pertain to their current teaching concerns. The point of the TIP project was to develop a hypertext data base that would make it easier for educators to find and use learning and instructional theory.

A major challenge in the project was to determine which theories to include (and exclude) from the data base. Theories were selected for inclusion based upon their relevance to human learning and instruction (particularly adult learning). All of the theories come from published literature (English language only). Theories that focus on animal learning, neuropsychology, learning disabilities, or teaching strategies are not included. The data base also does not include theories of learning that have limited scientific support or are primarily philosophical in nature (e.g., Dewey, Illich, Polanyi).

The TIP data base was initially implemented as a Hyperties data base for MS-DOS machines. Later, a multimedia (CD-ROM) version was developed, using HyperCard for the Macintosh. The multimedia version featured video clips of theorists explaining their work. The World Wide Web version of the data base contains the same text and graphics as the previous versions (updated over time), but not the video clips (which require about 250 MB). Once enough disk space is available on the current server (or a new server found), the full multime-

271

Table 1. Theories of learning and instruction included in the TIP data base.

Anderson, J. R.	ACT		Maltzman, I.	originality
Argyris, C.	double loop theory		Marton, F., & Entwistle, N.	phenomenonography
Atkinson, R.	mathematical theory			
Ausubel, D. P.	subsumption theory		Merrill, M.D.	component display theory
Bandura, A.	social learning theory		Miller, Galanter, & Pribram	information processing
Bransford, J. & CTGV	anchored instruction		Newell, A.	SOAR
Bruner, J.	constructivism		Newell & Simon	General Problem Solver (GPS)
Card, Moran, & Newell	GOMS		Norman, D. A.	modes of learning
Carroll, J. M.	minimalism		Pask, G.	conversation theory
Craik & Lockhart	levels of processing		Pavio, A.	dual coding theory
			Piaget, J.	genetic epistemology
Cronbach & Snow	aptitude-treatment interaction		Reigeluth, C.	elaboration theory
Cross, P.	adult learning		Rogers, C.	experiential theory
DeBono, E.	lateral thinking		Salomon, G.	symbol systems
Estes, W.	stimulus sampling theory		Scandura, J.	structural learning
Festinger, L.	cognitive dissonance theory		Schank, R.	script theory
Gagné, R. M.	conditions of learning		Schoenfeld, A.	mathematical problem-solving
Gardner, H.	multiple intelligences		Skinner, B. F.	operant conditioning
Gibson, J. J.	information pickup theory		Spiro, R.	cognitive flexibility theory
Guilford, J. P.	structure of intellect		Sternberg, R. J.	triarchic theory
Guthrie, E.	contiguity		Sticht, T.	functional context
Hull, C. L.	drive reduction theory		Thorndike, E. L.	connectionism
Knowles, M.	andragogy		Tolman, E.	sign/significate theory
Landa, L.	algo-heuristic theory		VanLehn, K.	repair theory
Lave, J.	situated learning		Vygotsky, L. S.	social development
Mager, R.	criterion referenced instruction		Wertheimer, M.	gestalt theory

dia version of TIP will be available on the Web. For futher discussion of the history of the project, see Kearsley (1995).

Use of the Data Base

Since being made available on the Web in 1995, the data base has been used extensively by educators and students around the world—who often send me e-mail about their interests. Actually, users often ask me for follow-up information on particular theories or concepts in the data base. While I would love to have the time (and the financial backing) to research and respond to these queries, I have to refer most people to the library. But it is fascinating to learn the variety of different purposes and backgrounds that users have in using the data base.

Many college instructors (including myself) make use of the Web site in classes—as a supplemental source for information on learning and instructional theories. Many of the projects in my graduate courses on educational technology (see the Web site for our program at: http://www.gwu.edu/~etl) require an analysis of the relevant learning theory for a specific instructional setting or activity; I encourage students to use the TIP data base for this purpose—although students will almost always need to consult primary sources (i.e., books/journals) to do a thorough analysis.

Table 2. Concepts and learning domains in the TIP data base.

Concepts	Domains
Anxiety	Aviation
Arousal	Computers
Attention	Concepts
Attitudes	Decision Making
Cognitive/Learning Styles	Engineering
Creativity	Language
Feedback/Reinforcement	Management
Imagery	Mathematics
Intelligence	Medicine
Learning Strategies	Military
Memory	Perception
Mental Models	Problem Solving
Metacognition	Procedures
Motivation	Reading
Productions	Reasoning
Schema	Sales
Sequencing of Instruction	Sensory-Motor
Transfer	Troubleshooting

The data base could also serve as the primary resource (an "electronic textbook") for a course on learning. Students can select or be assigned one or more theories and be asked to do further reading or analysis based on the information and references provided in the data base. (One day, I hope to ask a class to add new components to the data base as course assignments.) TIP is especially well-suited to comparative analysis of theories and concepts in learning and instruction because of the ease of browsing and searching.

While the primary purpose of the TIP project has been to provide a useful data base for practitioners and study tool for students, it has also been valuable for meta-theoretical analysis. For example, a study of the links among the theories and concepts in the data base indicated that the connections between ideas is minimal (Kearsley, 1993). These results suggest a significant lack of synthesis and commonality in theories of learning and instruction.

Organic and Evolving

Every month, there are new journal articles and books published which are relevant to the contents of the data base, and I am constantly revising the material based upon new work. So the data base is organic in the sense that it changes over time and continues to grow. Furthermore, data base users provide ideas and commentary on the contents, which results in changes and additions. So the data base evolves in response to input from its users.

Also, as time goes on, more of the newer source materials are available in online format, and I am looking forward to being able to include direct links from the TIP Web site to original sources. For example, the American Educational Research Association (AERA) is the single largest professional organization for those involved in learning and instructional theory in the U.S. Every year at the AERA conference, there are many presentations relevant to the TIP data base. Once the AERA proceedings and papers are available on the Web, I will be able to put links to them within the relevant TIP articles. Similarly, there are many workshops and publications of organizations devoted to specific learning/instructional theories included in the TIP data base (e.g., constructivists, behaviorists, gestaltists, etc.); when they make their materials available on the Web, they can also be directly linked.

This possibility of linking ongoing research to the TIP data base is very exciting because it makes learning and instructional theory much more accessible to everyone (i.e., all Web users). While there are many legitimate problems and issues with this domain of knowledge, there is no doubt that wider exposure of educators to theories of learning and instruction would ultimately result in improved teaching. The Web could play a significant role in helping to achieve this.

References

Kearsley, G. (1993, Spring). Hypertext as a tool for the metatheoretical analysis of learning theories: The TIP data base. *Journal of Computing in Higher Education, 4*(2), 43–56.

Kearsley, G. (1995, Autumn). Three generations of hypertext: Lessons learned from the TIP project. *Educational Technology Review, 4*, 33–37.

The Author

Greg Kearsley is a Professor, Department of Educational Leadership, Graduate School of Education & Human Development, The George Washington University, Washington, DC.

e-mail, World Wide Web
    kearsley@gwis2.circ.gwu.edu
    http://www.gwu.edu/~etl

SECTION IV

Delivering Web-Based Instruction

33

Computers and Connections, Servers and Browsers, HTML and Editors, and Other Helper Applications

Don E. Descy

The World Wide Web is a computer based medium. Our messages and files travel through computers, we access the Web using computers, we store our Web pages on computers, and we access Web pages residing on other computers that could be next door or around the world. Computers are hardware. Computers don't run all by themselves. They need and use instructions written by someone. These instructions are placed in the computer and tell the computer what to do and how to do it. These instructions are generally called software. If we are going to choose and use computer hardware and software effectively and efficiently, we must have a general idea about what hardware and software are available and the parameters which are designed into them.

Computers and Connections

The Internet was designed to be software driven. It was also designed to be hardware independent: It does not matter what kind of hardware you use as long as you use Internet software for your hardware configuration. Because the Web is hardware transparent, there are many different computer platforms on the Web. The most popular platforms are running the UNIX, DOS, Windows, and Macintosh operating systems (OS). Each OS has its own strengths and weaknesses, but they all do an adequate job. Some people swear by UNIX (or a DOS machine running a UNIX clone called Linux), others by Windows (or Windows NT), and still others by Macintosh operating systems. It is possible to choose software that will alleviate most of the deficiencies that the operating system may contain.

Once you have a computer, you will also need a modem. A modem allows your computer to talk with other computers through regular phone lines. One of the most important criteria to look for in a modem is the modem speed. Modem speed is measured in bits per second (bps). The faster the modem, the faster and more enjoyable your work on the Web. Most people recommend a minimum modem speed of 14.4 bps. I would recommend purchasing a 28.8 bps modem. Remember, the faster your modem, the faster information will be transferred to your computer. A fast modem saves time, and if you are paying by the hour, it will save you money.

Now that you have a computer and a modem, it is time to obtain a connection to the Internet. There are several ways to go about this. The first is by using a commercial online provider. There are two types of commercial providers. The first is the gateway service provider. Examples of these are America Online, Prodigy, and CompuServe. Basic service through one of these providers will be as low as $10 a month. This will buy you a specific allotment of time on-line and (usually) a toll free number. If you subscribe to one of these services, you may have to put up with certain restrictions: limited (by number and size) e-mail and the use of only the services and software provided by the service. Most gateway service providers will give you their software and 10 free hours of service. It is possible to try them all for free!

The second type of Internet service provider, and the one that I would recommend, is the type that gives you full Internet access. These Internet service providers provide the software (though you can download or use your own), and a direct Internet connection for a set amount of time each month. In many parts of the country it is possible to purchase unlimited Internet access for under $20 a month!

In some areas it is also possible to obtain dial-in service through a local school or college. If this is a possibility, you want to make sure that the school or college also provides SLIP or PPP access software. This software enables you to have a full Internet connection, including all of the graphical wonders of the World Wide Web.

Servers and Browsers

Two pieces of software are needed to present and view a World Wide Web page. These two pieces are the "server" software and the "browser" software. Server software resides on one computer and allows individuals to access Web pages that also reside on that computer. Browser software is the software needed to access the server and view the Web page.

The server software used depends on the computer containing the Web pages. Unless the server software is on the computer on your desk (as mine is), choice of computer and software is usually in the hands of your service provider or system operator. If you are using a Macintosh, you will probably want to use MacHTTP or its big brother (sister?) WebSTAR. GNNserver is popular on Windows NT, HTTPD on UNIX and Linux, and, of course, Netscape makes a variety of servers for everything from DEC to SUN computers.

The browser is the software that resides on your computer and allows you to access and display a Web page. Some people call browsers "viewers." All browsers are different and all browsers display Web pages a little bit differently. The same brand name of browser displays the same Web pages differently depending on the computer platform (i.e. DOS, Windows, Macintosh). For an almost complete list containing information on 60+ browsers, go to: http://www.why-not.com/company/browser_a2z.htm

The simplest browser is Lynx. Lynx is a text-only browser. No matter which Web page is accessed, Lynx users will only see text. There are still people who use Lynx (2% of Web users). It is fast and efficient, but much of the interesting information on the Web is lost. Lynx is the browser supported on many mainframe computers.

The vast majority of people use a graphic browser. A graphic browser is one that can display graphics as well as text. There are scores of graphic browsers, but only four or five of them are in common use. At the time of this writing, these include Netscape Navigator (used by 84% of Web users), Microsoft's Internet Explorer (used by 7%), the America Online browser (3%), Quarterdeck Mosaic (2%), and NCSA Mosaic (1%). Since most people use the Netscape browser, most Web pages are written so that they display optimally on this browser. Keep in mind, though, that the popularity of Web browsers may be short lived—at one time many people referred to the World Wide Web as "Mosaic" because that was the browser that everyone used...and Bill Gates has vowed that Internet Explorer will "bury" Netscape. The latest statistics on browser use can be found at http://www.why-not.com/company/browser_stats.htm

HTML and Editors

The magic of the World Wide Web is HyperText Markup Language (HTML). World Wide Web documents are written in HTML. It is not a computer programming language and, contrary to popular belief, it is not difficult to master. I know of 3rd graders who have produced nice World Wide Web pages.

HTML is a 'markup' language. It is a series of marks (words between < and > symbols), called tags, that tell browsers how and where to display the text and graphics. For example, <center> tells the browser to center the text that follows this tag. </center> tells the browsers to stop centering the text. <blink> causes text following it to blink, </blink> stops the blinking, and <p> tells the browser to skip a line and start a new paragraph. Most bookstores stock several books describing HTML. Great information is also available on the World Wide Web itself. A useful location to start your Web search is http://www.yahoo.com/Computers_and_Internet/Software/Data_Formats/HTML/Guides_and_Tutorials/

Many people write HTML documents by hand, inserting the tags as they go. All you need is a regular word processor or text editor that can save your files in a TEXT or ASCII format (see Descy, 1995a, 1995b, 1996).

An alternative approach to writing HTML is through the use of HTML editors. HTML editors are software programs that insert the tags for the writer. There are two basic types of editors. One type simply adds tags to the text. After the text is written, the text to be altered is highlighted. One of several menus is usually selected and the attribute desired (center, blink, make a link, etc.) is chosen. At this point, the HTML editor encloses the highlighted text within the desired tags. It is surprisingly very simple. Typically you have to open up a browser to view the work that is created. There are many good HTML editors. HTML Assistant, BBEdit, HTML-Editor, and HTML Web Weaver are popular Macintosh editors; HTMLed, Web Wizard, and HTML Author are popular Microsoft Windows editors; and HotMetal, tkHTML, and Tex2RTF are popular among UNIX users.

The second type of HTML editor is a WYSIWYG (What You See Is What You Get) editor. This shows you the page as you are working on it. Adobe PageMill is an example of a popular WYSIWYG HTML editor. WYSIWYG editors are easy and fun to use. PageMill, though popular, changes some tags in the documents that it constructs.

HTML editors are very popular and easy to use. They allow people to produce World Wide Web pages with little effort. However, editors do have several drawbacks. One has to do with Web pages that don't seem to display the text or graphics the way the designer intends (a common problem for all!). By relying on the HTML editor, and not learning any of the HTML tags, the user is unable to do even simple trouble shooting. A second drawback relates to the set of tags that the HTML editor is able to insert. No HTML editor is able to insert all of the scores of tags that are available. Granted, many of the unavailable tags are either not frequently used or can't be read by all browsers. However, many of the missing tags add polish and a professional look to a Web page. New tags are being introduced each month. It would be impossible for HTML editors to keep up. Given the drawbacks of the editors and the ease of learning HTML, I would recommend learning some basic HTML before relying on editors to construct your pages. Information and lists of HTML editors can be found at: http://www.yahoo.com/Computers_and_Internet/Internet/World_Wide_Web/HTML_Editors/

Other Applications

The World Wide Web is made up of text and images. It is also made up of audio and video. Each of these different file types require different application software to display, hear, or view.

As faster and move efficient forms of text, graphics, video, and sound files are developed, even newer applications are needed. The protocols (rules) that govern the Web are classified as an open standard. Open standards allow for the addition of new applications and data formats (such as Apple's proposed 3D data format). Most Web browsers allow these applications to be added to them as they are developed.

The most common, or standard, graphic file formats supported by Web browsers are JPEG (Joint Photographic Experts Group), GIF (from CompuServe), and XMP (X bitmap). There are other graphic file formats including: DIB (Device Independent Bitmap), TGA (Targa), TIFF (Tagged Image File Format) and PCX (PC Paintbrush). To view these, Windows users may download Image Alchemy or Paint Box Pro, Macintosh users may want JPEG View or LView Pro, and UNIX users may need a utility such as XV.

Increasingly, digital video is being incorporated onto Web pages. Previous limitations such as large file sizes and high bandwidth (amount of data being transferred) required by digital video are now being overcome by new means of file compression and higher speed modems. The increased need for such applications because of the increasing popularity of video conferencing is spearheading development.

There are presently three popular digital video formats: AVI (Audio Video Interleave) from Microsoft, QuickTime from Apple, and MPEG from Motion Picture Experts Group. QuickTime and MPEG are cross platform data formats. AVI is supported by Microsoft Windows.

At present AVI is only supported on Windows platforms. It is an interesting format in that AVI laces sound and picture data together much like a zipper. Sparkle and Popcorn are QuickTime viewers for the Macintosh and QuickTime may be viewed on a Windows platforms by using the QuickTime Player.

Digital sound has been on Web pages since the development of the first Mosaic browser. WPlay and Wham are very popular Windows applications, SoundMachine is a Macintosh favorite, and UNIX for X Windows or Open Windows sound files are supported by audiotool. In order to hear a sound using one of these applications, the whole sound file must be downloaded first and then decompressed before it is played. This may take several minutes for very large audio files when using slow modems. Some 3-minute sound files have taken as long as 30 minutes to download!

One of the hottest forms of Web technology is called Audio Streaming. Audio Streaming applications start to decompress sound files and play them immediately *as they are being received!* This dramatically speeds up the process and allows for such things as 'live' concerts and radio broadcasts. Currently, the hottest Audio Streaming technology comes from Progressive and is called RealAudio. Audio files must be saved in RealAudio file format, served to the Web using special RealAudio server software, and played using a RealAudio player. For more information, see: http://www.realaudio.com/

Another very popular application is Adobe Acrobat. Adobe is fast making its Acrobat Portable Document Format (PDF) the Internet standard. PDF allows the document to be saved with its format unchanged. This makes it is possible to view documents saved in the PDF format in their original WordPerfect or PageMaker format. All that is required is an Acrobat Player. Acrobat further allows files to be printed out as an identical copy of the original Web document. For more information, see: http://www.adobe.com/Acrobat/Acrobat.html

One of the newest applications is ShockWave. It allows interactive/multimedia documents created with Macromedia Director to be viewed on a standard Web browser. With ShockWave technology, it is possible to incorporate elements onto a Web page that actually move and respond when clicked on! For more information, go to Macromedia's Web site: http://www.macromedia.com/

New programming languages are continually being developed. Some may replace HTML and others may be used in conjunction with HTML. The two fastest rising stars among new languages are Java and VRML (Virtual Reality Markup Language).

Java is a streamlined programming language created by Sun that creates applications that are platform-independent. Java is not a markup language like HTML, but rather a programming language like C++. The only thing that Java requires is that the browser have an 'interpreter' application that reads the Java code. Programs written in Java do not have to worry about finding the proper application on the browser to run them. The actual applications needed are downloaded with the Java script, run the Java script, and disappear. For more information on Java, go to Sun Microsystem's Web site: http://java.sun.com/

One of the newest languages to be used on the Web was developed by Silicon Graphics and is called VRML. VRML creates 3D worlds on Web pages that can be maneuvered through as one would walk around a room or building. VRML also allows for links within this environment. These links can take the viewer to other VRML lands or regular Web pages. Two good places to look for information on VRML are: http://www.paperinc.com/wrls.html and http://vrml.wired.com/

Placing information on the World Wide Web is easy and fun. New and improved World Wide Web servers, browsers, editors, languages, and helper applications are appearing each and every day. The very best place to find information is on the Web itself. Search for information. Search for applications. Ask people and enjoy!

References

Descy, D. E. (1995a, October). All aboard the Internet: Making a World Wide Web home page. *TechTrends, 40*(5), 9–11.

Descy, D. E. (1995b, Nov./Dec.). All aboard the Internet: Adding graphics to your World Wide Web page. *TechTrends, 40*(6), 9–11.

Descy, D. E. (1996, April). Create your own home page: A step-by-step guide. *Technology Connections, 3*(2), 19–21.

The Author

Don E. Descy is Associate Professor, Library Media Education Department, Mankato State University, Mankato, Minnesota.

e-mail, World Wide Web
descy@vax1.mankato.msus.edu
http://www.lme.mankato.msus.edu/ded/don.html

34

Interacting in History's Largest Library: Web-Based Conferencing Tools

Steve Malikowski

Hundreds of courses from dozens of colleges are currently available exclusively over the Internet (Globewide Network Academy, 1996; Malikowski, 1996), and this number is likely to grow quickly. A Web-based course is similar to a traditional course in that students still read textbooks, watch videos, submit homework, take exams, and interact with other class members. Typically, such courses have learning materials on a Web page, and class members interact "off the Web" through an electronic mail list. Mailing lists have been used because the software to use them, a listserv, is free and people are familiar with using mailing lists. In recent years, however, software has become available that allows students and teachers to interact in a time-independent fashion using the Web. This software is referred to as Web-Based Conferencing (WBC), and some implementations of it are freeware. One of the advantages of WBC is that it allows Web-based courses to have course content and interaction in history's largest library—the World Wide Web.

General Description of WBC

WBC is like an e-mail list or a news group in that it is easy to add information to a discussion and view information that others have added. Figure 1 is a representation of one freeware implementation of WBC called Conferencing On the Web or COW (Klavins, 1996).

To the student, WBC is nothing more than another Web page. For example, a student may find the hyperlink "Class Discussions" on the main class Web page. Selecting such a link takes the student to a "hotlist" like the one in Figure 1. Many WBC systems use hotlists to enable users to select which conferences they want to monitor. Students need not monitor all conferences in a course because some conferences are dedicated to small group work. The number to the right of each conference in a hotlist is the number of messages in the conference. The discussions in Figure 1 have the following purpose:

1. **Discussion with Professor**
   Membership in a discussion can be restricted, so each student can have individual interactions with the instructor. Of course, e-mail messages could also be used for this purpose, but using WBC allows for consistency in class interactions and allows Web-resources—such as pictures, sounds, and hyperlinks—to be included in the discussion.

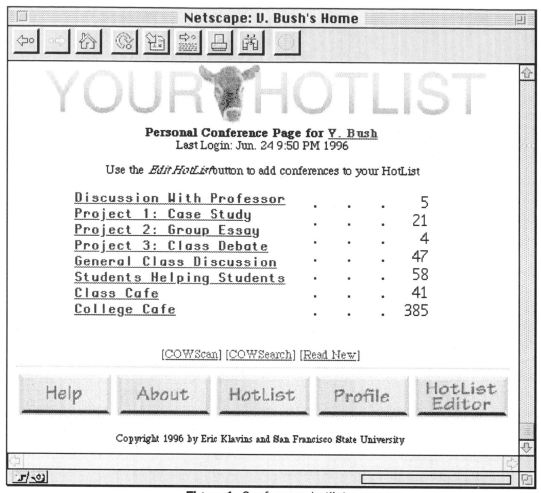

Figure 1. Conference hotlist.

2. Project 1: K–12 Case Study

3. Project 2: Group Essay on Collaborative Learning

4. Project 3: Class Debate

   All the projects listed above are small-group, collaborative learning exercises.

5. General Class Discussion

   An instructor uses this discussion to make class announcements, respond to frequently asked questions, and provide Web resources related to the class, or any other information that does not fit into other discussions.

6. Students Helping Students

   In traditional classrooms, students often create their own study groups. A topic like this allows the same activity in an online learning environment.

7. Class Cafe

   Teachers experienced with online learning emphasize the importance of fostering social cohesion in an online class (Bates, 1995; Gilbert, 1996; Harasim *et al.*, 1995). A surprising level of cohesion can occur by using conferencing (Rheingold, 1993), as long as the opportunity for non-class related interaction is promoted.

8. **College Cafe**

If Web-based courses and conferencing grow only a small fraction as fast as the Web itself, it is likely that other people at your school are using or interested in using WBC. By contacting such people, an additional social and academic resource can be added to your course.

Students follow hypertext links in a hotlist to get to a discussion, similar to that in Figure 2. This figure also shows how a HTML can be used for a note. To continue with the library analogy, this allows library resources to be directly inserted into a discussion. To add to a discussion, a student adds text or HTML into a form, selects a "preview" button, and decides to add the note to the discussion by selecting a "post" button.

Not all implementations of WBC use the format described here, but some type of structure is always implemented to keep conversations focused and easy to navigate.

WBC Compared to Other Computer Mediated Communication

Forms of computer mediated communication most similar to WBC are e-mail lists and newsgroups. WBC has distinct advantages over these forms of communication (December & Randall, 1994). An advantage it has over e-mail lists is that discussions tend to be more fo-

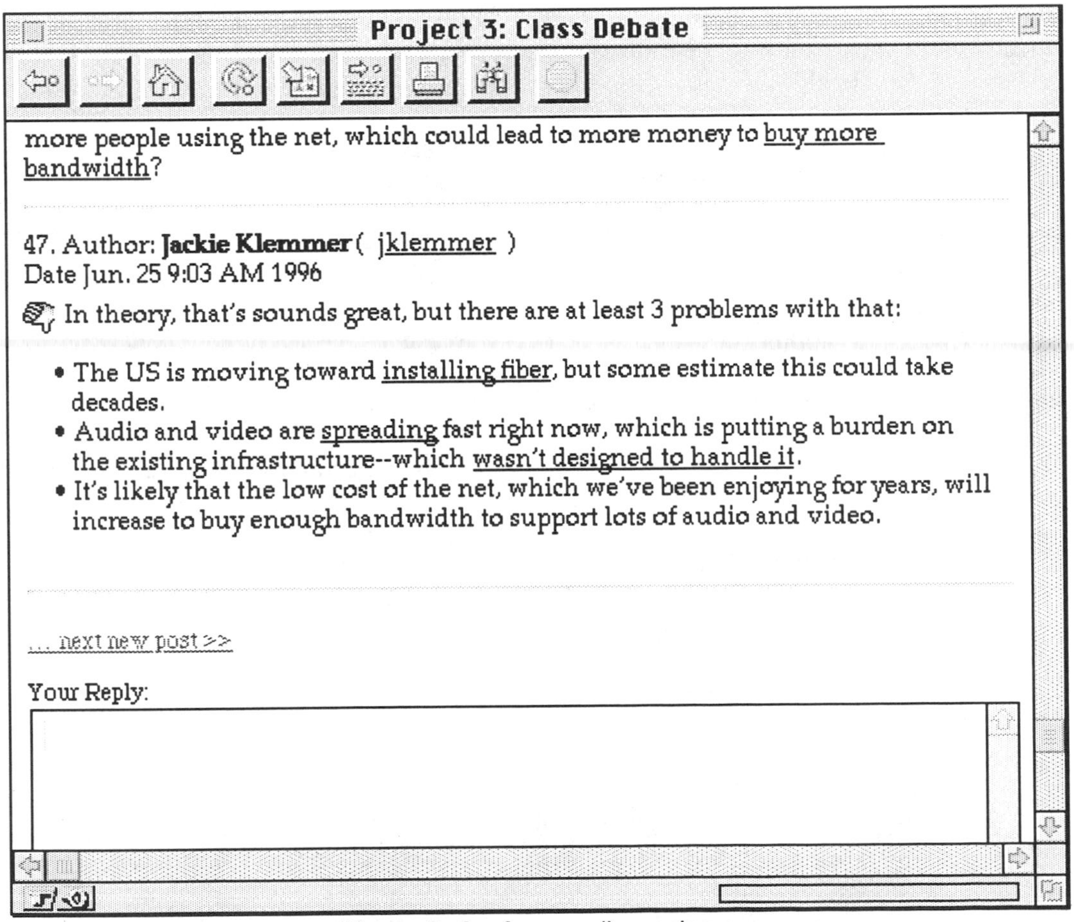

Figure 2. Conference discussion.

cused because of the structure implemented in WBC. The primary means of structure in an e-mail list is the use of different subject lines, or "threads." This structure makes multiple discussions manageable, as long as there are only a few discussion threads. If there are several threads, however, the discussion becomes convoluted—like talking with someone who often changes the subject. Unfortunately, multiple discussions often occur in electronic communication (Harasim *et al.*, 1995; Hiltz & Turoff, 1978; Rohfeld, 1995), so some form of structure becomes important. The structure implemented in WBC allows discussions to occur in separate conferences or topics. Of course, discussions in WBC can still become unfocused, but with this structure in place, teachers have resources to keep discussions focused. Last, in contrast to WBC, e-mail lists have little or no "sense of place." Since all users access a single computer in a conferencing system, they can feel as if they share a single place, or even community (Hiltz & Turoff, 1978; Rheingold, 1993). This sense of place can be helpful for class cohesion.

Unlike e-mail lists, newsgroups allow separate discussions, but WBC has some notable technical advantages. Newsgroups send all their messages to the local Internet service provider of each participant. For example, the news server at Indiana University (IU) contains hundreds of newsgroups for people to view. Unfortunately, only those with a computer account at IU can view these newsgroups. In order for students from the University of Minnesota (U of M) to interact with students from IU, the U of M must have duplicates of the same hundreds of newsgroups on its news server, and only those with an account at the U of M can access these newsgroups. This same duplication is required for any college or Internet service provider that wants to allow its students or customers to interact using newsgroups. This massive redundancy uses considerable server hard disk space and other system resources (December & Randall, 1994).

One way to resolve this issue is to purge newsgroups regularly. For instance, messages older than one month are often purged from all newsgroups to release resources from the server, such as hard disk space, for other purposes. This makes managing newsgroups easier, but it also means that the history of a discussion is lost. If a final exam is based on general or specific class discussions, additional technical support will be needed to assure that the discussions are not purged.

Purging discussions also removes the opportunity for analysis by scholars. Disciplines that may have an interest in such analysis include anthropology, education, history, linguistics, sociology, and any other discipline that analyzes some element of human interaction, whether the analysis concerns how people interact or the topics they are discussing.

The e-mail lists have a similar problem with redundancy and maintaining the history of a discussion. Instead of each participant viewing a single copy of each message, e-mail lists send a redundant copy of each message to each participant. The history of a discussion in an e-mail list is difficult to obtain, so when someone joins the list, he or she cannot read what is already been discussed. In such cases, the new participant may bring up issues that have already been resolved.

Since the discussions in a WBC system generally reside on a single computer or Web site, which users visit, redundancy is greatly reduced, and the history can be viewed by anyone with the proper access privileges. If the size of a conference becomes cumbersome, resources can be transparently distributed to other computers. This should not be confused with distributing redundant copies of a discussion across multiple computers, which is the case with newsgroups. In this case, the distribution is a unique link to a resource on the Internet, and not a redundant message.

Constraints of WBC

Like any distance learning technology, WBC has inherent constraints as well as the resources that have been described. An intuitive constraint is that students will not feel as if they are really part of a class when all they see of other class members is their text on a computer screen. This is especially important when the value of social interaction is considered in the learning process. It has been well established that the opportunity for students to interact, both formally and informally, is an important part of learning (Astin, 1993; Johnson & Johnson, 1984; Keith *et al.*, 1993).

There are a few options in dealing with this constraint of WBC. The most simple answer is to make a strong effort to have students meet in person or through interactive video or audio, Internet-based or otherwise, at some time during the course. When this is done, such live interaction often occurs at the very beginning of a course for a social and technical orientation (Levin, 1995). Another means of becoming more familiar with a teacher or classmates is to use interactive text chat, which is less expensive and thus more readily available than interactive audio or video. The shareware "Netscape Chat" is available from Netscape's Web site, and may support this need. The growth of the Web also makes it likely that some students in a class will have their own home page. Students visiting the Web pages of other students is another means of building

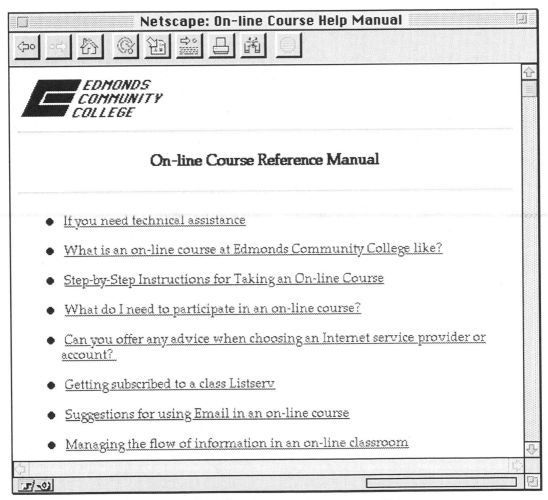

Figure 3. Online course reference manual.

cohesion in a class. Most implementations of WBC have a feature in which any note that a person posts has a link to his or her home page. If students do not have a home page, the teacher might require students to post a picture and description of themselves to the discussion. If students do not have a digitized picture of themselves, they could send a print to the teacher, who is likely able to digitize the picture. Having said this, a consideration of using pictures is that without them, student credibility is based solely on the content of his or her words and not on attractiveness, age, race, or other superficial traits (Baldwin, 1995). At any rate, it is likely that the best solution to the issue of class cohesion is a combination of the issues described above.

Even when live interaction or pictures of students are not available, computer conferencing can create a very cohesive classroom environment. Tony Bates (1995) describes this phenomenon based on his experience with courses that used computer conferencing, but were not Web-based, as the sole medium for student interaction. One of his experiences was with the course DT200: *An Introduction to Information Technology: Social and Technological Issues.*

> Associated with the removal of social isolation, computer conferencing can result in strong emotional involvement for learners in the process of learning and communicating with others, which is unusual not only in distance learning, but often in conventional education .... For me, DT200 was the first time in nearly 20 years at the Open University when I felt I was in direct contact on a regular basis with students.

Another constraint of WBC is availability and familiarity with technology (Paulsen, 1995). Put simply, many people have yet to use the Web for the first time. Of course, this situation is changing fast, but when using WBC for online learning, the instructor should be prepared to help new users. This includes patience in working with those new to the Web and providing technical resources. These resources may be traditional materials, such as printed materials or video tapes, or if students have some access to the Web, a Web site can be created for this purpose. Edmonds Community College in Lynnwood, Washington provides an Online Course Help Manual (Edmonds Community College, 1996), as shown in Figure 3, that is a good example of online resources that can be available.

Selecting a WBC System

Before reviewing WBC systems, it is important to establish that the technical resources and staff are available to support such a system. Generally, if a college or department has its own Web site, it should have the resources to maintain a WBC system. If these resources are not available, consult a local Internet service provider about maintaining a WBC system at their site.

Similar to reviewing any technology, specific and general issues regarding usability and technology must be considered. The remainder of this essay will describe these issues. David Woolley, a pioneer in computer conferencing, maintains a Web site listing many WBC systems (http://freenet.msp.mn.us/~drwool/Webconf.html). Applying the issues described below to the WBC systems listed at Woolley's site should satisfy many WBC needs for online learning.

Specific Issues

As mentioned earlier, one specific feature to consider is whether a WBC system has the ability to have a hotlist that a user or instructor can configure, as shown in Figure 1. Hotlists make it easy for students and teachers to specify which conferences or topics they want to monitor. Initially, it may not seem important to have such hotlists because discussions for online courses may seem relatively small. Sometimes this may be the case, but just as easily, discussions in online courses can grow at a surprising rate. For example, it is a good idea to require a minimal number of student postings each week (Harasim *et al.*, 1995; Paulsen, 1995). If a class has 20 students and each student is required to make 3 postings each week, the math is simple yet significant. For a 15 week semester, that totals 900 messages. If each topic averages 50 messages, that would be 18 topics—which is a lot for each student to monitor. Given the social cohesion that often occurs in an online course (Bates, 1995; Gilbert, 1996; Harasim *et al.*, 1995), students are likely to start their own topics as well.

WBC systems vary as to how they list the number of new messages. If this feature is available, new messages are referenced either to an individual user or to a general date (December & Randall, 1994). A "user-referenced" method classifies messages as being new if an individual user has not yet read them. The system used in Figures 1 and 2, COW, uses such a technique. A "date-referenced" method classifies messages as being new if the messages have been posted within a predetermined number of days. For example, all messages less than a week old might be considered as "new," regardless of whether or not a user has read them.

A specific issue that is more technical in nature is if or how much HTML can be included in a discussion response. Some WBC systems allow all HTML tags to be included. Others allow only links to other Web resources (URLs). Students are rapidly becoming familiar with HTML, so this feature has much potential. Unfortunately, problems may arise out of this potential, such as WBC postings that are difficult to understand (December & Randall, 1994). Some Web pages are difficult to understand or view because they use too many graphics, text sizes, or other multimedia elements. WBC responses using HTML can have this same problem. Because of this, it is advisable to require conservative use of HTML when it is supported in a WBC system.

Another technical issue is whether a WBC system can provide an instructor with detailed information about student activity. This information could include the following:

- Which students are enrolled in the class.

- Which topics a given student is enrolled in.

- How many messages each student has posted in a given topic.

General Issues

The most notable general issue is the fundamental structure of a WBC system. Systems use either a "star" or "tree" structure (Quarterman, 1990), as shown in Figure 4. The conferencing system described earlier, COW, is an example of a star structure. In this structure, the center of the star is the main conference Web site. Multiple conferences are listed around the center of the star. Farther out from the center of the star are subconferences or topics. Farther out still are the specific messages within a topic.

In a star structure, the only messages visible within a topic relate to the topic, as shown in Figures 2 and 4. This is in contrast to a tree structure, where individual messages and topics can appear together at any place in a conference, like an e-mail list. In a star structure, additional comments are added to the end of a discussion, as shown in Figure 2, which resembles most other forms of human interaction (December & Randall, 1994). A disadvantage of a star structure is that since all messages are added to the end of a discussion, responses to a message must be referred to instead of placed immediately after the message—which can happen in a tree structure.

In the tree structure shown in Figure 4, the center of the tree is the main conference Web page. Figure 5 is a specific implementation of a tree structure called HyperNews, which, like COW, is freeware (LaLiberte, 1996). In a tree structure, a response can be added to any other note in the system. A topic is generally considered to be a place on the tree where several messages follow, as shown in Figure 4. An inherent feature of tree structures is that a heading for each message is available, but this feature also occurs in some star structures. As Figure 5 shows, HyperNews also allows an icon to be associated with a response. Headers and icons

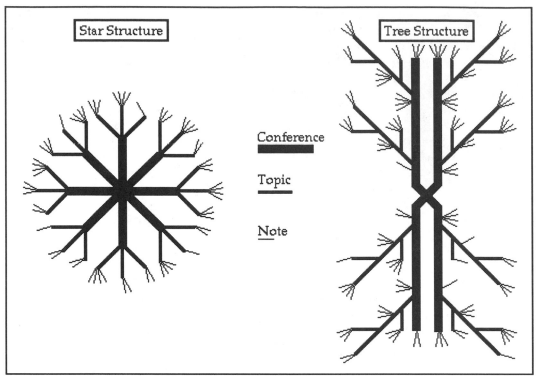

Figure 4. Star and tree structure.

are very appealing features of tree structures, but with them comes the loss of other appealing WBC features, such as hotlists and user-referenced new messages. It is likely that tree-structures do not usually implement hotlists or user-referenced new messages because it is difficult for a WBC system using a tree-structure to determine what is a topic and what is a message. A system cannot count what it cannot determine. Another disadvantage of a tree structure is that it can have a difficult growth path because discussions grow horizontally as well as vertically. If a class were to have the 900 or more messages described earlier entered into a tree-structure, the conversation would likely lose structure and clarity. A teacher could move topics in a tree structure to new locations, but this adds additional work for the teacher and can leave students wondering where their topic went.

Another general issue of WBI systems is enrollment. Enrollment is important because it is advisable to allow only students, and not anybody surfing the Web, to participate or view class discussions. Most systems allow students to enroll themselves, but not all systems allow "batch" enrollment. With batch enrollment, an existing electronic database of student information—such as names, passwords, and e-mail addresses—can be entered into the system at once. If no batch enrollment is available, information for each student will have to be entered individually (Propst, 1996).

A technical issue to consider is whether the system is scaleable. That is, can it maintain hundreds or thousands of postings as well as it handles dozens? Conferencing systems can collect many postings for such reasons as additional courses being offered online and expanded use of a conferencing system, such as for faculty and staff interaction. Of course, postings can be deleted after they become less active, but this removes the possibility of referring back to previous discussions for academic research, understanding why a particular decision was made, adding to discussions that have long been idle, or as mentioned earlier, using previous

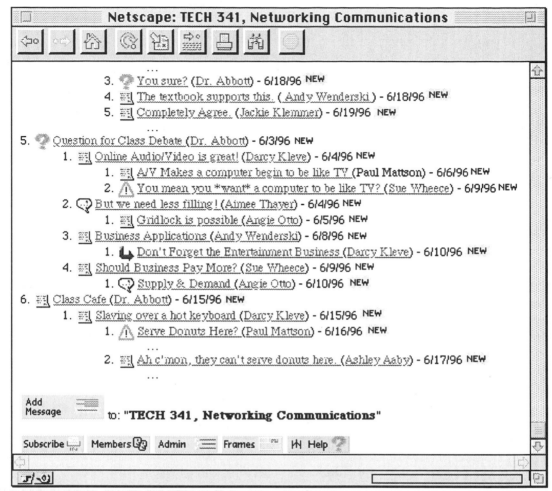

Figure 5. Tree structure discussion.

discussions to review for an exam. The only way to find out if a WBC system can handle many postings is to install the system and give it a lot of postings. This leads to the final technical consideration for a WBC system. You will need to test the WBC systems that appeal to you to see if they work well on your particular computer system. Unfortunately, compatibility can be a problem; therefore, select a couple of Web-based conferencing systems that appeal to you, in case your first selection cannot be implemented for technical reasons (Propst, 1996). Essentially, this means thoroughly testing a system before using it. Like any software, a WBC system that looks good after a few hours of use can look very different after a few weeks or months of use.

WBC Systems Dedicated to Online Learning

Recently, WBC systems have been created for the specific purpose of offering courses over the Web. These applications offer much promise, but since they are new, limited information is available regarding their implementation. Examples of such systems are the *Virtual-U Education System* and *Web Course in a Box*. In addition to having a WBC system, these packages include resources such as the following:

- Automated resources for creating course Web pages and conferences.

- Detailed information about student activity.

- Online evaluation tools.

- Class management tools.

Additional information about the *Virtual-U Education System* can is available (http://kochab.cs.sfu.ca:8000), and additional information on the *Web Course in a Box* is available as well (http://madduck.mmd.vcu.edu/wcb/wcb.html). Since conferencing is an important element of systems such as these, the issues described in this chapter still apply to WBC systems dedicated to WBI.

Conclusion

With the Web's explosion of popularity, it is not surprising that it has evolved into a central place for course resources and interactions. Presumably, it will become even more conducive to online learning with further development of WBC systems dedicated to this purpose. Fortunately, there are a variety of WBC systems that can accommodate the technical and financial resources of most schools interested in offering such courses. When selecting a WBC system, here are some key issues to consider:

Does the system:

- use a star or tree structure?

- include hotlists?

- support any or most of HTML?

- handle hundreds of notes as well as it handles dozens?

- classify new messages with reference to users or to a fixed date?

- provide the teacher with information regarding student activity?

- provide a header or icon for each message?

- allow batch enrollment?

- work well with your technology?

There are a lot of issues to consider when selecting a WBC system, and like most software selection, you never get all the features you want in a single system. When selecting a system, realize that the system you select will be the basis for the Web-based courses in your school or department. Therefore, it is important to get as many of the features that meet the needs of your courses as possible.

Even before the Web was created, courses were offered over the Internet using computer conferencing (Bates, 1995; Harasim *et al.*, 1995), and research was conducted on these courses. Some of this research, as well as descriptions of past and present online courses, is available on the Web. A Web site dedicated to these and other issues related to online learning is available (http://ezinfo.ucs.indiana.edu/~smalikow/courses.html). In this respect, WBI already has a history from which future teachers using online instruction can learn as they further develop this promising field.

References

Astin, A. W. (1993). *What matters in college? Four critical years revisited*. San Francisco: Jossey-Bass.

Baldwin, G. (1995). Computer-mediated communication and American Indian education. In Z. L. Berge & M. P. Collins (Eds.), *Computer mediated communication and the online classroom* (Vol. I, pp. 113–136). Cresskill, NJ: Hampton Press.

Bates, T. (1995). *Technology, open learning, and distance education*. London: Routledge.

December, J., & Randall, N. (1994). *The World Wide Web unleashed*. Indianapolis, IN: SAMS Publishing.

Edmonds Community College. (1996). *Online courses: Web pages, descriptions, and information* (http://www.edmonds.ctc.edu/cce/edol.htm).

Gilbert, K. (1996, April). Unpublished interview regarding online learning with Dr. Kathleen Gilbert, Associate Professor, Dept. of Applied Health Science, Indiana University.

Globewide Network Academy. (1996). *Globewide Network Academy Catalog* (http://www.gnacademy.org).

Harasim, L., et al. (1995). *Learning networks: A field guide to teaching and learning online*. Cambridge, MA: MIT Press.

Hiltz, S. R., & Turoff, M. (1978). *The network nation: Human communication via computer*. Reading, MA: Addison-Wesley.

Johnson, D. W., & Johnson, R. T. (1984). *Learning together and alone*. Englewood Cliffs, NJ: Prentice-Hall.

Keith, H. et al. (1993). *Distance education: New perspectives*. London: Routledge.

Klavins, E. (1996). *Conferencing on the Web* (http://thecity.sfsu.edu/COW2/).

LaLiberte, D. (1996). *Instructions for using HyperNews 1.9B5.x* (http://union.ncsa.uiuc.edu/HyperNews/get/hypernews/instructions.html).

Levin, J. A. (1995). *Organizing educational network interactions: Steps toward a theory of network-based learning environments*. Paper presented at the annual meeting of the American Educational Research Association, San Francisco.

Malikowski, S. R. (1996). *Web-based courses* (http://ezinfo.ucs.indiana.edu/~smalikow/courses.html).

Paulsen, M. F. (1995). Moderating educational computer conferences. In Z. L. Berge & M. P. Collins (Eds.), *Computer mediated communication and the online classroom* (Vol. III, p. 8). Cresskill, NJ: Hampton Press.

Propst, K. B. (1996, June). Unpublished interview regarding online learning at Indiana University with Dr. Kathryn B. Propst, Project Coordinator at the Indiana University Teaching and Learning Technologies Lab, Indiana University.

Quarterman, J. S. (1990). *The matrix: Computer networks and conferencing systems worldwide*. Bedford, MA: Digital Press.

Rheingold, H. (1993). *The virtual community: Homesteading on the electronic frontier*. Reading, MA: Addison-Wesley.

Rohfeld, R. W. (1995). Moderating discussions in the electronic classroom. In Z. L. Berge & M. P. Collins (Eds.), *Computer mediated communication and the online classroom* (Vol. III, p. 14). Cresskill, NJ: Hampton Press.

Acknowledgment

The author would like to thank David Woolley for his valuable input to the writing of this chapter.

The Author

Steve Malikowski is a Graduate Assistant in Instructional Systems Technology at Indiana University, Bloomington, Indiana.

e-mail, World Wide Web
  smalikow@indiana.edu
  http://ezinfo.ucs.indiana.edu/~smalikow

35

Web-Based Search Engines

Cleborne D. Maddux

Although search engines represent a step forward in improving the teaching and learning potential of the World Wide Web, they are less than perfect and are thus the source of additional frustration and problems for some users. Although they vary greatly in quality, search engines present the following problems:

Since search engines make use of previously constructed databases, none include all of the documents or sites on the Web.

There are no search engines that are completely up-to-date, and it can take weeks or months for a specific site to be included in the database for any one search engine, while other sites may not ever be found and included.

Although searching for sites dealing with one-word topics can be relatively simple, the syntax for more complex searches varies greatly from search engine to search engine.

The online data about how the database is constructed, the number of documents in the database, the syntax for use in complex searches, and other data and help screens vary greatly in quality and completeness from search engine to search engine. Thus, it is difficult to choose the best search engine for a particular task, and learning to use any one search engine can be difficult and time consuming.

It is common for features and search strategies claimed in online help screens to be inoperative.

Search engines change frequently. Thus, users who have come to depend on certain features or who have learned productive search strategies may suddenly find that they are no longer available or have changed drastically. This is a major problem. Those who maintain search engines must understand that to many users, *stability* may be as important or more important than are specific features and strategies. This is particularly important for teachers, who do not have vast amounts of time to devote to periodic study of search engines, and to students, whose academic problems and learning styles demand the security of consistency.

Those search engines that include rating schemes for a subset of sites in their databases seldom provide complete and accurate information about the qualifications of reviewers, how objectivity is maintained by a commercial site, how sites are chosen for evaluation, and the exact criteria used for the various rating schemes. Therefore, it is often impossible to make an intelligent judgment about the usefulness or accuracy of the rating system.

This chapter will provide a summary of a small number of popular search engines. Included will be information that is available online in the various search engine help screens, as well as information gleaned from experience in use of the engine. A search for the word "dyslexia" will be performed with each search engine reviewed, and the number of "hits" reported.

Although space will not permit a comprehensive review of every search engine, it is hoped that a summary and evaluation of a representative few will help users become aware of important features to look for in search engines, and to select one or more for further study.

HOTBOT
http://www.hotbot.com/

This is a relatively new commercial search engine, developed by Inktomi and HotWired Ventures LLC (a subsidiary of Wired Ventures) in February of 1996. It was difficult to find online general information about the search engine, and the help feature could be considerably improved by making this information easier to find. It is available currently by clicking on the Inktomi logo at the top of the page, but could not be found in the FAQ (Frequently-Asked Questions) section or in the general help section.

Clicking on the Inktomi logo gives the user access to information punctuated with hyperbole such as the following quotation in which we are told that HotBot "offer users the largest, freshest, most flexible Web search database on the planet." The text goes on to claim that HotBot is the only search engine capable of indexing every word on the Web, a claim also made by some other search engines, as we will see. The text goes on to claim that the database includes over 50 million documents and that HotBot is the only search engine with the capacity to keep up with the Web's growth in the near future. It further asserts that the search engine is designed to index 7 million pages a day, thus updating its database with every document on the Internet about once a week. In an apparent contradiction, the FAQ includes a paragraph, dated June 5, 1996, in which it is stated that the "weekly Web scouring" will begin "soon." There are repeated instances of claims that are made for features that have not yet been implemented. Examples include the promise of a button to toggle off the frames feature, and a "lighter" version of HotBot containing fewer images for faster loading.

The user interface is easy to understand and simple to use. The initial screen presents a blank field for the user to type in a *search string*. A field just above is set to the default of searching the Web "for all the words," but a drop down menu can be used to change the field to read "any of the words," "the phrase," "the person," "the URL." By clicking on the word "Modify," users are presented with options to require or prohibit words, phrases, persons, or URLs. By clicking on the word "Expert," users may choose to limit searches by date, by type of media, and by geographic area. In addition, they may choose the number of hits to view (10, 25, 50, 75, or 100).

Hits are presented as hot links followed by the first few lines of the document, and are assigned a score from 0% to 100% based on the likelihood that they will be useful. These scores are based on results of comparing the search string to the site based on the number of times the string appears in text, whether or not the search string appears in the title, a ratio of the number of times the string appears in text compared to the total number of words in the document, and whether or not the search string appears in the keywords for the site.

There were 9,637 "hits" to the search string "dyslexia."

Evaluation: HotBot is a relatively new search engine with excellent potential. Planned features are incomplete, and the help screens and descriptions should have the "hype" toned down considerably. The frames toggle needs to be implemented, and the help feature needs a good descriptive paragraph or two. Searches are easy to conduct, and the "Modify" and "Expert" features make it easy to perform advanced searches. At present, this search engine offers no features such as news or quality assessment of sites. Its strength is the database, which consists of the entire text of all pages included.

ALTAVISTA
http://www.altavista.digital.com/

AltaVista began in 1995 and is maintained by Digital Equipment Corporation. Like Hot-Bot, AltaVista indexes the entire text of included Web pages and newsgroups. Online information asserts that the database includes 30 million pages found on 275,600 servers. Also included are three million articles from 14,000 Usenet news groups. The search engine is accessed over 16 million times per weekday.

Users may choose to search the Web or Usenet discussion groups, and results can be displayed in Standard, Compact, or Detailed format. Simple searches can employ quotation marks so that words are treated as a required phrase, plus or minus signs can require or prohibit the words they precede, and an asterisk is a wild card symbol that will find matches of variant spellings or derived words ("spell*" will match "spelling," "spelled," etc.) Advanced searches can also make use of operators such as "and," "or," "near," and "not." In addition, users may designate specific words. Then, documents containing these words will be listed first. Also, users may list two dates and the search will be restricted to documents created in that time frame.

There were over 4,000 hits to the search string "dyslexia."

Evaluation: AltaVista is a premier search engine that makes use of advanced technology. Like HotBot, its database is huge and every word of every page is indexed. This is a definite advantage over most search engines, which typically index only those words in the title, the first few paragraphs, etc. The syntax of simple and advanced searches is easy to learn and logical, and the scoring criteria used to determine which hits will be listed first produces efficient results. AltaVista can search Usenet postings, and can even be used as a Usenet reader, since the database contains every word of every posting. There is a toggle to turn off graphics for those with a text-only browser—a feature that will be used by many schools that do not yet have a graphical interface capability.

YAHOO
http://www.yahoo.com/

Yahoo ("Yet Another Hierarchical Officious Oracle") began in 1994 as a non-commercial project of two graduate students at Stanford University. Today it is one of the most popular of all search engines. YAHOO is a commercial venture that is used more than 9 million times each day. The company claims its service is the second most accessed site on the Web (second only to the America Online site).

Web searches can be conducted in the entire database or in any of 14 hierarchical categories, including EDUCATION. Each of these categories includes numerous subcategories (38 subcategories in education, for example). Users who click on "Options" on the main YAHOO search screen can choose to search either the Web, Usenet news groups, or e-mail addresses. They may also elect to specify a Web page time frame (created in the last 1 day, 1 week, 1 month, or 3 years), search for ALL keywords entered or at least ONE of the keywords, choose to treat key words as SUBSTRINGS or as COMPLETE WORDS, and display "hits" 10, 25, 50, or 100 to a page.

Yahoo also includes one of the most complete repertoires of excellent auxiliary services such as news reports, sports stories and scores, and a host of others. A rating system is also used, and sites deemed "excellent" are marked with an eyeglass icon; the word "Xtra" next to a category or subcategory indicates that a related news story from the Reuters news feed is available.

Yahoo also maintains a special search engine for children 8 to 14 years of age. There is a link to this search engine, called "Yahooligans," or it can be accessed directly (http://www.yahooligans.com/).

A search for "dyslexia" produced 34 "hits."

Evaluation: Although Yahoo is probably the most popular of the search engines, its database has not been as large and complete as those compiled by search engines such as AltaVista. (AltaVista indexes every word of every page on the Web, rather than sampling titles, URLs, etc.) Soon before this chapter was written, Yahoo announced plans to use the AltaVista search service in the near future, while retaining the Yahoo format and features. When this is accomplished, Yahoo may be the best choice of all among search engines.

MAGELLAN
http://www.mckinley.com/

Named for the famous explorer, Magellan is a relatively new search engine whose distinguishing feature is its rating system for a large subset of documents in its database. Magellan users may search for "hits" in Web sites, FTP and gopher servers, newsgroups, and Telnet sessions, and may elect to search Magellan's 26 categories or its entire database.

The ratings are done by Magellan employees (Magellan is a product of the McKinley Group) and are on a scale from 1 to 30. They are derived by adding the points assigned for each of three categories including depth, ease of exploration, and net appeal. This point total is then transformed into the 1 to 4 star rating system as follows: 28–30 = 4 stars; 22–27 = 3 stars; 13–21 = 2 stars; 1–12 = 1 star.

Online helps are clear and complete. Users can search the entire database or elect to search only those sites that have been evaluated. Both simple and complex searches can be carried out, and plus and minus signs can require or exclude words from sites found. Hits are listed as hot links with brief descriptions. Reviewed sites can be identified because of the presence of one to four red stars. Those sites that the Magellan staff has identified as containing no mature material are marked with a green light icon.

Magellan also includes a full array of auxiliary features including news reports, sports stories and scores, a "people finder," weather, and lists of outstanding sites.

A search for the word "dyslexia" produced 586 "hits," only three of which were rated.

Evaluation: The idea behind Magellan's rating system is excellent. Unfortunately, only a very small subset of documents in the database have undergone this evaluation, as can be seen in the dyslexia example. Only three of the 586 "hits" had been rated.

One disadvantage is the presence of an option called "Search Voyeur," which produces a list of 20 randomly selected searches currently being carried out by Magellan users, and these frequently include some adult topics.

If the number of rated sites can be increased greatly while maintaining a large percentage of documents in the main database, Magellan could emerge as a strong contender and a good choice for teachers and students.

The Author

Cleborne D. Maddux is Professor, Department of Counseling and Educational Psychology, College of Education, University of Nevada, Reno.

e-mail, World Wide Web
   maddux@unr.edu
   http://unr.edu/homepage/maddux/

36

Evaluation Guidelines for Web-Based Course Authoring Systems

L i s a   H a n s e n   a n d

T h e o d o r e   W .   F r i c k

Introduction

The potential to use the Web for delivering instruction appears to be good. Historically, authoring systems such as Plato, TenCORE, ToolBook, and HyperCard have allowed developers to create instructional programs for specific computers. We can now do similar kinds of things with the Web for instruction, with the major advantages being that courseware is no longer platform dependent, and is accessible through the Internet.

To create Web materials, we presently use text editors, graphics programs, and CGI scripts. What would be ideal is a set of integrated software tools which make this whole design process as easy as it has become with tools such as Authorware, ToolBook and Hyper-Studio on personal computers.

This chapter may be useful for course instructors or classroom teachers who are looking for a WBI authoring tool. We present guidelines for evaluating such tools as they become available for creating Web-based instruction (WBI). Instructors will be making decisions about which tools to purchase, and these decisions will be driven by a variety of factors. We provide a set of questions to help you decide which program will work best for your situation. Also, we provide a set of representative tasks that can be used to evaluate software under consideration.

Information, Interaction, Assessment, and Course Management

We have found it useful to think about WBI in four areas: presenting information, providing human interaction, assessment of learning, and course management.

Information is the content made available for learning during the course. It can be in the form of printed text, lectures, videos, demonstrations, simulations, etc. Presenting information is the Web's strong suit. This is what the Web was originally designed to do, especially through hypertext or hypermedia formats.

Human interaction is that component of a course where students and instructors talk with each other. Interaction can be in the form of face-to-face class discussions or through other means, such as electronic mail or writing notes on paper. This is an important part of most learning environments; students need to communicate with the instructor and other students. The Internet (and the Web) make it possible for such communication to not be bound

299

by time and space. Such communication is asynchronous. Two people do not have to be at the same place and time to carry on a conversation.

Assessment is the third aspect that is important in instruction. Teachers need to know how well students have learned, and so do students themselves. The Web shows promise here as well. Similar to stand-alone computer authoring tools, it is possible to create quizzes and tests of student learning. Such assessment can be computer-based or computer-mediated. Computer-based assessment is when the computer does the grading; computer-mediated assessment is when the computer is used as the conduit between student and instructor. This component is what sets apart WBI from conventional computer-mediated assessment, because it can occur at a distance. The conduit is the Internet.

Course management pertains to administrative tasks such as student enrollment, keeping records on student progress, giving grades, creating student transcripts, etc. Historically, some of these clerical tasks have been done by teachers themselves, and others done by administrative support staff. The Web makes it possible to integrate or at least interconnect some of these activities. For example, when students register for a college course, a WBI course login and e-mail distribution list could be created automatically for an instructor. Similarly, when the instructor turns in grades, these could be seamlessly added to administrative records and student transcripts.

Remember the Old

The use of programs to develop, deliver, and manage computer-based instruction is not new. PLATO was one of the earliest and most successful of authoring systems (Woolley, 1994), and is especially relevant now:

a. PLATO was not simply a development tool; PLATO was also used to deliver the instruction and manage courses.

b. Interaction with the mainframe computer was used for assessment.

c. PLATO incorporated a Notes system that allowed for interaction between instructor and user (Woolley, 1994).

TenCORE, ToolBook, HyperCard, Authorware, and Director are examples of course authoring tools that emerged as the personal computer market grew, with courseware being distributed on computer disks and CD-ROMs. Now, with the advent of networks and the Internet, centralized delivery of instruction at a distance is again appearing, as it has for 30 years on PLATO (now Novanet).

Consider the New

New authoring programs are on the horizon that will make development on and for the Web a simpler process. Already, programs are being created that streamline the development process, automating or shortening the time it takes to do simple actions (see Table 1).

However, for the Web to become the primary delivery format for instruction, programs must be created that allow for integrated development of all aspects of a Web-based course.

Finding the new. Searching Alta Vista, Lycos, Open Text, and Yahoo for the next great authoring tool yielded tens of thousands of hits, none of which produced a single integrated program. We found several instances of methods created by institutions; for instance, *SCALE*, at the University of Illinois at Urbana-Champaign, is an organization that has developed a way to streamline the development process, using a variety of helper tools (Oakley, 1996). However, the most commonly found item was a tool that performed one task or another, but not all elements.

Table 1. A brief list of Web development tools and resources.

Web Page Creation

- Inter Network's Home Page Creation Center
  http://www.inetw.net/lib/start.html

- Web-Lint HTML Checker
  http://www.indiana.edu/~mgrwww/tool_guide_info/web-lint.html

- The Webmaster's Page—List of graphics programs
  http://miso.wwa.com/~boba/masters1.html#10

- HTML Converters
  http://www.w3.org/pub/www/Tools/Filters.html

Electronic Communication

- FirstClass for Macintosh
  http://www.writer.yorku.ca/files/fc/mac.html

- WebNotes for Windows
  http://www.inetw.net/lib/start.html

Creating Online Assessment

- Learn to Write CGI-Forms
  http://www.catt.ncsu.edu/users/bex/www/tutor/index.html

- Carlos' FORMS Tutorial
  http://robot0.ge.uiuc.edu/~carlosp/cs317/cft.html

Administration

- Shareware CGIs
  http://128.172.69.106:8080/cgi-bin/cgis.html

- West
  http://www.west.ie

General

- The Webmaster's Page
  http://miso.wwa.com/~boba/masters1.html

- WebReference—Developer's Corner
  http://www.webreference.com/dev/

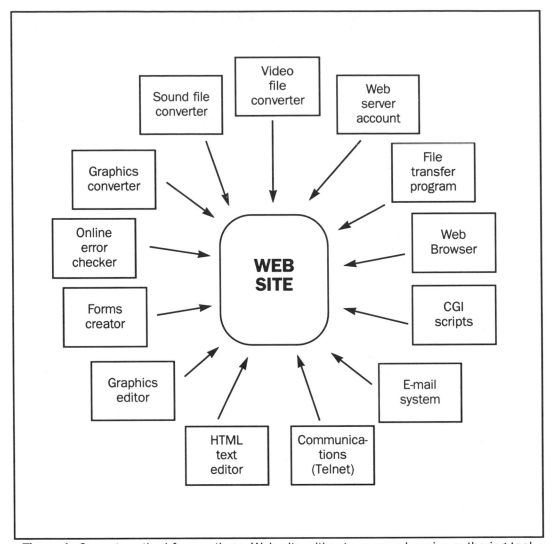

Figure 1. Current method for creating a Web site without a comprehensive authoring tool.

(Figure 1 represents some of the most basic programs used for Web design. Each box represents a separate program that is often used in creating a multimedia Web page.) For instance, West is a program that streamlines the administration of a Web-based course, but does not appear to provide development assistance. An example of an integrated authoring tool being created is *Web-CT* (Goldberg *et al.*, 1996).

Which Should We Choose?

Before a decision can be made about which authoring tool to use to develop WBI, one must carefully consider the way the course will be conducted. Is it primarily presentation of information, with limited discussion or tests? Will most interaction be done as part of a graded test or quiz, or will there be extensive dialogue? Knowing what aspects your course will emphasize can assist in the final decision. Next, consider the following questions when deciding which program to obtain:

How proficient is the developer in creating Web-based materials? This will strongly influence your choice. Are you buying a program for a highly skilled campus Web development team affiliated with Computer Services, or are you looking for something that a sociology instructor, who is not a computer expert, can use? The level of expertise of Web developers varies widely. If you expect instructors to do the WBI development, you should avoid purchasing a system that is primarily CGI scripting (i.e., computer programming).

How difficult is the suite of programs to learn? If possible, get an evaluation copy of the software and try it out. A program should have an interface that gets even the novice developer up and running in a few minutes. Ideally, a tutorial or step-by-step development option should be provided, rather than simply a collection of tools with no obvious starting point.

Does the program come with sufficient documentation, on-line help, and support? If the program does not have easy-to-use print and on-line manuals and a help system, consider one that does.

How much does the program cost? Price plays a major part of any software purchasing decision, and should be considered here as well. There are many free programs that can do certain parts of Web development very well. Be willing to pay for extraordinary capabilities, not simple HTML scripting.

Is the program Web-based or platform-dependent? If your instructors are working on one platform (all Macintosh, for instance), a program that is system-specific may not be a problem. A cross-platform program is better, since it allows for a variety of computers to be used as needed. The best alternative, however, may be a program that actually resides in Web space, can be accessed from any type of machine, and does not require instructors to always work in one place.

Does the authoring tool perform all of the functions needed to create all aspects of the planned course? An authoring tool should let you create every aspect of your proposed on-line course. This includes the elements of information, interaction, and assessment, as outlined above. Specific components of a Web-based course are used as benchmark tests, described below.

How well does the program convert components from other multimedia programs? A good program should allow an instructor to incorporate existing materials from other programs into the new on-line course. Certain browsers, such as Netscape, offer plug-in options, which many multimedia programs are providing. These plug-ins jump the user out to a player version of an application (i.e., HyperCard Player, RunAPM) which automatically launches a certain file. This does not fully integrate non-Web multimedia, but does offer one option for use. Ideally, an authoring tool should convert items from a multimedia program into a format that can be directly accessed from the Web.

How much of the development work does the program do for you? This issue is important for those people planning to develop many courses, or who do not have the time or inclination to decide every aspect, especially visual design issues, which are often time-consuming. A good program should provide step-by-step creation methods, templates, clip art graphics, sample Web pages that can be adapted for individual use, automatic generation of CGI scripts, and basic instruction for creating standard components.

What Can It Do?

There are many methods for evaluating software. Many books about computer-assisted instruction contain checklists of things to do (for instance, Azarmsa, 1991, p. 47). The simplest way to evaluate software for comparison purposes is to create and conduct a series of benchmark tests. We have determined that the following tasks cover most activities done while creating WBI. See Figure 2 for a sample form that can be used for evaluation.

Create a basic Web page. There are many HTML editors and Web page development tools available. A good WBI tool should incorporate basic HTML development. For this test, include the following items on your page and note how you created them:

  a. Title (Did you use HTML, or did the program designate it?)

  b. Header (Did you use HTML, or is the development tool WYSIWYG?)

  c. Navigation tool or tools (Did you use HTML and have to test your own links? Did the program prompt for graphics to use as navigation buttons? Did the program begin to create some sort of flowchart or hierarchy in order to organize multiple pages?)

  d. Graphic (Were you able to edit or create a graphic within the program, or were you only able to import from a support program?)

Create or convert a multimedia document (graphics, sound, video). At this time, multimedia components of Web pages are external files in a variety of formats that are supported with varying degrees of success by the helper programs the Web browser accesses. A WBI authoring tool should allow the instructor to:

  a. Import text documents with minimal loss of formatting or odd symbols.

  b. Convert graphics into formats compatible with Web standards (i.e., GIF, JPEG).

  c. Convert sound files into a usable Web format.

  d. Convert video files into a usable Web format.

Establish a means of asynchronous communications. A WBI authoring tool should either provide a communications system or incorporate an existing system (i.e., FirstClass, WebNotes). Here, see if the tool in question can:

  a. Create a form for asking questions of the instructor.

  b. Create a page that allows students to leave public messages for the group (this page would be similar to a Web-based newsgroup or bulletin board).

  c. Create a method for the instructor to post a response to a student question from within the system (although e-mail would be a simple alternative if this cannot be accomplished).

  d. Incorporate an existing Web-based communications system, such as WebNotes.

Create a test; create an assessment item. A good Web authoring tool should have the capability to create tests, quizzes, and guided practice with feedback. It should:

  a. Take the instructor through creating the assessment interface (i.e., a form for multiple choice tests; a Web page with a dialogue box for short answers and a response area; a form which will be submitted to the instructor for grading; a page that streamlines electronic file transfer of papers or other documents from student to teacher and back again; a self-assessment response form; an adaptive test with feedback for both students and instructor).

  b. Generate the CGI script that will be used to grade, examine, and provide feedback without direct instructor involvement.

Program Name: _____

Cost

   Single: $ _____

   Multi (# _____): $ _____

   Site license: $ _____

Support

   Manual: _____

   Online: _____

   800-number _____

Training

   Tutorial: _____

   Demo: _____

Development Platform(s)

   Windows: _____

   Macintosh: _____

   UNIX: _____

Contains

   Page templates   _____

   Forms templates   _____

   Wizards (step-by-step creation tools   _____

   CGI scripts _____

   Clip art   _____

   Media converters _____

Performance [1–Poor → 5–Excellent]

TASK	QUALITY OF PRODUCT					EASE OF USE				
1. Create basic Web page.	1	2	3	4	5	1	2	3	4	5
2. Convert media.	1	2	3	4	5	1	2	3	4	5
3. Create and use an asynchronous conference.	1	2	3	4	5	1	2	3	4	5
4. Create quizzes.	1	2	3	4	5	1	2	3	4	5
5. Perform course administration.	1	2	3	4	5	1	2	3	4	5

Figure 2. A sample form for evaluating WBI authoring tools.

c. Create the files that contain the results from tests or other interactions that the instructor would like to examine; these files should also be automatically forwarded to the appropriate location, such as the instructor's e-mail account.

Perform course management. An authoring tool should provide a simple method for allowing the instructor to keep track of who is accessing the site, what they are doing, and when they did it. Administration of the Web site is extremely important when students are paying for the privilege of attending this "virtual classroom."

Conclusion

Creating a Web-based course is not a simple task, and the tools for creating it are hard to find. The elements of information, interaction, assessment and course management should all be addressed by a WBI authoring tool if it is to become a standard for development. Determining the computer competency level of the instructor, the support offered by the authoring tool distributors, the costs and capabilities of the program, and the amount of work the program does for you are all elements you should consider when choosing an authoring tool. Also, using the benchmark tests of creating basic pages, creating usable multimedia elements, establishing interaction elements, creating assessment elements, and creating administration tools, will enhance your evaluation. A good WBI authoring tool will combine all of these tasks into one unified process.

References

Azarmsa, R. (1991). *Educational computing: Principles and applications*. Englewood Cliffs, NJ: Educational Technology Publications.

Goldberg, M., Salari, S., & Swoboda, P. (1996). World Wide Web course tool: An environment for building WWW-based courses (http://www.5conf.inria.fr/fich_html/papers/ P29/Overview.html).

Oakley II, B. (1996). SCALE: Sloan Center for Asynchronous Learner Environments (http://www.scale.uiuc.edu/scale/index.html).

Woolley, D. (1994). PLATO: The emergence of online community (http://www.xxlink.nl/plato.htm).

The Authors

Lisa Hansen is a Ph.D. Student, Department of Instructional Systems Technology, School of Education, Indiana University, Bloomington, Indiana.

e-mail, World Wide Web
lchansen@indiana.edu
http://copper.ucs.indiana.edu/~lchansen

Theodore W. Frick is Associate Professor, Department of Instructional Systems Technology, School of Education, Indiana University, Bloomington, Indiana.

e-mail, World Wide
frick@indiana.edu
http://education.indiana.edu/ist/faculty/frick.html

37

Using a Web-Based Course Authoring Tool to Develop Sophisticated Web-Based Courses

Murray W. Goldberg

Introduction

Placing educational material on the Web in the form of static notes and assignments is a relatively simple and quick task now, given the help provided by HTML editors and converters. Prior to using the World Wide Web as an educational tool, many educators had already created electronic copies of their course notes, or at the least, hand-written copies. The process of converting such notes to a World Wide Web-based form ranges from nearly automatic (for electronic copies) to tedious but easy (for hand-written copies). However, generating this kind of educational resource (course notes and assignments on the Web), while useful, vastly under-exploits the potential of the World Wide Web as a teaching resource. Much more is possible.

At UBC in the Department of Computer Science, we have developed a World Wide Web-based educational resource for our third-year course on the fundamentals of operating system design, CPSC 315 (Goldberg, 1996). This resource is intended to be used either as a complement to the existing lecture-based course, or as a self-contained distance alternative to a lecture-based offering.

This resource for CPSC 315 is a comprehensive learning environment containing more than just course notes and assignments. Examples of the tools available for student use include the following:

- *A bulletin-board for communication among all course participants.* This is a wonderful resource allowing for course discussions, questions regarding course material and assignments, and course announcements. Its advantages are tremendous, including greatly enhanced student inclusion and participation in the course.

- *A real-time chat facility.* This allows for the holding of real-time typed conversations. TAs can hold office hours this way without the need for students or the TA to travel to campus.

- *A searchable course glossary.* The glossary contains terms defined for the course and is searchable via prefix string. Terms are also linked directly from the notes to the glossary, so a student reading the notes can click on a term to access the definition for that term.

- *Online, timed quizzes.* Quizzes can be delivered to the students via the World Wide Web. The time a student spends performing the quiz is measured and recorded, and the results are submitted back to the TA for grading.

- A *student annotation facility.* Students can make permanent, private notes and associate any such note with a page of course content for future reference.

- *Student self-evaluation.* Interactive multiple-choice questions are associated with each page of course notes. Students make their selection, and an indication of correctness, along with an explanation of why their selection was correct or incorrect, is returned.

- *Course reference material.* Each page of course content has a linked "reference tool." Clicking on this tool provides a list of several related texts, images of their covers, and a page listing that directs the student to the pages that relate to the course notes currently being viewed.

This resource has proven to be very successful both as a supplement to an existing lecture-based course and as a stand-alone World Wide Web-based distance course.

The problem with this resource, however, was that it was very expensive and time consuming to create. The interactivity in the resource is based on CGI scripts written in PERL. These were all written from scratch, and required experienced programmers and a fair amount of time. Approximately twelve months of full-time programming and World Wide Web-development were involved for one experienced programmer. Given this kind of cost, sophisticated World Wide Web-based educational resources will not proliferate.

After completing this resource, we were presented with the opportunity to do the same for a set of other science courses. We would be able to create these courses more quickly than the first because of the experience gained in CPSC 315, and because we could reuse some of the software we had written for CPSC 315. Still, it would have been difficult for others to capitalize on our experience or incorporate our software modules into their courses. Thus, instead of working on those science courses directly, we decided to create a World Wide Web-based course authoring environment that anyone could use—WebCT (Goldberg & Salari, 1996). WebCT stands for World Wide Web Course Tools. Its goals were as follows:

- it should be easy to use and require no technical expertise on the part of the course designer;

- it should be World Wide Web-based, both in terms of delivery of the completed course, and in terms of the user interface presented to the course designer;

- it should provide all the tools listed above for CPSC 315, as well as many other tools useful in an educational setting; and

- it should allow the development of an educational resource for a course similar in scope and depth to that of CPSC 315 in roughly one-eighth to one-tenth the time taken to create CPSC 315.

WebCT is now in active use at UBC and elsewhere. In our experience, we have found that we have met our goal of a greatly reduced development cycle for World Wide Web-based educational resources, and that these resources are far more interactive and malleable than their predecessors. The remainder of this chapter provides an overview of WebCT.

World Wide Web Course Tools (WebCT)

WebCT is a tool that facilitates the creation of sophisticated World Wide Web-based educational environments. WebCT requires minimal technical expertise on the part of the developer of the educational material and on the part of the student.

The content of a course is provided by the course developer or designer. Interactivity, structure, and educational tools are provided by WebCT. WebCT, as well as allowing the incorporation of a set of educational tools in a course, also allows for the manipulation of the layout and look of the course.

What Interface Is Provided by WebCT?

WebCT is entirely World Wide Web-based, both for the student and for the course designer. A single Web server running the WebCT software is used both for course creation and delivery. Students wishing to interact with course material, and designers wishing to create new courses or modify existing courses use a Web browser to connect to the WebCT server.

Depending on the class of user connecting to a course, a different view will be presented by WebCT. For example, if a course designer signs on, he or she will be presented with a view that allows for both viewing and modification of the course. A student, on the other hand, is presented with a view that only allows for the viewing of a course (except in the case of student presentation areas, where the student is allowed to actually update particular areas).

The interface for all classes of user, like most Web-based resources, is a graphical point-and-click interface. As a brief example, say the course designer wishes to include a course bulletin-board in his or her resource, and make it accessible from the main home page for the course. To do so, the designer would go to the home page and click the button that says "add...." This would present another set of buttons, among them one titled "Course Tool." Pressing that button would present the designer with a list of tools to select from. The designer would then click on the bulletin-board tool. Having done so would automatically add a bulletin board to the course for communication among course participants, and would place a button on the course home page, allowing students to access the bulletin-board. Using WebCT, we can do in three mouse clicks what it took us two months of programming (to create a bulletin board from scratch) to achieve for CPSC 315.

What Does a WebCT-Created Course Look Like?

WebCT courses begin with a main course home page. This home page is configurable in a variety of ways, and provides links to course content, features, and tools. Supplementary home pages (called tool pages) can also be created and linked to from the main home page. This allows for greater structuring flexibility (see Figure 1).

Course content comes in two forms—individual content pages, and paths of content. Any number of both are allowed. A single page of content is useful for items like course outlines or schedules. Course paths organize pages into both a linear and hierarchical relationship. These allow easy sequential or direct access to course content for the student.

Each page of content has the designer's contribution in the main frame and a tool bar at the top. The tool bar provides buttons for navigation and for access to all course and page-related tools and features.

What Course Tools Can Be Included in a Course?

There is a large set of tools that can be incorporated into any course for the student to use. There are also a set of features designed to be used by the course designer that allow him or her to measure progress and manage the course.

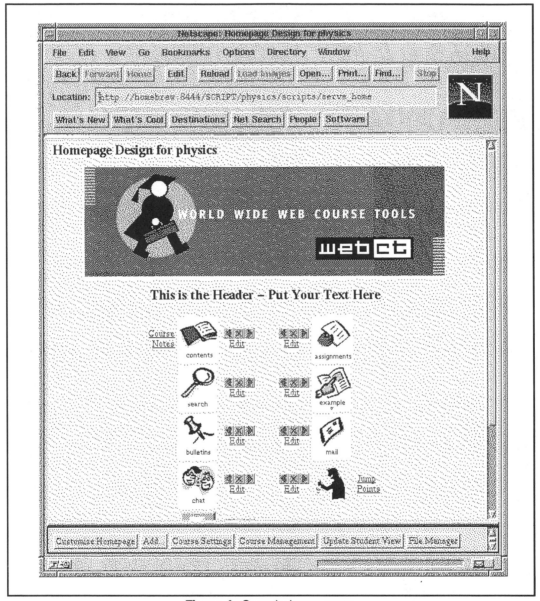

Figure 1. Sample home page.

First, all of the tools listed above for CPSC 315 can be included in any WebCT course through a few mouse clicks. These tools can be made accessible via the course home page, a supplementary tool page, or from any page of course content. To recap, these tools are the bulletin-board for communication among all course participants, a real-time chat facility, a searchable course glossary, online, timed quizzes, a student annotation facility, student self-evaluation, and a course reference material tool.

Other tools that can be incorporated for student use include the following:

- *Electronic Mail.* An electronic mail facility can be added to a course allowing one-to-one message transfer among course participants. Like the bulletin-board, messages can be searched for based on the sender, content and the date of sending.

- *Shared, Interactive White Board.* This is a collaborative tool that allows groups of students to create and edit a document in parallel over the Internet. Text and drawing are supported. Created documents can be saved for later re-editing, display, or printing.

- *Student Presentation Areas.* WebCT allows the designer to designate links which serve as the document home page link for student-generated Web pages. For each link, the designer can give authoring privileges to a single student, a group of students, or to the entire class.

- *Searchable Image Archive.* The course author can upload images to be included in the course. WebCT allows the association of annotations and free text with each image. Students can search for images based on these. Thumbnail versions for the matching images are presented which can be clicked to present the full version.

- *Automatic Indexing and Searching.* This tool allows the automatic creation of an index of course content and terms. The designer can define a set of words that he or she would like to appear in the index. WebCT dynamically creates an index which points to pages that contain that word. If the students do not find the term they are looking for in the index, they can enter their own term. A new index entry will be dynamically created showing the course pages where that term occurs.

- *Grade Tool.* Each student can view his or her own marks as entered by the designer. The student also has access to minimum, maximum and average marks for each course component. Students also have online access to the comments and grades for each online quiz written and marked.

- *Context Maintenance.* WebCT remembers the activities of each student during each session with a course. This way, when a student returns to a course after, say, not looking at it over a weekend, WebCT will automatically place the student at the point where he or she last left off during the previous session. This places the student back in a familiar course context and facilitates a faster return to learning.

There is also a set of tools that assists the course designer in managing the activities of a course in progress. These are as follows:

- *Student Progress Tracking.* Progress tracking pages allow the designer to monitor student progress in the course. Indicators such as date of first and last access, time spent on system, percentage of pages visited and more are available. An indication of course participation by way of the bulletin board is also available in terms of number of original and follow-up postings, and percentage of articles accessed.

- *Course Tracking.* This allows the designer to view statistics on individual pages of content. This includes the total number of accesses to, and on average the duration of access to each course page.

- *Timed Online Quizzes.* As mentioned above, quizzes can be written by the designer and delivered online on a predetermined day. A status page available to the marker indicates for each student whether that student has not yet begun, begun but not yet completed, or completed the quiz. A completed quiz, along with an indication of how long the student took to complete the quiz, is available to be marked online. Once marked, the grade assigned is automatically entered into the WebCT grade database and, along with comments, is made available to the student.

- *Student Management Tool.* This allows the course designer to add individual students or an entire class to a WebCT course (allowing them to sign on). Student passwords can be reset. This tool also maintains a grade database. Grades from quizzes are automatically entered into the database. Grades for external activities can also be entered. Finally, WebCT can compute a final grade (via weightings or a formula) and make a student's grade available to that student.

- *Course Look and Feel.* Courses can be customized in terms of several attributes. For example, the layout of the links on the home page can be displayed as one or two columns. The color schemes of the home page and content pages are configurable by the designer.

Defaults can be chosen, and overridden for individual pages. Likewise, a default set of tools can be made available from every page of content. This, too, can be overridden for individual pages. Two sets of icons are available to be chosen by the course designer, one providing a formal look, the other providing a more casual look. WebCT also provides a set of built-in images that can be used, for example, as course banners. If none are suitable, the course designer can upload his or her own. Finally, a counter can be added to any page that records and displays the number of accesses to that page.

Conclusion

Our experience with WebCT has been very positive and has spurred the development of Web-based courses at UBC. Its use is just now beginning to reach outside UBC, and we look forward to having WebCT facilitate World Wide Web-based course development at many institutions.

References

Goldberg, M. (1996, Feb.). CALOS: an experiment with computer-aided learning for operating systems. *Proceedings of the 27th SIGCSE Technical Symposium on Computer Science Education.*

Goldberg, M. (undated). First results from an experiment in computer-aided education for operating systems (http://homebrew.cs.ubc.ca/papers/calos-res).

Goldberg, M., & Salari, S. (1996). World Wide Web—Course Tool: An environment for building World Wide Web-based courses. *Computer Networks and ISDN Systems, 28,* 1219–1231.

The Author

Murray W. Goldberg is Instructor and Senior Faculty Advisor, Department of Computer Science, University of British Columbia, Vancouver, Canada.

e-mail
goldberg@cs.ubc.ca

38

The Creation of a Web Site

Richard J. Voithofer

Introduction

The students who attend the University of Wisconsin (UW) Hospital School are all special education students in the sense that they all present unique educational needs, depending on the nature of their medical treatment, as well as their individual learning styles and academic levels. In a typical school year, the hospital school, staffed by teachers from the Madison Metropolitan School District, educates over 200 students whose attendance varies from a few days to several months. Disrupted by treatments and complications presented by their illnesses, the children's lives are not conducive to any "standard curriculum."

Often more important to these students than learning a unit in a curriculum or mastering a particular skill is maintaining a connection with peers outside the hospital and having access to resources that help them complete work assigned by their regular teachers. The World Wide Web provides an appropriate vehicle and context to address both these specific needs. The Web site presented in this chapter (http://danenet.wicip.org/mmsd-it/hospital/index.html) was designed to help students at the Hospital School fulfill their interpersonal needs by coordinating a keypal project with peers at other Madison schools, as well as provide specific curricular activities and resources to develop research skills using the Internet and the World Wide Web.

The hospital school site exists as part of an integrated Web site for the entire UW Children's Hospital. This chapter will address issues surrounding the planning, installation, implementation, and revision of this Web site, balancing a discussion of instructional design issues with technical considerations.

The Students at Hospital School

The students who attend the University of Wisconsin hospital school because of extended treatments for life threatening illnesses confront difficult emotional and physical challenges while often feeling isolated from their peers. They repeatedly express a desire to stay connected with peers and friends outside the hospital. Yet, in between hospital visits, when they do come in contact with peers at their regular school or friends from their community, they are often misunderstood as a result of the physical and emotional consequences of their treatment (i.e., hair loss, depression, etc.). They find it uncomfortable to relate to peers who remember them as they were before they were treated for their illness. Electronic mail provides a more non-judgmental means of communicating with peers at their home school and other schools, reducing the awkwardness that may exist in traditional face-to-face interactions.

While older students (i.e., late elementary and middle school) can find a variety of topics to discuss via e-mail, younger students often need structure and guidance in the nature of their communications. This guidance can be created through the World Wide Web. More recent versions of HTML[1] implement a feature called "forms"[2] that provides a helpful means of structuring and administering keypal projects.

Anticipating the return to their regular lives, students in the hospital school are concerned with keeping up with their school work. This includes completing reports and research papers that require access to reference library materials that do not exist at the hospital school. While the Internet and the World Wide Web provide a vast, constantly growing, storehouse of information, it remains difficult to find appropriate, relevant, and accurate materials, especially for younger students who lack more sophisticated search skills. In order to separate the wheat from the chaff on the Internet, students must learn the features and idiosyncrasies of the major search engines.[3] The ability to use Boolean expressions in order to refine search criteria is often helpful.

While exploring the efficacy of employing the World Wide Web as a means of administering these two activities, interviews revealed that the students had a positive attitude towards the World Wide Web and enjoyed using computers. Important to the successful implementation of any technology-based learning experience is the learner's attitude towards the technology. Because of varying degrees of limited mobility, the students at the hospital school are comfortable with computers as a result of spending a large amount of their free time playing computer games and accessing the Internet. Many already use the Internet to do research for school projects, yet their research capabilities are unsophisticated in the sense that they can do a simple key word search but often cannot refine that search.

Planning

Aesthetic and Technical issues

An early design criterion prescribed creating a site that satisfied the content goals established, as well as exhibited sound graphic design principles including (a) grouping of related items, (b) the use of white space to allow the eye to rest, (c) consistency, and (d) the use of color as a means of orientation. These aesthetic goals are satisfied in the design by using color *and* text as a means of orienting the user. Whenever the user is presented with a menu of places to navigate within the site, each menu option is rendered in a unique color. This color is kept consistent throughout subsequent screens within that particular menu choice.

Because the hospital school site is subsumed under the UW Children's Hospital site, it was important to create an interface and aesthetic that is consistent throughout both sites. Attention is paid to offer users an easy way to orient themselves and jump to desired sections. Buttons and/or hot text[4] are provided in frequent intervals throughout each screen, reducing the amount of scrolling needed to reach a navigation point.

Hardware Issues

The primary hardware resources in the hospital school are two Apple PowerMac 5300 computers with 16 megabytes of RAM and 1 gigabyte hard drives. These computers provide sufficient computing power and video display capability to render the most sophisticated and graphical Web pages. The connection to the Internet for these computers is provided by direct TCP/IP[5] access using an Ethernet[6] connection allowing fast downloading of World Wide Web resources like graphics. Taking only these two factors into consideration, it would have been possible to design a site that incorporated numerous graphics and even integrated multimedia such as digital sound and video. However, because access to resources at potential partner schools vary in relation to computing power and speed of Internet access, including some schools restricted to slower 14,400 baud[7] modem access, the site contains fewer, lower resolution graphics.

Software Issues

Despite the proliferation of World Wide Web browsers, Netscape remains the dominant browser[8] used to access resources on the World Wide Web. In planning for this project, research of the Madison Metropolitan School District revealed that most partner schools have Netscape version 1.2 loaded on computers with Internet access, with an upgrade to version 2.0 becoming a district policy within a few months of production. During the planning of the site, version 1.2 was the most stable on both IBM compatible and Macintosh platforms.

Even after deciding on the use of a particular browser, a designer must still pay attention to the version of the browser selected. With each browser version comes new features and new HTML tags that are not interpreted by earlier browser versions and often cannot be read by browsers[9] produced by different companies. Hand in hand with new features generally comes greater hardware requirements. Deciding on a browser and a version is a design decision that should be agreed upon early in the planning process.

CGI and Java

A plain HTML document remains static much like a text file that doesn't change. The Common Gateway Interface (CGI) is a standard for interfacing external applications with information servers like Web servers. A CGI program is executed in real-time, so that it can output dynamic information, allowing for more interactivity between the user and the Web server. Writing and/or implementing CGI scripts generally requires a certain degree of expertise in administering World Wide Web resources. Because one of the goals of the project was to allow teachers at the hospital school with a minimum of HTML programming experience to update the pages and add information,[10] CGI was not used during the initial phase of the project. Because CGI scripts are useful in formatting the output of HTML forms, they still may be employed to help administer the keypal project. Table 1 provides the reader with Internet resources to help in determining the efficacy of using CGI scripts for a specific project.

Java is a powerful, platform-independent, general-purpose programming environment for creating applets[11] and applications for the Internet and represents the future of creating more complex interactivity on the World Wide Web. When using a Java-compatible browser to view a page that contains a Java applet, the applet's code is transferred to the user's system and executed by the browser, providing more opportunities to interact with a Web-based lesson and for the lesson to provide more context-sensitive feedback. Java was a new technology

Table 1. Internet CGI resources.

URL/Internet Address	Description
http://www.best.com/~hedlund/cgi-faq/	An introductory guide to CGI
http://hoohoo.ncsa.uiuc.edu/cgi/intro.html	Another introduction to CGI
http://hoohoo.ncsa.uiuc.edu/cgi/forms.html	Decoding Forms with CGI: an important implementation of CGI
http://www.perl.com/perl/index.html	Information about the PERL programming language used to create CGI scripts
comp.infosystems.www.authoring.cgi	Newsgroup for discussions about CGI

Table 2. Internet Java resources.

URL/Internet Address	Description
http://java.sun.com/	Good source of Java information offered by Sun Microsystems, Inc., the creators of Java
http://www.gamelan.com/	Directory and registry of Java resources
http://www.javaworld.com/	IDG's magazine for the Java community
comp.lang.java	Newsgroup for discussions about the Java language

during the design process, and because of the technical difficulty of implementation at the time, was not employed in this project. Nevertheless, Java's movement towards widespread acceptance throughout the Internet community makes it an important consideration for those designing instruction on the World Wide Web in the future. Table 2 provides resources on the Internet to learn more about Java

Balancing the Agendas of Multiple Stakeholders

Because the UW Children's Hospital and Hospital School site represent both the Madison Metropolitan School District and the University of Wisconsin Children's Hospital, it was necessary to create a site that followed the guidelines of both institutions and would still be motivating for the students who accessed it. The UW Children's Hospital asked that a "modified date" be placed on each page as well as a contact e-mail address for the content creator. The Madison Metropolitan School District requested that links be made to specific sections of its own home page. It was necessary to consult representatives from both institutions during the design process.

Because of general inexperience with placing information on the Internet, institutions are often unclear about their Internet policies. Up-to-date design and technical information must always be communicated to management and administrative personnel in order to maintain clear expectations between all stakeholders. Sustaining consistent, clear communication between the design team and both institutions proved invaluable in averting misunderstandings and balancing the agendas of both institutions.

Implementing

Prototyping

Because of the ease of creating and modifying HTML, it was beneficial after completing the initial design to test prototypes of sections of the project with students and teachers. Rapid prototyping allowed the students in the hospital school to become co-designers of the hospital school site. For example, students expressed a desire to publish their computer artwork, short stories and poetry on the World Wide Web. Because this addition was implemented early in the production process, it was easy to incorporate their ideas into the site. This shared ownership increased their enthusiasm about the site and provided motivation to use the site more often.

Installing

Early in the installation phase, teachers helped students, especially younger ones, understand the unique characteristics of accessing the World Wide Web before using the resources provided in the site. Knowing the attributes of a particular resource on the World Wide Web, like a search engine, may not always be enough of an understanding for successful implementation of instruction on the World Wide Web. Slow download times, Web servers not accepting connections, or dead links[12] can quickly lead to decreased motivation. For younger students, it can be frustrating to wait for a connection to a site or for larger graphics to download.

To address these issues, teachers provided brief introductions to students based on two criteria: (1) degree of student's World Wide Web expertise and (2) student's age level. Teachers helped students understand where they might experience frustration and offered suggestions to address these areas. For example, students were taught to use the "stop" button on their browser when they had attempted to load a particular page and there was no response after a minute. Students were introduced to the limitations of the medium as well as the potential benefits. After these introductory sessions, teachers worked with students on an individual basis, the most common form of teacher/student interaction in the hospital school.

Updating and Revision

It was important in the creation of this Web site to make it easy for teachers to update the site themselves. Updates included being able to add students' work to the Web page or make adjustments to specific portions of the site like adding another partner school in the keypal section. To facilitate the updating of the site, the HTML code was kept as simple as possible and the code was well documented. Comments were inserted frequently to indicate to anyone updating a page what function a particular part of the code carried out. The teacher who was assigned to update the page took two courses on the World Wide Web and writing HTML offered by the Madison Metropolitan School District. The school district maintains an ambitious agenda to provide teachers with resources and training to publish course material and student work on the World Wide Web.

A helpful tool during the revision process is placing a counter on each Web page that students can access on the site. A counter is a piece of software that keeps track of the number of times a particular page is accessed. A counter can usually be readily set up by the site's Webmaster,[13] using a CGI script. This information allows those carrying out revisions to track usage and ask students more focused questions when performing formative analysis. For example, if the designer notices that a particular page is being accessed infrequently, students can be asked specific questions about that page, including factors such as the look of the page, content, and ease of navigation.

Conclusion

After one has decided that the World Wide Web is an appropriate delivery vehicle for instruction, it is important to maintain a balance between understanding technical hardware and software considerations and following sound instructional design principles. This was addressed primarily through front-end analysis of the students at the University of Wisconsin Hospital School and attending to the hardware and software resources available to the primary users of the site.

During production and revision, one often realizes many opportunities to make additions and improvements to this type of learning environment. The ease of writing HTML increases this temptation. Nevertheless, one must always be able to distinguish the 'nice to have' from the 'need to have' additions and features during these processes. A clearly written design document agreed upon by all stakeholders serves as an important touchstone during the later phases of implementation, updating, and revision.

Notes

1 HTML—<u>H</u>yper<u>T</u>ext <u>M</u>arkup <u>L</u>anguage is a markup language that is used to construct documents that can be viewed by World Wide Web browsers like Netscape (see http://www.netscape.com) and Mosaic (see http://www.ncsa.uiuc.edu/SDG/Software/Mosaic/NCSAMosaicHome.html). A browser is a program that translates html into structured screens called pages that contain text, graphics, links to other pages on the World Wide Web, and various media including sound, video, and animation.

2 forms—This HTML feature allows users to input information into a Web page by entering text and/or selecting check boxes and radio buttons to make selections in a list.

3 Search Engines—Search engines are electronic databases or collections of Internet accessible sites. Most search engines can be queried by a user and then return a number of responses. Engines search for specific topics and/or specific Internet tools such as ftp sites. Some of the search engines are updated by people, while others are maintained by computers that periodically search the Internet for new sites.

4 hot text—In HTML, it is possible to make a word or group of words clickable so that when selected with a mouse click, one is linked to a another section of the site or a completely new site.

5 TCP/IP—TCP/IP is the communication protocol used to transfer digital information over the Internet.

6 Ethernet—Ethernet is a communication protocol used to allow computers to exchange digital information over a local area network (LAN). Although faster speeds are emerging, the standard speed of an Ethernet connection is 10 megabits per second, significantly faster then the fastest modem connections.

7 14,400 baud—This represents a particular speed (i.e., 14,400 kilobits per second) at which a modem is capable of downloading digital information. The lower the baud rate, the slower the connection.

8 See http://facs.scripps.edu/browsers.html and http://www.wishing.com/Webaudit/browsers_totals.html for up-to-date statistics showing a proportional break down of browsers used to access specific high traffic areas on the World Wide Web.

9 If one is uncertain of the browser that will used by the users of site, it remains important to maintain the most common HTML standards (see http://www.w3.org/pub/WWW/MarkUp/).

10 The site was designed and produced by a team outside the UW Children's Hospital. The team then trained representatives from each hospital department in the maintenance and updating of the pages.

11 applet—A Java applet is a Java program that can be included in an HTML page, much like an image can be included.

12 dead links—Dead links are links that are no longer active. Home pages are removed from the World Wide Web for any number of reasons, and when they are removed, all the pages that are linked to the removed page are not notified or automatically updated. It remains important before creating a link to a particular page to make certain that it is stable. Some good indications of the stability of a link include if it is consistently updated and/or a visitor counter indicates a large amount of traffic.

13 Webmaster—The Webmaster is the individual in charge of maintaining a Web server. The Webmaster carries out administrative functions on a Web server, including the creation of accounts, as well as maintaining the hardware and software integrity of the server.

The Author

Richard J. Voithofer is with the Educational Communications and Technology Program, University of Wisconsin-Madison.

e-mail
    rjvoitho@students.wisc.edu

39

Holistic Rapid Prototyping for Web Design: Early Usability Testing Is Essential

Elizabeth Boling and Theodore W. Frick

Overview

You want to design a Web site that will organize access to courses or programs that your organization offers, or one that serves as the "front door" to all the Web pages for your school, college, or company. Maybe you have already created several Web pages, even whole sets of pages for individual courses or training programs, and they look pretty good.

Now that you are getting ready to tackle the design of an entire Web site, however, you recognize that it may be difficult to anticipate the needs of everyone who will use the site, and probably difficult to get timely feedback about what works and what doesn't once the site is on the Web. Your urge is probably to sit down at a computer, learn a couple of the new Web tools that promise great results, and start producing pages.

When you design your own Web site, we recommend that the first thing you do is to start on paper, not on a computer. Create holistic paper prototypes very early in the process and test them out with the people you expect to actually use your site. A holistic prototype contains the entire top-level structure of your Web site, and enough strands to exemplify its primary features. Creating a holistic prototype is important because features that might work well in isolation, or in small sets of pages, do not necessarily add up to a good Web site design. Testing early in the process is important so that you have time to correct problems and so that structural changes are still relatively easy to make.

Why Create a Web Site in the First Place?

Before you create any prototype, of course, you will have answered several key questions:

- What problem are you trying to solve? Will another method solve it more easily?

- How will putting parts of your courses on the Web benefit your students? What does use of this kind of technology allow your students to do that could not be done before in some other way?

- Do the students in your courses and programs have convenient and easy access to the Web? If they don't, they won't be able to use your Web materials, and you should be focusing on an alternative way of providing information.

319

The answers to these questions are different for every situation, and only you can answer them for your situation. Providing you have solid justification for using technology, and infrastructure to support your students' use of the Web, the next step is to prototype your site.

The Basic Process: Start on Paper; Make a Prototype, Test and Revise; Then Build Your Site

For efficient Web site development that avoids the most errors possible and offers the most of what your users want, we recommend that you:

- create holistic, paper prototypes very early in the process;
- test the prototypes on the actual people who will use your site;
- revise your design; and
- then build the site on the computer.

What Is a Holistic Prototype?

A holistic prototype contains the entire top-level structure of your Web site, and enough strands to exemplify its primary features; for example, multi-page documents, search functions, and different information formats (maps, tables, image maps, forms, lists, text-only documents). This kind of prototype is a hybrid between the "horizontal" prototype, which represents all elements but none in detail, and the "vertical" prototype, which represents detailed functionality for only one path that a user might take (Nielsen, 1993).

Why Paper?

Creation of Web pages is relatively fast and easy, so it may seem that you should create a rapid prototype on the computer and not waste effort on a redundant paper product. While electronic prototyping may work well enough for small sets of Web pages, our experience suggests that paper prototyping is a more effective approach, and ultimately a more efficient one for large sites, simply because paper prototyping offers benefits that electronic prototyping does not (Rettig, 1994).

Hands on. The creation of a paper prototype requires that designers put their hands on the information they are organizing—literally. We have found it useful to put individual "pieces" of information on index cards. For example, in the redesign of the top-level information structure for the School of Education at Indiana University-Bloomington, we began with a needs analysis. We found out what questions are asked frequently when people call the school or visit in person, and we put each question with its answer on an index card—350 cards in all. Then we sorted those cards into groups with common themes, making new cards with the "theme" labels. From these groups, we derived the paper prototypes of our top-level Web pages. The activity of cutting and pasting, reading and re-reading, and sorting and stacking the index cards forced everyone who was involved to get closely acquainted with content of the planned Web site (Frick, Corry, Hansen, & Maynes, 1995).

Portability. Paper prototypes are portable; they can be used in test sessions where there are no computers, which usually means that time and location of sessions are more flexible than they would be for electronic prototypes. We put our paper prototypes into a three-ring notebook with dividers with labeled tabs. When we conduct a usability test, the subject can view only one "page" at a time, choose a link, and skip directly to the "next page" by check-

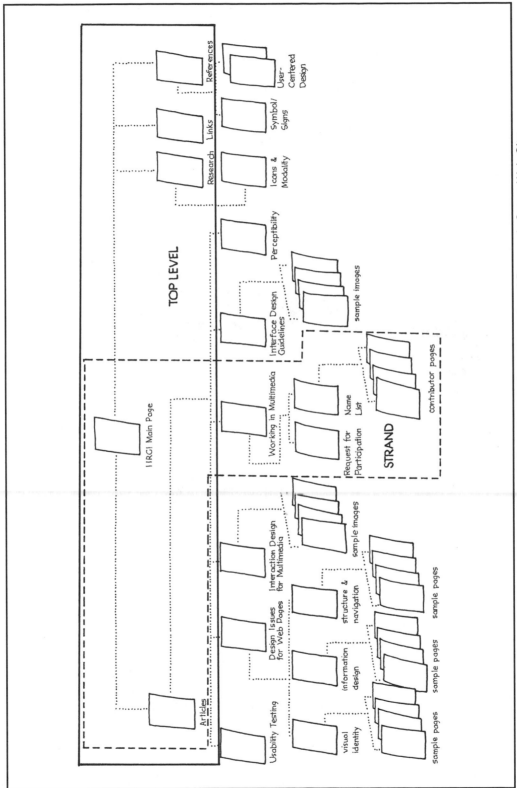

Figure 1. "Top level" and "strand" from the Interface Interest and Research Group Web Site.

ing the labeled tab on the divider. You can conduct usability tests with a notebook like this virtually anywhere that you and a subject can sit down together.

Draft form. Paper prototypes seem inherently less "finished" or "real," than do electronic prototypes. Your subjects may feel more comfortable working with paper prototypes, and criticizing them than they would if the Web pages seemed to exist already. Designers themselves are more willing to scrap a paper prototype that isn't working and start over than they are to throw away a large set of electronic files and start from scratch.

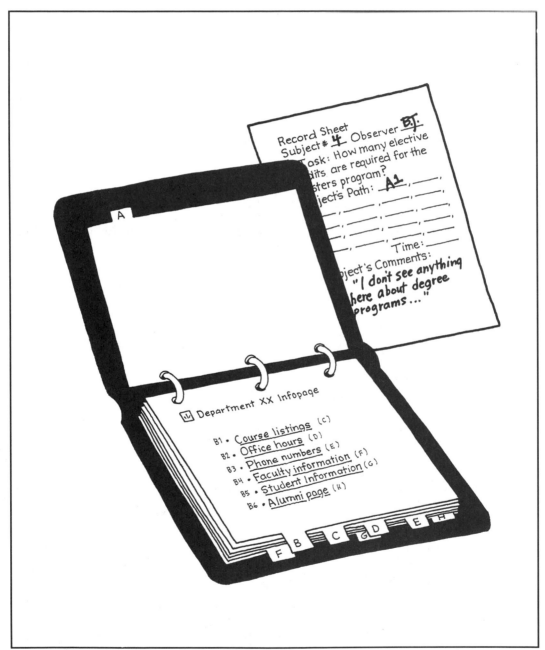

Figure 2. Paper prototype in a notebook with corresponding record sheet.

How Is a Test Conducted?

Prototype testing may be conducted in as many specific ways as there are projects, but you can follow a fairly standard pattern in testing your holistic paper prototype and be assured of useful results.

1. **Design the test.** You will not be developing new methods for this test, but you will have to decide on several basic components of your tests: the target population profile (from which you will identify your subjects), the tasks you will ask subjects to complete, the number of sessions you will conduct, and the method you will use to record your observations.

2. **Identify and recruit your subjects.** The temptation is to ask your friends or colleagues to be your subjects, but these people probably don't fit the profile of your target population (Boling & Kirkley, 1996). When members of the target population are not available, match their critical characteristics as closely as possible. What's critical? If nothing else, computer experience (particularly Web experience), prior knowledge of the content, and learning context (age, reading level, profession, motivation toward the content). Most of the time your target population is not homogenous; some may have a lot of computer experience, while others have none. When you recognize such disparity, you should define several profiles and find subjects to match each profile. Choose subjects whose characteristics are very similar to those of the eventual users. If your course is usually full of college sophomores who have taken two semesters of calculus, with about 75 percent men, then you need to find eight typical sophomores with the calculus prerequisite, where six are males and two are females. You do not need a large number of subjects to identify the most serious problems with your materials (Lewis, 1994; Virzi, 1992).

3. **Conduct test sessions under authentic conditions.** When you conduct a session, normally you will do this with one subject at a time. Ahead of time, you should have identified authentic tasks that you expect your target population to do. You are likely to have to make some compromises in authenticity when you test rapid prototypes, but do not compromise authenticity of tasks. These tasks can be very basic, such as finding the course Web site at your institution, logging into the course Web site, finding the syllabus, finding the answer to a frequently asked question, etc. Do not assume that your students will be able to do these tasks "because they are so easy and obvious." Some examples that could be relevant to the advanced calculus course: find the course syllabus; when is the mid-term exam?; find the quiz for chapter 3; read the instructor reply to a class question on _____; ask the instructor a question outside of class; and so on. When authentic conditions are not available, be sure that you make one key condition authentic by providing only the amount and type of support the subject would ordinarily get in using this site. If the people using your Web site are at home alone with no one to call for help when they get stuck, then they should not be able to ask for any help during the test session. If you will be giving your students a handout covering basic Web navigation, then your test subjects should get this handout, too (Gomoll, 1990).

What Will Usability Testing Tell Me?

Testing your prototype with authentic users and tasks will uncover big problems in the design of your site so that you can fix them before the site becomes active. During the test sessions you should watch for the times when people have trouble with:

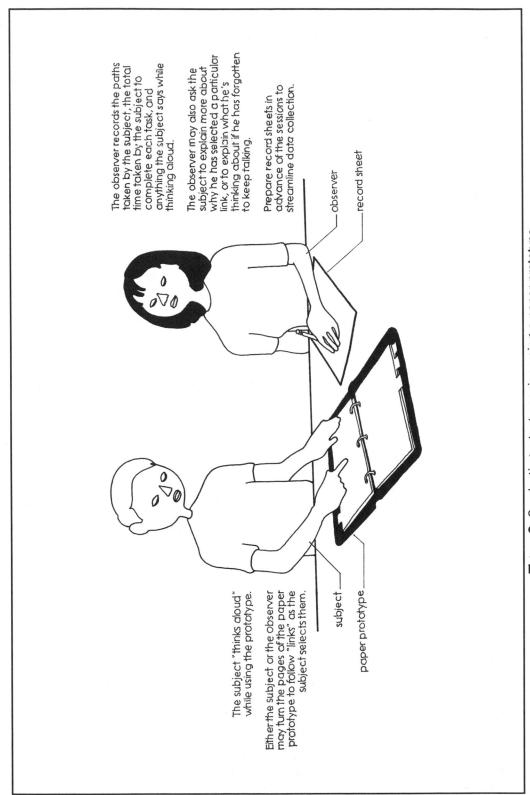

The subject "thinks aloud" while using the prototype.

Either the subject or the observer may turn the pages of the paper prototype to follow "links" as the subject selects them.

subject

paper prototype

The observer records the paths taken by the subject; the total time taken by the subject to complete each task, and anything the subject says while thinking aloud.

The observer may also ask the subject to explain more about why he has selected a particular link, or to explain what he's thinking about if he has forgotten to keep talking.

Prepare record sheets in advance of the sessions to streamline data collection.

observer

record sheet

Figure 3. Conducting a test session using a paper prototype.

- simple errors in the content of the site;
- differences in vocabulary between you and the users of your site;
- links or paths which made sense to you but are now confusing them;
  - correct paths followed with lack of confidence;
  - missed paths;
  - incorrect paths followed with confidence;
  - incorrect paths followed in desperation.

Like a good detective, you need to figure out what's important to attend to and what you can ignore while you are making these observations. If subjects consistently ignore a useful link for a certain task, the reason may not be immediately obvious. It may have to do with language or expectations that were established earlier in your materials and are inconsistent with what is currently in front of them. You need to encourage your subjects to continue to "think aloud" (Gomoll, 1990). You need to ask them questions when you don't understand what they're doing, and actively listen to what they say. Remember, you're looking for problems or errors and for patterns of error that repeat from one subject to the next. Testing may also help you predict problems that you can't fix because of existing technical or organizational constraints, or simply because you don't know what to do about them. For example, in usability tests conducted on the current Indiana University Bloomington Web site in 1995, we discovered that no one had been designated to provide information for a few key areas that users wanted to know about. We had no choice but to create placeholders for those areas until arrangements could be made to put the information online.

Testing will not tell you that your design is successful. Common sense can tell you that if you see four or five people struggle with the same problem, the problem probably does exist. However, just because you see four or five, or even ten, people use your pages successfully you can't assume that everyone will do so. The most you can conclude is that you are unable to predict any problems based on these observations (Boling, 1995).

What Problems Might I Expect with This Kind of Testing?

As with any other process, part of the value lies in the skill with which you complete the prescribed steps. Even as a novice, you can get valuable design direction from prototype testing if you avoid a few common pitfalls.

Observation problems. Becoming a good observer may take some practice. Be sure both to watch what subjects do during usability tests, and to listen to what they say when they "think aloud." Interject a question here and there, asking the subjects to clarify what they just did instead of assuming that you understand their motivation or frame of mind.

Being your natural, helpful self. If they wouldn't have you by their side when they attempt to use your site in real life, you must not ruin the authentic context of the test by helping them out during the test. Learn to say, "What do you think you should do?" in a friendly, helpful tone, and then wait.

Blaming the subject. Don't. The problem is with the design, not the subject. Don't even let subjects apologize for failing to do some of your tasks. Encourage them to spot errors or problems, and reinforce them when they do!

Becoming a "test-junkie." Sometimes people find usability testing so eye-opening that they are paralyzed in design, unwilling to make any decision that is not tested. Go ahead and apply your design judgement, the best guidelines you can find, and your own experience to the

Figure 4. Ask the subject what he's thinking; don't assume you know.

design and redesign of your prototypes—these are still valuable tools, and they will keep you from wasting time building and testing truly terrible prototypes.

How Will I Use This Information?

Once the sessions are complete, it is tempting to start revising your design immediately. By conducting a systematic debriefing, though, you can make sure you have considered all your findings and that you are actually fixing the right problems. These general steps will help you make sense of the data from your tests:

1. Combine all observations from everyone who conducted sessions.

2. Sort the observations, combining similar ones and noting their frequency.

3. Diagnose the observed errors. What may be wrong with the design that caused these errors to occur?

4. Prioritize the design problems and decide what revisions will be made.

5. Note interdependencies (parts of the design that weren't a problem but which will have to change because of the planned revisions).

PRIORITY	CHARACTERISTICS	EXAMPLES
LEVEL 1 ... must fix	users get stuck and cannot recover	browser crashes documents are missing or garbled text disappears
LEVEL 2 ... should fix	users may get stuck but manage to recover	confusing links, terms, graphics or text visibility problems glaring errors in spelling or factual information slow-loading graphics, sounds, etc. missing information
LEVEL 3 ... would be nice to fix	doesn't cause a lot of problems but reduces overall quality of the site or results in negative comments	minor typographical errors in text blocks "ugly" graphics
LEVEL 4 ... fix when and if the other problems are corrected	most people won't even notice, but we know it's there	small spacing problems extra pixels "floating" in a graphic

Figure 5. Method of prioritizing problems diagnosed from user test data.

Conclusion

After you have completed one or more rounds of prototyping, testing, and revision for a site using paper, it is important to test your electronic version of the site. Features like scrolling windows, the browser's "Back" button, and input fields on forms may cause their own problems for your target population, and an electronic prototype is the only way to find that out. By this time, though, you can tackle those problems knowing that your information structure is solid and understandable for the people who are going to use it.

Related URLs:

> http://www.indiana.edu/~iirg/index.html
> http://education.indiana.edu/ist/faculty/iuwebrep.html
> http://www.sun.com/sun-on-net/uidesign/usabilitytest.html

References

Boling, E. (1995). Usability testing for Web sites (http://www.indiana.edu/~iirg/ARTICLES/usability/usability.main.html).

Boling, E., & Kirkley, S. (1996). Helping students design World Wide Web documents: Part I: Planning and designing the site. *HyperNEXUS, 6*(1).

Frick, T., Corry, M., Hansen, L., & Maynes, B. (1995). Design-research for the Indiana University Bloomington World Wide Web: The "Limestone Pages" (http://education.indiana.edu/ist/faculty/iuwebrep.html).

Gomoll, K. (1990). Some techniques for observing users. In B. Laurel (Ed.), *The art of human-computer interface design* (pp. 85–90). Reading, MA: Addison-Wesley.

Nielsen, J. (1993). *Usability engineering.* Boston, MA: AP Professional.

Rettig, M. (1994). Prototyping for tiny fingers. *Communications of the ACM, 37*(4), 21–27.

Lewis, J. (1994). Sample sizes for usability studies: Additional considerations. *Human Factors, 36*(2), 368–378.

Virzi, R. (1992). Refining the test phase of usability evaluation: How many subjects is enough? *Human Factors, 34*(4), 457–468.

The Authors

Elizabeth Boling is Assistant Professor, Department of Instructional Systems Technology, Indiana University, Bloomington, Indiana.

e-mail, World Wide Web
eboling@indiana.edu
http://copper.ucs.indiana.edu/~eboling/home.html

Theodore W. Frick is Associate Professor, Department of Instructional Systems Technology, Indiana University, Bloomington, Indiana

e-mail, World Wide Web
frick@indiana.edu
http://education.indiana.edu/ist/faculty/frick.html

40

Training Teachers, Faculty Members, and Staff

Sharon Gray

Effective training is critical to successful implementation of Web-based instruction (WBI). Three major factors impact the effectiveness of training: (1) the role of computers, as envisioned by teachers and adminstrators, in enhancing the learning environment; (2) training delivery and time allocation; and, most importantly, (3) access of the institution and the individuals within the institution to the World Wide Web.

The first factor concerns the mindset of teachers and administrators. At a basic level, computers are used as *productivity tools* in conjunction with word processor software to create handouts, banners, certificates, and memos or in conjunction with spreadsheet or gradebook software to create and maintain gradebooks. Computers enhance the learning environment by freeing the teacher to spend more time on teaching/learning tasks and less time on bookkeeping.

At a more advanced level, computers are used as *delivery systems* to access educational CD-ROMs or in conjunction with presentation software. At this level, computers enhance the learning environment by making delivery of traditional pedagogy more appealing, by illustrating concepts and relationships more effectively and by providing access to more extensive sources of information.

At the most advanced level, computers are used as *cognitive tools* for collaborative learning projects, for exploring the wealth of information that is available on the Internet via the World Wide Web, and as a means of acquiring higher-order thinking skills.

The second factor concerns training delivery. The two opposing approaches are using outside consultants versus using in-house experts. The consultant approach often means hiring an outside expert for a day-long workshop where various pieces of hardware and software are demonstrated (sometimes hardware and software that the district doesn't even possess). Such demonstration only serves to pique interest. While a valuable and necessary step, demonstration *does not* equal training. There will not be a lasting internalization of skills.

The second approach, encouraging the development of in-house experts and mentors, can either mean hiring a full-time technology coordinator or simply encouraging individuals to become experts on particular pieces of hardware or software. One person may become an expert on HyperText Markup Language (HTML), another on World Wide Web graphics and browsers, one on World Wide Web video and audio, another on collaborative learning using the World Wide Web, and finally another on World Wide Web-based resources. These in-house experts are self-selective; they find their niche of expertise based upon their own in-terest. The key is to make teaching faculty members and staff aware of the existing and developing experts so those experts become known as resources for all faculty members. This can be done by distributing a regularly updated list. Such a list also serves to acknowledge and reward faculty members who have invested their time, thought, and energy to developing expertise.

Another advantage of cultivating in-house experts and mentors is that teachers are seen as more credible resources than non-teachers for providing information about utilzing technology in teaching. It is important to forewarn faculty members, however, that a valuable source of help might be students. This can be a threatening concept for any teacher who is afraid of appearing to know less than the students about a particular topic, or for a teacher who clings to the out-moded concept of teacher as active dispenser of knowledge and students as passive vessels to be "filled up." Young people, having grown up alongside the new technology, are not as likely to be intimidated by it as are adults. The young readily adapt to the technology's changing nature, and many will be amazingly adept at using the World Wide Web when they step into the classroom. (The fact that they may know how to do some things and how to get to some places the teacher doesn't want shared with the rest of the class is a topic for another chapter!)

Another element of the second factor is the attitude of administration toward training and time allocation. Does the district expect its faculty members to be trained on their own time or does it provide release time for training? Expecting faculty members and staff to be trained on their own time will mean that only those who are truly devoted and already have an interest will pursue training. This approach also fosters a certain resentment on the part of faculty members toward the administration. On the other hand, providing release time for training demonstrates that the district values the training and realizes its potential for improving the learning environment.

Finally, the third factor concerns institutional and individual access to the World Wide Web. Access can range from one computer in a lab setting connecting to the World Wide Web via a modem, to all teachers having computers connected on a local area network (LAN) which is connected to the World Wide Web via a 56 kilobyte line, a T1 line, or even fiber. A computer in a lab setting means access is limited, and access through a modem means access is slow—14.4 and 28.8 are fast for text-based transfer, but painfully slow for World Wide Web graphic-based transfer. Limited, slow access presents obstacles which many faculty members will not attempt to surmount. If the lab must be booked to use the World Wide Web, and then the access that is achieved is slow, the Web may be used as a vast library by a few devoted teachers and their students, but it will probably not be incorporated in a more meaningful way. More extensive access, on the other hand, presents opportunities that faculty members readily discover and share. Faculty members can easily use the World Wide Web for their own and their students' research, as well as for professional communication.

For WBI training to be effective, all three factors—role of computers in education, training delivery, and access—must be addressed. The role of computers must be seen as going beyond simply being productivity tools or delivery systems to being cognitive tools. In-house peer experts and mentors must be cultivated and provided with adequate release time, and their availability must be made known to all teaching faculty and staff. All teachers must have direct access to the World Wide Web, ideally through a high-speed link on a local area network.

Before initiating a faculty training program, it is helpful to perform a needs assessment. (An annual assessment will highlight progress and bring to light developing needs.) To bring a faculty member "up-to-speed" regarding the integration of the World Wide Web into the learning environment, training must first break the barrier of faculty's unfamiliarity with (and in some cases, phobia of) computers and move them to the stage of using computers as productivity tools. This is done through gentle exposure to computer technology, stressing the time-saving potential and ease of use. This *must* be done "hands-on" to be effective. It is extremely important that those providing such exposure and training maintain a positive, supportive attitude rather than a critical or condescending posture.

Once faculty members have reached this first stage, they can be trained to use computers as delivery systems (accessing CD-ROMs and projecting presentation software presentations.) Faculty members "show-and-tell" times are a good way of demonstrating to all faculty members what a few faculty members have discovered and are implementing.

Once they have reached this second stage (and occasionally without having reached this stage, but rather bypassing it), faculty members can be encouraged and trained to use computers as cognitive tools. They can learn to design group-based, collaborative projects wherein students learn to work together to achieve a common goal. They can learn to design research-based individual and group projects wherein students learn to tap the vast resources available on the World Wide Web, and to discern credible from non-credible World Wide Web resources. And they can design projects wherein students learn to organize information in a systematic, predictable manner for others to access. It is these sorts of projects that truly begin to harness the power of the World Wide Web for education. Faculty members arrive at this third stage by becoming aware of what others are doing on the World Wide Web.

Information sheets (sometimes erroneously called "cheat sheets") are an excellent resource and should be developed by in-house experts and distributed to all teaching faculty members and staff. These sheets should include log-in instructions, lists of useful World Wide Web sites, and the phone numbers and e-mail addresses of individuals to contact for answers to questions. Other helpful resources are technology periodicals such as *Educational Technology, Electronic Learning, Teaching with Technology*, and *Tech Trends*. They should be made available in the teachers' lounge or some other casual, central location.

The perceived barrier between "techies" and "non-techies" is an unproductive one and need not exist. Many teachers who would not have considered themselves "techies" are managing to very effectively incorporate the World Wide Web into their teaching. With the World Wide Web, Internet access technology has matured to such a point that the user interfaces are graphical and intuitive and not nearly as intimidating as they were 5–10 years ago. The technology itself is becoming transparent. The technical aspects of computers and the Internet do not need to be mastered to effectively use computers and the World Wide Web in education. The key is to stress that effective use of the World Wide Web in instruction rests with good teaching skills.

For more information on training teachers, faculty, and staff on WBI, a lesson plan on Internet Basic, course outline and reading list for Society and the Internet (a course taught completely over the Internet which deals with the impact of the Internet on society,) and a list of WBI resources (including sites with examples of effective uses of WBI), visit our home page (http://www.briar-cliff.edu/www/userhp/gray/gray.htm).

References

Coffee, R. (1993). Teacher experts: Two districts' perspectives of success. A presentation at the National School Board Association's 1993 Technology + Learning Conference.

Phillips, W. L. (1996). Electronic connections: An opportunity for a pedagogical shift. *Education Journal, Eastern Illinois University College of Education and Professional Studies, 25*(1).

The Author

Sharon Gray is Director of Instructional Technology, Briar Cliff College, Sioux City, Iowa.

e-mail, World Wide Web
  gray@briar-cliff.edu
  http://www.briar-cliff.edu/www/userhp/gray/gray.htm

41

Institutional Perspectives on Organizing and Delivering Web-Based Instruction

Vivian Rossner and Denise Stockley

Introduction

Universities today face a number of internal and external pressures to become actively involved in educational applications of new technologies. These pressures include increasing public access to information technology, government funding priorities for initiatives that support the development of distributed learning networks, increasing competition for students who no longer need to be present on a university campus, and the need to provide cost-effective, high-quality education to greater numbers of students. Because of these pressures, the strongest impetus for change now confronting educational institutions comes from two directions: first, the necessity to practice fiscal restraint in the face of government cutbacks in funding, and second, the need to keep pace with the rapid growth and development of advanced technologies in order to remain competitive with other institutions. Implementation of Web-based instruction can easily get caught between these conflicting realities. The use of sophisticated interactive technologies provides a viable means to educate greater numbers of students with limited institutional resources, and at the same time, it is a very costly undertaking. Here, we discuss the implications of this situation for implementing Web-based instruction in the university setting.

At the public university level, the impact of economic restraint is primarily felt through government directives requiring increases in numbers of full-time equivalent students without, at the same time, providing for the extra costs that such a demand entails. Consequently, universities are now in the process of assessing the potential impact of this directive on faculty teaching loads and research responsibilities. At issue is the need to find ways to use limited financial resources to meet the instructional needs of increasing numbers of campus and off-campus students without sacrificing established institutional practices of excellence in scholarship and teaching. To meet this challenge, many universities are now exploring the potential benefits of using powerful, Web-based interactive technologies as a means to provide pedagogically viable solutions to difficult instructional problems. Over the past decade, Web-based instruction has come to be seen as an important and effective means to provide sustainable, high-quality instruction to more students, without necessarily requiring an appreciable increase in numbers of faculty (see, for example, Harasim, Hiltz, Teles, & Turoff, 1995; Hiltz, 1994; Laurillard, 1993). The ability to implement and make maximal use of these technologies, however, requires reconfiguring key sectors of the university community in order to build the technological infrastructure and support systems needed to accommodate Web-based instruction. In this chapter, we first discuss how a coordinated vision for technological change can effectively guide this process, and second, point to the obstacles that must be overcome to ensure that the means to preserve long-term sustainability of network teaching are put in place.

The Need for a Vision

According to Gilbert (1996), a vision of technological change should begin with the straightforward realization that the institution concerned has a stated mission and a related set of shared values concerning the teaching, research, and administrative functions that must be served by the new technology. To ensure that newer Web-based modes of instruction are implemented in accordance with the goals and objectives of the institution's mission, the expertise and support systems needed to promote it must also be part of the overall strategy. General acceptance of network teaching and learning practices take time. The sooner these practices are perceived to be as effective and viable as traditional practices, despite the differences, the better placed the institution becomes to meet the external and internal demands for change placed upon it.

The acceptance of technology-based instructional practices is facilitated by having two methods of implementation occur simultaneously. First, the ways to use Web-based instruction as an enhancement and extension of more traditional campus-based teaching should be put within reach of members of the university community who want to experiment with it. In this way, Web-based instruction is integrated with more traditional instructional practices. Second, learning via the Web should also be promoted as a self-contained means to deliver university programs entirely over the Internet. These would be virtual programs designed to meet the needs of students who may only access the campus and its resources through the Web. Ideally, then, two systems of instruction would emerge, one complementary and one parallel, to campus-based teaching. Faculty may choose to work in one way or the other, both, or neither if they prefer face-to-face instruction. Timely implementation of Web-based integrated and parallel instructional systems may prove to be one of the best means possible to ensure that the same values of excellence embedded in traditional instructional practices will also be transplanted into the newer, technology-based modes of teaching.

Building integrated and parallel instruction systems requires a concerted effort among carefully coordinated sectors of the university community be formally established. Key requirements include the following:

- assurance of support from the senior administrative level;

- the commitment to put in place an easily accessible campus-wide technology "backbone" that supports Web-based instruction within and beyond the campus;

- extending current library facilities to include the online library;

- designing a system that allows students to register via the Web;

- designing a system that allows faculty and students to access any campus-based server containing information relative to their work;

- supporting researchers experimenting with hardware, software, and models of instruction that enhance Web-based teaching and learning;

- requesting input from existing faculty and professional technical people with Web expertise;

- developing support systems that provide training in the educational uses of interactive technologies;

- providing on-going technical and pedagogical support for faculty and students working on the Web; and

- committing adequate, long-term base budget financial support for Web-based instruction.

The first condition for the satisfaction of these factors is that they must be recognized as key requirements, and recognized as a cohesive package. The second condition is the presence of institutional commitment guided by a shared vision and strong, centralized leadership. In the absence of commitment and leadership, the in-house competition for limited resources could lead to a disintegration of the entire process into an ad hoc series of campus-wide developments, each having little or no awareness of the activities of the other. Such an undesirable state of affairs would create a situation where the potential for duplication of effort is both real and costly, and the resulting inequity of access to resources may be difficult to avoid and even more difficult to correct.

Implementing the Vision

Catalysts to university expansion toward adopting large-scale support for Web-based instruction are more likely to come from external, rather than internal, sources. These may take the form of requests from the public or private sectors to provide specialized programs that can be offered in the workplace or at home. In many instances, however, it is governments that offer universities, colleges, and school districts designated funds to establish distributed learning networks. Whatever the source, opportunities for funding are usually competitive. In our estimation, larger shares of government funds are more likely to be awarded to institutions that present integrated or "flagship" proposals rather than a variety of smaller requests from individual members of the university community.

Developing flagship proposals that reflect the integrated needs of the university requires administrative direction and commitment to a coordinated effort that includes the active participation of academic and technical units, the library, and other units that provide instructional support services to all Faculties; for example, a Center for University Teaching or a Center for Distance Education. In this way, proposals will comprise specific, but related, requests for funds to begin implementing or expanding the campus-wide technological backbone, an online library, and development of software that addresses the university's ability to implement cross-platform uploading and downloading of Web-based multimedia courses, assignments and projects, or Web-based interactive conferencing systems. Multimedia labs that draw upon these resources in order to provide faculty training and support, and mount, market, monitor, and evaluate Web-based multimedia curricula should also be established.

The need to develop an integrated funding proposal itself can act as a catalyst to campus-wide assessments of the technological status-quo, but this may also arise from pressures within—particularly the realization that the institution must remain competitive with others accessing the same funding sources and the need to remain competitive with them to attract the best on- or off-campus students. University task forces comprising representation from key units can be set up to take account of the existing situation, receive input from the community, and to assess current developments in the public and private sectors in order to make recommendations to senior administrators on appropriate directions to pursue.

Costs

It is a certainty that recommendations to "retool" the entire university backbone, update classrooms and lecture halls, place computers on faculty member's desks, build or expand the online library and the multi-media lab, and coordinate campus-wide resources, to name a few, will be extremely costly. Green (1995) makes the observation that institutions cannot afford to "build or maintain a technological infrastructure on year-end funds or 'budget dust.' " While implementing the initial infrastructure may take place using discretionary funds, the ongoing ability to sustain, update, and expand technological resources requires the commitment to provide adequate recurring funds drawn from the institution's base budget.

Fortunately, Web-based instruction itself can become an important source of revenue to the university, as many prospective students from private and public institutions are willing to pay differential fees to access university study in the home or workplace, whatever their geographical location. Thus, strong leadership and coordinated efforts on the part of the university community can implement much more than an up-to-date, well-serviced technological infrastructure. Such efforts are bound to start a positive momentum between the university and the wider community—that fosters the continuous intake of the financial resources needed to develop and sustain high-quality academic programs that, in turn, attract the very students willing to pay for the convenience of access implemented to meet their own particular needs.

Conclusion

We have suggested that for Web-based instruction to be successfully implemented in ways that preserve traditions of excellence and sustainability, institutions need to develop a clear, multi-faceted vision of what it is possible to do within the constraints of their own particular communities. Web-based instruction provides exciting opportunities for universities to introduce sophisticated, interactive technologies into more traditional and familiar instructional settings. These technologies will allow for greater dissemination of information and greater access to knowledge for participants within and beyond the university community.

References

Gilbert, S. (1996). Making the most of a slow revolution. *Change, 28*(2), 10–23.

Green, K. G. (1995). Paying the digital piper. *Change, 27*(2), 53–54.

Harasim, L., Hiltz, R. S., Teles, L., & Turoff, M. (1995). *Learning networks: A field guide to teaching and learning online.* Cambridge, MA: The MIT Press.

Hiltz, R. (1994). *The virtual classroom: Learning without limits via computer networks.* Norwood, NJ: Ablex.

Laurillard, D. (1993). *Rethinking university teaching: A framework for the effective use of educational technology.* London: Routledge.

The Authors

Vivian Rossner is Director of the University Centre for Network Learning, Simon Fraser University, British Columbia, Canada.

e-mail
    vivian_rossner@sfu.ca

Denise Stockley is a doctoral candidate at Simon Fraser University, British Columbia, Canada.

e-mail
    denise_stockley@sfu.ca

42

Legal Implications of Intellectual Property and the World Wide Web

Stanton M. Zobel

Since the advent of the printing press and Gutenberg's movable type, publishing houses—in concert with governments—have been the "keeper of the keys" of information distribution. The intense resource requirements of production, reproduction, and distribution of printed materials ensured, if not a monopoly in terms of corporate players, at the very least a severe handicap to the wide distribution of ideas by individuals. But the plasticity of digital documents and the advent of World Wide Web access level the playing field, affording individuals with no experience in publishing an immediate world-wide audience for their ideas, and importantly, no publishing house need be involved.

This situation accelerates the free communication of content, yet developers of World Wide Web documents labor within an historical and legally defined framework. Concepts such as intellectual property, copyright, and fair use doctrines must be considered by every developer. Without the benefit of the legal expertise of a publishing house, it is essential that we become familiar with such legal responsibilities.

"Copyright is essentially a system of property. The province of copyright is communication" (Strong, 1994, p. 1). Very often, producers of information feel compelled to protect their intellectual property and use the strong arm of the law to accomplish it effectively. Yet, as Nicholas Negroponte states in *Being Digital*, "Copyright law is totally out of date. It is a Gutenberg artifact" (p. 58). Indeed, it was shortly after Gutenberg's innovation (1455) that the evolution of legal principles dealing with the exclusive use and production of ideas via text were codified. The earliest were called Royal Patent Grants, in force in Venice in the 15th century and in England in the 16th century. For the most part, modern copyright law in Western societies is based on England's Statute of Anne, enacted in 1710. With the exception of changes resulting from the development of media such as movies, radio, and musical recordings, these laws have changed very little over nearly three centuries.

The explosive adoption of digital technology and Internet publication is exerting enormous stress on the existing system that sets governments, publishers, educational institutions and individuals scrambling to adapt current law to the new exigencies of electronic communication. These pressures of intellectual property and its reproduction can be identified all over the globe. A recent technological development at Oxford University enables a computer and its programs to "re-devise" the tonality and style of a musical artist in original works. Producers and artists are very concerned with issues of performance and compensation relating to this new development. The U.S. government is even now squabbling with the People's

Republic of China over entire factories dedicated to "pirating" software and music CD-ROMs. The U.S. House of Representatives Internet Law Library (http://www.pls.com:8001/his/53.htm) provides an excellent exposure to the complexity and diversity of international legal issues and the Internet.

This emerging legal discussion traverses the entire continuum of thought from the purely compensation-based ownership model to those which hypothesize that inherent to the new electronic infrastructure "...will be 'information rights,' a new concept of human rights that will supplement, and in part replace, property rights" (Kumon & Aizu, 1994, p. 318).

Central to the discussion of copyright is the First Sale Doctrine. "Under this doctrine, the copyright owner's right to distribute a particular copy is limited to the first time he or she sells or otherwise disposes of that specific copy" (Smedinghoff, 1996, p. 181). Hence, the purchaser of a work has the right to give away or sell his or her copy, but is not allowed to make or retain a copy for himself or herself. The implications of this practice for the World Wide Web are paradoxically simple and complex.

At the most simplistic level, we can assume that a publisher on the Web desires that his or her work be consumed by others. But publication does not necessarily release the work to be claimed and retransmitted by consumers of that information without proper citation or compensation. First Sale would have it that a consumer can retain or transmit a single copy, but if a consumer of that information retransmits the document to a listserv, for example, or even his or her own Website, he or she encounters the possibility that hundreds or thousands of people, as they browse the Web, automatically generate an electronic copy within their own machines. Hence, copyright infringement may be taking place simply by the posting the information to a network site.

The paradox and complexity of the issue is stated succinctly by William J. Mitchell in *City of Bits* (1995):

> Most importantly perhaps, one person's use of a file or some application software need not interfere with or prevent another's use of the same resource. Land is different: if I build on a lot, then you cannot.... So, even are books and videotapes: if I check out a copy of some work from the library, then other users cannot. By contrast, the digital resources that are available in cyberspace do not have to be scarce resources. And it is a queer kind of property that can be valuable without being intrinsically scarce. (p. 136)

If we add the concept of Fair Use, which dictates the use of copyrighted materials without payment of royalties, the legal landscape becomes more opaque:

> In infringement suits the two great principles of copyright law almost invariably clash: on one hand the need to protect the financial interests of creators, to make it worth their while to create; on the other hand the need to make each person's addition to the sum of human art and knowledge available for the use of all. From this second principle has evolved the concept of "fair use" of copyrighted materials. (Strong, 1994, p. 162)

Fair use considerations generally focus on the commercial effect of the resulting work on the original. Moreover, fair use is critically bound to the nature of use of the material. In educational environments, publishers and owners of information are generally more lenient in their demand for compensation than commercial sites. But their rightful concern is that the document be restricted in terms of the amount of time the documents are available and the potential audience of distribution. Hence, the use of copyrighted materials on a World Wide Web educational site first should be cleared with the original publisher. The secondary World Wide Web publisher should plan that the materials can be used for only one term and that access to those materials is password protected.

When printed materials were the major source of information distribution, it was relatively easy to discern copyright infringement. Without exception, widely-distributed printed materials carried both copyright notice and identification of the owner. In today's world, however, copyright ownership is not so easily defined.

In many countries, all information in fixed form is copyrighted; handwritten notes, listserv and newsgroup communications, digital images, video and audio files, as well as traditionally printed books, newspapers, and magazines are protected by copyright law. In some cases, a single work must be regarded as having multiple copyright considerations.

The next time you peruse a printed magazine, look with a critical eye at a graphic presentation. Obviously, the publisher of the magazine is sure to own many of the rights to that graphic, but not necessarily all of them. If the graphic portrays an individual, that individual may be involved because of his or her rights to privacy and publicity; both rights are legally defined. If a designer was employed in the production of text seen on the page, that designer may retain rights to the choice of font and placement of text on the page. If a graphic artist digitally manipulated a photograph, both the photographer and the artist may retain rights to their intellectual property.

If the media is a video or audio clip, the situation becomes even more involved. In this case, a developer may need to explore the release of rights retained by producers, directors, each of the actors, music directors, performers, writers, and composers. Overall, obtaining permission to reproduce a clip of either of these types of information can be overwhelming to the individual developer:

> We are schizophrenic about the treatment of information in our society. Although we like to talk about living in an information age and an information society, we have yet to begin to comprehend the consequences of this shift, much less to accommodate it. (Branscomb, 1994, p. 184)

I am not a lawyer, nor am I dispensing legal advice. The purpose of this chapter is rather to emphasize that the state of legal practice as it relates to electronic distribution is in flux. Neither the legal system nor World Wide Web developers nor nominal owners of original works are on solid footing when determining copyright infringement. Therefore, all World Wide Web developers should familiarize themselves with federal law relating to copyright, intellectual property, and fair use. Most countries have Websites detailing the particular nuances of their laws. Additionally, the Internet itself provides a wealth of information and discussion relating to intellectual property (see http://dmc-umn.tc.umn.edu/staff/stan).

There are individuals and groups which maintain that developers of online documents should not pay tribute to current legal practices. Their efforts are directed toward expanding the usage of online resources and contributing to the free exchange of information in a developing, online, world-wide community. Their rationale is that if we push the legal boundaries now, while the Internet is still young, these practices will become the de facto standard of Internet communications. At the other end of the spectrum are those who consider all information privately owned and capable of generating income and status for its originators. According to their view, the legal system should fully protect that work from unauthorized, uncompensated usage. Most of us are somewhere between these two extremes.

Each developer must be informed about and comfortable with the copyright issues of the references he or she uses to convey his or her unique message. But by acknowledging the fact that each developer presents a unique approach and unique conclusions, each developer should recognize that credit for the original work is deserved—and credit should be given.

On-line information relating to copyright, fair use, and intellectual property can be obtained on the Web (http://www.dmc.tc.umn.edu/service/stan.html).

References

Branscomb, A. W. (1994). *Who owns information?* New York: Basic Books.

Kumon, S., & Aizu, I. (1994). Co-emulation: The case for a global hypernetwork society. In L. M. Harasim (Ed.), *Global networks: Computers and international communication.* Cambridge, MA: MIT Press.

Mitchell, W. J. (1995). *City of bits.* Cambridge, MA: MIT Press.

Negroponte, N. (1995). *Being digital.* New York: Alfred A. Knopf, Inc.

Smedinghoff, T. J. (1996). Online rights of copyright users. In T. J. Smedinghoff (Ed.), *Online law: The SPA's legal guide to doing business on the Internet.* Reading, MA: Addison-Wesley.

Strong, W. S. (1994). *The copyright book* (4th ed.). Cambridge, MA: MIT Press.

The Author

Stanton M. Zobel is Academic Distributed Computing Services/Principal User Services Specialist, University of Minnesota, Minneapolis, Minnesota

e-mail, World Wide Web
stan@boombox.micro.umn.edu
http://dmc.tc.umn.edu/service/stan.html

43

Implementing Web-Based Instruction

Karen Rasmussen, Pamela Northrup, and Russell Lee

Introduction

Organized instruction delivered on the World Wide Web is increasing as educational institutions and students gain access to the Information Superhighway. The World Wide Web offers both providers and consumers of education a unique opportunity to participate in distance education and learning activities. Stand-alone, online distance education projects are typically tailored toward the adult learner; this discussion emphasizes Web-based instruction (WBI) for the learners.

There are critical issues that involve the implementation of instruction over the World Wide Web. Successful implementation involves the elements of Security, Connectivity, Communication, and Troubleshooting, the SCo²T model (see Figure 1 on the next page). Consideration and use of the SCo²T model enables instructors to implement instruction in the most efficient way possible. Consideration of these elements prepares the instructor to actively respond to learners and to meet unexpected events. The components of the SCo²T model may be examined in any order; however, examination of each component is required in a successful implementation plan.

Security

Security issues have two foci: (1) access and (2) registration. This component of the SCo²T model has broad ramifications in the implementation of WBI for the instructor, learner, and institution.

Access

The concerns related to access involve the inclusion of protection factors such as a password and the ability to locate, either accidently or purposefully, inappropriate materials. With the openness of the World Wide Web, unless home pages are password-protected, anyone can access a page, and this characteristic is seen both a benefit and a drawback (Futoran, Schofield, & Eurich-Fulcher, 1995; Shotsberger, 1996). Instructors may choose to password-protect their home pages so that only registered students may access them.

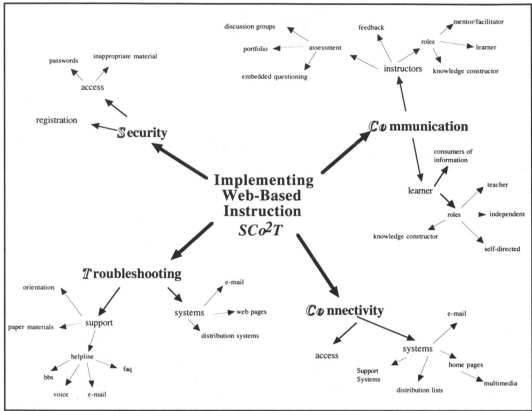

Figure 1. Implementing Web-based instruction, the SCo²T Model.

Registration

Implementation issues related to registration include the number of learners and their location. Through an active registration system, the instructor has a clear idea of who is participating in the class. Many colleges and universities have a system for online registration or an 800 number for dial-up registration. Given that the purpose of distance learning is to serve remote audiences, this factor plays a key role in successful student enrollment and tracking students throughout the length of the course.

Communication

A critical component in implementing WBI is communication. With learners dispersed at remote locations, their only common communication system is the WBI course. Communication in WBI courses may be conducted via e-mail, discussion groups, knowledge databases, real-time shared whiteboarding, and audio, as in "Cool Talk," or video communication as available through CU-SeeMe, or other desktop video communication protocol. This exciting paradigm shift promotes the new roles of instructor and learner as collaborators and knowledge constructors between instructors and learners or learner-to-learner.

Instructor

Feedback. In WBI, instructors and other students provide feedback to learners through shared WBI discussions. Whether the instructor or student is the mechanism of feedback, class interactivity is promoted through these discussions. Unlike the traditional classroom, feedback is not always immediate and personal. Depending on the number of students, it may not always be feasible for the instructor to provide each learner with individual responses to questions and problems. In these cases, general feedback to the class as a whole may be provided. Responding to the class as a whole is efficient and may answer another learner's unasked question.

Roles. Through WBI, the instructor must maintain a variety of roles to facilitate the learning process. The primary paradigm shift moves the instructor from direct deliverer of information to a mentor and guide. Instructors must design learning communities that require learners to be self-directed knowledge constructors. In addition, instructors must become equal learning partners in the virtual learning communities, yet serve as guides to assist students in all areas proposed by the SCo²T model (Sherry, 1996). Many colleges and universities are beginning to explore problem-based learning as a design scheme for WBI.

Assessment. In any learning environment, the instructor's evaluation of a student's performance is of utmost importance to that learner. In WBI, students written responses are assessed based on their clarity, relevance to the topic, and the traditional elements of comprehension, analysis, synthesis, and evaluation (Bloom, 1956). Students may be assessed using a variety of methods including testing, responses to individual and group discussion questions, and development of portfolios.

Learner

Consumers of Information. In WBI, learners are continually presented with a vast array of information. Many adult learners already possess cognitive and metacognitive strategies for handling and organizing information into memory, while others possess inadequate cognitive strategies (Taylor, 1992). Building a repertoire of cognitive strategies to promote knowledge construction for WBI is critical in making learners consumers of information.

Roles. To facilitate effective WBI, the role of the learner must change substantially from that found in a traditional classroom. Although the learner can remain a passive participant in the learning process, to fully participate in WBI, the learner must develop skills to fulfill the roles of teacher, independent, self-directed learner, and constructor of knowledge. Through active participation, learners begin to provide feedback to other learners, again enhancing interactivity. The learner must possess the flexibility to move through all of the roles found in the new paradigm.

Connectivity

Although the determination of how learners will connect to the learning environment will take place in the design and development of WBI, connectivity issues continue to be important to the implementor of WBI. As WBI is implemented, instructors must monitor the use of different systems and facilitate individual access to the instruction. For example, students accessing WBI through a commercial provider such as America Online may have different issues from students accessing through private providers, state educational providers (e.g., FIRN and TENET) or university providers.

Communication Systems

There are four main communication systems that may be used in WBI: electronic mail, distribution lists, home pages, and special communication programs, such as Integration, CoolTalk, or CONSTRUE (Lebow, Wager, Marks, & Gilbert, 1996). Each of these systems may be used alone or in combination.

Electronic Mail. Electronic mail, or e-mail, is a process by which individuals communicate through a personal computer. The personal computer is connected to a local area network, modem, or other configuration that permits access to mail services. Electronic mail permits the sender and receiver to communicate at times that are convenient for both. This communication protocol permits all involved parties to participate in active discussions. Electronic mail may be involved in presenting information to students, conducting class discussions, and assessing student performance.

Distribution Lists. Closely linked to electronic mail is the concept of distribution lists. With a distribution list, one piece of mail can be sent easily to all of the subscribers to the list. As with electronic mail, distribution lists may be used to present information, conduct class discussions, and assess student performance.

Home Pages. Home pages are the foundation of Web-based instruction. Home pages provide instructional material, organization, and links to other sites or mail systems. The process of creating a home page is quite simple. The programming language, HTML, is based on simple text documents that can be created through any word processing system. In these text pages, commands, or tags, are added to instruct Internet Browsers (e.g., Netscape, Mosaic, Internet Explorer) how to format the text. Also contained in the text are links to graphics, movies, and sound. There are many software packages (e.g., PageMill, SiteMill) and word processors (e.g., newer versions of ClarisWorks, MS Word, WordPerfect) that have templates and instructions on how to create home pages.

Support Systems. Programs enhancing the interactivity and organization of the World Wide Web are continually in production and distribution. One program, entitled Interaction, is a Macintosh-based product that permits learners to participate in discussions on the World Wide Web, rather than through an electronic mail or distribution list service. Through this program, instructors can post questions, guide discussion, and organize discussions in threads or general topics. These discussions can be accessed through the World Wide Web for review by instructors and learners.

Troubleshooting

In order for WBI to be successful, there must be a well-defined and structured process to support the student when questions about the instruction or assignments arise. A proactive view toward troubleshooting alleviates learner and instructor frustrations. There are times, however, that problems will arise that cannot be solved by the instructor or learners. At these times, technical assistance must be obtained from the local computer support center. Other questions should be able to be resolved by the instructor or learner.

Systems

Electronic Mail and Distribution Lists. For problems associated with an individual student or the class as a whole, e-mail or distribution lists can be employed to disseminate correct information. In cases where the learner cannot receive mail, other contacts such as telephone, fax, or traditional mail may be used for problem resolution.

Home Pages. The use of informational home pages, such as class syllabus, assignments, and grading methodology can be created on Web pages to prevent learner misunderstanding of course requirements. Additional references or associated Web links to other homes pages can be provided to assist the learner in resolving specific questions about access or other frequently asked questions.

Support

Orientation. If at all possible, it is important to conduct an initial orientation session before the online class is scheduled to begin. During this orientation session, the instructor may discuss the processes involved in WBI. This discussion is especially beneficial for those students who have never participated in WBI. In the orientation session, the instructor may assign or record appropriate e-mail addresses and ensure that all students are properly registered for the class.

Paper Materials. Printed class materials should be created to assist learners in accessing the courses and providing learning strategies for distance learners. In addition, a troubleshooting guide may include operating procedures, recommended hardware configurations, or other start-up information.

Help Line. A variety of help line activities can be employed to assist learners in their distance education experience. Help Lines may be full-time staffed, part-time staffed, or staffed online. Help Lines can also consist of bulletin boards services (BBS), e-mail support, database of frequently asked questions (FAQ), or fax support. A staffed Help Line would consist of a person or persons available to address troubleshooting questions raised by the student regarding connectivity or course content. Help Line facilities most often provide an 800 phone number for users to call with their questions. An unstaffed or partially staffed Help Line may be supplemented by a electronic BBS where notes are posted for students to retrieve general information about a course, or for downloading specific device drivers for printers, etc. Another form of Help Line support is FAQ, or frequently asked questions. In a FAQ, commonly asked questions are posted in a database, with common resolutions to those questions.

Conclusion

Through WBI, instructors and learners should actively participate in the learning process. Through a variety of strategies, instructors challenge learners to explore a new paradigm of learning. Instructors must also embrace this new paradigm to ensure that learners gain the most benefit from WBI. Implementing WBI using the SCo^2T model provides instructors with the techniques and skills required to be successful.

References

Bloom, B. S. (1956). *Taxonomy of educational objectives.* New York: Longman.

Futoran, G. C., Schofield, J. W., & Eurich-Fulcher, R. (1995). The Internet as an educational resource: Emerging issues of information access and freedom. *Computers in Education, 24*(3), 229–236.

Lebow, D., Wager, W. W., Marks, P., & Gilbert, N. (1996). CONSTRUE: Software for collaborative learning over the World Wide Web. Paper presented at the AECT Collaboration and Distance Education Conference, Tallahassee, Florida.

Sherry, L. (1996). Issues in distance education. *International Journal of Distance Education, 1*(4), 337–365.

Shotsberger, P. G. (1996). Instructional uses of the World Wide Web: Exemplars and precautions. *Educational Technology, 36*(2), 47–50.

Taylor, P. S. (1992). Effects of prior strategy use, motivation, and locus of control when using embedded cognitive strategies in daily work and posttest performance for minority students. Unpublished dissertation, Florida State University.

The Authors

Karen Rasmussen is an Assistant Professor in the Instructional Technology program at the University of West Florida in Pensacola.

e-mail, World Wide Web
  krasmuss@uwf.edu
  http://www.uwf.edu/~coe

Pamela Northrup is Coordinator of Instructional Technology and Assistant Professor in the Instructional Technology program at the University of West Florida in Pensacola.

e-mail, World Wide Web
  pnorthru@uwf.edu
  http://www.uwf.edu/~coe

Russell Lee is Director, Educational & Training Programs in the Instructional Technology program at the University of West Florida in Pensacola.

e-mail, World Wide Web
  rlee@uwf.edu
  http://www.uwf.edu/~coe

44

Management of Instructional Materials and Student Products in Web-Based Instruction

Ronald D. Zellner

Today's classrooms reflect increases in computer-based teaching/learning activities, a growing reliance on network resources, and a profusion of distance education formats. Technology related classes incorporate computer-based activities, creating a need for efficient distribution of instructional materials and parallel electronic methods of collecting, storing, and evaluating student products. In addition, many conventional classes are incorporating such electronic media for both faculty and student activities. Web-based resources now provide faculty with tools to more efficiently manage instruction and communication with their students. Such resources are necessary in distance education formats, but also offer important adjuncts to campus-based classes. When adding such management features to courses, it is important to not compromise the course objectives or the students' performance. As electronic products are already a component of most technology classes, course integrity should be more easily maintained. While conventional courses can benefit first from the inclusion of electronic production activities, they then can experience the added benefits of Web based delivery of materials to and from students.

Distance education classes must rely on some degree of Internet resources in order to maintain instructional activities. These resources may be available during class meetings through online classroom facilities. In addition, today's formats rely on students having home, school, or work computers which provide constant Internet access between classes. Campus-based classes can incorporate intranet/Internet access to instructional resources through dedicated classroom computer facilities and campus-wide, networked labs. In addition, home and dorm computers are relied on to access Internet and telecommunications resources. Their inclusion is not based on a distance delivery need, but on a desire for efficiency, flexibility, cost reduction, and convenience for students and faculty.

Distribution of Instructional Resources to Students

Types of Instructional Materials

Print based materials (e.g., syllabi, work sheets, directions, graphics, readings, tests, etc.), may still provide the most appropriate means of delivering instructional materials . However, utilization of elements such as color graphics, hypertext, and multimedia (e.g., QuickTime movies) create a need for managing electronic materials. Print materials can also be easily distributed electronically. Benefits to be experienced through Web-based distribution of such materials include:

- Paper use and student/institution costs are reduced.

- Lost class time is reduced.

- Students can obtain updated copies of materials throughout the course.

- Materials can be easily replaced if lost.

- Materials can be made available from alternative, cumulative sources, such as other students, conferences/discussion groups, etc.

- Materials may be included which may already be on another course Web page or any Web site throughout the world.

In both local and distance formats, actual outcomes of the distribution process should be considered. For example, if the students in a large class print out the Web-based course syllabus for the convenience of a paper copy (this is not unreasonable), we may simply be substituting more expensive, less efficient printing and should consider providing paper copies. Web-based back-ups can still be made available throughout the semester.

Electronic instructional materials such as files, templates, electronic workbooks, etc., typically provided on a disk or server, may also be distributed using Web-based resources. Materials may be downloaded as files, or may be part of the Web page itself. Downloading provides more freedom through off-line assignment completion, allowing more options for where and when to work. Connect times are also reduced, which is important as more students are connecting through Internet providers and university connections are becoming crowded. Stand-alone utilities may also provide a great deal more power than Web-based resources; however, this distinction is becoming less prominent every day. For example, a resource is now available which serves HyperCard stacks directly over the Web, allowing the direct use of instructional stacks locally or through cross-platform Internet access. Resources such as Cyberdog now provide instructor designed interactive environments containing browsers that can link directly to the appropriate Web sites to automatically access information or deliver student products. Such flexible, interactive software is rapidly changing the scope of Web-based course support resources.

Performance and evaluation materials (essays, objective exams, etc.) may also be accessed and completed via Web-based resources. Access must be protected with passwords and student rosters to insure confidentially and accuracy. While this provides no total assurance of honesty, there is no risk above that of any homework assignment. Relative access to such materials may also be controlled by the software so that only certain students can obtain certain resources and only during prespecified periods of time.

By also using Web-based resources for local distribution, rather than regular laboratory networking, we standardize the software, resulting in minimal training needs, reduced cost, and reduced disk storage space while providing both local and Internet access to the same set of materials. Cross-platform access to resources is supported, allowing access from different labs and student computers. However, there are parallel client-server software and networking utilities which have some added advantages over Web-based resources. In my courses, I also rely on a First Class server with network and modem access for functions such as conferencing and archiving that are are currently more convenient than on Web-based resources.

Methods of Distribution

Text and graphics materials may be best accessed through screen display without actually transferring the source files. Such direct display may be the best mode based on the nature of the material and the complexity of the graphics, especially in relation to student home disk storage requirements or in relation to laboratory computers which are serving many students in a variety of courses.

Often students need something to take away from the Web session, including full copies of the instructional materials, follow-up worksheets, parallel text materials, student generated notes, and ancillary resources. Copies of the text and graphics components are readily made by utilizing cut-and-paste functions available on standard Web browsers. In addition, downloading an entire, undisplayed document to the student's computer for later access or interaction will often be the preferred option. Built-in FTP capabilities allow this to be readily accomplished on a Web page or by accessing an FTP server containing large numbers of documents. Access to these files could also have password and date restrictions for security purposes. Downloading files reduces the need to be at a networked computer to complete assignments and avoids problems incurred when there are network problems.

Web resources which can access data base files, such as File Maker Pro, provide even further advantages to instructors and students alike. Rather than dealing only with intact files, accessing instructional materials (e.g., study questions, reference lists, assignment descriptions) which are stored and organized in a data base file can simplify both storage and retrieval processes. Also, data base file access allows students to access information such as the instructor's grade book to get convenient, current feedback on evaluations and scores. Proper security measures are required to insure confidentiality and integrity of the records.

Instructor initiated delivery is another consideration for distribution of resources. Materials for specific purposes or for individuals or groups of students may be sent at any time the instructor desires. Examples include communications, exams, feedback, annotated projects, etc. This may be accomplished by placing the information in special sections of Web pages which are accessible to only those individuals, in a protected data-base record/field, or e-mailed directly to the individuals as part of a message or attached file. This delivery option assures on-time awareness or access of the material, and can provide verification of receipt by the student.

E-mail software such as Eudora and Claris Emailer can also initiate the delivery of messages or files through automatic response features. For example, unit two discussion questions may be automatically sent to a student as an automatic response to the delivery of his/her unit one answers. In another option, hot links (URLs) can be embedded within the e-mail text that can be clicked to quickly connect the student directly to a desired Web-based resource.

Collection and Management of Student Products

Types of Materials to Be Collected

The materials to be collected from the students will vary with the type of course content and delivery format (classroom or distance), but will likely fall into the following categories: communications, assignments (papers, data from interactive workbooks, etc.), exams, and projects.

Methods for the Collection of Student Products

E-mail. E-mail communication is becoming a component in a wide variety of university courses. While distance delivery formats dictate a need for such communication, local classes will also benefit from its inclusion. The material to be conveyed can be included as part of the actual message text as attachments, allowing for delivery of student text, graphics, audio, hypertext, etc. This product variety extends the range of courses to which these techniques can be applied. For example, in a foreign language course, student audio files may be created at home and submitted in this manner for evaluation, feedback, and archiving.

E-mail functions may be integrated as part of the Web resource itself or accessed through adjunct systems and software. Mail accounts for each student will be necessary and may come from university computer services, state agencies, or private providers. The most appropriate source will depend on the student and the course delivery format.

Message management. Collecting, sorting, and responding to messages can consume a great deal of faculty time, especially when attachments are included. It is important to require students to utilize a standard list of subject labels for their messages so that the instructor can sort and categorize them efficiently and respond accordingly. E-mail software such as Eudora or Claris Emailer provide features such as hierarchical folders/mailboxes and automatic filters for managing and archiving messages. Drag and drop features simplify sorting that is done by the instructor. When messages are generated within Web pages, rather than directly from student e-mail accounts, resources can create appropriate subject labels (combining student name, section, content, etc.) so that the receiving e-mail software can be configured to easily sort and store them.

Attachments may not yet be filtered, but are automatically downloaded and stored in a specified folder; periodic changing of this folder can separate groups of attachments according to the date or time they are received. Once large numbers of files are collected, support resources are available which simplify the sorting process. For example, I use AppleScript Droplets, which accepts a folder full of student files, extracts information from the file names (assignment code, section number, and name/ID) and quickly sorts the files into a series of corresponding folders. This operation is invaluable, especially in large classes with multiple sections and many assignments.

Web page resources. Web page resources, primarily text boxes, can present topic content, questions, discussion items, etc. Text boxes can also be provided which provide space for students to enter responses to such materials. Similarly, text boxes, buttons, or pop-up menus can provide specific category or multiple-choice input formats. Point-and-click operations can be included to easily deliver the student's input as part of e-mail messages which are pre-addressed to the instructor. Predetermined message subject labels with student information (name, ID, section, etc.) allow sorting by visual inspection or automatic e-mail filters.

Data base resources. Web page generated input can also be delivered directly into a data base file on the faculty server. This format provides for much easier management of the content, as many related responses can be collected and automatically placed into a file organized by combinations of relevant identifiers (e.g., class, section, name, question number, or assignment title) rather than as a large collection of independent messages or attachments. Since the material is organized into a hierarchy of files, records, and fields, the management is greatly simplified. Related fields for recording scores and comments can be added for grading, providing a comprehensive file with both student work and faculty evaluations. Parts of this file can then be accessed by the students for daily Web access to their grades and performance feedback. This integration with data base utilities provides additional powerful resources to the management of Web-based instructional materials. The use of data base publish and subscribe features gives faculty even greater accessibility to the information maintained on the server.

FTP. FTP servers can be set up for access by students to download resources from a library of files. FTP functions can also be built into Web pages to allow easy delivery in the opposite direction; files which currently reside on the students' disks are copied to the server. This function provides the convenience to the student of working off-line (non-networked computers, computers with special software or hardware, etc.) with the ease of product delivery to a prespecified location. This Web-based format does not necessarily provide the security of a return address for verification of the sender as when sent as attachments via e-mail accounts; however, this concern is no worse than in traditional paper copy delivery of student products. Resources such as NetPresenz easily add this functionality to Web pages.

File Formats. While file transfer capabilities are of major importance in collecting the students' products, additional consideration must be given to file compatibility so they may be readily examined and evaluated by the instructor. Often, it may be appropriate to require that work be done on specific software as when course objectives must be met which can only be accomplished on that software. This is more likely to occur in technology courses where the software development is a major objective. At other times, the software may be only a means of accomplishing necessary course goals and it may be important to allow students the freedom to work in environments of their choice. In this case, faculty members still need the ability to adequately review such a variety of student product formats. Students may copy text materials into e-mail messages or submit ASCII text versions of their files. These alternatives do not always allow for any formatting and may limit the students' abilities to express themselves, however, some e-mail software packages such as Eudora Pro now allow text formatting within messages.

Students can also be instructed to save and submit translated versions of their work using translators which are built into their utilities. For example, ClarisWorks can save in alternate formats for various software and for either Macintosh or DOS platforms. Universal translators such as Rich Text Format can also be used. Faculty can also call on their own translators when opening a file from a different source. In some cases, mass translation can be easily accomplished through drag and drop functions with utilities or translators. Finally, a number of universal document readers (e.g., Acrobat Reader) are now available which can be incorporated to ease these compatibility issues. If file standardization or compatibility is not available for some reason, conventional print copies of the product may be submitted directly or by means such as fax.

General Concerns

Understanding the functions and operations of Web-based resources becomes especially important as more general courses, in which neither the instructors nor the students are technology experts, utilize Web-based formats. Trained personnel will need to assist in establishing such procedures. Support personnel trained in instructional design and developmental techniques will be necessary to develop Web pages and assist faculty in their use; technical personnel will be needed to maintain the networks and servers. The general compatibility between Web page development tools and faculty productivity software should help support staff members create and update the necessary Web-based resources, as well as provide interested faculty with the opportunities to develop and maintain their own materials.

Good instructional practice should not be sacrificed in order to provide instruction using these features. Standard principles of instructional design and educational psychology should be incorporated into any Web-based course design. References such as Mood (1995) or Moore and Kearsley (1996) should be consulted for considerations and concerns related specifically to distance delivery formats. Ryder and Hughes (1997) provide a good general review of Internet resources and developmental processes. Similarly, Shelly, Cashman, and Jordan (1996) have a good general guide to working with Internet resources and Krol (1996) has provided a very comprehensive guide to Internet resources. The Internet itself contains invaluable information on the "bells and whistles" that are available to educators who are designing Web-based materials. A quick search for the resources, mentioned above will quickly provide ample information, guidance and demonstration materials to any interested developer.

References

Krol, E. (1996). *The whole Internet user's guide and catalog.* Sebastopol, CA: O'Reilly & Associates.

Mood, T. A. (1995). *Distance education An annotated bibliography.* Englewood, CO: Libraries Unlimited.

Moore, M. G., & Kearsley, G. (1996). *Distance education: A systems view.* Belmont, CA: Wadsworth Publishing Co.

Ryder, R. J., & Hughes, T. (1997). *Internet for educators.* Upper Saddle River, NJ: Prentice-Hall.

Shelly, G. B., Cashman, T. J., & Jordan, K. A., (1996). *The Internet: Introductory concepts and techniques.* Danvers, MA: Boyd & Fraser Publishing.

The Author

Ronald D. Zellner is Associate Professor and Coordinator of the Educational Technology Program, Department of Curriculum & Instruction, Texas A&M University, College Station, Texas.

e-mail
    zellner@tamu.edu

45

Testing Learner Outcomes in Web-Based Instruction

DeLayne Hudspeth

Background

Because Web-based instruction typically provides a great deal of participant and system interaction, expectations and priorities concerning learning methods and course outcomes are different from those in a traditional course, in which the printed text book and library resources represent a stable base of knowledge. New sources of knowledge may shift the objectives of a course. Course outcomes can also change as students with different goals and backgrounds join an online course. Subsequently, without formal discussion and agreement as to what should be scored, counted, or judged, both the teacher and learner can become confused when learning outcomes are to be assessed.

Testing of learner outcomes is defined as a series of data and information points, collected during a course of study, which measure the student's ability to satisfy course requirements, which are usually communicated in the form of assignments. Data to judge learner progress can be derived from response to: direct questions; directions to demonstrate, integrate, or otherwise show learning; project outcomes; and a variety of guided opportunities. Test-like questions can be embedded within instructional processes and may serve to provide feedback to the student as well as to assess major milestones.

Characteristics of Learning Environment

Although the Web will spawn an increasing array of formal and informal instruction, the discussion that follows on effective testing assumes an adult learner in a computer-based, online environment with Netscape or a comparable browser. A formal curriculum defines the content of the course, which can be used for degree credit, CEUs, or to prepare for a professional certificate of some sort. I further assume that a syllabus provides the learner with goals and objectives, a schedule and description of what is expected from the learner, and at least a partial list of print and non-print resources. Increasingly, this list will include site locations and navigational directions rather than the name of a book or data source. Typically, a learner will respond to an assignment, and a remote instructor will provide both process feedback and knowledge of results.

With the possible exception of security, most of the historical problems of distance testing can be easily resolved. We know that the traditional forms of testing, such as essay or multiple choice tests, can be remotely administered and quickly scored with computers and telecommunication software. Although these arcane forms of testing have little relevance for most Internet-based learning, traditional tests can sometimes be used profitably by students to determine if enabling skills have been mastered, such as recall of vocabulary, definition of key terms, or association of important elements.

We have somewhat less experience in remotely measuring higher levels of learning (such as with case studies and complex simulations), but the issue is usually that of acquiring adequate resources rather than any doubt that remote assessment can be accomplished. Perhaps most important is that design of remote instruction with highly interactive tools such as the Internet includes provide frequent points at which learning can be assessed. Many times a short self-administered test can be downloaded as a practice test with the next download providing the correct answer set. Some instructors also ask for feedback concerning the test itself, which is beneficial to both learner and the instructor.

Cheating

In some environments, security is a concern. Is the *student* actually doing the work? Except when life and safety issues are involved, the solution to adequate security is essentially to reduce the need and desire to cheat. Elements of online instruction where test security needs are absolutely minimized include:

- The course is carefully designed with clearly stated outcomes perceived by the learner as useful and desirable.

- Assignments are judged by the learner to be relevant, and assignment resources have been assessed for availability, currency, and usability

- Help is available from friendly, credible, and efficient sources.

- Enabling knowledge and skills are flagged, tested, and supported.

- Learners have some control over nice-to-know material, examples, non-examples, and other support information.

- Tests and assessment points are flagged and provided frequently and feedback is either built into an assignment or provided within 24 hours.

- For longer (multi-week) courses, a progress map is provided so that the learners see how far they have progressed and how many subjects they have yet to master.

The purpose of this list is to define an environment so that the learner enters into a desirable, exciting learning experience where the he or she wants, and is able, to achieve course outcomes without the need to cheat. In this environment, the learner is typically more interested than the instructor in effective online tests.

Tests Based on Types of Learning

At least two factors interact in the design of effective assessment of learning: the type of learning involved and the purpose of the test. Various models or schema exist for describing different types of learning. The importance of having some method of discriminating types of learning is, first, that the testing method be consistent with the level and type of learning involved, and, second, that the judgment and marking system be both consistent and useful, especially to the learner.

Gagné and Briggs (1979), for example, describe several types of learning, such as intellectual skill, cognitive strategy, information, attitude, and motor skill. If the learning objective being addressed involves classification (an intellectual skill), then an appropriate test situation is to provide concepts which should be classified, usually within some conceptual framework. However, if the objective is for the learner to integrate prior learning and use a higher order rule, then a case study might well be used to represent a problem-solving situation where synthesis and evaluation could be demonstrated.

A different scheme is used when types of knowledge are organized with conceptual tools, such as concept and hierarchy maps, frames, and other methods of defining relationships between curriculum elements (see West *et al.*, 1991). Again, the type of learning dictates the conditions of testing. If the type of learning involves categorization, then testing would involve the placement of instances into types or categories.

Many frameworks exist which provide alternate approaches to instructional design and hence to the assessment of learning outcomes. Mapping, for example, in its many forms of semantic mapping, information mapping, networking, or framing, represents a method which defines different types of learning. Again, scoring of answers must be with a system consistent with how the learner acts in response to an assignment.

Purpose of Testing

The purpose of testing also interacts with the design of tests. If a test or test-like activity is for the purpose of providing feedback, then questions and choice points for each instructional objective should be created, specific to that objective. Although different instructional strategies suggest different feedback mechanisms, the selection and timing of feedback points is usually apparent, based on transition between major teaching points. A variety of question types should be used to maintain interest (factual, directive, reflective, etc.), and choice points should have a direct relationship to the type of objective and level of learning involved. Immediate feedback is usually provided based on the premise that immediate knowledge of results enables the learner to proceed with less confusion and higher motivation than if feedback is delayed. However, with higher levels of learning (problem solving, evaluation), immediacy seems to be not as important, and some delay may even be beneficial to the learner.

With the possible exception of self-testing for enabling objectives (vocabulary, recall of formulae), a traditional multiple choice or essay final exam is inappropriate for most Web-based learning, in part because of the extreme variability of instructional resources. Also, a wide range of differences can be anticipated in terms of the cognitive skills, motivation and entry knowledge of learners, their skill in using the resources which the Web represents, and how the course content relates to the learner's current job or academic program requirements especially if the learner is located in a different college or university. Subsequently, a culminating test needs to take these variations into account.

As noted above, perhaps the most important factor which affects testing is that in a Web-based environment, the content base may change by the nanosecond. Whereas text and reference books are designed with great deliberation and use reasonably stable data and concepts, many Internet courses may well want to capitalize on databases, rules, news, policy statements, and other types of information that are volatile. Further, some of these resources are difficult to name and cite, given that the learner may have located some critical material on the 612th line of a downloaded document that has neither source nor author attached. How, indeed, can the instructor ask reasonable test questions if the source of content knowledge is elusive and changes frequently? New testing paradigms are needed to assess and document learner outcomes in a Web-based instructional environment.

Learning Contract

Although just-in-time education provides the best instructional model for online testing (see Hudspeth, 1992), the conventional notion of a contract, held between the instructor and learner, may prove to be a useful mechanism for the transition between traditional and Web-based instruction. The basic elements of a contract is that of an understanding, between two or more persons, concerning a relationship of benefit to both parties. The proposed Learning Contract could be an integral part of the course syllabus. A typical syllabus might include:

- Description and contextual discussion of the course.
- Teaching objectives (written from the instructor's viewpoint) in terms of both "must know" and "nice to know" content.
- Typical assignments (papers, projects, and other deliverables, described from the learner's viewpoint). For example, "By the fifth week, write and submit a three column article which describes your understanding of the historic and current-day tensions between the Irish and British. This paper must include reference to the issues of X, Y, and Q. See your checklist for how this article will be judged."
- Housekeeping announcements such as URLs, hot-line numbers, course schedule requirements, word processing preferences, etc.
- A written agreement, a learning contract, which defines what the instructor is proposing and what the student agrees to do. The initial syllabus might describe 20 possible assignments of which the learner must provide the first six or eight (the "must know" content), but could select another six or eight "nice to know" outcomes from an extended list. The final list could reflect individual interests or different career backgrounds. Perhaps two or three unique outcomes could be negotiated with the instructor. If a grade system is used, then a predetermined number of points could be required for a specific grade.

The advantage of a contract is that while the outcomes to be demonstrated by the learner are carefully described, the means and methods used to achieve these outcomes need not be. Thus, the rich potential of Internet resources can be used with a great deal of flexibility.

Conclusion

Multiple reasons exist for moving to new means and methods of assessing learner outcomes in an Internet environment. The highly interactive nature of the medium, the volatility and currency of information, remote access of instruction and instructional resources—these and many other reasons suggest that new and innovative approaches are needed. Within the context of effective testing, both to provide feedback to the learner and in terms of judging achievement, a learning contract is recommended.

References

Gagné, R. M., & Briggs, L. J. (1979). *Principles of instructional design* (2nd ed.). New York: Holt, Rinehart, and Winston.

Hudspeth, D. (1992). Just-in-time education. *Educational Technology, 32*(6), 7–11.

West, C. K., Farmer, J. A., & Wolff, P. M. (1991). *Instructional design: Implications from cognitive science*. Boston: Allyn and Bacon.

The Author

DeLayne Hudspeth is Associate Professor, Area of Instructional Technology, College of Education, University of Texas at Austin.

e-mail, World Wide Web
   delayneh@tenet.edu
   http://edb518g.edb.utexas.edu/WWW_Directory/bylastname/HUDSPETH.html

46

Using Internet-Based Video Conferencing Tools to Support Assessment

James M. Laffey and Jon Singer

Traditional models of schooling view education (teaching, learning, and assessment) as a closed or fixed system. Understanding and competency are bound to subject matters which are presented by teachers and text books and acquired by students. In this model, assessment is simply matching how well the students' representation matches that of the teachers. Often the student is tested on recall or recognition. New educational standards challenge this old model and call for problem solving, inquiry, and learning by doing meaningful and authentic tasks. For example, the *National Science Education Standards* call for students learning science to be actively engaged in inquiries that are interesting and important to them (NRC, 1996, p. 13). The new standards call for students to be resourceful problem solvers and inquirers who construct personally meaningful understandings of the world through authentic tasks which integrate the curriculum and go beyond the bounds of traditional classroom practices. This view of learning as an open and constructive process requires new methods of assessment to provide valid measures of learning outcomes.

Performance based assessment, often relying on portfolios of outcome and process artifacts, is the new challenge for educational assessment. How to assess students' understanding and competency through their performances on authentic and contextually meaningful tasks which require not just the recall of knowledge but judgment about the use of knowledge? Grant Wiggins (1993) provides some guides to what makes a task authentic, and thus worthy of performance assessment:

- An engaging and worthy problem of importance.
- Faithful representation of the contexts (constraints, options, and resources) encountered in a field of study or real life practice.
- A real problem which is non-routine and multi-stage.
- Demystified criteria and standards which allow for thorough and accurate self-assessment and self-adjustment.
- Interactions between the assessor and assessee requiring justification of answers and allowing follow-up and probing.

For the past year, an award from the National Science Foundation to Project MOST (Laffey, 1995) has enabled a group of educators from the University of Missouri-Columbia (MU) and high schools in Missouri to implement learning systems of open inquiry and test new approaches for assessment. Our educational goal is for students to learn to work and inquire as scientists, mathematicians, and engineers. The teaching model challenges students with an opportunity to do a personally meaningful project and supports them with resources and advanced technology. This has led to exciting projects which go beyond the capacity of any individual teacher to provide guidance, let alone assessment. Students have found instructional support and guidance through the use of mentors, often via the Internet. We also saw an opportunity to use the Internet to bring expertise from outside the classroom to bear on assessment of student projects. The remainder of this chapter describes what we have learned about using Internet-based tools, primarily video conferencing, to assess and support student projects which go beyond the expertise of the classroom teacher or of any single individual.

Students in Project MOST classrooms have individual e-mail addresses and access to Internet browsing, and build Web pages to present their project work and outcomes. Students are able to use modeling, visualization, simulation, and programming tools to support project research and improve problem solving. These technology tools are a rich set of resources and provide for powerful and flexible communication. In an effort to implement a structured review, support, and assessment, we initiated a series of video conferences in the spring of 1996.

The test sites were two high schools, a large suburban school and a smaller school from a rural community. Project MOST placed a Silicon Graphics Indy workstation at each site and a third Indy was set up at the MU College of Education. The high schools each have 384K connections and MU uses a T1 line. Videoconferencing was established using the InPerson conferencing software which comes with the Indy systems.

The basic video conference model involves the interaction of three principal parties: (1) a group of students, (2) the classroom instructors, and (3) an "outside source." The term "outside source" refers to a population located beyond the daily environment of the school (e.g., university faculty or students, professionals from a hospital or engineering firm, or possibly students from another school). Each video conference has three distinct phases, a planning period, the actual conference, and a post-conference phase. By alternating these phases and the roles of the participants, the video conference can be an extremely powerful tool for supporting and assessing student learning.

Planning Phase

The first phase of any video conference is the planning phase. It is during this time period that the instructor(s) determine the curricular and logistical parameters of the conference and prepare the participants for their roles. Among the logistical concerns is timing. The quality of the conference connection is highly related to the volume of Internet traffic. We found that conferencing in the early morning supported the best connection. The late morning to early afternoon (11:30–1:30) was the worst time period. We also found that a "practice conference" was needed to work out logistics and support good participation. The practice conference should be held during the same time period as is planned for the actual conference. A minimum 20 minute session is necessary to determine if audio and video quality deteriorate. If a lengthy video conference is to be utilized (over 40 minutes), it may become necessary to periodically break the link and re-establish. Breaking and re-establishing the conference link generally takes less than a minute, especially if a pre-arranged process has been discussed. The instructor may want to plan for natural breaks (e.g., between scheduled presentations) to re-establish the conference links.

The instructor(s) needs to determine and communicate the educational purpose for the conference. The instructor needs to determine if the video conference will: (1) focus upon assessment of student knowledge, (2) be primarily concerned with providing support for learning, or (3) a combination. The second curricular parameter the instructor needs to determine is the roles that each party is to have in the video conference. Are the outside source going to be primarily an information source, inquisitor, or passive judge? Are the students going to present information to the outside source, field questions, or listen to information from the outside source? And finally, is the instructor going to be a moderator, evaluator, or even be present?

Selecting the appropriate software and peripherals is also important. Does the software only need to support the audio-visual, people-to-people connection, or is a white board or "extra" window for screen sharing necessary? We got by with just people-to-people audio-visual, but see the need to provide for other input and sharing. The practice sessions should test the quality and outcomes of your microphones, lighting, and camera angles. We seem to always underestimate the need for high quality microphones which can be worn by individuals (for group presentations). We also found that our "traditional" educational model of shooting a video camera at a line-up of students (for a group presentation) had them acting like convicts in a line-up rather than the interesting group of people we know them to really be. Creating less formal arrangements is highly recommended.

We also found that having the students provide the outside source and the instructor with a preview of their presentations led to better conferences. The preview should include the key goals or objectives of the students' presentations. The preview could be in the form of a paper, concept map, or outline, and should be sent electronically (e-mail with needed attachments) to the outside source with sufficient time for review. The instructor should provide the outside source and the students with the criteria for the assessment. This may be a generic rubric which illustrates the criteria. The outside source may then review the material (assessment criteria and presentation previews) and develop a set of questions to ask the students. These questions may then be sent back to the students and instructors. The questions can then be reviewed by the students and be used as a guide for the conference.

Conference

The instructor connects with the outside source and makes introductions. The first student or student group gives a brief presentation. The outside source asks a question off the prepared list. The student responds and the outside source either follows with a related question, or if satisfied with the response, proceeds to the next question off the list. Ideally, the conference becomes an interactive exchange following the scripted questions, but also creating new dialog based on the interchange of ideas. During the exchange, the instructor can take notes or fill out a planned assessment checklist on the student(s). This process is repeated for the next student(s).

Post-Conference

The instructor goes over the assessment criteria for the first student with the outside source. The outside source provides input on the level of understanding of the student(s), and the instructor evaluates the information based upon his or her knowledge of the students' capabilities and level of experience. The instructor notes any specific examples (positive or misconceptions) to bring to the student(s) attention. The process is repeated for the next student(s). Depending on the scheduling, this final assessment process may have to be held at a later time; however, the closer to the actual event, the better. Student responsibility during the post-conference component is also very important. Students should reflect upon their perceptions of the conference. This reflection can be a self-analysis of what they felt they did well and what they felt they could have done better. Students can also be assigned to prepare a similar analysis of a peer. These reflections should be turned in to the instructor approximately two to three days after the conference. Sufficient time needs to pass for the student to reflect upon the activity, but not too long that the conference begins to lose relevance for the student.

Using a Series of Video Conferences

Perhaps the most powerful use of video conferencing for assessment is when the conference is used to provide scaffolding for an in-depth investigation and assess conceptual growth. This is best facilitated when the outside source is seen as interested in the outcomes of the work, perhaps even being a customer for the student project. Ideally, a series of video conferences can be implemented. The conference planning phase will require additional attention, since several conferences need to be scheduled. The conferences should be scheduled so they can maximize support for the students, and are not necessarily evenly spaced during the course of the project. The first conference needs to be relatively early in the learning unit, preferably at a point where the student(s) has already begun to formulate a research agenda or has begun some initial background research. Subsequent conferences should be scheduled during the middle and at some point near the end of the learning unit.

Conclusions

Our experience in employing Internet-based video conferences for supporting project-based learning and assessment has been encouraging. The conferences become exciting events. The bottom line is that the student project gets better because of the conference interaction, and the teacher is supported in making sense of the students' efforts and accomplishments. We recognize that Internet-based video conferencing for the average classroom, with low bandwidth connections and without technical support, may still be too hard and too frustrating. We need enough bandwidth to create a personal feel to the interchange and to make the session dynamic. We need technology which gives the same performance and reliability we have come to expect from word processors or spreadsheets. These technology limitations will be overcome in the near future, and the challenge of using the Internet and video conferencing to support assessment will rest on the creativity and expertise of educators.

References

Laffey, J. (1995) Project MOST: Building a new educational community to support project-based learning using the Internet. *Proceedings of AACE World Conference on Education Multimedia and Hypermedia*. Charlottesville, VA: Association for the Advancement of Computing in Education.

National Research Council. (1996). *National science education standards*. Washington, DC: National Academy Press.

Wiggins, G. P. (1993, Nov.). Assessment: Authenticity, context, and validity. *Phi Delta Kappan*, 200–214.

The Authors

James M. Laffey is Associate Professor in Education and Co-Director for the Center for Technology Innovations in Education, University of Missouri-Columbia.

e-mail, World Wide Web
cilaffey@showme.missouri.edu
http://www.tiger.coe.missouri.edu/~most/index.html

Jon Singer is a Research Assistant, Project MOST, University of Missouri-Columbia.

47

Evaluating Learning Networks: A Special Challenge for Web-Based Instruction

Jason Ravitz

Evaluation can play a critical role in the development of World Wide Web-based instruction. Educational researchers are encountering both unprecedented opportunities and challenges with the advent of new technologies and educational practices. Large-scale educational projects using networks have emerged, bridging communities, institutions, time, and distance. The challenge for evaluators of such projects is to keep up with a dynamic, geographically distributed range of activity and to somehow organize, analyze, and learn from it. Adequate structures for evaluation must be put in place in order to understand and evaluate network-based educational projects as they grow over time. This chapter summarizes various issues and strategies concerning the analysis of network-based interactions and proposes one strategy to facilitate the evaluation of learning networks and their impacts. The Interactive Project Vita approach proposed here would provide improved organization and opportunities for the discussion of individual and group work.

Background

As more and more people gain access to networks within educational settings and increase their capacity to provide information and communicate via the World Wide Web, major changes in educational practices are expected. Kozma and Quellmalz (1996) provide an excellent overview of how the federal government and private agencies have initiated programs to improve education using the growing National Information Infrastructure (NII). They also provide an excellent overview of evaluation issues for these networks.

Developers of Internet-based projects are working with tools that afford rich opportunities for educational experimentation and delivery. Emergent communications technologies permit the creation of what Curtis (1995) calls "social virtual reality," which has the following characteristics:

- two- or multi-way communications,
- a shared context across distances,
- a rich structure,

- flexible participation, and

- a shared permanent record (Curtis, 1995; Ravitz, 1995)

While Curtis is not discussing the Web per se (he is a pioneer of multi-user domains, or MUDs), today the Web is increasingly capable of supporting rich forms of interaction such as those he describes (for example, see Diversity University at http://du.org). With the advent of sophisticated Internet-based tools using the World Wide Web, one can structure information so that it provides different views of work over time according to the interests of the user. Three aspects of the Web that will be discussed later in this chapter include: (1) a geographically distributed hypertext structure, (2) change over time, and (3) conversation and the social construction of knowledge.

Educational Innovations

This chapter is concerned with evaluating uses of such networks, particularly educational networks built on principles of collaboration and the social construction of knowledge (Chang, 1994; Harasim, 1990; Koschmann, 1995; Ravitz, 1995; Riel, 1994). To a significant extent, the goals of these projects are different from the goals of traditional instruction that focuses on individual performance measures. The scope of the projects and the variety of people participating in them require us to address more complex issues involving systemic change accompanied by multiple variables that complicate the determination of causal and comparative factors (Kozma & Quellmalz, 1996).

The key challenge addressed in this chapter is that these networked projects are often dynamic, active, and constantly changing. They incorporate various activities by participants who are geographically distributed and who are using online materials in ways that may not be anticipated (or even seen) by project developers. Additionally, the amount of data that is potentially generated in an online environment is a cause of concern that should be addressed in the design of projects and their evaluation.

Reigeluth (1995) discusses the shift that is taking place as we move towards an information paradigm of education. Romiszowski and Ravitz (in press) refer to this as a "conversation" paradigm, indicating the increased role of communications among participants. This paradigm stands in contrast to the traditional instructional paradigm, which is characterized by standard performance objectives and teacher-delivered instruction. As research moves from an instructional paradigm to a more conversational or information intensive paradigm, the "loss of control" over content creates, if not a problem, at least an added layer of complexity for designers and evaluators.

Finally, it is not only the educational projects that are changing, but also the Internet technologies on which they are founded. This presents additional opportunities for evaluation but also confounds the process as well. Therefore, to some extent, evaluations of learning networks must concern themselves with both the medium and its use (Riel & Harasim, 1994). More advanced technologies, for example, allow for the threading of discussions and input from participants via the Web. They may also offer users greater control in setting their communication within a context, e.g., by adding their thoughts to a concept map (Bereiter, 1996; Trochim, 1989).

Strategies for Evaluation

In their important paper entitled "Research Perspectives on Network Learning," Riel and Harasim (1994) discuss assessment issues in three main areas: network design and structure, social interactions, and individual learning outcomes. First, they state, an assessment of the design and structure of a networked project must take into account the size of the learning groups, the types of leadership provided, and the tasks undertaken by the participants. Second, an assessment of the social interactions that occur online must address such things as discourse analysis of messages, patterns of individual participation, response times, and varying involvement by individuals and groups throughout stages of the project. This often includes ethnographic approaches to discourse analysis that tell more about patterns of participation. Third, and perhaps most important, an assessment must take into account the educational outcomes for the students involved in the experience. How did the interactions change the participants? What was the effect of network-based learning on the students' skill level? The answer to these questions requires complex before-and-after analysis and comparison of treatments which are beyond the scope of this chapter.

Ultimately, in the view of Riel and Harasim (1994), a successfully designed networked environment is one that meets group needs, as indicated primarily by sustained activity and use. Riel and Harasim (1994) indicate that systematic observations, feedback from the user, and computer data can be used to examine the design of networks. Evaluation can be conducted by observing behavior coupled with reports of behavior, e.g., through written logs of participants, questionnaires, and computer data logs. However, these measures of the effectiveness of a network's design may not tell us if the network is successful in terms of learning outcomes or interaction patterns.

Social interactions on networks can also be analyzed in terms of the "climate" of interaction, as suggested by Allan Collins (personal communication). Climate involves the extent to which participants in the project feel comfortable taking "risks" in terms of communicating their ideas. This is consistent with the work of McKinley (1983), who describes the central element of trust in collaborative learning groups. In a networked environment, what happens inside the learner mentally and emotionally is important. Learners must be afforded the opportunity to express inner conflict and to struggle with new ideas using the network. "A free exchange of ideas, opinions, and feelings is the lifeblood of collaborative learning" (p. 16). Thus one important component in the evaluation might be the extent to which ideas are encouraged, generated, and expressed freely.

The issue of learning outcomes is increasingly being addressed, particularly in the context of needing new systems for alternative assessment (CRESST, 1996). Riel and Harasim (1994) list a variety of learning outcomes that are supported by the educational use of networks, including improved writing and communication skills, problem-solving, and attitudes toward learning, e.g., choosing to work on questions that do not have easy answers. Romiszowski and Ravitz (1997) provide analyses of impacts reported from users of computer-mediated communications (CMC) in education.

In sum, evaluators of Web-based instruction have an opportunity to explore educational applications using a new and evolving medium. This work requires the consideration of appropriate research methods and assessment strategies (Figure 1). A more detailed discussion of methodological issues, such as online survey research (Babbie, 1990), transcript/content analysis of messages (Levin *et al.*, 1990), portfolio review (CRESST, 1996), experimental designs and comparative analysis (Kozma & Quellmalz, 1996), and research methods for evaluating academic networked services (McClure & Lopata, 1996), is beyond the scope of this chapter, although any of these methods will be included in a comprehensive evaluation plan.

Summary of Research Issues and Strategies

Issues:
- the medium vs. the use

- design & structure (size, leadership, shared tasks)

- social interaction (discourse analysis, flexible participation, climate)

- outcomes (writing, problem-solving, retention, motivation, attitudes)

- sustainability/continued use

Strategies:
- user testimonials ("It was great.")

- volume of activity (1000 messages, 100 Web hits/day for 2 months)

- log books—self-reporting (what I/we did today....)

- discourse analysis (Jason said, Jill responded, Bob asked...)

- task phase analysis (what's planned, implemented, completed, and by whom)

- research teams (investigate similar themes across contexts, interdisciplinary teams)

- surveys & interviews (baseline data, reported benefits and activities, reactions)

- unsolicited feedback from users/public response (e.g., via e-mail, letters, phone)

- case studies & observation (rich description of participants in individual settings)

- expert reviews

Figure 1. Summary of research issues and strategies for evaluating learning networks.

Interactive Project Vita

Unless an adequate structure is put in place, as a project grows it becomes more and more difficult to understand and evaluate. The remainder of this chapter presents the Interactive Project Vita (IPV) as a design option that would help make information available to the evaluator by supporting the following processes:

- soliciting and keeping a record of new project ideas and their continued development

- helping learners and teachers submit portfolios of their work for review

- creating discussion archives around critical issues

- soliciting expert and peer feedback regarding participants' ideas and work

These processes are some ways the Web is being used to advance new types of learning and assessment.

As mentioned previously, there is a risk that large-scale online efforts, like any large research and development effort, will overwhelm the visitor with complex information and activity, a situation that can prevent an evaluator from understanding the scope and effectiveness of a project (Smith & Florini, 1993). What is needed is an overarching structure, a unifying mechanism that gives an overview and provides access to the component parts of a project.

Easily translating into a Web-based environment, the Project Vita approach (Smith & Florini, 1993) can provide a big picture, a "frame" (West *et al.*, 1991) that facilitates the efforts of evaluators (and others) to understand the parts, to "analyze their value comprehensively and holistically" (Guba & Lincoln, 1983), and to selectively give their attention to the project sub-components as per their interests.

- "The Project Vita has been used effectively as a basis of reports and briefings to project staff, boards of directors, advisory committees, site review teams, funding monitors, and interested audiences and visitors" (Smith & Florini, 1993, p. 52).

- The Project Vita gives "an indication of the order of magnitude of project impact, the possible range and spread of its effect, and the types of influence the project might have" (p. 51).

Although the Project Vita was not originally considered in terms of online work, the Internet seems to epitomize what Smith (1983) has called a "specialized application," i.e., an innovation that supports the development of new evaluation methods and theory. The proposed Interactive Project Vita strategy would adapt the above strategy to take advantage of key features of Web: (1) a geographically distributed hypertext structure, (2) change over time, and (3) conversation and the social construction of knowledge, as discussed below.

Using the Web's Hypertext Structure

The Project Vita is not so much a data collection mechanism as an organizing tool. The idea springs from the personal Curriculum Vita, a resume, which identifies, categorizes, and updates noteworthy work undertaken by an individual over time. The idea is to adapt this to the project level so that activities across geographically distant sites are categorized and presented appropriately in the context of a larger effort.

This approach takes advantage of a networked hypertext structure to illustrate significant project activities across sites. Given such information management during the course of a project, the evaluator's job may be greatly facilitated. The Online Internet Institute (http://oii.org), for example, is structured in terms of People, Processes, and Products, thereby organizing the representation of who is participating, what they are doing, and what the results of their work are during each course session.

Care must be taken that the display of activities presents actual student work and provides ways to determine the quality of the educational process (CRESST, 1996), as opposed to superficial reporting. "The inquirer must observe the facts as they normally occur, not as they are contributed in an artificial context" (Guba & Lincoln, 1983, p. 325). Therefore, the presentation of work should include pointers to actual project work, i.e., participants' products placed on the Web.

The AT&T Learning Circles project (http://www.att.com/education/lcguide/), developed by Margaret Riel, is organized around phases of activity which allows for the analysis of group participation over time and ultimately displays finished work in the form of a Computer Chronicles Newspaper categorized by type of project (Riel, 1990).

Presenting the Evolution of Project Work

Assessment of change over time is an important feature that the IPV can document. The evolution of an individual's or group's progress can be used instructionally and as a progress marker for students, teachers, and program evaluators (CRESST, 1996). By referring to a record of progress over time, an evaluator may be able to analyze the stages of development of a project (Riel & Harasim, 1994) as activities take place at different locations and possibly "measure intermediate products and partial results that can be used to trace indirect causal connections" (Kozma & Quellmalz, 1996).

For example, the collection of classroom project ideas, proposals, and completed project work (called "Toe, Wade, & Dive") as developed by Interactive Frameworks, Inc. (formerly Duggan Associates) for the Discovery Channel's Focus on the Promised Land Web site (http://school.discovery.com/learningcomm/promisedland/teachandlearn/toewade/) can provide a record of progress at different locations. This unifying structure can be used to assess and compare the evolution of projects at different locations.

Using the Discussion Component of the Internet

Finally, the "interactive" aspect proposed as part of the IPV means that the work displayed would be subject to scrutiny and discussion by others via networked interactions. In addition to providing a mechanism for structuring and presenting work over time, the Web allows evaluative discussion to take place between developers, peers, and evaluators. "Criteria for judging quality could be shared and debated, and judgments of quality could be deliberated in multiple electronic arenas. Judgments could be directly linked to the artifact being judged, with confirming and dissenting commentary attached" (Kozma & Quellmalz, 1996).

Unless the items on the Web undergo scrutiny by people who have a stake in the project, the use of a Project Vita approach risks emphasizing quantity over quality (e.g., 10 curriculum units developed by teachers, but these may not be implemented successfully). One reason to pursue discussion about the presentation of project work is that we are interested not only in the products, but also in "the meaning and interpretation people ascribe to them" (Guba & Lincoln, 1983, p. 318).

Summary

In an educational project that involves classrooms or learners in different states or countries, it is nearly impossible to keep track of all the activities taking place around a project, particularly those occurring offline. To some degree, new technologies such as the World Wide Web and threaded discussion mechanisms provide program developers and evaluators with opportunities to try to manage the complexities of geographically distributed projects. Important work is taking place using all of the other strategies discussed throughout this paper.

The proposed IPV is still an experimental idea, and it always will be a partial solution to handling the complexities of evaluating a learning network. Before we can draw conclusions about its success, there are many important issues to address. What is the effect of the Vita on project participants and evaluators? Will it be perceived as a distraction from the real work of learning, or as a central part of the learning process? People may express discomfort at highlighting their work in such a way that invites critical review (McKinley, 1983); they may use the IPV to put the best face on their work and ignore any problems. Further, only positively motivated participants may contribute to the evaluation effort, resulting in the omission of the perspective of those with negative experiences.

To address these possible limitations, the IPV approach should be tested as a part of a larger evaluation strategy that includes additional measures such as those described throughout this paper. In the end, the strategies discussed in this paper, along with new strategies that take advantage of the medium of instruction to deliver evaluation data, will increasingly be available for study and use by educational researchers and instructional designers.

Additional discussion and pointers to related work and projects are are available online (http://nsn.bbn.com/Ravitz/ipv.html).

References

Babbie, E. (1990). *Survey research methods* (2nd ed.). Belmont, CA: Wadsworth.

Bereiter, C. (1996). AECT presentation on the CSILE project. Indianapolis, IN.

Chang, E. (1994). Investigation of constructivist principles applied to collaborative study of business cases in computer-mediated communication. Unpublished doctoral dissertation, Syracuse University.

Center for Research on Evaluation, Standards, & Student Testing (CRESST). (1996, Spring). Creating better student assessments. In *Improving America's Schools: A Newsletter on Issues in School Reform* (http://www.ed.gov/pubs/IASA/newsletters/).

Collins, A. (1995, Oct. 29). Personal communication.

Curtis, P. (1995). Lecture, Northeastern University, Boston, MA.

Guba, E. G., & Lincoln, Y.S. (1983). Epistemological and methodological bases of naturalistic inquiry. In G. F. Madaus, M. Scriven, & D. Stufflebeam (Eds.), *Evaluation models: Viewpoints on educational and human services evaluation* (pp. 311–333). Boston: Kluwer-Nijhoff Publishing.

Harasim, L. M. (1990). Online education: An environment for collaboration and intellectual amplification. In L. M. Harasim (Ed.), *Online education: Perspectives on a new environment* (pp. 229–264). New York: Praeger.

Koschmann, T. (1995). Paradigm shifts and instructional technology. In T. D. Koschmann (Ed.), *CSCL: Theory and practice of an emerging paradigm.* Mahwah, NJ: Lawrence Erlbaum Associates.

Kozma, R., & Quellmalz, E. (1996). Issues and needs in evaluating the educational impact of the National Information Infrastructure. Paper commissioned by the U.S. Department of Education's Office of Educational Technology (http://www.ed.gov/Technology/).

Levin, J. A., Kim, H., & Riel, M. M. (1990). Analyzing instructional interactions on electronic message networks. In L. M. Harasim (Ed.), *Online education: Perspectives on a new environment* (pp. 185–214). New York: Praeger.

Madaus, G.F., Scriven, M., & Stufflebeam, D. L. (Eds.). (1983). *Evaluation models.* Boston: Kluwer-Nijhoff Publishing.

McClure, C. R., & Lopata, C. L. (1996). *Assessing the academic networked environment: Strategies and options.* Washington: Association of Research Libraries for the Coalition for Networked Information.

McKinley, J. (1983). Training for effective collaborative learning. In R. M. Smith (Ed.), *Helping adults learn how to learn. New Directions for Continuing Education, No. 19.* San Francisco: Jossey-Bass.

Ravitz, J. (1995). Building collaborative online communities for K–12: Observations concerning networking theory and practice. Proceedings of the Mid-continent Institute's Fourth Annual Innovations in Education Conference, Minot State University, Minot, ND., November 9–12 1995, pp. 71–83 (http://www.npac.syr.edu/users/jravitz/Ravitz_Paper_8_95.html).

Reigeluth, C. (1995). Systemic Change: What is it and why is it needed? *Patterns*, ASCD Systems Thinking and Chaos Theory Network Newsletter, January, 1996, pp. 7–9. An excerpt from C. M. Reigeluth (1994), The imperative for systemic change. In C. M. Reigeluth & R. J. Garfinkle (Eds.), *Systemic change in education.* Englewood Cliffs, NJ: Educational Technology Publications.

Riel, M. (1990). A functional analysis of educational telecomputing: A case study of learning circles. Paper presented at the Annual Meeting of the American Educational Research Association, Boston, MA.

Riel, M. (1994). Learning communities through computer networking. In J. Greeno & S. Goldman (Eds.), *Thinking practices: Math and science learning.* Hillsdale, NJ: Lawrence Erlbaum Associates.

Riel, M., & Harasim, L. (1994). Research perspectives on network learning. *Machine-Mediated Learning, 4*(2–3), 91–113.

Romiszowski, A., & Ravitz, J. (1997). Computer mediated communications. In C. R. Dills & A. J. Remiszowski (Eds.), *Instructional development paradigms*. Englewood Cliffs, NJ: Educational Technology Publications.

Smith, N. L. (1983). The progress of educational evaluation: Rounding the first bends in the river. In G. F. Madaus, M. Scriven, & D. L. Stufflebeam (Eds.), *Evaluation models* (pp. 381–392). Boston: Kluwer-Nijhoff Publishing.

Smith, N. L., & Florini, B.M. (1993). The Project Vita as a documentation and evaluation tool for large-scale research and development projects. *Evaluation and Program Planning, 16*, 49–53.

Trochim, W. (1989). An introduction to concept mapping for planning and evaluation. In W. Trochim (Ed.) *Evaluation and Program Planning, 12*, 1–16 (http://trochim.human.cornell.edu/research/epp1/epp1.htm).

West, C.K, Farmer, J. A., & Wolff, P.M. (1991). *Instructional design: Implications from cognitive science*. Boston, MA: Allyn and Bacon.

The Author

Jason Ravitz is a Researcher, BBN Educational Technologies, Cambridge, Massachusetts.

e-mail, World Wide Web
    jravitz@bbn.com
    http://idde.syr.edu/HTML/Ravitz/home.html

48

Formative Evaluation of Web-Based Instruction

Greg W. Nichols

Introduction

Formative evaluation is conventionally performed in a local setting where developers and students are easily brought together to complete their task. However, as the Web is ideally suited to distance delivery, it is reasonable to assume that the target population is remotely located. This can present a considerable degree of impracticality associated with using conventional evaluation methods.

If the Web is to be used to deliver instruction, then the professional instructional developer should consider how to evaluate the still forming materials from a distance. Further, as Web-based instruction is an individualized method, the focus should logically be on "one-to-one" tryouts, as opposed to small group or classroom tryouts.

Major Discussion Points of This Chapter

I will begin by discussing the cost aspect of using conventional formative evaluation techniques on the Web. Then a key difference between conventional and Web-based instruction, namely access to instructor assistance, will be highlighted. I will attempt to show how it may impact significantly on the formative evaluation process. In this regard, the requirements for developers to build in "compensating measures" and for evaluators to check their effectiveness will be a recurring theme. Finally, a number of techniques for conducting formative evaluation at a distance (i.e., over the Web) will be presented.

Cost of Using Conventional Techniques

Conventional formative evaluation is a hands-on, communication intensive process, with the tryout learner and evaluator working closely together (i.e., in the same place). While it is possible to still conduct the process in this manner with Web-based instruction packages, it is likely to be more expensive since "typical" learners and evaluators will have to be brought together. If they are remotely located, and possibly spread out across the country (perhaps across the world), the impracticality of bringing them together will be reflected in a significant cost factor.

Given the natural tendency to skimp on formative evaluation under the best of conditions, the additional cost can only serve to further discourage developers from the process. Thus, to be viable, a formative evaluation process for Web-based instruction materials must not add greatly to the cost side of the equation.

Difference Between Conventional and Web-Based Instruction

In addition to cost, it is also important to consider a fundamental difference between conventional instruction and Web-based instruction which can have a significant effect on learning. Conventional instruction benefits from access to instructor assistance to supplement planned learning activities. In the same vein, where instruction is largely dependent on technology, the availability of assistance to overcome equipment "glitches" can be an important factor.

First, consider the scenario where the evaluation process is conducted in the close personalized manner typical of conventional one-to-one tryouts. It is important to be aware of the natural tendency of a developer or instructor to provide numerous small insights to the tryout learner during formative evaluation. Romiszowski refers to these as "short cuts" (1986). While the resulting atmosphere of mutual cooperation can benefit the one-to-one tryout process, it can come with an undesirable side effect. The problem with "assisting" the learner over the rough spots in the program is simply that the program is not being proven to be able to stand alone. This is not as important with conventional instruction, because it is likely that an instructor's assistance will also be available when the final course is delivered. There is much less likelihood, however, that personal instructor assistance will be available with Web-based instruction.

If, on the other hand, the tryout is conducted at a distance over the Web, then the chances of inadvertent instructor assistance being provided is much less. Use of the distance approach places a much greater demand on the quality of the formative instructional materials and the evaluation process itself. However, the resultant faith in the integrity of the evaluation data will be much higher, and the quality of the final product should also be much greater.

Instructor assistance is often not "written in" to conventional programs, but is nevertheless an invaluable and integral aid, perhaps circumventing otherwise disastrous results for students experiencing difficulty. In Web-based instruction, compensating measures for the lack of direct instructor assistance must be "written in" to the program, and tested during formative evaluation to ensure that they are effective.

For example, the materials may have to have more branches, or be written for a lower common denominator of student ability. Supplementary references may have to be selected with greater care, and immediate availability to students guaranteed. Web-based materials, perhaps from professional institutions not associated with the instructional program, may be used in this regard. Special arrangements with the course provider's library may be essential in order to overcome the variability of "local" lender's offerings. A Web-based interface to the library should probably be available and complemented with electronic transmission of materials, "overnight" courier delivery or "faxing-back" of documents.

Another area where instructor assistance can be quite important is in the technical realm. Student unfamiliarity with equipment could easily bring learning to a complete stop if not for the timely aid of the instructor. Rather than taking extraordinary measures to complete the tryout, compensating measures, such as a permanent technical support "hot-line," should be in place and tested during the formative evaluation.

In summary, if the target population is remotely located, then access to "conventional" assistance when the final version of the course is implemented will not likely be great. To ensure the validity of the results, formative evaluation of Web-based instruction packages must be conducted without reference to conventional assistance that will not be available with the final product. It should, however, check that compensating measures have been incorporated and that they work as planned.

Web-Based Formative Evaluation Techniques

I will now discuss some techniques to assist in conducting formative evaluation from a distance.

It is assumed that the developer and the tryout learner are not co-located. The program may have been developed by a professor at the University of Calgary, while tryout learners may be located in New York, Toronto, Vancouver, and Dallas. While techniques such as video-conferencing or tele-conferencing could be used to monitor the tryout, there still exists a potential for excessive instructor assistance that would not be available with the final production version of the course.

Perhaps the best way to reduce unintended influences when carrying out one-to-one tryouts is to use the Web itself as the communications medium for feedback and questions. As the course will eventually be delivered over the Web, it is much more reasonable to expect that instructor assistance similar to that provided during the tryout will also be available with the final version of the course.

The most obvious implementation of this would be e-mail. There is very little development overhead associated with placing an e-mail comment capability on every screen of the instructional program. The required software is either integral to the Web browser, or if not, it is available as a separate program. It can be used by the student to correspond with the instructional staff as well as with other students taking the same course. Figure 1 provides an example.

Web browsers will automatically address the message to the developer and can even, if the developer so designates, insert a "subject" line specifying the precise screen that the student is viewing when sending the message. The student need only click on the "Comments" icon to launch an e-mail message to the developer. Unlike forms (discussed later), no programming is required to add this capability. Of course, nothing comes without a price, and the fact that comments need to be typed could be a discouragement to some learners.

While e-mail has a delivery time often measured in minutes, it is not intended to be a "real-time," or "live" communications medium, i.e., a message sent will likely not be read immediately by the addressee. Other software known as "talk," "chat," or "conferencing" sys-

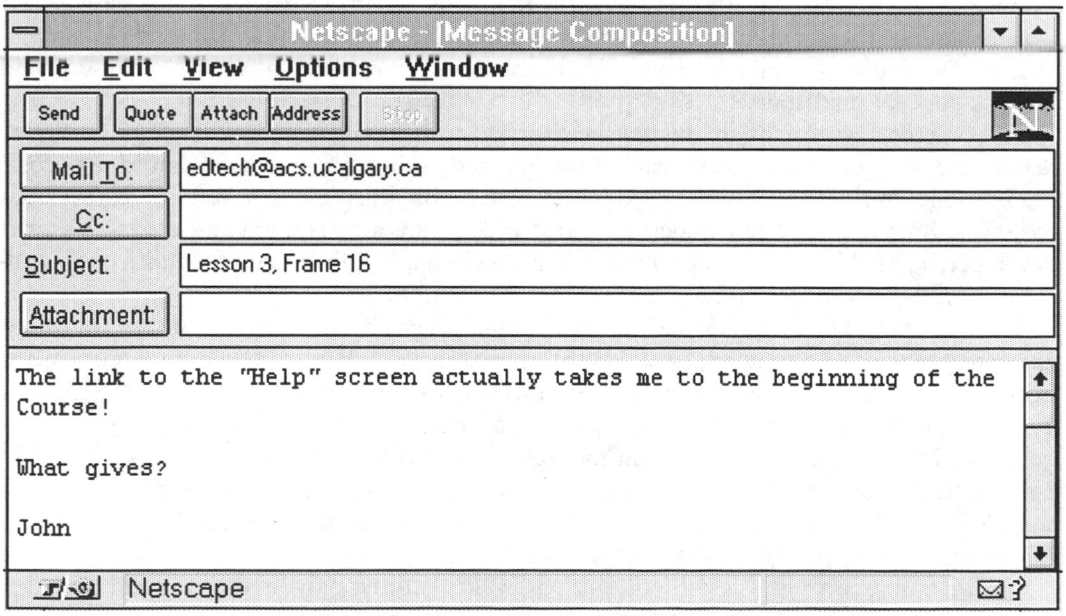

Figure 1. Critical comment using an e-mail message from tryout student to evaluator.

tems will allow close to "real-time" communications. It is possible to set up live text based discussions between the learner and the developer.

Talk utilities are perhaps most suited to one-to-one discussions and are already built-in to some multi-user operating systems such as UNIX. As many university systems are UNIX based (e.g., the University of Calgary uses a derivative known as AIX), talk has particular applicability at no extra capital cost. The developer and student need only log-in (via Telnet for example), start the utility, and conduct their discussion. The talk utility presents a split screen with the developer, for example, using the top half and the student using the lower half. Both parties can see each other's comments, essentially as they are being typed.

As the UNIX type of talk utility is not generally built-in to Web browsers, it will likely not be possible to include it as an integral window of the course presentation screen. However, it is easily run as a co-resident program which does not require a separate telephone line. Hence, the reasonably astute student can arrange his or her screen so that both the course and the talk utility are visible at the same time. In other words, it is a little inconvenient, but not a great deal.

The advantages of using the talk utility are the very close approximation to real-time one-to-one communications, and the low cost. Any problems with the course can be immediately communicated to the developer. Through a question and answer process, the developer can get a fuller appreciation of the situation. Note that talk limits discussions to only two people at a time, and both parties must already be online at the same time or a talk session cannot be started. By online, I mean actually logged-in to the host UNIX system, which is an additional step beyond that normally followed to start up a Web browser. If previously arranged, then this is not a major obstacle. These impediments, however, do suggest that the technique is less likely to be used in the production version of the course, and hence use of it during formative evaluation may not be advisable.

Chat software is similar to the talk utility, but is a more recent tool intended for use on the Internet. Unlike talk, which is a multi-user operating system tool (e.g., UNIX), chat should provide more seamless integration with course screens. As it can be used with more than two users at the same time, its applicability to discussion groups in the production version of the course is more likely. Certainly if the intent is to incorporate these types of online discussions into the course, then chat is the way to go with the formative evaluation. Under these circumstances, the subject of undue instructor or peer assistance is no more of an issue than it would be for a conventional course.

Conferencing systems are discussed elsewhere in this book; hence I will not go into great detail here. Not dissimilar from chat software, conferencing systems permit multi-user communications, but with additional capabilities such as organizing and searching for previous messages. Both chat and conferencing systems will require a certain amount of set-up by the developer, a possible disadvantage. However, it should not be too difficult to launch either utility as an integral window in the course presentation screen.

Up to this point, I have looked at options which might be used in place of the discussions and interviews of a conventional evaluation. Another typical data gathering instrument is the questionnaire. The Web-based adaptation of this is known as a "form."

Forms may have "radio buttons" allowing a single selection much like a multiple choice question, "check boxes" which permit multiple selections from a number of choices, and finally a "text entry box," which permits full sentences and paragraphs to be typed in. Once completed, the learner then clicks on a "submit" button to electronically send the form to the evaluator. Figure 2 provides examples.

The online form is a useful tool, but one which is often only used at the end of a program to report on the course in its entirety, i.e., much like a summative evaluation. A problem

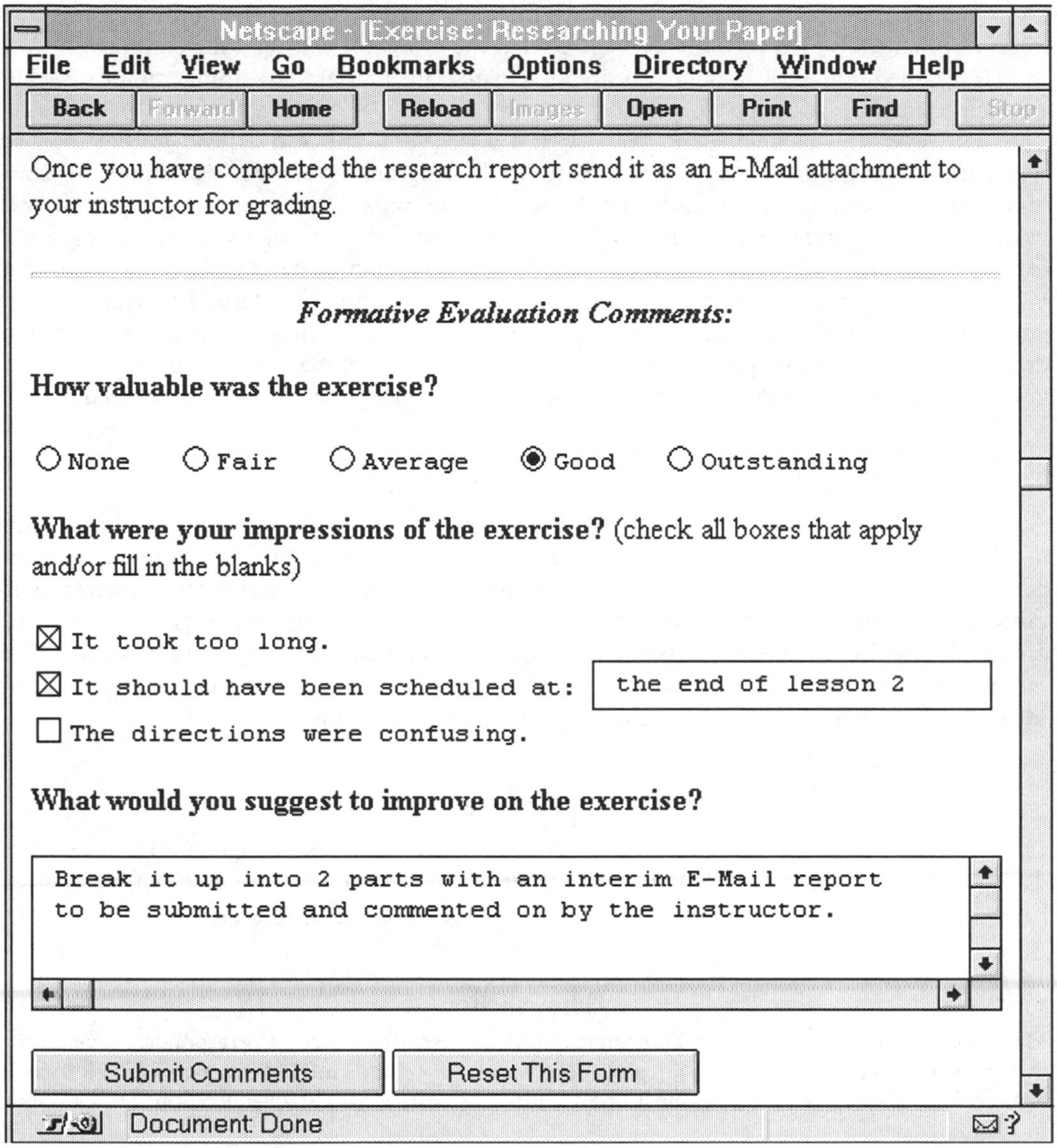

```
┌─────────────────────────────────────────────────────────────────────┐
│ ─    Netscape - [Exercise: Researching Your Paper]        ▼  ▲       │
├─────────────────────────────────────────────────────────────────────┤
│  File   Edit   View   Go   Bookmarks   Options   Directory   Window   Help │
├─────────────────────────────────────────────────────────────────────┤
│ │ Back │ Forward │ Home │  │ Reload │ Images │ Open │ Print │ Find │ │ Stop │ │
├─────────────────────────────────────────────────────────────────────┤
```

Once you have completed the research report send it as an E-Mail attachment to your instructor for grading.

Formative Evaluation Comments:

How valuable was the exercise?

○ None   ○ Fair   ○ Average   ⦿ Good   ○ Outstanding

What were your impressions of the exercise? (check all boxes that apply and/or fill in the blanks)

☒ It took too long.

☒ It should have been scheduled at: `the end of lesson 2`

☐ The directions were confusing.

What would you suggest to improve on the exercise?

```
Break it up into 2 parts with an interim E-Mail report
to be submitted and commented on by the instructor.
```

┌──────────────────────┐   ┌──────────────────────┐
│   Submit Comments   │   │   Reset This Form   │
└──────────────────────┘   └──────────────────────┘

Document Done

Figure 2. Critical comment using an e-mail message from tryout student to evaluator.

with this type of methodology is that timely (fleeting?) comments may be long forgotten by the time the learner completes the program. The natural tendency with a "one shot" evaluation of a complete program is to build a large and cumbersome form which covers all the bases. Although well intentioned, this discourages learners from taking adequate time to consider each and every question.

The online form can, however, be easily adapted for one-to-one tryout purposes. Pertinent questions can be placed at the end of each frame of a module to permit timely comments to be sent. For example, the developer may have tried out a new technique on a particular screen to which learner reaction might be mixed. A simple "radio button" question may be used asking simply: "Do you find this technique useful? Very much, Somewhat, Not at all."

The form can be programmed to have the particular screen title or number to which it refers automatically sent with the message so that the evaluator can read the comment in context. If a large number of respondents are anticipated, then a database application can be developed to manage and report on the data.

However, this technique can carry with it a large amount of overhead in that the host server usually needs to have a form handling "CGI" program developed. CGI stands for common gateway interface, which, in layman's terms, is the software programming aspect of Web development. As this is not generally within the skill base of the typical instructional developer, external assistance will usually be required. If a very simple implementation is intended, then inexpensive software is available which will essentially capture the data and forward it as an e-mail message to the developer. However, managing these numerous small messages can quickly become a very tedious and error prone process. Finally, if a database is anticipated for large numbers of respondents, then a database application also needs to be developed.

Summary

As the Web is likely to grow significantly as an important medium for delivering instruction, it is important to develop suitable formative evaluation techniques. A key difference between conventional and Web-based instruction programs is the degree of access to instructor assistance. I have shown how this can impact on the formative evaluation process, and have recommended the use of the Web itself in order to maintain the integrity of that process. The requirements for developers to build in compensating measures and for evaluators to check their effectiveness is a key requirement for Web-based instruction.

References

Clark, R. E. (1994). Assessment of distance learning technology. In E. L. Baker & H. F. O'Neil, Jr. (Eds.), *Technology assessment in education and training*. Hillsdale, NJ: Lawrence Erlbaum Associates.

Romiszowski, A. J. (1986). *Developing auto-instructional materials*. London: Kogan Page.

The Author

Major Greg W. Nichols is Training Development Officer, Canadian Forces. Correspondence concerning this chapter should be addressed to Greg Nichols, who is now completing a Master of Education in Educational Technology at the Department of Educational Research, Faculty of Education, The University of Calgary, Canada.

e-mail, World Wide Web
   gwnichol@acs.ucalgary.ca
   http://www.ucalgary.ca/~gwnichol

49

Factors to Consider When Evaluating a Web-Based Instruction Course: A Survey

Badrul H. Khan and Rene Vega

Introduction

The World Wide Web has become one of the most popular approaches of accessing information on the Internet. Because of the Web's capability of linking a variety of information and communication formats, Web-based instruction is becoming an increasingly prevalent method for delivering instruction. In this chapter, the results of a small, cross-sectional survey are given. This survey was conducted to sample which factors educators consider important when evaluating a Web-based course.

The survey was conducted between the months of July and August of 1996. Because of this brief time period, responses to this survey were minimal (24). The survey consisted of the following two questions:

(1) Please identify yourself by checking one or more of the following:

_____ I have taken a course on the Web.

_____ I have developed a course on the Web.

_____ I have taught a course on the Web.

(2) List the criteria you would consider when evaluating the effectiveness of any Web course.

Resources

The survey was posted on the following four listservs, which generally are involved in the discussion and promotion related to the technology of learning and instruction:

(1) AECT-L (Association for Educational Communications and Technology)

(2) WWWEDU (World Wide Web in Education)

(3) WWWDEV (World Wide Web Development)

(4) MEDIA-L (Media Literacy)

Participants

Participants were individuals who subscribed to the above mentioned listservs. Please note that some of the participants were either students, instructors, course developers, or a combination of two or three roles.

Student	6
Instructor	1
Course Developer	8
Student and Developer	2
Student and Instructor	1
Developer and Instructor	3
Student, Developer, and Instructor	3
Total number of Participants	**24**

Criteria Considered in Evaluating Web-Based Course Effectiveness

After all the responses were collected, they were ranked from the most to least frequently cited criteria for evaluating the effectiveness of a Web-based course. The following lists are some responses given by the participants, in order of frequency of occurrence.

1. Were the course objective(s) clear and achievable?

2. In terms of interactivity, did the course:
   - contain more required activities for the user than optional activities?
   - give feedback on choice or input?
   - provide access to instructor or other students (e-mail, listserv, chat rooms, and on-line conferencing)?
   - use the Internet phone to give additional instructional support?

3. In terms of the quality of content, was the course:
   - accurate?
   - interesting?
   - appropriate to discipline?
   - appropriate to method of distribution?

4. In terms of structure, did the course:
   - have good navigational design?
   - have a complementary structure of similar, print-based materials?
   - have a reasonable metaphor for organization (hierarchical, linear, etc.)?

5. In terms of accessibility, was the course:
   - on a stable system?
   - written in simple HTML or a similar, user-friendly protocol?
   - clear, and did it use effective language?
   - limited in coding errors?

6. Did the course provide application of content to practice?

7. Could student usage be followed for evaluation of effectiveness?

8. Was there proper technical support (hardware and software)?

9. In terms of a "hook," did the course have:
   - illustrations?
   - games or puzzles?
   - a questionnaire with feedback or scoring?

10. Was reasoning for using the Web suitable?

11. Did the material provoke insightful class discussion?

12. Was the effectiveness of training determined in terms of achieving the course objectives?

13. What was the level of participation by students?

14. What was the number of one-to-one communications with the instructor?

15. Did the architecture of the site facilitate students' ability to discern relevance in an ocean of information?

16. Did the course have a built in timeline: Were there space/time restrictions?

17. Was navigation easy?

18. Were the icons that were used for navigation consistent and well defined?

19. Did the course contain built-in methods for students' reports (e.g., progress reports, online learning contracts, etc.)?

20. Was there an opportunity for the students to provide informal feedback and evaluation concerning their thoughts on the learning experience?

21. Were a number of different learning styles addressed?

22. Was there asynchronous learning for individual student progress?

23. Did the course explicate the circumstances and background of a situation in a coherent and cohesive way?

24. Did the Web-based instructional system provide the instructor with a vehicle for integrating the broader themes of the course?

25. How did the course help students learn to process information?

26. Was the material easy for students to access? (download time, access to computer lab, materials)

27. What advantage did the use of this technology offer over more traditional methods?

28. Did the instructor provide net access to a reliable Web server?

29. Did the course take full advantage of the capabilities of the medium?

30. Were there clear screen layouts and relevant links to subject on hand?

31. Was the design of links consistent with the knowledge that the course was intended to impart?

32. What was the number of peer-to-peer relationships developed by students?

33. What added value does hypertext bring to this course topic?

34. Did the instructor have programming skills?

35. Did the course take advantage of the powers of being online (i.e., something beyond just long pages of text)?

36. Was the security of the course adequate?

Summary

The Web has changed the ways in which many people access, interpret, and apply information. There are several methods of learning through the Internet. Initially, an effective course on the Web seems to be evaluated much like a traditional classroom course. Not only should the objectives be clearly stated and a well organized outline provided, but also interactions among peers and instructors should be systematically incorporated into the course design. A Web-based course should be designed to address a variety of learning styles. The Web design itself should be constructed in a logical, user-friendly, and meaningful manner.

This survey was not intended to generate a comprehensive list of critical factors in Web-based instruction. It was the intent of the survey to create a list of concerns that students, developers, and instructors have regarding Web-based instruction.

Acknowledgment

We would like to thank Michael J. Sullivan for reviewing the survey described in this chapter.

The Authors

Badrul H. Khan is Assistant Professor and Coordinator of the Educational Technology graduate program at the University of Texas at Brownsville.

e-mail, World Wide Web
    khanb@utb1.utb.edu
    http://www.utb.edu/~khanb/khan.html

Rene Vega is a graduate student in the Educational Technology Program at the University of Texas at Brownsville.

SECTION V

Case Studies of Web-Based Courses

50

Existing Web-Based Instruction Courses and Their Design

Brenda Bannan and William D. Milheim

Introduction

As is evidenced in other chapters in this book, the World Wide Web is becoming a major source for educational material delivered to learners who prefer (or are required) to learn apart from a traditional classroom. While the educational potential of this medium is just beginning to be realized, its utilization will certainly increase over time as larger numbers of educators and learners see the significant value in this type of instruction.

However, while there is tremendous potential for this type of learning, there is also a significant need to describe these Web-based courses in terms of their overall instructional design characteristics, rather than defining each course only by the specific content it provides. Without this organizational process, courses will be perceived and categorized based primarily on their subject matter, rather than the instructional strategies and tactics used for the delivery of the educational material.

The specific purposes for this categorization process of Web-based courseware include the following:

1. To describe the overall design characteristics of a specific course, including its basic instructional model (e.g., classroom vs. online) and the conceptual learning theory represented by its design (e.g., objectivist vs. constructivist, learner-centered vs. program-centered).

2. To describe its general instructional methodology, including strategies such as the transmission of course content, the facilitation of student learning, fostering student collaboration and participation (including the development of various Web-based resources), role playing, and modeling of previous student work.

3. To describe various course attributes related to Web-based delivery, including items such as e-mail, listservs, the creation or utilization of Internet links, as well as various multi-user domains (e.g., MUDs, MOOs, MUSHs).

Based on the factors described above, the current authors suggest a framework for analyzing and describing educational Web-based materials. This framework consists of three dimensions, including *Overall Design, Instructional Methods,* and *Instructional Activities,* that can be used to describe various course components. This model and its three major components are described below, including examples from current Web-based courseware.

Overall Design

Designing any type of instruction involves determining the overall instructional approach and the theoretical or pedagogical basis for that approach, as well as the potential strategies or methods and corresponding instructional activities. When designed appropriately, these elements result in the significant engagement of the student in the learning process.

As with any new delivery medium such as the World Wide Web, a tendency exists to focus on design strategies based only on the technological capabilities of the medium, rather than the goals of the lesson, the needs of the learner, and the nature of the task involved (Rieber, 1994). Therefore, consideration of these core instructional elements become even more important when designing instruction for this new medium.

Existing courses delivered via the World Wide Web and examined through a framework of basic instructional elements necessary for effective design demonstrate a broad continuum of approaches and philosophies, methodologies, and instructional activities. Existing courses range from classroom-based instruction, including information posted on the World Wide Web as an alternative delivery mode for information presented in class; through classroom-directed learning supplemented with specific Web-based activities; to courses delivered totally online, relying on Web-based resources as a full delivery mechanism for course interaction. The structure of these courses should be based upon underlying theoretical concepts related to specific beliefs concerning how learning occurs.

Bednar, Cunningham, Duffy, and Perry (1992) strongly advocate identifying and applying a particular theory of learning when designing instruction. In Web-based instruction, the deliberate selection of a particular theoretical position provides the necessary basis for corresponding instructional methods.

Two primary schools of thought have emerged in regard to learning theory and the design of instruction that relate to the overall instructional utilization of Web-based courses. The objectivist and constructivist viewpoints offer drastically different positions on how knowledge is represented, how meaning is created, and therefore how learning occurs. Briefly, objectivist philosophy holds that information in the external world is mind-independent and can be characterized in objective, concrete terms which are transmitted or communicated from the instructor to the student. In contrast, constructivists believe that the individual student builds an internal and personal representation of knowledge which is indexed by his or her unique experiences (Bednar *et al.*, 1992). In Web-based instruction, the design of objectivist lessons may be represented by the posting of content organized by the instructor and delivered to the student; while constructivist design of the same course would include multiple opportunities for the student to synthesize, organize, and restructure information as well as creating and contributing his or her own resources.

An additional theoretical consideration for the design of courses on the World Wide Web involves the control of learning activities. Student-centered learning is demonstrated by students selecting and sequencing educational activities as well as creating their own learning opportunities and satisfying their own learning needs (Hooper & Hannafin, 1991). In contrast, program-centered activities involve courses which are highly structured and organized by course designers for the student to later follow, with participation by the student often being prespecified by the instructor and designed to ensure mastery of particular content. Each of these theoretical frameworks significantly impact the resulting educational methods which are utilized for instructional delivery on the World Wide Web.

Table 1. General instructional methods useful for Web-based instruction.

General Method	Purpose	Implementation
Dissemination	Information Distribution	1) Posting of course information.
		2) Organizing accessible Web-based resources and links.
		3) Providing transcripts of student Web-based exchanges.
		4) Providing links to digital text (e.g., online literary resources).
		5) Similar to traditional lecture format.
Facilitation	Student Assistance	1) Providing guidance, directing discussion, suggesting possible resources, fielding questions, etc..
		2) Accomplished through electronic dialogue using e-mail, listservs, or computer conference capabilities.
		3) Establishing parameters and conducting Multi-User Dialogue (MUD) environments.
Inside Collaboration	Student Communication	1) Provision of a supportive environment for asking questions, clarifying directions, suggesting or contributing resources, and working on joint projects with class members.
		2) Supported by activities such as e-mail, listservs, computer conference discussions, and MUD environments.
Outside Collaboration	External Interaction	1) Invitations to external personnel to participate in computer conferences.
		2) Provision of Web-based links to external resources.
		3) Allowing access to MUD environments.
		4) Traditional methods, including use of external speakers and guest lecturers.
		5) General participation of the wider electronic community.
Apprenticeship	External Expert Guidance	1) Guidance from an outside expert for a particular learning task.
		2) Can be provided through e-mail, listservs, or computer conferencing activities.
Generative Development	Content Generation	1) Assimilation, interaction, and synthesize of information through the creation, organization, or reorganization of specific content.
		2) Specific activities can include the development of original Web pages, as well as contributing or commenting on digital text.
Role-Play	Simulated Role Portrayal	1) Facilitated through MUD environments where instructors create a multi-user space with a central theme, characters and artifacts.
Modeling	Behavior Modeling	1) Ranges from modeling behavior in electronic environments to providing samples of relevant coursework.
		2) Provision of guidance for interactions in simulated environments such as MUDs.
		3) Posting of sample interactions, assignments, and projects on the Web to provide the necessary modeling for expectations of course requirements.

Instructional Methods

In addition to the several overall instructional approaches that can be used for the delivery of Web-based course materials, there are also a number of specific instructional methods that should be considered for this form of instruction. While many of these activities can be used in a variety of course delivery modes, they are particularly useful for courseware including a significant Web component. Table 1 shows a number of these general instructional methods and specific utilization suggestions for their use in Web-based courseware.

Instructional Activities

Involving the World Wide Web in course design affords both traditional forms of instructional activities and some unique forms of interpersonal exchange. While not all student activities are facilitated directly through the Web, the majority of activities involve online types of interaction, which are supported through directions or resources posted on the Web. Traditional forms of instructional activities may include posting of course information, reading of papers and/or literary works available through digital text, and asynchronous discussion-based facilities such as electronic mail, listservs and computer conferencing.

Other forms of exchange capitalize on the unique attributes of the Web and other online interpersonal tools. One of the most obvious attributes of the hypertext environment of the Web is the linking of additional resources for students to explore, such as related Web pages, databases, tutorials, and software. Unique Web-based activities include preserving and posting student discussions which take place in listservs and conferencing and real-time interaction among students, using Multi-User Dialogue (MUD) tools which provide a collaborative social environment for role-playing and social interaction concerning a specific topic or challenge. A description of the purpose and implementation of many of these activities is shown in Table 2.

Web-Based Course Examples

Many examples of current courses are available on the Web, representing various types of communication and potential interaction between instructors and students. Courses reviewed here were selected primarily from education and technology-related disciplines as samples of varying instructional approaches, philosophies, activities, and methodologies. Reviewed through observation of only what was available online, the courses were examined for evidence of the instructional elements outlined in the earlier sections of this chapter.

Other courses with additional types of strategies and methodologies can also be found on the Web. Examples of overall collections of sites highlighting courses with significant World Wide Web involvement include The World Lecture Hall (http://www.utexas.edu/world/lecture/), Web Based Courses (http://ezinfo.ucs.indiana.edu/~smalikow/courses.html) and a collection related to the World Wide Web Development Listserv (http://www.unb.ca/web/wwwdev/c3.html).

The following specific examples represent a continuum of Web-based courseware, ranging from the use of the Web as a simple information resource to the significant use of this immense resource. Each of these courses can be accessed directly from the URL shown in the text or from the authors' home page for this chapter (http://www.personal.psu.edu/faculty/wdm2/chap23.htm).

Situated Cognition (*University of Connecticut*). This doctoral seminar is an example of utilizing the World Wide Web on a limited basis, where the Web is used simply as an alternative mode for the distribution of class-related information. Supporting in-class activities, the use of the Web in this course seems to represent the classroom-based model of instruction and an objectivist philosophy emphasizing the simple distribution and transmission of information.

Table 2. Specific instructional activities associated with Web-based instruction.

Specific Activity	Purpose	Implementation
Posting Information	Information Delivery	1) Distribution system for syllabi, handouts, or other course-related information.
		2) Directions describing how to subscribe to one or more class-based listservs.
Electronic Mail	Course Interaction	1) Asynchronous communication between instructor and students
		2) Facilitation of questions and answers.
		3) Submission of coursework.
		4) Completion of electronic forms.
		5) Facilitation of course surveys, evaluations, and other course-related activities.
Listservs	Group Communication	1) Asynchronous class discussions.
		2) Directions concerning various course activities.
		3) Submission of assignments and proposals for feedback.
		4) Overall peer support.
		5) General instructor guidance.
Link Resources	Links to Web Sites	1) Readings as well as supplementary or enrichment information.
		2) Access to related databases, tutorials, or software for course-based activities.
Contributed Links	Student Generated Links	1) Permits students to automatically add their own Web links to the overall course site.
Multi-User Dialogues	Real-Time Interaction	1) Text-based environments providing collaborative environments for social interaction.
		2) Facilitation of innovative role-playing among class participants in a dynamic, electronically-constructed world.
Computer Conferencing	Group Discussion	1) Used to facilitate discussion on particular topics.
		2) Use of connected text messages and responses stored as threads.
		3) Creation of a hierarchical tree-like structure to reflect a conversational pattern.
		4) Generally instructor-led.
Electronic Community	External Participation	1) Participation from individuals outside of a formal class.
		2) Posting messages, initiating topics, and contributing personal links.
		3) Can provide valuable multiple perspectives from the external electronic community.
Records of Exchange	Capture of Dialogue	1) Capturing and posting of text dialogue from listservs or computer conferencing exchanges.
		2) Provision of a record of interaction for later viewing and analysis.
Digital Text	Access to Literary Works	1) Placement of classic and other literary works on the Web for downloading or reading.
		2) Provision of immediate access to poetry, papers, presentation notes, etc. for incorporation into course activities.
		3) Commentary feature permits students to insert comments into particular text passages.
Web Page Creation	Develop Web Sources	1) Involves students in synthesis of instructional Web-based content.
		2) Actual creation of Web resource by individual students.
Posted Projects	Shared Project Examples	1) Provision of shared examples of in-progress or completed projects, papers, and other student work on the Web.
		2) Used for modeling, discussion or review.

In this course (http://yoda.ucc.uconn.edu/users/youngm/sitcog.html), the Web is utilized as a method of disseminating information by providing course objectives and requirements, student assignments, topic outlines, and a reading list.

Educational Technology (*San Francisco State University*). This course represents a more comprehensive example of the classroom-based, objectivist model. At this site (http://user www.sfsu.edu/~pfresina/), the instructor uses both dissemination and facilitation methodologies in providing an extensive collection of handouts for each class session, as well as using electronic mail support and the creation of Web-based forms to solicit student questions and comments.

Western Civilization (*Boise State University*). This course also represents a classroom-based model for utilizing the Web and another example of the objectivist model of teaching where the course is primarily program-centered (http://www.idbsu.edu/courses/hy101/class.htm). However, in this case, the instructor provides an online lecture which includes the significant use of Internet links to assist in the appropriate chunking of the course information and the provision of student readings (as digital text) to support classroom material. This site also provides Internet-based links to various library resources as well as study questions for student use. Finally, the use of inside collaboration strategies are supported through the provision of transcripts of student interactions which focus on various subjects related to the course content.

Applied Educational On-Line Technologies (*University of New Brunswick*). This instructional site (http://cnet.unb.ca/nbco/ed5365/) delivers instruction through a totally online, constructivist model. While course expectations are clearly spelled out, the philosophy of this type of course is that students learn by doing through a student-centered approach, including activities such as proposals submitted via e-mail, Web page development, projects posted on the Internet site, and reflective student papers. Communication among students and faculty at this site is carried out through computer conferencing and a variety of listservs which also serve as the primary channel of facilitation by the instructor.

Computers and Writing Conference Classroom Distant Spaces and Education (*University of Texas at Austin*). This site (http://www.cwrl.utexas.edu/cw/index.html) provides further information describing how Web-based courses can be offered through a variety of innovative approaches. Although not a specific course, this resource serves as a discussion center for Web-based pedagogy and innovative methods, describing online courses and including succinct descriptions concerning how to provide Web-based courseware within a learner-centered constructivistic or social constructivistic framework. Specific methodologies demonstrated and described at this site include the utilization of role playing and MUDs, the development of Web pages, processes related to reading and commenting on digital text, the use of inside collaboration techniques (e.g., class listservs), and outside collaboration methods such as providing access to participants both inside and outside of a class so that they can contribute relevant links and personal comments to Web-based courseware.

Rhetoric of Epic Narratives (*University of Texas at Austin*). Finally, this site (http://www. cwrl.utexas.edu/~babydoll/coursematerial/spring96/index.html) allows students to explore various constructed environments based on particular themes such as ancient Greece or Rome through the use of MUSE or MUD-based technology. The instructional facilitation is controlled by the instructor who creates the overall situation while students role play various characters provided within the setting. While students interact with the environment and the artifacts within it, they develop new relationships with the provided scenarios and become deeply engaged with the material. Outside of the constructed world, students can further analyze their own (or other) responses through accessing the records of student exchanges that are posted during the course.

Conclusion

Delivering instruction using the World Wide Web is becoming increasingly popular, both as an adjunct to traditional classroom-based education and as a stand-alone platform for the delivery of entire courses. Although still somewhat in its infancy, these methods are being demonstrated in many discipline areas from K–12 education through graduate study.

While these methods are increasing in general utilization, the Web-based courses do require a systematic approach to various issues, including overall design, instructional methods, and instructional activities, in order to provide effective instructional interactions for the faculty and students who choose this form of education. It is hoped that the general discussion of these concepts and the examples provided above will assist instructors, researchers, and course developers in their pursuit of quality Web-based courseware.

References

Rieber, L. (1994). *Computers, graphics, and learning.* Madison, WI: Brown & Benchmark.

Bednar, A. K., Cunningham, D., Duffy, T. M., & Perry, J. D. (1992). Theory into practice: How do we link? In T. M. Duffy & D. H. Jonassen (Eds.), *Constructivism and the technology of instruction: A conversation* (pp. 17–34). Hillsdale, NJ: Lawrence Erlbaum Associates.

Hooper, S., & Hannafin, M. J. (1991). The effects of group composition on achievement, interaction, and learning efficiency during computer-based cooperative instruction. *Educational Technology Research and Development, 39*(3), 27–40.

The Authors

Brenda Bannan is Assistant Professor of Instructional Technology, College of Education, George Mason University, Fairfax, Virginia.

e-mail, World Wide Web
    bbannan@gmu.edu
    http://gse.gmu.edu/files/bannan.htm

William D. Milheim is Assistant Professor of Instructional Systems, Penn State Great Valley, Malvern, Pennsylvania.

e-mail, World Wide Web
    wdm2@psu.edu
    http://www.ed.psu.edu/dept/ae-insys-wfed/insys/Faculty/milheim.htm

51

Introducing Online Educational Alternatives into K–12 Worlds

Diana D. Derry

Introduction

This chapter is written for administrators or faculty interested in exploring the possibility of introducing K–12 online educational alternatives into their existing district-wide curriculum. The intent of this chapter is to provide those moving in a similar direction with resourceful insight into the opportunities and challenges they may encounter, and fundamental strategies and methods for pursuing their own online educational alternatives. We start with the road we traveled and the experience we have gained in the process. We hope it will prove useful to those entertaining new possibilities.

Brief History

In the fall of 1995, Jefferson County Public School District began to explore innovative ways to utilize its evolving district technological infrastructure to better serve students and faculty. The first step, familiar to those already in a K–12 world, was to *conduct a formal assessment*. The assessment was undertaken with the hopes of exploring and discovering academic directions that would enable the District to expand its educational vision and implementation to enable more students to successfully complete their high school education.

Beginning with the numerous 'special' and 'at-risk' populations, we were able to identify a number of educational needs, common to many programs, that were not being adequately met. The common concern reiterated by administrators and faculty was that traditional education could no longer meet the needs of students who were not able to adhere to a traditional format. These administrators were seeking educational choices in the form of a core curriculum, including electives, that was not bound to an institutionalized schedule (time/day/semester) or traditional delivery format (traditional classroom). They believed that more students would complete their education if they had access to what was required of them.

Based upon these initial assumptions and findings, we recommended the introduction of Web-based instructional (WBI) alternatives as the most appropriate distance learning direction. We advocated that WBI would achieve the following:

1. Web-based instruction can transcend the traditional boundaries of education, creating learning and teaching environments that better address the needs of those individuals who have fallen outside the conventional realms of education.

2. Web-based instruction can infuse the traditional educational scheme with an energy, a vision, and a pragmatic realization of how educational ideals can work collaboratively with innovative technologies to attain goals that have long been out of reach.

3. Web-based instruction can be cost-effective and revenue-producing sources for a K–12 District.

4. Web-based instruction is not a panacea, but it can offer more choice and opportunity to a greater variety of student and faculty populations.

Moving according to the above contentions, we began to seriously explore how Web-based instruction should be developed and implemented. Our aim was to design and deliver an alternative that would reach all populations served by the District, not just those labeled as 'special' or 'at-risk.'

Because many of the special programs had been involved from the beginning with the formal assessment, we found that we had already begun *to build our online initiative from the ground-up*. The direction of our initiative had been determined by realistically defined educational realities and a common voice. The relationships and rapport critical to clarifying program vision and implementation were already well formed. And at the heart of this understanding was a commitment to fully explore how online educational alternatives could be introduced into the District and meet the needs of all.

Program Development

From each of these programs, we were able to *form our initial design teams* for the development of Web-based courses. The purpose of the 'design' team was to unite a strong variety of experiences and perspectives, with educational agendas as the central impetus, and innovative technologies as the medium. The objective of a design team was to create educational content that was of the highest caliber and to deliver it using the most savvy technologies available.

The design teams were comprised of self-recruited individuals who were able to bring a critical resource to the product development. These individuals consisted of discipline-specific experts, Web-design professionals, program administrators, standards-based education consultants, and educational technologists. Our goal was to fuse the critical elements of both education and technology in a manner that would clearly model how a district can safely meld the numerous and oftentimes disjointed educational initiatives and efforts throughout its jurisdiction to create true systemic change.

In order to successfully carry out this charge, we needed to address and fulfill the criteria set forth by a number of educational agendas already underway at different levels in the district. By identifying and respecting these standards and expectations, we were able to roughly sketch the parameters for our initial online course design and development. It was this step that enabled us to know from the outset what our challenge involved and the ways we might go about realizing it.

In addition to the input of people and entities from within our own district, we also began to work closely with outside agencies, industries, and organizations. The reason for initiating these relationships was twofold: (1) to ensure that work-world realities were introduced into our educational content, and (2) to strengthen our program base for future expansion and possible working partnerships. We wanted to move away from the conventional isolation that many educational institutions work from. Instead, we wanted to operate from a large and diverse base of input; not just from our own perspectives.

The Look of a Web-Based Course

The online courses that we have developed attempt to incorporate a number of technologies. The Web constitutes the classroom's virtual environment, where essential content resources are housed. In addition to these finite resources, students have access to the infinite and always evolving resources of the Web. To complement and bring alive the contents of this 'static' domain, we integrate both asynchronous and synchronous forms of communications and interactions through basic e-mail capacities, group mailing lists, and real-time online office hours, consultations and classroom discussions.

Course instructors are guided in specific methods and strategies for facilitating a course online. We expect our online educators to possess specific technological competencies in addition to their discipline-specific expertise. To successfully facilitate an online course, we have identified specific professional criteria we require. These include the following: (1) appropriate content knowledge and experience; (2) competence and savvy with technologies required to deliver the course successfully, i.e., e-mail; real-time communications; list management; and Web-page maintenance; (3) ability to introduce and manage both synchronous and asynchronous communications and interactions; (4) openness to emerging technologies and ways to apply them to online educational environments.

Because technology is a critical component of Web-based instruction, embedded in our thinking was the assumption that all involved would learn to master the current technologies we were introducing. Our belief was that in order to fully utilize any specific technology, we must first clearly comprehend its capacities and limitations. Instead of racing from one technology to the next, we decided it was important to exercise available technology to its fullest educational advantage, and from there begin to move toward the integration of newer technologies. For those involved in online education, we discovered that professional upgrade is a constant state.

Although technology plays a critical role, the success of a Web-based course lies in the way the instructor and students approach and interact with the finite content of the course and the infinite territory of the Web. This is truly where Web-based instruction transcends the traditional educational formats. Students now have access to a number of resources right at their fingertips. If they learn how to explore and manage the availability of this knowledge, they can experience a very new kind of independent learning. In addition, if teachers shed their old paradigms that espouse teaching as the dissemination of knowledge, they can operate from a new paradigm that allows for the exploration and construction of knowledge, in a constant and evolving dynamic.

Moving Along Parallel Fronts

Successful program development requires the energies and input from a wide array of levels, programs and populations. A diverse mix will ensure a strong anchoring upon which to build and expand the initiative. (And it is an initiative until it gains enough maturity, through development and experience, to become a program.) Furthermore, it is the variety of needs and expectations brought together that help unfold and *clarify a vision common to all*. Listening to each separate voice enables one to hear the possibility of a united effort that can successfully introduce unprecedented educational realities into K–12 worlds.

As our program began to unfold, gradually and with great perseverance, we discovered that its impact was being felt in many realms. The paradigms we had long embraced were undergoing a subtle and interesting metamorphosis. We were beginning to feel more open towards the possibilities, both those that were clear and present and those we had yet to discover. It was more acceptable to challenge all we knew and had taught according to. In addition, we were discovering ways to introduce the agendas of numerous educational initiatives simultaneously.

In a single Web-based course, we were attempting to integrate district content standards, alternative assessment formats, the latest technologies (crucial to work-world realities and future educational environments), and sensitivity toward gender and culture. We advocated that online educational environments, especially Web-based, could pull together the separate efforts of a district into a nice mosaic that revealed a clear and cohesive vision.

The Possibility of Tomorrow

We believe that the introduction of online educational alternatives serves many purposes. Foremost, it should push educators to rethink their conception and delivery of teaching and learning. It should also encourage students to rethink the role they exert to ensure their own learning. And, finally, it should force K–12 schools and districts to rethink their educational missions and examine new ways to deliver their services. We believe 'rethinking' is what leads to the internal change that precedes true external, systemic change. Without the rethinking, change will merely be cosmetic and ephemeral.

A district can begin to generate change at all levels by addressing the needs of its administrators, faculty, staff, and students through technology. It is short-sighted to think that time is on your side. And it is a disservice to those you serve if you choose to wait. The possibility of tomorrow is today.

The Author

Diana D. Derry is Distance Education Consultant, Jefferson County Public School District, Denver, Colorado.

e-mail
diderry@jeffco.k12.co.us

52

Virtual Worlds as Constructivist Learning Tools in a Middle School Education Environment

Carlos R. Solís

Computers networks have opened new doors and ways to deliver up-to-the-minute information from around the world to the classroom. In the minds of many, they represent the latest step in a revolution that will bring education to new levels. However, up to now, just like the television and movies, the promise of information technology revolutionizing education remains largely unfulfilled (Soloway & Pryor, 1996). One reason for this is that while World Wide Web information reaches the classrooms at amazing speed and in incredible volumes now, it remains a two-dimensional medium, just like books. Furthermore, it often is used in a passive learning system and therefore does not change the way we learn.

Computer generated virtual worlds offer a radical new way to deliver information to users. For the first time in history, a single medium allows users to receive, in a single packet, information about space, relationships, scale, and time. It allows users to penetrate the medium and interact with the information. Students can use this medium to travel to places that are inaccessible because of time, distance, or physical constraints, such as inside the human body, the surface of the moon, or the molecular space in chemical structures (Smith *et al.*, 1995; Tapscott, 1996), and analyze information from an infinite number of perspectives that match their learning and analytical styles. Furthermore, it ensures to the authors of such information packets that the intended concepts are delivered as they were intended without having to rely on the user's abstraction capabilities for it to be compiled.

McCraw *et al.* (1995) argue that information technology achieves its highest level of success in the classroom when it is coupled to thematic instruction. In addition, they show that thematic instruction in this context has to be carried out in conjunction with a student-centered teaching style. Student-centered learning, as discussed by Norman and Spohrer (1996), relies on groups of students being engaged in active exploration, construction, and learning through problem solving, rather than in passive consumption of textbook materials.

The purpose of this chapter is to present a case study of the educational use of virtual reality worlds as learning tools in a middle school environment. Instructors used a constructivist approach to present the students with a carefully chosen and delimited problem within a thematic unit. The problem had to be solved around the construction of a virtual environment.

The Context

This project was carried out at the Rice School/La Escuela Rice, in Houston, Texas, as part of a middle school elective course which was taught throughout the spring of 1995. Over 120 students participated in this course, which was team taught by a teacher who specializes in gifted and talented education and by the author. The participants were a part of a multiage group of sixth through eight graders. The objectives of the course were:

- to enhance learning by integrating computer technology into a learner centered environment, through which students could express their constructions of knowledge;

- to enrich children's learning experiences by working cooperatively in a school/university partnership to develop student centered, culturally diverse, developmentally appropriate, and technology integrated curricula;

- to foster child-directed projects using developmentally appropriate software as vehicles for children's engagement in learning; and

- to provide the teacher with an opportunity for professional development through extended interaction with computer technologies integrated into thematic instruction.

The Rice School/La Escuela Rice is a kindergarten through eighth grade school that was set up as a collaboration project between Rice University and the Houston Independent School District. This school is unique because of its tremendous emphasis on computer technology and networking. Every student at the Rice School/La Escuela Rice has a network access, full Internet access through the more than 800 computers deployed throughout the facilities, and an electronic mail account.

Learning and exploration were centered around Galileo Galilei's life. In this collaborative effort between Rice University's Center for Technology in Teaching and Learning (http://cttl.rice.edu) and The Rice School/La Escuela Rice (http://www.rice.edu/armadillo/Rice), students used The Galileo Project (http://www.rice.edu/Galileo) as the starting point for exploration. This extensive World Wide Web resource is an example of the electronic studio concept developed at Rice University. It was created under the direction of Dr. Albert van Helden in an effort to provide users of all ages with a hypertextual information source about Galileo and the science of his time. This resource has successfully been used as a foundation system for undergraduate education at Rice University.

The course, called Galileo's Web (http://www.rice.edu/armadillo/Rice/Galileo), was run like a workshop. Students had access to a variety of learning activities to motivate and engage them in a constructive process. Projects were developed to cover multiple disciplines, and participants had access to a variety of 'off the shelf' technology tools to help them implement their plans. Work was carried out in a variety of learning situations, such as cooperative learning groups, student-teacher collaboration, and independent pursuits. The use of technology in this course was combined with more traditional activities, such as visits from experts in the field and consultation of other media such as books and movies.

The Process

One of the activities carried out in Galileo's Web was a team contest to design a home for Galileo. The design had to take into account this individual's particular needs and the time in which he lived. Winning designs would then be translated into virtual worlds. Even though a blueprint of Galileo's Villa, Il Gioiello, is available on the World Wide Web (http://es.rice.edu/

ES/humsoc/Galileo/Villa/index.html), this information was kept from students so that their designs would not be influenced by exposure to this resource.

The problem presented to the students was similar to one that would be presented to a firm of architects in the real world. In each class of approximately 30 students, teams of five to six people had to be formed. Each team had to design a home suitable for Galileo using the following rules:

- each team member was in charge of designing one of the rooms;

- each team member had to produce a blueprint for a room;

- all rooms had to be drawn using the same scale;

- room·floor plans had to match for door positioning; and

- each team member had to provide a content resource for the room. This resource could be a short paragraph describing the room's usage and purpose. Students could also provide a World Wide Web URL related the purpose of the room (e.g., a URL to an astronomy site describing Jupiter's moons could be supplied with the observatory).

Teams agreed on a common set of rules that would be used in the development of the project. They had to agree on the rooms that they considered to be the most important for this house. Furthermore, they had to agree on a common scale and positioning of elements such as doors, since all the created pieces had to be matched at the end of the project. Their knowledge of Galileo's life and endeavors was essential since it would be reflected in their choice of rooms and in the creation or selection of resources associated with their construction. Because different team members were in charge of different areas of the villa, cooperation and integration were essential to make the final product a seamless creation.

Students worked individually and cooperatively. Computers were assigned to students in two ways, depending on the execution phase that they found themselves in. They were provided with individual access to the World Wide Web when they were gathering resources for the project. However, during the virtual world construction phase, one computer was made available to the team. At this point students had to work together, taking turns in the realization of the project.

The World Wide Web and virtual reality models were used as part of the learning process with the focus not being on technology, but on learning, information processing, content development and concept acquisition. Therefore, students were not subjected to having to learn the VRML coding language. Instead, they used a graphical interface that would produce the code for their creations. Along the way, students moved from a conceptual, abstract world through a two dimensional path to finish in a virtual three dimensional environment.

At the beginning of the process, students held planning sessions to agree on the ground rules of their collaboration. After that they worked individually on the design of the rooms using pencil and paper. Each of them accessed the World Wide Web in search of resources to be associated with the rooms they were building, or used a WYSIWYG HTML editor to write up the content resource. Team members came together again to assemble the set of blueprints and present their project for judging.

The virtual reality worlds were put together using Paragraph International's Virtual Home Space Builder (http://www.paragraph.com). This MS Windows based program uses a graphical interface that allows the user to create virtual reality worlds for distribution over the World Wide Web. One of its more important features is that it allows the student to concentrate on the creative process and content rather than having to deal with a steep learning curve inherent to learning VRML coding. Furthermore, it allows users to assess their work and thought processes by providing immediate graphical feedback about their efforts. The user can create objects, manipulate colors and textures, and place pictures and graphic elements within worlds. It also allows the user to define resources associated with graphic elements and to define World Wide Web links associated with those environments. This program is simple to use, but simplicity comes at a cost. It can only create objects that are derived from blocks. Still, with enough imagination, blocks can be manipulated in numerous ways so that creations can be complex.

Other programs that offer graphical interfaces for the creation of virtual worlds, such as Virtus VRML (http://www.virtus.com) and Pioneer (http://www.caligari.com), were considered because of their power and capabilities. However, Virtual Home Space Builder was chosen because of its ease of use and low hardware requirements.

The Outcome

Over 20 projects were submitted as part of this effort. Designs were judged blind with respect to team members. Four of the designs were translated into virtual worlds (http://www.rice.edu/armadillo/Rice/Galileo/Villa/Worlds). Three of them are one floor dwellings; one has a two level observatory (Figure 1). Solutions were varied with respect to the geometry of the general building layout. All worlds were either colored or textured, and students learned not only how to produce walls, doors and windows, but created items such as tables, chairs, bookshelves and telescopes. All these items were, in one way or another, derived from blocks that were subsequently carved in creative ways. In the process of conception to creation, teams had to adapt to the limitations imposed by the virtual reality tools chosen for this program. Because they designed their villas without prior knowledge of those limitations, blueprints had to be modified. This required students to show flexibility and adaptability to overcome obstacles.

By working in computer generated worlds, students mastered construction skills in very short times and concentrated on the creative aspects of project development rather than spending prolonged times on tasks such as cutting and pasting of cardboard and balsa wood. In addition, this project offered teachers and students the opportunity to become contributors to the global learning community by distributing their projects through the World Wide Web.

At the end of the project, students were happy with the opportunity to have participated in this unique project. Some expressed the desire to extend the process and start on the cre-

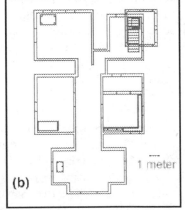

Figure 1. Screen captures of (a) Virtual villa #3 and (b) the modified blueprints of the villa, including scale.

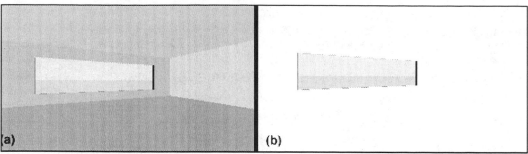

Figure 2. Two screen captures of the same virtual room showing in (a) how shades of gray help in the perception of space and how in a world of no shadows and textures (b) the same space appears as a flat surface.

ation of other virtual worlds. Many realized that a project like this had moved them, in a virtual environment, through a system that closely resembled the process in the real world.

The integration of technology and thematic instruction promoted divergent, creative and critical thinking in this group. In the process of developing a virtual world students developed skills and learned concepts in individual ways. Nevertheless, cooperation, the application of mathematical skills, the acquisition of knowledge related to the history of science and astronomy, conflict resolution and project development were all part of a common foundation acquired. Furthermore, virtual worlds allowed students to explore concepts that would not have been easily accessible, if at all, in the classroom. They were able to explore relationships in space, explore the effects of shading and light, and key elements in our ability to perceive three dimensions (Figure 2). Virtual reality constructions also fostered experimentation since students could engage in building and removal of walls at the touch of a key, and could design without the limits imposed by the laws of gravity.

One of the goals behind the development of projects like this is to create a reusable educational resources. Reuse can come from teaching the same units again or from using the same tools and gained experiences to rapidly prototype similar courses. We are currently examining the application of virtual worlds in units built around the Mayan civilization, the Egyptian pyramids, and the solar system. All of these themes have a multidisciplinary appeal that make them perfect for a constructivist, student centered learning system.

Negroponte (1995) states that one of the ideas behind virtual reality "is to deliver the sense of being there." In this project, participating students could have gained a lot by just being there and visiting Galileo's virtual villa (http://www.rice.edu/armadillo/Rice/Galileo/Villa/Worlds/Oldvilla/galileo.wrl). However, they gained more by constructing it. To use another Negroponte (1994) directive, students did not dissect it, they built it.

Acknowledgments

I would like to express my gratitude to The Rice School/La Escuela Rice and in particular to Kathy Heath, a special projects teacher at the Rice School/La Escuela Rice, for her help, cooperation and patience during this process and for allowing me to work with her students. Dina Montúfar-Solís and Leslie Miller read the initial manuscript and helped to greatly improve it. This project was made possible thanks to Compaq Computer's generous donation of 1,100 computers to The Rice School/La Escuela Rice.

References

McCraw, P. A., Meyer, J. E., & Tompkins, R. S. (1995). Technology integration and thematic instruction in a school/university partnership. *Journal of Computing in Childhood Education, 6*(1), 43–57.

Negroponte, N. (1994). Learning by doing: Don't dissect the frog, build it. *Wired, 2*(7).

Negroponte, N. (1995). *Being digital*. New York: Alfred A. Knopf.

Norman, D. A. & Spohrer, J. C. (1996). Learner-centered education. *Communications of the ACM, 39*(4), 24–27.

Smith, D., Boyd, R. & Scott, A. (1995). *Virtus VRML toolkit*. Indianapolis: Hayden Books.

Soloway, E. & Pryor, A. (1996). The next generation in human-computer interaction. *Communications of the ACM, 39*(4),16–18.

Tapscott, D. (1996). *Digital economy: Promise and peril in the age of network intelligence*. New York: McGraw-Hill.

The Author

Carlos R. Solís is with the Center for Technology in Teaching and Learning, Rice University, Houston, Texas.

e-mail, World Wide Web
solis@rice.edu
http://www.rice.edu/~solis

53

Virtual Experiments and Group Tasks in a Web-Based Collaborative Course in Introductory Electronics

Lucio Teles and Tim Collings

Introduction

This chapter discusses the design of an online version of an introductory course in electronics offered by the Department of Engineering Science, Simon Fraser University. The course is delivered on Virtual-U, a Web-based conferencing system for educational applications. Students can access a "virtual lab" and conduct group work to develop competence in introductory electronics.

As the campus student population increases, the existing lab cannot accommodate the growth and give all students lab time to do experiments. At the same time, the Department of Engineering Science makes ENSC 125 available to transfer students, those who come from other colleges and typically need the prerequisite skills taught in ENSC 125.

ENSC 125, Electronics I, is a prerequisite course which currently is offered only on campus with face-to-face course sessions and individual hands-on work in the laboratory to conduct experiments and explore the use of electronic equipment. Every week, students have three one-hour lectures and regular hands-on work in the electronics lab.

These issues led the instructor of ENSC 125 to explore the option of offering a Web-based version of the course as an alternative to the physical lab through virtual instrumentation in an "online lab." The concept of "virtual labs," where students analyze, simulate, and test basic electronic circuits, promises to enhance the course and to reach additional off-campus students. Collaborative tasks should foster the development of teamwork practices, a needed skill for a professional engineer. The software used for the delivery is Virtual-U, developed at Simon Fraser University.

The Virtual-U Web-Based Conferencing System

Virtual-U is a World Wide Web-based application customized for the design, delivery, and enhancement of post-secondary education. The main goal is to provide a flexible framework to support advanced pedagogies based on principles of active learning, collaboration, multiple perspectives, and knowledge building (Harasim, Calvert, & Groeneboer, 1996).

Virtual-U operates on an Internet network browser and offers asynchronous communication features to allow participants to contribute at their most convenient time, overcoming constraints of time and distance. Virtual-U has the core functionality of a computer conferencing system (VGroups) for asynchronous delivery and has tools to facilitate the instructor's task: Course Structuring Tool, GradeBook, and System Administration Tools.

The Course Structuring tool allows educators to design complete courses and put them online. The course template that is created includes instructor's information such as office hours and e-mail address, course syllabus and timetable, and activities such as readings, assignments, and tests.

The VGroups conferencing system allows the instructor to create conferences or sub-conferences, to define the subject, structure, and participants for each conference, to allow students to take on roles as moderators, participants, or observers, and to insert multimedia elements such as video and animation into messages.

The GradeBook manages students' grades for each course delivered with Virtual-U. When a course is submitted, a GradeBook database is automatically created with a class list of students and all of the assignments and tests to be completed during the term. Grades can be entered and edited. The GradeBook displays customizable color charts of student and class performance, supports quantitative and qualitative grades, and offers encryption security to protect sensitive information.

The System Administration Tools assist system administrators in installing and maintaining the Virtual-U Education System for functions such as creating and maintaining accounts, defining access privileges, creating courses, and keeping usage statistics. As Virtual-U runs on the Web, it works with plug-ins and home pages that enhance its functionality.

The goal of the Virtual-U software is to enable educational practices for knowledge building through group work, the support of the instructor and peers, and active individual work.

Engineering Science 125: Introductory Electronics

ENSC 125 is an introduction to electronics and covers topics such as properties of electrical circuits, frequency response, properties of LCR circuits, diodes, transistors, fundamentals of electrical measurements of non electrical quantities, transduction theory, and instrumentation. ENSC 125 is a prerequisite for course ENSC 222-5, Electronic Design I.

ENSC 125 is offered to both transfer and first year students who enter the Department's program. Students take ENSC 125 in their first year to have an introduction to analysis and design, as well as a stronger preparation for the first co-op work term. Students are given 24-hour lab access to pursue projects that are more open-ended and less structured than those in traditional schools.

Learning with Virtual Instrumentation and Collaboration: Pedagogy and Activities

The combination of self-directed learning, peer collaboration, lab experimentation, and instructors' support is a powerful model that relies on "learning by doing" with an active hands-on component. This model is a form of "situated learning," as the context is identified as playing a major role in the knowledge building process.

Brown, Collins, and Duguid (1989) developed the concept of situated learning to emphasize the role of the context, the activity, and the culture in the production of knowledge:

> For centuries, the epistemology that has guided educational practice has concentrated primarily on conceptual representations and made its relation to objects in the world problematic by assuming that, cognitively, representation is prior to all else. A theory of situated cognition suggests that activity and perception are importantly and epistemologically prior—at a conceptual level—to conceptualization and that it is on them that more atten-

tion needs to be focused. An epistemology that begins with activity and perception, which are first and foremost embedded in the world, may simply bypass the classical problem of reference—of mediating conceptual representations. (p. 41)

The collaborative social interaction that takes place in the appropriate context promotes learning:

> Learning, both outside and inside school, advances through collaborative social interaction and the social construction of knowledge . . . Throughout most of their lives people learn and work collaboratively, not individually, as they are asked to do in many schools. (p. 40)

The new design for ENSC 125 supports the concept of situated learning, which is implemented through exploration and experimentation in "virtual labs" where students explore the same concepts and experiments through "virtual instrumentation" and share results with peers and the instructor.

Students use a collaborative approach and rely on peers to obtain support via computer conferencing and e-mail. Through the system, students can access peers and electronics experts, or search through various remote databases for information.

The additional software packages, Electronics Workbench and MathCad, allow students to complete their assignments in virtual experiments.

Course Design

Students taking ENSC 125 have the following requirements: They need access to a computer that runs Netscape 2.0 or above, a minimum of 14.400 modem, access to Netscape, and an Internet account. In addition, they need the Electronics WorkBench and MathCad software packages.

ENSC 125 Online is composed of 14 conferences, each with a specific purpose: Social, Team, MathCad, EWB, Week 2, Week 3, Week 4, Week 5, Week 6, Week 7, Week 8, Week 9, Week 10, and Exam.

Each session was named after the week (Week 6, 7, 8, etc.), and each week's conference has a Theory and a Practice subconferences. Students use FTP to post their assignment files (EWB and MathCad) to a site where they are downloaded by peers and the instructor.

Students are expected to log on many times a week to contribute to the discussion, to respond to questions, and to pose new questions. The final exam is conducted face-to-face, and proctors are used for those students who can not come to campus.

The Virtual Experiment

The new design provides students with the tools to complete assignments in a "virtual lab" environment using software for circuit analysis (MathCAD), circuit simulation (Electronics WorkBench), and circuit prototyping (LabLink). Using LabLink, the student constructs the circuit and tests it using "virtual instrumentation" running on the host computer that is connected to the real circuit through a hardware applications interface. Students are encouraged, at the end of the course, to build the circuits and test them using real equipment found on a traditional electronics lab bench.

Collaborative Tasks

Some of the tasks given to students are based on collaboration and information sharing as students share assignments, insights into their weekly experiments, and pose questions to their peers based on the weekly virtual lab experiment.

Implications for Design and Research

This new instructional and delivery model raises new questions which need to be investigated: how does virtual learning compare with the traditional face-to-face classroom learning, what are the implications of using "virtual instrumentation" compared to instrumentation in the campus lab, what is the role of peer learning and collaboration in virtual environments, and what are the best instructional designs to explore the potentials of this new technology for learning?

References

Brown, J., Collins, A., & Duguid, P. (1989). Situated cognition and the culture of learning. *Educational Researcher, 18*(1), 32–42.

Collings, T. (1994). *Basic electronics engineering.* Burnaby: Department of Engineering Science, Simon Fraser University.

Harasim, L., Calvert, T., & Groeneboer, C. (1996). Virtual-U: A Web-based environment to support collaborative learning and knowledge building in post secondary courses. Unpublished.

Harasim, L., & Teles, L. (1994). Interactive group learning using communication networks. In A. Stahmer, L. Van den Brande, & T. Rivet (Eds.), *The Canada-European Union Workshop on New Media Learning Technologies: Perspectives on developing an international collaborative learning for flexible and distance learning.* Ottawa: The Canada-European Union Workshop.

Hiltz, R. (1994). *The virtual classroom.* Norwood, NJ: Ablex.

Teles, L., & Laks, A. (1993). The virtual interactive environment for workgroups: A broadband educational application. *Proceedings of Multimedia Communications 93*, University of British Columbia.

The Authors

Lucio Teles is Co-Director, University Centre for Network Learning, Simon Fraser University, British Columbia, Canada.

e-mail, World Wide Web
teles@sfu.ca
http://www.cde.sfu.ca/teles

Tim Collings is with the Department of Engineering Sciences, Simon Fraser University, British Columbia, Canada.

e-mail
collings@cs.sfu.ca

54

The Use of the World Wide Web in Teaching Foreign Languages

Kathryn A. Murphy-Judy

Introduction

FACT #1: However much English dominates as the language of information delivery on the World Wide Web, it remains a fact that the Web is global and functions multilingually. (Look at *http://info.isoc.org:80/images/mapv14.gif* for a map of Internet use in the world.)

FACT #2: The Web promotes self-instruction. One example: Despite scores of books on HTML and Web design available in stores and libraries, all one needs to know in order to get started and to progress from neophyte to expert is on the Web already. (See *http://www.eff.org/papers/eegtti/eegttitop.html* for a list.)

Do these two Web facts intersect? Is it currently possible to learn enough about a foreign language on the Web to be able to access and use information in a non-native language? If not, is it possible to construct effective language acquisition sites geared to that purpose? And finally, is the Web or, for that matter, any other electronic medium, appropriate to language learning and acquisition? The intent of this writing is not to posit definitive answers, but rather to suggest possible directions in thinking about these questions and, perhaps more importantly, to offer strategies for gaining access to the multilingual riches of the Web and using it in pedagogically sound ways.

Most Web sites are written in the developer's language of choice; they are not intended for foreign language instruction. There is, as well, a growing number of sites specifically designed to foster Foreign Language (FL) education. Such sites include dictionaries, grammar instruction, and testing, as well as elaborate acquisition activities and feedback. One can also find a plethora of listings of language-specific sites. Whether intentionally designed for language learning or not, they all provide a wealth of language education materials *but only* once inserted into a carefully prepared learning environment. The thrust of this article targets the types of preparation that lead to sound language instruction.

In order to use Web materials effectively, the user (a teacher or a self-directed learner) has to have a clear idea of how one goes about learning a second language and the use to which such learning will eventually be put. Foreign language education runs the gamut between meta-learning about the language (meta-grammar, philology, lexicography, for example), which FL educators refer to as "learning," and using the language for communication, called "acquisition." Few sites are designed to assess learning styles, degree and types of previous knowledge, and motivational factors, and therefore do not provide learners with guideposts to second language learning or acquisition (see my site: http://www.fln.vcu.edu/Intensive/LearningStrategies.html). For the moment, then, the Web does not yet provide the fundamental pedagogical resources for completely self-directed language education.

Good foreign language sites and preparatory materials take certain learning factors into account. In current foreign language education, five skills are set forth as both the modes of communication and the competencies that a language user must acquire. The skills are: listening, reading, writing, speaking, and cultural knowledge. Proficiency in these skills is determined according to the standards developed by the American Congress of Teachers of Foreign Languages (ACTFL). They are: novice, intermediate, advanced, superior. Sites should be prepared to target one or more of the five skills at a given proficiency level. Furthermore, the learner should be allowed a choice of sites from which to learn/acquire the language in various learning styles (global/analytic; auditory/visual/tactual, for example).

Below is an overview of the types of sites and activities that can be configured to promote foreign language education in each of the five skills. I have included general ideas for preparing the materials either in class or as a Web-based assignment. Basically, they stress the notion that any learning activity in a skill needs a pre-task work-up, followed by the task, and ending with assessment or enrichment activities.

Reading

Most Web information is currently text-based. Reading, therefore, is the primary skill that one can hone on the Web. Still, preparing students for texts and texts for students is critical. The preparatory materials need to respond to a learner's proficiency level such that the reading stretches the learner to $i + 1$ (Krashen's formula for language acquisition, where i = the learner's current language proficiency status and $i + 1$ is just beyond her grasp). Pre-reading activities may be Web-based (Web searches in the thematic area of the reading, searches for and discussion of images that provide background for the reading) or classroom activities like in-class discussion and vocabulary work-ups, presentation of some of the more difficult sentences, film clips, overhead projections, or the dissection of the problematic grammatical and syntactical elements. Such orientations can be (re)iterated on a Web page introduction that contains a link to the actual reading.

Reading theory in Second Language Acquisition (SLA) supports a concurrent top-down and bottom-up approach to reading strategies (Alderson & Urquhart). Such an approach provides a global and an analytic learning process. By using both, the learner is afforded easy access to new material through her dominant learning style and reinforcement through the other.

As part of the process of reading, the learner should be aware of the variety of reading strategies. He or she should also have online access to reading aids (dictionaries, grammars, notes), but should be encouraged to progress through the reading with as few digressions as possible. There is evidence to support the theory that listening to recordings while reading improves listening and speaking skills and may facilitate understanding and retention for auditory learners (Carbo, Dunn, & Dunn, 1986). Thus, access to simultaneous oral renditions of the text may stimulate all-around language acquisition for some learners. Note that this is not the case for all learners. Recordings can be delivered by audio cassette or accessed on screen from a digital audio file. The learner/teacher needs to weigh the complication of running two different machines (computer and cassette player) with the time it takes to load digital audio files in order to decide which medium is most appropriate and efficient for the immediate learning situation.

Besides cognitive and psycholinguist concerns, the teacher/learner needs to keep certain physical factors in mind. Some learners have a hard time reading computer screens (it has to do with the ocular neuroreceptor's reaction to backlit screens); they might be encouraged to make a paper copy and to read from it, keeping the computer alongside for the interactive help. Other disturbing factors can be the temperature of the room and the ambient lighting (Carbo *et al.*, 1986). It has been my experience in teaching in a computer lab situation for three years that cold temperatures (a frequent status given the need to keep the computers cool) and excessive heat (besides damaging to the machines) can prevent learning in even the best laid lessons.

Once the reading is accomplished, it is time to determine what the learner has understood from the reading and to underscore specific details of the text. This can be accomplished through Web forms (cloze exercises, multi-choice questions), discussion, further tasks that depend upon a specific understanding of the text, an essay, or other written testing.

Writing

Writing involves different preparatory strategies but maximizes the interactivity of the Web. Through the use of forms and e-mail, students can submit short texts to the teacher, fellow students, specialists in some field, or native speakers. Elsewhere, there are chat sessions (like the Internet Relay Chat or cgi/JavaScript run chat groups), MOOs (MUD Object Oriented), and MUDs (Multi-User Domains). The teacher can also set up long-term projects for which students create their own Web sites in the target language or contribute to a class Web project. Through process writing, the learners eventually produce a quality writing sample worth Web exposure. It is important to organize feedback so that students learn to edit their own drafts. If the student's writing is not directly addressed to the teacher, for example, e-mailing to other students or a native speaker, the teacher can request that she be cc'd. Then again, not all writing has to be corrected; research on the use of Daedalus has shown that task of writing by itself engages the learner in articulation in the target language, which then promotes language acquisition.

Listening

To improve listening skills, one can engage in listening comprehension over the Web. The quality of sound files, however, needs to be assessed by the instructor, especially since the contextualization of face-to-face speech or video may be lacking. The Web allows both audio files and full motion video. Such files, once prepared through pre-listening activities, can be downloaded and used in listening tasks. The teacher should keep in mind that audio and video downloads are often time-consuming. Students can be assigned their pre-listening work while the file(s) are downloading, or given some other activity during that time.

Speaking

And, finally, regarding speaking, the Web is not yet a wonderful locus for live discussion. Nevertheless, the technology is there (CU-SeeME, for example) and eventually will be a staple in our teaching toolbox (Crogger, 1994). In the meantime, what teachers can do to encourage oral skill production is to design activities in the other skills such that students work together in pairs or teams. This way learners approach the material in the target language and often will find it too difficult to switch between languages. All Web work can be prepared or followed up by discussions, oral presentations, role-playing, or question and answer sessions. Through proper classroom/lab logistics and lesson preparation, all Web materials can (and should) be used to stimulate classroom discussion and interactions in the target language.

The Future of Foreign Language Education on the Web

What still needs to be done is for an omnibus production group to develop a vast integrating site that allows the teacher or learner to select from a menu of options (proficiency level, skill, grammatical function, lexical arena, learning style proclivity) in order to discover and use materials. Each lesson would contain pedagogical hints and strategies. Directions for tasks would serve self-paced learning and learners could even choose a path through the materials based on responses to a series of learning level and style instruments. Eventually learners could learn in virtual classrooms, teaming up with learners and teachers from across the globe. (For the beginnings of such a group, see http://www.fln.vcu/FLOWWW/home.html).

The Web bases of multilingualism and self-directed learning do, indeed, intersect. At this moment I would say that it is not possible to learn enough of a foreign language on the Web to become proficient in anything beside reading. This status, however, given the infancy and current limitations of the Web, is not insurmountable. As facilities and delivery improve, it will become simple to offer comprehensive language instruction over the Web.

A caveat: Language acquisition even over the Web entails interactions with live language acquisition professionals. Furthermore, language is dialogic; it is in constant flux as are its users and learners. There will never be a time when the various sites will not need re-thinking, re-working, and updating.

For more information on these topics, please consult:

http://www.fln.vcu/FLOWWW/home.html

http://www.fln.vcu/SLAT/home.html

http://www.fln.vcu.edu.edu/murphy-judy/FR500s96.html#readFrench

http://www.fln.vcu.edu/murphy-judy/FRE500/summer/ReadGenesis.html

References

Alderson, J. C., & Urquhart, A. H. (Eds). (1984). *Reading in a foreign language*. New York: Longman.

Carbo, M., Dunn, K., & Dunn, R. (1986) *Teaching students to read through their individual learning styles*. Englewood Cliffs, NJ: Prentice-Hall.

Crogger, R. (1994, July/Aug.) On the Internet: CU-SeeMe video conferencing over the Internet. *Syllabus*, 3(7), p. 22.

Dixon, R. (1992). *The strategies of the successful listener: Classroom implications*. ERIC: ED 345 553.

Krashen, S. D. (1985). *The input hypothesis: Issues and implications*. New York: Longman.

The Author:

Kathryn A. Murphy-Judy is Assistant Professor, Department of Foreign Languages, Virginia Commonwealth University, Richmond, Virginia.

e-mail, World Wide Web
   kmurphy@cabell.vcu.edu
   http://www.fln.vcu/faculty/kmj.html

55

Interactive World Wide Web-Based Courseware

Peter A. Santi

Introduction

The Internet is quickly becoming an inexpensive and reliable source of information for students and instructors. The preferred method for Internet navigation is by World Wide Web browsers such as Netscape and Internet Explorer. These browsers allow users to obtain information from eye-pleasing text and graphical images called Web pages. Web-based instruction (WBI) is an attractive medium for delivering information to students; however, its present major limitation is its lack of interactivity. The purpose of this chapter is to describe one implementation of threaded discussion forums and a chat room for WBI using the Interaction conferencing software (http://www.ifi.uio.no/~terjen/interaction/).

Course Overview

This course is an honors level, 2-credit colloquium called "Animal Research for Human Health" and will be offered in the 1996, Fall quarter at the University of Minnesota. The purpose of the colloquium is to examine issues concerning the use of animals for biomedical research. The class meets as a group for one hour a week and over the Internet for five hours a week. Class materials include a syllabus, study guide, and a computer user account for access to the course and the Internet.

The Web pages were developed using Adobe PageMill software. The course runs on an Apple Power Macintosh 7100 computer using the Webstar World Wide Web server, and the discussion forums and a chat room are provided by Interaction software. Development and maintenance of the World Wide Web aspects of this course are well within the capabilities of a computer-literate but non-programmer instructor.

The basic structure of the class consists of the presentation of new topics every week by the instructor in class. Each topic is further explored by the student through hypertext links to supplementary information on the course Web pages. During the week, students read the hypertext material and participate in a discussion forum that the instructor has created relating to the topic. During the first part of the following class period, the students demonstrate that they have learned the material in sufficient detail by taking a short written quiz. This is followed by a summary discussion of the previous week's topic and then concludes with an introduction to the next week's topic. The final requirement of the class is a written position or analysis paper, using information obtained from the Web.

Course Contents

A portion of the first class period is devoted to accessing and using the course and the Internet. Fortunately, the University of Minnesota provides all new students with an orientation session that describes Internet browsing and e-mail. The course materials include a course syllabus, study guide, and Web pages.

The course syllabus includes the course title, credits, prerequisites, assignments, and grading policy. This information is also posted on a Web page, and for many Internet classes presently on the Web, this is the extent of the Internet part of the class. However, Web pages containing only the class syllabus should not be considered WBI.

The course study guide contains the instructor's background and e-mail address, location and availability of computer laboratories, how to access and use the World Wide Web and the course, course objectives, suggestions on how to successfully complete the course, assignments, grading, and printouts of the Web pages for each lesson. The study guide also contains space so that the student can write notes about the hypertext link reading material necessary for completing the learning objectives of the unit and pass the classroom quiz. A major advantage of using hypertext links for information is that it need not be copied and distributed to each student. The major disadvantage is that not all the information needed for a course is available through hypertext links. However, this is rapidly changing as authors make more of their information available by publishing it on the World Wide Web. The study guide is also posted on a Web page so that students can refer to this material online.

The Web pages covering each week's topic include the title, objectives/tasks to be learned, an introduction to the topic, hypertext links to information, a discussion forum for that topic, and access to a course chat room. In order to coincide with the classroom experience, each new topic will be posted weekly, rather than all at once. One Web page will be devoted to ideas and hypertext links for preparation of the final position or analysis paper.

Interactivity

The Web pages also provide a means for the instructor, students, and experts at distant locations to interact. Two levels of interactivity are provided: discussion forums and an informal chat room.

Each week the Web page contains a case study that is related to the topic. Each student is required to post at least one comment to the discussion forum concerning the case study. The case study always proposes a question that cannot be answered simply and requires knowledge and analysis of the topic. Guest experts are also encouraged to read and post comments in the discussion forum. As each participant's comment on the case study is posted on the Web page, the student's understanding and the knowledge base of the course is enriched. It is suggested that each student post his or her comment on the case study after reading other comments posted to the forum to avoid redundancy. Class participants are free to write as many comments on the case study or on other participants' comments as they wish. Although the software allows the forums to be moderated by the instructor before they are posted, it is hoped that this will not be necessary. After the comments are posted to the forum, editing or deletion of the comments can only be done by the instructor.

Since this has been designated as a private member's forum, each participant must log in to the forum with a valid user name in order to be able to read and write comments. The participant's user name will be automatically added to the discussion forum comment for author identification. However, a participant may initially choose a username (known to the instructor) to allow him/her to express his or her ideas more freely to other participants. This is particularly important if the person feels that his or her viewpoint is a minority opinion.

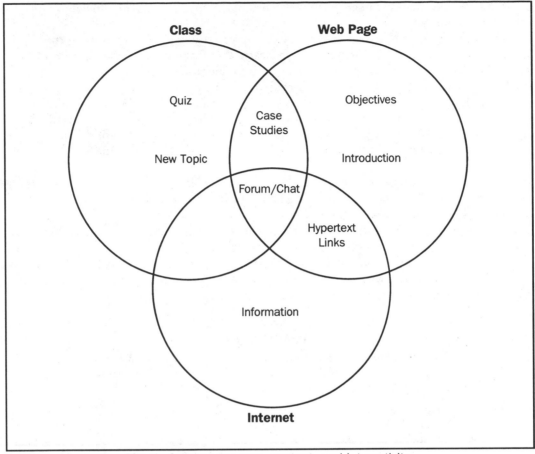

Fig. 1. Course structure, content, and interactivity.

Another form of interactivity among the class participants is through the informal chat room. In contrast to the discussion forums, which relate to a specific topic, there is a single class chat room. Because the chat room can be updated at regular, frequent intervals over the Web, it is possible for participants to engage in text-based "conversations" about the course when both participants are both "logged-in" at the same time. These conversations are written to the chat room sequentially as they are received, even if more than one participant is conversing. Although this may be confusing for some participants, it does allow for the possibility of pseudo, real-time question and answer sessions. It remains to be determined by experience whether the chat room offers a substantial benefit to the course. The course structure, contents, and interactivity are summarized in the following figure (Figure 1).

Final Paper

One of the greatest assets of the World Wide Web is the availability of a vast amount of information that had either been unavailable or difficult to obtain. On the negative side, much of the information on the Web is of dubious quality, since it has not been peer-reviewed and it may exist only temporarily. However, using World Wide Web browsers, students can collect information from reliable sources, such as the state and federal government and trade publications. This information can be quickly searched, filtered, and compiled into a new and useful document.

Two examples of class papers that could only practically be produced using the World Wide Web are described. The first example concerns the tracking of a Minnesota State Legislature bill which seeks to prevent the use of animals for biomedical research/education. The animals are usually dogs and cats that have been seized by animal control officers and are scheduled for euthanasia. The Minnesota State Government has developed Web pages (http://www.leg.state.mn.us/) that allow a user to track the passage of any bill through the House and Senate. Without access to this information provided on the World Wide Web, a student would have to make one or more trips to several state offices in order to compile the information for the paper.

The second example concerns a search of a newspaper archive for articles concerning animal rights activities at the University of Minnesota. The student newspaper, the Minnesota Daily, has provided a search engine and public access to its archives (http://www.daily.umn.edu/~online/). A student could determine a variety of facts about these activities, such as: the number of total articles, the number of articles/year, the peak year, and whether the articles favor, oppose, or present balanced views on the use of animals in biomedical research. Again, without the information being available on the Web, this paper would require considerably more time and effort to produce.

The Author

Peter A. Santi is Professor, Otolaryngology and Neuroscience, University of Minnesota, Minneapolis, Minnesota.

e-mail, World Wide Web
  santip@maroon.tc.umn.edu
  http://lions.oto.umn.edu/animal/arhh.html
  http://lions.oto.umn.edu/calhp/default.html

56

Teaching Literature on the World Wide Web

D a v i d   D o w l i n g

"Not many creatures can spin webs. Even men aren't as good at it as spiders, although they think they're pretty good and they'll try anything."

(E. B. White, *Charlotte's Web*, 1952; New York: HarperCollins, 1980, p. 60)

It's no good doing a Web search for my subject, because you'll turn up 680,614 entries for webs on Lycos, and 16,513 for spiders. There is an etymological as well as an entomological link between spiders and texts, because a text is literally something 'woven' (from the Latin texere, to weave), so my dictionary gives the first definition of "texture" as "the process or art of weaving." But here is where the analogy becomes unhelpful. A spider weaves a web out of its own being, and then waits for something to be caught in that web. Then it eats it. But when we use the World Wide Web, we are the visitors. Does this mean we will get eaten? To stay alive on the Web as a visitor (if that's possible) is to follow systems not our own. The Web is composed of linked nodes, and both the nodes and their links have been made by someone else. We are enmeshed at every point: As in a supermarket, our choices as 'free consumers' are only between the products someone else has chosen to put on the shelves. Our only real choice is whether to stay in the store—on the Web—or leave. But we can't not stay stuck on the Web, because what constitutes those spaces in the Web, the territory on either side of the information highway? It's a void, and if we fall into it, we fall through the net and through the cracks, out of the system—we wipe out. So it's not for nothing that the searcher Lycos chose a spider which doesn't use a web at all but runs around on the ground. 'Webcrawler's' little beast starts to look decidedly uncomfortable, perching on its surfboard with magnifying glass in hand, because it can only examine (and for how long?) what is in front of its nose, where the wave or the link is taking it. As a metaphor for knowledge acquisition, then, this cluster of images is very unsatisfactory. The user is no spider, the galaxy of sites no web. Only by shifting our paradigm of web and searcher/spider can we usefully approach the subject of teaching on the Web.

When Vannevar Bush wrote the seminal essay on hypertext in 1945, he had a rudimentary 'information retrieval' model in mind: "One cannot hope thus to equal the speed and flexibility with which the mind follows an associative trail, but it should be possible to beat the mind decisively in regard to the permanence and clarity of the items resurrected from storage" (Bush, 1945). But as Frank Smith observes, "Information theory loses its utility once we get inside the head" (Smith, 1988, p. 247) because the brain makes shapes out of these bits of information. Because knowledge involves seeing patterns or theories from above (if only temporarily), 'hypertext' seems to me an appropriate language and concept by which to create Web-based instructional programs. As educators, we try to enhance the mind's capacity to work associatively, to create, and to feel. We try to affect what Bush calls the "intricate web of trails carried by the cells of the brain." The question is: Can we spin good webs on the computer to enhance the webs in our brains—webs that are more than playgrounds on the one hand, and filing cabinets on the other? Especially when, as Laurillard notes, "The display of a network makes it explicit but does not make it known. The student still has to do a great deal of work to internalize its structure and interpret its meaning, just as they do with the implicit structure of text" (Laurillard, 1993, p. 124). I believe there are ways, but we must become 'spin doctors' to create them.

Unfortunately, there is a simplistic but widespread fear about computers, that they "strengthen the belief that objective data is, in fact, knowledge, and cannot express the tacit (in Polanyi's sense) as opposed to the explicit dimensions of knowledge. Those aspects of knowledge and knowing that cannot be organized into discrete components cannot be programmed" (Benyon & Mackay, 1993). Even so strong an advocate for hypertextuality in English literature studies as George Landow has to acknowledge "the tendency of hypertext to atomize documents into separate lexias..." (Landow, 1994, p. 15). It is understandable that a non-performative epistemology would see computers as running aground on this reef of compartmentalization. But by careful programming which takes full account of time and space, Polanyi's 'tacit' knowledge or the 'halo' of significance can be evoked on screen—and along with it, rich reading experiences. The metaphor I would like to use is a different kind of web, one which is curved around areas of significance—fields of force, if you like—where clusters of ideas and relationships are held in resonance and comprise a useful if temporary 'home' for a student to explore. The web is temporarily warped around a concept to form a context. This is my image of the 'hyper-environments' which Cumming and Sinclair (1991) say are "needed in schools," and which will result from our careful conceptual architecture: "for writers of the new dialogue, the task will be to build, in place of a single argument, a structure of possibilities" (Bolter, 1991, p. 117).

Much thinking about computer literacy these days tends to valorize the performative aspects of the screen user or manipulator. There's a lot more to do than just turning pages, what with all those buttons to push, and icons to click. Books like Brenda Laurel's *Computers as Theater* (1992) have already popularized this aspect of computer literacy. I act, and the 'computer' acts back—this involvement is of a different order from mere 'entertainment,' a word whose etymology betrays its essential quality of "holding" one "between" oneself and something else. Ryan (1994) theorizes that by planning the computer interface carefully, we might avoid placing the user in this limbo-land of 'holding between.' Instead, we might orchestrate a movement or dance between the user's immersion in the program ('doing') and the user's ability to step back and interact with it ('knowing what you're doing'): "These modes of interactivity have yet to solve the problem of design, but they point the way toward a solution of the conflict between immersion and interactivity: turn language into a dramatic performance, into the expression of a bodily mode of being in the world."

The sense of the computer as the other player must therefore be taken into account at the most fundamental level when one creates a hypertext. Good design is based on knowledge of how the human eye and brain take in information. As McLuhan (1994) says, "The effects of technology do not occur at the level of opinions or concepts, but alter sense ratios or patterns of perception steadily and without any resistance. The serious artist is the only person able to counter technology with impunity, just because he is an expert aware of the changes in sense perception" (p. 18). Derrick de Kerckhove (1995) argues that children habituated to watching television see differently from literate children: "They seem to glance at things, looking at them several times as if they were compiling a picture to make sense of the page" (p. 15). Since most of us are television watchers, how are we conditioned to seek for information on a computer screen? How do we reconcile our print and visual literacies? What makes a full screen an effective screen?

There are some fairly obvious rules here, such as the difference between how and what we see at the center of a computer screen, and at the edges of our peripheral vision. The apparently trivial choice between a 'dissolve' or an 'iris close' transition to another screen, for example, can be crucial to that moment in a student's reading experience when he or she is deciding its sense or its penetrability. The 'dissolve' suggests a close connection between two different screens by making one screen of text fade out and into the next, while an 'iris close' makes the contents of the screen appear to be swallowed up by the next screen. As well as carrying a heavy semiotic load, the time taken for the shift to happen may be designed so that it is exactly the number of seconds required for the brain to 'chunk' a unit of information, since "the chunk capacity of short term memory has been shown to be in the range of five to seven. Fixation of information in long term memory has been shown to take about five or ten seconds per chunk" (Simon, 1989, p. 221). This temporal dimension should always be an aspect of reading as performance, which is programmed into the software. For example, while HyperCard may be slower than some other applications, those very pauses between operations can become essential spaces in which the critical activity can take place—in the user's mind, rather than on screen (Dowling, 1992, p. 180). The learning experience is just that, an experience as much in time as in space. The grasping of a principle involves negotiating the dissonance or conceptual space between one site and another, until you can 'see' the sites by sensing their relative positions. 'Understanding' means knowing what you're standing under, not being lost in cyberspace. A simple example is teaching the fact that the last stanza of Blake's "The Tyger" is the same as the first, with the exception of one word. In my program, a student can click a button which activates the first stanza so that it slips across the page and slots into position at the end of the poem, bottom right (the single word, "can," winks as it finally changes to "dare"). This exercise in time and space conveys the dramatic effect of Blake's almost-repetition far more vividly than my telling the student that this is the case. The movement from one site to another, the disclosure of what was imminent, can promote an experience which is in no way 'thinned out' in space or time.

These principles can also work with longer texts. Students have difficulty conceiving of a novel as a unified machine with a structure, but provided they are willing to read a long text on screen (which has its own challenges of convenience and visual comfort), we can devise strategies which will lead the student to become familiar enough with the landscape of a novel to test his or her reading against other possibilities, and against various markers in the text which may have been missed. The computer's resources can help us to lead a student to experience the text's power because, as Riffaterre (1994) has argued, the hallmark of complex literature is that it actually delimits choice rather than expands it: "intertextuality, a structured network of text-generated constraints on the reader's perceptions, is the exact contrary of the reader-generated loose web of free associations that is hypertextuality" (p. 781). This is not to say that the 'meaning' is transparent, but rather that meaning is generated by a vivid and vibrant oscillation between various established points. That oscillation may be momentarily 'spelled out' for the student by a hypertextual gloss or maneuver, which "underscores the main point(s) of the text by making explicit those data that are only implied or presupposed by the text, thus defining their relevance" (p. 786). By marking up or dramatizing the text in this way, we encourage the student to both create and critique what Wilde (1981) calls the "horizon of assent," or the shifting boundary of possible outcomes of the story. As in more sophisticated computer games, the student's own responses should feed back and modify the range of future commentaries available: "Computers can be programmed so that 'facts' retrieved in one window on a screen will automatically cause supporting and opposing arguments to be retrieved in a halo of surrounding windows" (Kay, 1995, p. 155). As programmers, we can encourage more complex maneuvering within the text and between the text and other files, so that users may approach the more complex knowledge which comes from an oscillation or reverberation between possible meanings. Our technology may not yet allow us to create these half meanings or tentative linkages that are involved in more complex meanings, but Ryan's idea of a theater of instruction remains a useful ideal. For example, we can pre-construct hypertexts with virtual communities of interpreters. A user can then select one of these personae and follow that character's adventures with the text, thereby getting a sense of someone else's force-field, or arrangement of the web of possible significance. Figure 1 shows how I arranged this for my Blake project. Each stanza of the poem is surrounded by the students, as if sitting at their desks in a seminar room. There is an empty chair, where the user may choose to sit and join in. Elsewhere in the program these students have introduced themselves, their beliefs, their workstations, what their rooms look like, and so on. Here they are making comments on the text, either in class (indicated by the raised hand) or privately to themselves (some of them are shy!). Clicking on those icons takes you to their notes, which may consist of quotations from library books with their own reactions attached. The user of this program is therefore privy to several stories of reading which debate not only with one another in the classroom, but also with absent critics by means of notes. It's a kind of MUD (Multi-user dungeon), except that the task is not to free the princess or grasp the treasure, but to explicate a text. These links can also be accomplished on the World Wide Web using HTML. In fact, on the Web, virtual users can be replaced by real users, and the drama of learning can really begin.

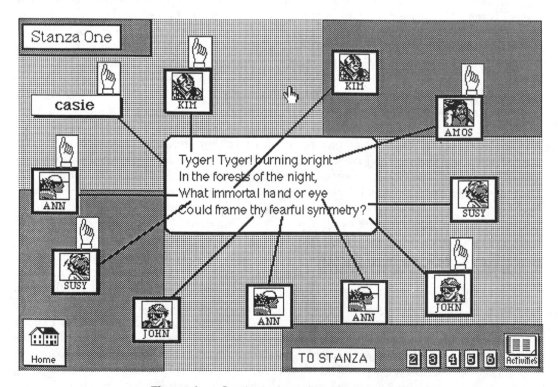

Figure 1.   Students in a discussion group.

I've been suggesting a theory of computer-aided instruction which will promote in the student a theoretical or top-down understanding, i.e., knowledge, rather than information. To do so, I've had to search for new metaphors, because what I'm describing is not simply the selective tagging which anyone marking up a text produces. The tags must surround the text or the idea without smothering it; they must provide threads out of confusion without over-simplifying; they must encourage a top-down view which does not censor out problematic links; and they must operate in an aesthetically pleasing and pedagogically useful way while preserving the rhetorical complexity of the text. As the rhetorician Lanham (1993) says, "As near as I can make out, we're going to need a new rhetoric of the arts and letters . . . which applies some bottom-up evolutionary thinking to the radical mix of word, image, and sound that is implicit in digital technology."

The learning web is temporary, sufficient for now, but tomorrow we may build another one. Learning on the computer has precisely this temporary feel to it, the kind of feel that gives Italo Calvino's citizens their certainty: "Now I will tell how Octavia, the spiderweb city, is made. . . . Suspended over the abyss, the life of Octavia's inhabitants is less uncertain than in other cities. They know the net will last only so long" ("Thin Cites #5," Italo Calvino, *Invisible Cities*). Nevertheless, as educators, we must not shirk our duty as possessors of authority, for "in the validation of information, the university will become more important than ever. With the explosive growth in the production of knowledge, society requires credible gatekeepers of information" (Noam, 1995, p. 249). Instructors might better be imaged not as gatekeepers policing the interface, but as Maxwell's kindly demon-usher resisting the entropy of the web system, sorting information into temporarily more useful compartments or packets of knowledge.

If it is to continue to be valued, the relationship of instructor and student will be based on usefulness rather than personality or institutional authority. What it presumes is the instructor's devotion to individual students, especially those who fail to perceive our fields of force, and wander off on a far strand towards an imaginary minotaur with no Ariadne to help them back. But "In this age of networked intelligence, do our students interest us enough?" (Pychyl, 1996). Far from freeing us from teaching responsibilities, the new technology will engage us with students more intimately than ever before. Even the most sophisticated monitoring mechanism won't explain exactly what is going on to every student, so there must always be the opportunity for an instructor to intervene in real time, and in one-on-one situations. The spin doctor may not be surfing, but she should be ready to make house-calls.

References

Benyon, J., & Mackay, H. (Eds.). (1993). *Computers into classrooms*. London: The Falmer Press.

Bolter, J. D. (1991). In G. Landow & P. Delaney (Eds.), *Hypermedia and literary studies*. Cambridge MA: MIT Press.

Bush, V. (1945, July). As we may think. *Atlantic Monthly* (http://www.csi.uottawa.ca/~dduchier/misc/vbush/as-we-may-think.html).

Cumming, A., & Sinclair, G. (1991). In G. Landow & P. Delaney (Eds.), *Hypermedia and literary studies*. Cambridge, MA: MIT Press.

de Kerckhove, D. (1995). *The skin of culture*. Toronto: Somerville House.

Dowling, D. (1992). Authoring for English literature in HyperCard: Where in the world is Blake's Tyger? *Hypermedia, 4*(3), 171–196.

Gelertner, D. (1991). *Mirror worlds*. New York: Oxford University Press.

Kay, A. C. (1995). Computers, networks, and education. *Scientific American* (Special issue: The Computer in the 21st Century), 148–155.

Landow, G. P. (1994). What's a critic to do? Critical theory in the age of hypertext. In G. P. Landow (Ed.), *Hyper/text/theory*. Baltimore: Johns Hopkins University Press.

Lanham, R. A. (1993). *The electronic word*. Chicago: University of Chicago Press.

Laurel, B. (1991). *Computers as theater*. Reading, MA: Addison-Wesley.

Laurillard, D. (1993). *Rethinking university teaching*. London: Routledge.

McLuhan, M. (1994.) *Understanding media*. Cambridge, MA: MIT Press.

Noam, E. M. (1995). Electronics and the dim future of the university. *Science, 270.*

Pychyl, T. A. (1996, May). Thoughts on technology and education: Teaching and learning in the age of networked intelligence (http://quarles.unbc.edu/ir/pychyl.html).

Riffaterre, M. (1994). Intertextuality vs. hypertextuality. *New Literary History, 25,* 779–788.

Ryan, M. L. (1994). Immersion vs. interactivity: Virtual reality and literary theory. *Postmodern Culture,* 5(1) (http://www.village.virginia.edu/pmc/issue.994/ryan.994.html).

Simon, H. A. (1989). In R. E. Horn (Ed.), *Mapping hypertext*. Lexington, MA: The Lexington Institute.

Smith, F. (1988). *Understanding reading*. Hillsdale, NJ: Lawrence Erlbaum Associates.

Wilde, A. (1981). *Horizons of assent: Modernism, postmodernism, and the ironic imagination*. Baltimore: Johns Hopkins University Press.

The Author

David Dowling is Professor and Programme Chair of English, University of Northern British Columbia, Canada.

e-mail, World Wide Web
   dowling@unbc.edu
   http://quarles.unbc.edu/ideas

57

Using the World Wide Web to Support Classroom-Based Education: Conclusions from a Multiple-Case Study

Brian S. Butler

The World Wide Web has received a great deal of attention as a distance education technology. It enables instructors to provide individuals who cannot participate in traditional classes with access to a wide array of educational materials. However, most education still takes place in a classroom environment. Thus, it is important to consider how the World Wide Web can be used to support classroom-based education.

Most experimentation with the World Wide Web in the classroom has been conducted by innovators, who are both technologically savvy and comfortable with the uncertainty of adapting a new technology to their situation. The results of these experiments are typically presented as case-studies or workshops. To synthesize these studies or effectively participate in the workshops, an individual often must have significant background information about applying technology in the educational setting. Consequently, these presentations are most useful for other innovators.

However, mainstream educators typically have different concerns; they are more skeptical about benefits, more concerned about costs—both time and money—and less certain about how the new technology can be effectively used in educational settings. Two crucial questions are: What is the real contribution of the new technology in the classroom? How can an educator constrained by time and money effectively apply it? If the capabilities of the World Wide Web are to be widely used in education, these questions must be addressed in a way that is accessible to the mainstream educator.

Drawing from a set of case-studies, we have created the following conceptual framework for understanding how the World Wide Web can be used to support classroom-based education. It involves categorizing uses of the World Wide Web in classrooms in one of three ways (see Figure 1 on the following page).

This framework provides a conceptual structure for organizing examples and issues that arise when considering use of the World Wide Web in the classroom. The remainder of this chapter elaborates the framework with examples drawn from six undergraduate and graduate courses which used the World Wide Web in different ways, ranging from supporting particular activities to providing all course materials online.[1] We conclude with applications of the

---

[1] The online materials for these courses are available: http://www.gsia.cmu.edu/bb26/

417

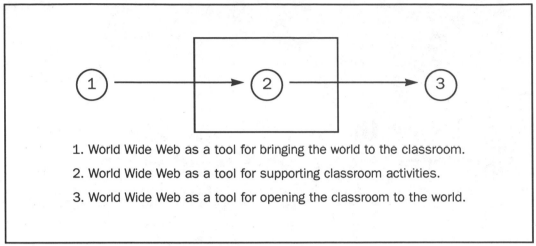

Figure 1. General conceptual framework.

framework to instructional technology planning, teacher education, and instructional technology research and development.

World Wide Web as a Tool for Bringing the World to the Classroom

Educators are often faced with the problem of finding and using information from many sources outside the classroom. The World Wide Web provides new information resources that can be used by both students and instructors in the classroom. Online resources include:

General Topic-Oriented Information Collections

On the World Wide Web there are many collections of information on topics ranging from information systems (e.g., ISWORLD: http://www.isworld.org/isworld.html) to medieval studies (e.g., Labyrinth: http://www.georgetown.edu/labyrinth/). These resources can be used by instructors when developing lectures, supplemental readings, or assignments. Because the materials are publicly available, students can also be encouraged to use online resources for course projects.

Time Sensitive Information Sources

Due to the length of the publishing cycle, many traditional sources cannot provide examples and details about recent phenomena. The World Wide Web provides instructors with access to information sources that are more dynamic, enabling them to incorporate more recent examples into the course materials. For example, we prepared an assignment that asked business students to examine the marketing literature for new software products. This assignment required that they apply concepts from the class to understand and evaluate systems which did not exist when the textbook was published.

It might be argued that these resources are of little value to instructors dealing with subjects where the core materials and phenomena do not drastically change over time. However, instructors can use recent newsworthy situations to illustrate concepts or test students' understanding. The World Wide Web is a useful source of these examples through both formal news services (e.g., Reuters news service: http://www.yahoo.com/headlines/) and informal topic-oriented "news" sources.

Archives of Discussion Groups and Other Online Communities

Materials from these archives can be used to introduce students to issues that are of direct concern to a larger community. By exposing students to a variety of perspectives extracted from discussion archives, we can show how topics which textbooks present as sterile academic debates are actually the concerns of real people. For example, to illustrate the issues that arise during organizational re-structuring, we provided students with links to announcements and discussions from an organization's publicly available internal archives. These materials demonstrated the problems and illustrated how different individuals had different perspectives and concerns.

Access to Phenomena of Interest

The World Wide Web can provide students with access to the phenomena that are the focus of many courses. A business strategy or marketing instructor might use the World Wide Web to provide examples of information systems supporting competitive strategy. For example, Security APL (http://www.secapl.com/) is a financial services firm which has used the Internet to offer free stock quotes. After attracting a large "audience," the firm began to offer a collection of online financial services. This illustrates how a firm can combine marketing, operations, and information systems to develop a new market.

The World Wide Web is also a source of non-technical phenomena, including medieval manuscripts and artwork (e.g., Beowulf manuscript: http://www.uky.edu/~kiernan/BL/kportico.html), astronomical phenomena (e.g., Galileo satellite's visit to Jupiter: http://www.jpl.nasa.gov/galileo/), or data describing recent economic situations (e.g., FCC bandwidth auctions: http://www.fcc.gov/). These World Wide Web resources enable instructors to introduce students to the real focus of an area—the things that intrigue participants in the field—rather than relying on generalized examples and second-hand descriptions.

Issues

1. It is not clear that students derive significant benefit from simply having access to large, unstructured collections of information. For example, in one course I provided a link to a large collection of materials about the U.S. government's process re-engineering efforts. However, most students ignored this resource; they were not sure what was relevant. Students often lack the background knowledge required to effectively make use of large collections of information. To address this, instructors may choose to provide guided entry points in the form of supplemental hypertext cover pages.

2. The World Wide Web does not provide equal coverage of topics. When searching for online materials, it is tempting to assume that there is good information available about every topic. Instructors and students need to consciously manage the time spent collecting World Wide Web materials and remember that a short trip to the library may be more productive than many hours searching the World Wide Web.

3. In the classroom, the World Wide Web is one of several competing media. Students get information through textbooks, lectures, e-mail, paper handouts, and personal contact with instructors and other students. In this 'competitive' environment, students choose how they will allocate their attention and time. Thus, I have found that in courses which used the World Wide Web to provide online copies of paper administrative documents, there is almost no student use of the online resources. In contrast, if crucial materials are available only online, students are more likely to use both the required and optional online materials.

World Wide Web as a Tool for Supporting Classroom Activities

The World Wide Web can also be used to manage information and activities that are contained within the classroom. Uses of the World Wide Web within the classroom include:

Supporting Administrative Functions

The World Wide Web can be used to distribute course materials such as assignments, lecture notes, and supplemental readings. Providing these materials online reduces administrative problems associated with managing and distributing paper copies. Online materials also provide students with greater access to materials, both during and after the course. In conjunction with electronic mail, the World Wide Web can facilitate management of assignments. Finally, World Wide Web forms provide a basic mechanism for administering course evaluations.

Student Projects

Technology oriented projects. The World Wide Web provides a set of interface and network capabilities. Thus it is a valuable laboratory for teaching technical skills related to creation and maintenance of complex information systems. Technology projects may also involve developing cost estimates and plans for creating Internet applications and the necessary technical infrastructure. In either case, technical projects use the World Wide Web to familiarize students with the development and management of hardware, software, and telecommunications technology.

Design oriented projects. One of the strengths of the World Wide Web is that users with minimal understanding of the technological infrastructure can use the hypertext distribution capability. Using HTML, it is possible for students with minimal experience and no programming skills to create prototype systems or complex hypertext documents. Students can focus on design and content creation. In contrast to the technology oriented projects, design projects emphasize applications and help students understand how to effectively use the World Wide Web.

Resource oriented projects. Users with no HTML skills and limited access can still use the information resources that are available through the World Wide Web. Resource oriented projects develop students' ability to find, evaluate, and use complex information resources.

While projects often incorporate aspects of these three types, instructors designing World Wide Web-based projects should identify a primary focus. Clearly defining the project helps students to allocate time and attention, while allowing the instructor to evaluate the educational contribution of the World Wide Web project.

Support and Creation of Innovative Classroom Activities

Instructors can also use the World Wide Web to create systems that support new classroom activities. For example, using the World Wide Web forms facilities, I developed an auction system which students in an object-oriented software design class used to buy and sell software objects. This system provided students with a new context for developing and using software components. The World Wide Web is a powerful tool for creating interactive courseware, while avoiding many of the difficulties associated with software development.

Instructors can also use the World Wide Web to indirectly support classroom activities. For example, the creation of materials needed for experiential exercises may be simplified with World Wide Web-based utilities. Furthermore, using the World Wide Web to distribute results from classroom exercises enables instructors to design units integrating in-class exercises, lectures, and assignments based on further consideration of the results. The World Wide Web provides an infrastructure that enables instructors to manage classroom activities more effectively.

Issues

1. Students often use the World Wide Web as a document distribution system, not an on-line document system. Most students print some or all of the online materials. This is consistent with previous reports of online documentation (Horton, 1990). Thus, claims that the World Wide Web use reduces materials costs are questionable.

2. Extensive use of the World Wide Web affects student use of other materials. In courses which rely on the World Wide Web, student use of other online facilities, such as electronic bulletin boards, may be significantly reduced, and students may interact less with the instructor. Educators should consider how using the World Wide Web affects students' use of materials and interaction with instructors and other students.

3. Most World Wide Web utilities support the creation of arbitrary World Wide Web documents. However, these general tools provide little assistance for the tasks which arise when using the World Wide Web in the classroom. Instructor using the World Wide Web must maintain a complex set of materials that change over time. Routine actions could be supported with specialized tools. Education-specific 'toolboxes' of forms and scripts would enable instructors to use the World Wide Web more effectively without becoming familiar with the details of the technical infrastructure.

4. World Wide Web materials and activities must be integrated into the course. If the World Wide Web is used as an independent addition, its contribution will be minimal. Publishers provide materials that help instructors integrate textbooks with assignments, lectures, and other activities. Likewise, instructors must design World Wide Web resources which fit with and contribute to the educational goals of the course.

World Wide Web as a Tool for Opening the Classroom to the World

By making it possible to easily 'publish' materials, the World Wide Web opens the classroom to others, including the following:

Other Educators

In most universities, faculty members rarely discuss teaching materials and activities (Boice, 1992). The World Wide Web makes it possible for instructors to 'observe' a range of techniques and content. World Wide Web-based materials provide educators with access to more teaching resources than are typically available within a single university.

Other Students

During and after a course, online materials can be used by students considering the course, students in other courses looking for additional information or review, and professionals interested in a particular topic. Through the World Wide Web, these 'shadow students' can take advantage of the materials long after the formal classroom activities are finished.

The Instructor

The World Wide Web server logs and sign-in forms provide instructors with information about how students use the online materials. By considering how supplemental materials are used, it is possible to identify topics that are of interest to students. Well-designed online materials provide feedback, which helps instructors evaluate and improve the course.

Issues

1. Providing students with the capability to make materials public (i.e., publish) is not the same as teaching student how to publish. Students rarely have experience as active participants in public 'discussions'; hence, they may not consider issues such as quality, content appropriateness, and intellectual property. Instructors who place students in the public eye on the World Wide Web may encounter unanticipated challenges as students experiment with public communication.

2. Designing reusable online materials is a difficult design problem. Structuring materials as topical modules, even within single lectures, simplifies selective reuse of course materials. However, creating materials for current students and developing materials that can reused by other are different projects each requiring a significant investment of time and effort. Managing the amount of time spent developing materials for redistribution helps to ensure that the immediate needs of students are met.

Applications of the General Framework

The discussion above elaborates a framework for characterizing use of the World Wide Web in the classroom. This model can be used to guide use of the World Wide Web, serve as the basis for educating instructors about the use of the World Wide Web, and direct further research about World Wide Web support for classroom-based education.

Using the Framework as an Instructor

Instructors can use this model as a guide for planning the use of the World Wide Web and developing realistic expectations. The framework can be applied as follows:

- Briefly describe current activities or activities that might be added to the course. This may be done independently or by identifying relevant activities from each general category.

- Place each activity within the model. Some activities will be best characterized by a single category. Others may involve subactivities that fall into different categories.

- Use examples and issues from the relevant categories as the basis for evaluating and planning the use of the World Wide Web for supporting each activity.

The framework can be used in conjunction with the extensive literature, both off- and online, which considers educational uses of the World Wide Web. By focusing on educational activities, not the World Wide Web itself, this model improves the chances that instructors will be able to realistically assess the costs and benefits of using the World Wide Web in the classroom. It also encourages instructors to evaluate the use of the World Wide Web for supporting particular activities rather than implying that the World Wide Web can support every aspect of the classroom. Successful practical frameworks must provide instructors with a basis for planning focused application of the World Wide Web.

Using the Framework as a Basis for Instructor Education

For the use of the World Wide Web to become widespread, the concerns of non-innovators must be addressed. This requires that the results of instructional technology experiments be presented in a way that is accessible to non-technical educators. The preliminary framework supports this goal by emphasizing non-technical issues, benefits, and costs that are likely to arise. Furthermore, this framework provides a structure for generalizing the lessons learned from individual cases by providing a representation of the implicit understanding that innovators develop through personal experience. With this model, educators are better equipped to assess the potential contribution of the World Wide Web in the classroom. Presentations and discussions that help instructors develop this understanding are as important as instruction about specific technical skills. Juxtaposing this framework and technical skills instruction prepares educators to intelligently plan, execute, and evaluate the use of the World Wide Web in their courses.

Using the Framework as for Instructional Technology and Research

Development of the Internet and the World Wide Web increased opportunities for applying communication technology in the classroom. It also prompted growing interest in the design, use, and impact of these technologies in educational setting. The framework presented here is an early step in the development of a model of the classroom as an bounded social communication system. Questions about the use and impact of information technology investigate the consequences of altering the infrastructure of an education-oriented social system. Studies in communications, organizational studies, and information systems address similar questions. This framework serves as a lens through which these studies can be viewed and used to inform future educational technology research.

Conclusion

The World Wide Web provides significant benefits when applied in the classroom. At the same time, instructors, trainers, developers, and researchers need to recognize that the World Wide Web has limitations. Everything that is feasible is not necessarily useful, and everything that is useful is not necessarily feasible. The framework presented here is a first step in the development of a systematic understanding of how the World Wide Web can be effectively used to support classroom-based education.

References

Boice, R. (1992). *The new faculty member: Supporting and fostering professional development.* San Francisco: Jossey-Bass Publishers.

Horton, W. K. (1990). *Designing and writing online documentation: Help files to hypertext.* New York: John Wiley & Sons.

The Author

Brian S. Butler is with the Graduate School of Industrial Administration, Carnegie Mellon University, Pittsburgh, Pennsylvania

e-mail, World Wide Web
bb26@andrew.cmu.edu
http://www.gsia.cmu.edu/bb26/

58

Astronomy Instruction Using the World Wide Web

Siobahn M. Morgan

stronomy is considered to be one of the oldest sciences, and is a popular topic for all levels of students and the general public. When Comet Shoemaker-Levy 9 impacted into the clouds of Jupiter in July of 1994, NASA's Jet Propulsion Laboratory Comet Website became an information and image archive for the event. From July 8 to 31, 1994, there were nearly 2 million accesses to the site, with an average transmission of 2 gigabytes per day. To date, the site has had more than 7.6 million accesses (Baalke, 1996). Similar high numbers can be seen at other NASA Websites, as well the Websites of the Space Telescope Science Institute, universities, and astronomy clubs.

Due to the "hands-off" approach in astronomy, there has always been a need for relaying images to students and the public, as well as explanations and demonstrations of complex phenomena. Previous to the introduction of the World Wide Web, astronomy resources for instructors had been mainly in the standard media, often provided by book publishers as incentives for adopting textbooks. These include video tapes, slides, overhead transparencies, and laserdiscs. CD-ROMs started to appear in the early 1990s as another method of providing images. All of these forms of media are hampered by obsolescence. This is particularly true in recent times due to the Hubble Space Telescope, frequent Space Shuttle missions, and the Magellan mission to Venus.

The World Wide Web has removed many of the obstacles that have plagued instructors of astronomy by providing up-to-date images, as well as information about the latest discoveries. Several instructors have provided their students with course information at local Web sites, as well as providing them easy access to new information via links to national and international archives. Also, due to the increased use of digital imaging systems, such as charge-coupled device (CCD) cameras, it is much easier to produce images that can be accessed online. Resources currently available for all levels of education will be reviewed, and examples of currently used World Wide Web-based instruction and outlines of future World Wide Web-based astronomy instruction will also be discussed.

Resources

The easiest way to find astronomy links related to education is to check the AstroWeb site, which includes links to the majority of astronomy sites around the world and tests most of the links daily. There is a special section devoted to Educational Resources. Another main resource can be found at the AstroEd site (Cairns, 1996). There are several pages devoted to educational resources, as well as a compact list of interesting sites.

Amongst the main online resources for astronomy education are those found at various NASA sites. These include images from current and past missions, as well as press releases, fact sheets, and teaching resources. The main site for education at NASA is the Spacelink Program, which provides resources to educators, including text, software, graphics and images. This includes lesson plans for not only astronomy, but also general science, math, and technology, as well as interdisciplinary topics. This site also has information on NASA's own educational policies and guidelines. The Quest site, NASA's Interactive Initiative K–12 Webpage, allows students the opportunity to use the Hubble Space Telescope, or to communicate with researchers in Antarctica (Federman *et al.*, 1996). Previous projects involved lessons centered around the arrival of the Galileo spacecraft at Jupiter, and the chance to learn about the robotic exploration of other worlds. Most of these activities provide lesson plans and teacher resources dealing with the various fields of study. Also located at this site is a very comprehensive listing of online educational resources, including school networks, museums, and university sites.

A valuable resource available from NASA is their large archive of images. One of the most comprehensive collections is at the Jet Propulsion Laboratory site, Welcome to the Planets. The site includes images of not only planets, but also moons, comets, asteroids and the Sun. Details about previous space missions and a glossary are also included. This site can act as a supplement to an astronomy text by providing a great number of images, and thorough information about each object. A similar site is the Views of the Solar System site located at the Los Alamos National Lab (Hamilton, 1994). This site provides not only pictures, but also detailed information and a large glossary page for obscure terms.

The Hubble Space Telescope site (O'Dea *et al.*, 1996) can provide educators with the latest information in astronomy research. While most of the data and images may be more appropriate for secondary school and college students, the large image archive provides excellent detailed pictures not available in most text books. There is also a collection of animation clips that can be downloaded.

Another large online resource is available through the Students for the Exploration and Development of Space. This site includes a massive image archive of the solar system, as well as multiple images of nebula and Messier objects. There is also an extensive collection of software available.

World Wide Web Astronomy Curricula Packages

Current examples of astronomy World Wide Web curricula are as simple as lecture notes provided online, and as complex as student Web page editing. Several examples of each are discussed here.

The Center for EUV Astrophysics has developed several online instructional units, primarily for K–12 students in the Earth and Space Sciences (Hawkins, 1996). Some of these have grown out of teacher in-service programs, and others are part of larger collaborations with NASA, museums, and research centers. The online lessons and lesson plans include studying the weather on Mars, understanding the operation of the Extreme Ultraviolet Explorer satellite, the properties of light, and constellations. There are also resources available for designing World Wide Web lesson plans, including graphics and animation.

Getting students involved in making their own Web pages is another way to enhance the learning process. An example of this is seen at the Dalton School in New York, where students create Web pages as part of their astronomy course. For each section of the curricula, the students, working in groups, are assigned tasks which must be included in the design of their Web pages. The students in this case gain not only a knowledge of astronomy, but also insight into traversing the maze of Internet resources, and writing skills. A similar system can be seen in an astrophysics course at the Illinois Mathematics and Science Academy (Moyer, 1996), where students are assigned various tasks in the design of a Web page for specific projects.

Several college/university instructors have developed paperless courses by putting their course material on Web pages. This includes not only syllabi, but also lectures, homework, and virtual textbooks. One example of this can be seen at the University of Oregon's Electronic Universe Project (Bothun, 1995), where entire physics and astronomy courses are presented electronically.

Foundations for Future Astronomy Projects Using World Wide Web

Remote Observing with Online Telescopes

One aspect of astronomy that is an important part of the curricula is the observation of the sky. However, in instances of poor local viewing conditions, the wonders of the heavens may not be easily accessible to all. This problem can be overcome by using online telescopes, which are available to all Internet users. Currently there are only a few such systems, but they have already provided research opportunities for high school students. The University of Iowa Automated Telescope Facility (Mutel, 1996) provides access to a 7 in. aperture telescope, with a CCD camera. The University of Bradford provides access to an 18 in. aperture telescope, and CCD camera (Cox, 1995). The University of California at Santa Barbara operates a remote 14 in. telescope with a CCD camera and provides several lab exercises suitable for high school or college students (Remote Access Astronomy Project, 1996).

Outlines of Astronomy Activities Using World Wide Web

Elementary school students. One of the most effective exercises for these grade levels is to provide students with pointers to image archives—particularly the ones dealing with the solar system. Links to images of other planets can lead to discussions of comparative planetology and descriptive exercises. Questions that may be of use in astronomy Web exercises include:

1. Which planet is most similar to the Moon?

2. How are the near and far sides of the Moon similar? How are the two sides different?

3. What features on Mars are similar to features on the Earth?

4. What would it be like to stand on the surface of Venus?

5. How much bigger is Jupiter than the Earth?

6. Which planets have rings?

7. Which planet has the most moons?

8. What do the moons of Mars look like?

9. Where is the largest volcano in the solar system?

10. How are the Martian volcanos like the Hawaiian islands?

Middle school students. A greater range of images can now be used, particularly those for stars, nebulae, and galaxies. Image comparison and analysis can lead to insight into the nature of light and qualitative descriptions of physical phenomena. This level of students may also be introduced to robotic telescope use, primarily to obtain their own images. As they learn to manipulate these images they will gain insight into "what doing science is all about." Questions that may be directed to students at this level include:

1. Why does an x-ray image and a radio telescope image of the same object differ? What does this tell you about the physical characteristics of the object?

2. What is the current status of the SOHO spacecraft? The Galileo spacecraft?

3. What is the latest discovery from the Hubble Space Telescope?

4. What is new/controversial/important about this study?

5. How can sunspot images be used to determine the rotation rate of the Sun? What other motions must be taken into account?

6. Based upon the variety of galaxy shapes, what scheme can you use to classify them?

7. Based upon the way the black hole warps space, what would you expect to happen if you had two black holes near one another? Could you possibly navigate a spacecraft past them?

8. What is the difference between the Crab Nebula and the Ring Nebula? How were they formed? What will eventually happen to them?

High school and college students. With a greater knowledge of math, they can use the images to answer more quantitative questions. They may also make use of various online databases to obtain not only images, but also spectra and photometric data. Advanced high school students and interested college students can also participate in observing projects using one of the available online telescopes. Such projects can include searches for supernova in distant galaxies, measuring the brightness of a asteroid to determine its size, or following the pulsations of a variable star to determine its period and variability type. Even the observations of the familiar planets and their moons can provide insight into physical phenomena, such as the variation in the features of Mars or the changing brightness of Io or Iapetus. Questions that may be asked of these students include:

1. Based upon the angular size of this nebula, its distance and its age, what is its rate of expansion?

2. Using the spectra obtained, determine the distance of this galaxy, and use that information to determine the age of the Universe?

3. Compare the light curve features of a Cepheid with an RR Lyrae star. How are they different? Why might they be different?

4. What does the presence of these particular spectral features tell us about the characteristics of this star?

5. Using the COBE satellite images, explain how the variation in temperature of the cosmic background radiation leads to the formation of superclusters of galaxies.

Complex World Wide Web-Based Instruction: Use of Image Maps and Forms

In order to demonstrate certain phenomena, it is perhaps more advantageous to provide an interface that students can interact with to learn about astronomical phenomena. This includes the ability to ask questions, work out problems and select items on a screen. These require a greater knowledge of World Wide Web architecture and computer programming skills, but are well worth the effort. I have been able to produce some of these type of exercises for my college level students, but the concepts can be expanded to other groups of students. Examples include:

1. Image maps of planets or moons, with links to major features

2. Image maps of plots showing the relationships between various physical characteristics of stars or galaxies, with links which provide greater information. This could include the standard luminosity-temperature plot for stars with various stars plotted. Links would provide greater information such as star name, radius, and spectra time. Spectra of stars can also be displayed, and various key spectral features which are used in classifying them have links.

3. Image maps of star clusters with links for individual stars provided to allow students to compile a set of characteristics which can show stellar evolution, cluster distance, and/or cluster age.

4. Image maps of a galaxy shown edge on, with links which provide information about the motions, which can be used to derive the mass of the galaxy.

5. Image maps of galaxies in a cluster can be used with appropriate links to allow students to determine their distances, and therefore the age of the universe.

6. Interactive form programs can take information such as a star's radius and temperature and provide a luminosity, or, given a value for a person's weight, calculate what his or her weight would be on other planets.

7. Online quizzes and tests, usually implemented with multiple choice forms.

Conclusion

Web-based instruction in astronomy can provide a great deal of information to students, in a topic that is of general interest at all levels of education. Some of the projects highlighted here can be implemented with only a minimal amount of World Wide Web knowledge and work on the part of the instructor. With the increase in the amount of online data, this trend should grow dramatically.

References

AstroWeb Consortium. (1996). *AstroWeb: Astronomy/Astrophysics on the Internet* (http://fits.cv.nrao.edu/www/astronomy.html).

Baalke, R. (1996). *Comet Shoemaker-Levy Collision with Jupiter* (http://www.jpl.nasa.gov/sl9/).

Bothun, G. (1995). *The Electronic Universe Project* (http://zebu.uoregon.edu/).

Cairns, A. (1996). *AstroEd: Astronomy Education Resources* (http://www-hpcc.astro.washington.edu/scied/astro/astroed.html).

Cox, M. J. (1995). *Bradford Robotic Telescope* (http://www.telescope.org/).

Dalton School (1996). *Dalton Astronomy Home Page* (http://www.nltl.columbia.edu/Groups1/Astro/home.html).

Federman, A., Tanski, C., Hickson, N., & Wang, M. (1996). *Quest: NASA K–12 Internet Initiative* (http://quest.arc.nasa.gov/).

Hamilton, C. J. (1994). *Views of the Solar System* (http://bang.lanl.gov/solarsys/).

Hawkins, I. (1996). *CEA Science Education Home Page* (http://w3.cea.berkeley.edu/Education/).

Jet Propulsion Laboratory of the California Institute of Technology (1995). *Welcome to the Planets.* (http://pds.jpl.nasa.gov/planets/).

Moyer, E. Jr. (1996) *IMSA Astrophysics Home Page* (http://www.imsa.edu/edu/astro/).

Mutel, R. L. (1996). *University of Iowa Automated Telescope Facility* (http://inferno.physics.uiowa.edu/).

NASA Spacelink—An Electronic Information System for Educators (http://spacelink.msfc.nasa.gov/).

O'Dea, C., Paradise, D., Stevens, M., & Levay, Z. (1996). *Space Telescope Electronic Information Service* (http://www.stsci.edu/).

Remote Access Astronomy Project. (1996). *Remote Access Astronomy Project Remotely Operated Telescope* (http://www.deepspace.ucsb.edu/rot.htm).

Students for the Exploration and Development of Space Home Page (http://www.seds.org/).

The Author

Siobahn M. Morgan is Assistant Professor of Astronomy, Department of Earth Science, University of Northern Iowa, Ceder Falls, Iowa.

e-mail, World Wide Web
   morgans@uni.edu
   http://nitro9.earth.uni.edu/department/smm.html

59

Preparing and Managing a Course Web Site: Understanding Systemic Change in Education

Theodore W. Frick, Michael Corry, and Marty Bray

Overview

The first author led a doctoral seminar on "Understanding Systemic Change in Education" during the spring semester, 1995. The World Wide Web was used in this course to facilitate student learning of 60 complex systems concepts that were part of an educational theory.

The resulting Web products of these students and their instructor can be viewed at:

http://copper.ucs.indiana.edu/~ist/siggs.html

We encourage you to browse this site as you read. In this chapter, we share some of our experiences from this course, which may be useful if you are planning to use the Web in your teaching or research activities.

About the Course

One goal of the seminar was for students to learn structural and dynamic properties of systems in general. This was a necessary step in order to understand a theory of education that was developed by Maccia and Maccia (1966). We expect this theory to serve as the foundation for a planned computer simulation of educational systems.

Students in the seminar needed to learn the following properties of systems from Maccia and Maccia's SIGGS theory model. SIGGS refers to the integration of set, information, digraph, and general systems theory.

- **Basic SIGGS Properties.** Component, affect relation, information, selective information, system, negasystem, toput (system environment), input, storeput, fromput (megasystem environment), and output.

- **SIGGS Structural Properties.** System complete connectivity, strongness, unilateralness, weakness, disconnectivity, vulnerability, passive dependence, active dependence, segregation, interdependence, wholeness, integration, hierarchical order, flexibility, homomorphism, isomorphism, automorphism, compactness, centralization, size, and complexity.

431

 **Educational Systems Theory**

Welcome to the SIGGS home page. You will find information on a theory of education which was developed from a well-defined systems model. Both the theory and the model are complex, requiring considerable study for full comprehension. We hope that the SIGGS Web will help create a major paradigm shift in how people think about education. The SIGGS model is an integration of Set, Information, diGraph and General Systems theories.

- Overview
- Seminar on Understanding Systemic Change in Education
- Education system: an introduction
- Education theory: 201 hypotheses
- Basic SIGGS Properties
- SIGGS Structural Properties (configural patterns)
- SIGGS Dynamic Properties (temporal change)
- System: fundamental notions underlying SIGGS

Figure 1. The Educational Systems Theory Home Page.

- **SIGGS Dynamic Properties.** System environmental change, feedin, feedout, feedback, feedthrough, filtration, spillage, regulation, compatibility, openness, adaptivity, efficiency, size growth, complexity growth, selective information growth, size degeneration, complexity degeneration, selective information degeneration, stability, state steadiness, state determination, equifinality, homeostasis, stress, and strain.

Why the Web?

Hypertext appeared to be a useful medium through which students and others could learn these complex and abstract systems concepts. The World Wide Web permitted students in the class to access the SIGGS theory model from many places and from different kinds of computers, so it was the medium of choice.

Furthermore, this seminar was viewed as a step in the direction of eventually designing a computer simulation of educational systems change. Such a simulation must be based on valid rules. Maccia and Maccia's theory—with its 201 hypotheses—appeared to be a good starting place. Each of their hypotheses states a predicted relationship between two or more of the SIGGS properties. If empirically validated, the hypotheses could then constitute the expert system needed for the simulation. The research needed prior to the design of the simulation is expected to take a number of years and will require participation by many inquirers. By putting the SIGGS model, the Maccia and Maccia theory, and subsequent research findings onto the Web, we would make this knowledge accessible to people from all over the world who might be doing research to support or refute hypotheses in the theory.

The Web Was There—and Accessible

We could not have used the Web in this seminar if it were not accessible easily by both the instructor and the students. Fortunately, Indiana University has excellent computing facilities and support services. On the Bloomington campus there are numerous labs with computers connected to the Internet. IU also provides dial-up modems so that students and faculty can access the Internet from off campus.

IU provides a number of computers running the Unix operating system, which does Web serving and provides other Internet services. It is a relatively simple matter to establish departmental and personal computer accounts. Within those accounts a user can establish a directory for Web documents. As soon as documents are created in that directory, they immediately become part of the World Wide Web.

The course instructor chose to use a departmental account on a university computer. All the students in the seminar used the same account and put their Web documents under that account. The reason for doing it this way was that the departmental account will persist over time. If the Web documents were to reside in student accounts, those accounts would normally be deactivated after students graduate, and this would cause long-term maintenance problems.

Instructor Knowledge of the Web and Training Materials

The course instructor was an experienced computer user. He had designed numerous Web documents prior to the seminar, was fluent in HTML, and was experienced in other Web-related matters. In fact, he had been leading efforts in the department and School of Education to help them gain a presence on the Web. As part of that leadership, he and graduate students had developed training materials and job aids for learning to spin the web (Frick & Hansen, 1995).

While it is not necessary to be a computer expert to develop documents for the Web, prior instructor knowledge and experience with Web development prevented many potential problems from occurring in the seminar. And most importantly, the training materials were used in the class, so that students could learn the basics of Web development prior to collaboration on the SIGGS model.

Class Discussions about SIGGS Concepts

Before students in the class could begin creating the SIGGS Web site, they required a better understanding of the properties and hypotheses that form the foundation of the theory. During the first half of the course, the instructor led class discussions about the basics of various system properties, hypotheses, and real life examples of their application. In addition, the instructor and each student had access to e-mail and were on a class distribution list. This list was used to facilitate communication among everyone in the class. Correspondence included questions as well as new understandings and examples of applications of the theory.

As the discussions progressed, each member of the class began to have a better understanding of each of the SIGGS properties, hypotheses, and how they fit together as a whole. Ultimately, this helped the students gain a better understanding of educational and systemic change.

World Wide Web Training

Once the students in the class had developed a basic understanding of the SIGGS theory, it was important that they also understood the basics of creating a World Wide Web site.

There was a wide range of Web development experience among the students in the class. Therefore, the instructor taught the students the basics of using HTML and a simple Unix text

Educational Systems Theory

Property: <u>toput</u>

Definition:
> "Educational system <u>toput</u> is educational <u>system environment</u>." (p. 49)

Comments:
> That is, <u>toput</u> is a <u>negasystem</u> of at least two <u>components</u> with at least one <u>affect relation</u> which has <u>selective information</u>.

Illustration:

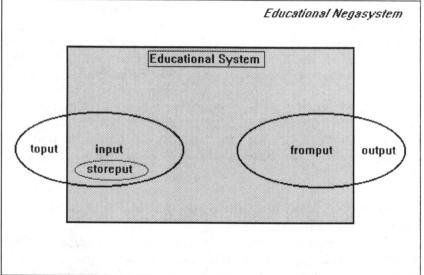

Figure 2. Part of a SIGGS Web Page for the Property 'Toput.'

editor to create Web documents. Many of the more experienced students used HTML editors to do their Web development work.

In addition to the guidance provided by the instructor, materials were used that had previously been developed by Frick and Hansen (1995). These materials took the user step-by-step through the development of a Web document. The materials were geared towards the facilities available to the students in the class.

Organizing the Web Site

Before students could begin creating SIGGS Web documents, it was important to organize the site. We needed to adopt conventions for naming files, since each needed to be unique, and those names were needed for the hypertext links that were created in HTML documents. For this to work, we needed to specify all file names in advance so that students could use this master list whenever they needed to create a link to someone else's Web document.

Second, the instructor created a template file on the Web, which can be found at:

http://copper.ucs.indiana.edu/~ist/template.html)

This template contains standard headings and subcategories. In addition, it includes place markers where SIGGS information could be added by the students. The template provided an easy way for students to "cut and paste" their information into the template with the result being their own SIGGS Web document. This helped to make the SIGGS Web documents consistent in appearance and structure.

A further issue concerned the graphics used in the Web pages. Each SIGGS Web page needed to include at least one graphic image to help illustrate a particular property. The students and instructor discussed the importance of consistency among the graphic images. We decided that each image should be not be wider than a typical 640x480 Web browser screen. In addition, we agreed that graphic images should use no more than 16 colors (4-bit color), which would result in quicker loading and viewing of the Web pages.

Paper and Web Prototypes

After agreeing on the organization of the Web site, each student was assigned five different SIGGS properties. The students first created paper prototypes for each of their assigned properties.

Students made paper prototypes to ensure their understanding of the SIGGS properties and the accuracy of their examples *prior* to publishing them on the Web. The instructor reviewed the paper prototypes and made suggestions for their improvement.

Next, students created prototype pages on the Web for each of their assigned properties. Again, once this process was complete, the instructor reviewed each of the Web documents to ensure their structure, organization, and accuracy. Any additional suggestions for change were then incorporated into the Web documents.

Review of Site and Better Understanding of SIGGS

After the students completed and revised their Web prototypes, they had the opportunity to review the entire SIGGS Web site. Many commented that this helped them to better understand the SIGGS theory, educational change, and systemic thinking.

The hypertext links among properties gave the students better accessibility to the relationships among properties and hypotheses in the SIGGS theory. To see the definition and examples of a property (e.g., toput), all they needed do was click the mouse on the word, and they would be automatically linked to the document which explained that property.

The other significant accomplishment by students in this course was to make a complex theory more understandable. We provided many commonplace examples in education systems to help the reader understand each system property. We also provided iconic representations to complement the abstract representations (definitions and examples). Finally, we created links to the hypotheses in the theory itself. The resulting SIGGS Web can be seen at:

http://copper.ucs.indiana.edu/~ist/siggs.html

Conclusion

The creation of the SIGGS Web site led to benefits not only for students in the class, but also for a larger audience interested in educational change. For the students in the class, the creation of the SIGGS Web site brought together a wide variety of concepts, insights, and opinions in a meaningful and orderly manner. For a larger audience, the benefit of the SIGGS Web site has been its accessibility. Before the project began, the theory was only available to those willing to go to the trouble of locating the original publication and ordering it.

As a result of student and instructor collaboration in the seminar, the SIGGS theory is now readily available to anyone with access to the World Wide Web. This has facilitated the theory's use by organizations such as the International Systems Institute at

http://www.clark.net/pub/nhp/isi/homepage.html

and by faculty at other universities who teach courses on educational systems. The SIGGS Web site is being used as a resource for the development of an educational simulation which, when completed, will help educators and others to envision new systems which can better meet the needs of an information society.

In a note to the first author, George Maccia and Elizabeth Steiner (who developed the SIGGS theory model) were delighted that this information is now available on the Web. They are now retired, leaving others such as ourselves to carry their research forward. The Web site which began in a doctoral seminar in 1995 is now available to the world.

References

Frick, T. (1993). A systems view of restructuring education. In C. Reigeluth, B. Banathy, & J. Olson, (Eds.), *Comprehensive systems design: A new educational technology* (pp. 260–271). Berlin: Springer-Verlag.

Frick, T., & Hansen, L. (1995). *Learning to spin the Web: Basic skills you need to create and use World Wide Web documents*. Bloomington, IN: Department of Instructional Systems Technology, School of Education, Indiana University.

Maccia, E. S., & Maccia, G. S. (1966). *Development of educational theory derived from three theory models*. Washington, DC: U.S. Office of Education.

Steiner, E. (1988). *Methodology of theory building*. Sydney: Educology Research Associates.

The Authors

Theodore W. Frick is Associate Professor, Department of Instructional Systems Technology, School of Education, Indiana University, Bloomington, Indiana.

e-mail, World Wide Web
  frick@indiana.edu
  http://education.indiana.edu/ist/faculty/frick.html

Michael Corry is a Ph.D. Candidate, Department of Instructional Systems Technology, School of Education, Indiana University, Bloomington, Indiana.

e-mail, World Wide Web
  mcorry@indiana.edu
  http://copper.ucs.indiana.edu/~mcorry/home.html

Marty Bray is a Ph.D. Candidate, Department of Instructional Systems Technology, School of Education, Indiana University, Bloomington, Indiana.

e-mail, World Wide Web
  lmbray@indiana.edu
  http://copper.ucs.indiana.edu/~lmbray/home.html

Author Index

Subject Index

NOTE: **Bold** page numbers indicate figures and tables. *Italics* page numbers indicate URL addresses.

Computer-Mediated-Communication (CMC), 32–34, 363, *See also* Communication; Conferences
  compared to computer conferencing, 32–33, 285–286
  and social presence theory, 104
Computers in the Classroom, 75
Computers and connections, 7, 12, 17, 62, 99, *See also* Access; Service providers
  connection speed issues, 240, 247
  human-computer interaction (HCI), 221–224
  language capabilities of, 86
  network computer (NC), 227–228
  physiological difficulties with, 405
  role in teacher training, 329–331
Computers as Theater, 412
Concept Mapping, 28
Concepts
  presentation of, 54–56
  in TIP database, **273**
Concerns-Based Adoption Model (CBAM), 112, **113–114,** 116
Conferences, *See also* Communication; e-mail
  affect on motivation, 102
  and Computer-Mediated-Communication, compared, 32–33, 285–286
  and e-mail, compared, 283–286
  interactive conferencing software, *407*
  student/group participation in, 70–72, 152, **154–156,** 170, **173**
  video conferencing, 357–360
  in Virtual-U system, 399–400
Conferencing tools, 6, 11, 152, 384–385, *See also* Tools
  Web-Based Conferencing (WBC), 283–292, **284–285,** *288*
Conferencing on the Web (COW), 283–292, **284–285**
  star structure and tree structure, compared, 289–291, **290**
Confidence, 232
  relation to motivation, 180–182
Conflict resolution, 71, *See also* Problem solving
Connections. *See* Access; Computers and connections
Connectivity, implementation considerations for, 343–344
Constructivism
  compared to instructivism, 53, 57, 381–382
    educational model for, **64–65**
    in pedagogical philosophy, 60
  compared to objectivism, 381, 382

  emphasis on case-based instruction, 122
  virtual worlds as constructivist learning tool, 393–397
  in Web-based instruction, 43, 45, 120, 191–203
CONSTRUE, 343
Consultant, compared to in-house expert, 329–331
Content, *See also* Curriculum
  affect of
    on student motivation, 69, 95, 99
    in Web-based instruction, 44–45, 83, 193, 239, 264
  analysis of, 50–51, 122, 376
  content linking, 256–257
  in course creation, 309
  cross-cultural considerations for, 87, 89, 91
  development of, 6, 163, 353
Context
  cultural relation of, 86
  maintenance of by authoring program, 311
  motivational, 179–180
  relation to
    knowledge, 121
    learning, 227, 267
Control
  and interactivity, 52, 82
  in learning environment, 68, 354, 382
  system control, 26, 240–241, 362
  vs. freedom, 130
CoolTalk, 342, 343
Cooperation. *See* Collaborative learning
Copyright, 337–*339*
Cost, *See also* Fees
  of authoring program, 303
  of literacy programs, 141–143
  of online course preparation, 308
  of technological materials, 77, 86–87
  of Web access, 16, 193
  for Web-based instruction, 78, 333–336, 348, 372, 390
Counter, for Web page, 317
Course authoring. *See* Authoring; Publishing
Course credit, 78, 400, *See also* Evaluation; Testing
Course materials, *See also* Instructional materials
  effect on student motivation, 94, 96–99
  interactive, *407–410*
  recommendations for, 356
  sharing of, 83
  templates for, 154
  for Web-based interactive course, 408–410
Course preparation, *See also* Curriculum

V

U